ENFORCEMENT OF FOREIGN JUDGMENTS

ENFORCEMENT OF FOREIGN JUDGMENTS

Edited by

DENNIS CAMPBELL

B.A., J.D., LL.M.

Member, Iowa State Bar and New York State Bar

PUBLISHED UNDER THE AUSPICES
OF THE
CENTER FOR INTERNATIONAL LEGAL STUDIES
SALZBURG, AUSTRIA

LLP

LONDON HONG KONG

1997

LLP Limited
Legal and Business Publishing Division
69–77 Paul Street
London EC2A 4LQ

SOUTH EAST ASIA
LLP Asia Limited
Room 1101, Hollywood Centre
233 Hollywood Road
Hong Kong

British Library Cataloguing in Publication Data
A catalogue record for this book is available from the British Library

ISBN 1–85978-123-3

Text set in 10/12pt Sabon by
Mendip Communications Ltd
Frome, Somerset
Printed in Great Britain by
Hartnolls Ltd
Bodmin, Cornwall

TABLE OF CONTENTS

Table of Cases vii
Table of International Legislation xvii
Table of Treaties and Conventions xxix
Contributors xxxiii

Chapter 1 – Introduction 1
Chapter 2 – Australia 3
Chapter 3 – Austria 25
Chapter 4 – Belgium 47
Chapter 5 – Canada 67
Chapter 6 – Cayman Islands 99
Chapter 7 – Denmark 125
Chapter 8 – England and Wales 137
Chapter 9 – Finland 161
Chapter 10 – France 169
Chapter 11 – Germany 179
Chapter 12 – Greece 199
Chapter 13 – Hong Kong 219
Chapter 14 – Ireland 231
Chapter 15 – Israel 245
Chapter 16 – Japan 263
Chapter 17 – Korea 283
Chapter 18 – The Netherlands 289
Chapter 19 – New Zealand 297
Chapter 20 – Nigeria 311
Chapter 21 – Norway 323
Chapter 22 – The Philippines 335
Chapter 23 – Portugal 343
Chapter 24 – Singapore 351
Chapter 25 – South Africa 363
Chapter 26 – Spain 379
Chapter 27 – Sweden 399
Chapter 28 – Switzerland 413
Chapter 29 – Taiwan 425
Chapter 30 – United States 435

Index 467

AUSTRIA

Austrian Supreme Court (OGH) 8, Ob 503/77 33
Austrian Supreme Court (OGH) EvBl 1973/53 29
Austrian Supreme Court (OGH) EvBl 1982/119 41
Austrian Supreme Court (OGH) EvBl 1984/133 27
Austrian Supreme Court (OGH) JBl 1957, 102 32
Austrian Supreme Court (OGH) JBl 1973, 321 38
Austrian Supreme Court (OGH) JBl 1988, 386 27
Austrian Supreme Court (OGH) JBl 1990, 328 30
Austrian Supreme Court (OGH) RdW 1988, 320 29
Austrian Supreme Court (OGH) RZ 1968, 73 33
Austrian Supreme Court (OGH) SZ 15/224 30
Austrian Supreme Court (OGH) SZ 24/232 34
Austrian Supreme Court (OGH) SZ 33/62 41
Austrian Supreme Court (OGH) SZ 50/25 31
Austrian Supreme Court (OGH) SZ 50/80 26
Austrian Supreme Court (OGH) SZ 51/17 30
Austrian Supreme Court (OGH) SZ 51/62 30
Austrian Supreme Court (OGH) SZ 54/11 31
Austrian Supreme Court (OGH) SZ 55/95 25
Avancini-Iro-Koziol, Bankvertragsrecht I 314 33

BELGIUM

Cass, 3 August 1848, Pas I, 358 47

CANADA

238344 BC Ltd *v.* Patriquin (1984) 57 BCLR 224 (CA) 80
Aero Trades Western Ltd *v.* Ben Hocum and Son Ltd (1974) [1975] 4 WWR 412, 51 DLR (3d) 617 (Man Co Ct) 77
Bank of Credit & Commerce International (Overseas) Ltd *v.* Gokal (1994) 99 BCLR (2d) 176 84
CIBC *v.* Brown (1986) 3 BCLR (2d) 270 (SC) 77
Clarke *v.* Lo Bianco (1991) 59 BCLR (2d) 334, 50 CPC (2d) 127, 84 DLR (4th) 244, (SC) 73
Clinton *v.* Ford (1982) 37 OR (2d) 448, 29 CP 30, 137 DLR (3d) 281 (CA) 72
Desert Place Inc *v.* Zigdon [1987] BCD Civ 3644–03 (Co. Cr) 71
Federal Deposit Insurance Corp *v.* Vanstone *et al.* (1992) 88 DLR (4th) 448 (BCSC) 71
Gacs *v.* Maierovitz (1968) 64 WWR 423; 68 DLR (2d) 345 (BCSC) 77
George Roberecht Seafoods Inc *v.* Island Fish Export Inc (1987) 43 DLR (4th) 157 (PEI CA) 77
Honolulu Federal Savings and Loan Association *v.* Robinson (1989) 64 DLR (4th) 551, 62 Man R (2d); affirmed [1991] 1 WWR 174, 14 RPR (2d) 315, 76 DLR (4th) 103, 68 Man R (2d) 311 (CA) (150 QB) 71
Hoopman Estate *v.* Imrie (1991) 57 BCLR (2d) 310 (BCSC) 76
Kaussen Estate, *Re*, 64 CBR (NS) 97, [1986] RJQ 268, 25 ETR 99, 64 CBR (NS) 97 (SC), affirmed (1988) 67 CBR (NS) 81, 12 QAC 39; sub nom Kaussen Estate (Bankrupt) *v.* Bayerische Hypotheken-Und Wechsel-Bank Aktiengesellschaft 47 DLR (4th) 626 (CA) 83
Malczewski *v.* Sansai Securities Ltd [1975] 1 WWR 462, 19 CBR (NS) 272, 49 DLR (3d) 624 (BCSC) 79
May *v.* Shell Co of Hong Kong [1981] 1 WWR 193 (BCCA) 77
McMickle *v.* Van Straaken (1992) 93 DLR (4th) 74 73
Minkler & Kirshbaum *v.* Sheppard (1991) 60 BCLR (2d) 360 (SC) 71
Mooney *v.* Orr (1994) 98 BCLR (2d) 318 78
Mooney *v.* Orr (1995) 100 BCLR (2d) 335 78
Morguard Investments Ltd *v.* De Savoye [1990] 62 BCLR (2d) 160; [1991] 2 WWR 217, 46 CPC (2d) 1 (SCC) 72, 73
Moshe-Cohen *v.* Hill Samuel & Co Ltd (1989) RJQ 2078 (CA) 96
Resorts International Hotel Inc *v.* Samuel Auerbach (1986) RJQ 2479 (CP) confirmed [1992] RJQ 302 (CA) 94
Richards *v.* Williams [1905] 11 BCR 122 74
Roglass Consultants Inc *v.* Kennedy *et al.* (1984) 65 BCLR 393 (CA) 72
Stoddart *v.* Accurpress Manufacturing Ltd (1993) 84 BCLR (2d) 194 71
United States *v.* Cassidy (1977) 79 DLR (3d) 63 (BCSC) 71

CAYMAN ISLANDS

Bank of Nova Scotia *v.* Emerald Seas Ltd [1984–85] Cayman Islands Law Reports 180 106
Ferrostaal AG *v.* Jones [1984–85] Cayman Islands Law Reports 143 108
Grand Court Cause 338 of 1988 105
Grand Court Cause 230 of 1989 .... 105, 106, 118
Kilderkin Investments Ltd (*by Clarkson Company Ltd, Receiver and Manager*) *v.* Player *and Six Others* [1980–83] Cayman Islands Law Reports 403 .... 106, 108, 117
Lake *v.* Cordoba Ltd (No 2) September 1990, Cayman Islands Law School Law Bulletin, p. 24 .... 102, 103
McAllister *v.* Tortuga Club (No 2) [1984–85] Cayman Islands Law Reports 411 100
Seymour *v.* Ebanks [1980–83] Cayman Islands Law Reports 252 113
Simmons (Trading as Simmons Enterprises) *v.* A and P Moxam, [1986–87] Cayman Islands Law Reports 175 114
Stewart (C) *v.* Ask Securities Limited [1986–87] Cayman Islands Law Reports 28 .... 103, 109
Thune and Roll *v.* Transocean Bank & Trust Co Ltd [1986–87] Cayman Islands Law Reports 358 108
Touche Ross and Company *v.* Bank Intercontinental Ltd [1986–87] Cayman Islands Law Reports 268 102

ENGLAND AND WALES

Abidin Daver, The [1984] 1 All ER 470 102
Allied Arab Bank Ltd *v.* Hajjar [1987] 3 All ER 739 301
Altertext Inc *v.* Advanced Data Communications Ltd [1985] FSR 21 16
American Cyanamid *v.* Ethicon [1975] AC 396 352
Anton Piller KG *v.* Manufacturing Processes Limited [1976] Ch 55 .... 16, 107, 142
Babanaft International SA *v.* Bassatne [1989] 1 All ER 433 106
Bayer AG *v.* Winter [1986] 1 All ER 733 301
Berliner Industriebank AG *v.* Jost [1971] 2 All ER 1513 298
Brinks-MAT Limited *v.* Elcome [1988] 3 All ER 188 301
Buchanan *v.* Rucker (1808) 9 East 192 113
Colt Industries *v.* Sarlie [1966] 1 WLR 440 101
Colt Industries *v.* Sarlie (No 2) [1966] 1 WLR 1287 113
Cook Industries Inc *v.* Galliher [1978] 3 WLR 637 16
Cretanor Maritime Co Ltd *v.* Irish Marine Management Ltd [1978] 3 All ER 164 301
Derby & Co Ltd *v.* Weldon (No 1) [1989] 1 All ER 469 106
Deutsche Schachtbau-und-Tiefbohrgesellschaft mbH *v.* R'As al-Khaimah National Oil Co [1988] 2 All ER 833 .... 107, 115
Emanuel *v.* Symon [1908] 1 KB 302 72
Judgment Debtor, A, *Re* [1939] Ch 601 7
Lister *v.* Stubbs (1890) 45 Ch D 1 301
Maharanee of Baroda *v.* Wildenstein [1972] 2 All ER 689 101
Mareva Compania Naviera SA *v.* International Bulk Carriers SA [1975] 2 Lloyd's Rep. 509 (CA) 14, 105, 141, 142, 301
Miliangos *v.* George Frank (Textiles) Ltd [1975] 3 All ER 801 .... 113, 155, 224
Nippon Yusen Kaisha *v.* Karageorgis [1975] 1 WLR 1093 141
Norwich Pharmacal Co *v.* Customs and Excise Commissioners [1973] 2 All ER 943 108
Nouvion *v.* Freeman (1889) 15 App Cas 1 247
Owens Bank Ltd *v.* Bracco and Another, *The Times*, 15 April 1991 156
Parkinson (Sir Lindsay) & Co Ltd *v.* Triplan [1973] QB 609 357
PCW (Underwriting Agencies) Ltd *v.* Dixon [1983] 2 All ER 158 301
Porzelack KG *v.* Porzelack (UK) Ltd [1987] 1 All ER 1074 234
Republic of Haiti *v.* Duvalier [1989] 1 All ER 456 106
Ridpath & Ridpath *v.* Zachner (1893) 9 TLR 538 304
Schorsh Meier GmbH *v.* Hennin [1975] 1 All ER 152 (CA) 154, 155
Siskina, The [1979] AC 210 .... 106, 118
Spiliada Maritime Corp *v.* Cansulex Ltd [1986] 3 All ER 843 .... 102, 103
Third Chandris Shipping Corporation *v.* Unimarine SA [1979] QB 645 .... 106, 118
Trendtex Trading Corp *v.* Credit Suisse [1981] 3 All ER 520 103
Wilder *v.* Wilder (1912) 56 SJ 571 304
Z Ltd *v.* A–Z and AA–LL [1982] 1 QB 558; [1982] 1 All ER 556 .... 236, 301

EUROPEAN COURT OF JUSTICE

De Cavel *v.* De Cavel (No 2) (Case 120/79) [1980] ECR 731 233
Denilauler *v.* SNC Couchet Frères (Case 125/79) [1980] ECR 1553 .... 63, 148
Gubisch *v.* Palumbo [1987] ECR 4861 233

FRANCE

Cour de Cass., Chambre Civile, 6 November 1979, *Clunet* 1980, 95, n. Ponsard, R. 1980, 588, n. Couchet, JCP 1984–23 171
Cour de Cass., Chambre Commerciale 30 May 1985, RCDIP. 1986, p. 329 n. Battifol 171
Cour de Cass., Munzer; 7 January 1964, *Clunet* 1964, 302; JCP 64, II, 13590 .... 172, 173
Cour de Cass., Simitch; 6 February 1985, RCDIP, p. 369 .... 172, 173
Paris Appellate Court, Giroux; RCDIP. 1978, p. 149 173
Paris Appellate Court, Mack Trucks; GP, 1972, 1, 209 173

GERMANY

EUGH, NJW 94, 1271 186
OLG Bremen, VersR 72, p. 250 187
OLG Frankfurt, OLGZ 93, 99 191
OLG Hamburg, GRUR 89, p. 1164 184
OLG Karlsruhe, Fam RZ 85, p. 805 185
OLG Koblenz, GRUR 89, p. 374 194
OLG München, NJW–RR 88, p. 1023 186
Supreme Court, BGH, WM 1991 et seq 179

GREECE

Judgment No 444/59 (Supreme Court), *Commercial Law Review*, 11, p. 210 216
Judgment No 15279/69 (Athens), Nov. 17, 1220 204
Judgment No 46/71, D 3, 297 (Evros) 207
Judgment No 542/71 (Piraeus) D 3, 291 217
Judgment No 72/72 (Piraeus) D 4, 187 216
Judgment No 6471/73 (Athens Appeal Court), *Shipping Law Review*, 2, p. 481 217
Judgment No 917/1974 (Piraeus) *Case Law Archives*, KE 575 216
Judgment No 1224/1975 (Supreme Court) 219
Judgment No 7960/1976 (Athens Appeal Court) 208
Judgment No 8783/1976 (Athens), *Commercial Law Revue*, 26, p. 610 201
Judgment No 137/77 (Supreme Court) Nov. 25, 1145 215
Judgment No 9931/1978 (Athens) Nov. 27, 1354 213
Judgment No 1079/81 (Supreme Court) Nov. 31, 194 209
Judgment No 2139/81 (Athens) Nov. 29, 723 203
Judgment No 12182/82 201
Judgment No 261/1983 (Volos) *Commercial Law Review* 34, p. 645 213
Judgment No 15674/83 (Athens) Nov. 32, 315 203
Judgment No 17037/89 201
Judgment No 9949/1991 (Athens) *Shipping Law Review*, 19, 436 213
Judgment No 3/1993 (Supreme Court) 208

HONG KONG

Caffall Brothers Forest Products Inc *v.* Chie Ku-yin, Trading as Sin Lie International Enterprises [1987] 1 HKLR 92 219
Tam Hing Yee *v.* Wu Tai Wai Civil Appeal No 118 of 1991: 19–21 November 1991 226

IRELAND

Campus Oil Limited *v.* The Ministry for Industry and Energy and Others (No. 2) [1983] IR 88 ... 235
Dennis *v.* Leinster Paper Company [1901] 2 IR 337 241
Fleming and Others *v.* Ranks (Ireland) Limited and Another [1983] IRLM 541 236
International Alltex Corporation *v.* Lawler Creations Limited [1965] IR 264 241

International Commercial Bank plc *v.* Insurance Corporation of Ireland plc and Meadows Indemnity Company [1989] IRLM 788 ... 234
Keenan Brothers Limited *v.* CIE (1963) 97 ILT 54 ... 235
Lynch *v.* Ardmore Studios (Irl) Ltd [1966] IR 133 ... 240
McDonnell *v.* McDonnell [1921] 2 IR 148 ... 241
Moore *v.* Attorney-General [1927] IR 569 ... 235
Ring (a bankrupt), *Re* [1869] IR 3 Eq 507 ... 235
Twomey (Dec'd), In the Goods of; O'Leary *v.* Stack (1800) 2 IR 560 ... 234
White *v.* Carroll [1897] IR 8 CL 296 ... 234

ISRAEL

BRA 156/73 Uniroyal *v.* Zion Ltd, PD 28(1), 229 ... 252
BRA 232/75 Ataba *v.* Ratsabi, PD 30(1), 477 ... 253
BRA 7/89 Rotem *v.* Nesher, PD 42(4), 683 ... 255
CA 565/62 Hirshenburg *v.* Hirshenburg, PD 16, 2851 ... 257
CA 219/64 Rozov *v.* Duda, PD 18(3), 412 ... 257
CA 121/65 Nechmad *v.* Bijou, PD 19(2), 578 ... 256
CA 364/65 Tabashi *v.* Shaki, PD 19(4), 104 ... 253
CA 72/69 Gross *v.* Express Service, PD 23(2), 807 ... 246
CA 703/70 Somech *v.* Ozer, PD 24(2), 799 ... 257
CA 146/72 Levi *v.* Goldman, PD 27(1), 321 ... 253
CA 512/73 Mery *v.* The Histadrut, PD 27(2), 670 ... 256
CA 551/73 Marioca Shipping Co *v.* Sela Insurance Co, PD 28(2), 136 ... 253
CA 577/74 Bank E.I. Britania *v.* Attorney-General, PD 29(2), 6 ... 261
CA 689/74 Basmat *v.* Eilat Municipality, PD 20(20), 281 ... 255
CA 173/75 Medinat Israel *v.* Ben-Zion, PD 30(1), 119 ... 261
CA 846/75 Onisson *v.* Deutsch, PD 30(2), 398 ... 255
CA 132/77 Genish *v.* Palmer, PD 32(2), 64 ... 255
CA 432/78 Weiler *v.* Chekaber, PD 34(2), 775 ... 251
CA 138/79 Tomer *v.* Levinsky, PD 35(1), 409 ... 261
CA 282/79 Dankner *v.* Spilsky, PD 36(1), 775 ... 250
CA 499/79 Ben-Dayan and Ors *v.* IDS International, PD 38(2), 99 ... 245, 246, 249
CA 603/80 Establishment Nahal *v.* Holiday Inns Inc, PD 35(3), 393 ... 253
CA 732/80 Arens *v.* Beit El, PD 38(2), 645 ... 253
CA 23/83 Jochimqak *v.* Kedem, PD 38(4), 309 ... 252
CA 555/84 Fucs *v.* Manchik, PD 39(3), 386 ... 248
CA 711/84 Discount Bank *v.* Fishman, PD 41(1), 369 ... 254
CA 558/85 Ilien *v.* Rothenburg, PD 40(1), 553 ... 253
CA 587/85 Stark *v.* Birnberg and Ors, PD 41(3), 227 ... 249
CA 40/87 Shukha *v.* Shukha, PD 41(3), 614 ... 256
CA 533/87 Hapoel Hamizrahi *v.* Wallach, PD 43(2), 864 ... 252
CA 257/88 Hochman *v.* Raveh, PD 38(3), 639 ... 248
CC: TA 2233/90 Okon *v.* Sachs (District Court), DCJ 1992 (A), 184 ... 256
CR 227/83 Goldberg *v.* Goldberg, PD 37(2), 778 ... 247
CR 4475, 4459/94, Solomov *v.* Sharabani (unreported) ... 258
HC 143/62 Schlezinger *v.* Minister of Interior PD 17, 225 ... 247
HC 42/64 Bank Hapoalim *v.* The Execution Office, PD 18(3), 116 ... 260
HC 635/79 Miller *v.* Miller, PD 34(2), 673 ... 247
HC 71/80 Sleich *v.* Arshied, PD 35(1), 100 ... 247
HC 268/80 Jensen Zohar *v.* Jensen, PD 35(1), 1 ... 247
HC 3914/92, Lev *v.* The Regional Rabbinical Council in Tel Aviv, PD 48(2), 491 ... 257, 258
R (Jer) 307/62 (District Court) Baruch *v.* Elias, DCJ 36, 107 ... 256
RA 246/85 Arad Insurance Co Ltd *v.* MBI Ltd, PD 41(1), 586 ... 254
RA 451/85 Adin *v.* Plato Sharon, PD 39(3), 303 ... 257
RA 383/86 Batarsa *v.* Iash, PD 41(1), 100 ... 254
RA 490/86 Johan *v.* McMillan, PD 40(4), 115 ... 253, 254
RA 10/87 Gadir *v.* Gaber, PD 41(5), 553 ... 256
RA 102/88 Ma'adanei; Avaz Hakesef *v.* Cent Or, PD 42(3), 201 ... 253
RCA 5242/95, Signal Electronics Services (1975) Ltd *v.* Denbar Ltd (handed down in September 1995; unreported) ... 258

JAPAN

Great Court of Judicature, 5 December 1933, 3670 Shinbun 16 ... 274

Osaka District Court, 9 October 1973 (Kansai Tekko Case), Final Judgment, 22 December 1977 .... 273, 278
Supreme Court, 27 February 1969, Minshu 23.2.441 279
Supreme Court, 28 November 1975 (Novo Industry SA), Minshu, 29.10.1592 264
Supreme Court, 4 October 1983, Hanji 1095/95 278
Tokyo District Council, 28 May 1970, 3 Kokusai torihiki hanreishu 538 274
Tokyo District Court, 20 July 1960, 11 Kaninshu 1522 274

KOREA

Supreme Court, 22 October 1981, 71 Da 1393 285

NETHERLANDS

Hof's-Gravenhage, 8 June 1982, NJ 1984, nr.407 291
Hoge Raad, 20 March 1913, NJ 1913, nr.636 294
Hoge Raad, 18 June 1915, NJ 1915, nr.891 294
Hoge Raad, 14 September 1924, NJ 1925 292
Hoge Raad, 25 January 1935, NJ 1935, nr.1509 295
Hoge Raad, 9 March 1939, NJ 1939, nr.1012 294
Hoge Raad, 15 January 1960, NJ 1960, nr.174 296
Hoge Raad, 7 January 1983, NJ 1983, nr.542 295
Pres.Rb.'s-Hertogenbosch, 12 June 1981, NJ 1981, nr.634 291

NEW ZEALAND

Bank of New Zealand *v.* Hawkins (1989) 1 PRNZ 451 .... 301, 309
Barton *v.* Wells, unreported, High Court, Auckland, CP 1233/87, 14 August 1987 304
Campion *v.* Campion (1986) 9 TCL 16/5; CCA (2nd) H-169 308
Club Mediteranée NZ *v.* Wendell [1989] 1 NZLR 216 300
Easton *v.* Hannan [1924] GLR 401 308
Ellison *v.* Bolton Enterprises Limited (1986) 10 TCL 4/6; CCA (2nd) H-128 303
Firth Concrete Industries Limited *v.* Duncan [1973] 1 NZLR 188 307
Hammond (D F) Land Holdings Limited *v.* Elders Pastoral Limited [1989] BC 2026; (1989) 12 TCL 42/5, 7 309
Hunt *v.* BP Oil Exploration Co (Libya) Ltd [1980] 1 NZLR 104 300
Hurst *v.* Alexander (1987) CCA (2nd) H-129 303
Hydrox Corporation Limited *v.* Moreau, unreported, High Court, Auckland, CP 2037/87, 7 December 1987 301
Jones *v.* Poffenroth, Smellie J, [1986] BCL 516; (1986) 9 TCL 16/5; CCA (2nd) H-167 308
Kuwait Asia Bank EC *v.* National Mutual Life Nominees Ltd (1990) 5 NZCLC 66, 509 (PC); [1989] 2 NZLR 43 (HC), 50 (CA) 300
Lewis *v.* Poultry Processors (Holdings) Limited (1988) 4 NZCLC 64, 508 303
Marac Finance Limited *v.* Martin [1988] BCL 304 308
Marketing Management Holdings *v.* NZI Securities Ltd [1989] BCL 1674 304
McConnell Dowell Constructors Limited *v.* Lloyd's Syndicate 396 [1988] 2 NZLR 257 300
Moffat *v.* Chambers [1989] BLC 2132 303
National Mutual Finance (1988) Ltd *v.* Shaw [1989] BCL 882 309
Neale & Haddow Limited *v.* Strawbridge [1984–1988] BCLD 1132 303
Nelson & Robertson Pty Limited *v.* Niue Products Limited, unreported, High Court, Auckland, A853/83, 31 August 1983 308
Nicholl *v.* Official Assignee [1966] NZLR 779 307
Obrist *v.* Reudi, unreported, Supreme Court, Hamilton, 14 July 1977 298
Pond *v.* Glover [1933] GLR 358 308
Proco Holdings Ltd *v.* C W Thompson [1989] BCL 350 304
Profile Developments Limited *v.* Contractors Bonding Limited [1989] BLC 559 303
Rapid Metal Development (NZ) Ltd *v.* Rusher (No 2) [1984–1988] BCLD 1005; (1987) 10 TCL 22/7 302–304
Steel *v.* Australian Guarantee Corporation (NZ) Limited, unreported, High Court, Auckland, CP 54/87, 5 June 1987 303
St Heliers Bay Coffee Lounge Limited *v.* Klass (1987) 10 TCL 41/4; CCA (2nd) A-17 304
Zietlow *v.* Simon, High Court, Auckland, CP 1336/91, 23 August 1991 301

NIGERIA

Alfred C Toepfer Inc of New York *v.* Edokpolor [1965] 1 All NLRP 292 316
Alhaja Bawaji Kuku (1991) 5 NWLRP 79 313
Anakwenze *v.* Louis Anneke & Ors (1985) Lose, pp. 41–61 318
Barzasil *v.* Visiononi Ltd (1973) NCLR 373 313
Bentworth Finance (Nigeria) Ltd *v.* Ibrahim (1969) NCLR 272 313
Gresham Life Assurance Ltd, *Re* (1973) NCLR 216 313
Macauley *v.* NAL Merchant Bank Ltd (1990) 4 NWLR 324 320
Murmansk State Steamship Line *v.* Kano Oil Olinnen Ltd (1974) NCLR p. 1 318
Nishiwaza Limited *v.* Strichand N Jethwani (1984) 12 SC, p. 234 321
Norwood (Nigeria) Ltd & Ors *v.* Tahiban GMBN (1988) 4 NWLRP 495 314
Raccah-Wahab (1958) NNLR 58 319
Somnar (Nigeria) Ltd *v.* Partenreederei M S Norwind & Anor SC 38/1986 p. 121 ..... 313, 314
Spiropoulous & Co *v.* Nigeria Rubber Co Ltd (1979) NCLRP 94 313
Swissair *v.* A C B Ltd (1971) INNLR 213 314
Vaswani *v.* Savalak (1972) 12 SC p. 77 315

THE PHILIPPINES

Arca and Javier *v.* Javier, 50 OG 3583 (1954) 337
BF Homes, Inc *v.* Court of Appeals, 190 SCRA 262 (1990) 342
Borthwick *v.* Castro-Bartolome, 152 SCRA 229 (1987) 337
Commissioner of Internal Revenue *v.* British Overseas Airways Corp., *et al.*, 149 SCRA 395 (1987) 336
Cu Unjienge Hijos *v.* Mitchell, 58 Phil. 476 (1933) 342
Eastboard Navigation Ltd *v.* Juan Ysmael & Co, Inc, 102 Phil. 1 (1957) 335
Facilities Management Corp *v.* dela Rosa, 89 SCRA 131 (1979) 336
Far East International Import & Export Corp. *v.* Nankai Kogyo Co, 116 Phil. 1053 (1962) 336
Home Insurance Co *v.* Eastern Shipping Lines, 123 SCRA 424 (1983) 335
Marshall-Wells Co *v.* Elser and Co, 46 Phil. 70 (1924) 335
Mentholatum Co *v.* Mangaliman, 72 Phil 524 (1941) 335
Nagarmull *v.* Binalbagan-Isabela Sugar Co Inc, 33 SCRA 46 (1970) 337
O'Brien *v.* del Rosario, 49 Phil. 657 (1926) 342
Perkins *v.* Benguet Consolidated Mining Corp, 93 Phil. 1034 (1953) 336
Querubin *v.* Querubin, 87 Phil. 124 (1950) 337
Rizal Commercial Banking Corporation *v.* Intermediate Appellate Court, 213 SCRA 830 (1992) 341, 342
Top-Weld Manufacturing, Inc *v.* ECED, SA, *et al.*, 138 SCRA 118 (1985) 336

PORTUGAL

Appellate Court of Oporto, 4 December 1986, *Colectânea de Jurisprudência*, 1986, Vol V, pp. 234 *et seq* 345

SINGAPORE

Bank of India *v.* Trans Continental Commodity Merchants Ltd & Another [1986] 2 MLJ 342 353
Cheah Wong Nyan *v.* Palaniappa [1935] MLJ 31 351
Hua Daily News Sdn Bhd *v.* Tan Thien Chin & Others [1986] 2 MLJ 107 352
KS Das *v.* P Suppiah [1988] 2 MLJ 445 352
Sun-Line (Management) Ltd *v.* Canpotex Shipping Services Ltd [1986] 2 MLJ 348 354
United Malayan Banking Corporation Bhd *v.* Soo Lean Tooi & Others [1984] 1 MLJ 47 351
United Overseas Bank *v.* Tjong Tjui Njuk [1987] 2 MLJ 295 351

SOUTH AFRICA

A list of commentaries on the subjects covered by Chapter 25 may be found in Schedule B on page 377

SPAIN

Constitutional Court Decision No 9/1981 of 31 March 1981 379

Constitutional Court Decision No 60/1982 of 11 October 1982 379
Constitutional Court Decision No 115/1984 of 3 December 1984 379
Constitutional Court Decision No 164/1984 of 17 December 1984 379
Constitutional Court Decision No 64/1988 of 12 April 1988 379
Supreme Court Decision of 30 June 1887 380
Supreme Court Decision of 25 March 1925 395
Supreme Court Decision of 23 April 1957 395
Supreme Court Decision of 21 May 1957 388
Supreme Court Decision of 20 June 1959 390
Supreme Court Decision of 19 December 1964 395
Supreme Court Decision of 10 July 1969 390
Supreme Court Decision of 23 March 1977 388
Supreme Court Decision of 25 February 1985 384
Supreme Court Decision of 3 July 1987 395
Territorial Court of Barcelona, 30 September 1985 382
Territorial Court of Burgos, 15 February 1983 .... 379, 380
Territorial Court of Caceres, 2 March 1975 382
Territorial Court of Madrid, 28 September 1966 382
Territorial Court of Madrid, 5 May 1977 382
Territorial Court of Madrid, 11 November 1981 380
Territorial Court of Majorca, 7 May 1968 382
Territorial Court of Oviedo, 8 May 1962 382
Territorial Court of Santa Cruz de Tenerife, 21 September 1962 380
Territorial Court of Seville, 9 December 1960 382

SWEDEN

Supreme Court (Högsta Domstolen), NJA 1956, p. 1 411
Supreme Court (Högsta Domstolen), NJA 1978, p. 593 412
Supreme Court (Högsta Domstolen), NJA 1983, p. 814 404
Supreme Court (Högsta Domstolen), NJA 1985, p. 879 412
Supreme Court (Högsta Domstolen), NJA 1991, p. 200 401
Supreme Court (Högsta Domstolen), NJA 1993, p. 182 402

SWITZERLAND

Civil Court of Basle, 1 February 1989, *Basler Juristische Mitteilungen* 1991, p. 31 417
Commercial Court of Zurich, 19 October 1990, *Blätter für Zürcherische Rechtsprechung*, vol. 89, Nr. 58 417
District of Geneva, 8 February 1990, *Semaine Judicaire*, vol. 112, p. 196 415
Federal Court (Bundesgerichterlicher Entscheid) BGE 97 I 683 420
Federal Court (Bundesgerichterlicher Entscheid) BGE 108 III 6 421
Federal Court (Bundesgerichterlicher Entscheid) BGE 109 Ia 53 422
Federal Court (Bundesgerichterlicher Entscheid) BGE 111 III 43 421
Federal Court (Bundesgerichterlicher Entscheid) BGE 112 III 47 419
Federal Court (Bundesgerichterlicher Entscheid) BGE 112 III 112 419
Federal Court (Bundesgerichterlicher Entscheid) BGE 113 II 102 420
Federal Court (Bundesgerichterlicher Entscheid) BGE 113 II 262 .... 413, 416
Federal Court (Bundesgerichterlicher Entscheid) BGE 113 III 2 421
Federal Court (Bundesgerichterlicher Entscheid) BGE 114 II 188 420
Federal Court (Bundesgerichterlicher Entscheid) BGE 115 II 67 414
Federal Court (Bundesgerichterlicher Entscheid) BGE 115 II 390 413
Federal Court (Bundesgerichterlicher Entscheid) BGE 115 III 45 421
Federal Court (Bundesgerichterlicher Entscheid) BGE 115 III 125 419
Federal Court (Bundesgerichterlicher Entscheid) BGE 115 III 148 413
Federal Court (Bundesgerichterlicher Entscheid) BGE 116 II 624 414
Federal Court (Bundesgerichterlicher Entscheid) BGE 116 II 631 417
Federal Court (Bundesgerichterlicher Entscheid) BGE 117 II 90 414
Federal Court (Bundesgerichterlicher Entscheid) BGE 118 II 188 418
Federal Court (Bundesgerichterlicher Entscheid) BGE 118 II 190 414
Federal Court (Bundesgerichterlicher Entscheid) BGE 120 II 85 417
Federal Court (Bundesgerichterlicher Entscheid) BGE 120 III 92 422

Federal Court (Bundesgerichterlicher Entscheid) BGE 1217 Ib 350 417
Supreme Court of the Canton of Zurich, 11 July 1989, *Blätter für Zürcherische Rechtsprechung*, vol. 88, Nr. 37 417
Supreme Court of the Canton of Zurich, 27 August 1990, *Blätter für Zürcherische Rechtsprechung*, vol. 89, Nr. 65 413
Supreme Court of the Canton of Zurich, 15 October 1990, *Blätter für Zürcherische Rechtsprechung*, vol. 89, Nr. 103 423
Supreme Court of the Canton of Zurich, 10 December 1990, *Blätter für Zürcherische Rechtsprechung*, vol. 89, Nr. 119 420

TAIWAN

High Court, Judgment (63) Tai Shang Tse No 426 431
High Court, Letter of Ruling (69) Wai Tiao Tze No 24039, 6 November 1980 432
High Court, Letter of Ruling (69) Yuan Tai-T'ing Tze, No 03938, 15 November 1980 432

UNITED STATES

Ackermann *v.* Levine, 788 F 2d 830 (2nd Cir 1986) 445
Al-Salamah Arabian Agencies Co Ltd *v.* Reece, 673 F Supp 748 (MDNC 1987) 457
Anderson Foreign Motors *v.* New England Toyota *et al.*, 475 F Supp 973 (D Mass 1979) 440
Atlas Chartering Services *v.* World Trade Group, 453 F Supp 861 (SDNY 1978) 460
Banco Nacionale de Cuba *v.* Sabbatino, 376 US 398 (1964) 435
Banque Libanaise Pour Le Commerce *v.* Khreich, 915 F 2d 1000 (5th Cir 1990) 442, 444
Bata *v.* Bata, 39 Del Ch 258, 163 A 2d 493 (Del 1960), cert denied 366 US 964 (1961) 443
CT Shipping Ltd *v.* DMI (USA) Ltd, 774 F Supp 146 (SDNY 1991) 455
Carl Zeiss Stiftung *v.* VEB Carl Zeiss Jena, 293 F Supp 892 (SDNY 1968), modified 433 F 2d 686 (2nd Cir 1970), cert denied 403 US 905, 91 S Ct 2205, 29 L Ed 2d 680 (1971) 447, 448
Carolina Power & Light Co *v.* Uranex, 451 F Supp 1044 (ND CA 1977) 456
Cheshire National Bank *v.* Jewett, 119 Mass 241 (1876) 439
Cunard, 733 F 2d 457 445
David L Threlkeld & Co *v.* Metallgesellschaft Ltd, 923 F 2d 245 (2nd Cir 1991) 459
De La Mata *v.* American Life Insurance Co, 771 F Supp 1375 (D Del 1991) 442, 444, 446–448
Deckert *v.* Independence Shares Corporation, 311 282 (1940) 440
Erie R R Co *v.* Tompkins, 304 US 64 (1938) 443
Ford Motor Company Limited *v.* M/S Maria Gorthon, 397 F Supp 1332 (D Md) 457
Genesco Inc *v.* T Kakiuchi & Co Ltd, 815 F 2d 840 (2nd Cir 1987) 457
Guinness-Harp Corp *v.* Jos Schlitz Brewing, 613 F 2d 468 (2nd Cir 1980) 460
Hager *v.* Hager, 1 Ill App 3d 1047, 274 NE 2d 157 (1971) 443
Hanson *v.* Denckla, 357 US 235 (1958) 446
Harrison *v.* Triplex Goldmines, 33 F 2d 667 (1st Cir 1929) 443
Hilton *v.* Guyot, 159 US 113 (1895) 442, 443, 445, 452
International Shoe Co *v.* Washington, 326 US 310 (1945) 446
Johnston *v.* Compagnie Generale Transatlantique, 242 NY 381, 152 NE 121 (1926) 443
Joseph Muller Corp Zurich *v.* Commonwealth Petro Chemicals Inc, 334 F Supp 1013 (SDNY 1971) 457
Klaxon Co *v.* Stentor Elec Mfg Co, 313 US 487 (1941) 443
McCreary *v.* CEAT, 501 F 2d 1032 (3rd Cir 1974) 456
McGee *v.* International Life Insurance Co, 355 US 220 (1957) 446
McLean Industries Inc, *Re* 68 BR 690 (Bankruptcy SDNY 1986) 463, 464
Meadows Indemnity Company Ltd *v.* Baccala & Shoop Insurance Co, 760 F Supp 1036 (EDNY 1991) 459
Mitsubishi, 473 US at 631; 105 S Ct at 3356 459
Moran *v.* Arcano, 1990 Dist, LEXIS 8161 (2 July 1990) 459
Moses H Cone Memorial Hospital *v.* Mercury Const. Corp, 460 US 1 (1983) 457
Mullane *v.* Central Hanover Bank & Trust Co, 339 US 306 (1950) 446
Newark Stereotypers' Union No 18 *v.* Newark Morning Ledger Co, 397 F 2d 594, cert. denied 393 US 954 (1968) 458
Nicol *v.* Tanner, 310 Minn 68, 256 NW 2d 796 (Minn 1976) 443
Nippon Emo-Trans Co Ltd *v.* Emo-Trans Inc, 744 F Supp 1215 (EDNY 1990) 439, 450–455
Overseas Inns SP PA *v.* United States, 911 F 2d 1146 (5th Cir 1990) 449
Panama Processes *v.* Cities Service Co, 796 P 2d 276 (Oklahoma 1990) 449
Pariente *v.* Scott Meredith Literary Agency Inc, 771 F Supp 609 (SD NY 1991) 444, 445, 449

Parsons *v.* Bank Leumi Le-Israel BM, 565 So 2d 2025 (Alabama 1990) 448, 449
Pioneer Properties Inc *v.* Martin, 557 F Supp 1354; appeal dismissed 776 F 2d 888 (DC Kan 1983) 457
Sedco Inc *v.* Petroleos Maxicanos Maxican National Oil Co, 767 F 2d 1140 (5th Cir 1985) 457
Société Nationale Algérienne Pour La Recherche, La Production, Le Transport, La Transformation et La Commercialisation des Hydrocarbures *v.* Distrigas Corporation, 18 *Collier Bankruptcy Cases* (2nd Series) at p. 865; Civil Action No 86–2012–Y (D Mass 1987) 465
Somportex Limited *v.* Philadelphia Chewing Gum Corp, 318 F Supp 161 (ED Pa 1970); 453 F 2d 435 (3rd Cir 1971); cert denied 405 US 1017 (1972) 443, 445
Sprague *v.* Rhodes Commodity Corporation, 566 F 2d 861 (2nd Cir 1977) 457
Svenska Handelsbanken *v.* Carlson, 258 F Supp 448 (D Mass 1966) 444
Tahan *v.* Hodgson, 662 F 2d 862 (DC Cir 1981) 445, 449
Teradyne Inc *v.* Mostek Corp, 797 F 2d 43 (1st Cir 1986) 440
Tonga Air Services Ltd *v.* Wayne-Fowler, 1992 Wash, LEXIS 78 (Supreme Court of Washington State Appeal No 58057–0—Opinion dated 26 March 1992 444
Venezuelan Meat Export Co *v.* United States, 12 F Supp 379 (DC Mid 1935) 443
World-Wide Volkswagen Corp *v.* Woodson, 444 US 286 (1980) 446

TABLE OF INTERNATIONAL LEGISLATION

AUSTRALIA

Admiralty Act 1988 (Commonwealth)
- s. 4(2)(c)(3)(u) ... 17
- s. 29 ... 17, 18
- s. 34 ... 18

Arbitration Act 1990 (Qld)
- ss. 4(1), 33, 53(1) ... 13

Bankruptcy Act 1966 (Commonwealth) ... 19, 21
- s. 29 ... 21, 22
  - (2)(a)(b)(5) ... 21
- s. 33 ... 20
- s. 44(1) ... 19
- s. 104(3) ... 20

Bankruptcy Rules
- r. 195B ... 21
- Sched. 5 ... 21

Commercial Arbitration Act 1984 (NSW)
- ss. 4(1), 33, 53(1) ... 13

Commercial Arbitration Act 1984 (Vic)
- ss. 4(1), 33, 53(1) ... 13

Commercial Arbitration Act 1985 (Tas)
- ss. 4(1), 33, 53(1) ... 13

Commercial Arbitration Act 1985 (WA)
- ss. 4(1), 53(1) ... 13

Commercial Arbitration Act 1986 (ACT)
- ss. 4(1), 33, 53(1) ... 13

Commercial Arbitration Act 1986 (NT)
- ss. 4(1), 33, 53(1) ... 13

Commercial Arbitration Act 1986 (SA)
- ss. 4(1), 33, 53(1) ... 13

Commonwealth of Australia Constitution Act 1990
- s. 51(xxix) ... 3

Constitution Act 1867 (Qld) ... 3
Constitution Act 1889 (WA) ... 3
Constitution Act 1902 (NSW) ... 3
Constitution Act 1934 (SA) ... 3
Constitution Act 1934 (Tas) ... 3
Constitution Act 1975 (Vic) ... 3
Conveyancing Act 1919 (NSW) ... 19
Conveyancing and Law of Property Act 1884 (Tas) ... 19

Corporations Law ... 19–21
- Chap. 4, Pt. 4.1, Div. 2 ... 22
- Chap. 5 ... 20
- s. 220 ... 20
- ss. 345, 350(14)(15) ... 22

Corporations Law—*cont.*
- s. 427(1) ... 19
- ss. 460(2), 465A(b), 471B ... 20
- s. 537 ... 18
- s. 580 ... 21, 22
- s. 581(2)(a)(b)(3)(4) ... 22
- ss. 588G, 592 ... 21

Corporations Law Regulations
- regs. 5.6.11, 5.6.39–5.6.56 ... 20
- reg. 5.6.74 ... 22
- Form 535 ... 20

Federal Court Rules, Ord. 72 ... 7
Foreign Judgments Act 1962 (Vic) ... 4
Foreign Judgments Act 1971 (SA) ... 4
Foreign Judgments Act 1973 (NSW) ... 4

Foreign Judgments Act 1991 (Commonwealth) ... 4–10, 13, 14, 19
- Pt. 2 ... 4
- s. 3(1) ... 4, 6, 9, 13
- s. 5 ... 4
  - (1) ... 4
  - (2)(3) ... 5
  - (4) ... 4, 6, 14
    - (b) ... 6
  - (5) ... 6
  - (6) ... 5, 7
  - (8)(a)(b)(c)(10) ... 6
- s. 6(1) ... 6
  - (b) ... 6
  - (2) ... 7
  - (3)(5)(6)(a)(b) ... 6
  - (7) ... 5
    - (c) ... 7
  - (8)(a)(15) ... 7
- s. 7(2)(a) ... 7
    - (iv) ... 8
  - (b) ... 10
  - (3)(a) ... 9
    - (iii) ... 8, 9
  - (b)(c) ... 9
  - (4)(b) ... 8, 9
    - (c) ... 8
  - (5) ... 9
- s. 8 ... 7
  - (d)(e) ... 6
- s. 9 ... 10
- s. 10 ... 5

Foreign Judgments Act 1991 (Commonwealth)—*cont.*
s. 13 8
s. 18 6
(1) 5
s. 19 5
(a)(b) 5
Foreign Judgments (Reciprocal Enforcement) Act 1962 (Tas) 4
Foreign Judgments (Reciprocal Enforcement) Act 1963 (WA) 4
Foreign Judgments (Reciprocal Enforcement) Act 1980 (NT) 4
Foreign Judgments (Reciprocal Enforcement) Ordinance 1954 (ACT) 4
Foreign Judgments Regulations 1992 (Statutory Rules No. 321 of 1992) 4, 5
Foreign Proceedings (Excess of Jurisdiction) Act 1984 (Commonwealth) 4
Insurance Act 1973 (Commonwealth)
s. 116(3)(6) 23
International Arbitration Act 1974 (Commonwealth) 8, 10–13
Pt. II 10
III 10, 11
s. 3(1) 10, 11
(3) 11
s. 7 10
(1) 10, 11
(2)(3)(4) 12
(5) 11
s. 8 10
(5)(7) 12
ss. 9, 19 12
s. 21 13
s. 30 11
ss. 34(a), 35(2) 13
Sched. 2 11
Law of Property Act 1936–1980 (SA) 19
Property Law Act 1958
s. 101(1)(c) 19
Property Law Act 1969–1979 (WA) 19
Real Property Act 1990 (NT) 19
Real Property Ordinance 1925 (ACT) 19
Reciprocal Enforcement of Judgments Act 1959–1981 (Qld) 4
Service and Execution of Process Act 1901 (Commonwealth) 3
Service and Execution of Process Act 1992 (Commonwealth) 3, 7
ss. 21, 105, 105(1) 4
Statutory Rules 1993 No. 143 5
Statutory Rules 1994 No. 283 5
Statutory Rules 1995 No. 35 5
Trade Practices Act (Commonwealth)
s. 46A 298

AUSTRIA

Bankruptcy Act (KO)
arts. 7(1)(2), 102 *et seq.* 41
art. 109 42
Business Corporation Act (GmbHG)
art. 42(4) 34
Cartel Act (KartG)
art. 52 34
Cheque Act (SchG)
art. 59(2) 34
Civil Procedure Code (ZPO)
arts. 57 *et seq.* 41
art. 57 .... 27, 28
(2) 28
art. 59 28
art. 402(2) 36
Code on Court Jurisdiction (JN) 25, 27
art. 41(3) 35
arts. 65–76, 75(1) 26
art. 81 .... 27, 39
art. 83 39
art. 83c 25
arts. 86a–101, 86a, 87 26
art. 88 25
(1) 26
(2) 25, 26
arts. 89, 91 26
art. 92a 25, 26
art. 92b 26
art. 93 .... 25, 26
art. 94 26
art. 96 .... 25, 26
art. 97 26
art. 99 25–27
art. 104 25
Copyright Act (UrhG)
art. 81 34
Enforcement Act (EO) 27, 30, 34
art. 1 29
lit 5 38
arts. 35, 36 41
art. 44 40
art. 78 36
arts. 79 *et seq.* 38, 39
art. 80 39
lit 3 39
art. 81(1) 32
art. 82 39
art. 84(b) 40
arts. 85, 86a 38
art. 262 31
arts. 290 *et seq.*, 294a 33
art. 296 .... 32, 33
(1) 32
arts. 370 *et seq.*, 370 .... 29, 37
arts. 371, 372 *et seq.* 37
arts. 376–377 38
arts. 378 *et seq.* 29
art. 379 30
(2) lit 1 30
lit 2 .... 30, 32
(3) 31, 35
lit 1 .... 31, 34
lit 2 31
lit 3 .... 31, 33
(4) 32

Enforcement Act (EO)—*cont.*
art. 381 lit 1 32
lit 2 .... 30, 33
art. 382 32
art. 385 37
(2)(3) 31
art. 387 27
arts. 388(1), 389(a) 35
art. 390 .... 28, 31, 35
(2) 31
(3) 36
art. 391(1)(2) 35
art. 393(1) 37
(2) 36
art. 394 36
(1)(2) 37
art. 395 35
art. 397 36
(1) 35
Patent Act (PatG)
art. 147(2) 34
Private International Law Act (IPR–G) 29
art. 4 29
Unfair Competition Act (UWG)
arts. 21, 24 34

BELGIUM

A List of Treaties and Conventions with Recognition and Enforcement as a Primary subject matter can be found on page 53
A List of Treaties and Conventions where Recognition and Enforcement is a Subsidiary issue can be found on page 54
Bankruptcy Law 63–64
art. 546 65
Code of Civil Procedure 47
Constitution
art. 191 47
Judicial Code 48–50, 58
art. 17 .... 50, 51
arts. 18, 18(2) 50
art. 19, al. 2 55
art. 570 52
art. 584 56
arts. 622–638, 624 47
art. 851 .... 48, 49
arts. 1025 *et seq.*, 1035 *et seq.* 56
art. 1148 61
art. 1389 48
art. 1413 57
art. 1414 58
art. 1415 .... 58, 59
arts. 1422–1428, 1429–1444 59
arts. 1445–1460 60
art. 1445 .... 49, 60
art. 1461 .... 50, 60
arts. 1467–1480 60
art. 1467, al. 2 49
arts. 1468, 1481–1488 61
art. 1482 48
art. 1483 49
art. 1719, al. 3 48
Law of 14 January 1993 59

CANADA

Bankruptcy and Insolvency Act, SC 1992, c.27 .... 82, 83, 86–88
ss. 2, 121 86
Bankruptcy Code
Chap. 11 88
Bill 38, 1992, c.57 (Quebec)
s. 170 92
British Columbia Supreme Court Rules
r. 47 82
Canada Shipping Act, RSC 1985, c.S–9 84
Canadian Judgments (Enforcement) Act SPEI, 1994 c.5 (Prince Edward Island) . 67
Civil Code of Lower Canada 94
art. 1220 96
Civil code of Quebec 92
art. 2730 98
art. 2822 96
art. 3083 93
art. 3129 95
art. 3148 93
art. 3155 94
arts. 3157, 3158 92
art. 3161 96
Combines Investigation Act, RSC 1985, c.C–34 85
Companies' Creditors Arrangement Act, RSC 1985, c.C–36 88
Competition Act, RSC 1985, c.19 85
Court Order Enforcement Act, RSBC 1979, c.75 .... 74, 75, 77, 79–81, 84, 85
s. 31(6) 76
Creditor Assistance Act, RSBC 1979, c.80 .. 81
Currency Act, RSC 1985, c.C–52
s. 13 74
Enforcement of Canadian Judgments Act, SBC, 1992 c.37 (British Columbia) 67
Evidence Act 74
Family Relations Act, RSBC 1979, c.121
Pt. 4.1 86
Foreign Arbitral Awards Act, RSBC 1985, c.74 .... 85, 86
Foreign Extraterritorial Measures Act, RSC 1985, c.F–29 85
International Commercial Arbitration Act, RSBC 1986, c.14 .... 85, 86
Law and Equity Act, RSBC 1979, c.224
s. 36 82
Quebec Code of Civil Procedure 94
arts. 178–180 95
art. 178 93
arts. 733, 734 97
art. 785 93
arts. 948 *et seq.*, 950 96
Transitional Law (Quebec) 92
art. 6 95
Uniform Reciprocal Enforcement of Judgments Act 75, 85

CAYMAN ISLANDS

Arbitration Law 1974
s. 22 113

Bankruptcy Law (Revised) 116
  ss. 2, 18, 34(1)(2)(3), 36 116
Companies Law (Revised)
  ss. 93, 94, 98, 100 117
Confidential Relationships (Preservation) Law 1976 107–109
  s. 2 107
  s. 3 .... 107, 122
    (2)(b)(i)(iii)(iv) 107
      (c) 109
  s. 3A 107–109, 122, 123
Court of Appeal Law 1975 99
Court of Appeal (Amendment) Law 1984 (Law 10 of 1984) 99
Evidence Law 1978
  s. 8 108
Foreign Arbitral Awards Enforcement Law (Law 30 of 1975) 113
  s. 5 113
Foreign Judgments Reciprocal Enforcement Law 1967 .... 111, 112
  Pt. 1 .... 111, 112
  s. 3(1) 111
  ss. 4(1), 6, 6(2) 112
Foreign Judgments Reciprocal Enforcement Law (Revised) 1976 110–112
  Pt. 1 113
  ss. 3(3), 7, 8 112
Fraudulent Dispositions Law 1989 110
Grand Court (Civil Procedure) Rules
  rr. 13–15 121
  r. 13 .... 101, 103
    (1)(3) 101
  rr. 14, 15 101
  r. 23 113
  r. 46 108
Grand Court Law 1975 (Law 8 of 1975) 99
  s. 13 .... 101, 102
    (1) 118
  ss. 14–19 .... 101, 119
  s. 20 .... 103, 118
    (2) 100, 104
Judicature Law 1975 114
  ss. 34–41, 42 114
  s. 46(3), 56(1) 115
Law 26 of 1979 .... 107, 122
Legal Practitioners Law 1969
  ss. 3, 4 100

DENMARK

Administration of Justice Act
  s. 478 .... 129, 130
Bankruptcy Act 127
Registration Act 126

ENGLAND AND WALES

Administration of Justice Act 1920 .... 145, 147
  Pt. II 111, 146
British Nationality Act 1981
  Scheds. 3, 6 221
Cayman Islands (Appeals to the Privy Council) Order 1984 99
Cayman Islands (Constitution) Order in Council 1972 100
Charging Orders Act 1979
  s. 2 152
Civil Jurisdiction and Judgments Act 1982 ... 138, 145, 146, 149
  ss. 5, 8(2), 18(7) 146
  s. 25 144
    (7) 143
  ss. 41, 42 138
  Scheds. 6, 7, 10, para. 1(2) 146
Civil Jurisdiction and Judgments Act 1991 . 156
Cyprus Act 1960
  s. 2(1) 222
European Communities Act 1972 154
Evidence (Proceedings in Other Jurisdictions) Act 1975 143
Foreign Judgments (Reciprocal Enforcement) Act 1933 .... 4, 111, 145–147, 149, 150, 155–157
  Pt. I 146
  s. 1(2A)(b)(c) 146
Foreign Judgments (Reciprocal Enforcement) Bilateral Treaties made under the 1933 Act. A list of these Orders can be found on page 157
Insolvency Act 1986 .... 153, 154
  s. 126 159
  s. 285(3) 158
Reciprocal Enforcements of Judgments (Canada) Order 1987 (S.I. 1987 No. 468) 150
Rules of the Supreme Court
  Ord. 11 .... 103, 139
  r. 1 103
    (1) 139
      (m) 103
  Ord. 13 103
  Ord. 23 104
  Ord. 30, r. 1 118
  Ord. 71, r. 28(1)(a)(i) 149
    r. 33(3) 150
Statutory Instrument 1985 (S.I. 1985 No. 1994) 111
Statutory Instrument 1989 (S.I. 1989 No. 1936) 155
Statutory Rule and Order 1933 dated 10 November 111
Supreme Court Act 1981 105
  s. 37 .... 105, 118
    (1) 118
Supreme Court of Judicature (Consolidation) Act 1925 101

FINLAND

Execution Act (Ulosottolaki)
  ss. 3(1), 7 161
Law 1991/1065 of 22 July 161
Law 1991/1066 of 22 July 161

Procedural Code (Oikeudenkäymiskaari) 164
s. 7 161
s. 12(4) 162

FRANCE

Civil Code
arts. 14, 15 170
Law No. 91–650 of 9 July 1991 ... 169, 171, 174, 176, 177
art. 89 171
Nouveau Code de Procédure Civile
arts. 42(1)(2), 46, 46(3), 48 170

GERMANY

Bankruptcy Act
para. 14 195
Civil Code (BGB)
para. 24 182
Code of Civil Procedure (ZPO) 179, 180
para. 5 181
para. 13 183
para. 17 .... 182, 183
paras. 20 *et seq.*, 21 183
para. 23 .... 179, 183, 191
paras. 29, 32 183
paras. 217, 226 I 190
para. 261 III 2 184
para. 274 III 190
para. 293 184
paras. 294, 294 II 187
para. 317 I 190, 191
para. 321 191
para. 328 .... 182, 195, 196
paras. 511, 545 II 190
para. 567 I 188
para. 722 .... 195, 196
I 196
para. 723 .... 195, 196
para. 802 183
paras. 916 *et seq.* 180
para. 917 I 185, 186
II 179, 185–187, 194
para. 918 183
para. 919 .... 182, 183, 186
para. 920 II 187
para. 921 I 188, 189
II 187
para. 922 I 188
II 189, 191
III 188
para. 923 .... 190, 191
paras. 924 I, II 2, 926 I 189
para. 927 194
II 195
paras. 928 *et seq.* 191, 193
para. 928 193
para. 929 I 191
II 191, 192, 194
III 191, 192
paras. 930, 930 I 3, 930 III 193

Code of Civil Procedure (ZPO)—*cont.*
para. 932 194
para. 934 I 191
paras. 935 *et seq.*, 940 180
para. 945 189
Introductory Law to the Civil Code (EGBGB)
para. 7 181

GREECE

Civil Code 199, 208, 209
art. 4 199
arts. 1257–1345, 1262, 1263, 1265–1266 208
arts. 1274, 1276, 1277, 1323(2) 209
Civil Procedure Code 199, 200, 209
arts. 3, 22 200
art. 25 .... 200, 201
arts. 27, 29, 30, 31, 31 3, 33, 34, 35 200
art. 40 .... 200, 201
arts. 162, 163, 164 211
art. 166 216
arts. 649, 682–703 201
art. 682 202
art. 683 202
(3) 200
art. 684 202
art. 686 205
art. 687(1) 203
art. 688 204
art. 689 201
arts. 690–691 205
art. 690 202
arts. 691, 2, 3 205
art. 692 1–5 203
art. 693 204
art. 695 202
arts. 696 1, 3, 697, 698, 699 204
art. 700(1) 203
(2) 203, 212
arts. 704, 705(1) 211
art. 706 209
arts. 707, 710, 711 206
art. 712 207
art. 712 2 206
art. 713 207
art. 714 206
art. 715(1)(4) 207
(5) 208
arts. 716(1), 717, 719 206
art. 725 210
arts. 728, 729(3)(5) 212
art. 731 .... 211, 212
art. 732 212
arts. 737–738 213
arts. 861–866 217
art. 921 207
arts. 946–947 212
arts. 975, 976 215
arts. 982–990 207
arts. 986, 1047 217
Commercial Code
art. 537 215
Constitution 199

Constitution—*cont.*
art. 20(1) ... 199
(2) ... 203
Law Decree 1059/71 ... 208
Law Decree 4007/1959 ... 213
Law 429/1974 ... 213
Law 841/1978 ... 213
Law 1099/1980 ... 213
Law 1149/1981 ... 213
Law 1184/1981 ... 213
Law 1242/1982 ... 213
Law 1323/1983 ... 213
art. 23(2) ... 213
Law 1450/1984 ... 213
Law 1548/1985 ... 213
art. 32(b) ... 213

HONG KONG

Bill of Rights Ordinance 1991
art. 8 ... 226
Foreign Judgments (Reciprocal Enforcement) Ordinance (c.319) ... 219–224, 229
s. 3 ... 221, 222
s. 9 ... 221, 222
(1) ... 222
Foreign Judgments (Restriction on Recognition and Enforcement) Order ... 222
Interpretation and General Clauses Ordinance (c.1) ... 221
Judgments (Facilities for Enforcement) Ordinance (c.9) ... 219–224, 229
Rules of the Supreme Court
Ord. 14 ... 220
Ord. 23 ... 220
Ord. 44A ... 225, 229
Ord. 49B ... 225, 226
Ord. 71 ... 222–224

IRELAND

Bankruptcy Act 1988 ... 239
s. 11(i)(a) ... 240
Circuit Court Rules 1950
Ord. 2(e) ... 237
Ord. 37 ... 238
Companies Acts 1963–1990 ... 233
Companies Act 1963
ss. 213, 214, 215, 284, 285 ... 239
Companies Act 1990
s. 123 ... 239
Court Orders Acts 1926–1940 ... 237
Courts Act 1981
s. 6(a)(i) ... 237
Courts (Supplemental Provisions) Act 1961
s. 45(1) ... 236
Jurisdiction of Courts and Enforcement of Judgments Act 1988 ... 231, 233, 240–242
Title III, s. 1 ... 241
arts. 26, 27, 27(4) ... 241
art. 45 ... 234
Sched. 5, Pt. I, Pt. III, para. 4 ... 232
Jurisdiction of Courts and Enforcement of Judgments Act 1993 ... 231, 240–242
Maintenance Act 1994
s. 22(a) ... 241
(b) ... 240
Maintenance Orders Act 1974
s. 12 ... 234
Rules of the Superior Courts
Ord. 9, r. 1 ... 233
Ord. 11 ... 233, 234
r. 1(a)(e)(i)(ii)(iii) ... 233
Ord. 11(A) ... 233
r. 6 ... 234
Ord. 29 ... 234
Ord. 50, r. 6 ... 235

ISRAEL

Arbitration Law 1968
ss. 16, 29 ... 253
Bankruptcy Ordinance ... 260
s. 3 ... 260
s. 5 ... 259
Bankruptcy Ordinance (New Version)
ss. 91–94 ... 260
Basic Law: Human Dignity and Liberty ... 257, 258
Civil Procedure Regulations 1984 ... 252, 259
r. 4 ... 251
rr. 352–359 ... 250
rr. 360–375, 360(4) ... 253
r. 376 ... 256, 257
r. 383 ... 257
r. 390 ... 255
r. 500 ... 252
r. 519 ... 251
Companies Ordinance
ss. 257, 266 ... 261
Dissolution of Marriage Law ... 252
Execution Law 1967
s. 22 ... 258
s. 51 ... 255
ss. 53–60 ... 256
s. 81 ... 257
Foreign Judgment Enforcement Law 1958 ... 245
s. 1 ... 246
s. 3 ... 246, 250
ss. 4, 5 ... 248
s. 6 ... 249
(a)(3) ... 246, 249, 250
(b)(c) ... 249, 250
s. 8 ... 246
s. 10(a) ... 250
s. 11 ... 248
(a)(b)(c) ... 249
Pledge Law 1967
s. 18 ... 257
Protection of Salary Law 1958 ... 254
Real Estate Law 1969
s. 90 ... 257
Women's Equal Rights Law (SH, 1951, 248)
s. 2 ... 247

JAPAN

Anti-Monopoly Law 264, 268–270
Bankruptcy Law 1922 (Law No. 71 of 1922)
art. 70 277
Civil Action Preservation Law (Minj Hozen Hou, Law No. 91 of 1989) ... 263, 266, 271, 277
art. 12 271
(1) 268, 269
(3) 272
art. 13 272
(1)(2) 272
arts. 19–20 272
art. 20 .... 267, 272
(2) 267
art. 21 272
art. 23 267
(1)(2) 267
art. 37 274
(1)(5) 274
Civil Code (Minpou) 264
arts. 2, 36 264
art. 85 271
art. 86 271
(2)(3) 271
art. 467(2) 278
art. 709 279
Civil Enforcement Law 266
art. 24 274
(3) 274
arts. 112, 122 272
Code of Civil Procedure (Minj Soshou Hou) ... 264, 266, 268
arts. 1–20 269
art. 1 269
art. 2 .... 270, 271
(2) 270
art. 4 .... 270, 271
arts. 5–20 270
arts. 5, 6, 10 270
art. 22 .... 268, 270
(1) 269
art. 23 269
(2) 269
art. 27 270
art. 45 264
art. 51 265
art. 89 279
arts. 107, 109, 110(2), 112, 114 265
art. 200 .... 273, 274
(1)(2)(3) 273
(4) 274
art. 267(2) 272
arts. 737–747, 755–765 266
Commercial Code
arts. 9, 10, 63(3), 64(1), 64(2), 188(2)2, 188(2)8, 479 270
Court Law (Saiban Hou)
arts. 24(1), 33(1)(i) 269
Foreign Exchange and Foreign Trade Control Law 274

KOREA

Arbitration Law 286
Code of Civil Procedure 283, 285–288
arts. 107, 112 285
art. 203 .... 285, 286
arts. 696–713, 714–723 283

NETHERLANDS

Bankruptcy Act (Faillissementswet)
art. 23 296
art. 33(2) 295
Burgerlijke Rechtsvorderingsverdragen 1954
art. 17 290
Civil Code (Burgelijk Wetboek)
arts. 3:299, 3:300 293
Code of Civil Procedure (Wetboek van burgerlijke rechtsvordering)
art. 86 294
art. 126 289
art. 152 290
arts. 289, 292 291
art. 350(1) 294
arts. 353, 414 290
art. 430(2) 293
(3) 294
art. 431 292
art. 432 294
art. 434 295
art. 435 293
(1) 294
arts. 436–447, 439(1), 440, 445 294
art. 446 295
art. 447 291
art. 448 .... 291, 294
art. 463 295
(1) 295
arts. 464, 466, 470, 474 295
arts. 475d–475f, 491–500 294
art. 491 293
art. 502(1) 294
art. 506(2) 295
arts. 514–529, 562a–582 295
art. 563(2) 294
arts. 585–611 293
art. 589 295
art. 598 293
art. 599(1) 294
art. 611a–i 293
art. 700(1)(3) 291
art. 701 290
art. 703 291
art. 709 291
(1)(3) 291
(4) 290
art. 710 291
(1)(2) 291
arts. 711(1), 714, 718, 725 291
art. 985 *et al.*, 985–994 292
arts. 985, 986, 987, 988(2), 989, 990 292
art. 992 293
Judicial Organisation Law (Wet op de Rechterlijke Organisatie)
arts. 1, 38–42, 53, 54 3°, 69, 91, 94 289

NEW ZEALAND

Commerce Act 1986 ... 7
ss. 36A, 98H, 99A ... 6
Companies Act 1955 ... 310
District Courts Act 1947
ss. 96, 96A ... 310
District Courts Rules 1948
rr. 244A–W, 264–278A, 579(a)(b) ... 310
District Court Rules 1992 ... 310
Pt. X, rr. 564–668 ... 310
High Court Rules ... 297, 298
Pt. VI ... 304
r. 131 ... 300
r. 219 ... 299
r. 220 ... 299, 300
r. 224 ... 299
r. 236B ... 301
r. 331 ... 302, 303
(1) ... 302, 303
(3) ... 303
rr. 335, 437, 547 ... 304
rr. 548, 549, 550, 551, 552 ... 305
r. 556 ... 309
(2)(c)–(e) ... 309
(3) ... 309
r. 558 ... 305, 309
r. 567 ... 302, 308, 309
rr. 570, 573, 574 ... 307
r. 576 ... 308
r. 578 ... 307
rr. 579, 579(c)–(e), 580(2)(a), 581, 582, 583, 584, 585, 586 ... 306
r. 588 ... 308
rr. 606, 608, 610 ... 305
Insolvency Act ... 310
Judicature Act 1908
s. 16 ... 300
s. 56 ... 298
Law Reform (Miscellaneous Provisions) Bill 298
Limitation Act 1950
s. 4(1) ... 298
Reciprocal Enforcement of Judgments Act 1934 ... 298
Pts. I, IA ... 298

NIGERIA

Arbitration and Conciliation Decree 1988 .. 317
s. 1(2) ... 317
s. 4(d) ... 316
ss. 31(1)(2)(3), 32, 51, 52, 52(2), 54 ... 317
Sched. 2 ... 317
Bankruptcy Act 1979, s. 43(1) ... 322
Civil Procedure Rules ... 313
Constitution of the Federal Republic of Nigeria 1979 ... 311
ss. 42, 236 ... 312
s. 251 (I–III) ... 317
Evidence Act ... 319
Exchange Control Act 1962 ... 316
Foreign Judgments (Reciprocal Enforcements) Act 1960 ... 315
Foreign Judgments (Reciprocal Enforcements) Act 1960—*cont.*
s. 3(1) ... 316
s. 12(1) ... 315
High Court (Civil Procedure) Rules, Imo State
Ord. 16 ... 319
Ord. 23 ... 321, 322
High Court (Civil Procedure) Rules, Lagos State
Ord. 3, r. 4 ... 320
Ord. 10 ... 320, 321
r. 1 ... 320, 321
rr. 2, 3 ... 321
Ord. 47, r. 2 ... 318
Judgment (Enforcement) Rules ... 318
National Office of Industrial Property Act 1979 ... 316
s. 4(d) ... 316, 317
s. 5(2) ... 316
s. 6(2) ... 317
ss. 7, 8 ... 316
Sheriffs and Civil Process Act ... 318
Sheriffs and Civil Process Law ... 318
s. 71 ... 318
Sheriffs and Civil Process Law, Imo State
s. 52.05 ... 318

NORWAY

Civil Procedure Act ... 332
Chap. 13 ... 324
s. 32 ... 324, 325
s. 168a ... 325
s. 182 ... 324
Enforcement Act 1992 ... 323, 326
Chaps. 14, 15 ... 329
s. 4–1(f) ... 326
ss. 4–15, 4–17 ... 325
s. 7–2, 11–2 ... 324
s. 14–1 ... 328
s. 14–2 ... 330
s. 14–3 ... 329
s. 14–6 ... 329, 330
s. 14–7 ... 331
s. 14–8 ... 332
s. 14–11 ... 333
s. 14–12 ... 330
s. 14–13 ... 331
ss. 14–14, 14–15, 14–17 ... 333
s. 15–2 ... 329

THE PHILIPPINES

Civil Code ... 340
arts. 2236–2251, 2242(2), 2243 ... 341
Corporation Code ... 335
ss. 123–126, 123, 133 ... 335
Insolvency Law (Act No. 1956) ... 341
ss. 3, 9 ... 341
s. 59 ... 342

Labour Code
art. 110 341
Presidential Decree No. 902–A (PD 902–A) ... 341, 342
s. 5 341
s. 6(c) 342
Rules of Court
r. 39, s. 50 336
r. 57, s. 1 337
ss. 2, 3, 4, 8, 12 338
ss. 15, 16 339
r. 59, ss. 1, 3, 4, 7, 8 340

PORTUGAL

Civil Code
art. 403, No. 1 348
Civil Procedure Code 1939
art. 4 343
Civil Procedure Code 1961 343
art. 2 346
art. 65, No. 1 al.(d) 346
arts. 381 *et seq.* 343
art. 382, No. 1 345
al.(a) 344
arts. 384, Nos. 2, 3, 386 345
arts. 388, No. 1, 393 348
arts. 396, No. 1, 397 No. 4 347
arts. 400, Nos. 1, 2, 401, 401, Nos. 1, 3 . 344
arts. 402, 412, No. 1 348
art. 421 347
arts. 423, No. 2, 424, Nos. 1, 2, 425, 614, 622, 819, 822 348
art. 1198, No. 1, 1205, Nos. 1, 2, 1315 .. 349
Code of Judicial Costs 344

SINGAPORE

Arbitration Act (cap. 10) 355
Arbitration (Foreign Awards) Act (cap. 10A) 352, 353, 355
ss. 5(1)(2), 6, 7(2)(3)(4) 356
s. 20 355
Bankruptcy Act 359, 361
s. 74(1) 360
s. 76(3)(6)(ii) 359
ss. 105(1)(2), 106(1)(2) 360
Companies Act (cap. 50)
ss. 255(1)(2), 258 360
s. 260 361
ss. 262(3), 291(6)(a) 360
s. 299(1) 361
(2) 360
ss. 334(1)(2), 335(3) 361
Reciprocal Enforcement of Commonwealth Judgments Act (cap. 264) 352–354
s. 2(1) 353
s. 3 353
(1)(2) 353
(3)(a)(c) 354
s. 5(1) 353
s. 6 352
Reciprocal Enforcement of Commonwealth Judgments Act (cap. 264). *A list of the countries to which this Act has been extended can be found on page 355*
Reciprocal Enforcement of Foreign Judgments Act (cap. 265) 352, 354
s. 2(1) 354
s. 3(1) 354
(2)(a)(b)(3) 355
s. 4(1) 354
(3)(4) 355
s. 5(1)(a)(b) 355
s. 8 352
s. 9(1) 354
Rules of Court
Ord. 14 .... 351, 352
Ord. 29 352
r. 10 357
Ord. 30 359
rr. 1(1)(2)(3), 2, 4 359
Ord. 45 357
Ord. 46 357
r. 4(1)(2)(3) 357
(4) 358
rr. 6, 14–21, 24 358
Ord. 47 357
Ord. 49, rr. 1, 2, 3, 4, 5, 7 358
Ord. 50 358
r. 1(1)(2) 359
Ord. 67, rr. 2, 3 356
r. 9 357
Supreme Court of Judicature Act (cap. 322) 351
ss. 15, 16, 17 351

SOUTH AFRICA

Insolvency Act (No. 24 of 1936) 373
Protection of Businesses Act 1978 (No. 99 of 1978) 368, 370
s. 1(a) 367
Reciprocal Enforcement of Civil Judgments Act 1966 (No. 9 of 1966) 367
A list of other relevant South African legislation can be found in Schedule A to Chap. 25 on page 376

SPAIN

Act No. 96/1966 of 23 July 1966 on the Competence of Municipal or Local Judges
ss. 1428, 1429 382
Act No. 8/1980 of 10 March 1980 (Labour Act)
s. 32 397
Act No. 34/1984 of 6 August 1984 382
Act No. 6/1985 of 1 July 1985 on the Judiciary
ss. 7, 21.1 .... 379, 387
s. 56 385

Act No. 7/1985 of 1 July 1985 on the Rights and Freedoms of Foreign Citizens in Spain
s. 29.1 ... 379, 387
Act No. 19/1985 of 16 July 1985 on the Bill of Exchange and Cheque
ss. 66–68, 96, 153 ... 389
Act No. 36/1988 of 5 December 1988 on Arbitration
ss. 52 *et seq.* ... 390
Act No. 31/91 of 30 December 1991 ... 392
Act No. 10/1992 of 30 April 1992 on Urgent Measures of Procedural Reform ... 382, 388
Chattel Mortgage Act, ss. 1, 2, 19, 52 ... 395
Civil Code ... 381
s. 8.2 ... 383, 387
s. 27 ... 379, 383
s. 28 ... 387
ss. 1587 *et seq.* ... 395
s. 1785 ... 382
s. 1815 ... 390
ss. 1921 *et seq.* ... 396
s. 1922 ... 396, 397
ss. 1923, 1926, 1927 ... 396
Code of Civil Procedure ... 381
ss. 51, 71 ... 383
s. 153 ... 391
s. 191 ... 390
s. 369 ... 384, 385
s. 374 ... 384
ss. 376 *et seq.* ... 391
ss. 381, 385, 421, 476 ... 390
s. 488 ... 394
s. 499 ... 382
s. 534 ... 379, 380, 387
s. 600 ... 383, 385, 386
s. 601 ... 386
s. 692, 728, 919 ... 390
s. 921 ... 392
s. 922 ... 394
ss. 924, 925, 926 ... 391
ss. 927, 928 ... 392
s. 949 ... 391
ss. 951 *et seq.* ... 387
s. 951 ... 384, 385, 390
s. 952 ... 384, 385
ss. 953, 954 ... 384, 386
s. 955 ... 385, 386
ss. 956, 957 ... 386
s. 958 ... 387
ss. 966, 968, 1007, 1010, 1069, 1175, 1179 ... 393
ss. 1273, 1277 ... 398
ss. 1378 *et seq.* ... 396
ss. 1378, 1381 ... 397
s. 1382 ... 398
ss. 1397 *et seq.*, 1400.1, 1400.2, 1401 ... 382
s. 1405 ... 383
s. 1409 ... 393
ss. 1411, 1416 ... 383
ss. 1417, 1427 ... 390
s. 1429 ... 387–389, 395
ss. 1435 *et seq.* ... 387
Code of Civil Procedure—*cont.*
ss. 1435, 1436 ... 392
s. 1439 ... 388
s. 1440 ... 388, 392
s. 1442 ... 392, 393
s. 1445 ... 388, 393
s. 1447 ... 388, 393, 395
ss. 1450, 1453 ... 393
ss. 1459, 1460 ... 388
s. 1462 ... 389
ss. 1463 *et seq.*, 1468, 1469 ... 388
ss. 1472, 1473, 1474 ... 389
s. 1476 ... 382
ss. 1477.1, 1481–1531, 1481, 1482, 1483 394
s. 1513 ... 395
ss. 1532 *et seq.* ... 391
ss. 1535, 1537, 1541, 1543 ... 394
ss. 1544, 1545, 1549, 1550 ... 389
s. 1687 ... 391
s. 1722 ... 381, 382, 390
s. 1803 ... 382
Code of Criminal Procedure
s. 281 ... 379
Commercial Code ... 381
ss. 98, 196, 208, 276, 320, 340, 372, 375, 376, 511, 580, 667, 704, 730 ... 397
ss. 876, 908 *et seq.*, 912 ... 396
ss. 913, 913.1, 913.2–5, 914.1 ... 397
Constitution
s. 24.1 ... 379, 387
Instrument of 13 April 1977 ... 379
Instrument of 26 September 1979 ... 379
Real Estate Mortgage Act of 8 February 1946 ... 381
s. 25 ... 397
s. 42.1 ... 382
ss. 50, 51, 63 ... 397
s. 86 ... 393
ss. 104, 126, 127, 129, 130–135, 131.1–3 395
s.131.15 ... 396
s. 138 ... 395
s. 168 ... 397
Real Estate Mortgage Act Regulation of 14 February 1947
s. 199 ... 393
Suspension of Payments Act of 26 July 1922
ss. 113 *et seq.* ... 396
s. 1100 ... 397

SWEDEN

Arbitration Act ... 401, 410
Bankruptcy Act ... 411
Chap. 2, s. 9 ... 411
Code of Judicial Procedure (Rättegangsbalken) ... 400, 403, 405, 407
Company Names Act ... 407
Copyright Act ... 407
Enforcement Code (Utsöknignsbalken) ... 410
Chap. 16, s. 10 ... 408
International Railway Traffic Act ... 410
Maritime Act
Chap. 4 ... 408

TABLE OF TREATIES AND CONVENTIONS

Accession Convention 1978 231
Accession Convention 1982 231
Accession Convention 1989 .... 231, 232
Arrest Convention 1952 (Brussels) 330
art. 7 408
Austrian/Finland Convention on the Recognition and Enforcement of Civil and Commercial Judgments 1986 .... 161, 169
Austrian/German Bankruptcy Convention, art. 14 41
Austrian/German Enforcement Treaty, arts. 8–10 29
Berne Convention on International Transport of Goods by Railway 1970 (CIM) 384
s. 56 197
Berne Convention on Transport of Passengers and Baggage by Railway 1970 (civ) 384
s. 52 197
Brussels Convention of 19 June 1948 331
Brussels Convention 1967 331
Brussels Convention on Recognition and Enforcement of Foreign Judgments in Civil and Commercial Matters 1968 .... 30, 37, 38, 49, 53, 62, 63, 83, 135, 138–141, 143, 145–148, 155, 156, 162, 169, 172, 186, 197, 213, 214, 231–234, 240, 241, 292, 294, 297, 349
art. 1 .... 148, 231
(2) 231
art. 2 .... 169, 232, 291
art. 3 .... 170, 191, 291
art. 5 .... 138, 232
(1) 170, 232
(3) 170
art. 6(1) 170
art. 13 .... 138, 139
art. 16 .... 138, 232, 234
(1) 232
(a) 232
(2) 232
art. 17 .... 138, 139, 170, 234
art. 18 138
art. 20 147
Brussels Convention on Recognition and Enforcement of Foreign Judgments in Civil and Commercial Matters 1968—*cont.*
art. 21 233
art. 22 146
art. 24 .... 140, 141, 144, 236, 347, 348
art. 25 .... 62, 140, 214
art. 26 146
art. 27 .... 147, 149
(1) 147
(2) 62, 147
(3) 147, 148
(4) 148
art. 28 147–149
s.29 147
arts. 31–49 147
art. 31 .... 149, 197
art. 32 149
art. 33 .... 48, 149
art. 34 .... 147, 149, 151
art. 35 151
art. 38 .... 49, 149
art. 40 150
art. 46 149
art. 47 149
(1) 149
arts. 55, 56(1) 53
art. 57 .... 54, 150
art. 59 150
Canada/United Kingdom Convention for the Reciprocal Recognition and Enforcement of Judgments in Civil and Commercial Matters (1984, SC 1984 c.32) 83, 84
Convention concerning Decisions on Child Support (Hague 1958) 416
Convention on Immunity for State-owned Vessels 1926/1934 331
Convention on Precautionary Attachment of Aircraft (Rome 1933) 331
Convention regarding Marital Separation and Divorce (Hague 1970) 416
Copenhagen Convention on Recognition and Enforcement of Judgments in Civil and Commercial Matters in Scandinavia 1977 .... 161, 166, 167

EC Judgment Convention. *See* Brussels Convention on Recognition and Enforcement of Foreign Judgments in Civil and Commercial Matters 1968.
European Convention concerning International Commercial Arbitration (Hague, 21 April 1961) 197
European Convention on the Immunity of States 420
European Treaty for Protecting Human Rights and Basic Freedoms (Rome 1950),
art. 6 379
France-Quebec Agreement on the Entente between Quebec and France regarding Judicial Mutual Aid in Civil, Commercial and Administrative Matters, RSQ 1985, c.A–20.1, Sched.,
s. 1 92
Franco-Swiss Treaty of 1869/1935 422
Geneva Convention on International Commercial Arbitration 1961 384
Geneva Convention on International Transport of Goods by Road (19 May 1956) (CMR) 384, 403
s. 31 197
Greece/Germany Agreement relating to the Recognition and Enforcement of Judgments 1961 213
Hague Convention 1905 (Rélative à la Procedure Civile) 403, 416
ss. 17, 18, 19 251
Hague Convention of 5 October 1961 .. 385, 386
Hague Convention 1973 197
Hague Convention on Civil Procedure (1 March 1954) 162, 197, 265, 273, 384, 403, 415, 416
art. 17 .... 183, 324
Hague Convention on International Legal Aid (25 October 1980) 162, 403, 415, 416
Hague Convention on Notification or Transfer Abroad of Judicial and Nonjudicial Documents in Civil and Commercial Matters (15 November 1965) 386, 416
Hague Convention on the Service of Process Abroad 1965 104
Hague Convention on Taking of Evidence (18 March 1970) 416
International Convention on Civil Liability for Oil Pollution Damage 1969 84
International Treaty of Civil and Political Rights 1966,
art. 14 379
Israel/Germany Convention for the Reciprocal Recognition of Court Decisions in Civil and Commercial Matters and for the Enforcement of such Decisions 1977 .... 249, 250
Israel/Republic of Austria Convention for the Reciprocal Recognition and Enforcement of Judicial Decisions in Civil and Commercial Matters 1966 250
Israel/United Kingdom and Northern Ireland Convention providing for the Reciprocal Recognition and Enforcement of Judicial Decisions in Civil Matters 1970 250
Japan/UK Consular Convention,
art. 25 273
Japan/US Consular Convention,
art. 17(1)e 273
Lugano Convention on Jurisdiction and the Enforcement of Judgments in Civil and Commercial Matters 1988 ..... 25, 30, 37, 38, 138, 156, 161, 165, 171, 231, 240, 242, 349, 404, 405, 408, 409, 411, 416, 420–423
art. 3 .... 324, 422
art. 16 .... 39, 405, 406
paras 1.a, 3 423
art. 17, para. 1.b 422
arts. 21, 22 .... 156, 157
art. 24 .... 164, 348, 404
arts. 31 *et seq.* 410
art. 33 40
Maritime Liens Convention 1926 330
Maritime Liens Convention 1967 330
New York Convention of 20 June 1956 .... 240, 241, 403
New York Convention 1958 316
New York Convention on the Recognition and Enforcement of Foreign Arbitral Awards 1958 .... 10, 85, 86, 113, 161, 197, 286, 288, 295, 317, 326, 355, 384, 416, 456, 458, 459
art. II 458
(1) 11
art. III 458
arts. V, VI 459
Nordic Judgment Convention 135
Norway/UK Treaty of January 1931,
art. 11 324
Protocol to the Brussels Convention on Recognition and Enforcement of Foreign Judgments in Civil and Commercial Matters 1968,
art. II 150
Rome Convention on the Law Applicable to Contractual Obligations 1980 413
Rome Convention 1990 .... 240, 241
Spanish Bilateral Treaties: A list of these can be found at f/n 14 on page 380 and again at f/n 30 on page 384
Swiss Bilaterial Conventions: A list of these can be found on page 416
Treaty of Commerce, Friendship and Navigation between the ROC and the US 1948,
art. VII 431
Treaty of Rome,
art. 106 .... 154, 155

Treaty on International Railway Traffic (9 May 1980) 403
UNCITRAL Model Law on International Commercial Arbitration 1985 ..... 10, 11, 13, 85, 86
Chap. VIII 10
arts. 1(3)(4), 7(1)(2) 11
art. 8 13
UNCITRAL Model Law on International Commercial Arbitration 1985—*cont.*
(1) 11, 12
(2) 12
arts. 34(2), 35(2), 36(1) 12
Uniform Rules on International Transport 1980 416
Warsaw Convention 1929 .... 413, 416

CONTRIBUTORS

NIKOS ANAGNOSTOPOULOS: Lallis Voutsinos Anagnostopoulos, Piraeus, Greece
PETER M. ANDERSEN: Berning Schlüter Hald, Copenhagen, Denmark
MARION BARBIER: Jeantet & Associés, Paris, France
M. J. M. BENNETT: Webber Wentzel, Johannesburg, South Africa
MICHAEL C. BLACK: Barrister, Auckland, New Zealand
OLE BORCH: Berning, Schlüter, Hald, Copenhagen, Denmark
KNUT BOYE: Simonsen & Musæus, Oslo, Norway
ROBERT BYRD: Jeantet & Associés, Paris, France
CHRISTIAN CAMPBELL: Center for International Legal Studies Salzburg Austria
DENNIS CAMPBELL: Center for International Legal Studies, Salzburg, Austria
SHELLY CHEN: Attorney at Law, Taipei, Taiwan
JACQUELINE P. E. CONOLLY SMELLIE: Ritch & Conolly, Grand Cayman, British West Indies
PEDRO DE ALBUQUERQUE: Albuquerque & Albuquerque, Lisbon, Portugal
JOSEPH DOZIE: Dozie & Co, Owerri, Nigeria
ISMAËL EL MECKY: Van Benthem & Keulen, Utrecht, The Netherlands
MICHAEL A. FITCH: Russell & DuMoulin, Vancouver, Canada
JOHN A. GLACKIN: Gerrard Scallan & O'Brien, Dublin, Ireland
CHRISTIAN HERBST: Schoenherr Barfuß Torggler & Partners, Vienna, Austria
SAMUEL JARMAN: Daikin Industries Ltd, Kyoto, Japan
ROBERT J. KALER: Gadsby & Hannah, Boston, Massachusetts, USA
LENNART KANTER: Advokatfirman Cederquist, Stockholm, Sweden
KAREN KAO: Van Benthem & Keulen, Utrecht, The Netherlands
YOUNG MOO KIM: Kim & Chang, Seoul, Korea
RACHEL LEVITAN: R Levitan & Co, Tel Aviv, Israel
FRANCISCO ED. LIM: Angara Abello Concepcion Regala & Cruz, Manila, Philippines
CARYN MACKENZIE: Field Fisher Waterhouse, London, UK
MARIA-PIA MIDENBÄCK: Advokatfirman Cederquist, Stockholm, Sweden
ZEKE C. W. MOK: Deacons, Hong Kong
DAVID ROYLANCE: Middletons Moore & Bevins, Melbourne, Australia
CHRISTINE SARTINI VANDENKERCKHOVE: Pissoort & Sartini, Brussels, Belgium
PEGGY SHARON: R Levitan & Co, Tel Aviv, Israel
JÜRGEN J. SIEGER: Deringer Tessin Herrmann & Sedemund, Köln, Germany
ROGER P. SIMARD: MacKenzie Gervais, Montreal, Canada
SEI BEE TAN: Arthur Loke & Partners, Singapore

JENS TILLQVIST: Advokatfirman Cederquist, Stockholm, Sweden
DANIEL URECH: Hürlimann Urech & Uhlmann, Zürich, Switzerland
UWE UUSITALO: Castrén & Snellman, Helsinki, Finland
ANTONIO VINAL: Antonio Vinal & Co., Madrid, Spain
SANDRO VISINI: Hürlimann Urech & Uhlmann, Zürich, Switzerland

CHAPTER 1

INTRODUCTION

The increasing tempo of international commerce—sales, licensing, joint ventures, mergers, acquisitions, and lending—yields a by-product in addition to profit: debt.

When a transaction goes sour, creditors—both judgment and pre-judgment—often find that the assets which they must pursue are outside their own jurisdictions. The solution is not merely to perfect a domestic judgment against a foreign debtor, nor to succeed in executing that judgment abroad. The most important step is to ascertain the whereabouts, the extent, and the accessibility of the debtor's assets and to preserve those assets pending judgment. Indeed, the very act of identifying and securing assets often provides a vital leverage in stimulating settlement and compromise, sometimes eliminating the need to proceed to judgment.

This book seeks to set out the basic parameters which govern the strategies and remedies available to the foreign creditor in various jurisdictions.

In the following chapters, each author has traced the steps necessary for a foreign creditor to begin the process of securing assets in his or her jurisdiction.

The basic questions, of course, are how available are the domestic courts to foreign creditors and foreign litigants and what requirements for the posting of a bond or other security for costs are imposed on the foreign party. If the courts are not readily available, the tracing of assets may prove to be a futile exercise at best; if the costs of proceeding are high, they may weigh against any effort which might be undertaken in a foreign jurisdiction—and indeed will influence both parties in any settlement negotiations.

Given the availability of the courts and that costs will not be a bar to proceeding, the foreign creditor must determine the degree to which his title to the debt—through final judgment or otherwise—must be perfected in his jurisdiction in order that he proceed abroad. And he must ascertain, as well, the nature of pre-judgment or provisional remedies which are available—attachment, seizure, injunction, judicial mortgage or pledge, or writ of execution—and the procedural steps required for the appropriate remedy.

The foreign creditor also must be aware of the impact that the debtor's bankruptcy or composition may have on his claim, if only from the standpoint of using the threat of bankruptcy to force the debtor to settlement.

Finally, the prudent creditor will determine whether his rights—and/or those of the debtor—may be affected by international conventions or multilateral or bilateral treaties.

It is hoped that the following chapters, by providing a survey of each of these issues, will serve as a useful starting point for any creditor—and creditor's counsel—in pursuing claims abroad. Obviously, "starting point" is a key phrase here. The material herein does not purport to substitute for the advice and guidance of local counsel, and any reader is cautioned that the expectation from any survey such as this should be of assistance in forming the right questions, not in ascertaining the correct answers.

Center for International Legal Studies
Salzburg, Austria

DENNIS CAMPBELL

10 September 1996

CHAPTER 2

AUSTRALIA

INTRODUCTION

The Commonwealth of Australia comprises six states, two mainland territories, and several external territories. The Australian legal system originates from a United Kingdom common law background. There is a federal court system (with defined jurisdiction) and, in addition, the states and major territories have their own courts. The High Court of Australia sits as the final appeal court, with jurisdiction over constitutional and other matters from inferior federal and state courts.

The Commonwealth was formed through the federation of the Australian states (then known as colonies) in 1901. As individual entities, the Commonwealth of Australia, the six states and, to a lesser extent, the mainland territories, are politically and legally autonomous.

Each part of the Commonwealth of Australia has been described as a foreign jurisdiction *vis-à-vis* each other part of the Commonwealth[1] and, as a result, judgment enforcement law applies as between the states and the territories as it does in relation to judgments from foreign countries.

Under powers contained in the state and Commonwealth constitutions,[2] legislation has been enacted to enable the enforcement of judgments of the courts of the states and territories elsewhere within Australia, to enforce judgments of foreign courts within Australia, and to enforce foreign arbitral awards and agreements.

ENFORCEMENT OF AUSTRALIAN JUDGMENTS IN OTHER PARTS OF AUSTRALIA

The enforcement of Australian judgments in other parts of Australia is governed by the Service and Execution of Process Act 1992 (Commonwealth). This Act replaced the Service and Execution of Process Act 1901 (Commonwealth) and provides that a judgment of any court of any state or part of the Commonwealth may be enforced in any other state or part of the Commonwealth, by the registration and then enforcement of that judgment, unless any person against whom the judgment has been

1. *Pezet* v. *Pezet* (1947) 47 SR (NSW) 45.

2. Commonwealth of Australia Constitution Act 1990, s. 51(xxix); Constitution Act 1902 (New South Wales); Constitution Act 1975 (Victoria); Constitution Act 1867 (Queensland); Constitution Act 1934 (South Australia); Constitution Act 1889 (Western Australia); Constitution Act 1934 (Tasmania).

entered successfully applies to the court in which the certificate of judgment is to be registered for a stay of proceedings.[3]

The registrar of the court to which the application for registration is made "must register the judgment" if it is proper on its face.[4]

Upon registration in another Australian jurisdiction, a judgment has the same force and effect in that jurisdiction as if that judgment had originally been made in that jurisdiction, and may thereafter be enforced in accordance with the procedures of the courts within it.

ENFORCEMENT OF FOREIGN JUDGMENTS WITHIN AUSTRALIA

In 1991 the Commonwealth enacted legislation to enable the execution of foreign judgments in Australia by registration in Australian superior courts. The Foreign Judgments Act 1991 (Commonwealth) ("the Act") became effective from 27 June 1991.[5] The Act was introduced with a view to facilitating "international enforcement of Australian judgments by providing an efficient and effective regime for enforcing foreign judgments in Australia".[6]

The Act is substantially based on the superseded scheme of uniform legislation of the States and Territories,[7] which was based, in turn, on the Foreign Judgments (Reciprocal Enforcement) Act 1933 (UK). The class of judgments registrable under the Foreign Judgments Act 1991 (Commonwealth) is broader than the class of judgments that was registrable under the uniform legislation.

The Act provides for the registration in superior courts of Australia of judgments given by certain courts in other countries in defined circumstances. The main criterion is that the courts of the other country in which the judgment was given would afford substantial reciprocity in their treatment of the judgments of superior courts of Australia.[8]

The Act applies primarily to money judgments of superior courts of countries specified in the Foreign Judgments Regulations 1992.[9] Regulations have been made extending the application of the Act to judgments of certain specified inferior courts of

3. Service and Execution of Process Act 1992 (Comm.), s. 105.

4. *Ibid.*, s. 105(1). Registrars have no jurisdiction to decline to register a sealed copy of a judgment which is proper on its face: *Ex Parte Penglase* (1903) 3 SR (NSW) 680.

5. Except for s. 21 (which amends the Foreign Proceedings (Excess of Jurisdiction) Act 1984 (Comm.)) which came into operation on 27 October 1991.

6. Owen F. L. Jones, *The New Commonwealth Foreign Judgments Legislation* (Attorney-General's Department, Canberra, Australia). See also Australian Law Reform Commission Report No. 80 (1996) *Legal Risk in International Transactions.*

7. New South Wales: Foreign Judgments Act 1973; Victoria: Foreign Judgments Act 1962; Queensland: Reciprocal Enforcement of Judgments Act 1959–1981; South Australia: Foreign Judgments Act 1971; Western Australia: Foreign Judgments (Reciprocal Enforcement) Act 1963; Tasmania: Foreign Judgments (Reciprocal Enforcement) Act 1962; Northern Territory: Foreign Judgments (Reciprocal Enforcement) Act 1980; Australian Capital Territory: Foreign Judgments (Reciprocal Enforcement) Ordinance 1954.

8. Foreign Judgments Act 1991 (Comm.) Part 2—"Reciprocal Enforcement of Judgments"; s. 5 is headed "Application of this Part on the basis of reciprocity of treatment".

9. *Ibid.*, s. 5(4) and (1). "Country" is defined to include any region of a foreign country, and any region under the protection of, or the foreign policy control of, a foreign country: s. 3(1).

such countries, however.[10] As at 31 October 1995, the courts of 31 countries had been prescribed under the regulations.[11] Further, regulations may be made extending the application of the Act to non-money judgments of specified courts.[12]

Once registration of a foreign judgment has been effected in an Australian court, that judgment is regarded as having the same force and effect as if it were a judgment of the registering court.[13]

The effect of the Act is that the only means of enforcement in Australia of a judgment to which the Act applies is by proceedings under the Act for registration of the judgment.[14] The intention of the Act is to prevent enforcement by commencing proceedings in respect of such foreign judgments at common law. Whilst the intention might also be to prevent commencing proceedings in Australia in anticipation of a judgment being given in proceedings in a foreign jurisdiction, the Act does not specifically preclude any interim action in equity (such as a *Mareva* injunction), as discussed below.

Transitional provisions

Judgments that were registered under the superseded uniform state and territory legislation (i.e. before 27 June 1991) continue to be generally governed by the provisions of the uniform legislation.[15] The Foreign Judgments Act 1991 (Commonwealth) provided a transition period of two years (i.e. to 27 June 1993), during which judgments of the courts of countries which had not been prescribed for the purposes of the Act were registrable under the superseded uniform legislation, providing that they met the criteria for registration under the state or territory act.[16] Where a judgment is not registrable under the Act or under state or territory legislation, common law procedures for enforcement of foreign judgments may remain.

10. *Ibid.*, s. 5(3). The Foreign Judgment Regulations (Statutory Rules 1992 No. 321, as amended by 1993 No. 143, 1994 No. 283, 1995 No. 35) have specified the following inferior courts: each District Court of New Zealand; the County Courts of England, Wales, and Northern Ireland; the Sheriff Courts of Scotland; the Provincial Courts of Alberta, British Columbia, and Manitoba; the following Swiss courts: Bezirksgerichte, Erstinstanzliche Gerichte, Arbeitsgerichte, and Mietgerichte; and each District Court of Taiwan, China.

11. The Foreign Judgments Regulations 1992 (Statutory Rules 1992 No. 321 as amended by 1993 No. 143, 1994 No. 283, 1995 No. 35 and 1996 No. 145) have specified the following countries: Alberta, Bahamas, British Columbia, British Virgin Islands, the Cayman Islands, Dominica, The Falkland Islands, Fiji, France, Germany, Gibraltar, Grenada, Hong Kong, Israel, Italy, Japan, Malawi, Manitoba, Montserrat, New Zealand, Papua New Guinea, Singapore, Solomon Islands, St Helena, St Kitts and Nevis, St Vincent and the Grenadines, Seychelles, Sri Lanka, Tonga, Tuvalu, and the United Kingdom. Various courts are set out in these regulations which are to be taken to be superior courts of these countries, however s. 5(2) of the Act provides that the omission of a court from these regulations "is not taken to imply that the court is not a superior court for the purposes of the Act".

12. Foreign Judgments Act 1991 (Comm.), s. 5(6). No such regulations have been made as at 31 October 1995.

13. *Ibid.*, s. 6(7).

14. *Ibid.*, s. 10.

15. *Ibid.*, s. 19(a).

16. *Ibid.*, ss. 18(1), 19(b). Judgments registered according to this provision continue to be regulated by the uniform legislation: *ibid.*, s. 19.

Registration of judgments

In order to be registered pursuant to the Foreign Judgments Act 1991 (Commonwealth), the judgment must be a judgment of a prescribed court[17] and must be a judgment:

1. under which an amount of money is payable[18];
2. which was given in a prescribed court[19];
3. which is final and conclusive[20];
4. which was made within six years of the application for registration[21];
5. which has not already been wholly satisfied at the date of application[22]; and
6. which is enforceable in the country of the original court.[23]

With two exceptions, only judgments dated later than the day on which the regulation prescribing the relevant court for the purpose of the Act came into force are registrable.[24] The first exception is for judgments of New Zealand and United Kingdom courts, which are registrable under the Act any time after its commencement, regardless of when they were made.[25] The second exception relates to judgments which were registrable under the uniform legislation immediately before the regulation prescribing the relevant court came into force.[26]

Previously, "judgment" has been defined to include final or interlocutory judgments or orders of courts in civil proceedings and orders of courts in criminal proceedings for the payment of compensation or damages to an injured person. In addition, the definition includes arbitral awards of a country which have become enforceable in a court of that country as a judgment.[27]

If a judgment satisfies the above conditions, it *must* be registered by the appropriate Australian court.[28] According to P.E. Nygh, however, "the court must refuse to register a judgment if it appears from the facts deposed to or from admissions made on

17. Foreign Judgments Act 1991 (Comm.), s. 5(4)(b).

18. Judgments for fines and penalties are excluded as are judgments for taxes of countries other than New Zealand and Papua New Guinea: s. 5(4), *ibid.*, s. 3(1) see definition of "enforceable money judgment".

19. *Ibid.*, s. 5(4)(b).

20. A judgment in interlocutory proceedings may be final and conclusive, and a judgment may be final and conclusive even though an appeal is pending, or the judgment might still properly be the subject of appeal, in the overseas country: *ibid.*, s. 5(5).

21. *Ibid.*, s. 6(1). Where the judgment has been the subject of an appeal, the date of the last judgment is taken to be the relevant date: s. 6(1)(b). The six-year period may be extended by order of the registering court: s. 6(5).

22. *Ibid.*, s. 6(6)(a).

23. *Ibid.*, s. 6(6)(b).

24. *Ibid.*, s. 5(8)(a), (b), and (c).

25. *Ibid.*, s. 5(8)(d).

26. *Ibid.*, s. 5(8)(e). The effect of this exception is to exclude from the operation of the requirement in s. 5(8)(a), (b) and (c) judgments of the superior courts of the following countries, which were prescribed by regulations which came into force before the end of the two-year transition period provided for by s. 18 of the Act: The Bahamas, British Columbia, British Virgin Islands, Cayman Islands, Dominica, Falkland Islands, Fiji, France, Germany, Gibraltar, Grenada, Hong Kong, Israel, Italy, Japan, Manitoba, Montserrat, Papua New Guinea, St Helena, St Kitts and Nevis, St Vincent and the Grenadines, Seychelles, Singapore, Solomon Islands, and Tuvalu. Judgments of such courts are registrable under the Foreign Judgments Act 1991 (Comm.) (provided that they were made within six years of the application for registration: s. 6(1) and that the country in question is one to which the relevant state or territory statute applied).

27. *Ibid.*, s. 3(1). Judgments in proceedings which involve the determination of s. 36A, 98H, or 99A of the New Zealand Commerce Act 1986 are specifically excluded from the operation of the Act: s. 5(10).

28. *Ibid.*, s. 6(3).

the application for registration that the judgment, if registered, is one which upon application by the judgment debtor the court would be bound to set aside".[29]

The appropriate court for registration of a judgment is generally the Supreme Court of a state or territory. If the application of the Act is extended by regulation to prescribed non-money judgments under section 5(6), the appropriate court would be the Federal Court of Australia. Judgments in proceedings involving the New Zealand Commerce Act 1986 may be registered either in the Federal Court of Australia or in the Supreme Courts of the states and territories.[30]

A judgment creditor is also entitled to have registered its reasonable costs of obtaining registration, and any interest due under the law of the original court up to the date of registration.[31] Once registered, interest accrues on the judgment according to the law of the registering court.[32]

Once registered in an Australian court, a judgment can thereafter be registered in other Australian courts under the Service and Execution of Process Act 1992, referred to above. Such a judgment is regarded as having the same force and effect as a judgment of the first Australian registering court, unless an order has been made for a stay of enforcement of that judgment.[33]

Once a judgment has been registered, there are a number of methods of execution available to judgment creditors, including warrants of execution, warrants of possession, attachment of debts, attachment of earnings, appointment of a receiver or liquidator, garnishee proceedings, and sequestration. The procedure to be adopted will depend upon the nature of the asset that is subject to the execution order and the debtor in question. In addition, it may be possible to have a court order to wind up a corporate judgment debtor or to commence bankruptcy proceedings[34] against an individual.

Stays of enforcement and setting aside registration

The Foreign Judgments Act 1991 (Commonwealth) expressly provides that the registering court may order a stay of enforcement of a registered judgment, pending the determination of an appeal, where an appeal has been lodged, or where the judgment debtor is entitled to and intends to lodge an appeal. Such an order must be made on the condition that the appeal be pursued expeditiously, or that the appeal be brought within a time prescribed by the court. Such an order may be made conditional on the judgment debtor providing security for costs.[35]

In certain circumstances, the Act requires the registering court to set aside the registration.[36] The judgment *must* be set aside where the court is satisfied that:

29. *Re Word Publishing Co. Pty Ltd* [1992] Qd R 336, as noted in P.E. Nygh, *Conflict of Laws in Australia* (Butterworths 1995, 6th ed.), p. 165.

30. Foreign Judgments Act 1991 (Comm.), s. 6(2). Order 72 of the Federal Court Rules regulates the procedure for the registration of foreign judgments in that Court.

31. *Ibid.*, s. 6(15).

32. *Ibid.*, s. 6(7)(c).

33. *Ibid.*, s. 6(8) and (9).

34. *Re A Judgment Debtor* [1939] Ch 601; *Re McGilvray* (1986) 66 ALR 181, as noted by P.E. Nygh, *op. cit.*, p. 169 footnote 62.

35. Foreign Judgments Act 1991 (Comm.), s. 8.

36. *Ibid.*, s. 7(2)(a).

1. the judgment is not, or has ceased to be,[37] one to which the Act applies, or was registered in contravention of the Act;
2. the judgment was registered for an amount greater than the amount payable under it at the date of registration;
3. the judgment debtor did not receive notice of the original proceedings in sufficient time to enable a defence of the proceedings and the judgment debtor did not appear;
4. the judgment was obtained by fraud;
5. the judgment has been reversed on appeal or otherwise set aside in the courts of the country of the original court;
6. the rights under the judgment are not vested in the applicant for judgment;
7. the judgment has been discharged or wholly satisfied; or that
8. enforcement of the judgment would be contrary to the public policy.

The registration of a judgment must also be set aside where the foreign court had no jurisdiction in the circumstances of the case.[38] The Act provides detailed provisions as to the interpretation of this requirement.

As a starting point, the Act sets out three situations in which the foreign court will be taken not to have had jurisdiction for the purposes of the Act, namely:

1. if the subject matter of the judgment was immovable property situated outside the country of the original court; or
2. if the judgment debtor was entitled to sovereign, diplomatic, or consular immunity, and did not submit to the jurisdiction of the court[39]; or
3. with two exceptions, if the bringing of proceedings in the foreign court was a contravention of an agreement between the parties as to jurisdiction for the resolution of the relevant dispute. The exceptions are:
   (a) Where the judgment debtor voluntarily submitted to the jurisdiction of the court.[40] If this is the case, the foreign court is not deemed to have acted without jurisdiction.
   (b) Where the proceedings related to an action which was neither an action *in personam* nor an action *in rem*, as defined, and the foreign court exercised a jurisdiction which would have been entitled to recognition under the law of the forum apart from the Act. If this is the case, the foreign court is not deemed to have acted without jurisdiction.

If the matter of jurisdiction is not determined by the application of these three tests, the Act provides further guidelines according to whether the judgment is based on a cause of action *in personam*, an action *in rem*, or an action which falls into neither category.

Proceedings in connection with matrimonial matters, the administration of the estates of deceased persons, bankruptcy or insolvency, the winding up of companies, mental health, or the guardianship of infants are specifically excluded from the

37. Provision is made for regulations revoking the application of the Act to the courts of countries where there is no substantial reciprocity of those courts' treatment of money judgments of Australian superior courts: *ibid.*, s. 13. However, nothing in this section affects the enforcement, under the International Arbitration Act 1974 (Comm.), of an award.

38. *Ibid.*, s. 7(2)(a)(iv).

39. Foreign Judgments Act 1991 (Comm.), s. 7(4)(c) as interpreted by P.E. Nygh, *op. cit.*, p. 169.

40. If the judgment debtor was a defendant in the original proceedings, the judgment debtor must have submitted to the jurisdiction of the court before the commencement of proceedings in order for this exception to apply: *ibid.*, s. 7(4)(b), s. 7(3)(a)(iii).

definition of "action *in personam*".[41] P.E. Nygh considers that these matters fall within the third category, actions which are neither actions *in personam* nor actions *in rem*, to the extent that they are expressed in monetary terms.[42]

If the action is found to be an action *in personam*, the foreign court is deemed by the Act to have had jurisdiction in the following circumstances[43]:

1. the judgment debtor voluntarily submitted to the jurisdiction of the foreign court[44];
2. the judgment debtor was a plaintiff or counter-claimed in the original proceedings;
3. the judgment debtor was a defendant in the original proceedings, and the judgment debtor resided in, or in the case of a corporation, had its principal place of business in, the foreign country when the proceedings were instituted;
4. the judgment debtor was a defendant in the original proceedings, and those proceedings related to a transaction effected through the judgment debtor's office or place of business in the foreign country;
5. an amount of money is payable in respect of New Zealand tax under the judgment.[45]

A judgment debtor is not to be taken to have voluntarily submitted to the jurisdiction of the foreign court merely as a result of having made submissions as to the jurisdiction of the foreign court, or as a result of having done no more than was necessary in order to protect or obtain the release of property which was, or was threatened to be, seized or encumbered in the original proceedings.[46]

If the action is found to be an action *in rem* concerning movable or immovable property, the foreign court is deemed to have had jurisdiction if the property was in the foreign country at the time of the original proceedings.[47]

If the action is neither an action *in personam* nor *in rem*, the obscure wording of section 7(3)(c) of the Act has the effect, according to P.E. Nygh, that judgments which determine such actions "are entitled to recognition if the foreign court exercised a jurisdiction which would have been entitled to recognition under the law of the forum apart from the Act".[48]

In addition to these circumstances, a judgment *may* be set aside if the registering court is satisfied that the dispute in the original proceedings had been the subject of a

41. *Ibid.*, s. 3(1).

42. P.E. Nygh, *op. cit.*, p. 169. The example given is an order for the payment of money by way of property settlement made in proceedings ancillary to proceedings for divorce: see *Van der Kreek* v. *Van der Kreek* [1980] FLC 90–810.

43. Foreign Judgments Act 1991 (Comm.), s. 7(3)(a).

44. If the judgment debtor was a defendant in the original proceedings, the foreign court will not be deemed to have had jurisdiction unless the judgment debtor submitted to the jurisdiction of the court before the commencement of proceedings: Foreign Judgments Act, s. 7(4)(b), s. 7(3)(a)(iii).

45. *Ibid.* "New Zealand tax" is defined by s. 3(1) to mean: "tax or other similar charge of a similar nature payable under the laws of New Zealand, and includes additional or other tax payable, by way of penalty, interest, or otherwise, because of a contravention of any of those laws or of a requirement made under any of those laws."

46. *Ibid.*, s. 7(5).

47. *Ibid.*, s. 7(3)(b).

48. P.E. Nygh, *op. cit.*, p. 168.

final and conclusive judgment by another court having jurisdiction in the matter, prior to the date of the judgment of the original court.[49]

The Act provides that the court must re-register a judgment where its registration was previously set aside because it was registered for an amount greater than that payable at the date of registration. When re-registered, the judgment will apply only to that amount owing at the date of the application for re-registration. In addition, a judgment which had previously been set aside because at the date of the application for registration it was unenforceable in the country in which it was given, may be re-registered if the judgment subsequently becomes enforceable in that country.[50]

ARBITRATION

The International Arbitration Act 1974 (Commonwealth) ("the Arbitration Act") incorporates the provisions of the 1958 United Nations Convention on the Recognition and Enforcement of Foreign Arbitral Awards (Part II of the Act), and the UNCITRAL Model Law on International Commercial Arbitration 1985 (Part III of the Arbitration Act) ("the Model Law"). The Arbitration Act provides for the recognition and enforcement of agreements and awards in Australia by enabling parties to such agreements or awards to apply to Australian courts for stays of actions brought in breach of them.[51]

The Arbitration Act applies only to arbitration agreements entered into after 12 June 1989 between parties having a connection with a country which is a party to the Convention.[52]

Part II of the Arbitration Act applies to foreign arbitration agreements if the arbitration agreement is governed by the law of a Convention country[53] or the arbitration agreement is governed by the laws of a country other than Australia or any Convention country, and at least one party to the arbitration agreement is Australia or a state of Australia or an Australian resident, the government of a Convention country

49. *Ibid.*, s. 7(2)(b).

50. Foreign Judgments Act 1991 (Comm.), s. 9.

51. International Arbitration Act 1974 (Comm.), ss. 7 and 8; Model Law, Chapter VIII.

52. International Arbitration Act 1974, s. 7(1). The following nations had acceded to or ratified the Convention as at 23 August 1995: Algeria, Antigua and Barbuda, Argentina, Australia (Australian external territories), Austria, Bahrain, Bangladesh, Barbados, Belarus, Belgium, Benin, Bolivia, Bosnia & Herzegovina, Botswana, Brunei Darussalam, Bulgaria, Burkina Faso, Cambodia, Cameroon, Canada, Central African Republic, Chile, China, Columbia, Costa Rica, Cote d'Ivoire, Croatia, Cuba, Cyprus, Czech Republic, Denmark (Faroe Islands, Greenland), Djibouti, Dominica, Ecuador, Egypt, El Salvador, Estonia, Finland, France (French external territories), Georgia, Germany, Ghana, Greece, Guatemala, Guinea, Haiti, Holy See, Hungary, India, Indonesia, Ireland, Israel, Italy, Japan, Jordan, Kazakstan, Kenya, Korea, Republic of, Kuwait, Latvia, Lesotho, Lithuania, Luxembourg, Macedonia, former Yugoslav Republic of, Madagascar, Malaysia, Mali, Mauritius, Mexico, Monaco, Mongolia, Morocco, the Netherlands (Netherlands Antilles, Surinam), New Zealand, Niger, Nigeria, Norway, Pakistan, Panama, Peru, Philippines, Poland, Portugal, Romania, Russia, San Marino, Saudi Arabia, Senegal, Singapore, Slovakia, Slovenia, South Africa, Spain, Sri Lanka, Sweden, Switzerland, Syria, Tanzania, Thailand, Trinidad and Tobago, Tunisia, Turkey, Uganda, Ukraine, United Kingdom (Belize, Bermuda, Cayman Islands, Gibraltar, Guernsey, Hong Kong, Isle of Man), United States of America (US external territories), Uruguay, Uzbekistan, Venezuela, Vietnam, Yugoslavia, and Zimbabwe.

53. It is noted that pursuant to s. 3(1) of the International Arbitration Act 1974 (Comm.), the definition of a "Convention country" excludes Australia. The intention of the legislators is to exclude the operation of the International Arbitration Act 1974 (Comm.) to arbitration agreements that are purely Australian (i.e., between Australian parties and governed by Australian law).

or part of a Convention country, a person who is ordinarily resident in, or a company that is incorporated or has its principal place of business in, a Convention country.[54]

The Model Law imposed through Part III of the Arbitration Act applies to international arbitration agreements made after 12 June 1989, or to earlier agreements where the parties have expressly agreed that the Model Law is to apply. Under the Model Law, the agreement must be for "international commercial arbitration".[55] The Model Law defines "international"[56] and specifies that the term "commercial" should be given a "wide interpretation so as to cover matters arising from all relationships of a commercial nature, whether contractual or not ...".[57]

There are other criteria to be fulfilled to determine if the Arbitration Act is applicable; the arbitration agreement must be in writing[58] and provide that "the parties undertake to submit to arbitration all or any differences which have arisen or which may arise between them in respect of a defined legal relationship, whether contractual or not ...",[59] concerning subject matter "capable of settlement by arbitration".[60] As to whether or not subject matter is arbitrable is a matter to be determined by the court to which any application is made. In exercising its discretion, the court can consider issues of public policy. Further, the arbitration agreement must not be null and void, "inoperative or incapable of being performed".[61] Again, this issue will be determined by the court in which the application is made.[62]

The arbitration agreement may be in the form of an arbitration clause in a contract or a separate agreement,[63] but the proceedings to which the application for a stay relate must concern the subject matter of the arbitration agreement.[64]

A party to an arbitration agreement to which the Arbitration Act applies may apply to a court in Australia for a stay of proceedings brought in breach of an arbitration agreement or award. In response to such an application, the court may order a stay of proceedings, or so much of the proceedings as involves the determination of the

54. International Arbitration Act 1974 (Comm.), s. 7(1); a company is deemed to be "ordinarily resident" in a country if it is incorporated or has its principal place of business in that country (International Arbitration Act 1974 (Comm.), s. 3(3)).

55. *Ibid.*, s. 30.

56. *Ibid.*, Art. 1(3), i.e. if the places of business of the parties are in different states, or the place of arbitration or the place in which a substantial part of the obligations of the agreement are to be performed is outside the state in which the parties have their places of business, or the parties have expressly agreed that the subject matter of the arbitration agreement relates to more than one country. In circumstances in which a party has more than one place of business, that place of business which has the closest relationship to the arbitration agreement or, if the party does not have a place of business, the party's habitual residence, will be deemed to be the place of business of that party (Model Law, Art. 1(4)).

57. International Arbitration Act 1974 (Comm.), Sched. 2, footnote 2, which provides examples of commercial transactions: "any trade transaction for the supply or exchange of goods or services; distribution agreement; commercial representation or agency; factoring; leasing; construction of works; consulting; engineering; licensing; investment; financing; banking; insurance; exploitation agreement or concession; joint venture and other forms of industrial or business co-operation; carriage of goods or passenger by air, sea, rail or road."

58. *Ibid.*, s. 3(1); Model Law, Art. 7(2); electronic means of communication which provide a record of the agreement, such as telex, are deemed to be included in the definition of "in writing".

59. Convention on the Recognition and Enforcement of Foreign Arbitral Awards, Art. II(1); International Arbitration Act 1974 (Comm.), s. 3(1); Model Law, Art. 7(1).

60. Convention on the Recognition and Enforcement of Foreign Arbitral Awards, Art. II(1); International Arbitration Act 1974 (Comm.), s. 3(1).

61. International Arbitration Act 1974 (Comm.), s. 7(5); Model Law, Art. 8(1).

62. *Oceanic Sun Line Special Shipping Inc.* v. *Fay* (1988) 165 CLR 197, *per* Brennan J at p. 225.

63. Model Law, Art. 7(1).

64. *Ibid.*, Art. 8(1).

matter, and may refer the parties to arbitration in respect of that matter.[65] The Arbitration Act provides that a party to arbitration in respect of that matter includes a reference to a person claiming through or under a party,[66] and it appears that the Arbitration Act may extend to the liquidator of a company or the trustee in bankruptcy of an individual.[67]

An order made by the court granting a stay of proceedings may be made on such terms and conditions as the court deems appropriate,[68] provided those terms are incidental to and not an extension or alteration of the arbitration agreement between the parties.[69] It follows, therefore, that if a foreign claimant were to seek to attach assets via Australian legal proceedings in a dispute that was subject to international arbitration, for example by way of a *Mareva* injunction, it would be open to the respondent to apply to a court to stay the legal proceedings. However, the court would have some discretion as to the terms of any stay and could, for example, order a stay only if the respondent provides acceptable security in respect of the amount in dispute.

Once a foreign arbitration award has been obtained, the procedural requirements to achieve recognition or enforcement of an award are based on the production to the court in which the application is made of a "duly authenticated original award or a duly certified copy thereof [and] the original arbitration agreement ... or a duly certified copy thereof".[70]

The International Arbitration Act 1974 (Commonwealth) provides that certain defences may be raised by a party to an arbitration award who seeks to resist the recognition and enforcement of the award. Defences include the incapacity of a party to the agreement, the invalidity of the agreement pursuant to the law to which the agreement is expressed to be subject, or, where no law is specified to govern the agreement, the law of the country where the award was made. Other defences include lack of notice or inability to defend the proceedings, or that the award made was beyond the scope of the arbitration agreement. A party could also contend that there exists an improper composition of the arbitral authority or that the procedure of the arbitration was improper, the matter was not properly arbitrable pursuant to the law of the country or jurisdiction in which the application is brought, or the enforcement of the award is contrary to public policy.[71]

In 1993 the Supreme Court of Queensland held that a foreign order will not be enforced if it is contrary to public policy, in the sense that it would not be made in the enforcing jurisdiction, particularly without undertakings as to damages and appropriate security, or if its enforcement might cause double jeopardy and be vexatious.[72]

65. International Arbitration Act 1974 (Comm.), s. 7(2); Model Law, Art. 8(1); arbitral proceedings may be commenced or continued, and an award may be made, notwithstanding that the issue may be pending before a court (Model Law, Art. 8(2)).

66. International Arbitration Act 1974 (Comm.), s. 7(4).

67. *Tanning Research Laboratories Inc.* v. *O'Brien* (1990) 64 ALJR 211.

68. International Arbitration Act 1974 (Comm.), s. 7(2) and (3).

69. *O'Brien* v. *Tanning Research Labs Inc.* (1988) 84 ALR 221, *per* Kirby J at p. 241, as discussed by P.E. Nygh, *op. cit.*, p. 158.

70. International Arbitration Act 1974 (Comm.), s. 9; Model Law, Art. 35(2).

71. International Arbitration Act 1974 (Comm.), s. 8(5) and (7); Model Law, Arts. 34(2) and 36(1). The circumstances in which the enforcement of an award will be deemed to be contrary to the public policy of Australia have been notably expanded by the Act as being when the award was induced or affected by fraud or corruption or when a breach of the rules of natural justice has occurred (International Arbitration Act 1974, s. 19).

72. *Resort Condominiums International Inc.* v. *Bolwell* (1993) 118 ALR 655 (Q Sup Ct., Lee J).

It appears that, in nearly all instances, the arbitration agreement will fall within the ambit of the Model Law.[73] It is thought that Article 8 of the Model Law will eventually replace all other alternatives as the method by which parties to arbitration agreements and awards may successfully obtain a stay of proceedings.[74]

Parties to arbitration agreements may also seek enforcement of awards pursuant to the Foreign Judgments Act 1991 (Commonwealth), which defines "judgment" to include "an award ... (other than an award given in a dispute of a kind referred to in paragraph 34(a) of the Arbitration Act or an award that may be enforced under subsection 35(2) of that Act) in proceedings on an arbitration conducted in, and under the law applying in, a country, being an award that has become enforceable in a court of that country in the same manner as a judgment or order given by that court".[75]

In circumstances in which the Arbitration Act does not apply, foreign arbitration awards and agreements will generally be upheld by Australian courts. This was confirmed by Mr Justice Street in *Joy Manufacturing Co.* v. *A.E. Goodwin Limited*,[76] who stated that "parties to international trade agreements should be able to be confident that, if they deliberately and advisedly stipulate for arbitration by a tribunal of their choice this stipulation will be respected".

The Commercial Arbitration Acts of the states and territories support this rationale.[77] Each such Act provides for the Supreme Court to exercise its discretion to grant a stay of proceedings which are contrary to an arbitration award or agreement[78] and to allow for the enforcement of an award made under an arbitration agreement in the same manner as a judgment.[79] The courts of the states and territories will not have jurisdiction in all circumstances, however, as would be the case if the foreign arbitration agreement is not in writing.[80]

EQUITABLE RELIEF

The common law courts in the United Kingdom, and elsewhere, have established that the laws of equity can be used to enforce foreign judgments, providing that the judgment of the foreign court, based on the laws of the country of the foreign court, is proper.[81]

Whilst it is a prerequisite for the enforcement of a foreign judgment at law that it be

73. P. E. Nygh, *op. cit.*, p. 184, refers to an agreement between the Australian branch office of a United States corporation and an Australian party, providing for arbitration in Australia in respect of a contract wholly performable in Australia which would not fall within Art. 8 of the Model Law but would be covered by the Convention. Note also that the parties themselves may exclude the operation of the Model Law (International Arbitration Act 1974, s. 21).

74. *Ibid.*

75. Foreign Judgments Act 1991 (Comm.), s. 3(1).

76. [1970] 1 NSWR 57 at p. 59.

77. NSW: Commercial Arbitration Act 1984; Vic: Commercial Arbitration Act 1984; Qld: Arbitration Act 1990; SA: Commercial Arbitration Act 1986; WA: Commercial Arbitration Act 1985; Tas: Commercial Arbitration Act 1985; NT: Commercial Arbitration Act 1986; ACT: Commercial Arbitration Act 1986.

78. NSW: s. 53(1); Vic: s. 53(1); Qld: s. 53(1); SA: s. 53(1); WA: s. 53(1); Tas: s. 53(1); ACT: s. 53(1); NT: s. 53(1).

79. NSW: s. 33; Vic: s. 33; Qld: s. 33; SA: s. 33; Tas: s. 33; ACT: s. 33; NT: s. 33.

80. NSW: s. 4(1); Vic: s. 4(1); Qld: s. 4(1); SA: s. 4(1); WA: s. 4(1); Tas: s. 4(1); ACT: s. 4(1); NT: s. 4(1).

81. W. R. White, "Enforcement of foreign judgments in equity", (1979–1982) 9 *SydLRev* 630.

for a fixed or ascertained sum of money, it has been suggested that this may not be required as a prerequisite to the enforcement of the judgment in equity.[82]

Other circumstances, including the risk of a judgment debtor absconding, or of his or her assets being removed from or disposed of within the jurisdiction, or otherwise disposed of so as to prejudice the plaintiff's ability to satisfy any judgment that might be obtained, gave rise to developments in English law, originating with the grant of the first *Mareva* injunction in the United Kingdom in *Mareva Compania Naviera SA* v. *International Bulk Carriers SA* in 1975.[83]

It took some little time for the interim relief concept of the *Mareva* injunction to be finally accepted in Australian jurisdictions. Initially some Australian courts expressed some reluctance about granting a *Mareva* injunction. At first, it was held in New South Wales that there was no jurisdiction to grant a *Mareva* injunction, but this position was reviewed on the basis of the court's inherent jurisdiction necessary for the administration of justice. To deny a *Mareva* injunction and thereby permit a defendant to remove assets would allow that defendant to abuse the court's process. As a result it can be accepted as a general proposition in Australia that a *Mareva* injunction can be granted.[84]

It would appear that decrees granting injunctive relief are not registrable under the Foreign Judgments Act 1991 (Commonwealth), since section 5(4) of the Act limits the scope of the Act to judgments under which an amount of money is payable. Although there is a provision under the Act for regulations extending the application of the Act to specified kinds of non-money judgments, no such regulations have been made.

In addition, Australian courts generally have power to grant orders for discovery of assets, including assets which are outside the jurisdiction[85]; in some instances some Australian courts have power to order discovery prior to the commencement of proceedings, although pre-action discovery is not common and must be obtained by an application to a relevant court with supporting material. A *Mareva* injunction is also available to parties seeking orders pursuant to arbitration,[86] although in Australia it has been considered that "as a general rule the applicant must show a vested and accrued cause of action".[87]

The availability of *Mareva* injunctions in the various state and federal jurisdictions within Australia has been confirmed in a number of cases brought before those courts,[88] but the courts have laid down various tests as to the grounds upon which such an injunction will be granted. By way of example, in Victoria the test as to

82. *White* v. *Verkouille* [1990] 2 Qd R 191.

83. [1975] 2 Lloyd's Rep. 509.

84. *Jackson* v. *Sterling Industries Limited* (1987) 61 ALJR 332, *per* Deane J at p. 336. See also *Ex Parte BP Exploration Co. (Libya) Ltd* [1979] 2 NSWLR 406; *Turner* v. *Sylvester* [1981] 2 NSWLR 29.

85. Robert Crawford, "The extra-territorial effect of *Mareva* injunctions—the sleeping giant in fairyland", (1990) 18 ABLR 28 at p. 36.

86. Mark Tedeschi, "The *Mareva* Injunction—An Update", (1985) 13 ABLR 236 at p. 240.

87. *Bank of Queensland* v. *Grant* [1984] 1 NSWLR 409, *per* Clarke J, as discussed in *ibid.* at p. 240.

88. High Court: *Jackson* v. *Sterling Industries Ltd* (1987) 61 ALJR 332; Supreme Courts: Vic: *Praznovsky* v. *Sablyack* [1977] VR 144, *Deputy Commissioner of Taxation* v. *Rosenthal* (1984) 16 ATR 159; NSW: *Riley McKay Pty Ltd* v. *McKay* [1982] 1 NSWLR 662; SA: *Devlin* v. *Collins* (1984) 37 SASR 98; WA: *Sanko Steamship Co. Ltd* v. *D.C. Commodities (Australasia) Pty Ltd* [1980] WAR 51, *Perth Mint* v. *Mickelberg (No. 2)* [1985] WAR 117; QLD: *Bank of New Zealand* v. *Jones* [1981] QdR 466; ACT: *Barisic* v. *Topic* (1981) 37 ACTR 1; as noted in Simpson, Bailey and Evans, *Discovery and Interrogatories* (Butterworths (Australia) 1990, 2nd ed.), p. 287; (Tas): *National Australia Bank Ltd* v. *Golden Sea Dragon (Hobart) Pty Ltd*, Supreme Court of Tasmania, Zeeman J, 4 September 1992.

whether a *Mareva* injunction is available is more strict, for instance, than in New South Wales.

In Victoria, the criteria necessary to obtain a *Mareva* injunction, laid down in *Deputy Commissioner of Taxation (Vic.)* v. *Rosenthal*,[89] was that "there must be evidence to show that the risk to the assets has materialised or will probably materialise".[90] More recently, in *Glenwood Management Group Pty Ltd* v. *Mayo*,[91] the Supreme Court held that to obtain a *Mareva* injunction the plaintiff must show, *inter alia*:

(a) that it has a good arguable case;
(b) that there are some grounds for believing that there is a risk that the defendant will remove its assets from the jurisdiction before judgment is satisfied (but the plaintiff does not show that the disposal of assets would be intended to frustrate a judgment); and
(c) that there is a danger of default if assets are removed from the jurisdiction.

In New South Wales, there must be a "real, not frivolous, risk".[92] In Queensland, the test is stricter than that laid down in New South Wales.[93] The Supreme Court of Western Australia referred to the following principle in relation to *Mareva* injunctions:

> Mareva injunctions should be granted, but granted only, when it appears to the court that there is a combination of two circumstances. First, when it appears likely that the plaintiff will recover judgment against the defendant for a certain or approximate sum. Secondly, when there are also reasons to believe that the defendant has assets within the jurisdiction to meet the judgment, in whole or in part, but may well take steps to design to ensure that these are no longer available or traceable when judgment is given against him.[94]

The South Australian Supreme Court Rules confirm that applications for *Mareva* injunctions may be made in that state. These rules set out the prerequisites which must be satisfied in order for that Court to grant a *Mareva* injunction. The prerequisites are that the applicant has a good, arguable and substantive cause of action in respect of which the court has jurisdiction; that there must be a real danger that the defendant's assets may be removed from the jurisdiction or otherwise disposed of so as to defeat any order or judgment which may be made; and, in the event that the defendant's assets are removed from the jurisdiction or otherwise disposed of, the plaintiff will be unable to satisfy the judgment by execution.[95]

In Australia, courts exercising equitable jurisdiction will generally lend assistance to the enforcement of a foreign judgment without requiring as a prerequisite that the foreign judgment be registered as a judgment of the local court.[96] For example, equity will generally assist by upholding a foreign appointment of a receiver to collect assets of an insolvent party within the local jurisdiction.[97] In general terms, either through

89. (1984) 16 ATR 159.
90. *Ibid.*, at p. 162.
91. [1991] 2 VR 49.
92. Tedeschi, *op. cit.*, p. 247.
93. See *Bank of New Zealand* v. *Jones* [1981] QdR 466.
94. *Perth Mint* v. *Mickelberg* [1984] WAR 230 at pp. 233–234, *per* Smith J, as discussed by Tedeschi, *op. cit.*, pp. 248–249.
95. Simpson, Bailey and Evans, *op. cit.*, p. 287.
96. *White* v. *Verkouille* [1990] 2 QdR 191 at p. 194, *per* McPherson J.
97. *White* v. *Verkouille* [1990] 2 QdR 191.

the exercise of equitable principles or the courts' inherent jurisdiction, interlocutory orders may be made to enable foreign claimants to obtain interim relief pending formalisation of proceedings.

Nevertheless, the local courts will primarily decide the nature and extent of the defendant's obligation pursuant to the order of the foreign court. If equitable relief granted in Australia has the effect of extending or altering the nature of the defendant's obligations, then the relief should not be granted.[98] Commentators have argued that an interlocutory injunction granted by a foreign court should be enforced in Australia unless and until it is altered by the foreign court.[99] Against this position, it has been contended in some instances that an interlocutory injunction (for instance, a *Mareva* injunction) should not be granted unless the underlying dispute is also within the court's supervisory jurisdiction.

In addition to *Mareva* injunctions, there is recognition in Australia that *Anton Piller* orders may be granted[100] in circumstances in which the applicant has a strong prima facie case and would otherwise suffer real and serious damage, and where there is a real possibility that the defendant may destroy incriminating documents prior to the determination of the matter to which they relate.[101] For example, orders have been made in various jurisdictions of Australia, in particular the Federal Court of Australia and courts in South Australia and Victoria, providing that a defendant supply on oath the names and addresses of persons from whom certain intellectual property was obtained.[102] In certain circumstances, the court may make ancillary orders requiring that the defendant (or its solicitor) provide undertakings.[103]

Anton Piller orders have been granted requiring that a foreign defendant allow access to premises located outside the jurisdiction for the purposes of inspection.[104] Due to the *in personam* nature of an *Anton Piller* order however, an order for inspection of premises cannot properly be made unless the foreign defendant has been duly served within the jurisdiction, or has submitted to the jurisdiction or leave has been granted to serve the defendant outside the jurisdiction.[105]

In support of *Mareva* injunctions and *Anton Piller* orders, applications for discovery and interrogatories, aimed at ascertaining the nature and extent of the defendant's assets, have successfully been made, notwithstanding that the subject matter of the dispute between the parties may not yet have been fully defined.[106] In

98. White, *op. cit.*, p. 640.

99. *Ibid.*, p. 646.

100. Commonwealth: *Simsek* v. *McPhee* (1982) 56 ALJR 277; Federal Court: *Polygram Records Pty Ltd* v. *Monash Records (Australia) Pty Ltd* (1987) 72 ALR 35; NSW: *BPA Industries Ltd* v. *Black* (1987) 11 NSWLR 609; Qld: *Chrysalis Records Ltd* v. *Vere* (1983) 43 ALR 440; SA: *Golf Lynx* v. *Golf Scene Pty Ltd* (1984) 59 ALR 343; Vic: *Television Broadcasts Ltd* v. *Reston Pty Ltd (No. 876 of 1988)* (18 March 1988, Murphy J); Tas: *Broadby* v. *Vecon Pty Ltd* [1982] Tas R 91, as discussed in Simpson, Bailey and Evans, *op. cit.*, p. 286.

101. As stated by the Court of Appeal in *Anton Piller K G* v. *Manufacturing Processes Ltd* [1976] Ch 55.

102. Federal Court: *Polygram Records Pty Ltd* v. *Monash Records (Australia) Pty Ltd* (1987) 72 ALR 35; SA: *Golf Lynx* v. *Golf Scene Pty Ltd* (1984) 59 ALR 343; Vic: *Rohm & Haas Co.* v. *Tayport Nominees* (Supreme Court, No. 4498 of 1982)—the order made in this decision was subsequently reversed because compliance with it would have exposed the defendants to prosecution for conspiracy to defraud. These cases are noted and discussed in Simpson, Bailey and Evans, *op. cit.*, p. 286.

103. *Golf Lynx* v. *Golf Scene Pty Ltd* (1984) 59 ALR 343.

104. *Cook Industries Inc.* v. *Galliher* [1978] 3 WLR 637.

105. *Altertext Inc.* v. *Advanced Data Communications Ltd* [1985] FSR 21 at pp. 26, 27, as discussed in Simpson, Bailey and Evans, *op. cit.*, p. 279.

106. Simpson, Bailey and Evans, *op. cit.*, p. 289.

Australia, such orders have also been made in respect of foreign assets.[107] However, these orders will usually be given subject to ancillary orders for security for costs and judgment by consent in circumstances in which there is evidence that the debtor has assets within the jurisdiction.[108]

The form in which an application for discovery of assets pursuant to a *Mareva* injunction or an *Anton Piller* order is framed is of importance. For instance, in the case of bank accounts, a general list of bank accounts which may be in the name of the defendant is insufficient. It is considered that the order for discovery should require the defendant to specify the precise name of the bank and branch at which the accounts are held, the account number, the name of the person, persons or company in whose name the account is held and the balance of the account as at the date of service of the order for discovery.[109]

In practice, a *Mareva* injunction (or any similar interlocutory injunction) can be obtained only by an application to an appropriate court. In the ordinary course of events, such an application would be made on an *ex parte* basis and would have to be supported by affidavit or other acceptable evidentiary material so as to satisfy the court that it is appropriate to grant the *Mareva* injunction. The party seeking the *Mareva* injunction will, in most cases, be obliged to give to the court undertakings to pay damages and costs in the event of the injunction application eventually being held to be ill-founded, and further, any *Mareva* injunction obtained on an *ex parte* basis may be the subject of an application by the affected party to set it aside.

In a situation where a foreign claimant protects its position (for example, by obtaining a *Mareva* injunction) pending the resolution of the dispute, the foreign claimant does not obtain any priority as a result of taking such protective steps. Consequently, if the defendant subsequently becomes insolvent, the foreign claimant's position will remain subject to the priority order of distribution of assets to creditors, with preferred and secured creditors being entitled to be paid before any balance is made available to unsecured creditors.

MARITIME CLAIMANTS

There are specific provisions that assist claimants in maritime matters. Pursuant to the Admiralty Act 1988 (Commonwealth), actions may be commenced *in rem* against a ship (or other specific property) to enforce a foreign judgment[110] or an arbitral award,[111] or to obtain security for a pending claim.[112]

By way of interim relief, a claimant may bring an action *in rem* against a ship (or other specific property) and by affidavit obtain on an *ex parte* basis an arrest warrant. Once the ship (or other specific property) is thereon arrested, the owner will have to

107. *Ballabil Holdings Pty Ltd* v. *Hospital Products Ltd* [1985] 1 NSWLR 155.
108. *Yandil Holdings Pty Ltd* v. *Insurance Co. of North America* (1986) 7 NSWLR 571.
109. *Ausbro Forex Pty Ltd* v. *Mare* (1986) 4 NSWLR 419, as discussed in Simpson, Bailey and Evans, *op. cit.*, p. 295.
110. Admiralty Act 1988 (Comm.), s. 4(2)(c).
111. *Ibid.*, s. 4(3)(u).
112. *Ibid.*, s. 29.

provide bail or security to enable the arrest warrant to be lifted or move to set aside the arrest warrant. Otherwise the arrested property will remain under arrest pending the resolution of the dispute and may in certain circumstances be sold on a court order.

There is no requirement on the claimant to give an undertaking in respect of damages at the time of obtaining the arrest warrant, although the arrest and holding costs must be guaranteed by the arresting party. However, in the event of a wrongful or unjustified arrest or an unreasonable demand for security, there may be an action for damages against the arresting parties under section 34 of the Admiralty Act 1988.

An arrest warrant may be sought notwithstanding that the parties are in dispute over an agreement that contains an arbitration clause and in relation to which the respondent would otherwise be entitled to obtain a stay of proceedings pending arbitration elsewhere. Section 29 of the Admiralty Act 1988 specifically allows the court to order that the release of arrested property be subject to specific terms, including terms as to security for the pending claim. The same provision also applies in the event the court considers that the dispute shall be determined by a court of a foreign country.

On an overall basis, Australian admiralty law and procedure is similar to that operating in the United Kingdom and in other common law-based countries, and a claimant obtaining an arrest warrant through Australian admiralty proceedings would be faced with the traditional admiralty priority positions and, unless third party security was obtained, would be in no better position as a result of the arrest process in the event of the debtor becoming insolvent.

INSOLVENCY

Effect of insolvency of Australian debtor

A foreign creditor may be unable to recover a debt because the Australian debtor is insolvent. If an Australian debtor is insolvent, a foreign creditor, like a local creditor, may make use of Australian insolvency procedures to seek to recover the debt.

These procedures include bankruptcy (if the debtor is an individual) or liquidation (if the debtor is a company), and the foreign creditor may be entitled to share with other creditors in the distribution of the debtor's assets through the bankruptcy or liquidation, as the case may be.

If the debt is secured, the creditor may have rights under the instrument creating the security, including the right to appoint a receiver over assets charged to the creditor.

A creditor appointing a receiver to the property of a corporation must notify the Australian Securities Commission[113] of that appointment within seven days,[114] and

113. The Australian Securities Commission is the statutory body which co-ordinates and manages the Australian uniform company scheme.

114. Corporations Law, s. 537.

must publicise the appointment in the *Commonwealth Government Gazette* within 21 days.[115]

The receiver's powers and duties are derived from the instrument creating the security, from the Corporations Law[116] and various state Real Property Acts.[117] The Corporations Law provides for the uniform and central co-ordination of and control over companies in Australia. The receiver will usually be empowered to take possession of and sell the debtor's assets and apply the proceeds in reduction of the secured debt.

Bankruptcy of an individual debtor under Australian law is governed by the Bankruptcy Act 1966 (Commonwealth) ("the Bankruptcy Act"). Bankruptcy proceedings are taken in the bankruptcy division of the Federal Court of Australia.

Under the Bankruptcy Act, a creditor may present a petition to the court against a debtor, seeking a sequestration order against the debtor's estate. The court has the discretion to make the order if the debtor has a sufficient connection with Australia, the creditor filing the petition is owed an ascertained debt of not less than A$1,500 by the debtor,[118] and the debtor has committed an act of bankruptcy within the six months preceding the presentation of the petition.

The return unsatisfied of a judgment is an act of bankruptcy. Accordingly, the return unsatisfied of a judgment registered under the Foreign Judgments Act 1991 (Commonwealth) would be an act of bankruptcy. The most common act of bankruptcy, however, is the failure to comply with a bankruptcy notice issued by the Court.

To obtain a bankruptcy notice, a creditor must have a judgment or court order (which includes a registered foreign judgment) in respect of the debt, and must file in the Court an authenticated copy of this judgment or order and the other supporting material required by rules made under the Bankruptcy Act. A time for compliance with the notice is then fixed and the notice issued.

The notice is in a prescribed form and demands payment of the debt. The creditor (which can include a foreign creditor) must have the notice served personally on the debtor. If the debtor does not comply with the notice within the required time, the debtor thereby commits an act of bankruptcy. Within six months after the debtor commits an act of bankruptcy, the creditor must file a petition and supporting material. The position must be served on the debtor personally.

At the hearing of the petition, the Court may make a sequestration order. The Court will not make such an order if the debtor can prove solvency or if the Court is satisfied there are no assets in the debtor's estate. If the petition is based on a judgment, and an appeal from that judgment on substantial grounds is pending, the court may adjourn the hearing of the petition.

115. *Ibid.*, s. 427(1).

116. The Corporations Law came into effect on 1 January 1991. Prior to this, the law relating to the governance of companies in each of the states and territories was comprised in codes which were substantially similar. However, management and co-ordination of the scheme prior to 1991 was conducted separately by each of the states and territories.

117. e.g., s. 101(1)(c) of the Property Law Act 1958 (as amended); see also (NSW): Conveyancing Act 1919 (as amended), SA: Law of Property Act 1936–1980; WA: Property Law Act 1969–1979: Tas: Conveyancing and Law of Property Act 1884 (as amended); NT: Real Property Act 1990; ACT: Real Property Ordinance 1925.

118. Bankruptcy Act 1966 (Comm.), s. 44(1).

discretion of the court". In the same case, Mr Justice Northrop stated that the Federal Court "may exercise such powers with respect to the matter [of bankruptcy] as it could exercise if the matter . . . had arisen within its own jurisdiction".[131]

Sections 580 and 581 of the Corporations Law are similar in nature to section 29 of the Bankruptcy Act. These sections provide that Australian courts must act in aid of the courts of prescribed countries,[132] and may act in aid of the courts of other countries[133] in relation to winding-up and insolvency proceedings, on receipt of a letter of request for aid from the foreign court, providing that the foreign court has jurisdiction over corporate insolvency and winding-up.[134] In these circumstances, a competent Australian court may exercise such powers with respect to the winding-up or insolvency as it could have exercised had the matter arisen in Australia.[135] Although the Australian court is required to act in aid of competent courts of prescribed countries if requested to do so, the form and degree of assistance are at the Australian Court's discretion.[136] Similarly, an Australian court may ask competent foreign courts "to act in aid of, and be auxiliary to, it" in the winding up and insolvency of bodies corporate (including foreign registered corporations).[137]

Recognition will generally be given in Australia to foreign liquidation orders made by courts of the country in which the foreign company is registered.[138] Provided the foreign jurisdiction has a significant connection with the foreign company and the exercise of the jurisdiction in the circumstances was proper and without irregularities, then Australian courts will recognise an order of a court of such a foreign jurisdiction.[139]

However, a foreign winding-up order is not, of itself, directly enforceable in Australia. It is necessary for a foreign liquidator to obtain a concurrent order from an appropriate Australian court in order to protect assets of the company located within Australia.[140]

Under section 350(14) of the Corporations Law, the local agent[141] of any registered foreign company[142] has an obligation to inform the Australian Securities Commission of any winding-up or liquidation order made against the company in the jurisdiction in which it is registered. An Australian liquidator may then be appointed by the court.[143]

131. *Ibid.*, at p. 138.
132. Corporations Law, s. 581(2)(a); Corporations Law Regulations, reg. 5.6.74 prescribes the following countries: Jersey, Canada, Papua New Guinea, Malaysia, New Zealand, Singapore, Switzerland, the United Kingdom and the United States of America.
133. *Ibid.*, s. 581(2)(b).
134. See further *ibid.*, s. 580 definition of "external administration matter".
135. *Ibid.*, s. 581(3).
136. Rosalind Mason, "Australian Liquidation of Foreign Companies and Recognition of Foreign Insolvencies in Australia: Some Aspects of Cross-Border Insolvency", (May 1994) 123 *Company and Securities Law Journal* 182 at p. 188.
137. Corporations Law, s. 581(4).
138. *Re Alfred Shaw & Co.* (1987) 8 QLJ 93, as discussed by A.D. Grace, "Law of liquidations: The Recognition and Enforcement of Foreign Liquidation Orders in Canada and Australia—A Critical Comparison", 35 ICLQ 664 at p. 683.
139. *Ibid.*, at pp. 683–684.
140. *Ibid.*, at pp. 685 and 701.
141. Corporations Law, s. 345 provides that each registered foreign company must appoint a local agent.
142. Corporations Law, Chapter 4, Part 4.1, Division 2.
143. The expression "Court" is defined in the Corporations Law to include the Federal Court, the Supreme Court of any state or territory of Australia, and the Family Courts.

Section 350(15) of the Corporations Law further provides that an Australian liquidator of a registered foreign company who is appointed by the court has obligations to advertise in Australia that the company is in liquidation, to invite creditors of the company to make their claims and to recover and realise the property of the foreign company in Australia. Thereafter, the Australian liquidator may pay the net amount so recovered and realised to the foreign liquidator of the company.

Only movable property of the registered foreign company can be taken by the liquidator.[144] In certain circumstances, it is possible that Australian courts may refuse to permit the payment to the foreign liquidator of the net proceeds of the winding-up of a registered foreign company. Such would be the case where the funds would become subject to a security interest which is deemed to be void according to Australian law,[145] or where an Australian statute specifically requires distribution of Australian assets to Australian creditors.[146]

Provided "the foreign liquidator is in a position to provide satisfactory undertakings, or security, authorised by the courts of the foreign jurisdiction, to distribute the funds in accordance with Australian domestic law", then the funds can be paid to the foreign liquidator.[147] Accordingly, Australian courts will ensure that they retain jurisdiction to determine the manner in which the funds resulting from the winding-up of a registered foreign company will be distributed.[148]

CONCLUSION

The law relating to the recognition and enforcement of foreign judgments, orders, and arbitral awards in Australia is largely codified, the common law assisting in the interpretation of the legislative provisions. The procedures for achieving recognition and enforcement of such judgments, orders and awards are set out in the legislation governing these matters. Provided the necessary prerequisites in relation to the applicability of each of the pieces of legislation are satisfied, foreign parties will be able to utilise the procedures available in an attempt to gain satisfaction from Australian defendants and debtors in respect of the judgment, order or award to which they are a party.

Similarly, the development of the law permitting interim injunctions and similar equitable rights (e.g., the *Mareva* injunction) enables protective steps to be taken by foreign claimants in appropriate situations.

DAVID ROYLANCE

144. E. Sykes and M. C. Pryles, *Australian Private International Law* (The Law Book Company Limited 1991, 3rd ed.), p. 401.

145. *Re Northland Services Pty Ltd* (1978) 18 ALR 684, as discussed by Grace, n. 138 *supra*, at p. 691.

146. e.g. s. 116(3) and (6) of the Insurance Act 1973 (Comm.): see *Re National Employers' Mutual General Insurance Association Ltd (in liquidation)* 15 ACSR 624 (Supreme Court of New South Wales, McLeland J).

147. Grace, *loc. cit.*

148. Grace, *loc. cit.*

CHAPTER 3

AUSTRIA

AVAILABILITY OF THE AUSTRIAN COURT SYSTEM TO FOREIGN CREDITORS AND LITIGANTS

General requirements

Foreign creditors may lodge actions and seek provisional/interim remedies at Austrian courts, provided the following requirements are met:

(1) International jurisdiction of such court.

(2) Jurisdiction *ratione loci.*

(3) Jurisdiction *ratione materie.*

The Austrian Code on Court Jurisdiction (JN) contains few statutory rules on the international jurisdiction of the Austrian courts. For money claims, there are no express rules on international jurisdiction. Venues which expressly allow suit against foreigners in Austrian courts are interpreted to define indirectly "international" jurisdiction (JN, Article 83c, intellectual property law claims; Article 88(2), claims of businessmen under their bills; Article 92a, venue of damage causation; Article 99, venue of asset location).

Prevailing opinion in Austria holds that Austrian courts may adjudicate only upon matters which have a "sufficiently close connection" with Austria (OGH/Austrian Supreme Court, SZ 55/95). Such connection is held to be indicated if in a particular case the JN provides for a specific territorial venue within Austria. Therefore, international jurisdiction will usually be affirmed if there is an applicable local venue against the defendant in Austria under the rules on jurisdiction *ratione loci.* With respect to certain venues (JN, Article 88, venue of performance of the contract; Article 96, venue of counterclaims; Article 93, venue of multiple defendants; Article 104, agreed venue) the courts have, however, examined in addition whether, under the particular circumstances of a certain case, the localising element which is decisive for the venue in Austria is a strong enough tie to establish Austria's interest in having its courts adjudicate the subject matter in question.

The Convention on Jurisdiction and the Enforcement of Judgments in Civil and Commercial Matters of 16 September 1988 ("Lugano Convention"), which Austria will soon ratify, allows a foreign plaintiff also to rely on the jurisdictional provisions of that Convention by establishing the "international jurisdiction" of Austrian courts in a certain matter.

Competence *ratione loci* is determined by the defendant's *general forum* (JN,

Articles 65–76), which ordinarily is the defendant's habitual residence. The general forum of companies (corporations and partnerships) is their seat. "Seat" is defined as the place where a company's activities are administered (JN, Article 75(1)).

The plaintiff may choose between the general forum of the debtor and special venues, if applicable. Such venues include (JN, Articles 86a–101, special laws):

(1) actions against federal and local entities which are represented by the Attorney-General's office: competent court at plaintiff's residence (JN, Article 86a);
(2) venue of (local) business establishment (JN, Article 87);
(3) venue of contract performance (JN, Article 88(1));
(4) venue of claims of businessmen under their bills (JN, Article 88(2));
(5) venue on bills of exchange (JN, Article 89);
(6) venue *rei sitae* (JN, Article 91);
(7) venue *loci delicti commissi* (JN, Article 92a);
(8) venue for disputes among shareholders and shareholder/company (JN, Article 92b);
(9) venue of co-defendants (JN, Article 93);
(10) venue of the main proceedings (JN, Article 94);
(11) venue of counter-action (JN, Article 96);
(12) venue of former general forum (JN, Article 97); and
(13) venue of assets (JN, Article 99).

Jurisdiction *ratione materie* is defined as follows: The Austrian court organisation provides for courts of general jurisdiction and specialist courts, for example commercial courts and labour courts. Courts of general jurisdiction in the first instance are district courts (*Bezirksgerichte*) and regional courts (*Landes/Kreisgerichte*). Jurisdiction of these two types of court depends on either the type of the claim or on the amount in dispute. In the absence of special jurisdiction, the regional courts decide on cases if the amount in dispute exceeds AS 100,000.

Vienna has specialised commercial courts which decide disputes concerning trade and commerce matters. These courts may consist of one judge or a panel of judges, including associate judges who are local businessmen. Outside Vienna, the regional and district courts also fulfil the function of commercial courts. Appeals from judgments of the district courts are heard by a panel of judges at the regional court. Final appeals against their judgments may be taken before the Austrian Supreme Court, which is located in Vienna. If the regional court/commercial court acts as court of first instance, appeals are heard by the regional court of appeals (*Oberlandesgericht*), and such decisions may be appealed to the Supreme Court.

Preliminary measures may be granted only by the ordinary Austrian courts and *not by arbitration courts* (OGH, SZ 50/80). The enforcement of the injunctive relief requires that an action is actually lodged at the agreed court of arbitration.

Selecting the proper Austrian forum

Actions combined with motions for injunctive relief

If a foreign plaintiff combines a motion for injunctive relief with a civil or commercial law action, i.e. main proceedings, the court of the main proceedings has jurisdiction.

The foreign plaintiff will primarily seek the general forum of the defendant, i.e., his habitual residence. There may, however, be other forums which prevail: realty disputes are within the exclusive jurisdiction of the court where the immovable property is located (JN, Article 81). If a debtor has no general forum in Austria, pecuniary claims may be lodged at the court in whose district debtor property is located, or in whose district the object, against which the action is directed, is located. The venue of assets is, however, only a subsidiary forum.

Assets under JN, Article 99, are those which may be economically exploited; the value of the assets must—according to court practice—be at least 10% of the claim value (OGH, EvBl 1984/133). The venue of assets applies not only to disputes between nationals and foreigners, but also to legal proceedings between foreigners in Austria (OGH, JBl 1988, 386).

The crucial question for the foreign plaintiff is, therefore, to define an applicable "territorial" venue of the defendant under the JN or under applicable international treaties (for example, CMR or Lugano Convention). If such territorial venue can be found, the jurisdiction of the Austrian court will usually be affirmed; in the absence of such venue, Austrian jurisdiction will most likely be denied.

Separate preliminary injunction proceedings

Venues for enforcement proceedings, including motions for injunctive relief which are not combined with a civil or commercial law action, i.e., main proceedings, are governed by the Enforcement Act (EO).

The following courts have jurisdiction to grant preliminary injunctions and to enforce them (EO, Article 387):

(1) During pending legal proceedings on the claim, the court of the main proceeding has jurisdiction.

(2) During the enforcement proceedings, the court which is to grant the enforcement has jurisdiction.

(3) Before main proceedings are lodged and between main and enforcement proceedings, the district court where the opponent has his general venue has jurisdiction; a subsidiary venue is the district court where the object to be attached is located, otherwise the district court of the residence or seat of the third-party debtor.

Certain special venues as described above—like the venue of assets under JN, Article 99—do not constitute a sufficient venue for injunction proceedings unless they are combined with a main action.

Requirement of a bond

Actions combined with motions for injunctive relief

If motions for injunctive relief are combined with a main action, the following applies to the main proceedings: pursuant to Article 57, Civil Procedure Code (ZPO), foreign plaintiffs must provide a security for costs *upon the request of the defendant*, unless applicable state treaties provide otherwise. There is no requirement of posting a judicial bond if the plaintiff has his habitual residence in Austria, or the Austrian decision on the award of trial costs is recognised in the country of the plaintiff's residence or if the trial costs are covered by sufficient real property located in Austria and owned by the plaintiff (further exceptions are provided for in ZPO, Article 57(2)).

The bond requirement under ZPO, Article 57, for foreign plaintiffs applies *only* if a civil law or commercial law action is lodged alone or combined with a motion for a preliminary injunction (for separate preliminary injunction proceedings, see below).

The defendant motion that the court require the foreign plaintiff to post a security for costs must be made at the first hearing or before the defendant joins the proceedings on the merits (ZPO, Article 59). The defendant must also specify the amount of security requested. The security may be in form of a cash deposit, bank guarantee or Austrian securities. The court order on the judicial bond may be appealed.

If the foreign plaintiff fails to post the bond within the term, the court will—upon the defendant's motion—declare the action of the plaintiff withdrawn; yet such withdrawal does not have the effect of a waiver of the claim on the merits.

Separate preliminary injunction proceedings

In separate preliminary injunction proceedings, foreign plaintiffs are not subject to the ZPO, Article 57, bond requirement. In injunction proceedings, foreign plaintiffs may be required to provide security like Austrian plaintiffs and only under the requirements of the Enforcement Act (EO, Article 390).

In injunction proceedings, the court may *at its discretion* require the creditor to provide security for damages which the opponent may suffer under an unjustified injunctive order. The court will in particular require such an EO, Article 390, bond if, in the court's opinion, the creditor has not provided sufficient evidence for his claim (see below).

Cost considerations

The party who loses the case must reimburse the successful party for all reasonable legal fees. This includes court fees and attorneys' fees, as calculated under the Austrian Tariff of Attorneys' Fees (RATG). If the plaintiff is only partially successful, the costs are divided between the parties *pro rata*.

The court fees are lump sum fees payable to the court in advance by the plaintiff upon commencement of a civil or commercial law action. If the claim in controversy has a value of AS 1 million, the court fees for the proceedings in the first instance are AS 13,520; for the proceedings in the second instance AS 19,880; and for the proceedings in the third instance AS 26,510. For claim values exceeding AS 5 million, the court fees are normally 1.2% of the claim plus AS 6,760 for the proceedings in first instance. The court fees for preliminary injunctions which are not combined with a main action in civil proceedings are 50% of each stated amount. Lump sum court fees for enforcement proceedings are AS 1,590 (movables) and AS 1,790 (immovables) for claim values of AS 1 million.

Attorneys' fees are governed by the RATG and the Autonomous Guidelines for Attorneys' Fees. Under the RATG, the fees are calculated on the basis of the claim value and the types of services rendered. Claims whose value cannot be measured in money have to be estimated. The client and his Austrian attorney may have a separate fee arrangement which might supersede the tariff. Time billing is mostly used for non-contentious matters. Litigation is normally billed under the RATG. Contingency fees are not allowed under Austrian law and bar rules.

PROVISIONAL AND INTERIM MEASURES

General

Preliminary measures require that the creditor alleges and provides evidence for his claim. Such claim may be a money claim, a claim to performance or to certain rights. Austrian courts must, in principle, have jurisdiction to either adjudicate the claim (see above) or to enforce it. Enforcement titles under EO, Article 1, include court judgments and settlements, arbitral awards and settlements, as well as notarial deeds (as to foreign judgments, see below).

No particular degree of perfection is required in the country of origin for the foreign claim or judgment to allow the foreign creditor use of the provisional or interim remedies provided by Austrian courts. Austrian and foreign creditors are subject to the same requirements (see below).

The substantive law applicable to a particular claim, which is not yet evidenced by the foreign judgment, is to be determined under the Austrian Private International Law Act (IPR-G). The conflict of law rules under the IPR-G, *inter alia*, detail the requirements of a valid choice of law agreement and the substantive law applicable in the absence of such choice.

Austrian courts are supposed to know all foreign laws (IPR-G Article 4: *iura novit curia*). However, to provide sufficiently convincing evidence to the court supporting his claim, the foreign creditor's motion must also include documentary evidence on the foreign law allegedly applicable (OGH, EvBl 1973/53). If a preliminary measure is extremely urgent, the Austrian court may apply Austrian law in evaluating the claim (OGH, RdW 1988, 320).

Types of preliminary measures

There are two types of provisional measures available to local and foreign creditors to secure their claims through the Austrian courts: *preliminary injunctions* under EO, Articles 378 *et seq.*, and *execution to secure a claim* under EO, Articles 370 *et seq.*

The principal difference between the two groups of measures is that motions for preliminary injunctions may be made by the Austrian or foreign creditor before an action is lodged, during legal proceedings and even during enforcement proceedings. The injunction may serve to secure money claims, and to ensure certain individual behaviour of the opponent, or to secure rights. Motions for execution to secure a claim, *inter alia*, require a (not yet enforceable) title (i.e., judgment or order) for a money claim rendered by an Austrian court. Since EO, Article 370, measures require a title by an *Austrian* court, the availability of these measures to foreign claimants may be of limited relevance. The limitation is, however, partly superseded by (bilateral) state treaties which allow the enforcement to secure claims on the basis of foreign enforcement titles (see, for example, Articles 8–10 Austrian/German Enforcement Treaty, BGB1 1960/105).

Preliminary injunctions under the Enforcement Act

Preliminary injunctions may be granted to secure money claims (EO, Article 379), or to secure other types of claim, if enforcement will otherwise be frustrated or substantially impeded, such impediment including the enforcement of the claim in a foreign country that has not ratified the Brussels or Lugano Convention (EO, Article 381, lit 1), or to prevent an impending act of violence or irreparable damage (EO, Article 381, lit 2). In the following paragraphs the first type of injunction, namely the preliminary injunction to secure money claims, is described in detail; the other types are briefly sketched.

EO, Article 379, injunctions (money claims)

REQUIREMENTS

The creditor (in the Austrian terminology of the injunction proceedings, the "endangered party") must file a motion for a preliminary injunction, providing evidence that:

(1) he has a money claim; and
(2) the collection of that money claim is *in concreto* subjectively endangered (EO, Article 379(2), lit 1), or the judgment would have to be enforced outside Austria (abstract endangerment, EO, Article 379(2), lit 2).

In concreto subjective endangerment under EO, Article 379(2), lit 1, is the probability that without the injunctive relief the opponent of the endangered party, i.e., the debtor, may defeat or substantially impede the collection of the money claim by damaging, destroying, concealing or transferring assets by sale or by other disposal of the assets, in particular by agreements with third parties. Since the endangerment must relate to certain actions of the opponent, the opponent's poor financial situation, a bankruptcy risk, etc., do not constitute sufficient *in concreto* subjective endangerment. The creditor must also not be secured by alternative—even better—means like a mortgage, or an enforceable title.

Abstract endangerment under EO, Article 379(2), lit 2, i.e., that the judgment would otherwise have to be enforced outside Austria, requires that the debtor does not have any assets in Austria other than the one(s) to be attached by the creditor (OGH, SZ 15/224). This applies to Austrian judgments which would have to be enforced outside Austria only (OGH, SZ 51/17). The nationality of the claimant and the debtor is irrelevant; injunctive relief under EO, Article 379(2), lit 2, may also be sought if the claims relate to an object in Austria of foreigners who live outside Austria (OGH, SZ 51/62).

Claims made in foreign proceedings may be secured by Austrian injunction proceedings, provided the foreign judgment may be acknowledged and enforced in Austria. In a recent decision, the Austrian Supreme Court held—against prior court practice—that the lack of enforceability of the preliminary injunction outside Austria does not hinder the injunctive relief being granted (OGH, JBl 1990, 328). This approach is consistent with the broad definition of "judgment" in the Lugano Convention, which includes interlocutory judgments which have not yet become final, as well as a number of orders and injunctions ordering provisional remedies.

The court may at its discretion require the creditor to provide security if—in the court's opinion—the creditor has not provided sufficient evidence for his claim (EO, Article 390). Insufficient evidence for the endangerment may not be substituted by a bond (OGH, SZ 50/25).

Even if the claimant has provided sufficient evidence for the claim and the endangerment, the court may—because of the circumstances of the case—still grant the injunction if the opponent's damage will be merely financial, but may make the grant dependent on the deposit of a security (EO, Article 390(2)).

The security under EO, Article 390(2), protects the opponent from any damages, including legal costs, he may suffer as a consequence of an unjustified injunctive order.

The security deposit may be in the form of cash, bank guarantee or Austrian securities. The amount of the security is in the discretion of the court; the bond may be required before the order is granted or during the injunction proceedings. An initially required security may also be increased during the proceedings (OGH, SZ 54/11). If the injunctive order is finally denied, the security deposit will be released to the opponent of the creditor upon his request.

TYPES OF PROTECTIVE MEASURES GRANTED BY THE COURT

In preliminary injunction proceedings to secure a money claim the court may grant only the following three types of relief (EO, Article 379(3)):

(a) *Order for attachment and administration of movable goods of the opponent of the creditor, including the deposit of money* (EO, Article 379(3), lit 1). This relief relates to money in particular. Money and other movables of the opponent will be deposited at the court to ensure that the money and/or the movables may serve the creditor for later enforcement of his claims. The creditor does not, however, acquire a lien on the movables, although other creditors may not enforce their claims on these movables held by the court (EO, Article 262).

(b) *Order prohibiting the sale or pledge of movable goods of the creditor's opponent* (EO, Article 379(3), lit 2). A sale or pledge violating such a prohibition under a court order is null and void, unless the third-party acquirer is bona fide: third parties may thus not validly acquire property rights or a contractual lien if they knew or must have known of the prohibition. The court order prohibiting the sale or pledge of the movables does not hinder third parties from enforcing their claims on the object(s).

(c) *Prohibitive order against third-party debtor*. Under EO, Article 379(3), lit 3, if the opponent of the creditor has a claim against a third party (third-party debtor), the court order enjoins the opponent from disposing of the claim, especially by cashing it in; the order also enjoins the third-party debtor from fulfilling his obligation towards the claimant's debtor or doing anything which might defeat or substantially impede the later enforcement of the creditor's claims. The attached claims may be money claims, claims for performance or claims for the release of objects.

This double prohibitive order does *not* provide a lien to the creditor; it does not protect against enforcement actions of other creditors into the attached claims. The prohibition rather makes the third-party debtor liable to the creditor for all damages resulting from a violation of the prohibition (EO, Article 385(2) and (3)). The third party may exclude liability by depositing the attached money or goods at the court, or by handing them over to a trustee appointed by the court. Please note that the third-party debtor may—by paying his debts or releasing any attached object to the creditor's debtor—validly fulfil obligations towards the creditor's debtor; the creditor is left with a damage claim against the third-party debtor.

Not within the scope of third-party debtor claim attachments are claims arising under certain commercial papers like bills of exchange, cash checks or savings books, as specified in EO, Article 296. These documents are treated as physical movables and must be seized as movables (see above) and deposited (EP, Article 296(1)).

From the aforementioned follows that money claims may not be secured by preliminary injunctions relating to the immovable assets of the opponent of the creditor. The prohibition of the sale, encumbrance or pledge of real estate, parts of real estate or related rights is also outside the scope of relief (EO, Article 379(4)), as is the administration of businesses (OGH, JBl 1957, 102).

EO, Article 81(1) injunctions (other types of claims)

REQUIREMENTS

Under EO, Article 381, lit 1, preliminary injunctions may be requested to secure claims other than for payment, being claims for other types of performance, toleration, or non-performance.

Since such claims may not be secured otherwise, a preliminary injunction may even be issued if there is a title for enforcement.

To obtain a preliminary injunction for specific individual claims under EO, Article 381, lit 1, the creditor must allege and provide evidence for:

(1) the individual claim, which must not be a money claim, and
(2) the danger of the claim being frustrated or substantially impeded.

An *in concreto* objective endangerment is sufficient, which is not dependent on the behaviour of the debtor: without the preliminary injunction the enforcement of the alleged claim, especially by a change of present circumstances, is likely to be defeated or substantially impeded.

As in EO, Article 379(2), lit 2, an abstract, and not an *in concreto*, endangerment is sufficient if the judgment would have to be enforced outside Austria.

TYPES OF PROTECTIVE MEASURES GRANTED BY THE COURT

Unlike preliminary injunctions securing money claims, which are limited to the three types of measures described above, the measures to secure specific non-money individual claims as named in the Enforcement Act are only descriptive (EO, Article 382). The court is free to impose other measures.

The most important measures the preliminary injunction may include are:

(1) a request to deposit attached objects which the opponent of the creditor holds at the court or with a court-appointed trustee;
(2) administration of movables or real estate, including businesses;
(3) retention arrest in which the creditor may keep objects of the opponent until after a final decision on the merits of the claim has been rendered;
(4) an order or a prohibition against the opponent of the creditor from taking specific action with respect to the attached object;

(5) a prohibition of the sale, encumbrance or pledge of real estate against which the creditor has lodged a claim;
(6) a prohibition of sale, encumbrance or pledge against any third-party debtor, and
(7) the arrest of the creditor's opponent. This is a measure of last resort. It requires, *inter alia*, that the opponent is escaping or trying to escape and, furthermore, that his escape would defeat the action. The creditor must provide sufficient evidence for both the claim and the endangerment.

EO, Article 381(2) injunctions (prevention of damages)

Preliminary injunctions under EO, Article 381, lit 2, are aimed at securing various (long-term) rights as long as they are in dispute. Such rights include property and other absolute rights (to a name, copyrights, patent rights), contractual rights (for example leases) or personal rights (marriage). Since that provisional relief does not seek to secure the enforcement of money claims of (foreign) creditors, it is not described in detail here.

Remedies as to particular assets

Funds in bank accounts/third-party debtor claims

Preliminary injunctions under EO, Article 379(3), lit 3, to secure a money claim may only block funds which are already credited to the account. Future funds may not be blocked (OGH 8, Ob 503/77), but require subsequent attachment petitions.

Preliminary injunctions prohibiting the debtor to dispose of bank funds do not extend to joint account owners who have sole signing power to the blocked account. Additional court action with respect to those joint owners must be taken (*Avancini-Iro-Koziol, Bankvertragsrecht I* 314).

The attachment of bank funds or claims the debtor has against third-party debtors is the most popular and efficient way to secure claims. This includes, *inter alia*, prohibition orders relating to bank guarantees and attachment of wage claims.

Enforcement against funds in a bank account on the basis of an enforceable title, e.g. under a foreign judgment, are also effected by a third-party prohibition to the bank. The difference to the preliminary injunction is that the enforcing creditor also acquires a lien on all deposits on the account.

With respect to other orders against third-party debtors, it is important to know, especially for the enforcement on the basis of (foreign) judgments, that Austrian law provides for a special regime of enforcement into wage claims (EO, Articles 290 *et seq.*), allowing the creditor to direct his motion even against unknown third-party debtors; the debtor's employer or pension fund is located with the support of the social insurance system (EO, Article 294a).

Savings books, bonds and commercial papers

The creditor may not block funds on a savings book or claims under commercial papers (EO, Article 296) by way of a preliminary injunction prohibiting the disposal of the funds under EO, Article 379(3), lit 3 (OGH, RZ 1968, 73; *Avancini, supra*,

493). However, upon the creditor's motion, savings books and commercial papers may be seized and taken into court custody under an EO, Article 379(3), lit 1, injunction order like other movables.

Enforcement against named savings books and commercial papers on the basis of (foreign) enforceable titles follows the rules of enforcement against movables; the enforcing creditor acquires a lien on the attached objects.

Prohibition against sale, encumbrance, or pledge of real estate

As described above, money claims cannot be secured by attaching the debtor's real estate. The grant of an injunction order prohibiting the sale, encumbrance, or pledge of real estate requires that the claim to be secured be a claim to that property or to related rights (OGH, SZ 24/232). When granted by the court, the prohibition to dispose of the real estate is recorded in the land registry.

Preliminary injunctions outside the Enforcement Act

Outside the Enforcement Act, special laws may provide for preliminary injunctions under different—lower—requirements than those under the Enforcement Act. This includes preliminary injunctions in copyright (UrhG, Article 81) and unfair competition (UWG, Articles 21, 24) matters. Cartel (KartG, Article 52), Business Corporation (GmbHG, Article 42(4)), Cheque (SchG, Article 59(2)) and Patent (PatG, Article 147(2)) Acts also provide for preliminary injunctions.

Procedure

Competent courts

The courts having jurisdiction to issue a preliminary injunction have already been described above.

Procedure

MOTION BY THE CREDITOR

The creditor seeking a preliminary injunction (attachment) must file a motion with the competent Austrian court. The motion is subject to the general formal requirements for court motions; it must specify why the court is considered to be competent, detail the claim to be secured, both as to its contents and value, and describe the endangerment to the claim. Finally, the motion must also include a particular request as to contents (type of protective measure) and term of effectiveness of the preliminary measure.

It is suggested that the motion be supported by evidence in the form of documents and affidavits; documents which are not in the German language must be supplemented by a certified translation of these documents into German by a sworn translator.

The creditor is limited to the three types of protective measures named in EO,

Article 379(3). However, he may request more than one or all of these measures at the same time if one single measure might not sufficiently fulfil the purpose of securing his claims.

Under EO, Article 389(2), the creditor may in his motion for the preliminary injunction name a certain sum, which would—in the opinion of the claimant—render the requested injunction unnecessary, if deposited by the debtor at the court. Even if the claimant does not name such sum—covering the value of the claim and the creditor's costs—the court shall prescribe such "release money", provided that appears sufficient to secure the claim (EO, Article 391(1)).

The deposit of the release money suspends the execution of the granted injunction. The opponent of the creditor may then request the lifting of the injunction.

THE COURT PROCEDURE

The court examines its jurisdiction for the matter *ex officio* (JN Article 41(3)). In principle, motions for preliminary injunctions are decided by a single judge (EO, Article 388(1)). The court decides on the basis of (readily available) evidence. Such evidence will primarily be documentary evidence; it might include the statements of informed persons, or of parties who are deposed or who submit their statements in writing.

The procedure is *ex parte*: the opponent of the creditor does not have the right to intervene. The court may, however, hear him (EO, Article 397(1)) before an order is handed down. By issuing an order the court may either reject the application for a preliminary injunction (on formal grounds), grant the injunction or deny the injunctive relief. Preliminary injunctions are served on the opponent and/or the third-party debtor, by physical delivery (EO, Article 395).

THE COURT ORDER

The court order on the preliminary injunction will include the following:

(1) identification of the secured claim;
(2) specification of the type of protective measure;
(3) term of validity (that term may be extended upon motion by the creditor), including a term of compliance for the opponent of the creditor, for example if he has to deposit objects;
(4) if the injunctive relief is granted and the creditor has not yet instituted legal or enforcement proceedings for his claims, the court will set a reasonable term (which might be extended) within which the creditor must initiate legal proceedings or, if he has an enforceable title, enforcement proceedings. If such court action is not taken by the creditor within the term, the court will lift the order *ex officio* or upon opponent's request (EO, Article 391(2));
(5) if applicable, specification of the amount of the "release money" which the opponent should deposit at the court to suspend the injunction order (see above);
(6) specification of a security deposit to be posted by the creditor (EO, Article 390), provided the claim was not sufficiently supported by evidence or the evidence was sufficient but other reasons necessitate a bond.

EXECUTION OF THE COURT ORDER

The court order granting injunctive relief allows certain protective measures, and also constitutes the title to enforce them. The enforcement is carried out *ex officio*. The enforcement of the order must be effected within one month; that term is particularly relevant if the enforcement is contingent upon a bond (EO, Article 390(3)) or a cost advance (EO, Article 393(2)) of the creditor. The enforcement of the order may also be suspended, for example because an appeal (*Rekurs*) is filed.

APPEALS

The creditor may lodge an appeal (*Rekurs*) against a court order denying the motion for a preliminary injunction (for details on appeal proceedings, see below).

The creditor's opponent may either file an appeal or an objection (*Widerspruch*), with the aim of lifting an injunctive order.

The appeal (ZPO, Article 402(2); EO, Article 78) term is 14 days. The appeal does not suspend the order unless it is successfully combined with a motion for suspension. The proceedings are written proceedings without a hearing. The appeal is decided by the appellate court. It must establish that the court of first instance should have reached a favourable decision with respect to the appellant on the face of the documents produced. No new facts may be presented.

The opponent of the creditor may lodge, in addition to the appeal, an objection (EO, Article 397) against the injunctive order, provided he has not been heard before the order was granted. The term for filing the objection is 14 days. The judge of first instance decides on the objection. The filing has no suspensive effect. There is an oral hearing. Grounds for the challenge of the order may be challenges to the amounts of the security deposit and/or release money, if applicable; alleged insufficient evidence, and the like.

The courts may reverse, amend or affirm the challenged injunction order.

There may still be appeal possibilities to the Supreme Court. The final appeal to the Supreme Court is excluded if the granting or denying order of the court of first instance was affirmed by the court of appeals.

Reversal or limitation of an injunctive order

The grounds for a reversal or limitation of an injunctive order are:

(1) if the term for filing legal proceedings or starting enforcement proceedings was not complied with by the creditor;
(2) if the creditor's security is or becomes excessive;
(3) if the conditions which lead to the order change and the injunctive order is no longer justified;
(4) if the opponent of the creditor posts sufficient "release money"; and
(5) if the claim of the creditor has been finally dismissed.

Costs, damages and penalties

The foreign creditor should be aware that injunction proceedings bear considerable cost risks for the unsuccessful claimant. Under EO, Article 394, the claimant is, *inter alia*, liable to the defendant for all damages which the defendant suffers under an injunctive order that proves to be unjustified. The liability is irrespective of fault of the claimant. Before preliminary measures are taken, the foreign creditor should make a careful risk evaluation with the support of Austrian counsel.The cost risks include costs of the proceedings, damages and, in exceptional cases, the risk of fines:

(1) The creditor seeking injunctive relief must initially bear the costs of the injunction proceedings, including the costs of certain protective measures (EO, Articles 385, 393(1)). The creditor has a claim for reimbursement of the costs of the injunction proceedings only if he succeeds in the main proceedings against the debtor. The debtor who successfully defeats an application for injunctive relief is entitled to reimbursement of reasonable costs.

(2) The creditor must reimburse his opponent for all damages which were caused by unjustified preliminary injunction. This is the case—
   (a) if the alleged claim of the creditor which was the basis for the injunctive relief has been finally dismissed;
   (b) if the application for injunctive relief has proven to be unjustified;
   (c) if the creditor fails to file an action to justify the injunctive relief (main proceedings or execution proceedings) within the term set by the court.

   The court determines the amount of damages at its discretion. The damage award may include lost profits. The final order on damages is enforceable against the assets of the creditor. The damage claims of the opponent of the creditor under EO, Article 394(1) do not require any fault (negligence) of the creditor but will be awarded irrespective of such fault.

(3) If a preliminary injunction was obtained wantonly, the creditor may be ordered by the court to pay a fine (EO, Article 394(2)).

Execution to secure a claim under EO, Articles 370 *et seq.*

As described above, motions for executions to secure a claim under EO, Article 370 require a (not yet enforceable) title, thus a decision or order, by an *Austrian court* on a money claim. International treaties may specifically allow such execution to secure a claim also on the basis of a title obtained in a foreign court (see above).

If the claimant provides a title under EO, Article 371, the court must allow the security attachment without evidence from the creditor that enforcement of his claim is in danger of being frustrated or substantially impeded, or will have to be enforced in a country which is not a member of the Brussels or Lugano Conventions. The "titles" under EO, Article 371, *inter alia*, are: judgments of first instance based on an acknowledgement of debt by the defendant, which nevertheless are appealed by the debtor; judgments based on default of appearance which were objected to; judgments confirmed by the appeals court when a final appeal is lodged; (appealed) judicial payment orders in summary proceedings. Moreover, there are certain appealed decisions of the courts of first and second instance where evidence on endangerment may be substituted by a security; orders in non-contentious proceedings and to secure alimony and rental payments (EO, Articles 372 *et seq.*) are subject to a special regime.

The types of protective measures available include the attachment of movables, liens on real property, the forced administration of immovables and other exploitable rights, as well as attachment of claims of the judgment debtor.

Generally, the procedure aims at obtaining attachments and liens. When the judgment title becomes final, the execution to secure a claim is *ipso iure* transformed into a regular enforcement proceeding (OGH, JBl 1973, 321).

The requirements for lifting the execution order securing a claim and on costs and damages are detailed in EO, Articles 376–377.

RECOGNITION AND ENFORCEMENT OF FOREIGN COMMERCIAL JUDGMENTS

General

Foreign judicial decisions, in particular money judgments, will in general be immediately enforced as if they were judgments by an Austrian court, provided reciprocity between the court of origin and Austrian courts is assured under state treaties or government orders. Under EO, Article 1, lit 5, settlements in civil and commercial matters are enforceable in the Austrian courts on the same basis as final decisions of these courts. Foreign judicial settlements are, therefore, subject to the same requirements of Austrian enforcement as foreign judgments. The following summary concentrates on money judgments.

Requirements

Recognition

In order to enforce his foreign money judgment in Austria, a judgment creditor must meet the requirements set forth in EO, Articles 79 *et seq.*, as recently amended to comply with the Lugano Convention. The law now provides for a uniform procedure under which foreign titles are declared enforceable within the Republic of Austria. The judgment creditor has to move for the issuance of an "enforceability order" (*Vollstreckbarerklärung*). The enforceability order is not restricted to judgments and instruments issued within the scope of the Brussels and Lugano Conventions, but can be issued for all foreign titles which are covered by multilateral or bilateral treaties to which Austria is a party.

Under the Lugano and Brussels Conventions, public instruments, court settlements, and civil and commercial judgments rendered in a member state must be recognised in the other member state without any special procedure. Recognition is thus *ipso iure*. Furthermore, in the event of a dispute, if recognition is itself a principal issue, the general procedure for enforcement may be applied. Both principles are now laid down in EO, Article 85, which is limited to civil and commercial matters. Matters relating to a person's status are not covered by its scope; the law will thus not change in this respect. The effects of a judgment issued abroad relating to a person's status must thus be treated as a preliminary question in deciding the matter. Upon taking effect in Austria, the Lugano Convention will supersede most bilateral treaties (except the treaties with Israel, Tunisia and Turkey; see Schedule 1).

EO, Article 86a provides that acts and documents issued by supranational organisations of which Austria is a member shall be deemed enforcement titles issued abroad. Enforceability in Austria thus requires the issuance of an enforceability order under EO, Articles 79 *et seq.*

Subject matter requirements

The existing subject matter requirements for the enforcement of titles awarded outside Austria are the following (EO, Article 80):

Reciprocity, which can be verified on the basis of state treaties or by a government order published in the *Austrian Federal Law Gazette* (BGBl). The only such order presently in effect relates to the Canadian province of British Columbia.

The foreign court's jurisdiction, which can be determined by applicable state treaties (Lugano Convention, Article 16) and Austrian jurisdictional principles. Austrian courts claim, *inter alia*, exclusive international jurisdiction over:

(1) disputes of rights relating to real property situated in Austria, including possession, easements and servitudes (JN, Article 81);
(2) disputes arising from the lease of Austrian realty (JN, Article 83), and
(3) certain disputes between corporations/companies and their shareholders/members and among the shareholders/members themselves, provided the registered office of the company is located in Austria.

The original court order which commenced the foreign proceedings resulting in the foreign title must have been timely served on the judgment debtor, either in his country of origin, or by means of mutual aid in legal matters, or in Austria by physical delivery.

The foreign title must be final, i.e., no longer subject to appeal. Enforceability in the country of origin is sufficient, if enforcement is sought in Austria under an Austrian government order (EO, Article 80, lit 3).

The enforceability order will nevertheless be denied if:

(1) the debtor did not have the possibility of being a party to the proceeding upon which the foreign title has been issued;
(2) the foreign title entitles the prevailing party to an action which is illegal or unenforceable under Austrian law; or
(3) enforcement of the foreign title violates Austrian *ordre public* or is *contra bonas mores* (such violation may be found, e.g., in cases of fraudulently obtained judgments).

Procedure

Competent courts

Under EO, Article 82, the district courts (see above) have exclusive jurisdiction to issue an enforceability order on the basis of foreign judgments. The venue is determined by the defendants general forum (habitual residence). Where a general venue cannot be found in Austria, jurisdiction as to the enforceability order will depend, e.g., on the location of the property at which enforcement is directed. The same court will—upon additional motion—issue the execution permit commencing the actual enforcement based on the concurrently issued enforceability order. However, before the enforceability order has become final, actual enforcement is limited to protective measures.

Filing the motion

The judgment creditor will file a motion for an enforceability order. This motion may be combined with the motion for the execution permit (*Exekutionsbewilligung*). The motion for the execution permit must spell out the requested means of enforcement (like, e.g., the compulsory auction sale of movables or lien and sale of movables). Under the Lugano Convention, Article 33, the procedural formalities for making the application are to be governed by the law of the state in which enforcement is sought. Other applicable multilateral conventions or bilateral treaties (see Schedule 1 below) may further clarify which documents have to be presented to the Austrian court by the foreign judgment creditor. In general, a duly certified and authenticated copy of the foreign title, and, if applicable, documents proving that the title is final and enforceable in the country of origin, will suffice. Foreign language documents must be accompanied by a certified translation (requirements are set forth in applicable state treaty) into German. If the motion satisfies all formal requirements, the execution permit will usually be issued within two weeks of filing. The Austrian court must not review the merits of the foreign title before issuing the order.

The effects of an enforceability order are not restricted to a specific enforcement proceeding, but may be relied on for all future motions for execution permits. Once final, the enforceability order makes the foreign title equal to an Austrian title (EO, Article 84(b).

Appeals

Enforcement is granted to the judgment creditor upon a motion without a hearing for the judgment debtor. When an enforceability order (combined with an execution grant) is served on the judgment debtor, he may lodge an appeal (*Rekurs*) to the Regional Appellate Court or an objection (*Widerspruch*) to the district court that granted the enforcement. The appeal must be brought within 14 days after service of the order or the permit. The objection, however, may be brought within one month after issuance of the enforceability order if the debtor has his habitual residence in Austria, otherwise within two months. The judgment creditor may take an appeal against a court order denying the execution permit or enforceability order.

The decisions on appeal and objection may be further appealed to the Supreme Court. Appeals may be combined with a petition to suspend the enforcement proceedings. The suspension will be granted if the judgment debtor is likely to suffer irretrievable damage due to the execution; the judgment debtor may be ordered to provide adequate security (EO, Article 44).

The judgment debtor may also try to defeat the enforcement by bringing actions based in EO, Articles 35 and 36 (*Impugnations/Oppositionsklage*).

Costs, interest, security

Applicants who are successful in the enforcement proceedings are entitled to reimbursement of the court fees and attorneys' fees as calculated under the applicable Austrian Tariff for Attorneys' Fees.

The judgment creditor is entitled to interest on the principal only if and to the extent the judgment of the court of origin provides for such interest.

ZPO, Articles 57 *et seq.* (security for costs, see above), does not apply in enforcement proceedings based on a foreign judgment. Security may be requested from the foreign judgment creditor only in those cases where an Austrian national would also be required to post a bond (for example, interim orders for enforcement).

IMPACT OF BANKRUPTCY OF THE DEBTOR

Preliminary injunctions combined with main proceedings

The filing of a bankruptcy petition stays pending legal proceedings against a debtor with the exception of proceedings relating to assets outside the scope of the bankruptcy estate (Bankruptcy Act (KO), Article 7(1)). The bankruptcy trustee, joint defendants and opponents of the debtor may choose to continue the proceedings (KO, Article 7(2)).

Pending preliminary injunction proceedings combined with a civil or commercial law action ("main action") are equally stayed (OGH, EvBl 1982/119).

The effect of a foreign bankruptcy proceeding on a domestic lawsuit against the debtor is governed by applicable international treaties on bankruptcy (see, e.g., Article 14 of the Austrian/German Bankruptcy Convention, BGBl 1985/233).

Separate preliminary injunction proceedings

After the opening of the bankruptcy proceedings, the court must not grant injunctive orders with respect to assets that are part of the bankruptcy estate. Whether already granted injunctive orders remain valid during the bankruptcy proceedings depends on the individual circumstances of the case.

Injunctions requiring certain behaviour of the bankrupt and/or third parties remain valid. Injunctions granting the attachment of assets which now belong to the bankruptcy estate become invalid; this is particularly true for injunctions securing money claims, provided no lien has been acquired by the creditor (OGH, SZ 33/62).

Filing of claims with the bankruptcy court

Foreign creditors may file their claims with the bankruptcy court like domestic creditors (KO, Articles 102 *et seq.*). The foreign creditor must name an Austrian representative as recipient for all notices in the proceedings. Timely filing is a prerequisite for participation in the distribution of the estate.

A claim is deemed allowed if the bankruptcy trustee does not challenge it as unfounded (KO, Article 109). If the trustee disallows a claim, the foreign creditor may lodge an action against the bankruptcy trustee within a certain term fixed by the bankruptcy court. The economic advisability of such civil action depends not only on the likelihood of successful action, but also on the amount of prospective recovery (expected pro rata share).

Composition proceedings

Composition proceedings do not affect granted injunctions or pending injunction proceedings.

CHRISTIAN HERBST

SCHEDULE 1

There follow lists of selected international agreements on the enforcement of foreign (money) judgments and arbitral awards to which Austria is a party.

Multilateral Conventions

1. The Geneva Protocol on Arbitration Clauses (1923) (1928 BGBl 57).
2. The Geneva Convention on the Enforcement of Foreign Arbitral Awards (1927) (1930 BGBl) 343).
3. The Hague Convention on Civil Procedure (1954) (1957 BGBl 91).
4. New York Convention on the Recognition and Enforcement of Foreign Arbitral Awards (1958) (1961 BGBl 200).
5. European Convention on International Commercial Arbitration (1961) (1964 BGBl 107) and Agreement on the Application of the European Convention on International Commercial Arbitration (1962) (1965 BGBl 19).
6. Convention on Jurisdiction and the Enforcement of Judgments in Civil and Commercial Matters (1988) (Lugano Convention) (not yet in force).

Treaties and Conventions Where Recognition and Enforcement Is a Subsidiary Issue

- International Convention on the Carriage of Goods by Rail (CIM) (1970 and 1980) (1974 BGBl 744 and 1985 BGBl 225).
- International Convention on the Carriage of Passengers and Luggage by Rail (CIV) (1961) (1974 BGBl 744).
- International Convention on the Contract for the International Carriage of Goods by Road (CMR) (1956) (1961 BGBl 138 and 1981 BGBl 192).
- Convention on the International Carriage of Goods by Rail (COTIF) (1980) (1985 BGBl 225 and 1988 BGBl 20).

Bilateral Treaties

Belgium (1959) (BGBl 1961/287).
Federal Republic of Germany (1959) (BGBl 1960/105).
Finland (1988) (BGBl 1988/118).
France (1966) (BGBl 1967/288).
Israel (1966) (BGBl 1968/349).
Italy (1971) (BGBl 1974/521).
Liechtenstein (1973) (BGBl 1975/114).
Luxembourg (1971) (BGBl 1975/610).
Norway (1984) (BGBl 2985/406).
The Netherlands (1963) (BGBl 1966/37).
Poland (1974) (BGBl 1974/79).
Spain (1984) (BGBl 1985/373).
Sweden (1982) (BGBl 1983/556).
Switzerland (1960) (BGBl 1962/125).

Tunisia (1977) (BGBl 1980/305).
Turkey (1930) (BGBl 1932/90).
United Kingdom (1961) (BGBl 1962/224 and 1971/453).

Government Order of Reciprocity

Canada (order of 28 September 1970).

SCHEDULE 2

Selected Laws

Enforcement Act (EO) RGBl 1886/79, as amended by BGBl 1995/519. Code on Court Jurisdiction (JN) RGBl 1895/111 as amended.
Civil Procedure Code (ZPO) RGBl 1895/113 as amended.
Private International Law Act (IPR-G) BGBl 1978/304.
Austrian Tariff on Attorneys' Fees (RATG) BGBl 1969/189 as amended.

Selected Bibliography

Angst, Jakusch, Pimmer, *Exekutionsordnung* (1989, 12th ed.).
Avancini, Iro, Koziol, *Bankvertragsrecht I* (1987).
Fasching, *Zivilprozeßrecht* (1990, 2nd ed.).
Konecny, *Der Anwendungsbereich der einstweiligen Verfügung* (1992).
Loewe, *Zwischenstaatlicher Rechtsverkehr in Zivilrechtsachen* (1984/87).
Mohr, *KO/AO/AnfO* (1990, 7th ed.).
Neumann, Lichtblau/Heller, Berger, Stix, *Kommentar zur EO* (1976, 4th ed.).
Rechberger/Simotta, *Exekutionsverfahren* (1989).
Rechberger/Simotta, *Zivilprozeßrecht* (1986, 3rd ed.).
Stohanzl, *JN/ZPO* (1990, 14th ed.).
Wiesbauer, *Internationales Insolvenzrecht* (1986).

Abbreviations

EvBl	*Evidenzblatt*
JBl	*Juristische Blätter*
RPflE	*Rechtspflegerentscheidungen*
RdW	*Recht der Wirtschaft*
RZ	*Richterzeitung*
SZ	*Sammlung Zivilsachen*

CHAPTER 4

BELGIUM

ACCESS OF FOREIGNERS TO BELGIAN COURTS

As a matter of principle, access to the Belgian courts is open to any foreign claimant.

In 1848, the Supreme Court considered the access to Belgian courts, as a right to any foreigner, issued from the *droit des gens* (Cass, 3 August 1848, Pas. I, 358). Moreover, this right is guaranteed by the Belgian Constitution.

New Article 191 of the Constitution provides that any foreigner located on Belgian territory may benefit from the protection granted to persons and to properties, unless exceptions are provided by law. Two exceptions have been created by Belgian statute:

(1) the *cautio iudicatum solvi* (see below); and

(2) some restrictions regarding the right to benefit from legal aid.

The territorial competence of the Belgian courts is ruled by Articles 622 to 638 of the Judicial Code (the Belgian Code of Civil Procedure). The basic principle is contained in Article 624:

> Except when the law expressly provides that a particular judge has jurisdiction, a suit may be lodged, at the plaintiff's discretion, with
>
> 1. the judge of the district where the defendant or one of the defendants is domiciled,
> 2. the judge of the district where one or more of the obligations in dispute arise, or ought to be performed,
> 3. the judge of the district where domicile has been contractually elected,
> 4. the judge of the district where the bailiff has verbally notified the defendant in his presence, if neither the latter nor any other defendant has a domicile in Belgium or elsewhere.

To this basic principle the law adds a long list of matters falling within specific territorial jurisdiction. However, these principles established by the Judicial Code have been superseded by a growing number of treaties concluded by Belgium which, directly or indirectly, regulate the jurisdiction of the Belgian courts in international litigation.

Election of domicile

Regarding access to Belgian courts, it should be noted that claimants (Belgian as well as foreign) must comply with Belgian laws that oblige the claimant to elect domicile for certain specific procedures before the Belgian courts.

By way of example and given the topic of the present report, it is worth noting that:

(1) The party who intends to ask the presiding judge of the court of first instance to declare an arbitral award enforceable in Belgium must elect domicile in the

without the court's preliminary permission, through a bailiff, funds, properties or other valuables, in the hands of any third person, which are owed to his debtor, upon production of an authenticated (drawn up by a public notary) or private deed.

(b) Further, Article 1461, relating to the distraint procedure (*saisie-gagerie/pandbeslag*) provides that landlords of houses, apartments and other premises are entitled to seize, without the preliminary permission of the court, the goods placed in the leased premises by the tenant, in the event of non-payment of rent by the tenant.

These above-mentioned provisional remedies can also be obtained through the courts. It must be stressed that the application of provisional remedies without the court's preliminary permission, although valid, is done at the creditor's own risk. This means that the debtor may be entitled to claim damages from the creditor if the provisional remedy was executed abusively and caused a loss to the debtor. It is therefore advisable to seek the court's preliminary permission in order to avoid such claims for damages.

Characteristics of the foreign claim

The Judicial Code does not provide for a special requirement as to the degree a foreign claim must be perfect in its jurisdiction of origin in order to sustain a procedure seeking provisional or interim remedies before the Belgian courts.

The Belgian courts are available to foreign creditors and litigants within the conditions as set out above.

As to the admissibility of a claim invoked by a foreigner under Belgian law, the same general conditions of admissibility of claims raised by Belgians apply.

The following conditions must be fulfilled in order for a claim to be declared admissible:

(1) The plaintiff must have an interest in the outcome of the procedure.
(2) The plaintiff must be a proper party, referred to in Belgium as *la qualité/hoedanigheid*.
(3) The plaintiff must have the legal capacity to act before the courts.

Interest

According to Article 17 of the Judicial Code, a claim cannot be admitted if the plaintiff has no interest in the outcome of the procedure. In short, if there is no interest, there is no legal action. The "interest" is any advantage or benefit to the plaintiff in putting forward a claim. This interest may not be of an immoral nature.

The interest must be concrete, personal, and direct. This means that the claim cannot be purely theoretical but must apply to a concrete situation which exists between the parties in the lawsuit.

Article 18 of the Belgian Judicial Code requires a present and immediate interest. This implies that a claim will not be admissible if the interest of the plaintiff is only a potential or future interest. This, however, does not mean that the damage must have already occurred. Article 18, paragraph 2, provides that a claim may be declared admissible if the procedure has been initiated in order to prevent the violation of a right which is threatened.

Quality

According to Article 17 of the Judicial Code, the plaintiff must be the proper party or have the *qualité* or *hoedanigheid* to seek collection of a claim before the courts. This requirement presupposes a link between the person introducing the claim and the right of action.

The following persons are considered, among others, as the proper persons:
(1) the holder of the right, and
(2) his legal or contractual representative or agent.

Legal capacity

According to the doctrine, the plaintiff must have the legal capacity to exercise his rights before the courts. As a general rule, all persons (physical or legal) which have the capacity to enter into contracts have the capacity to submit a claim to the courts.

Minors, convicts, and the insane, amongst others, do not have the required legal capacity to act before the courts. However, this legal capacity is considered by some authors as not being a condition of admissibility of the claim but rather a condition of nullity of the procedure.[1]

RECOGNITION AND ENFORCEMENT OF FOREIGN JUDGMENTS

A distinction should be made between "recognition" and "enforcement" of foreign judgments.

The question of recognition depends upon whether the judgment has the effect of *res iudicata* (*autorité de chose jugée/kracht van gewijsde*), whereas the question of enforcement depends upon the executory authority of that judgment (*force exécutoire/uitvoerbare kracht*). These notions are not defined in the law but have been established by case law and authoritative legal commentaries such as the following:

(1) The concept of *res iudicata* requires that a foreign judgment obtained in one state (state of origin) be recognised as producing the same effects and having the same authority in another (state addressed).
(2) The executive authority of a foreign judgment means that it can be enforced in Belgium. An *exequatur* is a leave order given by a Belgian court upon an application for leave to enforce a foreign judgment, an arbitral award or an authentic instrument obtained in another jurisdiction.

Except in matters relating to the status and legal capacity of natural persons, foreign decisions, as a general rule, have no effect in Belgium without an *exequatur*. There is,

1. A. Fettweis, *Manuel de Procédure Civile* (1985), p. 54.

however, a growing exception to this principle. Many international treaties provide that judgments rendered in the contracting state be recognised and declared enforceable automatically or be submitted to simplified proceedings in Belgium. It is therefore necessary in matters relating to the recognition or enforcement of a foreign judgment, to confirm that, among the many international conventions, there is no bilateral or multilateral treaty which could be applied to the judgment in question with regard to the jurisdiction of origin and the issue in question.

National law

The *exequatur* procedure, initiated by a writ of summons, is ruled by Article 570 of the Judicial Code.

> The court of first instance shall whatever the amount of the claim in question, rule on the application for *exequatur* of judgments rendered by foreign courts, in civil and commercial matters. Unless a treaty between Belgium and the country where the judgment was rendered, should be applied, the court shall, in addition to the matter at issue, verify:
> 1. that the judgment contains nothing which is contrary to Belgian principles of public policy or to the rules of Belgian public law;
> 2. that the right of defence has been respected;
> 3. that the foreign court has not assumed competence solely on the grounds of the claimant's nationality;
> 4. that according to the law of the country where the decision was rendered, it is considered to be a final adjudication;
> 5. that according to the same law, the authentic copy which is produced conforms to all the necessary formalities regarding authenticity.

Any judicial decision may be referred for *exequatur*, whatever its nomenclature (judgment, order, decree, decision).

It is useful to examine in detail the fourth condition set forth by the Belgian Code, i.e., that the foreign judgment has, under that foreign law, become a final decision (*force de chosé jugée/kracht van gewisjde*) in application of the principle of territoriality of procedural rules.

Strictly interpreted, the expression "final decision" means that the judgment is not subject to further appeal. Nevertheless, doctrine and jurisprudence provide a more flexible interpretation to the extent that they consider that a judgment may be entered for *exequatur* if, in the country in which the judgment was rendered, it is as enforceable as the *exequatur* which is requested in Belgium, even if it is not final.[2] Thus, a foreign judgment which is stated to be provisionally enforceable, notwithstanding any appeal, may be the subject of *exequatur* proceedings in Belgium, even if the avenues of appeal are still open.

Treaty law

A distinction must be made between the bilateral and multilateral treaties which deal with the recognition and enforcement of foreign decisions as a primary subject matter and the treaties where recognition and enforcement is a subsidiary matter.

2. Répertoire Pratique du Droit Belge, V° Exequatur, No. 37.

Although the following lists are long, they cannot be considered exhaustive.

Treaties and conventions with recognition and enforcement as a primary subject matter

(1) Belgium/France on Jurisdiction, the Validity and Enforcement of Judgments, Arbitration Awards and "Public" Documents (8 July 1899)*;
(2) Belgium/Netherlands on Territorial Jurisdiction of Courts, Bankruptcy, Validity and Enforcement of Judgments, Arbitration Awards and "Public" Documents (28 March 1925)*;
(3) Convention on Recognition and Enforcement of Foreign Arbitration Awards (26 September 1927);
(4) Belgium/Great Britain on Mutual Enforcement of Judgments (2 May 1934) (afterwards declared applicable to the Hong Kong Territory and New Zealand);
(5) New York Convention on the Recognition and Enforcement of Decisions Relating to Maintenance Obligations (20 June 1956);
(6) Belgium/Austria on Mutual Recognition and Enforcement of Judgment and Probative Instruments Relating to Maintenance Obligations (25 October 1957);
(7) The Hague Convention on Recognition and Enforcement of Decisions Relating to Maintenance Obligations towards Children (15 April 1958);
(8) New York Convention on Recognition and Enforcement of Foreign Arbitration Awards (10 June 1958);
(9) Belgium/Germany on Mutual Recognition and Enforcement of Judgments, Arbitration Awards and Public Documents in Civil and Commercial Matters (30 June 1958)*;
(10) Belgium/Switzerland on Recognition and Enforcement of Judgments and Arbitration Awards (29 April 1959);
(11) Belgium/Austria on Mutual Recognition and Enforcement of Judgments, Arbitration Awards, and Probative Instruments in Civil and Commercial Matters (16 June 1959);
(12) Belgium/Italy on Recognition and Enforcement of Judgments and Other Enforceable Instruments in Civil and Commercial Matters (6 April 1962)*;
(13) EEC Convention on Jurisdiction and Enforcement of Judgments in Civil and Commercial Matters (27 September 1968); and
(14) Belgium/Yugoslavia on Recognition and Enforcement of Decisions Relating to Maintenance Obligations (12 December 1973).

The most frequently applied convention is, of course, the Brussels Convention. The bilateral treaties above marked with an asterisk (*) have been superseded by the Brussels Convention by virtue of Article 55. However, in accordance with Article 56(1): "The Treaty and Conventions referred to in Article 55 shall continue to have effect in matters to which this Convention does not apply."

It should be noted that the Brussels Convention concerns civil and commercial matters but does not apply to:

(a) the status or capacity of natural persons, marriage régimes, wills or inheritance;

(b) bankruptcies, compositions or similar proceedings;
(c) social security; and
(d) arbitration.

The Brussels Convention does not waive bilateral and multilateral treaties with a more specific object (Article 57).

Treaties and Conventions where recognition and enforcement is a subsidiary issue

(1) The Hague Conventions on Civil Procedure of 17 July 1905;
(2) Geneva Convention of 19 May 1956 relating to Contracts for the International Carriage of Goods by Road (Article 31);
(3) Organisation for Economic Co-operation and Development (OECD) Convention, Paris, 29 July 1960 on Liability in the Field of Nuclear Energy (Article 13);
(4) Convention with Austria of 16 July 1969 on Bankruptcy (Article 9); and
(5) Convention on Mutual Aid in Civil and Commercial Matters with Algeria of 9 June 1970; Yugoslavia of 24 September 1971; Romania of 3 October 1975; Morocco of 30 April 1981; Germany of 29 November 1982 and Czechoslovakia of 15 October 1984.

INTERIM AND PROVISIONAL REMEDIES

Types of remedies

Under Belgian law, the following remedies are available:

(1) Interim or interlocutory remedies—Reference is made to the decisions determining an intermediate issue made in the course of pending litigation on the merits of the claim, which does not dispose of the case entirely. These decisions are rendered by the court, who makes a further ruling upon the merits of the claim, resolving the entire controversy.
(2) Provisional remedies—Reference is made to proceedings incidental to and in connection with a regular action, invoked before initiating the primary action or while the primary action is pending, in order to assure that the claimant's right will be preserved or that he will not suffer irreparable injury. The judge may grant the provisional remedy subject to the institution of a proceeding on the merits of the claim before the competent court, in Belgium or abroad, within a certain period.

The provisional remedies include:

(a) decisions rendered *en référé/in kortgeding* and those issued upon request by the presiding judges;
(b) remedies ordered by the judge of seizure: attachment of movable goods, attachment of immovable goods, garnishment, distraint procedure, attachment of vessels, and seizure description in patent and copyright litigation; and
(c) remedy ordered by the justice of the peace: affixation of official seals.

Procedure

Interim remedies

According to Article 19, al. 2 of the Judicial Code, the judge who makes a ruling on the merits of the case is entitled to order any preliminary remedy, before pronouncing his final decision on the matter, in order to:

(1) investigate the claim (e.g., order an expert survey); or

(2) provisionally regulate the situation between the parties.

The general and basic steps of a procedure on the merits before the Belgian courts are as follows:

(a) The procedure on the merits is generally initiated by way of a writ of summons to be served on the defendant(s) by a bailiff.

(b) The introductory document is recorded in the court register and a hearing date is fixed.

(c) At the initial hearing, either a hearing is postponed to a fixed date or the case is sent back to the court list without any hearing date (*renvoi au rôle/verzending naar de rol*).

(d) Then follows the exchange of documents (including documentary evidence) and submissions (arguments in writing) between counsel of the parties.

(e) When the case is ready to be orally presented before the court, a hearing is requested by the parties.

(f) After counsel have presented their oral argument, the court declares the closing of the debates.

(g) Judgment on the merits is normally rendered within one month of the closing of the debate.

At any of these stages, but before the court declares the closing of the debates, interim remedies can generally be rendered at the request of the party(ies) either already mentioned in the writ of summons or formulated later by way of submissions. However, the court may also, at its own discretion, render an interlocutory decision, especially if the judge wants to have recourse to some evidentiary measures. These include: documentary evidence, verification of handwriting, instruction called "falsified civil documents", hearing of witnesses, appointment of an expert, examination of the parties, party-oath, and viewing of the premises.

Although prima facie these measures do not seem to be of primary importance to a foreign creditor who seeks relief toward securing collection of a claim, one should bear in mind that these measures may be of some help to maximise the chances of having the claim declared founded by the court.

It should be emphasised that interim remedies are ordered by the judge who tries the merits of a claim. As is mentioned below, the other conservatory and provisional remedies are ordered by special judges who are not entitled to make a ruling on the merits of a claim.

Interlocutory judgments may be subject to appeal, but one should note here the effect of this appeal on the lawsuit itself, called the effect *dévolutif/devolutief*. This effect is considered to be one of the most important exceptions to the principle of the two-tier jurisdiction in Belgium. If an appeal is lodged against an interlocutory judgment, the appellate court will decide on all the grounds of the case and not only on the facts known to and ruled by the original judges in their interlocutory judgment. In this case, the court of first instance which rendered the interlocutory judgment will be prevented from ruling on the merits of the case, and therefore the parties will lose a tier of jurisdiction. As an exception to this, when the appellate court confirms an instruction measure (as listed above), it must send the case back to the court below.

Provisional remedies

PROVISIONAL AND CONSERVATORY REMEDIES ORDERED BY THE PRESIDING JUDGES

According to Article 584 of the Judicial Code, the presiding judges of the court of first instance, the commercial court, and the labour court have the jurisdiction to order any provisional remedy in case of urgency, with respect to matters within their jurisdiction.

The application may be made independently of any pending action and the relief granted does not prejudge the merits of the case.

Depending on the circumstances justifying the provisional remedies (urgency, extreme urgency, absolute necessity), which will have an influence on the type of introductory document, a distinction must be made between the procedure *en référé/in kortgeding* and the procedure by request.

Procedure en Référé—The so-called procedure *en référé/in kortgeding* is regulated by Articles 1035 *et seq.* of the Judicial Code.

The presiding judges of the court of first instance, the commercial court, and the labour court, depending on the nature of the matter, only have jurisdiction to hear cases where there is a degree of urgency. The notion of urgency is not defined by law. According to doctrine and case law, however, a case should be considered as urgent when loss or prejudice might occur if prompt measures are not taken. Whether the matter is urgent is left to the judge's discretion.

The procedure is adversarial and is instituted by writ of summons to be served to the defendant by a bailiff. The period of delay in which to summon the adverse party to appear at the hearing is a minimum of two days from the time of serving the writ. In case of extreme urgency, the presiding judge can authorise, upon unilateral request, a shorter period of delay within which to summon the adverse party to appear at the hearing.

The law provides that, in maritime matters, the plaintiff is allowed to summon the adverse party on any day, at any time, without any special permission.

The presiding judges make "provisional" orders which do not compromise the merits of a claim which may be *sub judice* in another court. Their orders may not have any influence on the decision of the judge who will rule on the merits of the case.

Decisions *en référé/in kortgeding* are immediately and provisionally enforceable, notwithstanding any appeal.

Procedure Introduced by Request—The procedure introduced by request (*requête/verzoekschrift*) is regulated by Articles 1025 *et seq.* of the Judicial Code. Only in the case of absolute necessity can a claim seeking provisional relief be initiated by unilateral request before the presiding judge of the court of first instance, the commercial court, or the labour court.

The procedure initiated by request is a fully unilateral procedure (instead of *référé*, which is an adversarial procedure). This means that the adverse party against whom certain provisional remedies are requested will not be summoned to appear before the presiding judge.

The presiding judge can order provisional remedies by way of unilateral decision (often used for investigation purposes). If he considers it necessary, he can convocate the parties involved for further explanation. The presiding judge pronounces his decision in closed chambers.

The decision given on unilateral request can be enforced immediately and provisionally, notwithstanding any appeal. Appeal against the decision must be lodged within a month of the notification of the decision.

The presiding judges of the court of first instance, the commercial court, and the labour court ruling *en référé/in kortgeding* in urgent matters or upon unilateral request in matters of absolute necessity, have jurisdiction to order:

(1) any necessary provisional remedy in order to prevent the occurrence of any damaging events;
(2) any conservatory remedy in order to safeguard certain rights, such as the establishment of an inventory, the deposit of certain documents or goods, the sale of certain goods, and the appointment of an administrator;
(3) any measure of investigation such as the appointment of an expert, ordering an expert survey to establish the damage, calculate the amount of damages and examine the cause of the damage;
(4) any necessary measures in order to protect certain rights, including the sale of abandoned movable goods;
(5) the hearing and examination of any witnesses, even with respect to a future dispute, it it has been established that, in case of postponement of the examination, the witnesses could not be further investigated;
(6) the provisional restitution of securities, stocks and shares, and bills of exchange; and
(7) the suspension of a certain event (e.g. an announced but unauthorised sale).

This list is not comprehensive, given the wide, if not unlimited, variety of decisions the presiding judges can render in matters of urgency.

CONSERVATORY REMEDIES BY THE JUDGE OF SEIZURE OF THE COURT OF FIRST INSTANCE

The judge of seizure is a judge of the court of first instance appointed to hear cases related to conservatory seizures and executory measures.

According to Article 1413 of the Judicial Code, every creditor is entitled, in case of urgency, to seek the court's permission to attach the seizable goods of his debtor. The creditor applies for a seizure order for distraint of assets (moneys in a bank account, real estate, goods) belonging to the defendant (debtor) so as to prevent the latter from disposing of them until a final judgment on the merits is obtained.

Two conditions must be satisfied for the conservatory seizure to be granted:

(1) The case must involve an element of urgency: the plaintiff must establish that he has the grounds for concern that recovery under a later court decision might be compromised by the present or future insolvency of his debtor (Article 1413 of the Judicial Code).

(2) The claim must be certain (i.e., there is prima facie evidence of a good claim), due (i.e., the obligation has already arisen), and for a determined amount or be capable of provisional evaluation (Article 1415 of the Judicial Code).

The claim must be initiated before the judge of seizure by unilateral request. The procedure is fully unilateral. This means that the party against whom conservatory measures are requested will not be notified of the request or summoned to appear before the judge of seizure.

The request must indicate the amount up to which the conservatory measure is sought.

The judge will act on the request within eight days from its filing.

Conservatory seizure is valid for three years. The judge may, however, reduce the duration in the case of conservatory seizure on movable goods.

If the creditor wants the conservatory seizure to be maintained beyond the three-year period, he is entitled to request a renewal of the seizure.

The order of the judge of seizure granting a conservatory seizure is served by a bailiff to the party against whom the seizure is requested (i.e., the debtor). The seized party has the right to make an appeal against this decision within one month after the order is served.

To lift the conservatory measures, the seized party can set up a guarantee, in the hands of the bailiff or of an appointed receiver, or at the *Caisse des Dépôts et Consignations/Deposito en Consignatiekas* (of the Ministry of Finance) (*cantonnement/kantonnement*).

The conservatory seizure can be transformed into an executory seizure after the attainment of a final court decision on the merits of the case.

The Belgian Judicial Code provides for several types of conservatory seizures:

(1) attachment of movable goods;
(2) attachment of immovable goods;
(3) garnishment;
(4) distraint procedure;
(5) attachment of vessels; and
(6) seizure description in patent and copyright litigation.

Various items of property have been declared by the Judicial Code as being exempt from seizure, including wages and salaries on a sliding scale.

It should be stressed that, in two cases, the Judicial Code provides that the claimant is exempted from asking the preliminary permission of the judge of seizure: the former is, therefore, entitled to seize through a bailiff's intervention in the cases of garnishment and distraint procedure (see below).

Furthermore, according to Article 1414 of the Judicial Code, any judgment, albeit a judgment which has not been declared as "enforceable notwithstanding appeal", is still equivalent to the authorisation to conservatorily seize assets up to the amount to which the adverse party has been declared liable.

If a party has been granted a judgment on the merits in Belgium, he need not ask for the preliminary permission of the judge of seizure to seize assets belonging to his debtor. The bailiff can seize the assets on the basis of the judgment.

It is worth examining the *validity of a foreign judgment*: to what extent may a foreign creditor, who has already been granted a court judgment on the merits of a claim under his jurisdiction but who is seeking to obtain conservatory remedies in

Belgium toward securing collection of that claim, use the foreign decision? This question does not receive a unanimous answer from the authoritative authors. According to some authors, a foreign judgment would be recognised as of the same value as the Belgian judgment. Therefore, a foreign decision would allow the claimant to attach assets of the debtor without the permission of the judge of seizure.[3]

A foreign judgment on the merits of a case can be invoked by a foreign creditor to sustain his request for conservatory remedies and to prove that his claim is certain, due, and for a determined amount (conditions required by Article 1415 of the Judicial Code). In this case, the foreign judgment can be considered as "documentary evidence", but it does not have the same value as a judgment rendered in Belgium.

On the other hand, according to the same author, if a treaty has been signed between the country where the invoked decision has been given and Belgium, regarding the mutual recognition and enforcement of their judgments, then the foreign court's decision can justify a conservatory seizure without the preliminary authorisation of the judge of seizure in much the same way as a Belgian court's decision, even if the foreign decision has not yet been declared enforceable in Belgium by way of *exequatur*.[4]

TYPES OF CONSERVATORY MEASURES

1. The procedure for *attachment of movable goods (saisie mobilière conservatoire/ bewarend roerend beslag*: Articles 1422–1428, Judicial Code) follows the general rules as mentioned above. The conservatory seizure can be carried out on all movable goods which are the property of the debtor, such as furniture, jewellery, machinery and other office equipment, goods.

As mentioned above, the conservatory attachment can be converted into an executory attachment when a final court decision has been rendered on the merits of the case.

The law of 14 January 1993 has created the possibility for the debtor whose assets have been conservatorily blocked and which will be sold afterwards in the framework of the executory attachment to sell them amicably. The proceeds of this sale will be allocated to his creditors.

The debtor must inform the bailiff of the proposals within 10 days following the notification of the executory attachment.

Should the creditors prove the insufficient asset of the proposal, the request of the debtor for amicable sale is set aside.

Payment is made by the purchaser into the hands of the bailiff.

2. *Attachment of immovable goods (saisie immobilière conservatoire/bewarend onroerend beslag*: Articles 1429–1444, Judicial Code) prevents the debtor from selling or mortgaging his immovable assets (real estate) and their accessories.

When filing the request, the claimant must annex a copy of the extract of the state register showing the number under which the real estate is registered by the administration and the name of the owner, as well as an attestation delivered by the mortgage office.

3. See Chabot-Leonard, *Saisies Conservatoires et Saisies-exécutions* (1979), p. 109. Other authors advocate a more restrictive interpretation.

4. De Leval, *Traité des Saisies* (1988), pp. 322–323.

The decision of the judge of seizure authorising the conservatory seizure of immovable goods must be registered at the mortgage registry office within a period of one month from its pronouncement. From the day of transcription of the conservatory seizure, the debtor cannot validly sell or mortgage the seized immovable assets.

3. *Garnishment* (*saisie-arrêt/derdenbeslag*: Articles 1445–1460, Judicial Code) can be either granted by the judge of seizure upon unilateral request or enforced by a creditor without any court's preliminary permission.

According to Article 1445, any creditor is entitled to seize, through a bailiff without the court's preliminary permission and upon production of a notarial or private deed, any conservatory funds, property, or other valuables in the hands of third persons which are owed to his debtor. In this case, the garnishment will be carried out at the creditor's own risk. The creditor may be sued for damages in the case of vexatious or ungrounded garnishment procedure.

The purpose of such a procedure is to prevent third parties paying moneys due to the debtor (or to deliver goods due to the debtor) and to block those moneys (or goods) in the hands of those third parties. Through this procedure, the creditor can secure collection of his claim immediately with third parties and not with his own debtor. By blocking the moneys and goods in the hands of a third person, these do not fall into the estate of the debtor.

The procedure involves three parties: the seizing creditor, the debtor, and the seized third party.

A copy of the decision of the judge of seizure granting the garnishment is sent by registered mail by the registrar of the judge of seizure to the claimant and to the seized third party. The garnishment becomes effective from the time of reception.

Within 15 days following the reception of the copy sent by the registrar, the seized third party must officially declare to the seizing party and to the debtor, by registered mail, which moneys and goods are due to the debtor and are subject to garnishment.

The decision of the judge, together with the declaration of the seized third party, must be notified to the debtor.

The seized third party may not dispose of the blocked moneys or goods.

If the seized third party infringes this interdiction, he can be declared as "debtor" of the seizing party and can be held totally or partially liable for the amount due.

Attachment of a bank account is a type of garnishment frequently used in Belgium.

4. Through the *distraint procedure (saisie gagerie/pandbeslag*: Article 1461, Judicial Code) landlords (foreign as well as Belgian) of houses, apartments and other premises are entitled to seize, without the preliminary permission of the court, the goods placed in the leased premises by the tenant, in the event of non-payment of rent.

However, this attachment, if done without the judge's permission, presents a risk: the bailiff in charge of the seizure must inform the debtor, at least 24 hours in advance, by way of a summons, of the intention to seize the property. Therefore, the debtor-tenant may remove his property before the bailiff returns the next day to draw up the report of seizure. Consequently, it is recommended that the landlord asks the permission of the judge of seizure. In this case, no special summons must be presented in advance by the bailiff.

5. *Vessel attachment (saisie conservatoire sur navires et bateaux/bewarend beslag op zeeschepen en binnenschepen*: Articles 1467–1480, Judicial Code) may be granted by the judge of seizure to secure collection of a maritime claim.

The maritime claims that can be guaranteed by such type of seizure are restrictively enumerated in Article 1468 of the Judicial Code. The seizure must refer to the allegation of a right or a claim for damages caused by a vessel, either by collision or otherwise, wages of captains, officers and the crew, and any maritime mortgage.

The conservatory attachment can be authorised on the vessel to which the maritime claim relates, or on any other vessel belonging to the same owner, at the moment the maritime claim has arisen.

6. Through *seizure description in patent and copyright litigation (saisie-description/beslag inzake namaak*: Articles 1481–1488, Judicial Code), the owners of patents and copyrights, or rights existing under the laws for protection of designs and similar laws can apply to the judge of seizure for leave to have an expert appointed to examine and describe in a survey:

(a) the equipment, machines and all objects purported to infringe the claimant's intellectual property rights invoked;
(b) the plans, documents, and other writings which establish the invoked infringement; and
(c) the equipment directly used for the manufacture of the purported infringing items.

It must be stressed that the expert has no authority to give an opinion as to the existence of the infringement; his role is limited to the complete description of the above listed objects and documents. This procedure will allow the claimant to gather the necessary information in order to decide whether or not to initiate an infringement proceeding and will avoid the disappearance of evidence.

The judge of seizure may also:

(a) enjoin the disposal of the infringing objects;
(b) attach these objects and the revenue that they may provide;
(c) appoint a depository; and
(d) affix seals.

The expert's report is filed with the registrar of the judge of seizure, and a copy is sent to the claimant and the purported infringer.

The claimant must initiate the infringement proceedings before the court of first instance within a month of the sending of the expert's report by the registrar.

If the claimant fails to start a procedure on the merits, the order of the judge of seizure has no effect *ipso iure*.

This seizure description presents a fundamental difference to the other procedures to be initiated before the judge of seizure: the judge may grant the measure to the claimant even if the case is not urgent.

It should be stressed that, in Belgium, infringement of copyright and rights existing under the laws for the protection of designs and similar laws can also be the object of a procedure before the criminal court. However, it is impossible for the victim of such infringement to take advantage of the seizure description as well as lodge a claim before the criminal court. He has to make a choice between the two different types of procedure and cannot accumulate them.

CONSERVATORY REMEDY ORDERED BY THE JUSTICE OF THE PEACE

Article 1148 of the Judicial Code provides for a special procedure called the affixation and lifting of official seals (*apposition et levée des scellés/verzegeling en ontzegeling*).

Each time a serious interest requires it, the affixation of seals on assets belonging to the common estate of a married couple, inheritance or joint estate can be requested by all creditors of the common estate, inheritance or joint estate, and all persons claiming rights with regard to the estate. This procedure can be a very efficient remedy, in that it prevents the alienation or the dispersal of assets and valuables.

The affixation of seals must be requested from the justice of the peace, either by unilateral request or orally (in the latter case, the declaration is recorded by the registrar of the justice of the peace).

The seals will be affixed within 24 hours from the time of the request. In case of urgency, the seals can be affixed on Saturday, Sunday, and public holidays.

A report of affixation of seals must be drafted. This document will contain a description of the objects which are not sealed and a detailed description of the objects upon which the seals have been affixed.

After obtaining a final and enforceable judgment establishing the definite rights of the parties, the lifting of the seals can be requested from the justice of the peace.

INFLUENCE OF INTERNATIONAL TREATIES

In general, the above-mentioned bilateral treaties and international conventions aim to facilitate access to the courts of the signatory countries to the citizens of other signatory countries, and provide for the recognition and enforcement of judgments, arbitral awards, and probative acts without any specific procedure or with a simplified procedure. These treaties and conventions facilitate collection on a claim in Belgium.

Given its importance and the frequent reference to the Brussels Convention, it is worth explaining the basic principles of this Convention and examining in more detail its application to provisional remedies, and therefore the value of those measures granted in a contracting state.

According to Article 25 of the Convention, "judgment" shall encompass any judgment rendered by a court or tribunal in a contracting state, whatever the judgment may be called, including a decree, decision, order, or writ of execution. It is commonly agreed that Article 25 includes provisional remedies.

The Brussels Convention has sanctioned the principle of the automatic recognition of a judgment rendered by a court in a contracting state (state of origin) in the other contracting states (states addressed) without any special procedure being required. If this recognition is challenged in the state addressed, the Convention has allowed for a proceeding to be initiated by the party who seeks the recognition of the judgment. However, a judgment shall not be recognised:

> Where it was given in default of appearance, if the defendant was not duly served with the document which instituted the proceedings in sufficient time to enable him to arrange for his defence. (Article 27(2))

The Convention allows for a simplified procedure to obtain *exequatur* from a court of a contracting state. According to authoritative authors, the *exequatur* can be refused for the same reasons as recognition. Moreover, it is subject to specific rules.[5]

5. Weser, *La Convention Communautaire sur la compétence judiciaire et l'exécution des décisions* (1975), Number 290.

Therefore, judgments rendered without the defendant having the opportunity to be heard and to prepare his defence cannot benefit from the recognition and enforcement system as provided by the Brussels Convention.

The European Court of Justice has expressly ruled that this principle also applies to provisional remedies.[6] To justify its decision, the court declared that the provisions relating to recognition and enforcement convey the intention of ensuring that the right of defence is respected throughout the legal proceedings. It is because of the guarantees which benefit the defendant in the proceedings held in the state of origin that the Convention is so "liberal" as to recognition and enforcement. Consequently, a provisional remedy can never be subject to recognition or enforcement in a state addressed if the defendant has not been heard or at least been given the possibility of defence in the state of origin.

One can conclude that a provisional remedy rendered in Belgium on an *ex parte* basis, such as conservatory attachment, could never be recognised in an EC member state on the basis of the Brussels Convention.

INFLUENCE OF BANKRUPTCY

It is useful to examine bankruptcy proceedings in Belgium as this may be of interest to foreign creditors who seek to enforce their rights in Belgium.

Bankruptcy is a proceeding organised by law that aims toward the collective enforcement of the estate of a trader in the interest of the creditors. Three conditions must be met in order to be declared bankrupt:

(1) The debtor must be a trader and a natural person or commercial company.
(2) The trader must have ceased to pay his creditors.
(3) The trader must be unable to obtain credit.

The bankruptcy is declared by the commercial court of the domicile or the registered office of the trader as soon as these three conditions are met.

Bankruptcy proceedings can be initiated in four ways:

(1) Debtor's avowal in bankruptcy (within three days after establishment of the conditions).
(2) Creditor's petition in bankruptcy.
(3) Court proceedings instituted by a creditor of the trader.
(4) At the commercial court's initiative.

The commercial court determines when the bankrupt ceased his payment (a maximum of six months before the bankruptcy declaration). The period of time fixed by the court is called the "suspect period".

The Bankruptcy Law provides for the nullity of some types of transactions carried out during this period and during the 10 days preceding this period, i.e.:

(a) unusual transactions;
(b) transactions concluded with a third party aware of the insolvency;
(c) late registration of a mortgage.

6. Case 125/79 *Denilauler* v. *SNC Couchet Frères*, 21 May 1980, *Recueil de Jurisprudence de la Cour*, 1980, pp. 1553 *et seq.*

A declaration of bankruptcy will have, *inter alia*, the following effects:

(1) The estate of the debtor will be allocated to the creditors; it is the principle of the unity (*unité/eenheid*) of the bankruptcy.

(2) The judge will appoint a trustee (*curateur/curator*) who will act for the general body of the creditors and manage the debtor's estate. The debtor is not allowed to manage his assets as from the day of the declaration of bankruptcy.

(3) Within a period fixed by the judge, the creditors must declare their claim by way of a declaration with the registrar of the commercial court that has declared the trader bankrupt. Should this period have expired, the creditor must summon the trustee to appear before the commercial court that has declared the bankruptcy, in order to have the court recognise the existence of the claim.

One of the basic principles of Belgian bankruptcy law—the equality of creditors—implies that the creditors' rights are "crystallised" on the day of the bankruptcy. As a matter of principle, the creditors whose rights are unsecured or secured by a general lien are not entitled to initiate proceedings against the debtor. They are entitled to sue the trustee in order to have their claim established by the court, but not to have the trustee condemned to pay an amount of money.

Even if the creditors' rights are sanctioned by a court, they cannot be enforced. All the measures provided by the Belgian law to enforce a right are suspended. Once more, however, Belgian law provides several exceptions: the creditor who is the first preferred mortgagee is still entitled to sell the immovable property of the bankrupt by public auction. In addition, the creditors whose claims are secured by a pledge or a warrant are also entitled to enforce their rights after their debtor has been declared bankrupt.

Even conservatory measures (such as attachment) are stopped on the date of the declaration of bankruptcy.

The interest on unsecured debts stops accumulating the day the bankruptcy is declared.

The statutes of limitation are *not* suspended by the bankruptcy proceedings.

The trustee is entrusted with the handling of the debtor's estate and the payment of the creditors in accordance with the priority of the claims as established by law. The trustee abides by the following legal rules concerning the payment of the claimants:

(1) The secured debts are paid before the unsecured debts.

(2) Among the secured debts, the law has established the following priorities:

   (a) the first paid are the claims legally guaranteed by a special security (i.e., immovable or movable property used to guarantee a claim), and

   (b) the second to be paid are the claims legally guaranteed by a general security (in this case, all the properties or all the properties belonging to a certain type (movable or immovable) guarantee all the claims of the same rank).

(3) Finally, the last to be paid are the unsecured debts. If the proceeds of the sale do not cover all the unsecured debts, the creditors are paid in proportion to the amount of their claims.

From a practical and international point of view, it is worth citing a provision of the

Bankruptcy Law that could help a foreign or Belgian creditor but which must be applied before the bankruptcy:

> The suppliers of machines, equipment, tools, and other professional equipment employed in industrial, commercial and artisanal firms, will benefit from a lien on the supplied material for a five-year period of time provided that a certified true copy of the invoice, even if not accepted, or of any document establishing the sale, is filed with the registrar of the commercial court within 15 days following the delivery of the goods. (Article 546 of the Bankruptcy Law)

This lien may be enforced even if the machines, tools, and other professional equipment are considered as part of the immovable property.

In case of conflict of law on liens, the applicable law for liens on specific goods is that of the country where the goods connected to the lien are located. In case of general lien, the applicable law is that of the country where the debtor has been declared bankrupt.

The claim of a foreign creditor can be accepted by the trustee as a secured claim, even if there exists no mutual treaty with this country, because the right to the lien is of "natural" essence.

The liens recognised by a foreign law are applicable in Belgium if they are not contrary to Belgian public policy.

CHRISTINE SARTINI VANDENKERCKHOVE

CHAPTER 5

CANADA

INTRODUCTION

There is no single, comprehensive code for the recognition and enforcement of foreign judgments in Canada. This is so because Canada has a federal system of government in which the primary power to legislate in relation to property and civil rights has been granted to the 10 Canadian provinces and two separate territories. Although the federal legislature has exercised a limited authority in specific areas impacting on creditors (such as bankruptcy and admiralty law), creditors' remedies (including those of foreign creditors) are generally dealt with pursuant to provincial legislation. The only federal court system for recognising judgments exists in relation to certain admiralty matters.

Further, because there is no national registration system for most types of assets and security interests, a creditor's attempts to enforce a judgment must be conducted separately in each province or territory in which it wishes to pursue a remedy. Although many of the provinces have enacted legislation addressing the reciprocation of judgments, such legislation, although similar in many respects, contains important procedural distinctions from province to province. Uncertainty for foreign creditors also results from the fact that the province of Quebec is a civil law jurisdiction, whereas the remaining provinces are common law jurisdictions. The result is that the general common law rules (which apply unless pre-empted by specific legislation in all of the other provinces and territories) do not apply in Quebec. There has been some recent debate in Canada calling for a revision to the law relating to the enforcement of judgments on a national basis and an endorsement of the principle of "full faith and credit" with respect to Canadian judgments. Although that debate has not yet led to national reform, it has produced legislation in Prince Edward Island (Canadian Judgments (Enforcement) Act SPEI, 1994 C.5) and draft legislation in British Columbia[1] which (if proclaimed) could be relied upon to register a judgment made in any other Canadian province or territory in British Columbia on the full faith and credit principle including, presumably, an order made in another Canadian jurisdiction recognising a foreign judgment. It is anticipated that other jurisdictions in Canada will follow Prince Edward Island and British Columbia's lead, with the result that the Canadian legislative framework for registering foreign judgments may be significantly changed from what applies at the present time.

1. Bill 21 (1992): Enforcement of Canadian Judgments Act, SBC, 1992, c. 37, received Royal Assent on 23 June 1992 and will come into force by regulation.

Notwithstanding all of the foregoing, this chapter will attempt to describe in general terms the rules which are appropriate at the present time to the common law jurisdictions, by referring primarily to the rules and legislative procedures which now apply in the province of British Columbia, since these are generally similar to those of other Canadian common law provinces. A postscript to this chapter by Roger P. Simard details the different approach which applies in the province of Quebec. Obviously, specific situations which arise for foreign creditors will have to be analysed in the context of the province where assets of the debtor are known to be situated.

It is also important to note that some of the provincial acts will recognise judgments of other provinces more readily than they will a judgment which is foreign to Canada, and it is therefore conceivable that registration of a foreign judgment in more than one province will become easier for a foreign creditor once its judgment is registered in the first Canadian province.

Finally, the discussion in this chapter is limited to unsecured claims of foreign creditors. If a foreign creditor succeeds in obtaining security from a Canadian debtor on a consensual basis (and assuming that the security is properly registered in accordance with the law of the appropriate Canadian province or territory), that security can be enforced in the province by the foreign creditor on the same basis and in the same fashion as a domestic creditor holding similar security, subject only to the possibility that the foreign creditor might be required by the courts to post security for the debtor's costs if the claim is defended.

AVAILABILITY OF CANADIAN COURTS TO FOREIGN CREDITORS

Generally, Canadian courts are available to a foreign judgment creditor seeking to enforce its judgment within Canada. Except for certain limited restrictions which are discussed below, there are no guiding policy considerations which constrain against the enforcement of foreign judgments. However, a foreign judgment has, of itself, no inherent right to recognition and enforcement in the Canadian common law provinces. A foreign judgment can only be enforced if it is recognised in a new and separate legal proceeding commenced by the foreign creditor in the appropriate provincial jurisdiction. Recognition and enforcement in turn depend upon an application of the common law conflicts of law rules as to the recognition of foreign judgments and special statutory provisions regarding the reciprocal enforcement of foreign judgments.

There is no concrete rule as to whether a foreign party seeking to enforce a claim within Canada must post a bond for costs. It is open to a judgment debtor in an action brought by a foreign judgment creditor to seek an order obliging the foreign creditor to post security for the judgment debtor's costs. However, whether such security will be required is entirely at the discretion of the court. The existence of reciprocal enforcement legislation in the jurisdiction in which the foreign judgment creditor resides has been taken as a factor favouring the refusal of such an order.

The only absolute restrictions on enforcing foreign judgments relate to judgments arising under certain types of foreign laws, such as penal laws, revenue laws, laws of a political nature or laws which are inconsistent with the fundamental public policy of the forum.

RECOGNITION PROCEDURE

At common law, a foreign judgment is viewed as a simple contract debt. There is no merger of the original cause of action upon the granting of a judgment in a foreign venue. Therefore, it is open to a foreign judgment creditor to sue either upon the foreign judgment or upon the original cause of action. It is also possible to continue in one action the alternative requests for recognition of the foreign judgment and a suit on the original cause of action.

Thus, a foreign judgment creditor has three possible means of seeking the enforcement of his foreign judgment in the Canadian common law provinces:

(1) to sue on the original judgment as a debt;
(2) to sue on the original cause of action; or
(3) to register the judgment under reciprocal enforcements of judgments legislation (if any) if the foreign jurisdiction is designated as a "reciprocating state".

Creditors holding foreign judgments will generally prefer to pursue the first or the third alternative in order to avoid having to relitigate the issues giving rise to the original judgment.

One final introductory point must be mentioned. Regardless of the enforcement procedure a foreign judgment creditor pursues, it is always open to the judgment debtor to contest the proceeding. There is no absolute guarantee that a person with a judgment from outside a province can avoid relitigating all or part of the claim or establishing that various procedures were followed to obtain the judgment, before steps may be taken to recover any of the money owed. In other words, the foreign judgment does not always take the judgment creditor very far. Often, the judgment creditor might be better advised to forgo obtaining the foreign judgment and instead proceed on the original cause of action in Canada in the first instance, particularly if the debtor is now resident in Canada or if the connection between the debtor and the foreign jurisdiction is tenuous.

Common law

When examining the recognition and enforcement of a foreign judgment within the Canadian common law provinces, one must distinguish between judgments *in personam* (which includes the category of money judgments) and judgments *in rem*.

The rules as to the recognition and enforcement of foreign judgments *in rem* are substantially different than those for judgments *in personam*. A judgment *in rem* is a judgment pronounced upon the status of some thing, subject matter or person, or the disposition of a thing, by a court of competent jurisdiction.

Generally speaking, a foreign judgment *in rem* relating to movables will be recognised and enforced in the common law provinces if the movables were situated in the foreign jurisdiction at the time of the commencement of the domestic proceedings. A foreign judgment *in rem* relating to immovables will be recognised if the immovables are situated in the foreign country. For purposes of the following discussion, references to judgments will be restricted to judgments *in personam*.

Proceeding on the original cause of action

In most of the common law provinces, the requirements for proceeding upon the original cause of action by a foreigner are substantially the same as those applicable to domestic litigants instituting an action, subject to the requirement that the court possess "jurisdiction" to hear the matter when dealing with a foreign element. If the Canadian court has "jurisdiction", a foreign claimant may begin an action and then proceed through the litigation process as would a domestic litigant.

The "jurisdiction" issue addresses the question of the required nexus between the province in which the proceeding is instituted and the action or the parties to justify the courts of that province adjudicating the dispute.

At common law, the "jurisdiction" of a provincial court depends upon service of the parties pursuant to the local rules of civil procedure or voluntary submission by the debtor to the jurisdiction of the court.

Service may be effected by one of two means. The first is personal service upon a party present in the jurisdiction. In respect of individuals, "presence" is not equated with residence or domicile. Even the most temporary presence will suffice for the purposes of service, provided that the presence was not involuntary. Service upon legal entities other than individuals may be effected pursuant to provisions of the local rules of court or the statute which created the entity in question. The second means of effecting service is service *ex juris*. Each province has enacted local rules of court governing the requirements that must be met to validly effect service *ex juris*. These rules vary substantially from province to province, and reference should be made to the local rules of court to determine if jurisdiction may be established on this basis. However, the underlying principle in all provinces governing the authority to effect service *ex juris* is a determination of when a sufficiently real and substantial connection exists between the issues and/or parties and forum to justify the assumption of jurisdiction over an absent defendant.

Once jurisdiction is established, a foreign claimant proceeding on the original cause of action proceeds as a domestic claimant would in conducting its case.

Proceeding on original judgment as debt

Proceeding on this basis will usually avoid the relitigation of all of the issues litigated or available to be litigated in the foreign court. In general, the recognition of a foreign judgment requires that:

(1) the judgment debtor has not already paid the judgment;
(2) the foreign court rendering the judgment had jurisdiction over the judgment debtor as defined by private international law conflicts rules;
(3) the enforcement of the foreign judgment will not violate domestic public policy;

(4) the judgment was not obtained by fraud; and
(5) the procedure adopted by the foreign court is not contrary to the requirement of natural justice.[2]

WHAT CONSTITUTES PUBLIC POLICY?

Canadian courts tend to take a broad view of what constitutes public policy at any particular point in time, restricting the principle to prevent registration of judgments involving issues of illegality and moral turpitude. In a recent British Columbia decision,[3] for example, the foreign plaintiff had been granted judgment in Nevada with respect to the defendant's gambling debt. The defendant was served in British Columbia but did not attend or attorn to the Nevada court's jurisdiction. The plaintiff then commenced an action on the gambling debt in British Columbia and relied on the foreign judgment as evidence of the debt. In defence, the defendant raised the immorality of gambling and argued that he was not resident in Nevada and did not submit to the Nevada court's jurisdiction. As regards the first defence, the court held that a foreign judgment resulting from an action which would not be successful if brought in British Columbia, does not mean that a British Columbia court will refuse to recognise the foreign judgment. Moreover, the court added that, in this day and age, gambling is not morally or fundamentally contrary to public policy. The court found that there was no evidence of fraud and accepted that the foreign judgment was conclusive evidence of the debt claimed to be owing. The court did not follow earlier jurisprudence in other Canadian provinces which refused to enforce judgments relating to gambling debts.

In a recent Manitoba case,[4] the court held that the provincial legislation which extinguished a mortgage debt where the mortgagee became the owner pursuant to foreclosure was not applicable to foreign judgments. Accordingly, where a plaintiff acquired title to foreclosed property in Hawaii, sold the property, obtained a judgment in Hawaii for its deficiency and then brought an action in Manitoba, judgment was granted notwithstanding that the debt would not be collectable in Manitoba if the property was situate there.

In another British Columbia case,[5] the British Columbia Supreme Court enforced a California judgment even though the California court had pierced the corporate veil. The court stated that piercing the corporate veil is not repugnant to British Columbia public policy. Most recently[6] the British Columbia Supreme Court held that just because the law of another country may be different from that of British Columbia, this is no reason not to enforce a judgment. The proper test was whether the foreign law was contrary to domestic conceptions of essential justice and morality or was inconsistent with the good order and solid interests of society. Accordingly, where

2. In British Columbia there is a further peculiar requirement that the judgment contain no "manifest error" as would result where, for example, the foreign court failed to recognise a payment by the debtor: *Federal Deposit Insurance Corp.* v. *Vanstone et al.* (1992), 88 DLR (4th) 448 (BCSC).

3. *Desert Place Inc.* v. *Zigdon* [1987] BCD Civ 3644–03 (Co. Cr).

4. *Honolulu Federal Savings and Loan Association* v. *Robinson* (1989), 64 DLR (4th) 551, 62 Man R (2d) affirmed [1991] 1 WWR 174, 14 RPR (2d) 315, 76 DLR (4th) 103, 68 Man R (2d) 311 (CA) (150 QB).

5. *United States* v. *Cassidy* (1977) 79 DLR (3d) 635 (BCSC).

6. *Minkler & Kirshbaum* v. *Sheppard* (1991) 60 BCLR (2d) 360 (SC) at p. 365 and *Stoddart* v. *Accurpress Manufacturing Ltd* (1993) 84 BCLR (2d) 194.

there were "echoes" of the Arizona community of property legislation in British Columbia laws relating to family assets, British Columbia will recognise a foreign judgment against a spouse based upon such legislation even though similar rights are not available under British Columbia family law legislation.

WHEN IS FRAUD A RELEVANT ISSUE?

The reference to a judgment obtained by fraud has been interpreted to mean "extrinsic" rather than "intrinsic" fraud. In a British Columbia case,[7] for example, the court concluded that "a judgment obtained by fraud may be impeached, but it is extrinsic fraud, that is, a fraud of the type which deprives a person of an adequate opportunity to present his case in court which will vitiate a judgment". Therefore, the defendant's allegations that the plaintiff filed fraudulent affidavits did not constitute "extrinsic fraud" as the defendant failed to show that he was deprived of the opportunity to dispute the plaintiff's case.

HOW DOES A FOREIGN COURT ACQUIRE JURISDICTION?

In most cases, the most important requirement for a foreign creditor is that of jurisdiction. There are five categories by which a Canadian court has traditionally found that a foreign court had jurisdiction over a defendant:

(1) where the defendant is a subject of the foreign country in which the judgment had been obtained;
(2) where the defendant was resident in the foreign country when the action began;
(3) where the defendant has selected a forum in which he is afterwards sued;
(4) where the defendant has voluntarily appeared; or
(5) where the defendant has contracted to submit himself to the forum in which the judgment was obtained.[8]

It is interesting, in this context, to note that an Ontario court has held that entering an appearance to a foreign proceeding for the sole purpose of protecting the seizure of property located in the foreign jurisdiction does not constitute a voluntary appearance.[9]

However, Canadian courts have recently expanded upon earlier case law which made it relatively easy for defendants simply to ignore foreign proceedings and then deny the jurisdiction of the foreign court when proceedings were commenced in Canada to enforce the foreign judgment. A 1991 decision of the Supreme Court of Canada[10] is a sweeping decision wherein the court clearly endorsed the proposition that the enforcement of judgments between Canadian provinces should be easier. The Supreme Court did not fully adopt the principle of full faith and credit. The test formulated by the Supreme Court of Canada in *Morguard* is whether a real and substantial connection between the jurisdiction of the foreign court, the transaction in respect of which it has granted judgment and the defaulting defendant is found such

7. *Roglass Consultants Inc.* v. *Kennedy, et al.* (1984) 65 BCLR 393 (CA).
8. *Emanuel* v. *Symon* [1908] 1 KB 302, 309.
9. *Clinton* v. *Ford* (1982) 37 OR (2d) 448, 29 CP 30, 137 DLR (3d) 281 (CA).
10. *Morguard Investments Ltd* v. *De Savoye* [1990] 62 BCLR (2d) 160 [1991] 2 WWR 217, 46 CPC (2d) 1 (SCC).

that "it was inherently reasonable for the foreign court to exercise the jurisdiction which it did exercise". This new test reflects a wholly new direction for the enforcement of judgments from other jurisdictions and arguably has swept away many of the antiquated rules of private international law.

The *Morguard* case concerned the enforcement of an Alberta judgment in British Columbia. However, in British Columbia, the *Morguard* principle is being liberally applied to recognise judgments obtained in jurisdictions outside of Canada. One of the first cases to consider *Morguard* involved an attempt to enforce a California judgment in British Columbia against a former California resident who never voluntarily appeared to the California proceedings and was not resident in California when the foreign action was commenced. Nevertheless, in that case,[11] and even though none of the tests noted above could be met by the foreign judgment holder, the British Columbia court held that the judgment could be enforced on the basis that "the substantial connection between the defendant and the state of California in the cause of action is of a kind which makes it reasonable to infer that the defendant voluntarily submitted himself to the risk of litigation in the state of California". A similar approach has been applied by the British Columbia Supreme Court in a number of cases where a foreign judgment was obtained on a default basis in a number of jurisdictions outside of Canada. In one case[12] the courts enforced a default judgment obtained in the state of California despite the defendant having never resided or operated a business in that jurisdiction. Still, the court found that by advertising its products in that state, it had voluntarily submitted itself to the risk of litigation in that jurisdiction.

Thus, a further category for jurisdiction relating to "voluntary submission to the risk of litigation" may have been added to the categories noted above, thereby making it easier for foreign judgments to be enforced in Canada and more difficult for defendants simply to ignore foreign proceedings.

WHEN IS A FOREIGN JUDGMENT FINAL AND CONCLUSIVE?

Once recognised, to be enforceable, a foreign judgment must be for a definite sum and be final and conclusive. "Definite sum" means a sum, other than for taxes or penalties, which can be ascertained by a simple arithmetical process. "Final and conclusive" means that the judgment must determine the rights and liabilities of the parties to it so as to be *res judicata* in the foreign jurisdiction where it has been pronounced. In other words, the court that granted the judgment must have no power to vary or rescind it. Thus, a judgment subject to appeal is nevertheless "final" if the pronouncing court cannot vary or rescind, even if an appeal is actually pending in the foreign jurisdiction. However, if appeal proceedings are pending at the time of the enforcement action, the court may order the action stayed pending the conclusion of the appeal.

If the above requirements are met, the court may grant judgment for the amount of the "debt" (the foreign judgment), and the foreign judgment creditor is then in the same position as a domestic creditor for the purposes of enforcement.

11. *Clarke* v. *Lo Bianco* (1991) 59 BCLR (2d) 334, 50 CPC (2d) 127, 84 DLR (4th) 244, (SC), following *Morguard Investments Ltd* v. *De Savoye*, *supra*, n.10.
12. *McMickle* v. *Van Straaken* (1992) 93 DLR (4th) 74.

Procedural issues

SERVICE

A debtor must be advised that proceedings are taking place against him. It is not necessary that service be personal service; service of the original proceedings may have been made substitutionally or outside the foreign court's territory. A complete lack of notice to the judgment debtor may amount to a denial of natural justice. A successful argument that the lack of service amounts to a denial of natural justice requires the judgment debtor to demonstrate not only that he was not served but also that the action did not come to his knowledge or notice.[13]

LIMITATIONS

Each province has enacted provisions respecting limitation periods within which actions must be commenced. In British Columbia, an action on a foreign judgment must be commenced within six years of the date of judgment, and an action on the original cause of action must be commenced within six years from the date the cause of action arose or the date that the plaintiff should have reasonably been aware that he had a cause of action.

COSTS

Costs in an action are awarded by the court in its discretion. Costs are usually awarded to the successful party to an action, and in British Columbia the normal tariff of costs which applies in most cases is intended to approximate one-half of the real financial cost of an action.

PROOF OF A FOREIGN JUDGMENT

The proof of a foreign judgment is governed by the Evidence Act of each province. Generally, these Acts provide that proof of a foreign judgment may be made by tendering a certified copy of the foreign judgment impressed with the seal of the foreign court. Where the foreign court has no seal, a copy of the foreign judgment must be certified as a true copy by a judge of the foreign court, who must affix his signature to the certified copy and attach a written statement to the effect that the foreign court has no seal. Several provinces restrict these provisions to specified other jurisdictions, requiring all others to be proved at common law, which means the authenticity of the seal must be proved.

CURRENCY

Section 13 of the Currency Act,[14] requires all money judgments issued by Canadian courts, including those obtained in an action on a foreign judgment, to be expressed in Canadian currency. Selection of the currency exchange date is determined by the court in the enforcement action. For example, in British Columbia the Court Order Enforcement Act[15] stipulates that the foreign judgment date shall be the conversion

13. *Richards* v. *Williams* [1905] 11 BCR 122.
14. Currency Act RSC 1985, c. C–52.
15. RSBC 1979, c. 75.

date. In other jurisdictions, the appropriate conversion date is determined in accordance with the common law. The present approach permits a court to choose one of several dates as the conversion date: the foreign judgment date, the date of commencement of the enforcement proceedings, or the date of the enforcement judgment. The date selected will be that which best affords justice to the parties or is the most recent reasonable date.

Canadian courts are reluctant to allow a foreign judgment debtor who has been evading his payment obligations to benefit from any currency exchange fluctuations. This attitude favours adopting a conversion date which maximises the gain available to the foreign judgment creditor. However, where a foreign judgment creditor has unduly delayed the commencement of his enforcement proceedings, Canadian courts may deny him currency exchange related gains associated with a later conversion date.

By statute

All provinces, except Quebec, have enacted legislation in almost identical form based upon the Uniform Reciprocal Enforcement of Judgments Act, promulgated by the Uniform Law Conference of Canada. The Court Order Enforcement Act is British Columbia's version of this Act.

This domestic legislation was originally intended to facilitate the enforcement of judgments from one Canadian province in another as if they were local judgments upon registration of the judgment in the enforcing province. However, many provinces have expanded the scope of the legislation so that judgment creditors from jurisdictions outside Canada can utilise the registration system.

In order for a foreign judgment creditor to proceed under the Court Order Enforcement Act, the Lieutenant Governor of British Columbia, by order in council, must have declared the jurisdiction in which the foreign judgment was obtained to be a reciprocating jurisdiction. Within Appendix A is the most recent list of jurisdictions which have been declared reciprocating jurisdictions for the purposes of the British Columbia Court Order Enforcement Act.

Generally, the Court Order Enforcement Act does not make foreign judgments to which it applies any less foreign or any more directly enforceable than before it was passed because it does not materially alter the conflicts of law rules applicable to the recognition of foreign judgments. The legislation expressly preserves the judgment creditor's right to bring an action on the judgment or on the original cause of action. The primary function of the legislation is to provide a cheaper and more expedient method for making effective those judgments which could otherwise be enforced under common-law conflicts rules.

Once registered, the judgment may be enforced as though it were a judgment rendered by the courts of British Columbia.

A "judgment" that may be registered under the Court Order Enforcement Act is a:

> judgment or order of a court in a civil proceeding, where money is made payable, and includes an award in an arbitration proceeding if the award, under the law in force in the state where it was made, has become enforceable in the same manner as a judgment given by a court in that state, but does not include an order for the periodical payment of money as alimony or as

maintenance for a spouse or former spouse or reputed spouse or a child of any other dependant of the person against whom the order was made.

The application for registration of the foreign judgment is made to the British Columbia Supreme Court and requires:

(1) The application for registration to be made within six years after the date of the foreign judgment.
(2) It may be *ex parte* where:
 (a) the judgment debtor was served personally with process; or
 (b) though not personally served, the defendant appeared to or defended it, or attorned or otherwise submitted to the jurisdiction of the court.
(3) Where the application is made *ex parte*, the proceedings are brought by originating application and must include:
 (a) a certificate issued from the original court and under its seal and signed by a judge or a clerk of the court;
 (b) a certified copy of the order; and
 (c) an affidavit setting out:
  (i) that the judgment creditor is entitled to enforce the judgment;
  (ii) that the judgment is not precluded from registration under the provisions of section 31(6) of the Court Order Enforcement Act;
  (iii) that the judgment debtor was duly served with process of the original court;
  (iv) that the original court had jurisdiction to grant the judgment;
  (v) the amount owing under the judgment; and
  (vi) the particulars of the judgment debtor.

Section 31(6) of the Court Order Enforcement Act precludes registration where:

(1) The original court did not have jurisdiction under its rules or the conflict of laws.
(2) The original court was without authority under the law in force in its jurisdiction.
(3) The judgment debtor neither carried on business nor was ordinarily resident in the foreign jurisdiction and did not voluntarily appear or otherwise submit during the proceedings to the jurisdiction of that court.
(4) The judgment debtor was not duly served with the process and did not appear even if ordinarily resident and carrying on business in the jurisdiction of the court.
(5) The judgment was obtained by fraud.
(6) An appeal is pending or the time for an appeal has not yet expired.
(7) The judgment ought not to be enforced as being for a cause of action that for reasons of public policy would not have been entertained by the courts of British Columbia.
(8) The judgment debtor would have a good defence if an action were brought on the judgment.

These provisions will be strictly enforced against a foreign creditor. In a recent British Columbia case,[16] a court considered the jurisdiction of a court in the state of Washington. In that case the plaintiff's husband was killed in an aeroplane crash in

16. *Hoopman Estate* v. *Imrie* (1991) 57 BCLR (2d) 310 (BCSC).

Washington. The defendant, a British Columbia resident, was the owner and pilot of the aircraft. The plaintiff obtained default judgment in Washington for wrongful death and was awarded more than $1 million in damages. The plaintiff then obtained an *ex parte* order for registration of the judgment in British Columbia, which the defendant applied to set aside. The court allowed the defendant's application to set the judgment aside on the grounds that the defendant never resided nor carried on business in Washington and did not appear or submit to that court's jurisdiction. The third test under the Court Order Enforcement Act noted above was therefore not met. The court refused to apply the Washington law which deems a defendant to have submitted to the jurisdiction of a Washington court where the defendant has committed a tortious act within Washington. The court rejected the plaintiff's submission that it is the law of the foreign jurisdiction which determines whether the defendant has attorned to the jurisdiction of the foreign court.

On the other hand, the expression "a good defence" has been narrowly interpreted to exclude defences available with respect to the original cause of action.[17] For example, the British Columbia court has held that the defence that a chattel mortgagee in British Columbia, unlike a chattel mortgagee in Alberta, cannot both seize chattels and sue for the deficiency was not a "good defence" to an action on the Alberta judgment.[18] The purpose of having legislation that expedites enforcement of foreign judgments is to avoid having to sue on the foreign judgment and having to relitigate the cause of action.[19]

An example of what constitutes a "good defence" in an action brought on a default judgment is a "manifest error perceptible on the face of the writ" such as what would occur where the amount of interest claimed in a writ leading to a foreign default judgment was in error.[20] Canadian courts have generally considered that the defence of a manifest error was only available to a judgment debtor seeking to set aside registration of a foreign *default* judgment.[21]

From the date of registration, the foreign judgment has the same force and effect as if it had been a judgment granted originally in the British Columbia Supreme Court at the date of the registration, and the judgment may be enforced as a judgment of the registering court subject to the limitation that any registration obtained under an *ex parte* order may not be proceeded upon prior to the expiration of one month from notice to the judgment debtor of the registration.

REMEDIES ON ENFORCEMENT

Once a foreign judgment is recognised, either pursuant to the common-law conflicts rules or by registration under some statutory provision, the remedies available to a foreign creditor are the same as those available to a domestic creditor.

17. *George Roberecht Seafoods Inc.* v. *Island Fish Export Inc.* (1987) 43 DLR (4th) 157 (PEI CA).
18. *C.I.B.C.* v. *Brown* (1986) 3 BCLR (2d) 270 (SC).
19. *Re Aero Trades Western Ltd* v. *Ben Hocum and Son Ltd* (1974) [1975] 4 WWR 412, 51 DLR (3d) 617 (Man Co Ct).
20. *Gacs* v. *Maierovitz* (1968) 64 WWR 423, 68 DLR (2d) 345 (BCSC).
21. *May* v. *Shell Co. of Hong Kong* [1981] 1 WWR 193 (BCCA).

Provisional and interim remedies

Although traditionally the common law provided little assistance to a creditor before a claim was reduced to judgment, the legislature and the courts have provided mechanisms to reinforce a claimant's position prior to judgment, so that presently, pre-judgment remedies are regularly available to a judgment creditor under Canadian law. These remedies are equally available to a foreign judgment creditor provided that the foreign judgment has been perfected, or a foreign creditor has commenced proceedings in Canada on the original cause of action.

Mareva injunction

A *Mareva* injunction is a particular type of interlocutory injunction which effectively freezes the assets of the defendant pending the final disposition of a proceeding or until further order of the court. In two recent decisions,[22] the courts have held that a defendant can also be prevented from dealing with any of his assets which are located outside of the jurisdiction. It is a very useful remedy, but one which is difficult to obtain except in exceptional circumstances.

The impetus behind the development of this remedy was the desire to protect a plaintiff from a hollow judgment caused by the defendant removing assets from the jurisdiction of the court so as to render himself "judgment proof".

It is difficult to enunciate a single clear test as to the threshold required to be met in order to obtain a *Mareva* injunction. However, it can be said that courts will demand that the plaintiff demonstrate a very strong case before a *Mareva* injunction is granted. The courts recognise the stifling and coercive nature of this remedy and the burdens and potential risks it imposes and will carefully scrutinise the merits of the plaintiff's case. Generally, the plaintiff must demonstrate real proof of a risk of loss, evidenced by such things as previous shady conduct, hiding or removal of assets to defeat creditors, and other similar untrustworthy actions.

The *Mareva* injunction applicant is under an obligation to make full and frank disclosure of all matters relevant to the assessment of the application and is required to provide an undertaking in damages supported by a bond or security so that if the main claim fails or the injunction is not justified, the defendant's loss resulting from the *Mareva* injunction may be made good.

Pre-judgment garnishment

This remedy in effect provides a plaintiff in an action with security for its claim by permitting it to attach amounts otherwise owing to the debtor from third parties. As with the *Mareva* injunction, it is an exceptional remedy inasmuch as the advancement of a claim of tenuous validity may deprive a defendant of funds which are rightfully his, pending the disposition of the action.

The remedy is available in some, but not all, of the Canadian common law provinces. Where it is available, in recognition of the onerous nature of this remedy, courts hold the applicants to strict compliance with the statutory procedures and requirements.

22. *Mooney* v. *Orr* (1994) 98 BCLR (2d) 318; *Mooney* v. *Orr* (1995) 100 BCLR (2d) 335.

A pre-judgment garnishing order is available in British Columbia on affidavit and by desk order (i.e., without an appearance before a judge) but is not available in respect of salary or wages.

Pre-judgment receivership

A court may appoint a receiver under its general equitable jurisdiction where it is "just and convenient". In collection situations, this test is met where it can be demonstrated that a receiver is necessary to preserve the debtor's property from some danger during the course of a lawsuit between the parties. The receiver is usually made the custodian of the property pending disposition of the action. A more detailed discussion of the role of a receiver is found below.

Post-judgment remedies

Garnishment

The garnishment procedure enables a judgment creditor to obtain an order compelling a third person, the garnishee, to pay into court to the benefit of the judgment creditor a debt which would otherwise be due to the judgment debtor. The process is implemented in British Columbia by affidavit and desk order and is therefore relatively cheap and simple. If successful it produces immediate cash rather than assets which must then be sold.

In British Columbia, the Court Order Enforcement Act provides that "debts due" are subject to garnishment, which by definition include "debts, obligations and liabilities owing, payable or accruing due and wages that would in the ordinary course of employment become owing, payable or due within seven days after the date on which an affidavit has been sworn".

Several important results flow from this definition. First, the claim of the debtor must be for a debt (i.e., it must arise from contract and not tort).[23] Secondly, at the time of the issuance of the order, there must be a debt owing, payable or accruing due. If the obligation to pay money is dependent upon conditions which may or may not be fulfilled, there is no debt due or accruing due.

In British Columbia, a creditor may garnish wages that are presently payable or are due within seven days of the date that the affidavit is sworn. Wages earned may be attached even if not yet payable as long as the judgment debtor has done everything to earn the money and merely has to wait and receive it, as this constitutes a debt accruing due.

The primary limitation of the garnishment procedure in British Columbia is that 70% of the net wages due from an employer to an employee are exempt from seizure or attachment under a garnishing order. A debtor or creditor may apply for an increase or decrease in the exemption, but in no case is the exemption to be greater than 90% nor can it reduce the wages of an employee to less than $100 (without dependants) and $200 (with dependants). Different exemptions will apply in other Canadian provinces.

A bank account of a judgment debtor may be garnished by serving the garnishing

23. *Malczewski* v. *Sansai Securities Ltd* [1975] 1 WWR 462, 19 CBR (NS) 272, 49 DLR (3d) 624 (BCSC).

order on the branch where the account is located. The garnishing order is applicable only in respect of that branch but will bind all accounts located there. Joint accounts are not subject to garnishment unless judgment against all joint depositors is obtained.[24]

Most provinces have enacted legislation which prevents garnishment of pensions, life insurance proceeds payable to a beneficiary other than the judgment debtor (including a life insured retirement savings plan), family allowance payments, workers' compensation payments, and unemployment insurance payments.

Execution against land

This remedy is available in all Canadian jurisdictions, with the exception that in some provinces a debtor's personal residence (or some portion of it) may be exempt from seizure. In British Columbia (where no exemption is available), execution against land is governed primarily by the Court Order Enforcement Act.

The Act provides that a judgment entered or obtained in the province may be registered against the title to specified land in any or all of the land title offices, and upon registration provides a means by which a judgment creditor may execute his judgment against the land in question. It is not possible in British Columbia to make a general filing of a judgment against all interests in land held by a debtor within the province; the specific parcel of land must first be identified.

A certificate of judgment registered against an interest in real property in British Columbia expires two years from the date of registration unless an application for renewal is made. If the certificate of judgment does expire, it may be re-registered, although it will be subject to any intervening registered charges.

Registration of a certificate of judgment in British Columbia creates a charge against the land and places the judgment creditor in a position to avail itself of the provisions in the Court Order Enforcement Act permitting the sale of the judgment debtor's interest in the property if the judgment is not satisfied.

The sale procedure is complicated and is carried out pursuant to a series of applications to the court; it ultimately results in a sale of the land by the court bailiff to satisfy the judgment.

In most cases, the judgment creditor commencing the enforcement proceedings has no priority over other judgment creditors, irrespective of the priority of his registration against the land. In British Columbia, there is an exception to this general rule in the case of sale pursuant to foreclosure proceedings commenced by a mortgagee whose security has priority over judgment creditors. In that situation, judgment creditors are paid in order of priority of registration.

Execution against goods and chattels

In all provinces, execution against goods and chattels is available to enforce the payment of a money judgment.

In British Columbia, to obtain execution against goods and chattels, one must first send a writ of seizure and sale with a copy of the judgment to the court registrar. The

24. *238344 B.C. Ltd* v. *Patriquin* (1984) 57 BCLR 224 (CA).

registrar then places the court seal upon the writ, signs it and then forwards it to the judgment creditor who forwards it to the court bailiff having jurisdiction where the goods and chattels are located. Once seizure is complete, the court bailiff will advertise the goods for sale, often with a reserved price, conduct the sale and distribute the proceeds.

Subject to the exemptions contained in the relevant provincial legislation, all goods, chattels, and effects of a judgment debtor are liable to seizure and sale. British Columbia permits an exemption for personal property of the judgment debtor up to a value of $2,000 that the judgment debtor selects within two days of seizure. Other provinces allow different exemptions and, as noted earlier, an exemption for the debtor's personal residence may also be available. A creditor should be careful to determine the appropriate exemption before considering any type of execution proceeding.

Priority of unsecured creditors

All Canadian jurisdictions have legislation to ensure that unsecured creditors are treated equally. These Acts are designed to prevent priority among unsecured creditors, and will generally provide a mechanism for the orderly distribution of the moneys realised as a consequence of execution proceedings initiated by a sole creditor among all creditors who have established a claim to the distribution.

In British Columbia, there are two means by which a creditor may establish a claim to the distribution. Upon a levy having been made by a court bailiff (a seizure and a receipt of money after the seizure), the court bailiff must enter notice of a levy having been made in a book of levies, available to the public, at his office. In order to establish a claim to the distribution of the levy, a judgment creditor must deliver to the court bailiff prior to the expiry of one month from the notice of levy being registered by the court bailiff:

(1) a writ of execution to the court bailiff as provided for in the Court Order Enforcement Act; or

(2) a "certificate" as provided for in the Creditor Assistance Act.[25]

A "certificate" is obtained by filing an affidavit of claim of debt. No formal judgment is required to support the claim. If the claim is not contested within 10 days after the day of service of the notice upon the debtor, the registrar may issue a certificate of claim. If the claim is contested, the claimant then applies to the court for an order allowing his claim and determining the amount and, if successful, obtains a certificate from the court.

The creditor who instituted the execution proceedings and those creditors who have delivered to the sheriff a writ of execution or a certificate, are entitled to participate rateably in the distribution of the proceeds of the levy.

Equitable execution

Most execution and garnishment remedies fail to encompass the full range of personal and real property which a judgment debtor may own. All of the Canadian common

25. Creditor Assistance Act, RSBC 1979, c. 80.

law provinces will provide remedies under the heading of equitable execution to expand the property available for execution to a judgment creditor.

EQUITABLE RECEIVERSHIP

A receiver is a person who has been appointed to take possession of property belonging to a third party. In British Columbia, the appointment of a receiver may now be accomplished by statute, under British Columbia Supreme Court Rule 47, which is an addition to the old equitable basis of appointment which has been preserved under the Law and Equity Act.[26]

Canadian courts generally take a fairly restrictive approach to the appointment of a receiver under their equitable jurisdiction. The following principles are generally applied when assessing whether a receiver ought to be appointed:

(1) A judgment creditor has no absolute right to the appointment of a receiver, it being a matter of judicial discretion.
(2) A receiver will not be appointed unless it is established that it is practically very difficult, if not impossible, for a creditor otherwise to obtain any fruits of its judgment; in other words, equitable execution will not reach assets already exigible or garnishable without impediment.
(3) In certain instances, courts will find "special circumstances" justifying the grant of a receiver. The most common examples of special circumstances are where the judgment debtor has left the jurisdiction or where the ordinary remedies which exist would be so expensive that no profit would result to the judgment creditor.

Upon appointment, a receiver takes charge of the management of the debtor's assets under direction by the court, on the terms the court orders and with the powers afforded him in the order of appointment.

CHARGING ORDER

The equitable charging order evolved because there was no execution remedy available to a judgment creditor who wanted to reach funds or assets owing to the judgment debtor which were in the court's custody. Appointment of an equitable receiver to collect such funds or assets was not necessary as the funds or assets were already in the court's possession.

The equitable charging order charges funds which are in the court's custody and in which the judgment debtor has a beneficial or legal interest at the time the order is granted. Typically, it is used to charge funds owing to the judgment debtor which are in court with respect to another action. Generally, the equitable charging order will be subject to existing legal or equitable claims on the funds.

Bankruptcy petition

Bankruptcy in Canada comes under federal jurisdiction and is administered under the Bankruptcy and Insolvency Act.[27]

26. Law and Equity Act, RSBC 1979, c. 224, s. 36, and the British Columbia Supreme Court Rules, rule 47.

27. SC 1992, c. 27.

A foreign creditor has the same status as a domestic creditor to file a petition under the Bankruptcy and Insolvency Act to cause an insolvent debtor to be made bankrupt. The only requirement is that the foreign creditor have a claim provable under the Bankruptcy and Insolvency Act. Moreover, a foreign creditor can file a petition in Canada notwithstanding the fact that the debtor has been declared bankrupt in the jurisdiction in which the creditor resides.[28] For a further discussion of the effects of bankruptcy upon a Canadian debtor, see below.

LEGISLATION AND TREATIES

As an alternative to proceeding on the foreign judgment or the original cause of action, a foreign judgment creditor may also pursue the enforcement of the judgment debt pursuant to several legislative schemes. In addition, there are some specific federal statutes which will limit, in specialised circumstances, the remedies normally available to a foreign creditor.

Reciprocal enforcement of judgments legislation

As discussed above, all Canadian provinces and territories (other than Quebec) have enacted legislation permitting designated foreign jurisdictions to make use of legislation originally intended to facilitate registration of judgments between provinces. A foreign creditor should always review the relevant statute in the province in question to determine whether or not the foreign jurisdiction is designated as a reciprocating state under the legislation of that province.

Canada–United Kingdom Convention

The main purpose of the Convention between Canada and the United Kingdom for the Reciprocal Recognition and Enforcement of Judgments in Civil and Commercial Matters (1984, SC 1984 C 32) was to prevent any adverse effects of the accession of the United Kingdom to the Brussels Convention of 27 September 1968, on Jurisdiction and the Enforcement of Judgments in Civil and Commercial Matters. The Brussels Convention required British courts to recognise and enforce judgments rendered by the courts of other European Community (EC) member states against domiciliaries of third states, even though they have been rendered on an extended rule of jurisdiction. The Convention, however, permits contracting states to enter conventions with a third state limiting this latter rule. The Canada–United Kingdom Convention expressly declares that the United Kingdom will not recognise judgments rendered against Canadians on an extended rule of jurisdiction.

The Canada–United Kingdom Convention permits United Kingdom judgments to be registered in the Federal Court of Canada or in the courts of such provinces as have adopted the necessary enacting legislation.

All provinces and territories with the exception of Quebec have to date adopted the

28. *Re: Kaussen Estate*, 64 CBR (NS) 97; [1986] RJQ 2683, 25 ETR 99, 64 CBR (NS) 97 (SC), affirmed (1988) 67 CBR (NS) 81, 12 QAC 39 [sub nom *Kaussen Estate (Bankrupt)* v. *Bayerische Hypotheken-Und Wechsel-Bank Aktiengesellschaft*, 47 DLR (4th) 626 (CA)].

necessary enacting legislation. In British Columbia, the Convention has been incorporated into the Court Order Enforcement Act.

In a recent decision of the British Columbia Court of Appeal,[29] it was held that where a judgment has been registered under the Convention, the equivalent provision of the Court Order Enforcement Act will not apply. This is significant in that it limits the grounds on which the debtor can defend the registration of a United Kingdom judgment. Provided that service was effected properly in the originating action, essentially the only defence available to the debtor will be to attack the originating court's jurisdiction in the originating jurisdiction. The debtor cannot defend the registration application on the basis that he has a good defence to the action, as would be the case if the judgment were being registered pursuant to the regular provisions of the Court Order Enforcement Act.

Federal court jurisdiction

As stated in the Introduction, admiralty law judgments are enforced in federal court rather than provincial courts. The court's jurisdiction includes claims for damages caused by ships and claims for losses or damages to goods in transit, and is equally applicable to domestic and foreign litigants. The jurisdiction also extends to claims relating to aircraft, whether domestic or foreign.

Where a judgment of a court of a state other than Canada that is a party to the International Convention on Civil Liability for Oil Pollution Damage of 29 November 1969, has been rendered with respect to civil liability for oil pollution occurring after 24 April 1989, the judgment creditor may apply to the Canadian Federal Court to have it registered in that court pursuant to the relevant provisions of the Canada Shipping Act.[30]

Registration depends upon:

(1) the applicant establishing a case for registration; and
(2) evidence that the foreign judgment is not under appeal and is no longer subject to appeal in the foreign state.

If the judgment debtor appears at the hearing of the application for registration, the court shall not order the registration of the foreign judgment if it is satisfied that:

(1) the foreign judgment has been fully satisfied;
(2) the foreign court acted without jurisdiction;
(3) the foreign judgment was obtained by fraud; or
(4) the defendant in the foreign action was not given reasonable notice and a fair opportunity to present his case.

A registered judgment is of the same effect as an ordinary judgment of the Federal Court, and all the normal remedies for execution may be pursued, provided that execution of the registered judgment shall not be issued until the expiration of 30 days after the judgment debtor has been served with a notice of registration of the foreign judgment, during which time the registration may be challenged.

The Act also contains provisions regarding preregistration interest, costs, conversion into Canadian currency and applications for a stay of execution.

29. *Bank of Credit & Commerce International (Overseas) Ltd* v. *Gokal* (1994) 99 BCLR (2d) 176.
30. Canada Shipping Act, RSC 1985, c. S–9.

US treaty

A convention exists between the US and Canada which directly addresses the recognition of foreign judgments and foreign administrators between those two countries. For reasons which are completely obscure, that convention has never been enacted by either country, and therefore no reciprocal legislation between the two jurisdictions exists.

Foreign antitrust judgments and orders

While, in principle, ordinary conflicts rules apply to the recognition and enforcement of foreign antitrust judgments and orders, the Federal Competition Act (formerly the Combines Investigation Act)[31] sets up a process whereby the Commission appointed under the Act can refuse to implement a judgment or order if its implementation would adversely effect competition or trade and commerce in Canada.

Similarly, the Foreign Extraterritorial Measures Act[32] authorises the Attorney-General of Canada to order that a foreign judgment not be recognised or enforced if the Attorney-General is of the opinion that its recognition or enforcement could adversely affect significant Canadian interests regarding international trade or commerce involving a business carried on in whole or in part in Canada.

In the case of a foreign judgment for a specified amount of money, the Attorney-General may, for the purposes of its recognition and enforcement in Canada, order that the amount of the judgment be reduced. This provision is aimed at US treble damages awards.

Foreign arbitration awards

As stated previously, all the common-law provinces and the two territories have adopted, with some modifications, the Uniform Reciprocal Enforcement of Judgments Act. In British Columbia, the statute adopting this Act is the Court Order Enforcement Act. In that Act, a judgment is defined to include an award in an arbitration proceeding if the award, under the law in force in the state where it is made, has become enforceable in the same manner as a judgment given by a court in that state. The requirements for enforcement and the defences available are the same as for foreign judgments. Where the legislation applies, it excludes resort to enforcement at common law. The requirement of jurisdiction in the Act is met if the arbitration agreement is valid by its proper law.

There are other methods of enforcing arbitration awards in Canada. British Columbia has two arbitration Acts which each adopt different international conventions. The Foreign Arbitral Awards Act[33] adopts the 1958 New York Convention, and the International Commercial Arbitration Act[34] adopts the 1985 UNCITRAL Model Law. These two conventions have also been adopted federally.

The Foreign Arbitral Awards Act applies to domestic as well as international commercial arbitral awards. Unlike the Court Order Enforcement Act, reciprocity is

31. Competition Act, RSC 1985, c. 19 (formerly the Combines Investigation Act, RSC 1985, c. C–34).
32. Foreign Extraterritorial Measures Act, RSC 1985, c. F–29.
33. Foreign Arbitral Awards Act RSBC 1985, c. 74.
34. International Commercial Arbitration Act, RSBC 1986, c. 14.

not required. Therefore, the state in which the foreign award was obtained need not be a party to the convention. Under the Act, arbitration awards are to be enforced in accordance with the rules of procedure in force in the place where they are relied upon or sought to be enforced. In general, awards are recognised and enforced almost automatically and without a review of the merits of the dispute.

Under the International Commercial Arbitration Act, an international commercial arbitration award can be enforced upon application to a competent court and is to be recognised as binding irrespective of where it was granted. The Model Law does not cover domestic commercial arbitration awards which are within the scope of the 1958 Convention, nor does it apply to non-commercial foreign arbitration awards which must be enforced at common law or pursuant to special provincial legislation.

Family maintenance orders

All of the provinces and territories have enacted reciprocal enforcement of maintenance orders legislation to simplify the procedure for enforcement of foreign maintenance or alimony orders. In British Columbia, the procedure is contained in Part 4.1 of the Family Relations Act.[35]

Two types of orders are covered by the legislation: final orders and provisional orders.

A final order is one made by a court that had jurisdiction over the respondent at the time the order was made. If the respondent moves to a reciprocating state, the order may be registered there and enforced as if it had been made in that state. A list of reciprocating states can be found in Appendix B.

A provisional order is one made by a court where the respondent is not subject to that court's jurisdiction. A provisional order cannot be enforced until confirmed by a court in the state where the respondent resides. This court can vary, confirm, or rescind the order, or can remit the matter to the court that made the provisional order.

IMPACT OF BANKRUPTCY

There are no provisions in the Canadian Bankruptcy and Insolvency Act which directly address the status of a foreign judgment creditor or a foreign representative upon the initiation of bankruptcy proceedings within Canada in respect of a judgment debtor. However, the Bankruptcy and Insolvency Act does not purport to apply only within the territorial limits of Canada. Hence, a creditor is defined in section 2 of the Act as "a person having a claim ... provable as a claim under this Act", and under section 121 "all debts and liabilities" of the bankrupt are "deemed to be claims provable in proceedings under this Act". Since the only requirement for proceeding under the Act is that the creditors must have a provable claim, foreign creditors are afforded the same rights under the Act as domestic creditors.

Under the Bankruptcy and Insolvency Act in its present form, upon the initiation of bankruptcy proceedings, no creditor may proceed with any remedy against the debtor or his property, or shall commence or continue any action, execution or other

35. Family Relations Act, RSBC 1979, c. 121.

proceedings for the recovery of a claim except those creditors holding security over the debtor's assets. In other words, there is a general stay of proceedings to provide for the orderly and fair distribution of the property of a bankrupt among his creditors. The result is that any foreign creditor who has obtained a judgment on the debt or original cause of action, or who has registered its judgment under reciprocal enforcement of judgments legislation, must prove its claim under the Bankruptcy and Insolvency Act provisions and line up with all the other unsecured creditors.

Further, bankruptcy proceedings take precedence over all judicial or other attachments, garnishments, certificates having the effect of judgment, judgments, certificates of judgments, executions, or other process against the property of a bankrupt, except those that have been completely executed by payment to the creditor. Any execution proceedings that are not complete, in that they have not resulted in payment to the judgment creditor, are stayed upon the commencement of bankruptcy proceedings. In addition, completed execution proceedings are still subject to review by a trustee in bankruptcy of a debtor if payment was made within three months of the date of bankruptcy (or one year if the parties are not at arm's length).

A trustee in bankruptcy is appointed to administer the bankrupt estate, and in due course, assets generated in the bankruptcy are converted to cash and distributed rateably amongst all of the unsecured creditors after payment of all priority claims.

In this context, a foreign judgment creditor must carefully assess the situation of the debtor before initiating bankruptcy proceedings, because in most instances there is rarely anything left for division among unsecured creditors after those who rank in priority to unsecured creditors have been paid. Priority claims under the Canadian bankruptcy system include secured creditors, trust claimants and various categories of preference creditors, including the bankruptcy administrator, employees, landlords, and the provincial and federal Crown.

The Bankruptcy and Insolvency Act also contains a provision which protects unpaid suppliers of goods to a bankrupt (or a company in receivership) by allowing them to reclaim those goods if they were supplied within 30 days of the date of the bankruptcy or receivership provided that the goods remain identifiable, unaltered and unsold. A foreign supplier would have similar rights to a domestic supplier.

The Bankruptcy and Insolvency Act also permits a debtor to file what is known as a "proposal in bankruptcy", whereby a plan of arrangement is presented and voted upon by the debtor's unsecured creditors and, at the option of the debtor, its secured creditors. Those creditors having a preference status must be paid in full; other secured and unsecured creditors are subject to having their debts compromised, provided that two-thirds in dollar value and a majority in number of each of the classes of creditors approve the proposal.

A more detailed discussion of this topic and the implications of the Bankruptcy and Insolvency Act is beyond the scope of this publication.

Foreign bankruptcy

There is no statutory rule in Canada which addresses the question as to what remedies can be invoked in Canada against a debtor where bankruptcy proceedings are outstanding against that debtor in some other jurisdiction. In general terms, Canadian courts will look to the principles of comity when considering the implementation of foreign insolvency orders. If foreign bankruptcy proceedings are recognised by the Canadian courts, then proceedings by individual creditors in Canada would likely be stayed in deference to the foreign bankruptcy proceedings.

Other insolvency statutes

In addition to the Bankruptcy and Insolvency Act, there are other Canadian statutes which provide remedies to insolvent entities and which therefore might impact upon foreign creditors. Most significant is the Companies' Creditors Arrangement Act,[36] a federal statute providing reorganisation relief to Canadian corporations. Where a debtor files for relief under that statute, claims of all creditors (including secured creditors) are usually stayed for whatever time is ordered by the court in order for a plan of rearrangement to be prepared and presented to the creditors for their collective approval. The process has sometimes been compared to what is available in the United States under Chapter 11 of the Bankruptcy Code, although the Canadian statute is significantly different.

Federal and provincial winding-up legislation also exists, and reorganisation remedies are available under federal and provincial corporation statutes which can impact upon creditors in some circumstances. All of these statutes apply equally to foreign and domestic creditors.*

MICHAEL A. FITCH

36. Companies' Creditors Arrangement Act, RSC 1985, c. C–36.
* Note: The above chapter reflects the law as at September 1995.

APPENDIX A

Court Order Enforcement Act of British Columbia

Jurisdictions declared to be reciprocating states for the purposes of this Act (as at 1 September 1995)

North America:

In Canada

- Alberta
- Manitoba
- New Brunswick
- Newfoundland
- Northwest Territories
- Nova Scotia
- Ontario
- Prince Edward Island
- Saskatchewan
- Yukon Territory

In the United States:

- Alaska
- California
- Colorado
- Idaho
- Oregon
- Washington

Europe

- Austria
- Germany
- United Kingdom

South Pacific:

In Australia

- Australian Antarctic Territory
- Australian Capital Territory
- Coral Sea Islands Territory
- Heard and McDonald Islands Territory
- New South Wales
- Northern Territory of Australia
- Queensland
- South Australia
- Tasmania
- Territory of Ashmore and Cartier Islands
- Victoria

APPENDIX B

Family Relations Act of British Columbia

Jurisdictions declared to be reciprocating states for the purposes of this Act (as at 1 September 1995)

North America:

In Canada

- Alberta
- Manitoba
- New Brunswick
- Newfoundland
- Northwest Territories
- Nova Scotia
- Ontario
- Prince Edward Island
- Quebec
- Saskatchewan
- Yukon Territory

In the United States:

- California
- Colorado
- Connecticut
- Idaho
- Kansas
- Maine
- Michigan
- Minnesota
- Montana
- Nebraska
- Nevada
- New Hampshire
- New Mexico
- New York State
- North Dakota
- Ohio
- Oregon
- Pennsylvania
- Vermont
- Virginia
- Washington
- Wisconsin

In the Caribbean:

- Island of Barbados and its dependencies

Africa:

- Republic of South Africa
- Southern Rhodesia

Europe:

- Isle of Man
- States of Jersey
- United Kingdom
- Germany
- Kingdom of Norway
- Bailiwick of Guernsey
- Gibraltar
- Austria

South Pacific:

In Australia

- Australian Capital Territory
- New South Wales
- Northern Territory of Australia
- Queensland
- South Australia
- Tasmania
- Victoria
- Western Australia

Territory of Papua and New Guinea

New Zealand (including Cook Islands)
Fiji

Asia:

Hong Kong
Singapore

POSTSCRIPT: THE PROVINCE OF QUEBEC

Introduction

This postscript will outline any significant differences between the law of the Province of Quebec and that which was noted with respect to the common law provinces. The outline of the preceding text will be followed, when possible, and sections dealing with matters of federal jurisdiction, or where the general terms are similar, will be omitted.

Important reforms regarding the law governing the recognition and enforcement of foreign judgments have been made as a result of the enactment of the new *Civil Code of Quebec* (CCQ) on 1 January 1994. These reforms have greatly facilitated such recognition and enforcement by virtue of the elimination of the requirement of legislative competence (Art. 3157, CCQ) and of examinations of the merits of the decision (Art. 3158, CCQ). As a result, decisions of foreign authorities will be treated no differently to those decided by authorities of other Canadian jurisdictions.

It is important to note, however, that section 170 of An Act respecting the implementation of the reform of the Civil Code[37] (the "Transitional Law") dictates that this more favourable regime is not applicable to decisions which were already rendered when the new legislation came into force, nor to procedures pending before foreign authorities at that time. As a result, it is necessary to outline the conditions for the recognition and execution of foreign judgments applicable both before and after the coming into force of the new legislation.

Availability of Quebec courts to foreign creditors

Quebec courts have no discretion and must order the posting of a bond by any plaintiff not domiciled in Quebec, if the defendant applies for one. French residents are relieved of this obligation pursuant to a France–Quebec agreement: the *Entente between Quebec and France regarding Judicial Mutual Aid in Civil, Commercial and Administrative Matters* (translation).[38] Bonds will be ordered against a corporation if its head office is outside Quebec, even if it is located elsewhere in Canada and even if substantial assets and offices are situated in Quebec. It is common for defendants to use and abuse this procedure to obtain delays.

37. Bill 38, 1992, c. 57.
38. RSQ 1985, c. A–20.1, Schedule, s. 1.

Recognition procedure

Civil law

Under the old law, Quebec courts did not automatically recognise foreign judgments. In order to execute a foreign judgment rendered prior to 1 January 1994, or rendered later on procedures pending on that date, a creditor must institute exemplification proceedings in a Quebec court. In the course of exemplification proceedings, a local debtor may invoke the now repealed Article 178 of the Quebec *Code of Civil Procedure*, which provided that "any defence which was or might have been set up to the original action may be pleaded to an action brought upon a judgment rendered out of Canada". Hence, a judgment or order rendered outside Canada may be re-opened and pleaded on the merits in Quebec.

For foreign judgments rendered after 1 January 1994, or later on procedures pending on that date, the onerous exemplification proceedings described above no longer apply. The new provisions of the Quebec Code of Civil Procedure, notably Article 785, simply require that "(a)n application for recognition and enforcement of a decision rendered outside Quebec is made by way of a motion. It may also be made incidentally, even in defence, if it comes within the jurisdiction of the Quebec court".

Article 3148 of the Civil Code of Quebec states that Quebec authorities have jurisdiction in personal actions where:

(1) the defendant has his domicile or his residence in Quebec;
(2) the defendant is a legal person (i.e., a corporation or partnership), is not domiciled in Quebec but has an establishment in Quebec, and the dispute relates to its activities in Quebec;
(3) a fault was committed in Quebec, damage was suffered in Quebec, an injurious act occurred in Quebec or one of the obligations arising from a contract was to be performed in Quebec;
(4) the parties have by agreement submitted to it all existing or future disputes between themselves arising out of a specified legal relationship;
(5) the defendant submits to its jurisdiction.

The Article further allows parties to agree to submit any disputes between them to a foreign authority. In addition, in cases of actions *in rem*, Quebec authorities will have jurisdiction when the property in dispute, whether movable or immovable, is situated in Quebec.

The issue of jurisdiction must, however, be distinguished from that of which law will apply to a specific dispute. Each kind of legal relationship has different rules which govern the issue of applicable law. For example, in the case of contracts, if no law is designated by the parties in the act, the law of the country with which the contract is most closely connected will apply. In cases of civil liability, the obligation to compensate for injury caused to another is governed by the law of the country where the injurious act occurred.

It is important to note that the new law has added a provision which further nuances the rules governing the issue of applicable law when a dispute has a foreign element. Article 3083 of the Civil Code of Quebec allows a party being sued in Quebec to raise the issue of capacity. It states:

> The status and capacity of a natural person are governed by the law of his domicile.
>
> The status and capacity of a legal person are governed by the law of the country under which

it was formed subject, with respect to its activities, to the law of the place where they are carried on.

Therefore, if the law of the party's domicile states that the party does not have the capacity to be sued, for example, then he may invoke this provision to prevent the action from being maintained in Quebec.

FOREIGN JUDGMENTS

The recognition and enforcement of foreign judgments was a matter of procedure under the old law, and was governed by the Code of Civil Procedure. In cases where the old law is applicable, the courts must refuse to enforce or recognise a judgment rendered outside Quebec where Quebec courts have exclusive jurisdiction on the subject matter, or if the foreign rule of law contradicts an imperative Quebec rule of law. The judgment to be enforced must also be definitive and final for the court to do so.

Under the old law, the defence raised in an exemplification proceeding must be one that could or should have been successful in the foreign jurisdiction, under the foreign law, even if the grounds were not raised there.

Under the new law, Article 3155 of the Civil Code of Quebec dictates that a Quebec court will recognise and declare enforceable any decision rendered outside Quebec, with the exception of certain enumerated cases, which are as follows:

(1) the authority of the country where the decision was rendered had no jurisdiction under the provisions of this Title (i.e., the recognition and enforcement of foreign decisions and jurisdiction of foreign authorities);
(2) the decision is subject to ordinary remedy or is not final or enforceable at the place where it was rendered;
(3) the decision was rendered in contravention of the fundamental principles of procedure;
(4) a dispute between the same parties, based on the same facts and having the same object has given rise to a decision rendered in Quebec, whether it has acquired the authority of a final judgment (*res judicata*) or not, or is pending before a Quebec authority, in first instance, or has been decided in a third country and the decision meets the necessary conditions for recognition in Quebec;
(5) the outcome of a foreign decision is manifestly inconsistent with public order as understood in international relations;
(6) the decision enforces obligations arising from the taxation laws of a foreign country.

The Quebec courts have borrowed many common law principles in developing the rules of recognition of foreign judgments. In that respect, a foreign judgment based on a gambling debt, which could not have been similarly decided under the *Civil Code of Lower Canada* given the unenforceability of such debts, was recognised by a Quebec court for the same reasons as in the common law decision.[39]

It is important to note that Quebec has enacted specific protective legislation with

39. *Resorts International Hotel Inc.* v. *Samuel Auerbach* (1986) RJQ 2479 (CP) confirmed at [1992] RJQ 302 (CA).

respect to damages resulting from exposure to raw materials originating in Quebec, with a view to avoiding exemplification of US litigation awards related to asbestos.

Article 3129 of the Civil Code of Quebec reads:

> The application of the rules of this Code is imperative in matters of civil liability for damage suffered in or outside Quebec as a result of exposure to or the use of raw materials, whether processed or not, originating in Quebec.

Prohibitive, punitive or exemplary awards relating to such damages, which would not be granted by a Quebec judge, cannot therefore be enforced in Quebec.

JUDGMENTS ALREADY RECOGNISED IN ANOTHER CANADIAN JURISDICTION

Under the old law, if the creditor had obtained a judgment in another Canadian jurisdiction, even by recognition of a foreign judgment, no defence available against the original action could be pleaded against the exemplification action if the defendant was personally served, or appeared in the Canadian action, except with respect to arguments concerning Quebec immovables and the jurisdiction of the Canadian courts on such property.

With respect to judgments to which the old law is applicable, it is necessary to prove that the judgment debtor was served in the Canadian court proceeding according with the domestic jurisdiction's rules of service, which must also be proven.

Under the new law, the distinction established by Articles 178–180 of the now repealed provisions of the Code of Civil Procedure between decisions rendered outside Canada and those rendered in the other provinces has been abolished. As a result, all decisions rendered outside Quebec, irrespective of their origin, will be accorded more favourable treatment given that exemplification procedures are no longer required, as discussed above.

PROCEDURAL ISSUES

(1) Proof of service is no longer necessary in a recognition proceeding unless it is raised in the plea.

(2) Under the old law, limitation periods ("prescription") on the original debt varied from one year to 30 years. The foreign procedure interrupts prescription, causing the delay to start again on the date of the judgment. A Quebec judgment, under the old law, was enforceable for 30 years. However, under the new law, it is prescribed by 10 years. Article 6 of the Transitional Law governs cases which straddle the coming into force of the new law. Given that the new law shortens the prescription period, the second paragraph of the article dictates that:

> Where (the new legislation) shortens a prescribed period, the new period applies, but begins to run from the coming into force of the new legislation. However, the period prescribed in the former legislation is maintained where it would in fact be extended if the new period applied.

Therefore, a foreign judgment rendered prior to 1 January 1994 would be enforceable for 10 years after that date, unless it would have been prescribed sooner had the 30-year period applied.

The limitation period on a foreign judgment was 30 years under the old law, and is similarly 10 years under the new law, since the latter dictates that the same rules of enforceability in the place of origin shall be equally applicable in Quebec.

(3) Costs awarded to the successful party are minimal.

(4) The Civil Code of Lower Canada states in Article 1220 that copies of the foreign judgment, under the seal of the foreign court or under the signature of the officer having the legal custody of the record of such judgment, make *prima facie* proof of the "contents" of the judgment, without any evidence of the seal or signature affixed to such copy or of the authority of the officer granting same being necessary.

Under the old law, once properly filed as evidence, the foreign judgment proved, *prima facie*, that the foreign court had jurisdiction, applied the foreign law and concluded properly on the merits of the claim. The defendant in the Quebec exemplification proceedings then has the burden of proving his defence to the contrary.

Under the new law, exemplification proceedings are no longer required, as discussed above. With regards to the rules of evidence applicable to foreign judgments, the first paragraph of Article 2822 of the Civil Code of Quebec provides that "(a)n act purporting to be issued by a competent foreign public officer makes proof of its content against all persons and neither the quality nor the signature of the officer need be proved".

(5) In cases where the old law is applicable, the rate of exchange at the date of the Quebec judgment is usually used to calculate the award, but a diligent creditor will obtain the benefit of the most favourable rate, as held in the case of *Moshe-Cohen* v. *Hill Samuel & Co. Ltd.*[40]

The new law in this regard provides more specific rules when applicable. The first paragraph of Article 3161 of the Civil Code of Quebec provides that:

> (w)here a foreign decision orders a debtor to pay a sum of money expressed in foreign currency, a Quebec authority converts the sum into Canadian currency at the rate of exchange prevailing on the day the decision became enforceable at the place where it was rendered.

By statute

Arbitration awards are enforced pursuant to Articles 948 *et seq.* of the Code of Civil Procedure, and no change resulted from the coming into force of the new legislation. Unless the arbitration award deals with a matter not subject to arbitration in Quebec, or if its recognition is contrary to public order, foreign arbitration awards will be recognised.

Article 950 of the Code of Civil Procedure reads:

> A party against whom an arbitration award is invoked may object to its recognition and execution by establishing that:
>
> 1. One of the parties was not qualified to enter into the arbitration agreement;
> 2. The arbitration agreement is invalid under the law elected by the parties or, failing any indication in that regard, under the laws of the place where the arbitration award was made;
> 3. The party against whom the award is invoked was not given proper notice of the appointment of an arbitrator or of the arbitration proceedings or was otherwise unable to present his case;
> 4. The award deals with a dispute not contemplated by or not falling within the terms of the arbitration agreement, or it contains decisions on matters beyond the scope of the agreement;
> 5. The manner in which the arbitrators were appointed or the arbitration procedure did

40. (1989) RJQ 2078 (CA).

not conform with the agreement of the parties or, if there was no agreement, with the laws of the place where the arbitration took place; or

6. The arbitration award has not yet become binding on the parties or has been set aside or suspended by a competent authority of the place or pursuant to the laws of the place in which the arbitration award was made.

In the case of subparagraph 4 of the first paragraph, if the irregular provision of the arbitration award described in that paragraph can be dissociated from the rest, the rest may be recognised and declared executory.

Remedies on enforcement

Provisional and interim remedies

Any claim, whether recognised by a foreign judgment or not, can benefit from provisional remedies before a Quebec judgment is obtained. Therefore, while exemplification proceedings in Quebec are pending in order to obtain a Quebec judgment for the recognition and enforcement of foreign decisions rendered before 1 January 1994, or procedures pending on that date, the provisional and interim remedies described below may be available.

SEIZURE BEFORE JUDGMENT AUTHORISED BY A JUDGE

Any property of a defendant can be attached by way of seizure before judgment on an *ex parte* application to a judge in chambers, pursuant to Article 733 of the Code of Civil Procedure, if there is affidavit evidence that it is reasonable to fear that, without this remedy, the recovery of the debt may be put in jeopardy.

Such seizures can be released on a motion within a short period, if the motives for seizure were false or insufficient. The burden of proof is on the plaintiff. This remedy is in fact maintained only in exceptional cases, involving acts amounting to fraud or if a flagrant disrespect for the law is shown.

SEIZURE BEFORE JUDGMENT AUTHORISED BY A COURT OFFICER

Even in the absence of fear for or peril to the claim, some specific debts give the creditor a right to obtain a seizure before judgment on specific property, on a simple affidavit application to a court officer. Article 734 of the Code of Civil Procedure provides for four types of property upon which such a seizure is possible:

(1) a movable property which the creditor has a right to revindicate;

(2) a motor vehicle which has caused damage to the creditor;

(3) a movable property upon the price of which the creditor is entitled to be collocated by preference and which is being used in such a way as to jeopardise the realisation of his prior claim; and

(4) a movable property which a provision of law permits the creditor to seize in order to assure the exercise of his rights upon it.

Post-judgment remedies

GARNISHMENT

Garnishment of any deposits, receivables, wages and amounts owing, present or future, due or not, can be effected by a simple writ prepared by the creditor's attorney, subject to restrictions for unseizable property.

EXECUTION AGAINST LAND

A creditor is entitled to register immediately a Quebec judgment against any specified land owned by the debtor, even before the expiry of the delay to appeal. Such registration creates a legal hypothec or mortgage against the land, ranked according to the date of registration.

A minimum debt of $10,000 is necessary to seize a personal residence. A writ of seizure is obtained and the sale is conducted by the court sheriff to satisfy the judgment.

SEIZURE OF MOVABLES

Upon the signature at court of a writ prepared by the plaintiff's attorneys, a bailiff retained by the plaintiff will seize and sell any property of the debtor, subject to some restrictions. In fact, Article 2730 of the Civil Code of Quebec provides that:

> Every creditor in whose favour a judgment awarding a sum of money has been rendered by a court having jurisdiction in Quebec may acquire a legal hypothec on the movable or immovable property of his debtor.

EQUITABLE EXECUTION

Equitable remedies are not available in Quebec.

ROGER P. SIMARD

CHAPTER 6

CAYMAN ISLANDS

INTRODUCTION

The Cayman Islands have emerged as a leading off-shore financial centre.

The object of this chapter is to examine, albeit only briefly, by virtue of its given scope, the law and procedure available to the foreign creditor or prospective civil litigant who might seek to trace, protect and recover assets within the Cayman Islands.

The Cayman Islands comprise three islands, namely, Grand Cayman, Cayman Brac, and Little Cayman. These islands are situated approximately 500 miles south of Miami, Florida, and approximately 180 miles west of Jamaica.

The islands are a colony of the United Kingdom and, consequently, the structure of the colony's courts and its legal system are substantially similar in practice to those of the United Kingdom.

The court structure of the Cayman Islands is composed of the Privy Council, the Court of Appeal, the Grand Court, the magistrates' courts, and the juvenile court.

The highest appellate court of the Cayman Islands is the Judicial Committee of the Privy Council. Appeals to that court are governed by Orders of Her Majesty the Queen-in-Council, the most recent of which is the Cayman Islands (Appeals to the Privy Council) Order 1984. Decisions of the Privy Council are binding on all courts of the Cayman Islands.

The next highest appellate body, the Cayman Islands Court of Appeal, was established by the Court of Appeal Law 1975, as amended by the Court of Appeal (Amendment) Law, Law 10 of 1984. Prior to 1984, the Court of Appeal of Jamaica served as the Court of the Appeal of the Cayman Islands.

The Grand Court of the Cayman Islands has a wide jurisdiction at first instance and is also the first appellate court for appeals from the summary courts. As a court of first instance, the Grand Court exercises original jurisdiction in all indictable criminal cases and in all civil cases involving claims of more than $2,000. Its jurisdiction and inherent powers were recognised, re-enacted, and expanded by statute in 1975 by the Grand Court Law 1975, prior to which time it exercised hybrid powers as a lower court and limited powers of a superior court of record. Since 1975, it has been entirely a superior court of record and, in addition to the jurisdiction expressed by statute, also exercises all the inherent jurisdiction as might be exercised by the High Court of Judicature of England and Wales.

At present, the judiciary comprises three Grand Court judges, including the Chief

Justice of the Cayman Islands.[1] The magistracy comprises the senior magistrate and one other magistrate.

It should be noted that practitioners before the courts of the Cayman Islands must be admitted to practise in the Cayman Islands, either generally or for a limited admission for a particular case, pursuant to sections 3 and 4 of the Legal Practitioners Law 1969. Generally, a barrister, solicitor, or an attorney who is qualified to practise within the Commonwealth is eligible to practise in the Cayman Islands, but such a person must also obtain the necessary licence to work in the Cayman Islands. The legal profession in the Cayman Islands is fused, and practitioners are referred to as attorneys-at-law.

The legal system of the Cayman Islands is based on the common law of England. A local legislature exercises internal legislative power by virtue of the Cayman Islands (Constitution) Order in Council 1972. To the extent allowed by the Constitutional Order in Council, the local legislature exercises the powers of Parliament, with the power of disallowance of its legislation being reserved to Her Majesty through a Secretary of State.

Responsibility for the external affairs of the colony are also reserved to Her Majesty's Government. As will be illustrated later, certain United Kingdom Acts have also been extended to the Cayman Islands by Order-in-Council made by Her Majesty the Queen-in-Council, thus becoming a part of the laws of the Islands.

In 1975, a number of statutes were passed by the local legislature which, to a certain extent, codified the common law. A number of these statutes, and rules made pursuant to them, sought to deal with the jurisdiction of the courts, the criminal procedure and penal provisions of the Islands, as well as matters of civil practice and procedure. However, regard is frequently still had to the practice and procedure of the High Court of England and to precedents decided by the English courts which are of great persuasive authority in the Cayman Islands.

By virtue of section 20(2) of the Grand Court Law, the practice and procedure of the High Court of England can be applied in the superior courts of the Cayman Islands. Section 20(2) reads as follows:

> (2) In any matter of practice or procedure for which no provision is made by this or any other Law or by any Rules, the practice and procedure in similar matters in the High Court in England shall apply so far as local circumstances permit and subject to any directions which the Court may give in any particular case.

The effect of this section has been considered in numerous local cases. It is now well accepted that United Kingdom practice and procedure will only be imported into local practice and procedure where there are no provisions in the local rules which deal with the particular aspect in question.[2] In other words, United Kingdom practice and procedure will not be imported to cure a defect in local legislation. However, even where local procedural provisions specifically exist, they would originally have been modified and adapted from United Kingdom provisions, and some provisions, although ultimately based on United Kingdom practice and procedure, would have been imported via Jamaica, of which the Cayman Islands were administratively and politically a part until 1962.

1. The incumbent is Sir Denis Malone, appointed in January 1990.
2. *McAllister* v. *Tortuga Club (No. 2)* [1984–85] Cayman Islands Law Reports 411.

AVAILABILITY OF COURTS TO FOREIGN LITIGANTS

It has already been observed that the jurisdiction of the Grand Court is substantially similar to that exercised by the High Court of England and Wales. Under this sub-title, the matter of the jurisdiction of the Grand Court requires wider treatment and entails a brief study of certain statutory provisions.

Section 13 of the Grand Court Law (Law 8 of 1975) reads as follows:

> 13. (1) The Court shall be a superior court of record and, in addition to any jurisdiction heretofore exercised by the Court or conferred by this or any any other law for the time being in force in the Islands, shall possess and exercise, subject to the provisions of this and any other laws of the Islands, the like jurisdiction within the Islands which is vested in or capable of being exercised in England by—
>
> (a) Her Majesty's High Court of Justice; and
>
> (b) the Divisional Courts of that Court,
>
> as constituted by the Supreme Court of Judicature (Consolidation) Act, 1925, and any Act of the Parliament of the United Kingdom amending or replacing that Act.
>
> (2) Without prejudice to the provisions of subsection (1), the Court shall have and shall be deemed always to have had power to make binding declarations of right in any matter whether any consequential relief is or could be claimed or not.

Sections 14–19 inclusive set out other areas of jurisdiction, for example admiralty, bankruptcy and matrimonial. These Sections are set out in Appendix 1 to this chapter.

Service of process and jurisdiction

The extent to which the courts are available to a foreign litigant or creditor depends upon the basic principle of jurisdiction, which is whether the prospective defendant is amenable to service of process on him.

There are, of course, certain persons who cannot be sued or who cannot sue, for example certain diplomats and enemy aliens.

Rule 13 of the Grand Court (Civil Procedure) Rules deals with service of original process on a defendant. This rule provides that, wherever practicable, service should be effected by delivering to the defendant a sealed copy of the originating process. However, in certain circumstances, the court can—upon application by the plaintiff—make an order for substituted or other service.

By virtue of rule 13(3), no process shall be served outside the jurisdiction without leave of the court.

Rules 14 and 15, respectively, deal with service of process in particular cases and the procedural requirements for an application for leave to effect substituted service under rule 13(1). An extract containing rules 13–14 inclusive is set out in Appendix 2.

Generally speaking, if the defendant is within the territory of the Cayman Islands, he is amenable to the jurisdiction of the court as he can be served with the original process of the court. It does not matter that his stay within the territory is limited.[3]

Thus, the basic premise of jurisdiction is whether the parties are amenable to the process of the court. There are, however, certain exceptions and conditions to this

3. See *Maharanee of Baroda* v. *Wildenstein* [1972] 2 All ER 689; *Colt Industries* v. *Sarlie* [1966] 1 WLR 440.

general rule. Some obvious exceptions would be if the acceptance by the court of jurisdiction may result in injustice, or the matter involves an action completely unconnected to the Cayman Islands. Other exceptions are discussed below.

Even if the defendant is properly served and before the court, he may be able to have the proceedings stayed if he can satisfy the court that a court in another jurisdiction is the more appropriate court in which to try the action.[4]

Some of the exceptions and the manner in which they apply were also illustrated in the local case of *Touche Ross and Company* v. *Bank Intercontinental Ltd.*[5] The plaintiff firm had sought an injunction to restrain the defendant bank from continuing proceedings it had commenced in Florida, on the basis that the courts of the Cayman Islands were the more natural and appropriate forum. It was held by the Cayman Islands Court of Appeal that the Cayman Islands were the natural forum for the determination of the issues of this case. The onus was on the defendant bank to show that the granting of the injunction to stay the proceedings in Florida would deprive it of a legitimate personal or juridical advantage, and the bank had failed to discharge this onus.

This case in the Cayman Islands was decided prior to the very helpful United Kingdom case of the *Spiliada Maritime Corp.* v. *Cansulex Ltd*,[6] which comprehensively reviewed the United Kingdom authorities and restated the principles that the burden of proof in applications for a stay of proceedings lay on the defendant, and the defendant must show not only that the local court is not the appropriate forum but that the other forum is more appropriate.

The House of Lords in the United Kingdom stated in *Spiliada* that the courts, in considering this question, should have regard to certain factors, for example the availability of witnesses, convenience and expense, the law governing the relevant transactions, and the place where the parties reside or carry on business.

Service outside the jurisdiction in support of Cayman actions

Similarly, the principles enunciated in *Spiliada* apply when the court is considering an application by the plaintiff for leave to effect service outside of the jurisdiction, as is often required when the subject matter of the suit is present within the jurisdiction but the defendant is not. However, in this context, the burden of proof would be reversed and on the plaintiff to show that the Cayman Islands are the appropriate forum for the action (see *Spiliada*). This would be so because the plaintiff would be seeking to establish that the Cayman Islands would be of proper forum in which to sue a defendant resident abroad.

These principles were applied in the local case of *Lake* v. *Cordoba Ltd (No. 2)*,[7] where the Cayman Islands Court of Appeal held that, although the provisions in rule 13 were sufficient to exclude the importation or incorporation of the English rule, nonetheless, the simplicity and generality of the provisions of rule 13 render the guiding principles as enunciated in the English cases and reviewed in *Spiliada* all the more helpful in determining whether the Cayman court was the more appropriate

4. See *The Abidin Daver* [1984] 1 All ER 470.
5. [1986–87] Cayman Islands Law Reports 268.
6. [1986] 3 All ER 843.
7. September 1990, Cayman Islands Law School Law Bulletin, p. 24.

forum. The court also held that leave for service abroad had been properly granted in the instant case.

Lake v. *Cordoba Ltd* is also authority for the principle that the Grand Court will not allow the importation of the practice and procedure contained in Order 11 of the United Kingdom Supreme Court Rules (Service of Process), because Order 11 is jurisdictional in nature, and adequate jurisdiction and procedural provisions exist in the Cayman Islands having regard to section 20 of the Grand Court Law and rule 13 of the Grand Court (Civil Procedure) Rules (rule 13, as earlier explained, deals with service of process). However, the Court of Appeal did state that account would be taken of Order 11, rule 1, of the United Kingdom Rules but that the court would not feel bound by this Order.

None of the dicta is to be taken as an expression of uncertainty either about the court's powers to order service of process abroad or about the manner in which the court will exercise those powers. At most, the dicta simply confirm that the manner in which and the circumstances under which these powers will be exercised are matters which will be influenced by the examples set by the English court. Thus, the precedents for application will be patterned on the United Kingdom examples but the basic powers of jurisdiction need not be imported. The local law and Order 13 suffice in that regard.

Thus, there can be no question that in an appropriate case the Cayman courts will accept jurisdiction over a party not physically present in its territorial limits and will make such orders for service of its process abroad as might be necessary for those purposes.

Apart from the general principle that jurisdiction will be exercised where the parties are amenable to service of process, if the parties have agreed to submit themselves to the court's jurisdiction, the court will respect the choice of court made by the parties.[8] However, even in these cases, the court may refuse to exercise jurisdiction where, for example, the contract governing the choice of jurisdiction is void or terminated by frustration.

It is also possible for the defendant to have the proceedings stayed on the ground of *forum non conveniens*, in which case the principles enunciated in *Spiliada* would be applied.[9]

The fact that a defendant (who is not present in the jurisdiction) has assets within the Cayman Islands by itself will not give the local courts jurisdiction over the action.[10] However, having regard to *Lake* v. *Cordoba Ltd*, the court will be prepared to accept jurisdiction where a foreign creditor has a foreign judgment or award which he seeks to enforce in the Cayman Islands in respect of assets located within the Cayman Islands against a debtor who is resident abroad.

8. *Trendtex Trading Corp.* v. *Credit Suisse* [1981] 3 All ER 520.

9. For a full factual illustration of the manner in which the court will examine the principles in the Cayman Islands of *forum non conveniens*, see *Stewart* v. *Ask Securities Limited*, the facts of which are dealt with below under the heading "Provisional and interim remedies".

10. By way of reference to the likely manner in which the Cayman court would recognise this principle, see Rules of the Supreme Court, Order 11, rule 1(m), and para. 11/1/25, *Supreme Court Practice*.

Service of process abroad under the Hague Convention

This Convention deserves special mention in this context because of the common scenario in which a litigant abroad needs to effect service on a defendant in the Cayman Islands or vice versa.

The Hague Convention on the Service of Process Abroad (1965) was extended by Order in Council to the Cayman Islands on 20 May 1970, and entered into force on 19 July 1970.[11]

Pursuant to this Convention, a foreign plaintiff who has commenced proceedings in another jurisdiction against a person within the Cayman Islands can serve notice of the proceedings on the defendant by transmitting a request for execution of service to the Secretary of State for Foreign and Commonwealth Affairs in London, for onward transmission to the office of the Governor in the Cayman Islands. The documents are required to be translated into English, where English is not the original language.

This procedure, while not serving to vest jurisdiction over foreign subjects in the Cayman Islands, enables the Cayman courts to assist a foreign creditor over a Cayman resident by effecting service in the Islands.

Security for costs

This is always a subject of concern when a foreign litigant seeks to bring an action.

There are no local provisions which deal with security for costs and, pursuant to section 20(2) of the Grand Court Law 1975, recourse is had to the practice and procedure of the High Court of England.

Pursuant to Order 23 of the Supreme Court Rules 1981, it is a matter of discretion for the court, and it is not automatic that a foreign plaintiff, when bringing an action in the Cayman Islands, will be required to put up security for costs, but it is highly likely.

The burden is on the defendant to prove that the plaintiff is ordinarily resident outside of the jurisdiction.

If the plaintiff has substantial property within the jurisdiction, then no security for costs will be required.[12]

Conclusion

In conclusion, it will be readily apparent that the Grand Court has the necessary jurisdiction to provide the foreign litigant with a proper forum for the trial of any action, including those requiring the resolution of issues of conflict of laws.

PROVISIONAL AND INTERIM REMEDIES FOR THE IDENTIFICATION, PRESERVATION AND RECOVERY OF ASSETS

The Grand Court has wide powers in equity and at common law, as well as by statute, to grant orders in aid of a cause to prevent dissipation of assets, for the search for and

11. *Practical Handbook on the Operation of the Hague Convention of 15 November 1965 on the Service Abroad of Judicial and Extrajudicial Documents in Civil or Commercial Matters* (Maarten Kluwer Internationale Uitgeversondernemning, Antwerpen-Apeldorn), p. 23.

12. See Order 23/1–3/4 of *Supreme Court Practice* ("White Book").

seizure of property, and for the detention, preservation and delivery up of assets. These powers are analogous to those exercisable by the High Court of England and Wales.

Two such types of orders which will be of direct interest in the context of this chapter are the so-called *Mareva* injunctions and *Anton Piller* orders. Brief reference will also be made in this context to the orders for discovery and tracing of assets.

The *Mareva* injunction

An injunction is a judicial remedy by which a person is ordered to refrain from doing or to do a particular act or thing. In the former case it is called a restrictive injunction, and in the latter, a mandatory injunction. An injunction is a remedy of an equitable nature.[13]

In certain circumstances, prior to the Supreme Court Act 1981 (UK), the court had specific statutory powers to grant injunctions, but it is not generally within the scope of this chapter to examine those circumstances. For present purposes, the focus will be placed on the *Mareva* injunction.

The *Mareva* injunction is a *quia timet* interlocutory order of the court, prohibitory in nature, and, although made *in personam*, operates *in rem* without creating rights *in rem*. It may be granted *ex parte* without notice to the defendant or potential defendant at any stage in an action in the Grand Court.[14]

A foreign plaintiff, like any other plaintiff, can obtain such an interlocutory order to preserve the assets of the defendant within the jurisdiction until the trial of the action. This type of injunction derives from the well-known case of *Mareva Compania Naviera SA* v. *International Bulkcarriers SA*.[15] In the United Kingdom, this principle is now embodied in statute by section 37 of the Supreme Court Act 1981. However, in the Cayman Islands, reliance is placed primarily on the case. Thus, the power to grant such an injunction in the Cayman Islands is an inherent power of the court. Notwithstanding the existence of this inherent power, the statutory powers vested by the Supreme Court Act 1981 have been held to have been received and applied in the Cayman Islands.[16]

As there are no local rules of procedure, regard would be had to the practice and procedure of the English High Court. An application would normally be made *ex parte* and supported by affidavit setting out the grounds for seeking the order. The plaintiff has to show that he has a good arguable case, that there is a risk of removal of assets by the defendant, and the plaintiff must give full and frank disclosure of all issues—those for as well as against his case. Failure to do so might result in the discharge of the order at a later date.

A foreign plaintiff might have to put up security for the usual undertakings as to damages, and similar principles are applied as in arguments on security for costs.[17]

Applications for *Mareva* injunctions are fairly numerous within the local courts

13. *Halsbury's Laws of England* (4th ed.), Vol. 24, para. 901.

14. See generally Order 29 of the *Supreme Court Practice* ("White Book") of the High Court of England and Wales, which applies in the Cayman Islands, and Richard N. Ough, *The Mareva Injunction and Anton Piller Orders—Practice and Precedents* (Butterworths 1987).

15. [1975] 2 Lloyd's Rep. 509.

16. Causes 230 of 1989 and 338 of 1988 of the Grand Court.

17. John Gatenby, *The Recovery of Money* (Longman Group UK Ltd 1989, 7th ed.), p. 31.

and, as already stated, the relevant case law of the United Kingdom has been consistently applied.

In the local case of *Bank of Nova Scotia* v. *Emerald Seas Ltd*,[18] the Grand Court held, applying the principles of the *Third Chandris*,[19] that the facts that the first and second defendants were foreigners within the jurisdiction (and thus not bound to remain for a trial or to maintain their assets within the jurisdiction) did not of itself warrant the injunction. That decision was notwithstanding the earlier dicta of Summerfield CJ in *Kilderkin Investments* v. *Player*,[20] to the effect that the risk of the removal of assets by the defendant from the jurisdiction might more readily be inferred from the circumstances in the Cayman Islands than in England. The learned Chief Justice stated (at p. 408):

> It may well be that this court will have to give further consideration to the application of this point in applications for a *Mareva* injunction in this jurisdiction as different considerations may arise from those in England. Where considerable sums of money are involved and the persons concerned have no strong ties to the Islands, or a company is involved which can easily fold or be stripped of its assets, the temptation to remove assets from the jurisdiction to escape the effects of a judgment of this court must be great. That temptation gives rise to a risk. Risk may be inferred from circumstances here which might not give rise to the same inference in England.

Although the learned Chief Justice's recommendations have not yet found complete acceptance in Cayman case law so as to make *Mareva* injunctions more readily obtainable than in the United Kingdom, nonetheless it was earlier accepted that a *Mareva* injunction would be ordered in a suitable case to restrain assets of the defendant within the jurisdiction and that the court would also be prepared to order disclosure of all of the defendant's assets.

Furthermore, having regard to the recent line of cases,[21] it would appear that the English courts are now more and more prepared to grant a worldwide *Mareva* injunction in exceptional cases. There are obvious difficulties in the enforcement of such orders, and the courts have qualified such orders by provisos to avoid affecting third parties abroad and to prevent oppression to the defendant by a multiplicity of proceedings.

In June 1990, the Grand Court granted a *Mareva* injunction having extraterritorial and worldwide effect.[22]

It is well established that, where the court does not have jurisdiction to try the matter generally, it will not grant a *Mareva* injunction.[23]

For the benefit of a creditor, it is clear that a *Mareva* injunction may be granted after judgment where there are grounds to believe that the debtor intends to dispose of his assets in order to avoid execution. In addition, a *Mareva* injunction granted prior to judgment may be extended after judgment to facilitate execution of the judgment, although such an injunction is not made solely for the purpose of enforcing a judgment.[24]

18. [1984–85] Cayman Islands Law Reports 180.
19. *Third Chandris Shipping Corporation* v. *Unimarine SA* [1979] QB 645.
20. [1980–83] Cayman Islands Law Reports 403.
21. *Babanaft Int. SA* v. *Bassatne* [1989] 1 All ER 433; *Republic of Haiti* v. *Duvalier* [1989] 1 All ER 456; *Derby & Co. Ltd* v. *Weldon (No. 1)* [1989] 1 All ER 469.
22. Cause 230 of 1989 of the Grand Court of the Cayman Islands.
23. *The Siskina* [1979] AC 210.
24. Order 29/1/23 *Supreme Court Practice*.

In relation to the enforcement of foreign judgments, there is at least one example of the courts in the United Kingdom granting a *Mareva* injunction in the case of the enforcement of a foreign arbitral award. Although the House of Lords on appeal discharged the injunction, nothing was stated which would put in doubt the principle that the court had jurisdiction to grant the injunction in the first place.[25]

Anton Piller orders

The *Anton Piller* order is also a *quia timet* interlocutory order of the court, but mandatory in nature and made *in personam*. Such an order is made upon *ex parte* application without notice to the defendant.

The *Anton Piller* order is a sobriquet acquired from the first case in the English courts in which an order of this type was granted (*Anton Piller KG* v. *Manufacturing Processes Limited*).[26] It is a form of discovery which has been likened to a search warrant. There are, however, important differences and safeguards. The consent of the defendant (respondent) is required before any search is conducted. There are other preconditions:

(1) There must be an extremely strong prima facie case in favour of the plaintiff.
(2) The damage to the plaintiff, potential or actual, must be very serious.
(3) There must be clear evidence that the defendants (respondents) have in their possession incriminating documents or things, and that there is a real possibility that they may destroy such material before any application *inter partes* can be made.

Where those preconditions are satisfied, the plaintiff is entitled by the order to search for articles which are or may be the subject of litigation, and for evidential material which may be relevant to the action or proposed action, and, if he finds it, to inspect it and remove it to the safekeeping of his solicitor (attorney) or the court, to prevent its destruction, alteration or concealment by the defendant (respondent).

Discovery and tracing of assets

The Cayman Islands, as one of the leading off-shore financial centres, has, as part of the foundation of its legal regime, strict laws of confidentiality. This confidentiality or secrecy is preserved by strict application of the Confidential Relationships (Preservation) Law 1976 ("the CR(P) Law"), as amended by Law 26 of 1979. Disclosure of "confidential information", as defined in section 2 of the CR(P) Law, is not permitted except with the consent of the principal pursuant to section 3(2)(b)(i); or in compliance with the directions of the Grand Court pursuant to section 3A, or in accordance with specific authorisation granted by the Governor in Council pursuant to section 3(2)(b)(iii) and (iv).

Sections 3 and 3A of the CR(P) Law are set out in Appendix 3. Section 2 reads as follows:

25. *Deutsche Schachtbau-und-Tiefbohrgesellschaft mbH* v. *R'As Al Khaimah National Oil Co.* [1988] 2 All ER 833.
26. [1976] Ch. 55.

"... confidential information" includes information concerning any property which the recipient thereof is not, otherwise than in the normal course of business, authorised by the principal to divulge;

It might appear at first blush, therefore, that a plaintiff or litigant would have difficulty in obtaining orders for discovery or tracing of assets within the Cayman Islands. However, it is well established that the Grand Court is prepared to make the necessary orders for discovery and in aid of tracing in certain circumstances.

In the local case of *Kilderkin Investments Ltd (by Clarkson Company Ltd, Receiver and Manager)* v. *Player and six others*,[27] there was an action brought in the Cayman Islands by the foreign receiver and manager appointed by the Superior Court of Ontario, Canada, to identify, preserve, and recover assets of the defendants within the Cayman Islands, as a result of an alleged fraud and breach of trust. An application for an order for the disclosure of assets was successful, and the Grand Court held

that the disclosure of the location and disposition of the trust funds would be ordered as a prima facie case of fraud and breach of trust had been established and it was the duty of the court to assist the plaintiff in every way recognised by law to trace, recover or preserve the assets. The Confidential Relationships (Preservation) Law did not inhibit the making of such an order, since if the information sought was confidential and the consent of the relevant principal was not obtained an application would have to be made under section 3A of the Law and any order made pursuant to that section would take precedence over any order made in the present proceedings.

Thus, an order under section 3A would be necessary as a final step to overcome the requirements of the CR(P) Law. The onus would be on the defendant or respondent (typically the holder of the confidential information) to seek and obtain such an order.

This case also dealt with the important issue of recognition of a foreign appointed receiver, and will be dealt with in more detail later when we come to consider the effect of bankruptcy (liquidations) on the recovery of assets.

Thus, it is clear from *Kilderkin* that the appropriate orders for discovery will be made, but these orders will be subject to the CR(P) Law.

In the local case of *Ferrostaal AG* v. *Jones*,[28] this principle was applied in considering an application for inspection of bankers' books under section 8 of the Evidence Law 1978.

Section 8 of the Evidence Law, which provides for the disclosure of bankers' books, was made expressly subject to the CR(P) Law, and the Grand Court held that the plaintiff would first have to make an application under section 3A of that Law before it might make disclosure in compliance with the instant order.

Another local case, *Thune and Roll* v. *Transocean Bank & Trust Co. Ltd et al.*,[29] dealt with discovery and the impact of the CR(P) Law on an order for discovery. In that case, the plaintiffs applied under rule 46 of the Grand Court (Civil Procedure) Rules for an order for discovery in respect of confidential information held by the first defendant bank concerning customers. An order was made for discovery by the court following the principles in the United Kingdom case of *Norwich Pharmacal Co.* v. *Customs and Excise Commrs*,[30] directing that the information should be given on

27. [1980–83] Cayman Islands Law Reports 403.
28. [1984–85] Cayman Islands Law Reports 143.
29. [1986–87] Cayman Islands Law Reports 358.
30. [1973] 2 All ER 943.

affidavit, but as the information was confidential the bank applied under section 3A of the Law for directions.

Although the bank made the application under section 3A, it argued that the court had no jurisdiction to hear the application under section 3A, as making discovery on oath (by affidavit) is not equivalent to giving information "in evidence" as contemplated by the section, as affidavits are only a form of pleadings.

The Grand Court held that it had jurisdiction, as an order for discovery on oath would amount to the respondent being required to give confidential information "in evidence" within the meaning of section 3A. Judge Hull said (at p. 363) in recognising the juxtaposition of the court's inherent jurisdiction with the provisions of section 3A:

> In my opinion, quite apart from section 3(2)(c), nothing in the Confidential Relationships (Preservation) Laws limits the jurisdiction of this court to order discovery in a legal proceeding. It would require express language or necessary implication to do so. It appears to me to be important that the court should be free in the first instance to make such orders as are proper, applying the ordinary principles that govern discovery and should be jealous in maintaining its jurisdiction to do so. There is nothing in the Law which expressly or by necessary implication limits that jurisdiction in the first instance.

Later (at p. 368) the learned judge continued by stating:

> Although I have expressed the opinion that nothing in the Confidential Relationships (Preservation) Law limits the jurisdiction of this court in the first instance to order discovery, the operation of the Law in relation to persons to whom such orders are addressed does affect their efficacy. I recognise that the distinction I have sought to make may in some cases be an academic one, i.e., in any case where on the section 3A application, the court, having heard the arguments against disclosure, then directs that it should not be made. Clearly, in that kind of situation it is desirable, if possible, that at the outset the court should have the opportunity to consider all aspects of the matter comprehensively, so that any order it makes will be fully effective at once and not merely conditional on the possibility that a direction will be given subsequently allowing disclosure by the person affected.

Another local case, which was a tracing action (and which was earlier cited as an illustration of the principles of *forum non conveniens*), requires full consideration here to show how these principles of discovery and tracing were applied.

C. Stewart v. *Ask Securities Limited*[31] involved a tracing action for the recovery of shares held by the second defendant as nominee for the first defendant which was a Cayman company. The plaintiff was the wife of the third defendant, and these parties were engaged in divorce proceedings in California.

Under Californian laws, the wife was entitled to one-half of the matrimonial property, and settlement was made on those terms. Subsequently, the plaintiff alleged that the third defendant had misrepresented the value of the shares, and she took legal action in California to rescind the settlement. Before that action was heard, the third defendant transferred the shares to the first defendant in return for an annuity.

It was alleged that the shares were registered in the name of the second defendant, a Bermuda company. The wife's applications in California for an injunction preventing any dealings with the shares was refused.

The wife then brought proceedings in the Grand Court of the Cayman Islands, seeking a declaration that she owned one-half of the shares and requiring the delivery

31. [1986–87] Cayman Islands Law Reports 28.

up of the shares. She also made a successful *ex parte* application for an injunctive order to prevent dealings in the shares pending the hearing of the action.

Subsequently, the defendants sought a stay of the proceedings on the grounds that California was the natural and appropriate forum for the action and the Cayman proceedings were a duplication of the California proceedings, and that the plaintiff could gain no juridical advantage by the Cayman proceedings. It was also argued that the plaintiff's action, being one of equitable tracing, was bound to fail as the first defendant was a bona fide purchaser for value without notice.

It was argued on behalf of the plaintiff that California was not the natural and appropriate forum as the first and second defendants were not parties to the action in California and, consequently, the Cayman proceedings were not a duplication of the California proceedings. It was further argued that the plaintiff could demonstrate that her action was not bound to fail as she could demonstrate that the first defendant was a purchaser for value with notice and the second defendant was a purchaser without value with notice.

The Grand Court held that the proceedings would not be stayed as the actions did not duplicate each other, and Cayman was the more appropriate forum as the first defendant was a Cayman company which exercised control over the shares.

The Cayman proceedings therefore allowed the plaintiff to pursue the tracing action as effectively as possible, especially since there was no evidence as to what recourse (if any) she might have against either the first or second defendants in California.

Discovery would also be ordered as there was a serious issue to be tried as against the first and second defendants. The court held that there were no public policy considerations having regard to confidentiality which would affect the order for discovery.

The Cayman Islands Court of Appeal subsequently upheld the decision of the Grand Court.

FRAUDULENT DISPOSITIONS LAW 1989

It should be noted that modern legislation which deals with fraudulent dispositions came into operation on 1 May 1990. The Fraudulent Dispositions Law 1989 provides that any disposition of property made with an intent to defraud and at an undervalue shall be voidable at the instance of the creditor thereby prejudiced.

The burden of proving an intent to defraud is on the creditor who seeks to set aside the disposition.

Actions or proceedings pursuant to this Law must be commenced within six years of the relevant disposition.

RECOGNITION AND ENFORCEMENT OF FOREIGN JUDGMENTS AND FOREIGN ARBITRAL AWARDS

In order to enforce a foreign judgment in the Cayman Islands, the creditor either has to enforce the judgment at common law or by registration under the Foreign Judgments Reciprocal Enforcement Law (Revised) 1976.

Part II of the United Kingdom Administration of Justice Act 1920 and the United Kingdom Foreign Judgments (Reciprocal Enforcement) Act 1933 have both been extended to the Cayman Islands by Orders in Council.[32] However, local enabling legislation to afford reciprocity was only enacted in 1967 with the passage of the Foreign Judgments Reciprocal Enforcement Law. This Law was subsequently consolidated and revised in 1976.

Under this Law, there is a scheme for the registration of foreign judgments. The provisions of this Law are almost identical to those contained in the United Kingdom Foreign Judgments (Reciprocal Enforcement) Act 1933.

The local Law operates so as to give the Governor (acting on the advice of the Executive Council) power to extend the provisions of Part 1 of the local Law to countries giving substantial reciprocity of treatment to judgments of the Grand Court of the Cayman Islands.

Pursuant to section 3(1), the Governor may by order direct that Part 1 of the Law shall extend to a particular foreign country, and the courts of the foreign country specified in the order are deemed to be superior courts of that country for the purposes of reciprocity.

In 1971, a number of orders were made which extended Part 1 of the Law to the Australian states of South Australia, Victoria, Western Australia, and Queensland. Further, on 8 May 1990, several more orders were made which extended Part 1 to New South Wales, Christmas Island, Norfolk Island, The Cocos (Keeling) Islands, Heard and McDonald Islands, Coral Sea Islands, Ashmore and Cartier Islands, the state of New South Wales in the Commonwealth of Australia, the Australian Antarctic, the Northern Territory, the Australian Capital Territory, the state of Tasmania in the Commonwealth of Australia, and the Commonwealth of Australia.

Peculiarly enough, no other orders have been made under this Law. The author understands that this is primarily because no other states have approached the Cayman Islands to obtain reciprocal enforcement of their judgments.

Although from 1920 the United Kingdom had recognised the Cayman Islands as a dominion whose judgments would be reciprocally enforced by the United Kingdom courts, research has not found any order of the Governor-in-Council in the Cayman Islands purporting to give reciprocity of enforcement to United Kingdom judgments. This appears to continue to be the case, even since the passage of the 1967 Cayman Islands legislation, which has been made effective by orders extending its operation (so far as research has revealed) only to the states mentioned above.

The non-recognition of United Kingdom judgments for the purpose of reciprocal enforcement in the Cayman Islands is all the more surprising as the scheme in the United Kingdom under Part II of the Administration of Justice Act 1920 has been extended to the Cayman Islands.

Equally surprising is the absence of reciprocal orders for the enforcement of United States and Canadian judgments.

In a report of the Commonwealth Secretariat commissioned in 1978,[33] the following observation was made:

32. Order 1985 (Statutory Instrument 1985 No. 1994) and Order dated 10 November 1933.

33. "Recognition and enforcement of judgments and orders and the service of process within the Commonwealth", *a report of a Working Meeting held at Basseterre, St Kitts, 24–28 April 1978*, p. 257.

The extensions (of reciprocal benefits) seem to have been the consequence rather of *ad hoc* decisions for particular circumstances and of energetic interest by a small number of law areas, such as Nigeria and New South Wales, than of a careful appraisal of commercial and trading activities or the migration of people.

Registration

By virtue of section 4(1) of the 1967 Law, a judgment creditor from a state reciprocally recognised may, at any time within six years from the date of judgment, apply to have the judgment registered in the Grand Court.

The judgment must be final and conclusive, in respect of a sum of money which is not a sum payable in respect of taxes, other similar charges, a fine or penalty, and the judgment must have been given after the order came into operation.

A judgment is considered to be final and conclusive even though an appeal is pending.[34] However, the registration of the judgment may be set aside or adjourned if the judgment debtor satisfies the Grand Court that he has an appeal pending or he is entitled and intends to appeal.[35]

The effect of such registration under Part 1 of the Law is that the judgment will be of the same force and effect as if it had been originally given in the Grand Court of the Cayman Islands.

If the foreign judgment is in a foreign currency, then the judgment shall be registered as if it were a judgment for such sum in Cayman Islands dollars at the rate of exchange prevailing at the date of judgment of the original court.[36]

Setting aside of registration of foreign judgments

The 1967 Law, as consolidated and revised in 1976, also contains detailed provisions for the setting aside of the registration of a judgment. Section 6, which contains the relevant provisions, largely embodies the common law principles which would prevent such judgment from being enforced. For example: on the basis that the courts of the country of the original court had no jurisdiction; that the judgment debtor did not receive sufficient notice of the proceedings to enable him to appear or defend the proceedings; that the judgment was obtained by fraud; or that the enforcement of the judgment would be contrary to public policy in the Cayman Islands.

Section 6(2) also sets out circumstances under which the original court is deemed to have had jurisdiction.

Once a judgment can be registered under the 1967 Law, the Grand Court cannot entertain any other proceedings in relation to that judgment.[37] In other words, once registration of the judgment of a foreign country is possible, then in order to enforce that judgment within the Cayman Islands, the judgment creditor can no longer rely on the common law principles of enforcement and must register the judgment under this Law.

34. Foreign Judgments Reciprocal Enforcement Law (Revised) 1976, s. 3(3).
35. *Ibid.*, s. 7.
36. Cayman Islands dollars $0.80 = US $1.00.
37. Foreign Judgments Reciprocal Enforcement Law (Revised) 1976, s. 8.

Recognition and enforcement at common law

As few countries have the benefit of the extension of Part 1 of the Foreign Judgments Reciprocal Enforcement Law (Revised) 1976, in most instances a foreign creditor will have to sue upon the judgment in the Grand Court, i.e., proceed by way of enforcement at common law.

As in the case of registration, the judgment must be final and conclusive, although it does not matter if an appeal is pending.[38]

The issue of jurisdiction is another important aspect of enforcement of a foreign judgment. The foreign court must have had jurisdiction over the defendant in accordance with the principles of jurisdiction applied by the Grand Court.[39] The defendant will normally be taken to have submitted to the jurisdiction of the foreign court if he either acknowledges service of the foreign court's process or agrees to submit to the foreign court's jurisdiction. However, appearance only to contest the proceedings will not be taken to indicate that the defendant has submitted to the court's jurisdiction.

The Grand Court of the Cayman Islands will not enforce a judgment which was obtained by fraud, is contrary to public policy, or if the judgment is founded on a cause of action which is not recognised in the Cayman Islands or relates to the penal or revenue laws of the foreign country.

Actions on foreign judgments should usually proceed quite quickly as the judgment creditor can apply for judgment (once the debtor has been served) under rule 23 of the Grand Court (Civil Procedure) Rules on the basis that the debtor has had no defence.

The foreign judgment may be in a foreign currency.[40]

In cases where a foreign creditor seeks to enforce a foreign judgment, he will usually be required to give security for costs.

The Foreign Arbitral Awards Enforcement Law

The Foreign Arbitral Awards Enforcement Law (Law 30 of 1975) gives effect locally to the New York Convention on the Recognition and Enforcement of Foreign Arbitral Awards, which was adopted by the United Nations Conference on International Commercial Arbitration on 10 June 1958.

Pursuant to section 5 of this Law, an award made in pursuance of an arbitration agreement in a territory of a state other than the Cayman Islands, which is a party to the New York Convention, shall be enforced in the Grand Court as if it was an award under section 22 of the Arbitration Law 1974 of the Cayman Islands.

A duly authenticated or certified copy of an award and the original or certified copy of the arbitration agreement must be produced to the court.

There are also provisions which allow a party to challenge the award on various grounds, for example that the party did not receive proper notice of the arbitration

38. *Colt Industries Inc.* v. *Sarlie (No. 2)* [1966] 1 WLR 1287.

39. *Buchanan* v. *Rucker* (1808) 9 East 192 (the English courts refused to enforce a Tobagan judgment where service had been effected only by posting the writ to the court house door in Tobago, an island the defendant had never visited).

40. *Miliangos* v. *George Frank (Textiles Ltd)* [1975] 3 All ER 801, which was considered in the local case of *Seymour* v. *Ebanks* [1980–83] Cayman Islands Law Reports 252.

proceedings or that the arbitration agreement is not valid under the law to which the parties subjected it.

The Law also gives the court power to stay proceedings in an action where the parties had agreed under the arbitration agreement to submit to arbitration.

METHODS OF EXECUTION OF JUDGMENTS

Generally, the methods of execution of judgments are the same as would be available in the courts of England and Wales.

In the Cayman Islands, the various methods are prescribed in the Judicature Law 1975, and include warrants of execution, summons for commitment, sale of land, summons of attachment, and warrants of possession. These will be briefly considered below in turn.

Warrants of execution

Sections 34 to 41 inclusive of the Judicature Law contain the provisions which deal with warrants of execution against goods belonging to a debtor.

Such a warrant may be obtained at any time after expiration of seven days from the judgment. Pursuant to such a warrant the bailiff may seize and take away any goods belonging to the debtor, with the exception of his or her family's clothes, bed, bedding, tools, and implements of his trade up to a value of $100. At the expiry of five days after the taking of the goods, they may be sold.

The bailiff can also seize cheques, bills of exchange, promissory notes and bonds, and the judgment creditor can sue in the name of the judgment debtor on such securities.

Sale of land

Pursuant to section 42 of the Judicature Law, if the court is satisfied that the judgment debtor has no sufficient goods which can conveniently be taken, the court may, on the application of a judgment creditor, make an order for the sale of the estate of the judgment debtor or his interest in any lands.

Such a sale is usually made by public auction but the court may for special reasons approve sale by private treaty.

If another person other than the creditor has a charge on the land, then that person shall be served with notice of the order and may attend the auction; and the benefit of the proceeds of sale will be distributed among persons found entitled thereto according to their respective priorities.

These provisions dealing with the sale of land were considered by the Cayman Islands Court of Appeal in the case of *Simmons (Trading as Simmons Enterprises)* v. *A. Moxam and P. Moxam*.[41] The Court of Appeal also prescribed guidelines as to the procedure to be followed in sale of land proceedings.

41. [1986–87] Cayman Islands Law Reports 175.

Summons for commitment

This is one of the most frequently used methods of enforcement of judgments. The judgment creditor obtains a summons for the debtor to appear and to be examined as to his means.

If the court is satisfied that the judgment debtor is wilfully refusing to pay the debt when it is in his power to do so, then the court may order that such debtor be punished by being committed to prison for a period not exceeding one year or until the debt is satisfied, if the judgment is not sooner satisfied.

By virtue of section 46(3), imprisonment under this Law does not operate to discharge the debt or deprive the judgment creditor of his right to levy execution against the debtor's goods or any other remedy.

Attachment

If the judgment creditor files an affidavit and statement of claim alleging that the judgment debtor is beneficially interested in any moneys, securities for money, goods, or other property (other than any interest in lands) in the custody or control of another person ("the garnishee"), the clerk of the court shall issue a summons of attachment.

As soon as the summons is served on the garnishee, it shall bind the property of the judgment debtor in the hands of the garnishee.

If the garnishee after service of the summons upon him knowingly and wilfully parts with the custody of the property or sells the property, he shall become liable to the judgment creditor.

The court can also order that the property be seized by the bailiff if it appears that there is reasonable cause to believe that the property is in danger of being removed out of the Islands.

For an examination of the circumstances and principles under which the English court (and, therefore, the Cayman court) would defer to an order of a foreign court in order to remove the danger to a debtor of double payment of a debt, see the judgment of the House of Lords in *DST* v. *Raknoc*.[42] In this case, the House of Lords held (among other things) that, as the debtor had established that it was exposed to a real risk of having to pay the debt twice, the appeal against making the provisional garnishee order absolute would be allowed, and the *Mareva* injunction granted in support of that garnishee order would be discharged.

Warrants of possession

Pursuant to section 56(1) of the Judicature Law, after any judgment affecting possession of land, the court may issue a warrant to the bailiff to give possession of the land as specified in the warrant and as the court may direct.

42. *Deutsche Schachtbau-und Tiefbohrgesellschaft mbH* v. *R'As al-Khaimah National Oil Co.* [1988] 2 All ER 833.

PERSONAL BANKRUPTCY AND CORPORATE LIQUIDATION

Usually, when insolvency is chosen as a means of recovery of a debt, the creditor is prepared to concede that all efforts to recover the entire debt have failed or are likely to fail. In all but the rarest cases, the creditor is, by choosing this means, conceding that he will be able to recover only a part of the debt.[43] Nonetheless, in an appropriate case, these means are available to a creditor in the Cayman Islands both *vis-à-vis* an individual debtor and a corporate debtor.

Special consideration should also be given to the impact insolvency might have upon the other recourses available to a creditor who might seek to use those other recourses for the recovery of a debt.

Personal bankruptcy

By virtue of the Bankruptcy Law (Revised), the Grand Court exercises jurisdiction upon application. Application is by petition to the court.

If the debt is not less than a statutory minimum ($40 at the time of writing), the creditor may present a bankruptcy petition based on an act of default deemed by the Law to be and included under the expression "acts of bankruptcy".

If satisfied that it is just so to order, the court may order that the affairs of the debtor be wound up and property administered under the Law of Bankruptcy.

These powers, by virtue of section 2 of the Law, are exercisable by the courts on the petition of any person who is a creditor, including a body corporate or a firm.

Section 34(1) of the Law provides:

> When a provisional or an absolute order has been made against a debtor, no creditor to whom the debtor is indebted in respect of any debt provable in bankruptcy shall have remedy against the property or person of the debtor in respect of such debt, except in manner directed by this Law.

Section 36 provides:

> When a provisional order has been made against a debtor, his property shall become divisible amongst his creditors in proportion to the debts provided by them.

There are further provisions which would be of interest to the foreign creditor who would be minded to seek provisional, interim or even final remedies against a debtor who is already subject to a provisional or an absolute order of bankruptcy. In this regard, section 34(2) provides:

> All proceedings to recover any such debt shall, if not already stayed, be stayed upon notice of such order being given in manner prescribed, but the Court may on application by any creditor or person interested, allow any proceedings commenced to be continued upon such terms and conditions as it thinks just.

Also of further significance, section 34(3) provides:

> The provisions of this section shall not affect the power of any secured creditor to realise or otherwise deal with his security in the same manner as he would have been entitled to realise or deal with the same as if the section had not been passed.

The court on granting a petition may appoint a receiver.[44]

43. John Gatenby, note 17 *supra*, Chap. 16, p. 171.
44. Bankruptcy Law, s. 18.

Corporate liquidation

Pursuant to section 93 of the Companies Law (Revised), a company may be wound up by the court if:

(a) the company has passed a special resolution requiring the company to be wound up by the court;
(b) the company does not commence its business within a year from its incorporation, or suspends its business for a whole year;
(c) the company is unable to pay its debts; or
(d) the court is of the opinion that it is just and equitable that the company should be wound up.

Section 94 sets out the circumstances in which a company is deemed to be unable to pay its debts. This includes the case where a creditor to whom the company is indebted either at law or in equity in a sum not less than $100 has served a demand on the company requiring the company to pay the sum due and the company has for a period of three weeks neglected to pay such sum.

As in the case of personal bankruptcy, application is made to the Grand Court by petition.

Pursuant to section 98, the court may at any time after the presentation of a petition for winding-up restrain further proceedings in any action, suit, or proceedings against the company.

Once the order has been made for winding-up, no suit, action, or proceeding shall be proceeded with or commenced against the company without leave of the court.[45]

The court will usually appoint a provisional liquidator early in the action, and later on an official liquidator will be appointed. Foreign appointed liquidators will be recognised in the Cayman Islands courts.

Kilderkin Investments v. *Player*[46]

The Cayman Islands Court of Appeal held that the Grand Court had jurisdiction (derived from that exercised by the High Court in England) to recognise in the Cayman Islands a receiver appointed by a foreign court if it were satisfied that there was a sufficient connection between the defendant company and the jurisdiction in which the receiver was appointed to justify recognition of the foreign court's order. Such a connection existed in this case as: (a) the second defendant was a defendant in the Canadian proceedings and had submitted to the jurisdiction of the Supreme Court of Ontario; (b) the second defendant company was incorporated in Canada; and (c) the second defendant carried on business in Ontario and the management of the company was located in Canada.

In this case, it was not necessary to consider the fourth test which was whether the courts of the jurisdiction where the defendant was incorporated would themselves recognise a foreign-appointed receiver as it was accepted that the Ontario courts would do so.

As there were no local rules dealing specifically with the procedure for the recognition of a foreign-appointed receiver and manager, it was held proper to follow

45. Companies Law, s. 100.
46. [1980–83] Cayman Islands Law Reports 403.

the procedure laid down for the appointment of a receiver within the jurisdiction and, in accordance with the terms of the Grand Court Law, sections 13(1) and 20, the English Supreme Court Act 1981, section 37(1), and the Rules of the Supreme Court, Order 30, rule 1, were received and applied.

In Cause 230 of 1989, earlier cited (Grand Court—In the Matter of a petition by the Acting Inspector of Banks for the Compulsory Winding-Up of a Company), the issue arose whether upon making an order for the compulsory winding-up, the court had jurisdiction to grant injunctive relief restraining a director and contributory of the company and his wife from disposing of their assets until further order. It was held (*inter alia*):

(1) Applying the principles in *The Siskina* and *Third Chandris* (both cited earlier) and by receiving the provisions of section 37 of the Supreme Court Act 1981 (United Kingdom), that the court had the power to grant the necessary injunctive relief being sought.

(2) The liquidator has a duty to protect the interest of creditors; he is a fiduciary whose office is an amalgam of statutory rules, agency and trust principles; one of his duties, as part of the general duty to collect the assets of the company, is to proceed against delinquent directors when he sees good ground for doing so; as such, the liquidator has a sufficient legal or suitable interest to apply for an injunction.

Conclusion

The foregoing provides a brief reference to some of the provisions and principles which apply in the Cayman Islands in the context of bankruptcy and liquidation. They are intended to identify the advantages and pitfalls which those recourses present to a foreign creditor.

JACQUELINE CONOLLY SMELLIE

APPENDIX 1. GRAND COURT LAW 1975, SECTIONS 14–19

Admiralty proceedings

14. The Court shall be a Colonial Court of Admiralty within the meaning of the Colonial Courts of Admiralty Act, 1890, of the Parliament of the United Kingdom and all proceedings in Admiralty shall be had and taken on the Admiralty side of the Court.

Bankruptcy jurisdiction Cap. 7

15. The Court shall continue to be the Chief Court of Bankruptcy and shall have and exercise all the jurisdiction and powers conferred on that court under the provisions of the Bankruptcy Law.

Mental incapacity

16. The Court shall have power to appoint guardians of the persons and estates of persons of unsound mind or suffering from mental illness and for that purpose to enquire into, hear and determine by inspection of the person the subject of such inquiry, or to examine on oath or otherwise the party in whose custody or charge such person may be, or any other person or persons, or use such other ways and means by which the truth may be best discovered.

Matrimonial jurisdiction Cap. 71

17. The Court shall have and exercise general jurisdiction in divorce and matrimonial causes and matters in accordance with the provisions of the Divorce Law.

Law and equity to be administered concurrently

18. In every civil cause or matter law and equity shall be administered concurrently. The Court in the exercise of the jurisdiction vested in it shall have the power to grant and shall grant, either absolutely or on such reasonable conditions as shall seem just, all such remedies whatsoever as any of the parties thereto may appear to be entitled to in respect of any and every legal or equitable claim or defence properly brought forward by them respectively in such cause or matter, so that so far as possible all matters in controversy between the said parties respectively may be completely and finally determined, and all multiplicity of legal proceedings concerning any of such matters be avoided. In all matters in which there is any conflict or variance between the rules of law and the rules of equity with reference to the same matter, the rules of equity shall prevail.

Counter claims and third parties

19. The Court shall have power, subject to the procedural requirements of any other law or any Rules, to grant to any defendant, in respect of any legal or equitable estate, right or title claimed or asserted by him, all such relief against any plaintiff as such defendant shall have properly claimed by his pleading and as the Court might have granted in an action instituted by the same defendant against the same plaintiff. The Court may also grant all such relief relating to or connected with the original subject of the cause or matter and in like manner claimed against any other person, whether or not already a party to the same cause or matter, who shall have been duly served with notice in writing of such claim pursuant to any Rules or order of the Court, as might properly have been granted against such person if he had been made a defendant to an action duly instituted by the same defendant for the like purpose. Any person served with any such notice shall thenceforth be deemed to be party to such cause or matter with the same right in respect of his defence against such claim as if he had been served in the ordinary way by such defendant.

APPENDIX 2. GRAND COURT (CIVIL PROCEDURE) RULES 1976, RULES 13–15

Service of original process

13. (1) Except where the defendant, in person or by his legal representative, undertakes to accept service or enters an appearance, originating process shall, wherever practicable, be served by delivering to the defendant a copy thereof sealed with the seal of the Court, but if the Court is satisfied, on application made by the plaintiff, that service cannot conveniently be so effected, it may make an order for substituted or other service, or for service of notice by advertisement or otherwise as may seem just.

(2) Substituted service may be ordered to be effected by delivery of the document—

(a) to some adult at the defendant's or respondent's known place of residence; or

(b) to some agent within the Islands of the person to be served, or to some other person through whom it appears to the Court that there is a probability that the document will come to the knowledge of the person to be served.

(3) No such process shall be served outside the jurisdiction without the leave of the Court, and no sub-process shall be issued without such leave, if it is apparent from the document that service outside the jurisdiction will be required. When leave to serve outside the jurisdiction is granted a copy of the order for such service shall be served therewith:

Provided that when leave is given for service of process outside the jurisdiction upon a person who is not a British subject nor within Her Majesty's dominions, notice thereof and not the process itself shall be served.

Service in particular cases

14. (1) The Court may give directions as to the person or persons to be served in cases where the defendant is an infant, a person of unsound mind, an official served in his official capacity, a corporation aggregate or any other special case in which no statutory provision has been made regulating service of process.

(2) Subject to any directions given by the Court in any particular case, service of the originating process in an action to recover land, may where the land is not in occupation and service cannot otherwise be effected, be made by posting a copy thereof in a conspicuous part of the property.

Application to the Court for substituted services

15. (1) Any application to the Court for leave to effect substituted service, service outside the jurisdiction or for directions for service in any special case shall be supported by affidavit setting out the grounds upon which the application is made.

(2) When leave for substituted service is granted and the court is satisfied that such service has been effected in accordance with the court's directions, the summons shall be deemed to have been properly served.

APPENDIX 3. CONFIDENTIAL RELATIONSHIPS (PRESERVATION) LAW, SECTIONS 3, 3A, AS AMENDED BY LAW 26 OF 1979

Application and scope

3. (1) Subject to subsection (2), this Law has application to all confidential information with respect to business of a professional nature which arises in or is brought into the Islands and to all persons coming into possession of such information at any time thereafter whether they be within the jurisdiction or thereout.

(2) This Law has no application to the seeking, divulging, or obtaining, of confidential information—

(a) in compliance with the directions of the Grand Court pursuant to section 3A;

(b) by or to—

(i) any professional person acting in the normal course of business or with the consent, express or implied, of the relevant principal;

(ii) a constable of the rank of Inspector or above investigating an offence committed or alleged to have been committed within the jurisdiction;

(iii) a constable of the rank of Inspector or above, specifically authorised by the Governor in that behalf, investigating an offence committed or alleged to have been committed outside the Islands which offence, if committed in the Islands, would be an offence against its laws; or

(iv) the Financial Secretary, the Inspector or, in relation to particular information specified by the Governor, such other person as the Governor may authorise;

(v) a bank in any proceedings, cause or matter when and to the extent to which it is reasonably necessary for the protection of the bank's interest, either as against its customers or as against third parties in respect of transactions of the bank for, or with, its customer;

(vi) the relevant professional person with the approval of the Financial Secretary when necessary for the protection of himself or any other person against crime; or

(c) in accordance with the provisions of this or any other Law.

Directions regarding the giving in evidence of confidential information

3A. (1) Whenever a person intends or is required to give in evidence in, or in connection with, any proceedings being tried, inquired into or determined by any court, tribunal or other authority (whether within or without the Islands) any confidential information within the meaning of this Law, he shall before so doing apply for directions and any adjournment necessary for that purpose may be granted.

(2) Application for directions under subsection (1) shall be made to, and be heard and determined by, a Judge of the Grand Court sitting alone and in camera. At least seven days' notice of any such application shall be given to the Attorney-General and, if the Judge so orders, to any person in the Islands who is a party to the proceedings in question. The Attorney-General may appear as *amicus curiae* at the hearing of any such application and any party on whom notice has been served as aforesaid shall be entitled to be heard thereon, either personally or by counsel.

(3) Upon hearing an application under subsection (2) a Judge shall direct—

(a) that the evidence be given; or

(b) that the evidence shall not be given; or

(c) that the evidence be given subject to conditions which he may specify where the confidentiality of the information is safeguarded.

(4) In order to safeguard the confidentiality of a statement, answer or testimony ordered to be given under subsection (3)(c) a Judge may order—

(i) divulgence of the statement, answer or testimony to be restricted to certain named persons;

(ii) evidence to be taken in camera; and

(iii) reference to the names, addresses and descriptions of any particular persons to be by alphabetical letters, numbers or symbols representing such persons the key to which shall be restricted to persons named by him.

(5) Every person receiving confidential information by operation of subsection (2) is as fully bound by the provisions of this Law as if such information had been entrusted to him in confidence by a principal.

(6) In considering what order to make under this section a Judge shall have regard to—

(a) whether such order would operate as a denial of the rights of any person in the enforcement of a just claim;

(b) any offer of compensation or indemnity made to any person desiring to enforce a claim by any person having an interest in the preservation of secrecy under this Law;

(c) in any criminal case, the requirements of the interests of justice.

(7) In this section, unless the context otherwise requires—

"court" bears the meaning ascribed to it in section 2 of the Evidence Law;

"given in evidence" and its cognates means make a statement, answer an interrogatory or testify during or for the purposes of any proceeding;

"proceeding" means any court proceeding, civil or criminal and includes a preliminary or interlocutory matter leading to or arising out of a proceeding.

The debtor's outstanding debts

According to Danish law, mortgaging of debtor loans is, in principle, simple. The act of giving security is the debtor's receipt of notice that the original creditor has transferred the right to payment to the new creditor (the lending or supplying company). When the debtor has received this information, the debtor is under an obligation to follow the instruction, and the debtor's possible omission to do so will have the result that the debtor may be held liable to pay the claim again to the new creditor. Although the system is easy to handle, I would not recommend that (particularly foreign) suppliers themselves receive claims, either as security or as payment. If there are or there will be free claims at disposal, I would recommend that the suppliers claim that the company itself uses the claims for financing, i.e., that a bank, against having the claims concerned assigned to it, provides a guarantee to the supplier.

In all the above situations, creditors supplying against additional security must be aware that a provision exists according to the Bankruptcy Act that such security shall be granted not later than simultaneously with the contracting of the debt, and the security act shall be performed without any delay. Any delay could mean that the right of security is made voidable in the event of a subsequent bankruptcy, with the effect that the security provided will fall to the estate and that the creditor will then have to be satisfied with his position as ordinary creditor.

INDIVIDUAL LEGAL PROCEEDINGS BY CREDITORS

Individual legal proceedings by creditors in Denmark are usually divided into three stages:

(1) The creditor will obtain a basis of execution by way of a judgment or certain other forms of recognition of debt from the debtor.

(2) The creditor will levy execution on the assets of the debtor.

(3) The creditor will sell the debtor's assets at an auction.

Obtaining a basis

In order to enforce a claim before the Danish courts, it is required that the creditor has a document which confirms the size and enforceability of the debt—in Danish legal terminology called a "basic document". The basic document may be:

(1) a judgment pronounced by a Danish court; or

(2) an instrument of debt signed by the debtor; or

(3) a decision made by an authority recognised by the Danish legal authorities.

(With respect to foreign decisions, reference is made to the text below relating to "Recognition of foreign court decisions".)

Judgment by a Danish court

The procedure to obtain a judgment from the Danish courts of law is as follows.

A writ of summons is submitted to the local court—normally in the court district in which the debtor is domiciled. Writs not exceeding DKK 500,000 are issued by the City Courts (lower courts) in one of the 82 court districts into which Denmark is divided. Proceedings involving writs of more than DKK 500,000, or if the case raises principal legal questions, may be instituted before one of the two High Courts: the Eastern High Court, with its seat in Copenhagen and having jurisdiction over the Islands, and the Western High Court, which has its seat at Viborg and embraces Jutland.

Usually, a case will be prepared through submission of two written pleadings from either party. Each party shall, in its pleadings, include its statement of claim and the allegations made in support of the claim. The parties shall, furthermore, produce to the court the documents on which each of them will rely in the proceedings and state what witnesses shall be heard at the trial. When both parties have submitted two written pleadings, the preparation is, in principle, considered concluded. A date of the trial is appointed. The hearing will always be oral. Foreign parties who find that they should give oral evidence as a party to the action or that foreign witnesses should be heard must take into consideration that such witnesses will be questioned during the hearing of the case in Denmark. Exceptionally, evidence may be given abroad by the Danish court forwarding a commission rogatory to a local foreign court requesting an examination in court of the witness or witnesses concerned.

When the trial is over, the court will usually ask the parties if they are interested in receiving a proposal for a compromise, and the court will then indicate—possibly after some deliberation—their decision on the matter. If both parties agree to finish the case on that basis, no actual judgment will usually be pronounced, but the parties will make a settlement in court, and it will have the same binding effect as if the decision was made by an actual judgment. If one of the parties does not accept the decision of the court, a request is made for a written judgment. This normally requires another one to three months, and it provides a possibility to appeal the case to a higher court.

An appeal of cases decided by the lower courts lies to the High Court. High Court cases are appealed to the Supreme Court.

Usually, it takes approximately 12 months to prepare a case before a lower court. Before the High Court, it is usually approximately 18 months. An appeal case in the High Court takes approximately nine months, and in the Supreme Court approximately six months.

Costs incurred in connection with cases before the Danish courts of law consist of court fees, costs, if applicable, to the opposite party if the case is lost, and fees for one's own lawyer. All three amounts are, in principle, calculated on the basis of the value of the subject matter of the action. The court fee consists of a basic fee of DKK 500.00 + 1% of the claim exceeding DKK 6,000.00.

The losing party in an action will usually, but not necessarily, be ordered to pay part of the successful party's costs. The amount thus awarded will, however, rarely cover the costs involved in going through with an action. Security may be requested of a foreign plaintiff at the institution of proceedings. Such security must correspond to the amount of costs that the plaintiff might have to pay to the defendant if the plaintiff loses the case. The size of the security is normally 2 to 4% of the principal amount, dependent on the nature of the case. However, no security can be requested to be provided if the plaintiff comes from a country which in a similar situation would not request a Danish national to provide security.

There exist no longer official scales with regards to the lawyer's fee, as the previous scales were abolished in the Spring 1996 pursuant to an order by the Danish Competition Authorities. According to the Danish Administration of Justice Act the lawyer's fee shall be considered reasonable. The time used, the obtained results, promptness etc. are facts determining the size of the fee; with regard to foreign clients, it is normal to charge a higher fee than the rate fee, if the lawyer can show that the foreign connection as such has involved more work in conducting the case than is normal in Danish actions (on account, e.g., of much foreign correspondence). Therefore, a creditor who is to go through with an action before the Danish courts should always obtain an agreement on which terms his lawyer may charge his fees.

In round figures, it should be expected that it will cost an amount corresponding to about 7.5 to 10% of the claim to proceed with an action before the Danish courts. In that amount are included fees in connection with translation of the basic documents. If the case requires an expert opinion, such costs must be added.

In simple debt collection matters, the procedure is of course simpler. Often, judgment is given due to the defendant's failure to appear in court or enter a defence. The time and costs involved in obtaining a basic document in such a situation is only a fraction of those explained above for contested actions.

Instruments of debt

If the debtor admits his debt, he will usually be willing to sign a voluntary settlement which has effect as an instrument of debt, in which the debtor confirms the debt and undertakes an obligation to pay interest on the debt and to settle the debt.

Instruments of debt issued in Denmark must be stamped by 0.3% of the principal.

In order to be used in the further process in the Danish debt collection system, it is recommended to have the document signed before two witnesses and to have it provided with the following endorsement: "Nærværende fundament kan danne grundlag for tvangsindrivelse, jfr. Retsplejelovens § 478. This document may form the basis of execution, cf. section 478 of the Danish Administration of Justice Act."

If the creditor retains a Danish lawyer to have the instrument of debt issued, expenses incurred in that connection will usually be between 1 to 2.5% of the claim, but the amount will also usually be added to the debt of the debtor.

Decisions made by other authorities

As a point of departure, Danish courts accept awards made by arbitration. It is a condition, however, that the arbitration is adequately composed and that it is based on a voluntary agreement between the parties.

Where in their contracts the parties have agreed to voluntary arbitration, such a decision is binding and will preclude both parties from later seeking a solution to the matter before the ordinary courts against the wishes of the other party. Conversely, two parties who agree may elect to institute the action before the courts if they wish so instead of the arbitration originally agreed on.

It is more expensive to proceed with an action by arbitration. One reason is that the judges of the arbitration tribunal must be remunerated by the parties. By tradition, no costs are ordered to be paid by the losing party to the successful party in a Danish arbitration unless very special circumstances speak in favour of this.

It should be expected that costs incurred in connection with arbitration in Denmark with three arbitrators could amount to 15 to 20% of the claim.

The advantages of an arbitration are the speed and the fact that the decision is not public. However, it must not be disregarded that there are no means of appeal of a decision reached by an arbitration.

Execution

Enforcement of money claims takes place through an enforcement court. This court is a division of the local lower court in one of the 82 court districts mentioned earlier.

The first step in an enforcement procedure is that the creditor requests the execution court to levy execution on some of the debtor's assets. By these proceedings, the creditor obtains a right through the decision of the court to demand that part of the debtor's assets be sold in order to obtain cover of the amount owed. By the same act, the creditor obtains a mortgage on the asset concerned.

In order to carry through execution proceedings, an application shall be forwarded with enclosed copy of the basic document which confirms the debt. As mentioned above, it may be, e.g., a judgment, an instrument of debt, or an agreement between the parties. In order for an instrument of debt or an agreement between the parties to be used to go directly to the enforcement court, i.e., by not having to obtain a judgment prior to the enforcement proceedings, it is required that the basic document carries an endorsement accepted by the debtor to this effect. The endorsement should read as follows: "Nærværende fundament kan danne grundlag for tvangsindrivelse, jfr. Retsplejelovens § 478. This document may form the basis of execution, cf. section 478 of the Danish Administration of Justice Act."

A basic document according to which the debtor confirms owing the amount, but without the above endorsement, cannot be used in the enforcement court and collection will, therefore, still require that the creditor first issues a writ of summons in order to obtain a judgment against the debtor. This process may easily delay proceedings by three to four months.

Enforcement proceedings may be carried out either by the debtor being summoned to appear before the enforcement court or by an officer of the court going out to the debtor's house or place of business and levying execution there. In very special cases, the enforcement court may decide that the police shall arrest and present the debtor in court, to question him about his financial situation and assets.

Depending on the nature of the matter—including the expectation that the debtor will fulfil his obligation to pay—the enforcement court may decide that the assets on which execution is levied shall be removed immediately and kept until an auction can take place.

Execution may be levied on practically all tangible assets, with the main exception of the necessities of life of the private debtor. A business debtor has almost no protection of the assets attached to his business.

Execution is levied for the purpose of selling the asset in question within a certain period of time at an auction. It is worth noting in this connection that the term of limitation, if applicable, of execution differs depending on the nature of the asset. A creditor who has obtained execution on chattels of the debtor is, therefore, forced to proceed with an auction within one year. Execution on real estate is time-barred after 20 years.

The execution is without legal effect if the debtor is declared bankrupt within three months after the date of the execution. In the event, the creditor must either return any payment received or accept that the assets on which execution has been made can be disposed of by the estate to the benefit of all the creditors.

The creditor who is to have execution levied for his account payable should expect that costs incurred in this respect (including a new court fee of approximately 0.5%) will usually amount to approximately 2% of the amount due.

Forced sales

Different procedures apply as to how a forced sale is to be implemented, depending on the nature of the asset. The sale of real estate usually occurs at a forced sale. It is more simple to realise operating plant and chattels. Similarly, it is essentially different as to how long it takes to carry through a forced sale. A forced sale of operating plant and chattels may be carried out immediately after it is established that the debtor is no longer able to pay and cannot offer an instalment arrangement which, must, however, not exceed 10 months unless the creditor accepts a longer arrangement. On account of delays in the courts as a result of many forced-sale cases, it should be expected that it takes six to nine months to carry out a forced sale of real estate.

It is important to note that, in two ways, it is relatively expensive to carry out a forced sale. First, significant costs are incurred by way of fees and dues in connection with procedure. Secondly, the prices obtained at a forced sale are most often substantially lower than in a sale in the open market. If at all possible, it often pays to try to obtain an agreement with the debtor about the terms of a voluntary sale. Such arrangement may be made, for example, by the creditor's lawyer obtaining a power of attorney from the debtor to realise the asset in question against settling the sales sum to execution creditors or other mortgagees.

Pre-trial attachment—interlocutory relief

A creditor who has reason to fear that a debtor is about to evade his payment obligations may ask the enforcement court to levy attachment. Attachment may be termed interlocutory seizure of part of the debtor's assets, and it is applicable until the time when the creditor has obtained a basic document (see above).

It is relatively difficult to make a Danish enforcement court carry through attachment. The creditor must be able to render it probable that the debtor is, e.g., about to leave the country or that a trader is making unusual realisations of his assets or in any other manner makes unusual dispositions.

The effect of the attachment is that the debtor is deprived of the possibility of disposing of the asset(s) on which the attachment is levied. Attachment may be effected by the assets being removed from the debtor, but usually it is done solely by the enforcement court giving notification that the attachment has been levied and that the debtor will commit a criminal act if he acts contrary to the attachment.

The weakness of the attachment is that any creditor who has already obtained a basic document can oust the creditor who has only an attachment. Furthermore, in the event of the debtor's bankruptcy an attachment is without legal effect, with the result that the estate can dispose of the assets for the benefit of all the creditors.

by the bankruptcy can still be claimed against the debtor. This rule, however, is not relevant to companies being liquidated, as a company by the end of the liquidation is dissolved. The creditor must, in this connection, pay attention to the fact that, with regard to a number of situations—including supply of goods—a rule of limitation exists, according to which a creditor who intends to maintain his claim for a period longer than five years will have to make the debtor recognise his debt or take out a writ of summons to obtain a judgment. A judgment or an instrument of debt is not time-barred until after 20 years at the earliest.

As mentioned above, the debtor is not discharged of the unpaid part of his debt after a bankruptcy. A discharge of debt may, according to Danish law, be established in two situations: in a compulsory composition or through rescheduling of debts. Rescheduling of debts is a process which is usually applied in connection with wage earners who have incurred debts so large that they have no possibility of paying them through their wages. The decision of a rescheduling of debts is made by the court and may, in principle, result in total extinction of the debt.

Before the court makes a decision about a rescheduling of debts, all creditors will have received notification of the financial position of the debtor, and they will have had an opportunity to speak about their stand on the proposal to reduce or clear away the debt. It should, however, be pointed out that the court can disregard objections from creditors.

Universal proceedings costs

It is most important to note that the bankruptcy petitioner is personally liable for the costs released by the bankruptcy. This should naturally be understood to mean that, first, the debtor's assets are issued, *inter alia*, to cover these expenses but, if the debtor does not own assets or if all the debtor's assets are encumbered by a third party's better right (for example, by way of non-voidable and valid mortgages), the expenses will be incurred by the bankruptcy petitioner.

In principle, there is no ceiling to these expenses, but usually the court will request that the petitioner provide security of DKK 20–30,000 to serve as payment for the preliminary examinations as to whether the debtor has any assets at all to be sold, and to serve as payment to the costs incurred in connection with the bankruptcy.

International bankruptcy

The five Nordic countries (Denmark, Sweden, Norway, Finland, and Iceland) have bankruptcy regulated in a common convention, in which the countries mutually respect suspension of payments or compositions. With regard to the rest of the world, Denmark has no effective conventions.

In relation to corporate bankruptcy estates, this problem is most often solved by the Danish authorities and courts furnishing the trustee with the necessary official certificates confirming that the trustee is authorised to sign with respect to the assets which may be held abroad. The trustee's ability to include the assets in the estate assets depends on the trustee's ability to convince either the foreign authorities in question or the bankrupt of the expediency of co-operation.

Conversely, it follows from the lack of conventions that Denmark does not generally recognise bankruptcy orders pronounced by other countries either.

RECOGNITION OF FOREIGN COURT DECISIONS

According to Danish administration of justice, the point of departure is that solely Danish decisions shall be respected. However, Denmark has acceded to a number of conventions, with the result that decisions made by a number of countries will also be respected.

The most important of these conventions are the following.

The European Community Judgment Convention

The European Community (EC) Judgment Convention guarantees mutual recognition of the participating member states with regard to all judgments and other court decisions made by the courts of the states comprised by the Convention, notwithstanding who are the parties of the case, the basis of venue, whether the decision is a judgment by default, and whether the case may be appealed. In such cases, the substance of the decision cannot be tried. Only the competence of the foreign court of law may by exception be tried. It must be assumed that the EC Convention thus provides that, if a creditor makes a request for attachment to be levied, he will be free to choose whether he wants the attachment levied by a Danish enforcement court according to Danish rules or by the possible foreign court where the dispute is pending or will be pending.

Similarly, the EC Judgment Convention provides that a compromise made before the court of the member state will have the same status as an actual court decision.

The Nordic Judgment Convention

The Nordic Judgment Convention corresponds in a number of areas to the EC Judgment Convention but is, however, different, e.g. concerning judgments by default, which are not recognised.

Outside the Conventions

Legal decisions of countries that are not signatories of the above two Conventions shall not immediately be recognised in Denmark. An exception is that the Ministry of Justice is authorised to recognise individual countries. For practical reasons, I will not list the individual recognitions which exist on this basis but must recommend that individual examinations be made in each case.

The fact that a court decision of a country is not recognised does not mean, however, that no importance is attached to it. The evidence from testimony of parties and witnesses presented before the foreign court, the evaluation of evidence made by the court, and often its legal application will be made the foundation of the Danish court's decision, unless information provided by the parties gives grounds to believe that the foreign judgment may be wrong. However, the decision cannot be enforced immediately but must be tried through an ordinary legal action.

It is of no importance whether the court decision is based on an agreement between the parties regarding venue. The decision will still have to be tried by a Danish court in order to be made a foundation for a basis of enforcement.

PETER M. ANDERSEN
OLE BORCH

CHAPTER 8

ENGLAND AND WALES

INTRODUCTION

This chapter examines the position of foreign creditors who seek provisional remedies or enforcement of judgments in England and Wales.

All references to England in the following text include Wales but not Scotland and Northern Ireland.

AVAILABILITY OF ENGLISH COURTS TO FOREIGN CREDITORS

The availability of the English courts to a foreign creditor, seeking to commence proceedings in the United Kingdom, requires consideration of the adjudicatory jurisdiction or competence of the English court to hear and determine those proceedings.

The English court has power to determine whether or not it has jurisdiction to adjudicate upon the merits of the particular case before it and, in so doing, the court must be satisfied as to the following: first, that the foreign creditor, the plaintiff, is a person at whose instance the court is prepared to exercise jurisdiction; secondly, that the defendant is a person over whom the court is able or is prepared to exercise jurisdiction; thirdly, that the subject matter of the case is one in respect of which the court is prepared to exercise jurisdiction.

The plaintiff

Any adult of sound mind has capacity to sue in his own name, but the fact of his residence outside the United Kingdom might give rise to certain procedural consequences. For example, foreign residence might render the plaintiff liable to provide security for the defendant's costs, and he will be required to give an address for service of documents within the jurisdiction. The issue of security for costs will be considered later.

A foreign corporation duly created according to the laws of a foreign state is recognised by English law as having legal personality and, so long as it continues in existence under the law of its incorporation, it may bring proceedings in its corporate name, provided that it acts in those proceedings through a solicitor.

If a partnership constituted according to foreign law has its own legal personality under that law, it may bring proceedings in the courts in its own name; but where a foreign partnership has no legal personality under that law, it can bring proceedings in its own name only if it has a place of business in the United Kingdom, whether or not it has its principal place of business outside the United Kingdom.

The defendant and the subject matter

For the court to be prepared to exercise jurisdiction over the defendant, there must exist a basis for the court's jurisdiction and the defendant must also have been properly brought before the court following service of the proceedings, and the defendant must be a person not immune from being sued.

The principles to be adopted depend upon whether jurisdiction is founded under the 1968 Brussels Convention on Jurisdiction and the Enforcement of Judgments in Civil and Commercial Matters ("the Convention") as enacted into English law by the Civil Jurisdiction and Judgments Act 1982 ("the 1982 Act").

The application of the Convention is confined to civil and commercial matters, but does not apply, *inter alia*, to bankruptcy, or to proceedings relating to the winding-up of insolvent companies or other legal persons. The jurisdictional rules in the Convention constitute a uniform code directly applicable in all the contracting states, the members of the European Union (EU). Switzerland, though not a member of the European Union, is within this group of states by virtue of the United Kingdom's ratification of the Lugano Convention in January 1992.

The general jurisdictional rule is that when a defendant is domiciled in a contracting state any proceedings against him must be brought in that state unless one of the Convention's other jurisdictional rules permits the bringing of the proceedings in another contracting state. Section 41 of the 1982 Act provides that an individual is domiciled in the United Kingdom if he is resident and the nature and circumstances of his residence indicate that he has a substantial connection with the United Kingdom. In the case of a company, section 42 of the 1982 Act will give the court jurisdiction if the defendant company was incorporated under the law of a part of the United Kingdom and has its registered office or some other official address there, or its central management and control is exercised there.

The English court will have jurisdiction over a defendant domiciled in another contracting state in the following circumstances:

(1) If the defendant submits to the jurisdiction of the English court by acknowledging service of the proceedings upon him, unless he does so solely to contest jurisdiction (Article 18 of the Convention) and no other contracting state has exclusive jurisdiction under Article 16 of the Convention, even if the parties have agreed under Article 17 that the courts of another contracting state are to have jurisdiction.

(2) If the proceedings relate to a contract, and the obligation in question was due to be performed in the United Kingdom (Article 5 of the Convention), unless the contract was a "consumer contract" within Article 13 of the Convention, in which case jurisdiction is dependent upon the consumer's domicile.

(3) If the English court has exclusive jurisdiction in one of the five separate categories listed in Article 16 of the Convention, irrespective of the defendant's domicile or of the defendant's submission to the jurisdiction of the courts of another contracting state under Article 18, or of a contractual

choice by the parties, under Article 17 of a different contracting state. These five categories of cases are all based upon the connections between the subject matter of the proceedings and a particular contracting state.

(4) If the English court has exclusive jurisdiction by virtue of an agreement by the parties that the English court is to have jurisdiction under Article 17 of the Convention, unless it is contrary to the provisions of Article 13 in the case of "consumer contracts" and unless the defendant submits to the jurisdiction of another contracting state other than solely to contest that state's jurisdiction.

Where the Convention does not apply

In circumstances where the Convention does not apply, there are three possible bases of jurisdiction.

Jurisdiction based on physical presence

The presence, however temporary, of the defendant in England and Wales at the time when he is served with proceedings is sufficient to found jurisdiction unless he has been induced by deception to come into the jurisdiction for the purpose of being served.

Jurisdiction based on consent

The English court will have jurisdiction over a defendant who, though outside the territorial limits of the English court, submits or is taken to have submitted to the jurisdiction. Most commonly, the defendant may submit by acknowledging service of legal proceedings without then contesting the court's exercise of jurisdiction, or he is party to a contract containing a choice of jurisdiction clause.

Jurisdiction assumed over a defendant outside the territorial limits

Under Order 11 of the Rules of the Supreme Court, the English court has a discretionary power to assume jurisdiction over defendants, regardless of their nationality, outside the territorial limits by granting to a plaintiff leave for service of proceedings outside the jurisdiction. On such an application for leave, the plaintiff must show that he has a good arguable case on the merits, that it is proper for the court to exercise its discretion, and that his case falls within one of the listed paragraphs of rule 1(1) of Order 11. For present purposes, the relevant paragraphs are those concerning:

(1) claims for relief in respect of a breach of a contract that was made within the jurisdiction, or was made by an agent within the jurisdiction on behalf of a principal residing out of the jurisdiction, or was governed by English law, or contained an English jurisdiction clause, and
(2) claims in respect of a breach committed within the jurisdiction of a contract made within or out of the jurisdiction.

Security for costs

A plaintiff who is "ordinarily resident" outside the United Kingdom may, on application to the court by the defendant at any stage of the proceedings, be ordered to provide security for the defendant's costs of the proceedings. There is no inflexible rule or practice that a plaintiff resident abroad will be ordered to give security but, as a matter of discretion, it is the usual, ordinary or general rule of practice of the court to require such a plaintiff to give security, because it is ordinarily just to do so. The court has a wide discretion, and will make such an order only if it thinks it just to do so, taking into account all the circumstances of the case, including the financial circumstances of the plaintiff, his prospects of success, any admissions made by the defendant, and the factors outlined below.

It is for the defendant to show that the plaintiff is "ordinarily resident" outside the United Kingdom and, whilst the test does not depend upon the duration of the residence, the residence must be more than occasional or temporary. Furthermore, whilst it is not enough to avoid providing security that the plaintiff is resident within the EU, the court will take that fact into account in exercising its discretion.

The court will also take account of the available procedures for the enforcement of judgments as between the parties. A plaintiff ordinarily resident in a country outside the EU and to which the Convention does not apply, will be ordered to give security. The enforcement procedure under the Convention, the principal object of which is to facilitate the enforcement of judgments across the national frontiers of states within the EU, is an important but not decisive factor to be considered by the court in exercising its discretion.

Security will not be required from a plaintiff, permanently residing outside the United Kingdom, if he has substantial real or personal property of a fixed and permanent nature located within the United Kingdom.

The amount of security awarded to the defendant is in the discretion of the court and will usually be based upon an estimate made by the defendant's solicitors of the costs likely to be incurred in the future. It is usual for security, when awarded, to be in the form of a specified sum of money paid into court by the plaintiff, but in special cases security may be ordered to be given by bond, with two independent and solvent sureties.

PROVISIONAL AND INTERIM REMEDIES

An interim or provisional remedy is a synonymous term for a wide range of orders made in the course of proceedings with a view to achieving interim protection. Such measures are ordinarily granted pending trial but they may also be granted pending an appeal or pending the execution of a judgment.

Article 24 of the 1968 Convention enables an application for interim relief to be made in the courts of one contracting state in which, under the Convention, the courts of another contracting state have jurisdiction as to the substance of the matter. Furthermore, in view of the wide definition of "judgment" in Article 25, an order for interim relief made in one contracting state is, in principle, enforceable in the other contracting states. It follows that the Convention permits the English courts to grant interim relief in aid of proceedings contemplated or pending in the courts of another contracting state. It also obliges English courts to recognise and enforce provisional and protective measures granted by the courts of other contracting states.

The remedies under Article 24 do not in themselves confer on the court any new power to grant interim relief, nor do they create any new type of relief. The English courts retain a limited discretion in deciding whether to accept or to decline jurisdiction in a case to which the 1968 Convention applies. Once the English court has accepted jurisdiction, either under the 1968 Convention or under other English rules, it still retains a discretion as to how it will exercise that discretion if the relief sought is itself discretionary. It has yet to be seen how far the English courts will extend the exercise of their jurisdiction, particularly where the interim order has an extraterritorial effect.

Types of interim relief

The types of interim relief which the courts may make are the following.

Interlocutory injunctions

An injunction is an order of the court requiring a party to do or refrain from doing some particular act. The injunction may be interlocutory or final, but where the application is made at an interlocutory stage, then the injunction would normally be until the trial of the action. The court grants an interlocutory injunction to minimise the risk of injustice to the applicant during the period before the merits of the dispute can be resolved and does not itself closely investigate the merits. In practice, however, once an interlocutory injunction is granted that will often have the effect of concluding matters.

The procedure for an interlocutory injunction is that proceedings must be commenced and the application is made by way of affidavit (i.e. sworn) evidence submitted to the court. The court will normally grant an injunction to preserve the original status quo in a situation in which there is a serious question to be tried, where damages will not adequately compensate for the alleged infringement, where the balance of convenience or the balance of justice supports the granting of an injunction, and the order may be made either unconditionally or on such terms and conditions as the court thinks fit.

The applicant will be required to give an undertaking to pay damages of any loss sustained by the other side by reason of the injunction should it be held at trial that the injunction was wrongly granted. A plaintiff who is outside the jurisdiction may be ordered to bring a sum of money into court or to provide other security.

Mareva injunctions

A *Mareva* injunction will be granted to prevent the party removing his assets from the jurisdiction, or from otherwise disposing or dealing with them within the jurisdiction so as to frustrate the enforcement of any judgment obtained in due course. The concept was first introduced in 1975 in the case of *Nippon Yusen Kaisha* v. *Karageorgis*[1] and the case of *Mareva Compania Naviera SA* v. *International*

1. [1975] 1 WLR 1093.

Bulkcarriers SA.[2] Prior to those decisions, it was held that a creditor could do nothing until judgment to prevent the debtor dealing with his assets as he wished. Such injunctions are important in the context of international litigation where the risk of assets being removed is greater than in domestic arbitration. They can be granted in relation to both domestic and foreign parties, and the remedy has not been restricted to commercial cases but has been used in the fields of intellectual property, personal injuries, matrimonial cases, and so on.

An application is made to the court for the granting of a *Mareva* injunction. As the application is normally urgent and surprise is required, it is usually made *ex parte*, that is without notice to the other side. The applicant must show he has a good arguable case and there is a probability that, if the injunction is not granted, execution of any judgment will be frustrated. The assets no longer have to be within the English jurisdiction but they must be identified to the court as precisely as possible. If it is sought to freeze a bank account, the branch of the bank and details of the account must be identified. The applicant must make full and frank disclosure of all matters within his knowledge that might affect the granting of the injunction and, if it is discovered that he has not been frank with the court, the injunction would normally be discharged. Again, the applicant will be required to give an undertaking in damages. The terms of the order normally allow the debtor to apply to vary or discharge the order; they will also allow him to take out legal costs from any frozen assets and normally provide for drawing an appropriate weekly amount for living expenses.

Anton Piller orders—"Search and seek orders"

These are orders requiring a party to permit the applicant's representatives to enter on to his property to search for and seek certain documents and property, so that they may be preserved until trial. The court has an inherent jurisdiction to make such orders and to order the detention and preservation of the subject matter and of the documentation. The relief is sought mainly in cases involving intellectual property rights.

The criteria for the granting of this relief were first laid down in the case of *Anton Piller KG* v. *Manufacturing Processes Limited*.[3] The applicant must show clear evidence that there is a risk that documents will be destroyed and that the defendant would ignore court orders. There must be a very strong prima facie case and the potential or actual damage to the plaintiff's interest must be very serious.

The application is made *ex parte* and sworn affidavit evidence is lodged with the court.

The appointment of a receiver

The court may appoint a receiver where it considers that disputed property is at risk and should be kept out of the possession of both parties until the issues between them have been resolved.

2. [1975] 2 Lloyd's Rep 509.
3. [1976] Ch 55.

Orders for preservation, inspection, or delivery up

The court has extensive powers to make orders relating to physical property, the subject matter of the dispute.

Orders for the interim payment of money

The court has general power to order a party to proceedings to make an interim payment as it thinks just.

Orders for obtaining evidence

Provisions for the obtaining of evidence are excluded from the definition of interim relief in section 25(7) of the 1982 Act, and that Act does not, therefore, permit them to be made in aid of proceedings in other contracting states. The term covers orders for the examination of witnesses, the production of real evidence, and probably also orders for discovery and orders for appointing a court expert, but an order may nonetheless be made under the Evidence (Proceedings in Other Jurisdictions) Act 1975.

Arrest in maritime claims

The court has power to issue a warrant for the property, usually a ship, against which proceedings are brought. The warrant is executed by the Admiralty Marshall, fixing the warrant to the property whilst it is within the limits of the territorial jurisdiction.

Extraterritorial effect of English interim orders

The decision of whether or not to grant interim relief is discretionary. In cases in which the court's order can only be put into effect outside the limits of the territorial jurisdiction, the exercise of discretion has been much influenced by considerations of respect for foreign sovereignty and difficulties of enforcement. However, the strength of these considerations is much reduced in the context of the 1968 Convention.

Until recently, a *Mareva* injunction would not be granted in respect of assets outside the jurisdiction. This area of law is now rapidly developing, and the courts are accepting that there are circumstances in which *Mareva* injunctions covering foreign assets will be granted. The courts are requiring certain safeguards by means of a proviso to ensure that third parties are not affected by the terms of the order, and the proviso may also be qualified in such a way as to enable a foreign court to give effect to the order within its own jurisdiction. It remains to be seen how the courts will interpret this area of expanding law between the contracting states to the Convention and other assets and jurisdictions.

Enforcement of interim order

A breach of an interim order may render a person liable for penalties for contempt of court. An undertaking in damages is nearly always required for the granting of an injunction, whether it be a *Mareva*, *Anton Piller*, or interlocutory injunction.

Interim relief in aid of proceedings in other contracting states

Applications for interim relief are based on the presumption that the dispute will end in a substantive hearing before the court (unless it is settled by agreement before then) and will lead to a final judgment. A plaintiff in proceedings before a foreign court against a defendant with assets in England might wish those assets to be preserved for the satisfaction of a judgment in the foreign court. Before the passing of the 1982 Act, the only way in which he could secure those assets was by starting parallel proceedings before the English court. He would then be entitled to the relief normally granted to plaintiffs before the English court. If it was not possible to start parallel proceedings, for example because the English court lacked jurisdiction, then there was no power to grant interim relief.

Article 24 of the Convention permits the courts of each contracting state to grant provisional and protective measures as are available under national law even if the jurisdiction over the substance of the case is allocated to another contracting state. Accordingly, the English courts can now grant interim relief where there are actual or contemplated proceedings in the courts of another contracting state. It is not relevant whether the jurisdiction of the courts of the other contracting state arises under the Convention's own rules or in some other way. Thus, an application for interim relief in aid of proceedings in another contracting state based on the exercise of exorbitant jurisdiction can be granted in England.

The question as to what types of interim relief can be obtained is difficult to answer with certainty. Section 25 of the 1982 Act provides that the court may grant any form of interim relief which it can ordinarily grant in proceedings relating to matters within its jurisdiction, except a warrant for the arrest of property or a provision for obtaining evidence. The exclusion of provisions for the obtaining of evidence prevents practical problems in relation to discovery and inspection of documents, for the classification of documents seized under an *Anton Piller* order which may be used for evidential purposes. It is arguable that a distinction has to be drawn between "obtaining evidence" and "protecting and preserving" evidence.

An application for interim relief under section 25 of the 1982 Act is made to the court. If the foreign proceedings have not been commenced it is necessary to show that the intended court will have jurisdiction and that there is a genuine intention to bring them. If the initial application is made *ex parte*, the initial order is not capable of recognition or enforcement in another contracting state until the defendant has had notice of it and had an opportunity to challenge it in an adversarial way.

Effect of foreign jurisdiction clause

Where the courts of another contracting state have exclusive jurisdiction over the substance of a dispute, there is no objection in principle to the English courts granting interim relief. What is less clear is whether the English courts would be willing to grant such relief if the jurisdiction agreement applied not only to the substance of the dispute but, either expressly or by implication, to proceedings for interim relief themselves.

RECOGNITION OF FOREIGN JUDGMENTS

Under English law, foreign judgments may be recognised and enforced in accordance with rules developed by the common law or in accordance with one of a number of statutory schemes which may apply to the judgment in question. Only if a foreign judgment is not so enforceable or entitled to recognition may fresh proceedings be brought on the original cause of action.

Judgments in civil and commercial matters given in one of the other contracting states to the 1968 Convention will usually be enforceable in England under the Civil Jurisdiction and Judgments Act 1982. Judgments given in the courts of a number of Commonwealth and colonial countries, and of certain European countries not parties to the 1968 Convention, will be enforceable under the Administration of Justice Act 1920 or the Reciprocal Enforcement of Judgments Act 1933.

Recognition and enforcement at common law

In order that a foreign judgment may be accorded recognition or enforcement in an action at common law, the following conditions (in addition to that of existence of jurisdiction of the English courts over the enforcement action itself) must be satisfied:

(1) The foreign court must be regarded as having possessed international jurisdiction according to the principles of English private international law.

(2) The foreign court must have been internally competent according to its own law.

(3) The foreign judgment must be final and conclusive, in the sense that it cannot be altered in later proceedings between the same parties in the same foreign court. The fact that the foreign judgment is open to appeal or that an appeal is actually pending in the foreign country does not prevent the foreign judgment from being held to be final and conclusive.

(4) In the case of enforcement, the foreign judgment must be for a fixed and definite sum of money, which would exclude, for example, a foreign decree of specific performance or an award of costs to be taxed.

(5) The foreign judgment must not have been obtained by fraud, either to the merits of the case or as to jurisdiction of the foreign court.

(6) Recognition or, as the case may be, enforcement of the foreign judgment must not be contrary to English public policy nor to natural justice.

Proceedings

The creditor brings an action in the normal way by serving a writ of summons on the defendant in which the foreign judgment is pleaded as the basis for the claim. If the defendant does not indicate it is contesting the claim by returning a form of acknowledgement of service, the plaintiff can file for judgment in default and does not have to serve the judgment or have it translated, certified or authenticated. If the defendant returns the acknowledgement of service, whether or not he also serves a defence, the plaintiff can apply for summary judgment and exhibit the foreign judgment.

Judgments under the 1968 Convention

The most far-reaching of the changes that the Civil Jurisdiction and Judgments Act 1982 and the Convention have brought to the enforcement of judgments in the English courts is the extension of the types of judgments which may be enforced. Article 22 provides a wide definition of "judgment" and includes the following types of judgments and orders given in other contracting states, by judicial tribunals of all levels, whether or not they can strictly be regarded as courts, so long as they are enforceable in the state of origin:

(1) money judgments and orders;
(2) non-money judgments and orders, for example foreign orders equivalent to injunctions, decrees for specific performance or for specific delivery of chattels;
(3) interim and interlocutory orders, so long as they govern the legal relations of the parties and do not merely arrange the further conduct of the proceedings;
(4) various forms of summary orders to pay debts, for example the French *injunction de payer* and the German *mahnbescheid*;
(5) orders for the payment of penalties imposed by the foreign court for non-compliance with court orders, for example the French *astreinte*;
(6) compensation awarded by the criminal court exercising civil jurisdiction;
(7) orders for costs; and
(8) foreign judgments awarding multiple damages.

Judgments in *ex parte* proceedings are excluded from the Convention recognition and enforcement regime, as are judgments on judgments (foreign judgments recognising or enforcing another foreign judgment). Section 18(7) of the 1982 Act expressly excludes such judgments from inter-United Kingdom enforcement provisions in Schedules 6 and 7 to the Act, and they are also excluded from the provisions of the Foreign Judgments Act 1933, under section 1(2A)(b) and (c) thereof, as substituted by the 1982 Act, Schedule 10, paragraph 1(2).

In so far as the judgments of foreign contracting states are concerned, section 5 of the Act is inapplicable. The latter prohibits enforcement in the United Kingdom of foreign judgments for multiple damages, under Part II of the Administration of Justice Act 1920 or Part I of the Foreign Judgments (Reciprocal Enforcement) Act 1933, or at common law. These matters are mainly directed against American antitrust legislation and judgments, but the fact is that they are applicable in relation to the specified judgments of any overseas country, the latter being defined under section 8(2) of the 1980 Act as any country or territory outside the United Kingdom other than one for whose international relations Her Majesty's Government in the United Kingdom is responsible.

Recognition of foreign judgments under the 1968 Convention

Article 26 of the Convention provides that a judgment given in a contracting state shall be recognised in the other contracting state without any special procedure being required. The Article identifies two types of situation in which the need for recognition may arise. First, if recognition is the principal issue in a dispute, application may be made to the High Court for a declaration of recognition of the foreign judgment by following the same procedure as is provided under the Convention for the enforcement of a foreign judgment (Articles 31–49 of the Convention). Secondly, if the question of recognition arises incidentally in proceedings the outcome of which will be determined by the decision of recognition, the court hearing those proceedings will have jurisdiction over that question.

Grounds for refusal of recognition and enforcement

One of the fundamental principles of the Convention is that, subject to limited exceptions, the enforcing court is not entitled to examine the merits of the case or the basis upon which jurisdiction was exercised by the court which gave the judgment. It is provided both in Article 29, in respect of recognition, and in Article 34, in respect of enforcement, that in no circumstances may the foreign judgment be reviewed as to its substance.

The principal grounds on which recognition and enforcement of foreign contracting states judgments must be refused are those contained in Articles 27 and 28 of the Convention. These grounds can be summarised as follows:

(1) Recognition or enforcement is contrary to public policy in the United Kingdom (Article 27(1)). It is a feature common to all schemes for recognition and enforcement that a court addressed is entitled to refuse to recognise or enforce a foreign judgment based on laws which are considered to be fundamentally immoral. The statutory schemes established under the Acts of 1920 and 1933 both contained provisions to this effect. The 1968 Convention is no exception to this general rule, although the circumstances in which recognition or enforcement of a judgment can be refused under the Convention for reasons of public policy are considerably narrower than under pre-existing law.

(2) Lack of due and sufficient service upon a defendant not entering an appearance (Article 27(2)). It is not necessary to show that the defendant had actual knowledge of the proceedings. The English court is justified in assuming that, following "due" service in accordance with the procedural law of the state of origin, the document came to the defendant's knowledge. The court is then to decide whether the time thereafter available to the defendant was sufficient in these particular circumstances. It should be noted that the periods allowed by the extra jurisdiction tables for returning the acknowledgement of service in corresponding English proceedings are considerably shorter than those allowed by the procedural rules of other contracting states. The English court is not bound by the time limits provided by the domestic law of the trial court, or by the fact that the trial court may be taken to have observed its obligations under Article 20 of the Convention and to have concluded that the defendant had had sufficient time to arrange his defence.

(3) A foreign judgment sought to be recognised is irreconcilable with an existing judgment of the United Kingdom in a dispute between the same parties (Article 27(3)). The conflicting judgments need not necessarily be in respect of the same cause of action as long as the respective proceedings were between the same parties. If the United Kingdom is the state addressed, the

effect of Article 27(3) is ordinarily to give priority to the United Kingdom judgment. However, it should be noted that if both judgments concern the same cause of action and the judgment in the United Kingdom was given after that which is being sought to be enforced, arguably it is the earlier judgment that should be recognised. Where a judgment sought to be enforced in England conflicts with a judgment given in another contracting state, the Convention is silent as to what should be done. It is suggested that priority should be accorded to that which was given in the proceedings which started first. The United Kingdom judgment need not itself fall within the scope of the Convention.

(4) The court of origin has, in order to arrive at its judgment, decided a preliminary question concerning the status or legal capacity of natural persons, rights in property arising out of matrimonial relationships, wills or succession in a way which conflicts with the rule of English private international law, unless the same result would have been reached by the application of English private international law (Article 27(4)).

(5) The judgment is irreconcilable with an earlier judgment given in a non-contracting state involving the same cause of action between the same parties, provided that the earlier judgment fulfils the conditions necessary for recognition in the United Kingdom.

(6) The judgment conflicts with the Convention's rules relating to insurance matters and consumers' contracts, or the rules relating to exclusive jurisdiction (Article 28).

(7) The judgment is not a judgment to which the Convention applies, in that its subject matter falls outside the scope of the Convention (Article 1). A judgment in a matter which was not civil or commercial within the meaning of Article 1 of the Convention would not be enforceable under it. Included under this head of objection would be judgments in respect of fines in criminal proceedings, or in respect of tax liabilities in another contracting state.

(8) The judgment is not one to which the simplified enforcement procedure of the Convention applies because it orders the taking of provisional and protective measures, it was made without the party against whom it was directed having been summoned or appeared, and it was intended to be enforced without prior service of the judgment on that party—the ground of objection is applicable to the attempted enforcement of orders for provisional and protective measures which have been made *ex parte*. It was decided by the Court of Justice in *Denilauler* v. *Couchet Frères*,[4] that this type of order was not enforceable under the Convention.

(9) The judgment is not a judgment to which the Convention applies, by reason of the operation of the Convention's transitional provisions. A judgment given in another contracting state on or after 1 January 1987 in proceedings which commenced before that date is only enforceable in the United Kingdom under the Convention if jurisdiction was founded on rules which accorded either with the jurisdictional rules of the Convention or with the

4. [1980] ECR 1553.

provisions of a Convention between the United Kingdom and the state of origin which was in force when the proceedings were instituted. The contracting states with which the United Kingdom has bilateral enforcement Conventions are Belgium, Germany, France, Italy, and The Netherlands.

(10) The judgment is not enforceable in the state of origin (Article 31). A provisionally enforceable judgment which is common in many of the contracting states is enforceable under the Convention. These judgments remain provisionally enforceable despite the bringing of an appeal. In such a case, the judgment creditor can apply to the English court for a stay of execution under Article 38. If enforcement has been stayed in the country of origin, the judgment is of necessity not enforceable there, and accordingly it cannot be registered in England.

(11) The judgment was not served on the person against whom it is to be enforced. Article 47(1) requires an application for registration to be supported by evidence that the judgment to be enforced is "enforceable and has been served". This requirement is repeated in the Rules of the Supreme Court.[5]

(12) The person by whom the application for registration was made is not an "interested party" (Articles 27 and 31). It is for the national law of the state of origin to determine what interest the applicant has in the judgment, but it is a question for interpretation under the Convention whether that interest is sufficient to give rise to the right to apply for enforcement in another contracting state. The equivalent provision under the 1933 Act (which is limited to the enforcement of money judgments) is "that the rights in the judgment are not vested in the person by whom the application for registration was made". The definition of an "interested party" in the 1982 Act could well be wider and might well include a person or a direct party to the original proceedings, who had an interest in the defendant obeying a court order to perform some non-money obligation.

(13) The procedural formalities laid down in the Convention or the Rules of the Supreme Court have not been complied with. The procedural requirements of the Convention concerning the making of the application for enforcement are set out in Articles 32, 33, 46, and 47. Although Article 34 provides that the application may be refused "only for one of the reasons specified in Articles 27 and 28", a challenge on procedural grounds may still be made. Furthermore, as Article 33 expressly provides that the procedure for making the application shall be governed in the law of the state in which enforcement is sought, a failure to comply with the requirements of the rules of the Supreme Court could equally be fatal to an application. Thus, a registration would probably be set aside on appeal if there were substantial defects or inconsistencies in the supporting documentation. The copy of the judgment must satisfy the conditions necessary to establish its authenticity in accordance with the law of the contracting state of origin. In the case of a judgment given in default there must be a document which establishes that the judgment debtor was served with the "document instituting the proceedings or with an equivalent document". If it appeared from the documentation that

5. RSC, Order 71, rule 28(1)(a)(i).

the judgment debt had been registered in an incorrect amount or that interest had been incorrectly calculated, or that the defendant's name had been incorrectly given in the judgment, there would also be strong grounds for setting aside the registration on appeal. If such matters became evident to the court when it was considering registration it might refuse to register the judgment, or, in some cases, it might adjourn the application to enable the documentation to be put in order, or it might refuse to entertain the application.

(14) The judgment was given in respect of a civil claim in, or dependent upon, criminal proceedings in which the defendant did not appeal and did not have the opportunity of arranging his defence in his absence (Article II of the 1968 Annexed Protocol).

(15) In a case in which the court of origin had jurisdiction only by virtue of a specialised convention, the requisite conditions for recognition and enforcement under that convention have not been fulfilled (Article 57).

(16) The court of the contracting state of origin assumed jurisdiction on an exorbitant basis over a person who was domiciled or habitually resident in a non-contracting state with which the United Kingdom has a convention pursuant to Article 59 of the 1968 Convention. The only relevant Convention is that with Canada.[6]

Appeals

Under Article 40 of the Convention, the judgment creditor may appeal against a refusal to order the registration of a judgment. The appeal is by way of summons *inter partes* to the judge in chambers. Although the Convention specifies no time limit for the bringing of an appeal against the refusal to register a judgment, the Rules of the Supreme Court require such an appeal to be brought within a month of the refusal of the application for registration. Further appeal by the judgment creditor is limited, as is further appeal by the judgment debtor, to a single point of law.

The grounds for an appeal by the judgment debtor against an order for registration are the same as for the refusal of recognition and enforcement, discussed below. Such an appeal is brought to a judge and is comparable to the application to set aside registration under the 1933 Act. The instituting of an appeal operates automatically to stay the execution of the registered judgment until the determination of the appeal. The summons must be served within one month of service of notice of registration of the judgment, or within two months of service of the notice, if it was served on a party not domiciled within the jurisdiction. If the party against whom judgment is given is not domiciled in a contracting state and an application for an extension of time is made within two months of service of a notice of registration, the Rules of the Supreme Court provide that the court may extend the period within which an appeal may be made against an order for registration.[7]

The summons should set out the grounds relied upon for appealing the order for

6. Reciprocal Enforcements of Judgments (Canada) Order 1987 (SI 1987 No. 468).
7. RSC, Order 71, rule 33(3).

registration and should be supported by an appropriate affidavit. Unless, at the hearing of the appeal, the judgment debtor can put forward sufficient grounds to challenge the registration, the judgment creditor may proceed to whatever method of execution may be appropriate as if the judgment were an original English judgment. If there are valid grounds for setting aside the registration of the judgment the court may not impose terms, such as the payment of money into court, as a condition of setting aside the registration.

As already mentioned, the grounds for an appeal by the judgment debtor against an order for registration are the same as for a refusal of recognition and enforcement. In addition to these grounds, there are some further aspects for an appeal.

Powers of the court on the hearing of the appeal

If a ground for setting aside the registration is established by the appellant, then the court has no discretion in the matter and must direct accordingly. If no ground for setting aside is established, then the appeal must be dismissed. The judgment may then be executed subject to the court's general powers to order a stay of execution in certain cases. The court also has power under the Convention to make execution conditional on the provision of security by the judgment creditor. The Convention makes it clear (Articles 34 and 35) that there must be no delay in dealing with the application for registration and appeal.

Effect of an appeal in the contracting state of origin

In most contracting states, a judgment is not enforceable until expiry of an appeal and the disposal of any appeal, unless the judgment has been declared to be, or is by law, provisionally enforceable. A judgment which is not enforceable in the state of origin may not be registered in England. If a judgment has been properly registered in England and if an "ordinary" appeal is brought in the state of origin, the registration continues to be valid, but the judgment debtor may apply to the English court for a stay of the proceedings. He may also generally do this where he merely intends to bring such an appeal, the time for so doing not having expired, but in this case the English court may impose a time limit for the bringing of a foreign appeal.

The power to grant a stay is discretionary, and it has been suggested by the European Court of Justice that a stay should be granted "whenever reasonable doubt arises with regard to the fate of the decision in the state in which it was given". If the effect of the appeal before the court of origin is to suspend the enforceability of the judgment in the state of origin, or if enforceability is suspended by order of the court of state of origin, then it is suggested that the English court should always grant the stay. The stay will normally be expressed to be until the determination of the appeal or until further order.

If an appellant fails to prosecute before an appeal with sufficient diligence, the judgment creditor will apply to the court for the stay to be removed. However, even if the order for the registration is eventually upheld, the court retains various powers to order a stay of execution which are more limited than the powers to order a stay of proceedings. A party may apply for a stay of execution by reason of matters which have been cured since the day of the judgment or, in the case of execution by writ of *fieri facias*, if the court is satisfied that there are special circumstances which rendered it inexpedient to enforce the judgment.

REMEDIES AVAILABLE TO FOREIGN CREDITORS

There are various remedies available to the foreign creditor. Which of those he uses will depend on which part of the court machinery he has used to try to recover his debt initially. The most usual method of debt recovery through the court is by obtaining judgment against the debtor in either the High Court or the County Court for lower sums of money. This process is not the subject of this chapter. Alternatively, the creditor may have used the threat of bankruptcy or liquidation to try to enforce payment. If this is the case, different remedies will be available to him.

The remedies listed below are those most commonly used by a creditor. This list is not exhaustive.

Seizure of chattels: writ of *fieri facias*/writ of execution

The mode of enforcing judgment by the seizure and sale of enough of the debtor's goods and chattels to satisfy the judgment debt is known as a writ of *fieri facias* (fi. fa.) in the High Court and a writ of execution in the County Court. A writ of fi. fa. and a writ of execution can be issued immediately the judgment becomes due, and usually no leave is required from the court.

In the High Court, the judgment debtor files at the court a formal request for the issue of a writ of fi. fa. (*a praecipe*), two copies of the writ of fi. fa., a copy of the judgment, and a fee. Execution of the judgment will be carried out by a court official.

Charging order

This method of enforcement provides the creditor with security for his debt. Moreover, having obtained a charging order absolute, should it prove necessary, the creditor can apply to the court for an order for the sale of the land charged so that the judgment can be satisfied out of the proceeds. This remedy is available in the High Court if the debt exceeds £5,000, and otherwise in the County Court.

Property which may be charged is specified by section 2 of the Charging Orders Act 1979, and includes land, stock other than building society stock, and unit trusts. The judgment creditor must have prima facie evidence that the debtor is the proprietor of such property if a successful application is to be made.

In the High Court, an application is made *ex parte* on affidavit to a master or district judge. A fee is payable on application, and if an order is made fixed costs are required. At the hearing the court may make an order to show cause (a charging order nisi). This will be served on the debtor along with a copy of the affidavit. It is then for the debtor to show the court why the order nisi should not be made absolute, and a further hearing will take place for this purpose. At this hearing the court may make the order absolute.

A charging order, whether it is a charging order nisi or absolute, should be served personally on the judgment creditor. In the case of land, details should also be registered at the District Land Registry.

Proceedings to enforce the charge are also available.

Garnishee order

Through garnishee proceedings, the judgment creditor can divert funds which stand to the debtor's credit in, for example, a bank or building society account, and obtain an order that these be used to satisfy the judgment debt. Both current and deposit bank accounts can be attached to the debt, as can building society accounts and post office accounts. No order will be made which would reduce below £1 the amount standing in the name of the judgment creditor in an account with a building society or credit union.

As with charging orders, the proceedings for obtaining a garnishee order are in two stages. First, an application is made *ex parte* on affidavit. At the hearing of this application the court may make a garnishee order nisi. This order will attach the debt due or accruing due to the judgment debtor and requires the garnishee (i.e., the bank or building society) to attend at the time and place specified and show cause why he should not pay the debt directly to the judgment creditor.

This order should be served personally on the garnishee. It should also be served on the judgment debtor, but there is no requirement that this should be done personally. At the subsequent hearing the court may make the garnishee order nisi absolute. The court may also make an order allowing the costs of the creditor and the garnishee.

Insolvency proceedings

A creditor can look to the court to have a debtor company wound up or an individual debtor made bankrupt. The threat of insolvency proceedings can prove to be effective. However, if a bankruptcy or insolvency order is made against an individual or a company, the creditor who has commenced these proceedings will be in no more favourable position than any of the other creditors of the company or of the individual bankrupt. The trustee in bankruptcy or liquidator's job is to collect in and redistribute the insolvent company's or individual's assets and not to favour the person who has initiated the proceedings in the first place.

Insolvency is not strictly a method of enforcement and is only brought into play if more conventional matters fail. With both individual and company insolvency, the Insolvency Act 1986 provides certain criteria which must be satisfied before proceedings may be begun. In brief, the criteria are as follows.

Individual insolvency

The debtor must be domiciled in England and Wales at the date of presentation of the petition or at any time within three years preceding the date of presentation of the petition, having been ordinarily resident in England or Wales, or carried on business in England or Wales.

The debt must be for £750 or more.

The creditor must show that the debt is one which the debtor appears unable to pay or to have no reasonable prospect of paying. The debtor is deemed unable to pay a debt if the debt is payable immediately or either:

(1) the creditor has served on the debtor a demand in the prescribed form requiring him to pay, secure or compound a debt and this has not been done within three weeks of service; or
(2) execution has been returned wholly or partially unsatisfied.

Company insolvency

Under the provisions of the Insolvency Act 1986, a creditor must have grounds for winding up a company. For the purposes of this chapter, the most likely ground to be invoked would be that the company is unable to pay its debts. The company is deemed to be unable to pay its debts if:

(1) a creditor for £750 or more has left at the registered office of the company a written demand for payment; and
(2) the company does not pay, compound or secure the debt within three weeks; and
(3) process of execution is returned wholly or partially unsatisfied; and
(4) it is proved to the satisfaction of the court that the company is unable to pay its debts.

The place of residence of an individual or the registered office of a company will determine the court which has jurisdiction. The procedure is determined by the Insolvency Act 1986.

INTERNATIONAL TREATIES

Treaty of Rome, Article 106

Each member state of the EU undertakes to authorise, in the currency of the member state in which the creditor or beneficiary resides, any payments connected with the movement of goods, services or capital and any transfers of capital and earnings, to the extent that the movement of goods, services, capital and persons between member states has been liberalised pursuant to this Treaty.

If need be, member states shall consult each other on the measures to be taken to enable the payments and transfers mentioned in the Article to be effected.

This was incorporated into UK law under the European Communities Act 1972, which provides that all EU legislation in areas where there would be conflict would override UK law, unless otherwise stated.

Thus, where an action for a debt or damages arises from the movement of goods, capital or persons, and is brought by a company established in a member state, the court may agree to give judgment in the currency of the member state.

This was followed in *Schorsh Meier GmbH* v. *Hennin*,[8] where it was held that the plaintiffs, who carried on their business in West Germany, were entitled to judgment in deutschmarks for the sum owing to them by the defendant, under Article 106 of the Treaty.

8. [1975] 1 All ER 152 (CA).

This judgment was further considered in the case of *Miliangos* v. *George Frank (Textiles) Ltd*,[9] although the plaintiff was a Swiss national and not from a member state of the EU.

The scope of the judgment in *Schorsh* v. *Hennin* was not entirely clear. Certainly, this case affected contract, but there was uncertainty as to how far it affected the rule in relation to damages for tort. The decision made was, in fact, doubted in *Miliangos* v. *Frank*. The majority of the House of Lords held:

> ... it is open to question whether Article 106 of the EEC Treaty is directly applicable to member states of the EEC, and it is doubtful whether that Article has any bearing on the question of the currency in which claims may be made in member states or whether it is relevant at all to the ascertainment of the date of conversion of such claims.

It is unclear just how much influence the Treaty has on the enforcements of judgments in the UK, despite the decision to uphold Article 106 of the Treaty in the *Schorsh* case. However, the effect of the EU on the enforcement of judgments in member states does not come, on the whole, through the application of the Brussels Convention of 1968.

Brussels Convention 1968

The Convention, which applies to all EU member states, was brought into force in the UK by SI 1989 No. 1936 and has had the full force of the law since then.

Parties to the Convention (as at 1995) are: Belgium, Denmark, France, Germany, Hellenic Republic, Republic of Ireland, Italy, Luxembourg, The Netherlands, Portugal, Spain, the United Kingdom, Finland, Sweden and Austria.

The Convention replaces bilateral treaties with the following countries, under the Foreign Judgments (Reciprocal Enforcement) Act 1933: Belgium, France, Federal Republic of Germany, Italy, and The Netherlands.

The Convention applies in civil and commercial matters, but does not extend, in particular, to revenue, customs, or administrative matters. The Convention also does not apply to:

(1) the status or legal capacity of natural persons, rights in property arising out of matrimonial relationships, wills and successions;
(2) bankruptcy, proceedings relating to the winding-up of insolvent companies or other legal persons, judicial arrangements, compositions, and analogous proceedings;
(3) social security; or
(4) arbitration.

An application for enforcement in England and Wales should be made to the High Court of Justice or, in the case of a maintenance judgment, to the magistrates' court, on transmission by the Secretary of State.

No security bond or deposit is required of a party in one contracting state on the ground that he is a foreign national or that he is not domiciled in the state in which enforcement is sought.

A party seeking enforcement shall produce:

9. [1975] 3 All ER 801 (CA).

(1) a copy of the judgment which satisfies the conditions necessary to establish its authenticity;
(2) in the case of a judgment given in default, the original or a certified copy of the document which establishes that the party in default was served with the document instituting the proceedings or with an equivalent document;
(3) documents which establish that, according to the law of the state in which it has been given, the judgment is enforceable and has been served; and
(4) where appropriate, a document showing that the applicant was in receipt of legal aid in the state in which judgment was given.

The Convention does not apply to any European territory situated outside the UK for the international affairs of which the UK is responsible, unless the UK makes a declaration to the contrary in respect of any such territory.

The use of this Convention was considered in the case of *Owens Bank Ltd* v. *Bracco and Another*,[10] but it was held that the Convention did not apply to proceedings for the recognition and enforcement of judgments of non-contracting states.

Lugano Convention 1988

The Lugano Convention is between the member states of the EU and the member states of the European Free Trade Association (EFTA).

The Convention was brought into force in the UK by the Civil Jurisdiction and Judgments Act 1991.

Parties to the Convention (as at 1995) are: Austria, Belgium, Denmark, Finland, France, Germany, Hellenic Republic, Iceland, Republic of Ireland, Italy, Luxembourg, The Netherlands, Norway, Portugal, Spain, Sweden, Switzerland, and the United Kingdom. This replaces bilateral treaties with Austria and Norway under the Foreign Judgments (Reciprocal Enforcement) Act 1933.

The applications for this Convention and its provisions are the same as those for the Brussels Convention. The existence of this Convention in no way prejudices the right to application by member states of the EU of the Brussels Convention. In no way does the Convention supersede the Brussels Convention. However, the Lugano Convention shall in any event be applied:

(1) In matters of jurisdiction where the defendant is domiciled in the territory of a contracting state which is not a member of the EU, or where a jurisdiction on the courts of such a contracting state is confirmed.
(2) In relation to a *lis pendens* or to related actions as provided for in Articles 21 and 22, when proceedings are constituted in a contracting state which is not a member of the EU and in a contracting state which is a member of the EU.
(3) Recognition or enforcement may be refused if the grounds or jurisdiction on which the judgment has been based differs from that resulting from the Convention and recognition/enforcement is sought against a party who is domiciled in a contracting state which is not a member of the EU, unless the judgment may otherwise be recognised/enforced under any rule of the law of the state addressed.

10. *The Times*, 15 April 1991.

Article 21

Where proceedings involving the same cause of action and between the same parties are brought in the courts of different contracting states, any court other than the court first seised shall of its own motion stay its proceedings until such time as the jurisdiction of the court first seised is established.

Where the jurisdiction of the court first seised is established, any court other than the court first seised shall decline jurisdiction in favour of that court.

Article 22

Where related actions are brought in the courts of different contracting states, any court other than the court first seised may, while actions are pending at first instance, stay its proceedings.

A court other than the court first seised may also, on the application of one of the parties, decline jurisdiction if the law of that court permits the consolidation of related actions and the court first seised has jurisdiction over both actions.

For the purposes of this Convention, actions are deemed to be related where they are so closely connected that it is expedient to hear and determine them together to avoid the risk of irreconcilable judgments resulting from separate proceedings.

Foreign Judgments (Reciprocal Enforcement) Act 1933

Various bilateral treaties have been formed with foreign countries under the auspices of this Act. Some of these have since been superseded by the Brussels and Lugano Conventions, including those with: Austria, Belgium, France, Federal Republic of Germany, Italy, The Netherlands, and Norway.

Those treaties that are still in force are those with:

Australian Capital Territory (SI 1955/559)
Guernsey (SI 1973/610)
India (SI 1958/425)
Isle of Man (SI 1973/611)
Israel (SI 1971/1039)
Jersey (SI 1973/612)
Pakistan (SI 1958/141)
Suriname (SI 1981/735)
Tonga (SI 1980/1523).

A creditor may apply to the High Court at any time within six years of the judgment being given (or in the case of an appeal, after the date of the last judgment given in the proceedings) to have the judgment registered in the High Court; and on such application the court shall, subject to proof of the prescribed matters (and other provisions of the Act), order the judgment to be registered.

A judgment shall not be registered if, at the date of the application:

(1) it has been wholly satisfied; or
(2) it could not be enforced by execution in the country of the original court.

Subject to the provisions of the Act with respect to the setting aside of registration:

(1) A registered judgment shall, for the purposes of execution, be of the same force and effect.
(2) Proceedings may be taken on a registered judgment.
(3) The sum for which a judgment is registered shall carry interest.

(4) The registering court shall have the same control over the execution of a registered judgment as if the judgment had been a judgment originally given in the registering court and entered on the date of registration.

Execution shall not issue on the judgment so long as, under Part 1, section 2 and the Rules of Court made thereunder, it is competent for any party to make an application to have the registration of the judgment set aside, or, where such an application is made, until after the application has been fully determined.

If, at the date of the application for registration, the judgment of the original court has been partly satisfied, the judgment shall not be registered in respect of the whole such payable under the judgment of the original court, but only in respect of the balance remaining payable at that date.

If, on an application for registration of a judgment, it appears to the registering court that the judgment is in respect of different matters and that the same, but not all of the, provisions had been contained in separate judgments, those judgments could properly have been registered in respect of those provisions aforesaid but not in respect of any other provisions contained in them.

In addition to the sum of money payable under the judgment of the original court, including any interest which by the law of the country of the original court becomes due under the judgment up until the date of registration, the judgment shall be registered for the reasonable cost of and incidental to registration, including the costs of obtaining a certified copy of the judgment from the original court.

IMPACT OF BANKRUPTCY

Under United Kingdom law, there are two types of insolvency: bankruptcy, which affects individuals, and liquidation, which affects limited companies.

Where a company is wound up (liquidation) or an individual is made bankrupt, the creditors may be divided into secured and unsecured creditors. Where a judgment has been obtained and registered in the United Kingdom, the creditor is deemed to be an unsecured creditor. Whereas secured creditors have an immediate right to the security upon which their debt is based, the extent to which unsecured creditors will recover their debt will depend upon the number of creditors and the value of the insolvent person's or company's assets.

As a general rule, the ability of a judgment creditor to execute his judgment against the judgment debtor will depend upon whether he has completed execution prior to the bankruptcy or winding-up order being made. After that time, he may no longer proceed in winding-up proceedings, and may only proceed with the leave of the court in bankruptcy proceedings. The following is a more detailed analysis of the position.

Bankruptcy

The effect of bankruptcy upon litigation is covered by section 285(3) of the Insolvency Act 1986. This section provides that, after the making of a bankruptcy order, no person who is a creditor of the bankrupt in respect of a debt provable in the bankruptcy shall commence any action against the bankrupt except with the leave of the court and on such terms as the court may impose.

Where the bankruptcy order is made after judgment but before execution of the judgment, the judgment creditor has no automatic right to commence execution proceedings against the bankrupt judgment debtor unless a debt is not a provable or bankruptcy debt. Where the bankruptcy order is made after execution has been commenced by the judgment creditor, the court may, upon the application of the trustee in bankruptcy, stay an execution commenced before the presentation of the petition or impose terms upon the continuation of the execution proceedings. However, where the execution is commenced after the bankruptcy order is made, the execution creditor must serve notice of the judgment on the bankrupt defendant's trustee and obtain leave to start execution from the court. Such leave may be given at the discretion of the court and on such terms as the court may think fit, or the action may indeed be stayed. Where execution has been completed, the trustee has no claim against the proceeds.

The question therefore arises as to the stage at which execution is deemed to be completed. This will vary according to the method of execution used. In particular, where a writ is issued for seizure and sale of the execution debtor's goods (writ of fi. fa.), the completion of the execution will be deemed to occur once the goods have been seized and sold. In the case of land, execution will not be completed until a charging order has been made or, in the case of a debt which has been "frozen" under a garnishee order, until payment of the debt has been received.

Winding-up

Once the winding-up order has been made against a company, no action or proceedings may be proceeded with or commenced against the company or its property except by leave of the court. This includes proceedings for the execution of judgments.

While the staying of all proceedings is automatic after the making of the order, the company's assets can also be protected during the interim period between presentation of the petition and the making of the winding-up order through the court exercising its power under section 126 of the Insolvency Act 1986 to restrain actions or proceedings against the company which are pending. Both applications may be made by the company or any creditor. However, in the absence of an order being made under section 126, the execution proceedings may be continued until a winding-up order is made.

Judgment creditors should, therefore, take steps to enforce their judgments as quickly as possible if there is any prospect of the company going into liquidation. If, either after the presentation of the winding-up petition or the making of the winding-up order, execution of the foreign judgment has been restrained or prevented, the judgment creditor will remain an unsecured creditor for the purposes of the winding-up procedure.

Procedure after bankruptcy or winding-up order

Once a winding-up or bankruptcy order has been made, the court will fix a time limit within which creditors are to prove their debts or claims; and the creditors who fail to prove in time, may be excluded from distribution made before their proof of debt.

Forms of proof of debt will be sent out by the liquidator to every creditor known to him or identified in the company's statement of affairs. Each creditor will complete the proof of debt form and return the same to the liquidator. The liquidator will consider the proofs and admit them for dividend, either for the whole of the amount claimed or for part of that amount, or, indeed, reject them in their entirety. If he rejects a proof in whole or in part, the liquidator must send the creditor a written statement of his reasons for doing so. A creditor who is dissatisfied with the liquidator's decision in respect of his proof may apply to the court for the decision to be reversed or varied. Such an application must be made within 21 days of receiving the liquidator's statement of his reasons for the decision taken.

Assuming that the proof of debt is accepted by the liquidator, the liquidator then proceeds to collection and distribution of the assets of the bankrupt or the wound-up company. Once the liquidator has paid the costs and expenses of the liquidation and paid all preferential debts or debts secured by floating charges, the outstanding balance will be used to defray the ordinary unsecured debts such as judgment debts. All creditors within this category stand on an equal footing irrespective of the chronological order in which the claims originated. The amount which the judgment creditor will therefore ultimately recover will depend upon the number of creditors, the amounts claimed by those creditors and the dividend arising from the company's assets.

CARYN MACKENZIE

CHAPTER 9

FINLAND

INTRODUCTION

This chapter aims to give foreign creditors a general overview as to the possibilities concerning the prevention, through rapid intervention, of the adverse party transferring, concealing, or destroying assets which are located in Finland where the creditor has not yet obtained a judgment subject to execution.

Actions with the object of securing a probable justified claim in advance or in the interim period will be referred to as provisional measures.

New laws concerning provisional measures were enacted in July 1991.[1] According to the new laws, the rules for the deciding of provisional measures are contained in section 7 of the Procedural Code (*Oikeudenkäymiskaari*) and for enforcement in section 7 of the Execution Act. Decisions concerning provisional measures are within the competence of the general courts at first instance.

ENFORCEMENT OF FOREIGN JUDGMENTS

According to section 3, paragraph 1, of the Execution Act, a foreign judgment or arbitral award can be executed if the law provides for it. Finnish law does not include any general legislation for the recognition and enforcement of foreign judgments, but Finland is a party to several international conventions which enable the recognition and enforcement of certain foreign judgments. For example, Finland is a party to the Lugano Convention on Jurisdiction and the Enforcement of Judgments in Civil and Commercial Matters of 16 September, 1988 (hereafter referred to as the Lugano Convention), the Copenhagen Convention on Recognition and Enforcement of Judgments in Civil and Commercial Matters in Scandinavia (1977), the New York Convention on Recognition and Enforcement of Foreign Arbitral Awards (1958), and the bilateral Convention between Austria and Finland on the Recognition and Enforcement of Civil and Commercial Judgments (1986).

The Lugano Convention is a parallel convention to the Brussels Convention of 27 September, 1968 on Jurisdiction and Enforcement of Judgments in Civil and Commercial Matters. The Lugano Convention came into force in Finland on 1 July, 1993.

Judgments to which international conventions cannot be applied are, however, not

1. 22 July 1991/1065 and 22 July 1991/1066.

totally insignificant. A foreign judgment may have an evidentiary effect in a Finnish trial.

FOREIGN PERSONS IN FINNISH COURTS

According to Finnish law all natural and juridical persons are capable of being parties in a civil procedure, regardless of nationality or residence. Furthermore, according to section 12, paragraph 4, of the Procedural Code, a foreign person who is not capable of conducting legal proceedings according to the laws of his or her native country can be heard in a Finnish trial if the person is capable of conducting legal proceedings according to Finnish laws.

A foreign plaintiff does not need to deposit a security for legal expenses because Finland is a party to the Hague Conventions of 1954 and 1980 which enable the enforcement in the member states of judgments where the plaintiff is obliged to perform legal expenses.

PROVISIONAL MEASURES

The principal rule in civil cases is that an execution is not possible before a judgment subject to execution is given by the court. The law concerning provisional measures is an exception to this principle rule because, with provisional measures, the creditor tries to prevent, through a quick intervention, the adverse party from transferring, concealing or destroying assets before he has obtained a judgment subject for execution.

Attachment

A claim on money and property can be secured in Finland by attachment, which is ordered by the Court of first instance. An attachment is enforced by the execution officer, who takes possession of the object which shall be secured, or deprives the adverse party of possession of the object in some other way.

If the creditor has a claim on money, the execution officer will attach movable and real property to such a degree as to ensure that the claim is secured.

General provisional measure

It may also be possible to secure claims on other rights than money or property.

First, the adverse party can be prohibited from taking or avoiding action through the threat of a fine. Secondly, the creditor can be entitled to do something or have something done at the expense of the adverse party. Thirdly, the property of the adverse party can be entrusted to a trustee. The general provisional measure can also provide other action necessary to securing the creditor's claim on a right.

Conditions for an order of provisional measures

The conditions for an order of provisional measures can be divided into positive conditions and negative conditions. Each of the positive conditions must be fulfilled, while none of the negative conditions need be in hand.

Positive conditions

CONDITIONS FOR SECURING A CLAIM ON MONEY

The applicant must submit evidence that he has a claim on money, which the adverse party can be ordered to pay by the court.

The claim on money does not need to be subject to court proceedings when applying for an attachment or an interdiction against sale or dispersion. Furthermore, the claim need not be mature when applying for provisional measures. The claim must, however, be mature when the substance of the matter is brought to court.

A court order means not only a judgment given at the regular civil trial or an arbitral award, but also payment orders resulting from a dunning process and payment orders resulting from a debt recovery process, according to present Finnish law.

There must also be a danger that the adverse party will transfer, conceal, or destroy the asset or act in a way that endangers the claim of the applicant.

CONDITIONS FOR SECURING A CLAIM ON PROPERTY

The applicant must submit evidence that he has a claim or a better right to a specific object or other property, which can be confirmed by a declaratory judgment.

There also must exist a danger that the adverse party will transfer, conceal, or destroy the specific object or other property, or that the adverse party will act in a way which endangers the right to the object or other property, e.g. the adverse party might establish rights which encumber the property, or damage or misuse the property in such a way that the value of the property is reduced.

CONDITIONS FOR SECURING OTHER RIGHTS

The applicant must submit evidence that he has another right than a claim on money or property which can be confirmed by a declaratory judgment.

There also must be a danger that the adverse party is acting or neglecting to act in a way that prevents or weakens the realisation of the right of the applicant. For example, if there is a dispute over a better right to a specific manufacturing process or to another business secret, there might be the danger that the adverse party will betray the secret to a third party. Furthermore, the adverse party might engage in a business from which he has promised to refrain or which is forbidden to the adverse party.

Negative conditions

SECURITY DEPOSITED BY THE ADVERSE PARTY

An attachment securing a claim on money shall not be enforced if the adverse party deposits an acceptable security with the execution officer. The adverse party might deposit a security when the application for provisional measures is already in hand.

EXISTING SECURITY

An obstacle to giving an order of provisional measures might be that the applicant already has an adequate pledge or a guarantee for the debt. A pledge and a guarantee are, of course, obstacles only if the coverage value of the pledge is sufficient and the guarantors are solvent and with good financial standing.

A provision regarding the reservation of title, when it is for securing a purchase money claim, differs from a pledge because the object of security is in this case in possession of the adverse party. Thus, if there exists a danger that the adverse party is going to transfer, conceal, or destroy the object of security, provisional measures are available.

A right of set-off might prevent the issue of an order or enforcement of provisional measures, providing the money claim of the adverse party is clear and uncontested.

These negative conditions are obstacles to an order of provisional measures only if the applicant has a money claim. If the applicant has a claim on property or other rights, the adverse party normally cannot prevent an order of provisional measures, although he has, for example, deposited a security or guarantee.

Proceedings for a provisional measure

The proceedings for a provisional measure comprise two stages: first, there has to be made an order of provisional measures, and, secondly, the order has to be enforced.

Applying for a provisional measure order

FORM OF THE APPLICATION

The application for provisional measures has to be presented in writing, unless the application is presented in court where the substance of the matter is in progress. If the trial of the subject matter is in progress, the application can be presented orally.

COMPETENT AUTHORITY

Deciding upon provisional measures is within the competence of the general courts of first instance. The competent court of relevance is the one where the substance of the matter is under proceedings. If the proceedings as to the substance of the matter are not yet in progress, the competent court is determined by the jurisdiction rules of the Procedural Code.

An exception to the above rule is Article 24 of the Lugano Convention. According to the Convention, an application for provisional measures may be made to the courts of a contracting state, even if, under the Convention, the courts of another contracting state have jurisdiction as to the substance of the matter.

EVIDENCE OF EXISTENCE OF THE CONDITIONS

The purpose of a provisional measure is to prevent, with a quick intervention, the adverse party from transferring, concealing, or destroying assets. Because the provisional measure has to be quick, the conditions are examined summarily. Full evidence of the claim is not required in the summary process. No full evidence of the existence of the danger of transference, concealment, or destruction of property is required. The claim will be examined in detail later, when the substance of the matter is in hand in a normal court process.

The applicant who is applying for a provisional measure has to submit evidence in support of his claim on money, property, or other rights. In legal practice, evidence is based on documentary evidence. If there is no promissory note, bill, or contract of sale, other written evidence may be allowed; for example, it may be enough to have a written evidence from the applicant's bookkeeper or accountant that the claim exists.

Evidence is not required to support the contention of danger because of the nature and urgency of the matter: a statement by the applicant that a danger exists is normally sufficient. If possible, the applicant should, however, refer to those circumstances from which it can be concluded that a danger exists.

HEARING OF THE ADVERSE PARTY AND TEMPORARY DECISION

The application cannot be accepted without giving the adverse party the opportunity of being heard. However, if the need of a provisional measure is urgent and the purpose of this action will otherwise be endangered, a provisional order is possible without having heard from the opposing party. An order made in this way is temporary until a hearing has been granted and the application has finally been examined.

When a temporary order is given, the applicant must pursue the application during a time limit set by the order, under penalty of forfeiture of the application.

Ordinary appeal

The time for appeal is 30 days from the day the party appealing has received the decision from the court of first instance. The place of appeal is the Court of Appeal. A decision of the Court of Appeal may be appealed to the Supreme Court within 60 days from the day when the decision by the Court of Appeal was given. An appeal to the Supreme Court requires permission.

Appeal does not prevent the enforcement of the measure. The court which deals with the case may, however, for special reasons, forbid the enforcement or order temporary suspension of enforcement.

Enforcement of a provisional measure order

An attachment is enforced by the execution officer. For an attachment or other provisional measure to be enforced, the applicant must deposit a security with the execution officer to cover the possible damages caused by the provisional measures. Normally a bank guarantee is required. However, the court of first instance may exempt the applicant from depositing a pledge or guarantee, if the applicant shows that he is unable to deposit a security and his claim is obvious.

Enforcement of a foreign provisional measure order

According to the Lugano Convention, any judgment rendered by a court or tribunal of a contracting state, irrespective of the terms used to define the decision, may be enforced in another contracting state. In view of this very broad definition, decisions ordering provisional measures also may be enforced under the Convention.

According to the Copenhagen Convention among Scandinavian countries and the bilateral Convention between Austria and Finland, only a decision which concerns the substance of the matter may be enforced in a contracting state.

Cancelling a provisional measure

If the conditions for a provisional measure order no longer exist, the provisional measure must be cancelled, i.e., the debtor has paid the debt which was secured by a provisional measure.

Provisional measure must be cancelled by the court where the substance of the matter is in hand. If the substance of the matter is not yet under court proceedings, cancellation must be decided by the court which initially ordered the provisional measure.

The execution officer is not allowed to enforce a provisional measure, and an already-enforced provisional measure must be cancelled if the adverse party is depositing a security. However, if the provisional measure is securing a claim on property or other rights, a security deposited by the adverse party does not cancel the provisional measure without the acceptance of the applicant.

Furthermore, the execution officer must cancel the enforcement of the provisional measure if the applicant requests it, or if the adverse party produces a statement given by the applicant or other evidence that the claim has been paid. The execution officer also must cancel the provisional measure if the applicant has not begun the process concerning the substance of the matter within the time limit set (see below), or if the provisional measure has been cancelled by a decision of the court. Finally, the provisional measure must be cancelled if the applicant has not continued his application in the given time limit after getting a temporary provisional measure order.

Expenses related to a provisional measure

The applicant is responsible for the expenses caused by the application and enforcement. When the substance of the matter is handled by the court, the court will also decide who is responsible for the expenses.

Compensation for damages

If the provisional measure has been unnecessary, the applicant is responsible for any resulting damages and the damages caused by the provisional measure.

The adverse party must initiate legal proceedings within one year from the day when the provisional measure was cancelled or a decision on an appeal was given, if he wants to claim on damages and expenses in the case.

Bankruptcy of the adverse party

According to Finnish law, bankruptcy of the debtor prevents an execution on the debtor's property. If an adverse party whose property has been put under provisional measures is declared bankrupt, it does not in principle prevent an enforcement or cancel the provisional measure. It might, however, be that the conditions for a provisional measure no longer exist, because the administrator of the bankrupt's estate takes possession of the debtor's property.

PROCEEDINGS ON THE SUBSTANCE OF THE MATTER

Time limit for commencing the trial

The trial proceedings must begin within one month from the day when the order of provisional measures was given. If the substance of the matter is to be conducted by arbitration proceedings, the applicant for provisional measures must present a demand to the adverse party within one month, asking that the arbitration agreement be applied. If an arbitration award is not given because of circumstances beyond the applicant's control, or if the arbitration award is null and void, or if the arbitral award will be reversed, the applicant must begin the proceedings at the general court of first instance within the time limit mentioned above. The time limit begins from the day when the applicant was informed of the obstacle concerning the arbitration, or from the day when the authorities considered the arbitral award null and void, or the court has reversed the arbitral award which has gained legal force.

The provisional measure will be cancelled if the proceedings concerning the substance of the matter have not commenced as required.

Foreign state jurisdiction

The Lugano Convention establishes rules of jurisdiction which are directly applicable in the contracting states. The basic principle laid down by the Lugano Convention is that proceedings brought against any person domiciled in a contracting state shall be brought before the courts of that state, irrespective of the defendant's nationality. Under the Lugano Convention, judgments rendered in a contracting state and enforceable in that state shall be declared enforceable and enforced in another contracting state upon application by a party.

If the proceedings as to the substance of the matter are commenced in a foreign country, according to the Lugano Convention it must be clear that the foreign court proceeding will be handled in the same way as in a Finnish court trial in respect of the provisional measures.

The Copenhagen Convention among the Scandinavian countries and the bilateral Convention between Austria and Finland do not include jurisdiction rules. However, according to these Conventions, judgments rendered in one contracting state may be enforced in another contracting state. In addition, according to these Conventions, there is nothing which prohibits the initiation of court proceedings in a contracting state if the judgment can be enforced later in Finland.

UWE UUSITALO

CHAPTER 10

FRANCE

INTRODUCTION

This chapter will focus on the following themes:

(1) Availability of French courts to foreign creditors and litigants.
(2) Enforcement of foreign decisions in France.
(3) Types of remedies available to foreign creditors and procedural steps involved in obtaining them under the 9 July 1991 law and its implementing decree of 31 July 1992.
(4) Impact of the debtor's bankruptcy on the provisional or interim remedies available to foreign creditors.

AVAILABILITY OF FRENCH COURTS TO FOREIGN CREDITORS AND LITIGANTS

French courts are available to foreign nationals without discrimination. In particular, there is no requirement for a bond to be posted by foreign litigants. Foreign creditors and litigants may have access to French courts either to institute an action on the merits or simply to secure or realise assets located in France.

Jurisdictional rules applicable to actions on the merits

French courts may take jurisdiction on a wide variety of grounds in application of French internal jurisdictional rules or, where applicable, in application of international conventions, and in particular, the Brussels Civil Jurisdiction and Judgments Convention (the Brussels Convention).

Jurisdiction of French courts for actions on the merits may be founded upon:

(1) ordinary jurisdictional rules;
(2) special jurisdictional rules; and
(3) exorbitant jurisdictional rules.

Ordinary jurisdictional rules

(a) *Place of domicile of the defendant.* The traditional rule is that the court of the place of domicile of the defendant has jurisdiction (Article 42, paragraph 1, Nouveau Code de Procédure Civile (NCPC); Article 2, Brussels Convention).

(b) *Place of performance.* In contractual matters, jurisdiction may also be founded upon the place of performance of the contract (Article 46, NCPC; Article 5, paragraph 1, Brussels Convention).

(c) *Place where the loss occurred or where the damage was suffered.* In tort claims, jurisdiction may be founded upon the place where the loss-causing event occurred or where the damage was actually suffered (Article 46, paragraph 3, NCPC; Article 5, paragraph 3, Brussels Convention).

(d) *Multiple defendants.* In a case with multiple defendants, the plaintiff may bring suit before the court of the place of domicile of any one of the defendants (Article 42, paragraph 2, NCPC; Article 6, paragraph 1, Brussels Convention).

Special rules

There are a number of jurisdictional rules which confer exclusive or optional jurisdiction in certain areas. In the context of the present discussion, the following might be noted:

(a) *Exclusive jurisdiction by subject matter.* If the action on the merits involves real estate, then the court in whose jurisdiction the property is located will have jurisdiction.

(b) *Exclusive jurisdiction by choice of the parties.* In commercial matters, the parties to a contract may provide for exclusive jurisdiction of a specific forum (Article 48, NCPC). The Brussels Convention provides for the possibility of contractual prorogation without any restriction as to the nature of the contract (Article 17, Brussels Convention).

Exorbitant jurisdictional rules

French courts may also take jurisdiction on the sole ground of the nationality of the plaintiff (Article 14, Civil Code) or the defendant (Article 15, Civil Code), unless prevented from doing so under a binding international convention, such as the Brussels Convention (Article 3 of which specifically excludes the application of Articles 14 and 15 of the French Civil Code to parties domiciled in a contracting state).

Jurisdictional rules applicable to provisional or interim actions

In the case where the target debtor owns property or has assets in France, a French court will, in application of well-established case law, take jurisdiction to order provisional or interim remedies over such goods or assets to the benefit of a foreign creditor.

Moreover, when such property or assets are in the hands of a third party (e.g. a bank) having domicile in France, or if the attachment can otherwise be effected in France through such third party, then French courts shall have jurisdiction to order provisional or interim remedies.

In the case of an attachment of assets held by a bank in France, the latter must declare the amounts deposited by the debtor, including those amounts deposited in its branches located outside France.[2]

Where provisional or interim remedies have been carried out in France, French courts will have exclusive jurisdiction to rule over the "validation" of such remedies even if the debtor is a foreign national with no domicile in France.

Moreover, since 1979, French courts have considered that they have jurisdiction to settle disputes concerning the existence of the debt claimed by the party seeking the provisional or interim remedy.[3]

The above-mentioned case law solutions were founded on reference to applicable provisions of present law which have been amended by the law of 9 July 1991. Such past solutions may very well be maintained by future case law applying the 9 July 1991 law, but this is not certain.

While the 9 July 1991 law provides (Article 89) that "a decree of the Conseil d'Etat shall determine the particular conditions of adaptation of the present law to assets, rights, and shares of French nationals residing outside France, as well as to the obligations they contracted in France, and in particular to the increased time limit on account of distance", it does not contain any provision concerning foreign nationals domiciled outside France owning assets, rights or shares in France (for foreigners domiciled in France, the general provisions of the law will certainly apply).

Jurisdictional rules applicable to enforcement measures

Pursuant to Article 9 of the decree of 31 July 1992, the court having territorial jurisdiction for enforcement measures is the court at the place of domicile of the debtor or the place of enforcement, at the choice of the plaintiff.

If the debtor's domicile is outside of France or is unknown, then the court having jurisdiction is the court at the place of enforcement.

ENFORCEMENT OF FOREIGN DECISIONS

The enforceability of a foreign decision in France will be a determining factor as to whether the claimant has access to enforcement measures, which require a *titre exécutoire* (defined under the 9 July 1991 law to include, *inter alia*, foreign acts and judgments declared to be enforceable by a decision not subject to appeal having the effect to suspend enforcement), or to provisional or interim measures, pending the obtention of an enforceable act or judgment.

French law distinguishes between recognition and enforcement of foreign decisions. Certain categories of judicial decisions, e.g. those dealing with civil status, nationality, matters involving child custody or property rights, require no enforcement *per se*, but their legal effects may nevertheless be recognisable in France. No special procedure is required to obtain such recognition. Other judicial decisions, such as money

2. Cour de Cass., Chambre Commerciale, 30 May 1985, RCDIP, 1986, p. 329, n. *Battifol.*

3. Cour de Cass., Chambre Civile, 6 November 1979, Clunet 1980.95, n. *Ponsard*, R. 1980, 588, n. *Couchet*, JCP 1984–23.

judgments or decisions directing some act to be done, do require enforcement. Such decisions are subject to a special procedure to be enforceable in France, referred to as *exequatur* proceedings.

From a business law standpoint of attacking or realising assets, the requirements for enforcement are of the most practical importance and, accordingly, the following discussion will concentrate thereon. The rules discussed below governing enforcement of foreign decisions are largely judge made and would be expected to remain valid under the new regime.

The enforcement of foreign judgments is a subject matter *par excellence*, to be treated by bilateral or multilateral conventions. France has entered into numerous such conventions, and hence a practitioner will initially have to determine whether any such convention applies. The Brussels Convention is of particular importance insomuch as it provides for quasi-automatic enforcement of decisions rendered by a European Union (EU) member state in the other EU member states where the Convention is in force.

The following discussion will briefly outline what are believed to be salient aspects of general French law.

Conditions for execution

A landmark decision of the Cour de Cassation, *Munzer*, rendered on 7 January 1964[4] held generally that domestic courts had no power to re-examine foreign judgments on the merits. Since that decision, the limited role of the French judge requested to enforce a foreign judgment has been to assure that the foreign judgment satisfies a number of conditions, which the Cour de Cassation listed in *Munzer*, i.e.:

(1) the foreign court had proper jurisdiction;
(2) the foreign court applied the proper law;
(3) the foreign decision is in conformity with French public policy; and
(4) the foreign decision is not in any way fraudulent.

The Cour de Cassation had also included a fifth condition in *Munzer*—the regularity of the foreign proceeding (due process)—but that condition was subsequently included in the notion of conformity with French public policy.

Jurisdiction of the foreign court or other authority

While in *Munzer* the Cour de Cassation specifically made proper jurisdiction of the foreign authority a condition of execution of that authority's decision in France, the court failed to specify according to what criteria such jurisdiction should be determined.

A more recent decision of the Cour de Cassation[5] sided in favour of a flexible approach already employed by the Paris Court of Appeals. In addition to the traditional requirement that the choice of jurisdiction be free from fraud, *Simitch* requires the absence of exclusive jurisdiction of French courts and a "characteristic link" with the place of foreign jurisdiction.

4. Clunet 1964, 302; JCP 64, II, 13590.
5. *Simitch*, rendered on 6 February 1985, RCDIP, pp. 369 *et seq.*, pp. 243 *et seq.*

The French court seised with enforcement proceedings will apply French jurisdictional rules to determine whether there exists exclusive jurisdiction of another forum which would preclude the adjudicating country's authority hearing the matter. The legal bases to determine whether jurisdiction is exclusive are varied, but in general terms exclusive jurisdiction may result from internal jurisdictional rules, agreement by the parties concerned, and international treaties.

The second condition specifically stipulated in *Simitch* is that the foreign court must have a characteristic link with the place where that decision was rendered. The term "characteristic link" is new in this context and has not yet been clearly defined by the courts, although some insight is given by two former Paris Appellate Court decisions[6] which had referred to a "sufficient link, i.e., the choice (of the foreign jurisdiction) was neither arbitrary, artificial, nor fraudulent".

Proper law

Another condition specifically noted in *Munzer*, by then traditionally applied, is that the French court seised with a request for enforcement of a foreign decision must ascertain that the foreign authority had applied the proper law according to French conflict of law rules.

Conformity with French public policy

Conformity with French public policy is a traditional condition for the enforcement of foreign decisions.

By virtue of what is referred to in French as the "attenuated effect" (*effet atténué*) of French international public policy, in order for French international public policy to effectively preclude enforcement of a foreign decision, that decision must be found to be contrary to a fundamental public policy rule. Owing to this "attenuated effect" of international public policy, the enforcement of foreign decisions is rarely denied on such grounds in business law matters.

Absence of fraud

In *Munzer*, the absence of fraud was set out as a separate condition for enforcement. The notion of fraud is vast and in most instances will overlap with one of the other conditions for enforcement, in particular the requirement that the foreign decision not be contrary to French international public policy.

Challenges to enforcing foreign decisions

In addition to those conditions for enforcement expressly cited in *Munzer*, there are a number of other grounds which may be raised to challenge enforcement which merit some brief comment.

Pursuant to French case law, a French decision which is contrary to a foreign decision on the same subject matter between the same parties may be a cause for denying enforcement of the foreign decision.

6. *Mack Trucks*, GP, 1972, 1, 209; *Giroux*, RCDIP, 1978, p. 149.

In order for a foreign judgment to be enforceable in France, French law also requires the foreign decision to be enforceable in the jurisdiction in which it was rendered. The enforceability of the foreign decision in its own jurisdiction is determined by the French judge in view of the applicable law of the foreign jurisdiction.

French law does not require that the foreign decision be final and conclusive but only that it be executable. Thus, for instance, if the foreign decision is subject to interim enforcement notwithstanding an appeal, it will still be enforceable in France.

REMEDIES AVAILABLE TO FOREIGN CREDITORS AND PROCEDURAL STEPS

The following discussion will outline the types of remedies available to creditors and the procedural steps involved in obtaining them under the 9 July 1991 law.

One of the main innovations of the new law is the creation of a specialised judicial authority, the *juge de l'exécution*. The *juge de l'exécution* has broad powers to rule on requests for recognition and enforcement of foreign decisions, and to authorise provisional or interim measures and to settle any disputes connected therewith.

The *Présidents* of the Tribunaux de Grande Instance (lower civil trial courts) are by statute designated as having the power to act as *juges de l'exécution*, but a *Président* may nevertheless delegate such powers to one or several judges of a Tribunal de Grande Instance. The *juge de l'exécution* may, should he so decide, refer the matter to a panel of judges of a Tribunal de Grande Instance.

A distinction may be made between provisional or interim measures, on the one hand, and enforcement measures, on the other hand.

Provisional or interim measures

The 9 July 1991 law provides for two types of provisional or interim measures:

(1) The *saisie conservatoire*, which can be used to secure any of the debtor's tangible or intangible movable property.

(2) The *sûreté judiciaire*, which can be used to secure the debtor's real estate, business, stocks, bonds, and other transferable securities.

Both the *saisie conservatoire* and the *sûreté judiciaire* require a prior authorisation from the judge, unless the creditor holds an enforceable instrument or decision (*titre exécutoire*) or a judicial decision, even if not yet enforceable in France.

Authorisation is granted through *ex parte* proceedings, either by the *juge de l'exécution* or, in the case where such provisional or interim action is aimed at securing a debt which falls under the commercial jurisdiction, by the presiding judge of the commercial court having jurisdiction where the action is taken.

To obtain authorisation, the creditor must, as under the previous regime, demonstrate that his claim "appears founded in principle" and that there exist "circumstances endangering the recovery of his debt". Present case law considers that the claim need not to be certain, nor liquid nor actually due if otherwise prima facie well-founded. There is no reason to believe that such case law will not be maintained under the new regime.

Once authorisation is obtained, the creditor must then institute or continue

proceedings in view of obtaining an enforceable decision, in the case where he does not already possess one.

The creditor who is in possession of an enforceable instrument or judicial decision establishing a liquid and due debt may proceed to the sale of assets which were secured through the attachment up to the maximum amount of his claim.

In the case where the attachment involves a liquid debt, then the requesting party, if in possession of a *titre exécutoire*, may demand payment. Payment shall be immediately executed on the attached debt up to the amount of the condemnation or up to the amount of the debt recognised or established by the judge.

Enforcement measures

Enforcement measures are only available to creditors who have obtained a *titre exécutoire*, e.g. a foreign judgment enforceable in France.

The principal relevant enforcement measures and the procedural steps to obtain them may be briefly described as follows:

Saisie attribution

The *saisie attribution* can be used by any creditor in possession of an enforceable decision establishing a liquid and due debt, to secure and sell assets held by a third party or obtain payments owed by a third party for the benefit of the debtor.

This enforcement measure is carried out by a bailiff (*huissier de justice*). The act served by the bailiff gives rise to the immediate obligation of the payment of the debt, up to the amount authorised, to the benefit of the requesting party. The third party forming the object of this enforcement measure becomes the substitute debtor to the requesting party up to the limits of his own personal obligation to the original debtor.

The amount forming the object of this enforcement measure must be paid within one month if there has been no challenge by the debtor before the *juge de l'exécution*.

In the event that there is a challenge before the *juge de l'exécution* within the one-month period, payment will be deferred unless the judge authorises payment pending the outcome of the challenge.

The third party forming the object of this enforcement measure has the obligation to declare to the creditor the extent and scope of its obligations to the original defendant as well as any terms and conditions thereof which may affect the debt, if such be the case, as well as any assignment of the debt, delegations or prior attachments. In the case where the third party is a financial institution, that institution shall be required to declare the balance of the debtor's account on the day of the attachment. However, within 15 business days the balance of the account may be modified to take into account transactions implemented prior to the attachment although having posterior effect.

Saisie-vente

The *saisie-vente* may be used to attach and ultimately sell any tangible movable property held by the debtor himself or by a third party.

In the case where the debtor is an individual and where the attachment must be carried out at his place of residence, the attachment must be carried out only as a last alternative, and shall therefore only be allowed in the event that the claim cannot be recovered by other means.

When the enforcement involves the debtor's place of residence, the *saisie-vente* must be preceded by a formal order, served by a *huissier*, to pay the debt. Such an order to pay must enjoin the debtor to communicate the name and address of his employer and references of his bank account.

The *saisie-vente* is followed by the forced sale of the movable property by public auction subsequent to a one-month period, running from the day of the attachment, during which the debtor may proceed to the out-of-court sale of the property.

Saisie des droits incorporels

This enforcement measure may be used to attach and ultimately sell any incorporeal rights, other than money debts, held by the debtor.

The 9 July 1991 law provides that only those claimants having filed a demand prior to the sale of the property forming the object of this measure may seek payment from the proceeds of the sale.

Saisie immobilière

The *saisie immobilière* provided under the former law remained unmodified under the 9 July 1991 law. This enforcement measure may be used by a creditor in possession of an enforceable decision to secure and ultimately sell real estate belonging to his debtor, and may also be used against a third party when the creditor benefits from a right stemming from a mortgage or privilege on real estate.

The actual procedure of the *saisie immobilière* is a rather complicated affair, the full details of which are thought to be beyond the scope of this discussion. In summary, this execution measure may be divided into two phases, the actual attachment followed by a procedure leading to the sale at a public auction of the property forming the object of the attachment.

The first step in this proceeding is the serving on the debtor of a formal notice to pay the debt, which notice is published at the *Bureau des Hypothèques*. As from the date of publication the property cannot be sold by the debtor-owner, nor may other rights on the property be attached thereon. The second phase of the procedure include extensive publicity and other formalities in preparation of the sale, followed by a special procedure for the actual sale by public auction.

IMPACT OF THE DEBTOR'S BANKRUPTCY

The opening of bankruptcy proceedings in France causes, *ipso facto*, individual proceedings against the debtor to cease. Thereafter, it is not possible to recover a debt outside the bankruptcy proceedings from the debtor's assets.

Further, in order to keep his debt alive, a creditor must declare it to the representative of the creditors within two months from publication of the bankruptcy decision in an official legal publication in France. This time limit is increased by two

months for creditors domiciled outside France. Should the creditor fail to submit a declaration of his debt within this time limit, the debt shall be extinguished unless the creditor has obtained special authorisation from the court to file late.

If any proceedings are pending at the date of the decision opening the bankruptcy proceedings, they will be adjourned until the creditor has declared his claim, then automatically reopened (with the participation of the representative of the creditors and, if necessary, the receiver), but solely in order to establish the justification of the claim and to fix its amount. Attachment proceedings which are pending but not finalised on the date of opening of bankruptcy proceedings will be null and void. There will be an automatic removal of all measures blocking the assets or the debts held or owed by a third party to the benefit of the bankrupt debtor.

Furthermore, even if the provisional or interim proceedings are finalised on the date of opening of the bankruptcy proceedings, such measures may be cancelled if the recording of the attachment was made after the date of suspension of payments. Such date of suspension of payments is fixed by the judge within a period of 18 months before the decision opening bankruptcy proceedings, taking into consideration the day on which the debtor was deemed to be insolvent.

CONCLUSION

Foreign creditors and litigants have available a wide array of means of securing assets in France. The French law of 9 July 1991, in effect as from 1 August 1992, and its implementing legislation attempts to strike a balance between a creditor's need to secure his debt expeditiously and the need to protect a debtor from unwarranted attacks.

ROBERT BYRD

CHAPTER 11

GERMANY

INTRODUCTION

The German law relating to provisional remedies to the benefit of a foreign creditor who seeks interim or provisional relief towards securing collection on a claim is contained in the Code of Civil Procedure (*Zivilprozeßordnung*, hereinafter ZPO), as amended, and the respective supplementing international multilateral and bilateral treaties.

In principle, German courts are available to foreign creditors and litigants to the same extent they are available to German plaintiffs/applicants. This also applies if the defendant/opponent is a non-German citizen/legal entity. As in the case of a German plaintiff/applicant, the prerequisite for any action is the existence of a German forum. For those cases in which the opponent does not live or reside in Germany and no other special forum (e.g. *forum delicti commissi*) exists, paragraph 23, ZPO, provides for a forum at the court where assets of the defendant/opponent or the subject matter of the action are located. It has, however, to be noted that this provision is interpreted restrictively by the German Supreme Court, in particular if the plaintiff/applicant is non-German.[1] Another notable qualification to the general rule that German courts are likewise available to foreign plaintiffs/applicants is contained in paragraph 917 II, ZPO, providing a presumption important for the obtaining of a writ of attachment which applies to the benefit of judgments rendered in German main proceedings only.

A foreign creditor wishing to enforce a claim against a German or non-German opponent may do so by commencing respective German main proceedings, by moving to have a foreign judgment declared enforceable in Germany, or, in both cases, by commencing preliminary injunction proceedings. The commencement of regular main proceedings in Germany is not a topic of this chapter and will, therefore, not be dealt with. The chapter will concentrate on setting out how a foreign creditor can obtain provisional relief, in particular with respect to securing a claim for the payment of money. In addition, the general principles concerning the proceedings whereby a foreign judgment is declared enforceable in Germany will be outlined.

1. BGH, WM 1991 *et seq.*: it is not sufficient for a forum pursuant to para. 23, ZPO, that there are assets within the jurisdiction of the court; para. 23, ZPO, requires a further and closer relationship of the case (e.g. its parties, subject matter) to Germany.

PROVISIONAL ATTACHMENT PROCEEDINGS (ARRESTVERFAHREN)

Types of preliminary attachment and other injunction proceedings

The ZPO distinguishes between two types of preliminary proceedings, namely:

(a) proceedings securing the enforcement of claims for the payment of money, irrespective of whether such claims are subject to a condition subsequent (*auflösende Bedingung*), to a condition precedent (*aufschiebende Bedingung*), unless the claim is worthless on account of the unlikelihood that the condition precedent will occur[2] or not yet due (*betagt*), and claims which are convertible into a claim for the payment of money (e.g. claim on account of a violation of representations and warranties) (so-called *Arrest* pursuant to paragraph 916, ZPO, provisional attachment); and

(b) proceedings securing all other kinds of claim (interim injunction/*einstweilige Verfügung*) pursuant to paragraph 935, ZPO.

The latter is subdivided into three categories:

(i) *Sicherungsverfügung*, securing interim injunction proceedings, for the purpose of securing claims which are not directed at the payment of money, such as claims for recovery or delivery of certain assets, claims for a declaration of intent, claims for ordering the other party to do or to refrain from doing something;

(ii) *Regelungsverfügung*, preliminary disposition injunction proceedings, for obtaining a preliminary decision on the status or (non-)existence of a certain legal relationship (*streitiges Rechtsverhältnis*) pursuant to paragraph 940, ZPO; and

(iii) *Leistungsverfügung*, interim performance injunction proceedings, pursuant to paragraph 940, ZPO, analogously directed at providing early satisfaction of claims in the very limited cases where it would be grossly inequitable to deny a right to preliminary satisfaction (e.g. a claim for providing maintenance).

All three types of interim injunction are governed by paragraphs 916 *et seq.*, ZPO, i.e., the basic rules for the obtaining of a (provisional) attachment and its enforcement and appeal are basically identical. Certain special rules are laid down in paragraphs 935 *et seq.*, ZPO, and, respectively, paragraph 940, ZPO, none of which will be dealt with here, since this chapter will examine the provisional attachment proceedings (*Arrestverfahren*) only, i.e., the obtaining of a writ of (provisional) attachment for the securing of a claim for the payment of money.

Requirements for obtaining a writ of provisional attachment (*dinglicher Arrest*)

As a rule, German procedural law does not distinguish or even discriminate against foreign plaintiffs/applicants.[3] Such parties are, therefore, free to bring preliminary injunction proceedings in Germany just as any German applicant might commence

2. Zöller, *Zivilprozeßordnung* (1995, 19th ed.), para. 916, annot. 7.

3. In preliminary injunction proceedings, the parties are called "applicant" rather than "plaintiff" and "opponent" rather than "defendant"; *Antragsteller* and *Antragsgegner*.

such proceedings against German opponents (individuals or companies residing in Germany), or—provided there is jurisdiction—even against a foreign opponent. For obtaining a writ of provisional attachment all general requirements for bringing an action must be observed, with due consideration of any peculiarities applying to preliminary injunction proceedings; the applicant's case must be properly stated, i.e., the facts on the basis of which the applicant feels entitled to a claim for the payment of money (attachment claim/*Arrestanspruch*); the facts justifying the issue of a provisional attachment (attachment reason/*Arrestgrund*) have to be given; and sufficient prima facie evidence for the attachment claim, as well as the attachment reason, must be presented.

Requirements for bringing provisional attachment proceedings

The main formal requirements are as follows.

LEGAL CAPACITY

Proceedings may be commenced only by a party (applicant) against another party (opponent) if both parties have legal capacity and thus the capacity to be a party to legal proceedings (paragraph 5, ZPO). Under German law, the following German parties have legal capacity and may, therefore, sue or be sued in Germany:

(a) any individual;
(b) any legal entity under public and private law[4];
(c) any commercial partnership.[5]

Due to lack of a legal capacity of its own, in a private partnership all partners must be sued in their capacity as members of the private partnership; a silent partnership cannot be sued; as to a "sole entrepreneur" (*Einzelkaufmann*), the owner must be sued, and as to a branch, the company to which the branch belongs must be sued.

A foreign party may sue or be sued in German courts if—according to the foreign party's national law—the foreign party has legal capacity and thus may sue or be sued under its respective national law.[6] In the case of a foreign company, the law of the country where the company's actual head office is situated applies.[7]

LIS PENDENS

The subject matter of provisional attachment proceedings involves the question whether the applicant has a right to have the later enforcement of his (alleged) claim provisionally secured by a writ of provisional attachment (i.e., not the question whether the applicant in fact does have a claim for payment). Accordingly, provided there is a basis for attachment, provisional attachment proceedings are admissible, irrespective of whether main proceedings are pending in a German or foreign court.

If, at the same time, preliminary injunction proceedings are pending in a foreign jurisdiction, such foreign provisional attachment proceedings would only prevent the

4. GmbH, AG, KGAG, and *Genossenschaft*.
5. oHG, KG and GmbH & Co. KG.
6. Para. 7, EGBGB—Introductory Law to the German Civil Code.
7. BGHZ 97, 269; Baumbach, Lauterbach, Albers and Hartmann, *Zivilprozeßordnung* (1995, 53rd ed.), para. 50, annot. 2.

bringing of respective German proceedings if the foreign writ of attachment rendered in such proceedings would be recognised in Germany and would thus result in *res judicata*.[8]

The bringing of further provisional attachment proceedings, despite the fact that such proceedings have already commenced in another German court, is not allowed, regardless of whether the prior proceedings have been commenced in the German court competent for the main proceedings,[9] or in a local court the competence of which is based only on certain assets of the opponent being located in such court's jurisdiction.[10]

RES JUDICATA

Distinction must be made between foreign and German orders and judgments in provisional attachment proceedings.

To the extent such foreign orders and judgments are recognised in Germany, the rule of *res judicata* applies.[11] If a German court has already rendered a decision, the following scenarios might occur:

(a) If the court has decided in favour of the applicant, such order may be used for attaching all German and non-German assets of the opponent, regardless of whether the decision was rendered by a local court the competence of which is based on certain assets being in its jurisdiction.[12]

(b) If the court has denied the issue of a writ of provisional attachment, the admissibility of new proceedings depends on why the former motion was not granted; *res judicata* applies if the first motion was dismissed for lack of an attachment claim, i.e., if the court ruled that the applicant did not have a claim for payment. Contrary thereto, new preliminary injunction proceedings for a writ of attachment may be brought on the basis of new facts regarding the grounds for attachment if the prior motion was dismissed on the grounds of lack thereof, or regarding the presentation of prima facie evidence concerning the attachment claim or the grounds for attachment if formerly dismissed on account of insufficient prima facie evidence.[13]

POSTING OF A BOND

All non-German citizens, regardless of whether they reside in Germany, and all non-German legal entities (companies with their seats outside Germany)[14] must put up security for the opponent's probable costs of the provisional attachment proceedings if the opponent so requests, and that regardless of the applicant's financial situation. But since a writ of provisional attachment is usually issued without the opponent being heard,[15] such security is often put up only on the opponent filing

8. See "Recognition and enforcement of foreign judgments", below.

9. Undisputed, for such court's order could be used to attach all assets of the opponent; see Baumbach et al., note 7 *supra*, para. 928.

10. Prevailing view: cf. Baumbach et al., note 7 *supra*, para. 919, annot. 6.

11. See para. 328, ZPO, and "Prerequisites for recognition of foreign judgments", below.

12. Para. 919, ZPO; cf. Baumbach et al., note 7 *supra*, para. 919.

13. Baumbach et al., note 7 *supra*, para. 322; *Arrestverfahren.*

14. Para. 17, ZPO; para. 24, BGB (German Civil Code).

15. Cf. "Obtaining a writ of provisional attachment", below.

an objection (*Widerspruch*) against the already-issued writ of provisional attachment.[16] The amount of security is determined by the court at its discretion. As a rule, the amount will be equal to the opponent's likely costs for all instances.[17]

A security, *inter alia*, need not be put up if there is no reciprocal duty on a German citizen in the applicant's country, or if it is excluded by international treaties such as the Hague Convention of 1954[18] or by bilateral treaties.[19]

The kind of security is determined by the court at its discretion. In general, the applicant must deposit the amount in cash with the court (*Hinterlegung*) or put up a corresponding bank guarantee, typically issued by a major German bank.

FORUM

Pursuant to paragraph 919, ZPO, a plaintiff may choose to file an application for a provisional attachment either with a court having jurisdiction for the main proceedings or with a court in the jurisdiction of which assets of the opponent are situated[20] or where the person to be arrested[21] lives. Other courts do not have jurisdiction (paragraph 802, ZPO).

Whereas, in the latter case, the competence of the court is determined merely by the location of the opponent's assets (actual place of movable assets; court of registry in the case of real property or other rights concerning real property; general forum of third party, if opponent's rights against such third party are to be attached), the situation is somewhat more complex in the former case. If the main proceedings are not yet pending, the court for the main proceedings is determined according to the general rules. Accordingly, all other forums are excluded if there is a binding agreement between the parties on the venue and jurisdiction; in all other cases, including those where the agreement in question provides for an arbitration clause,[22] the general rules on general or special forums apply: the general forum of an individual is at his permanent residence (paragraph 13, ZPO) and that of a legal entity at the company's seat (paragraph 17, ZPO).

Special jurisdiction relates to particular circumstances and provides for one or several additional forums (paragraphs 20 *et seq.*, ZPO):

(1) A person without a registered permanent residence may be sued in the court of his abode (paragraph 20, ZPO).
(2) All actions related to the business of a branch may be filed with the local court for the branch, irrespective of whether the company itself is domiciled in Germany (paragraph 21, ZPO).
(3) Further special forums are those of the place of performance of contractual duty or the commission of a tort (paragraphs 29 and 32, ZPO).
(4) The most important forum, if suing a non-German party in Germany, is provided under paragraph 23, ZPO, according to which a non-German party

16. Cf. "Proceedings without oral hearing"; Baumbach et al., note 7 *supra*, para. 110, annot. 7; Zöller, note 2 *supra*, para. 110, annot. 3.
17. Baumbach et al., note 7 *supra*, para. 112, annot. 4.
18. Cf. Art. 17 of the Hague Convention of 1 March 1954.
19. An overview concerning all countries is set out in Baumbach et al., note 7 *supra*, para. 110, supplement to para. 110.
20. Para. 23, ZPO; cf. "Introduction".
21. Cf. para. 918, ZPO, and "Requirements for a writ of preliminary attachment", below.
22. Zöller, note 2 *supra*, para. 919, annot. 3.

> may be sued in the German court in the jurisdiction where assets of the opponent or the subject matter of the action are located.[23]

If the main proceedings are pending in a German court, such court is deemed—for the purposes of filing an application for a provisional attachment—as the court competent for the main proceedings. Such competence is not affected by the main proceedings having been filed with a court without jurisdiction, or even by the main proceedings later being dismissed on the grounds that the court approached is not competent.[24]

Finally, it should be observed that German procedural law does not provide for special rules on the determination of an "international forum" for cases such as a German citizen/company intending to sue a foreigner, or vice versa, or where occurrences abroad or foreign property are at stake. Accordingly, the German rules on local jurisdiction set out above are also decisive for the question of international jurisdiction. If a German court considers itself the locally competent court, it also would consider itself the internationally proper forum.

Requirements for writ of preliminary attachment

The court will issue a writ of preliminary attachment (*dinglicher Arrest*) or a writ of personal attachment (*persönlicher Arrest*) if—on the basis of the facts presented and the supporting prima facie evidence—it is convinced that there is a valid attachment claim as well as a reason for attachment.

ATTACHMENT CLAIM (ARRESTANSPRUCH)

The application must state in sufficient detail all facts which form the basis for the applicant's claim for payment. The description must be detailed with respect to what events (e.g., facts which constitute a breach of contract or amount to a commission of tort) result in a claim for payment of the opponent and what the exact amount of the claim for payment is and what interest thereon is requested. It is not sufficient merely to allege the facts. The plaintiff further has to present prima facie evidence for these facts. The applicant has to convince the court that the facts as presented by him are probably true (*überwiegende Wahrscheinlichkeit*)[25]; full proof is not necessary.[26]

In cases where the claim raised is based on foreign law (e.g., the tort was committed abroad; the contract on which the claim is based provides for foreign law), it is disputed whether the applicant's duty to present prima facie evidence for his alleged claim also applies to the applicable foreign law. From a strictly theoretical point of view, it is correct to state that the applicant has to provide prima facie evidence merely for the underlying facts, whereas the law is to be applied by the court itself, regardless of whether the case is subject to German or foreign law.[27] In view of the urgency of provisional attachment proceedings and the court's obligation to decide as soon as possible, some argue[28] that the prima facie evidence requirement also should extend to

23. This provision is narrowly and restrictively interpreted by German courts, cf. note 1.
24. Baumbach et al., note 7 *supra*, para. 919, annot. 5; para. 261 III 2, ZPO.
25. Baumbach et al., note 7 *supra*, para. 294, annot. 1.
26. See "Requirements for a writ of preliminary attachment", below.
27. Para. 293, ZPO.
28. OLG Hamburg, GRUR 89, p. 1164.

the foreign law. From a practical point of view, it is strongly recommended that, in all cases involving foreign law, prima facie evidence is presented to the greatest extent possible. This can be done by attaching to the application legal articles (German or foreign, the latter to be translated by a sworn interpreter), by bringing an expert on the respective foreign law to the court when filing the application, or by attaching a sworn affidavit of a recognised expert.

Another scenario of interest here is one in which a foreign judgment or a German or foreign arbitration award has already been rendered in favour of the applicant and which is not (yet) enforceable in Germany. The presentation of such foreign judgment or arbitration award is another permissible means of presenting prima facie evidence for the applicant having an attachment claim, i.e., a claim for the payment of money.[29]

ATTACHMENT REASON (ARRESTGRUND)

The law provides for a general rule (paragraph 917 I, ZPO) and a legal presumption if the judgment is to be enforced abroad (paragraph 917 II, ZPO). In any case, it is, however, necessary that the applicant has a legitimate interest for bringing provisional attachment proceedings.

An attachment reason exists only if there is a substantial risk that enforcing the (possibly not yet obtained) judgment in the German or foreign main proceedings will not be possible, or will at least be substantially more difficult, if no provisional attachment is granted (paragraph 917 I, ZPO). Whether this is the case is to be decided from an objective, reasonable point of view; the personal view or opinion of the applicant is irrelevant.

There are no precise criteria as to under what circumstances the prerequisites of paragraph 917 I, ZPO, are met. The courts prefer, however, a restrictive construction, so that the existence of an attachment reason pursuant to paragraph 917 I, ZPO, is only seldom affirmed. Examples of sufficient grounds are if the opponent:

(1) squanders his assets;
(2) smuggles or dissipates substantial assets;
(3) gives up his residence without having his new domicile registered;
(4) is preparing to move abroad;
(5) assigns all his accounts receivables;
(6) begins "hiding" his assets; or
(7) suddenly encumbers all his real estate.[30]

There is, however, no sufficient attachment reason if the financial situation of the opponent is bad or worsening,[31] or if other creditors are attaching assets of the opponent.[32] A provisional attachment will be granted only if there is a particular worsening of the financial situation of the opponent or if the chances of enforcing a final judgment are substantially reduced. Whether that is so depends very much on the circumstances of the individual case. It is, however, to be decided on an objective basis, so that it is irrelevant whether the opponent acts dishonestly or whether the opponent is responsible for the facts resulting in the risk that the enforcement of a judgment might become impossible or substantially more difficult.

29. Baumbach et al., note 7 *supra*, para. 920, annot. 7.
30. See Zöller, note 2 *supra*, para. 917, annot. 5.
31. Baumbach et al., note 7 *supra*, para. 917, annot. 4.
32. OLG Karlsruhe, FamRZ 85, p. 805.

A writ of personal attachment (*persönlicher Arrest*) will be granted only if this is the sole means for securing the enforcement of the judgment in the main proceedings (paragraph 919, ZPO).

It is clear from the above example that it is very difficult to prove that an attachment reason exists pursuant to paragraph 917 I, ZPO, or even paragraph 919, ZPO. That is why the legal presumption of paragraph 917 II, ZPO, is of great practical importance. According to this provision, it is deemed to constitute an attachment reason if the judgment rendered in the main proceedings would have to be enforced abroad, i.e., outside Germany. If so, the court may not examine whether there is a substantial risk that the judgment may not be enforceable. The presumption also applies if:

(1) the opponent is a foreign company or a foreign individual living abroad;
(2) the opponent was abroad at the time the applicant "acquired" his claim; or
(3) both opponent and applicant are foreigners and live or reside abroad.[33]

Despite the seemingly clear wording of the presumption in paragraph 917 II, ZPO, two questions in connection with the European Convention on Jurisdiction and Enforcement of Judicial Decisions in Civil and Commercial Matters[34] (*EuGVÜ*) of 27 September 1968 have been disputed for years[35]:

(a) Only in 1994, did a decision by the EuGH[36] provide for an end to the long-disputed question, whether the presumption of paragraph 917 II, ZPO, also applies if the judgment rendered in the main proceedings is to be enforced in a member state of the European Convention. According to the EuGH decision, paragraph 917 II, ZPO, is not applicable any more in regard to member countries of the European Convention.
(b) According to prevailing opinion, the presumption of paragraph 917 II applies only to German judgments. Thus, if the main proceedings are either pending abroad or, if not yet pending, will have no German forum, the presumption of paragraph 917 II does not apply.[37]

The prevailing opinions cited above result in enormous difficulties in obtaining a provisional attachment order if the main proceedings do not take place in Germany: it is very hard to present sufficient prima facie evidence to the court to meet the requirements of paragraph 917 I, ZPO, or paragraph 919, ZPO, and the presumption of paragraph 917 II, ZPO, only applies in favour of judgments to be rendered in German main proceedings. Thus, an applicant having the choice between a foreign and German forum should carefully consider bringing the main proceedings in a German court (provided there is German jurisdiction for the main proceedings), if the obtaining of a writ of provisional attachment is decisive for securing his claim for payment.

Finally, it has to be observed that a writ of a provisional attachment will be issued

33. Baumbach et al., note 7 *supra*, para. 917, annot. 10.

34. *Übereinkommen der Europäischen Gemeinschaft über die gerichtliche Zuständigkeit und die Vollstreckung gerichtlicher Entscheidungen in Zivil- und Handelssachen vom 27.09.1968.*

35. Among the most recent of many publications are: Mankowski, "Zum Arrestgrund der Auslandsvollstreckung in § 917 II, ZPO", NJW 92, pp. 599 *et seq.*; Ericke, "Nochmals: Zum Arrestgrund der Auslandsvollstreckung in § 917 II, ZPO", NJW 92, pp. 602 *et seq.*; Thümmel, "Der Arrestgrund der Ausnahmsvollstreckung im Fadenkreuz des europäischen Rechtes", EuZW 94, 242 *et seq.*

36. EuGH, NJW 94, 1271; as to the former dispute see Baumbach et al., note 7 *supra*, para. 917, annot. 2; Zöller, note 2 *supra*, para. 917, annot. 15; dissenting Ericke, note 35 *supra*.

37. Zöller, note 2 *supra*, para. 917, annot. 15; Mankowski, note 35 *supra*, OLG München, NJW-RR 88, p. 1023, dissenting: Ericke, note 35 *supra*; Baumbach et al., note 7 *supra*, para. 917, annot. 13.

only if the applicant has a legitimate interest to take legal action.[38] Such legitimate interest is denied if the applicant already has sufficient security (e.g., retention of title with respect to the things the payment for which the applicant seeks), even if such securities are located abroad.[39] Thus, even if the prerequisites of the presumption of paragraph 917 II, ZPO (enforcement abroad), are met, no writ of provisional attachment will be issued if the opponent has sufficient assets in Germany and if there is no risk that the opponent could prevent the enforcement of the judgment rendered in the main proceedings.[40]

A further consequence is that no provisional attachment proceedings may be brought if the applicant already has obtained in the main proceedings a final judgment or a judgment which is enforceable without the need to put up security. If the judgment obtained in the main proceedings is, however, enforceable against security only, provisional attachment proceedings remain available.[41]

PRIMA FACIE EVIDENCE

As set out above, the applicant must present prima facie evidence to support the attachment (paragraphs 920 II and 294, ZPO). Due to the provisional character of such proceedings, it is not necessary to present full proof. It is, however, necessary that the written prima facie evidence offered (documents and sworn affidavits) are attached to the application and that the witnesses and/or experts whose testimony is offered are present when the application is filed and, if a hearing is scheduled,[42] are present at such hearing. Evidence which cannot be taken immediately is not admissible (paragraph 294 II, ZPO). Prima facie evidence, in particular, includes the presentation of documents, witnesses and experts, and sworn affidavits (*Eidesstattliche Versicherungen*). It is permissible to make reference to other court files or German or foreign judgments, even if the latter are not recognisable in Germany.[43]

If the applicant is not able to present sufficient prima facie evidence, the court nevertheless may issue a writ of attachment provided the applicant puts up security (usually in the form of a cash deposit with the court or a bank guarantee by a major German bank) covering all possible costs which the opponent might suffer on account of the provisional attachment.[44] As a practical matter, the court will usually issue a writ of attachment before the security has been put up but will order that the writ of attachment may be enforced only upon a certain security having been posted.[45]

The possibility to post security is a remedy only in those cases in which the prima facie evidence offered was not sufficient. In other words, if the alleged facts as presented by the applicant are not sufficient, i.e., the facts do not support an attachment claim and attachment reason, a writ of attachment may not be issued, regardless of any security.[46]

38. Undisputed. It is, however, disputed whether this requirement is part of the attachment reason or merely one of the general procedural prerequisites; cf. Zöller, note 2 *supra*, para. 917, annot. 10.
39. Baumbach et al., note 7 *supra*, para. 917, annot. 9; BGH NJW 72, p. 1044.
40. *Ibid.*, para. 917, annot. 11; OLG Bremen, VersR 72, p. 250.
41. Prevailing opinion: cf. Zöller, note 2 *supra*, para. 917, annot. 12.
42. Cf. "Proceedings without oral hearing", below.
43. See Zöller, note 2 *supra*, para. 920, annot. 10.
44. See para. 921 II, ZPO.
45. See Zöller, note 2 *supra*, para. 921, annots. 2–4.
46. See Baumbach et al., note 7 *supra*, para. 921, annot. 5.

Obtaining a writ of provisional attachment

Since it is at the court's discretion whether it decides on the application to issue a writ of attachment with or without an oral hearing, these two kinds of proceedings must be distinguished.

Application

In all cases, the applicant must file with the competent court[47] a written application (the other possibility provided by law—oral application to be minuted by the court—is almost never used), along with all prima facie evidence offered. The application must set out:

(1) the attachment claim, i.e., the facts on which the applicant's (alleged) claim for payment is based;
(2) the attachment reason, i.e., the facts justifying the granting of a preliminary attachment;
(3) the necessary prima facie evidence concerning the attachment claim and attachment reason; and
(4) the motion to order either that the entire assets of the opponent are declared to be provisionally attached (writ of provisional attachment/*Anordnung des dinglichen Arrestes*) or that the opponent himself is to be arrested (writ of personal attachment/*Anordnung des persönlichen Arrestes*).

Since the court may issue a writ without a prior oral hearing, i.e., without the opponent being heard,[48] it is strongly recommended that the writ of attachment be issued without such prior oral hearing. Such procedure, if successful, has a welcome "surprise effect" on the opponent. Moreover, the chances of obtaining a writ of attachment are obviously higher if the opponent is not heard. Such procedure also provides the possibility to discuss any problems or difficulties with the judge. If these cannot be solved, i.e., the judge cannot be convinced to issue a writ of provisional attachment, the applicant retains the ability to withdraw his application without the opponent ever learning of the applicant's attempt to obtain a writ of attachment.

Proceedings without oral hearing

If the court is of the opinion that the prerequisites for the issue of a writ of attachment are not met and the applicant does not withdraw his application,[49] the motion is dismissed by court order.[50] The opponent will not be informed of the decision.[51] The applicant may, however, appeal the order (*einfache Beschwerde*) pursuant to paragraph 567 I, ZPO.

If the court accepts that there is an attachment claim, attachment reason and that sufficient prima facie evidence has been presented, the writ of attachment will be

47. Cf. "Forum", above.
48. See para. 921 I, ZPO.
49. Cf. "Application", above.
50. See para. 922 I, ZPO.
51. See para. 922 III, ZPO.

issued but not served on the opponent *ex officio*.[52] This is to be done by the applicant[53] in order to be able to enforce the writ of provisional attachment.

The opponent may file an objection (*Widerspruch*) at any time, i.e., there is no deadline for such objection.[54] If an objection is filed, the court will order an oral hearing.[55]

The opponent also may respond by filing a motion that the applicant must commence main proceedings within a period to be determined by the court.[56] Such approach is to be recommended if it is difficult for the opponent to present prima facie evidence that there is no attachment claim or attachment reason. The main proceedings will result in the taking of full evidence and will offer a much better means for the opponent to present his defence, if the latter is very complex and difficult to prove in preliminary injunction proceedings. Although this would imply that the writ of attachment remains enforceable for the time being, this might be acceptable to the opponent if he has averted the enforcement of the attachment by putting up a security[57] and if the applicant is financially so sound that any later claim for damages can be successfully enforced by the opponent since the applicant will be liable for all damages suffered by the opponent as a result of an unjustified attachment.[58]

In view of the possibility that a court might issue a writ of attachment without a prior oral hearing, German legal practice has developed the "protective brief" (*Schutzschrift*). Such protective brief may be filed by the opponent with any competent court if the opponent expects that the applicant might try to obtain a writ of attachment without prior oral hearing. Such protective brief must set out why there is no attachment reason and/or no attachment claim and move that any possible motion to issue a writ of attachment be dismissed or not be granted without a prior oral hearing. The difficulties connected with such protective brief are to find the proper court (i.e., the court where the applicant will file his application) and to assume fairly correctly what facts establishing an attachment claim and attachment reason will be presented by the plaintiff. The first problem can be solved by filing identical protective briefs with all courts which might be approached by the applicant. The latter problem requires the opponent's lawyer to consider carefully what possible alternatives the applicant might have in presenting his facts and what possible prima facie evidence might possibly be presented by the applicant.

Proceedings with prior oral hearing

An oral hearing will be scheduled either if the court in its discretion[59] so decides or if the opponent, upon a writ of attachment having been issued, files an objection.[60] The

52. See para. 922 II, ZPO.
53. Cf. "Service of and periods for enforcement of writ of provisional attachment", below.
54. See para. 924 I, ZPO.
55. Cf. "Proceedings with prior oral hearing", below.
56. See para. 926 I, ZPO.
57. Cf. "Right to avert enforcement of writ of attachment", below.
58. See para. 945, ZPO.
59. See para. 921 I, ZPO.
60. See para. 924 II 2, ZPO.

date for an oral hearing usually is scheduled at short notice without the need for the regular period between service of summons and date of hearing to be observed,[61] in particular since the periods may be shortened upon application.[62]

If such an oral hearing is scheduled, it will be essential to have all prima facie evidence (including witnesses, experts, and documents) available at the hearing.[63] It is further recommended that the party be prepared for all unexpected new facts and means of prima facie evidence. Upon the oral hearing, the court will render its decision by judgment as follows:

(1) If no writ of attachment was issued before, the judgment will provide for such issue.
(2) If the writ of attachment was issued before the oral hearing took place on account of an objection being filed, the judgment will merely confirm the issue.
(3) In all other cases, the court will either set aside the former writ of attachment or, if not yet issued, dismiss the respective motion.

In all cases, the defeated party may file an appeal within one month.[64] Upon appeal, there is no further recourse to the Supreme Court.[65] Unlike an order, the judgment is served *ex officio* upon the parties.[66]

Right to avert enforcement of writ of attachment

Pursuant to paragraph 923, ZPO, the court, if granting a writ of attachment, is obligated to determine simultaneously an amount of money by the deposit of which with the court the opponent can move for suspension of the enforcement of the writ of attachment or, if already enforced, for the setting aside of all enforcement measures taken.

The amount of the security must cover the amount of the applicant's claim, any interest thereon, and a lump sum for legal costs.[67] Both parties may appeal the amount of the security as determined by the court.

The purpose of paragraph 923, ZPO, is to enable the opponent to provide sufficient security to the applicant so that, in exchange, the opponent can avoid or have set aside any enforcement measures taken in the meantime by the applicant. This is of particular importance since the writ of attachment does not limit the assets which might be attached or seized by the applicant on the basis of the writ of attachment, the reason being that it is not possible for the applicant or the court to know beforehand what value the seized assets might have and, if a favourable final judgment in the main proceeding is obtained, to what extent such assets may be realised to the benefit of the applicant. Thus, if the enforcement of the writ of attachment results in the seizure of assets in excess of the amount of security as determined by the court pursuant to paragraph 923, or if the seizure of assets is unbearable to the opponent for other

61. See para. 274 III, ZPO; Zöller, note 2 *supra*, para. 274, annot. 5.
62. See paras. 217 and 226 I, ZPO.
63. Cf. "Proceedings with prior oral hearing", above.
64. See para. 511, ZPO.
65. See para. 545 II, ZPO.
66. See para. 317 I, ZPO.
67. The costs for the provisional attachment proceedings are determined independently and must be paid by the opponent immediately, i.e., their payment cannot be suspended by the putting up of a security; cf. Baumbach et al., note 7 *supra*, para. 923, annot. 1.

reasons, the opponent is forced to put up a security in the amount determined by the court.

Although paragraph 923 provides only for the deposit of a cash amount with the court, it is accepted practice that the court may allow the opponent to put up a bank guarantee of a major (usually German) bank instead. A further possibility is for the parties to agree on the kind and amount of security.[68] A foreign opponent should be aware of the fact that the putting up of a security might be sufficient to create a special forum pursuant to paragraph 23, ZPO.[69] This risk exists, however, only outside the scope of the European Convention on the Enforcement of Civil and Commercial Judgments.[70]

If the court should fail to determine the amount of the security, this does not affect the validity of the writ of attachment. The parties are, however, entitled to move that the writ of attachment be supplemented pursuant to paragraph 321, ZPO.[71]

If the security is put up, the writ of attachment may no longer be enforced. To the extent enforcement measures have been taken, these are set aside.[72] It is to be noted, however, that the opponent remains obligated to pay the applicant's legal costs in connection with the obtaining of the writ of attachment[73] and that the court order as to the costs may still be enforced.[74]

Service of and periods for enforcement of writ of provisional attachment

A writ of attachment is enforced according to the general principles of German civil procedure to the extent paragraphs 928 *et seq.*, ZPO, do not provide otherwise.

The writ of attachment constitutes an executory title (*Titel*), which does not require a special certificate of enforceability (*Klausel*) unless the writ of attachment is to be enforced against a party different from the opponent,[75] by a party different from the applicant,[76] or abroad.[77]

Irrespective of whether the writ of attachment has been issued by means of an order which is not to be served *ex officio*[78] or by means of a judgment which is to be served *ex officio*,[79] it must be served on the opponent by the applicant in order to meet the deadlines of paragraph 929 II, III, ZPO.[80]

It is of great importance to note that, pursuant to paragraph 929 II, ZPO, the writ of attachment may be enforced no longer than one month after such writ of attachment has been issued[81] or has been served on the applicant.[82]

68. Cf. Baumbach et al., *ibid.*, para. 923, annot. 1A.
69. Forum of assets; cf. OLG Frankfurt, OLGZ 83, 99; Zöller, note 2 *supra*, para. 923, annot. 3.
70. Cf. Art. 3, EuGVÜ.
71. See Zöller, note 2 *supra*, para. 923, annot. 1.
72. See para. 934 I, ZPO.
73. Cf. note 67 *supra*, and "Cost of litigation", below.
74. See Baumbach et al., note 7 *supra*, para. 923, annot. 3; Zöller, note 2 *supra*, para. 923, annot. 1.
75. See para. 929 I, ZPO.
76. See para. 929 I, ZPO.
77. See para. 35, AusfG EuGÜbk; Baumbach et al., note 7 *supra*, para. 929, annot. 1.
78. See para. 922 II, ZPO.
79. See para. 317 I, ZPO.
80. Cf. paras. 166 *et seq.*, ZPO; Zöller, note 2 *supra*, para. 929, annot. 12.
81. After an oral hearing having been held; Zöller, note 2 *supra*, para. 929, annot. 5.
82. If an oral hearing has taken place, the order issuing the writ is to be served upon the applicant *ex officio*; see Zöller, *ibid.*, para. 929, annot. 6.

Contrary to the general rules, a writ of attachment may be enforced prior to its service on the opponent. The enforcement is, however, without effect if the writ of attachment is not served within one week after its enforcement and prior to the expiry of the one-month period set out in paragraph 929 II, ZPO.[83]

The purpose of the one-month period is to ensure that the writ of attachment is enforced as soon as possible, to warn the opponent, to prevent the building up of a "stock" of executory titles by the applicant, to inform the opponent about any writs issued against him in view of the fact that provisional attachment can be obtained in a simplified proceeding, and to avoid the possibility that a writ of attachment is enforced later although the circumstances have changed substantially in the meantime.[84]

Since enforcement measures might be time-consuming, it is recognised that it is sufficient for meeting the above deadlines if the applicant has commenced with the enforcement prior to the expiry of the said deadlines.[85]

Although it is sufficient for meeting the deadline of paragraph 929 II, ZPO, that the respective enforcement measures have been commenced and the applicant has done everything possible to consummate the enforcement, it also is recognised that only those enforcement measures which meet these prerequisites remain possible. In other words, it is not sufficient to commence one enforcement measure within the one-month period and to commence other enforcement measures only thereafter.[86]

If the one-month period is not met, the writ of attachment becomes inoperative *ipso jure*.[87] The writ of attachment then is set aside without a court examining its prerequisites, and any enforcement measures taken also are set aside. Moreover, all costs in connection with the attachment proceedings are borne by the applicant.[88]

Whether it is possible to obtain a new writ of attachment if the one-month period provided for in paragraph 929 II, ZPO, has been missed is disputed.[89] The admissibility of such new application depends on the local jurisdiction. Even if a new application is admitted, it must be noted that a "renewed" writ of attachment does not grant the priority of the former writ of attachment.[90]

Enforcement of a writ of attachment

It cannot be stressed enough that, since German civil procedure distinguishes between the issue of a writ of attachment on the one side and its enforcement on the other side, it is essential to observe the respective periods for enforcement. If not, all rights under the writ of provisional attachment are lost.[91]

The writ of attachment and its enforcement have the sole purpose of provisionally securing the applicant's alleged claim so that, if the applicant obtains an enforceable

83. See para. 929 III, ZPO.
84. Baumbach et al., note 7 *supra*, para. 929, annot. 2.
85. Zöller, note 2 *supra*, para. 929, annot. 11.
86. Baumbach et al., note 7 *supra*, para. 929, annot. 10.
87. *Ibid.* para. 929, annot. 2.
88. *Ibid.* para. 929, annot. 17.
89. *Ibid.* para. 929, annot. 17; Zöller, note 2 *supra*, para. 929, annot. 23.
90. Baumbach et al., note 7 *supra*, para. 929, annot. 17.
91. *Ibid.*, para. 928, annot. 1.

judgment in the main proceedings, such judgment can be enforced successfully. Accordingly, all enforcement measures are of a provisional character only, i.e., they are aimed at securing the applicant's position (priority) but do not give the claimant the right to satisfy his (alleged) claim by realising the securities so obtained.

Pursuant to paragraph 928, ZPO, the writ of attachment is to be enforced according to the general rules of civil procedure, unless paragraphs 928 *et seq.* provide otherwise.

Pursuant to paragraph 930, ZPO, movable properties are attached by seizure, which is effected by the bailiff's taking possession of the property, either by taking the goods away from the opponent/debtor, or by taking possession by means of fixing a bailiff's stamp (*Pfandsiegel*) to the seized goods or by attaching a notice of seizure (*Pfandanzeige*). The bailiff must take away from the opponent money, valuables, and securities. The same applies to other property if the opponent is likely to damage or remove it.

The bailiff may levy execution if the debtor's items of property are in the possession of the applicant himself or a third party, unless the third party refuses to consent. In the latter case, the applicant may attach the opponent's claim for recovery against the third party and then bring an action for recovery.

A valid seizure results in the attachment (*Verstrickung*) and an execution lien to the seized movable properties.

A realisation of the seized goods is not allowed. Paragraph 930 III, ZPO, provides, however, for an exemption to be granted by the court if the seized goods are likely to lose their value (e.g., fresh fruits) or if their retention would cause disproportionately high costs.

The applicant also is entitled to enforce the writ of attachment against the opponent's money claims (*Geldforderungen*), claims for the recovery or delivery of goods, or any other "economic rights" (*Vermögensrechte*). The applicant thereby becomes, for the purposes of execution, the creditor of the opponent's debtor, the garnishee.

In order to attach such money claims and other rights it is necessary to obtain an attachment order (*Pfändungsbeschluß*), to be issued by the court which has granted the writ of execution (paragraph 930 I 3, ZPO). The attachment order contains, *inter alia*, the specification of the alleged claim as to its creditor (opponent) and its debtor (garnishee) and the legal foundation of the claim. Such specification must be as precise as possible in order to be valid. If the applicant wishes to seize or "freeze" the opponent's bank accounts, the attachment order must set out the opponent's name, the bank's name, if possible the account number, and the legal relationship (e.g., banking contract or loan).

The attachment order is usually served on the debtor/opponent and the garnishee, but only service to the latter is essential. Again, on account of the provisional character of the writ of attachment, it is not possible for the applicant to obtain a transfer order (*Überweisungsbeschluß*) because this would constitute a realisation of the attached debt.

As regards the garnishee, his position is not weakened by the attachment. The debtor/opponent remains the holder of the claim so that the garnishee can plead all defences he could have pleaded against the debtor/opponent, e.g., set off. But, due to the garnishment order, the garnishee will no longer be discharged from his liability if he makes payments to the opponent after the garnishment order is served on him. Practically, this results in the garnishee making no further payment to the opponent.

The garnishee is, however, not under an obligation to declare, within two weeks after service of the attachment order, *inter alia*, whether he acknowledges the debt or whether he is prepared to make payments, whether other parties claim to be entitled to the debt, and whether there was a prior attachment for the benefit of other creditors.[92]

As regards real estate, paragraph 932, ZPO, provides that a compulsory security mortgage is to be registered in favour of the applicant. Again, it is not possible for the applicant to apply for a compulsory sale of the real estate until a final judgment in the main proceeding has been issued to his benefit.

In those rare cases where personal attachment has been ordered, the court may order that the opponent is to be arrested for a period not exceeding six months.

Setting aside writ of provisional attachment for changed circumstances

The possibility to appeal a decision whereby the issue of a writ of provisional attachment was denied, or to appeal its issue, as well as the opponent's option to request that the court set a deadline for the commencement of the main proceedings, have been set out above.[93] German civil procedure provides for an additional remedy, in particular for those cases in which the issue of the writ of attachment has become final[94] but the factual circumstances have changed in the meantime: Pursuant to paragraph 927, ZPO, the opponent may move for the setting aside of a writ of an attachment on account of (i) changed circumstances, or (ii) the offering of and putting up of sufficient security.

Changed circumstances may concern the attachment claim or the attachment reason. Examples regarding the falling-away of the attachment claim are:

(1) satisfaction of the claim by payment;
(2) rescission of law on which the attachment claim was based;
(3) the applicant's loss in the main proceedings.[95]

Examples regarding the falling-away of the attachment reason are:

(1) expiry of the period for the enforcement of the writ of attachment (paragraph 929 II, ZPO) without the applicant having enforced the writ,[96] or
(2) the possibility of enforcing the judgment in Germany so that the presumption of paragraph 917 II, ZPO,[97] no longer applies.[98]

Another foundation for a motion pursuant to paragraph 927 is the opponent's offering and actual putting up of sufficient security for the applicant's claim.

Since it is the primary purpose of paragraph 927, ZPO, to provide the opponent with a remedy to have a writ of attachment set aside after it has become final, a respective motion might not be possible if the opponent could also raise the change of circumstances in (still pending) appeal proceedings.[99] As regards objection-

92. See Zöller, note 2 *supra*, para. 930, annot. 3.
93. See "Proceedings without oral hearing" and "Proceedings with prior oral hearing", above.
94. See Zöller, note 2 *supra*, para. 927 annot. 1.
95. *Ibid.*, para. 927, annot. 5.
96. See "Service of and periods for enforcement of writ of provisional attachment", above.
97. See "Attachment reason (*Arrestgrund*)", above.
98. See Zöller, note 2, *supra*, para. 927, annot. 6.
99. Disputed: see Zöller, *ibid.*, para. 927; OLG Koblenz GRUR 89, p. 374.

proceedings (*Widerspruchverfahren*),[100] the opponent has a choice as to what kind of proceedings he wishes to bring.[101]

Competence lies with the court where the main proceedings are pending. In the absence of pending main proceedings, the court which has issued the writ of attachment is competent (paragraph 927 II, ZPO).

Opening of bankruptcy proceedings

If German bankruptcy proceedings are opened with respect to the applicant, the receiver will continue to exercise the applicant's rights in the attachment proceedings.

As regards bankruptcy proceedings with respect to the opponent, two circumstances must be distinguished:

(1) If a writ of attachment has been issued but not yet enforced when the bankruptcy proceedings are opened, the writ of attachment no longer can be enforced (paragraph 14, German Bankruptcy Act).

(2) If the applicant already has enforced the writ of attachment and obtained a lien (*Pfandrecht*) with respect to seized assets of the opponent, the applicant has a right to separate these assets from the bankrupt's estate (*Aussonderungsrecht*).[102]

Foreign bankruptcy proceedings, in principle, will be recognised in Germany, provided they do not interfere with German bankruptcy proceedings against the same bankrupt.

RECOGNITION AND ENFORCEMENT OF FOREIGN JUDGMENTS

German civil procedure provides for a dual system, i.e., recognition and enforcement must be distinguished from the obtaining and enforcing of a writ of attachment. The German judge examines, in the course of the enforcement proceedings, whether the foreign judgment meets the respective (negative) prerequisites set out in paragraph 328, ZPO, or, respectively, the applicable multilateral or bilateral treaties.

There is no particular procedure for the recognition of foreign judgments as such (apart from matrimonial matters). The foreign judgment is observed *ipso jure*, if the requirements for its recognition are met. Whether this is the case will be ascertained by the German court if proceedings for having the foreign judgment declared enforceable are brought pursuant to paragraphs 722 and 723, ZPO. Such proceedings are necessary since foreign judgments are not enforceable *per se*.

Prerequisites for recognition of foreign judgments

Paragraph 328, ZPO, defines the circumstances under which a foreign judgment is *not* to be recognised. These are[103]:

100. See "Proceedings without oral hearing" and "Proceedings with prior oral hearing", above.
101. See Zöller, note 2 *supra*.
102. See Baumbach et al., note 7 *supra*, Grundzüge, para. 704.
103. See Baumbach et al., *ibid.*, para. 328; Zöller note 2 *supra*, para. 328.

(1) The judgment has been rendered by a court belonging to a country the courts of which—according to German procedural law—did not have international jurisdiction for the case at hand.
(2) The writ of summons was not properly served on the defendant, or only with such delay that the defendant was prevented from defending himself properly.
(3) The foreign judgment is contradictory to another German or foreign judgment recognisable in Germany (*res judicata*), or is contradictory to another pending case (*lis pendens*).
(4) The foreign judgment violates basic principles of German law (*ordre public*).
(5) The foreign judgment has been rendered in a country which does not recognise German judgments (reciprocity).[104]

But, as set out above,[105] even if a foreign judgment is not recognisable in Germany, it still may be used as a means of presenting prima facie evidence that the applicant has an attachment claim.[106]

Prerequisites for enforcement of a foreign judgment

Foreign judgments are not enforceable *per se* and thus may be enforced only if declared enforceable pursuant to paragraphs 722 and 723, ZPO.

The German court competent for such proceedings is the court at the debtor's/defendant's domicile or residence or place of business. In the absence of such domicile or residence, the foreign plaintiff may turn to the court in the jurisdiction where assets of the debtor/defendant lie.

The foreign judgment will be declared enforceable if both of the following criteria are met (paragraph 722 I, ZPO):

(1) The foreign judgment must be final and binding according to the law under which it was rendered. Accordingly, the foreign judgment must be perfected in its jurisdiction of origin. A foreign judgment which is only provisionally enforceable may not be declared enforceable in Germany. The same applies, of course, to judgments or orders obtained in foreign interim and provisional proceedings.
(2) The recognition must not be excluded pursuant to paragraph 328, ZPO.[107]

As regards the subject matter of the proceedings, the German court will examine only whether the above criteria are met, i.e., it will not examine the merits of the case. It is, therefore, irrelevant whether the foreign judgment is correct, i.e., that the respective foreign procedural and substantive laws have been properly applied. It is to be noted that the debtor/defendant also may raise those objections against the claim as stated by the foreign judgment which have arisen only after the foreign judgment was rendered.[108]

104. The respective countries are set out by Baumbach et al., note 7 *supra*, para. 328, supplement.

105. See "Requirements for writ of preliminary attachment", above.

106. Prerequisite for obtaining of a writ of attachment; see "Requirements for writ of preliminary attachment", above.

107. See "Prerequisites for recognition of foreign judgments", above.

108. See BGHZ, 59, pp. 116 *et seq.*

The proceedings provide not only for the debtor being heard but also that the court may not grant leave for provisional enforcement of the debt as stated in the foreign judgment. This results in the proceedings being not only time-consuming and costly but also worthless, if there is a need for quickly attacking the German assets of the debtor. This, in turn, explains why provisional attachment proceedings might be of great importance in connection with the provisional enforcement of a foreign judgment.

Multilateral and bilateral treaties

The most important multilateral treaty is the European Convention on the Enforcement of Civil and Commercial Judgments, to which Germany, Belgium, France, Italy, Luxemburg, The Netherlands, Denmark, the United Kingdom, Eire, and Greece are signatories. Under this Convention, judgments are generally recognised, with the reservation of public policy and proper service of writ of summons. The Convention confines the debtor's right to formal objection against a decision which was rendered without his participation (Article 31). For further detail, reference should be made to the treaty itself and the respective German implementary law.[109]

The Hague Convention of 1 March 1954 provides for the enforcement of costs of legal proceedings.[110]

The Hague Convention of 2 October 1973 provides for special rules regarding the recognition and enforcement of maintenance judgments.

Other multilateral treaties include:

(1) International Convention on the Transport of Goods by Railway (CIM, section 56) of 7 February 1970;
(2) International Convention on the Transport of Goods by Road (CMR, section 31, number 3) of 19 May 1956; and
(3) International Convention on the Transport of Persons and Luggage by Railway (CIV, section 52) of 7 February 1970.

Bilateral treaties containing provisions regarding the recognition and enforcement of foreign judgments have been entered into with Switzerland, Italy, Austria, Belgium, Britain, Greece, The Netherlands, Tunisia, Israel, Norway, and Spain. To the extent these countries are also members of the European Convention, the provisions of the latter prevail over the respective bilateral treaty.[111]

RECOGNITION AND ENFORCEMENT OF FOREIGN ARBITRATION AWARDS

Respective multilateral treaties to which Germany is a signatory are the United Nations Convention regarding the Recognition and Enforcement of Foreign Arbitration Awards of 10 June 1958 and the European Convention concerning International Commercial Arbitration of 21 April 1961.

In addition, bilateral treaties providing for the recognition and enforcement of

109. See Baumbach et al., note 7 *supra*, pp. 2480 *et seq.*
110. *Ibid.*, pp. 2444 *et seq.*
111. *Ibid.*, p. 2481.

arbitral awards exist with Switzerland, Italy, the United States, Austria, Belgium, Greece, The Netherlands, the former Soviet Union, and Tunisia.[112]

COST OF LITIGATION

In Germany, costs follow the event, i.e., the loser must reimburse the successful party's costs and disbursements, in particular court and counsel's costs.

The litigation costs are laid down in various statutes. All computation relating to court costs and counsel's costs is made on the basis of the value of the disputed subject matter. Although the client may agree with his counsel that he is to be remunerated on an hourly basis (contingent fees are illegal *per se*), such agreement is binding *inter partes* only. Accordingly, the winning party may recover from the losing party only reimbursement of court and legal costs in the amount set out in the respective statutes. Costs exceeding these limits and resulting from an agreement with the lawyer retained are not to be reimbursed by the other party.

DR JÜRGEN J. SIEGER

112. *Ibid.*, pp. 2515 *et seq.*

CHAPTER 12

GREECE

INTRODUCTION

Obtaining security for a claim is equally as important as obtaining a favourable judgment on the main action. The attempts to obtain security may inevitably implicate foreign jurisdictions, and therefore it is material that a creditor has a basic idea as to the procedure and peculiarities of the jurisdictions in which he may apply for interim relief.

The Greek courts are generally open to provide interim relief to foreign creditors. Interim relief is afforded through the granting of any of the "security measures" provided for in the Greek Code on Civil Procedure.

In this chapter, the terms "security measures" and "interim relief" are used interchangeably.

AVAILABILITY OF GREEK COURTS TO FOREIGN CREDITORS

The Greek Constitution

Article 20, paragraph 1, of the Greek Constitution provides as follows: "Everybody is entitled to legal protection from the courts and is allowed to present before the courts his views on his rights or interests, in the way provided for by the laws." It is unanimously accepted by commentators and the judiciary that the above legal protection may be sought and granted either for obtaining a judgment on the merits of the case or for obtaining interim relief. Therefore, the Greek courts are, in principle, obliged under the Constitution to grant, when requested, interim relief to an applicant.[1]

The Greek Civil Code

According to Article 4 of the Greek Civil Code, "foreigners enjoy the same civil rights as Greek citizens". The word "enjoy" means that Greek law recognises the existence of a right and, furthermore, that Greek law allows the exercise of such right according, of course, to the provisions of the *lex causae*.[2] In the ambit of the exercise of a civil

1. Mitsopoulos, *On Civil Procedure* (1972), p. 79; Rammos, *Handbook on Civil Procedure III*, para. 542.
2. Krispis, *Private International Law*, p. 94; Vrellis, *Private International Law* (1988), p. 284.

right is included the right to apply to the court asking for legal protection. Furthermore, in the ambit of legal protection is included the right to apply to the court for interim relief. In view of the above, it may be said, as a general principle, that foreigners are, like Greek citizens, entitled to apply to the Greek courts, requesting interim relief for security of their civil rights.

The Greek Civil Procedure Code

According to Article 3 of the Civil Procedure Code (CPC), "The Greek courts have jurisdiction over Greek citizens and foreigners, provided they have jurisdiction (jurisdiction *ratione loci*) to try the case". The CPC sets out certain grounds on the basis of which the Greek courts have jurisdiction to decide on a case. (Once the jurisdiction of the courts is established, then the international jurisdiction of the Greek court is automatically established.) The main grounds upon which the jurisdiction of the Greek courts is established are the following:

(1) The domicile or the residence of the defendant (Article 22, CPC).
(2) The seat or the principal place of business of a body corporate (Article 25, CPC).
(3) The seat or the principal place of business of a body corporate in respect of company's disputes (Article 27, CPC).
(4) The situs of immovable property in case of disputes over this property or in case of a dispute over the lease of this property (Article 29, CPC).
(5) The domicile of the inheritor in the case of disputes over the inheritance (Article 30, CPC).
(6) The place of the court of the main action where a consequent action is instituted (Article 31, CPC).
(7) The place of the court first seized of the matter in respect of interrelated claims (Article 31, 3, CPC).
(8) The place of the court seized of the main action where a counter claim is introduced (Article 34, CPC).
(9) In the case of a claim arising out of a criminally punishable act, the place of the court where the act was committed (Article 35, CPC).
(10) The place where a contract was concluded or the place where a contract was to be performed in respect of disputes arising from a contract (Article 33, CPC).
(11) In respect of pecuniary claims against persons not having a domicile in Greece, the place where the defendant has assets or the property in question is situated (Article 40, CPC).
(12) The place where the security measure is to be executed (Article 683, 3, CPC).

May a foreign creditor apply for interim relief?

In view of the above, it appears that any foreigner, whether a physical person or a body corporate, is entitled to apply to the Greek courts requesting interim relief in the same way and to the same extent and degree as a Greek national, provided that the Greek court has jurisdiction on the basis of any of the grounds above. It should be further noted that the Greek courts shall grant interim relief to a foreign creditor irrespective of whether the litigants are foreigners, the main proceedings may be tried in Greece or before a foreign court or arbitration tribunal, or the substantive right in respect of which the Greek courts are requested to provide interim relief has been acquired by virtue of a foreign legal system or the domestic law. The following examples are useful:

(a) A Dutch company maintained a claim against a Greek company arising out of a sales contract. The Dutch company applied to the Athens court requesting the conservative attachment of any assets of the Greek company for security of its claim. The court granted the security measure requested by its Judgment No. 12182/82. The sales contract provided for Greek law and jurisdiction. The Athens court had jurisdiction, *inter alia*, on the basis of Article 25, CPC ("the seat of the defendant").

(b) An English bank maintained a claim against a Saudi subject arising out of a loan agreement. The agreement provided for English law and jurisdiction. The debtor was the legal owner of a flat in Athens. The bank applied to the Athens court asking leave to register a prenotation of hypothec against the flat for security of the English court proceedings. The Athens court, by its Judgment No. 17037/89, granted the security measure requested. The Athens court had jurisdiction on the basis of Article 40, CPC ("the respondent had assets in Greece").

Must a security be posted?

A foreigner seeking security for his claim from a Greek court is not required to lodge any form of security because he is a foreigner.[3] Of course, Article 649, CPC, provides that the Greek courts in granting interim relief may order the applicant to lodge a security. However, such a provision applies equally to foreigners and Greeks, and the Greek courts exercise such a discretion very exceptionally.

Sovereign immunity

Finally, in this respect, it is relevant to mention Article 689, CPC, which provides: "The application for security measures against a foreign state is inadmissible without previously obtaining the permission of the Minister of Justice." According to the prevailing view, the Article applies where the application is brought against the foreign state itself and not against foreign companies or enterprises owned or controlled by foreign states.[4]

SECURITY MEASURES UNDER GREEK LAW

The security measure is a form of legal protection afforded by the Greek courts through a special procedure (security measure proceedings), provided by Articles 682 to 703, CPC. The procedure is flexible and speedy, so that the creditor's claim may be secured in a satisfactory way at the earliest possible time.

3. Athens Court, Judgment No. 8783/1976; *Commercial Law Revue*, 26, p. 610.
4. Beis, *On Civil Procedure*, vol. V, p. 88.

Since the main proceedings on the merits of the case take a considerable time to be concluded, the need for obtaining security on a claim is of paramount importance, and therefore security is requested in most cases before the main proceedings are instituted. This has the advantage that several cases are settled after the security measure is granted by the court, since the litigants either accept the prima facie judgment of the court as a reflection of the true position of the case, or the debtor considers that the security measure granted against him is sometimes more onerous than the expectation of a favourable judgment for him on the merits of the case.

The basic characteristic of the security measures is that the legal protection afforded through them is provisional, since the secured right shall be fully and finally decided upon in the course of the main proceedings on the merits. Article 695, CPC, specifically provides that the judgment issued in the security measure proceedings creates a provisional *res judicata* and does not have any bearing on the main proceedings. This is why the prevailing view regards security measures, in principle, as an "accessory" to the main proceedings, in the sense that the aim of the "security measure" is the security of a claim pending its determination by the final court judgment.[5]

Who orders the security measures?

Security measures are ordered by the courts (Article 683, CPC). The one-member court of first instance is normally vested with the power to hear and decide on all applications for security measures. However, where the magistrates' court is competent to decide the merits of a claim, it is also competent to hear and decide on applications for security measures (the magistrates' court is, *inter alia*, competent to try cases where the amount involved does not exceed drs 1,000,000). Any other court (i.e., the multi-member court of first instance, the Court of Appeal, and even the Supreme Court, when trying a case on its merits) seized of the merits of a case is competent to hear and decide on an application for a security measure (Article 684, CPC).

Basic requirements for granting a security measure

For the Greek courts to grant a security measure, the applicant must satisfy two basic requirements:

(1) He has to establish an arguable case on the merits (Article 690, CPC).
(2) He has to show that there is an imminent risk to the eventual satisfaction of his claim, or an urgent need justifying the granting of the security measure requested.

The issue of the imminent risk or the urgent need are fundamental prerequisites for the court to grant a security measure. If the court finds that the claim of the applicant, although prima facie established, is not at risk or there is no urgent case, then no security measure shall be granted and the court will let the case be decided on the merits in the course of the main proceedings (Article 682, CPC).

5. Beis, *op. cit.*, vol. V, p. 6.

Inter partes hearing

The application for a security measure is heard by the court *inter partes*. This is based on a fundamental principle of Greek law (Article 20, paragraph 2, Greek Constitution), since no one may be condemned unheard. However, in exceptional cases whereby serious urgency or irreparable damage is imminent, the court may hear an application *ex parte* (Article 687, 1, CPC).

The court's judgment

The court is free to grant the most appropriate security measure, and it is not bound to grant that requested by the applicant (Article 692, 1, CPC). Furthermore, the court may consider that more than one security measure should be granted for the effective protection of the applicants' claim (Article 692, 2, CPC). The law gives a discretion to the court in granting security measures and, in so doing, it is expected that the court will exercise its discretion in such a way as to secure the applicant's claim by granting the less onerous measure for the debtor, provided such measure is effective (Article 692, 3, CPC).

As already mentioned, the security measure is not allowed to provide the applicant with full satisfaction of his claim, but should merely serve the need to secure the claim (Article 692, 4, CPC). Therefore, the court will, apart from certain exceptional instances, decline to grant a security measure if the applicant satisfies his claim by this measure.[6]

Article 692, 5, CPC, specifically provides that the security measures should not prejudice the rights of third persons, particularly in case the applicant's claim is conditional.

Execution of the judgment ordering a security measure

In general, security measures are executed in the way provided in respect of the execution of judgment issued on the merits (Article 700, 1, CPC). A copy judgment is sufficient for the purposes of the court bailiff, who, on the basis of that, proceeds to execute the judgment ordering a security measure (Article 700, 2, CPC).

Is the court's judgment granting a security measure final?

The judgment granting a security measure (or dismissing an application for a security measure) is not subject to appeal before the Court of Appeal or to any other of the three specific legal remedies provided for by the CPC, i.e.:

(1) opposition against a default judgment when the defendant was duly summoned to appear;
(2) appeal before the Supreme Court on legal grounds; or

6. Beis, *The Limits of Provisional Judicial Protection* (1980); Athens Court Judgment No. 15647/83, *Nomiko Vina*, 32, p. 315; Athens Court Judgment No. 2139/81, *Nomiko Vina*, 29, p. 723.

(3) application for reviewing a final judgment for certain reasons (Article 699, CPC).

However, since the judgment is of a provisional character, the CPC provides that it may be revoked either partly or in full in the following instances:

(1) Until the hearing of the main proceedings, the court which granted the security measure may revoke or amend the security measure granted, where there is a change of the factual background of the case justifying such revocation or amendment (Article 696, 3).
(2) The court competent to try the main action may revoke or amend the security measure granted (Article 697).
(3) Where a security measure was granted *ex parte*, the debtor may apply for the revocation or amendment of the security measure.

Where the security measure may have prejudiced the rights of a third party, such third party may request the revocation or the amendment of the security measure (Article 696, 1, CPC). It should also be noted that the court is bound to revoke the security measure if:

(1) a final (not subject to appeal) judgment on the merits has been issued;
(2) a final judgment on the merits has been issued and executed;
(3) a settlement has been agreed on the merits of the case; and
(4) it is after the expiry of 30 days from the suspension of the main proceedings (Article 698, CPC).

Security measures and the main proceedings

As mentioned above, the security measure proceedings are closely related to the main proceedings. Therefore the law expects that when a security measure is granted, the main proceedings, if not already started, will follow promptly. Article 693, CPC, provides that if the security measure was granted before the commencement of the main proceedings, the judge may fix a time for the commencement of the main proceedings of not less than 30 days. However, such a discretion is not exercised very frequently by the courts.

It should be mentioned in this context that with regard to three specific security measures (conservative attachment, judicial sequestration and provisional adjudication of a debt) the CPC specifically provides that the main proceedings should start within 30 days from the granting of the security measure. If the applicant does not commence the main proceedings within the time stipulated by the court or provided by the CPC, the security measure is *ipso jure* revoked.[7]

Security measure procedure

The applicant submits a written application to the court containing, *inter alia*, a brief but nevertheless comprehensive description of the factual background of the case, details as to the imminent risk or urgency, the amount involved in respect of any pecuniary claim, as well as the security measure(s) requested (Article 688, CPC).

7. Beis, *On Civil Procedure*, pp. 166–170; Athens Court Judgment No. 15279/69, *Nomiko Vina*, 17, p. 1220.

The presiding judge fixes the hearing date and orders the time and mode for summoning the respondent. The summoning may be made either by a court bailiff, or by telegram or even by telephone, depending on the urgency of the matter (Article 686, CPC).

At the filing of the application, either *ipso jure* or normally at the request of the applicant, the court may issue a provisional order with regard to the steps which should be taken until the issuance of its judgment on the application. The judge exercises such discretion where he considers that the time until the issuance of his judgment may prejudice the applicant's claim. Such order is normally granted *ex parte*, and it is valid until the issuance of the judgment (Article 691, 2, CPC).

At the hearing, both litigants argue their case before the judge, examine and cross-examine witnesses and submit their written pleadings with all supporting documents available. According to the established practice, the parties are given two to three days after the hearing date for submission of their files.

The judge is entitled to take into consideration any evidential material produced to him, and he is further allowed to collect himself evidence not submitted by the parties (Articles 690–691, CPC).

The judge issues his judgment at the earliest possible time. The judgment should, *inter alia*, mention the basic particulars of the claim secured and the particular security measure granted (Article 691, 3, CPC).

Third parties interested to intervene in the security measure proceedings may do so orally by entering an appearance at the hearing date (Article 686, CPC).

SPECIFIC SECURITY MEASURES

The security measures provided by Greek law are the following:

(1) conservative attachment;
(2) prenotation of hypothec;
(3) judicial sequestration;
(4) lodging of guarantee;
(5) provisional regulation of an affair/relationship;
(6) provisional adjudication of a debt; and
(7) seal, unseal, inventory, and public deposit.

Conservative attachment

The conservative attachment of property is a security measure granted by the court aimed at the "preservation" of the attached property until a final judgment is issued on the merits of the claim. This "preservation" is effected by the fact that the debtor is deprived of the administration of his attached property and, furthermore, he is prohibited to part with the attached property. The "conservative attachment" is ordered for the security of claims of a pecuniary nature.[8]

8. Beis, *op. cit.*, Art. 708, 396.

Property subject to conservative attachment

Conservative attachment may be ordered against any movable or immovable property, proprietary rights or claims, or any other property of the respondent, either in his hands or in the hands of a third party (Article 707, CPC).

Assets not subject to conservative attachment

Conservative attachment cannot be effected on property which is deemed unattachable according to the provisions on the "compulsory attachment of CPC" (such as, *inter alia*, goods for the personal use of the respondent and his family, food for three months, books, musical instruments, the salaries of the employees) or against goods which are liable to perish quickly (such as flowers, fruit, and possibly meat) (Article 710, CPC).

Conservative attachment of perishable goods

Perishable goods which do not perish swiftly as provided for in Article 710, CPC, are subject to conservative attachment. However, where the attached goods are perishable or their maintenance is expensive compared with their value, the court may order the sale of such goods. The sale proceeds are the subject of the attachment (Article 719, CPC).

How conservative attachment is effected

Conservative attachment of movable property or of proprietary rights is effected by a court bailiff. In particular, the court bailiff draws up a report of attachment in which he describes the goods attached and an estimate of their value. Copies of such report are served on the respondent and the competent magistrate (Article 711, CPC). A trustee of the attached goods is appointed at the time the attachment is effected (Article 716, 1, CPC). Usually the debtor is appointed as trustee for the goods, since he is normally in the possession of the goods. However, the court has discretion to appoint another person (Article 717, CPC). Where the attached goods are money, these are deposited with the "Deposits and Loans Fund" (Article 712, 2, CPC).

Conservative attachment of immovable property or proprietary rights on this property is effected by the service of the court's judgment on the respondent and on the Real Estate Registry of the place where the immovable property is situated (Article 714, CPC).

Conservative attachment of movables or claims in the hands of a third party is effected by serving on the third party the court's judgment on the basis, and in pursuance of which, that the movables or the claims are attached. The court's judgment should be accompanied by an order made by the applicant and addressed to the third party, to the effect that the third party should not deliver the goods or pay his debt—*pro tanto*—to his creditor (i.e., respondent in the security measure proceedings) and should not part with the goods or the debt in question until a final judgment on the merits of the case—between the applicant and the respondent—is issued.

In reply to the above order, the third party has a duty to make a "declaration" within eight days from the time he was served with the court's judgment and the order to the magistrates' court where he resides, stating clearly whether he possesses the goods or owes the debt. In the case of a "positive declaration", a period of inactivity follows until a final judgment on the main action is issued. In the case of a "negative declaration" or "non-declaration", the matter comes to an end. The applicant has the right to dispute the negative declaration, or non-declaration or untrue declaration of the third party, and he may also have a claim for damages against the third party in tort (Articles 712, 982–990, CPC).

Conservative attachment of a vessel or an aeroplane is effected by serving the court's judgment on the respondent and, in the case of a Greek flag vessel or an aeroplane registered in the Greek Registry, by serving on the appropriate Registry. The court's judgment should specify the particulars of the vessel or the aeroplane and the amount for which the attachment is ordered (Article 713, CPC).

Effects of conservative attachment

The effects of the conservative attachment are the following:

(1) Any disposal of the attached property (including sale, registration of hypothec, registration of pledge) by the respondent is forbidden and is, *ipso jure*, invalid *vis-à-vis* the applicant. In the case of conservative attachment of property or a claim in the hands of a third party, the delivery/disposal of the goods or the transfer, set off or discharge of the claim by the third party to the debtor/respondent is equally forbidden and is, *ipso jure*, invalid *vis-à-vis* the applicant (Article 715, paragraph 1, 4, CPC).

(2) The property attached, either movable or immovable, is put under a trustee. In case of attachment of money, negotiable instruments, or jewellery, these are deposited with the "Deposits and Loans Fund". In case of conservative attachment of vessels or aeroplanes, the sailing of the vessel or the take off of the plane is prohibited.

Conservative attachment on assets already attached

Article 921, CPC, specifically provides that conservative attachment or compulsory attachment is allowed to be effected on assets already conservatively attached. Furthermore, the prevailing view is to the effect that a conservative attachment can also be effected on assets already compulsorily attached.[9]

Conservative attachment and the main proceedings

The main proceedings on the merits of the case, if not already commenced, should be instituted within 30 days from the day the court's judgment ordering the conservative

9. Beis, *op. cit.*, vol. V, p. 387; Rammos, *Introduction to Civil Procedure*, II, p. 1861; Evros Court Judgment No. 46/71, D 3,297.

attachment was served on the respondent. If this period expires without the main proceedings having been commenced, then the conservative attachment loses, *ipso jure*, its validity (Article 715, 5, CPC).

Conservative attachment (freezing) of bank accounts

In theory, the conservative attachment of bank accounts may be effected by following the steps for attaching property in the hands of a third party. As outlined above, the third party, once the court's judgment and the order of the applicant is served on him, is obliged to make a declaration stating whether he possesses the goods so attached. In respect of attachment of bank accounts, the bank in its capacity as third party should declare to the applicant the details of the material account(s); in the case of a positive declaration, the attachment is effected. However, according to Law Decree 1059/71, bank accounts in Greek banks are confidential. Furthermore, the disclosure by banks of information concerning accounts to a third party is a criminal offence. (The disclosure is basically permitted in case of a criminal offence committed in Greece, provided such disclosure is necessary to the investigation and punishment of such offence.) In view of the above, the judiciary unanimously accepts that Greek banks (including foreign banks doing business in Greece) have no obligation to make any declaration with regard to the accounts kept by them. Therefore, Greek courts decline to order conservative attachment of bank accounts in view of the fact that the third party (i.e., the banks) is not allowed to make the necessary declaration.[10]

This view has been strongly criticised by many commentators, who agree that the conservative attachment of bank accounts is perfectly possible.[11] However, the situation, as it stands today, is to the effect that conservative attachment of bank accounts in a Greek or foreign bank operating in Greece does not appear to be possible.

Prenotation of hypothec

Right of hypothec under the Greek Civil Code

The hypothec is a proprietary right, provided by the Greek Civil Code (Articles 1257–1345), registered on a stranger's immovable property and aiming at the security of the creditor's claim through the auction of the property so burdened, in which (auction) the hypothec-ed creditor shall enjoy priority over other creditors.

Obtaining the right of hypothec

The right of registering a hypothec may be afforded to a creditor either by statute (Article 1262, Civil Code), or by final and enforceable judgment (including foreign judgments and arbitration awards declared enforceable in Greece), or by an agreement with the debtor (Articles 1263, 1265–1266, Civil Code).

10. Supreme Court Judgment No. 3/1993; Athens Court of Appeal Judgment No. 7960/1976.
11. Mitsopoulos, *op. cit.*, para. 13.

Security provided through registration of hypothec

The right of hypothec follows the property in the hands of any buyer of the property and, furthermore, where the hypothec-ed property is auctioned, the creditor enjoys priority in the auction proceeds over other creditors, who enjoy no priority or privilege.[12] Therefore, it is recognised that the hypothec is a good security for the creditor's claim.

Prenotation of hypothec under the Greek Civil Code

It is often the case that a creditor cannot secure his claim by registering a hypothec, since he may not have obtained a final judgment, or the statute does not afford to him the right of registering a hypothec, or his debtor does not consent to his registering a hypothec. In these circumstances, the creditor may secure his claim by registering a prenotation of hypothec on his debtor's immovable property.

The right of prenotation of hypothec is afforded to the creditor only by way of a court's judgment (Article 1274, Civil Code). It is a hypothec conditional on the obtaining by the creditor of a final judgment and the conversion of the prenotation into a proper hypothec within 90 days of obtaining the final judgment. Therefore, the prenotation of hypothec gives a right of expectation to the creditor to obtain a hypothec, which is considered as registered *ex tunc* (i.e., as from the time the prenotation was registered) once the above two conditions are fulfilled (Article 1277, Civil Code).

Prenotation of hypothec as security measure under the Code of Civil Procedure

As mentioned above, under the civil law the prenotation of hypothec is a proprietary right on immovable property. Under the provisions of the CPC, the prenotation of hypothec is a security measure ordered by the court for securing the creditor's claim in the way provided for in the preceding paragraphs relating to the hypothec. The court's judgment should always specify the amount for which the prenotation of hypothec is ordered (Article 706, CPC).

According to the prevailing judicial view, the prenotation of hypothec may be registered against immovable property belonging not only to the debtor but also to a third party, provided the third party gives his consent before the court.[13] The prenotation takes effect upon the registration of the court's judgment in the appropriate Real Estate Registry (Article 1276, Civil Code).

Conversion of prenotation of hypothec into hypothec

For the creditor to enjoy the security provided for by the prenotation of hypothec, he must convert the prenotation into a hypothec within 90 days from the issuance of the final judgment on the merits of the case. The conversion is a simple procedure (Article 1323, 2, Civil Code). Failing such conversion, the prenotation of hypothec is extinguished as a right.

12. Georgiadis-Stathopoulos, *Civil Code*, vol. VI, p. 419.

13. Georgiadis-Stathopoulos, *op. cit.*, vol. VI, p. 490; Supreme Court Judgment No. 1079/81, *Nomiko Vina*, 31, p. 194.

Judicial sequestration

Article 725, CPC

The CPC provides that the court can order as a security measure the judicial sequestration of movables or immovable property or an enterprise if there is dispute as to ownership, possession, or any other aspect in respect of such property.

Nature of claims secured by sequestration

Sequestration is ordered only if there is a dispute over the goods sought to be put under sequestration. In other words, judicial sequestration secures the parties' alleged and disputed rights over particular goods so that the successful plaintiff, in the main action, will be able to take possession or ownership of the goods sequestrated. Thus, the court does not have the power to replace the security measure of judicial sequestration even by the provision of a guarantee, since the other security measures are not good security for the applicant's right over goods but only through the goods (i.e., by their auctioning).[14]

Effect of sequestration

Judicial sequestration results in the removal of the sequestrated goods from the debtor's possession and their delivery to the custody of the sequestrator appointed by the court. It also prohibits the disposal of the goods by the debtor.[15]

The court's judgment

The court's judgment ordering the sequestration of goods should identify the goods and should also appoint a sequestrator, into whose custody the goods must be delivered. When the goods are capable of being deposited (money, negotiable instruments or jewellery) they are deposited with the "Deposits and Loans Fund". The court's judgment is immediately enforceable.

The sequestrator

The court may appoint as sequestrator any person at its absolute discretion. The applicant or the person in possession of the goods at the time the judgment is issued may be so appointed. Where an enterprise is put under sequestration, the court should appoint the debtor as sequestrator. The sequestrator may be replaced by a court order. The main duty of the sequestrator is to keep the goods until the final judgment is issued.

Provision of guarantee

The provision of a guarantee by the respondent, following a court's judgment, is recognised as a security measure for the satisfaction of the applicant's claim when a final judgment is issued.

14. Beis, *op. cit.*, vol. V, pp. 602–603; Tzifras, *On Security Measures* (1980), p. 224.
15. Beis, *op. cit.*, vol. V, p. 598; Tzifras, *op. cit.*, p. 214.

Nature of claims securable by guarantee

The provision of a guarantee is ordered by the court particularly for the security of claims of a pecuniary nature. It may also be ordered for security of other rights of the applicant (Article 704, CPC).

Form of guarantee

The guarantee, ordered by the court as a "security measure", may take the form of either a cash deposit or a deposit of shares/bonds, or the provision of a letter of guarantee by a bank, Greek or foreign, operating in Greece. The bank guarantee is, of course, the most usual form of guarantee (Articles 163, 164, CPC). In the case of cash and shares or bonds, these are deposited with the "Deposits and Loans Fund", and the appropriate receipts are submitted to the Secretary of the court which ordered the provision of a guarantee. The bank guarantee is submitted directly to the court's secretary. The court is not allowed to order any form other than a bank guarantee. However, the parties are free to agree on any form of guarantee, and such agreement may be sanctioned by the court (Article 162, CPC).[16]

Is the provision of guarantee an effective security measure?

The provision of a guarantee depends exclusively on the respondent, since there is no mechanism available to compel the respondent to provide a guarantee.[17] Therefore, applicants do not normally request such a security measure, preferring other types provided for by the law.

Replacement of other security measure by the provision of guarantee

Since the guarantee (if provided by the respondent) is the most attractive security measure, it is specifically provided in the CPC (Article 705, 1) that the court is bound, if requested, to substitute it for any measure ordered for the security of a claim of a pecuniary nature. Normally, court judgments ordering a security measure specifically provide for the respondent to substitute a guarantee.

Temporary regulation of a relationship

Article 731

Article 731 of CPC provides that the court may grant a security measure by ordering the respondent either to perform, omit, or tolerate the performance of a specific act.

PREREQUISITES FOR GRANTING AN ARTICLE 731 SECURITY MEASURE

The basic prerequisites for the granting of any security measure (i.e., establishing an arguable case on the merits and the existence of an imminent risk or urgent need for the granting of a security measure) should, of course, be satisfied. Regarding the first

16. Beis, *op. cit.*, vol. V, p. 274.
17. Beis, *op. cit.*, vol. V, p. 290; Tzifras, *op. cit.*, p. 115.

prerequisite, it should be shown that, under the *lex causae* of the case, the debtor has an obligation to perform, omit, or tolerate a specific act. In other words, the court may order the debtor provisionally to perform, omit, or tolerate a specific act only if he has the same obligation according to the substantive law.[18]

ENFORCEMENT OF THE COURT'S JUDGMENT

The court's judgment ordering the debtor to perform, omit, or tolerate a specific act is executed by the service on the debtor of a copy judgment with the written order of the applicant to comply with the contents of the judgment (Article 700, 2, CPC). If the debtor fails to comply with the contents of the judgment, the court normally provides that the debtor is subject to a fine and/or to personal detainment for up to one year (Articles 946–947, CPC).

Article 732

Article 732, CPC, provides that the court may grant, at its discretion, any security measure appropriate under the circumstances so that the right of the applicant may be secured or preserved, or an affair or relationship be adjusted or regulated. It has been realised that, in certain cases, the security measures provided for by law are not good and sufficient security for the applicant's rights, and therefore the law provides a very wide discretion to the court to grant the appropriate security measures under the circumstances.[19]

Like any security measure, the provisional relief ordered by the court on the basis of Article 732 (and Article 731 above) should not lead to the full satisfaction of the applicants' right.

Provisional adjudication of a debt

The law provides as a security measure the provisional adjudication of a debt to the applicant. In particular, in certain cases (Article 728, CPC), i.e., outstanding wages, compensation in respect of employees' accidents, claims for alimony between spouses, the court may provisionally adjudicate to the applicant up to half of the claim, prima facie established, provided that there is an urgent case, in that the applicant's welfare, life, or health may be at stake.

The enforcement of the court's judgment starts with the service on the debtor of a copy judgment. Twenty-four hours thereafter, the applicant may proceed to execute the provisional judgment in the same way as the final judgment. The law specifically provides that the amount provisionally adjudicated is not subject to conservative attachment, seizure, set off, or assignment (Article 729, 3, CPC).

The applicant must commence the main action on the merits within 30 days of the issuance of the court's judgment (Article 729, 5, CPC). If the court dismisses the main action, the applicant must refund the amount temporarily adjudicated.

18. Beis, *op. cit.*, vol. V, pp. 792–793; Rammos, *op. cit.*, para. 615, 1891.
19. Beis, *op. cit.*, vol. V, pp. 797–798; Tzifras, *op. cit.*, p. 254.

Seal, unseal, inventory, and public deposit

Whenever there is a real risk that goods (normally movables) may be stolen, embezzled, hidden, damaged, or replaced, the court may order, as a security measure, that such goods are sealed for the security of the applicant's right on the sealed goods. The court's judgment appoints the person to effect the seal (usually a notary public or magistrate) and the trustee of the sealed goods.

The practical result of the seal is that the sealed goods cannot be removed. However, according to the prevailing view, the sealed goods may change their legal status, i.e., be sold or pledged; this is the main difference compared with the security measures of conservative attachment and sequestration.

The step which normally follows the seal and unseal is the inventory of the sealed goods. The public deposit of goods capable of being deposited may follow the inventory or may be ordered as an independent security measure by the court (Articles 737–738, CPC).[20]

BILATERAL AGREEMENTS AND INTERNATIONAL CONVENTIONS

Enforcement of security measures outside Greece

The prevailing view is that Greek courts cannot grant a security measure if such measure is to be enforced abroad.[21] The reasoning is mainly based on grounds of comity, ineffectiveness of the order, and futility. The same applies *mutatis mutandis* in respect of orders of foreign courts sought to be enforced in Greece. The above is subject, of course, to any bilateral or international convention to which Greece is a party.

Bilateral agreements

Greece has signed agreements relating to the recognition and enforcement of judgments with the following countries: Yugoslavia (Law Decree 4007/1959); Romania (Law 429/1974); Bulgaria (Law 841/1978); Lebanon (Law 1099/1980); Hungary (Law 1149/1981); Poland (Law 1184/1981); the former USSR (Law 1242/1982); Czechoslovakia (Law 1323/1983); Syria (Law 1450/1984); and Cyprus (Law 1548/1985).

The agreement between Greece and Germany of 4 November 1961 has been overridden by the Brussels Convention of 1968. The agreement between Greece and Cyprus provides specifically that it does not apply in respect of court judgments ordering security measures (Article 32, b). The agreement with Czechoslovakia specifically provides that court judgments ordering security measures are recognised and enforced, provided that a similar security measure may be issued and enforced by the courts of the country of reception (Article 23, 2). The other bilateral agreements do not specifically provide for the recognition and enforceability of security measures.

20. Tzifras, *op. cit.*, p. 437; Beis, *op. cit.*, vol. V, p. 926.

21. Beis, *op. cit.*, vol. V, p. 47; Athens Court Judgment No. 9931/1978, *Nomiko Vina*, 27, p. 1354; Volos Court Judgment No. 261/1983, *Commercial Law Review*, 34, p. 645; Athens Court Judgment No. 9949/1991, *Shipping Law Review*, 19, 436.

The prevailing view, however, is that the agreements allow the recognition and enforcement of security measure judgments, under the strict condition that the security measure sought was granted *inter partes*.[22] There is no reported case on this issue.

The Brussels Convention 1968

Greece has signed the Brussels Convention of 1968 on Civil Jurisdiction and the Enforcement of Foreign Judgments, which came into force on 1 April 1989. Court judgments granting security measures are included in the meaning of "judgments", as provided in Article 25 of the Convention.[23] Therefore, foreign court judgments ordering security measures may be enforced in Greece as provided in the Convention, under the sole condition that the court judgments must have been issued *inter partes*. There is no reported case on this issue.

IMPACT OF DEBTOR'S BANKRUPTCY ON INTERIM RELIEF

A merchant (whether a physical person or a body corporate) may be declared bankrupt by the court, provided he has suspended his payments generally and permanently. The court appoints, *inter alia*, an official receiver who will be in charge of the bankruptcy procedure and the actual date of the suspension of the payments (the period between the date of suspension of the payments and the date of issuance of the judgment is called the "suspect period").

The main effects of the debtor's bankruptcy towards his creditors are:

(1) The creditors are deprived of their right to pursue their claims directly against the debtor and independently of the bankruptcy procedure; instead they can only satisfy their claim by the bankruptcy procedure and through the bankruptcy property.

(2) All creditors' claims following the debtor become due at the time the court declares the debtor bankrupt.

(3) The creditors' claims do not earn interest as from the issuance of the court's judgment.

(4) The receiver is bound to register a mortgage against any immovable property of the debtor in favour of the creditors.

Further to the issuance of the court's judgment, the receiver takes all the necessary steps to trace the assets of the debtor, and then he proceeds with the verification and admission of the creditors' claims. The bankruptcy procedure may be terminated either by the settlement of the creditors' claims or by the liquidation of the debtor's property and its distribution among the creditors.

Can a creditor obtain interim relief after bankruptcy?

After the bankruptcy of the debtor, the creditor cannot commence or continue any court proceedings against his debtor aiming at the satisfaction or the security of his

22. Beis, *op. cit.*, vol. V, p. 343.
23. Kerameas, Kremlis, Tagaras, *The Brussels Convention* (1989), p. 208; Beis, *op. cit.*, vol. V, p. 343.

claim. The creditor can only follow the steps provided by Greek law on bankruptcy in order to participate with other creditors in the bankruptcy procedure and satisfy his claim through the settlement agreed or through the liquidation of the debtor's assets.[24] However, those creditors whose claims are secured by a mortgage or pledge or who enjoy a "specific privilege" under Article 976, CPC, may pursue their claims outside the bankruptcy procedure and satisfy their respective claims in full.[25] Furthermore, creditors having claims which enjoy a "general privilege" under Greek law (Article 975, CPC) (i.e., claims such as those under employment contracts or for lawyers) must follow the bankruptcy procedure but enjoy priority over the other creditors in the satisfaction of their claims.

Effect of debtor's bankruptcy on an executed security measure

As a general rule, it may be said that the impact of the debtor's bankruptcy on security measures is closely related to the impact of the bankruptcy on the pursuance of the main action.

Conservative attachment

Once the debtor is declared bankrupt, a conservative attachment already registered against his assets becomes in essence ineffective. The whole property of the debtor (the bankruptcy property) is administered by the receiver, and therefore the conservative attachment serves no practical purpose.

Prenotation of hypothec

This security measure remains in principle unaffected by the debtor's bankruptcy. In particular, the creditor who has obtained a prenotation of hypothec on the debtor's immovable property at least 10 days before the "suspect period" is entitled to pursue his claim under the prenotation directly against his debtor, represented by the receiver, outside the bankruptcy procedure, and enjoy full satisfaction of the claim, in the same way as the creditor who has obtained a mortgage on the debtor's immovable property, subject to the timely conversion of the prenotation into a hypothec.[26] The prenotation of hypothec registered within the "suspect period" or within 10 days before it is *ipso jure* void towards the debtor's creditors (Article 537, Commercial Code).

Judicial sequestration

Where judicial sequestration has been ordered in respect of a dispute over the legal ownership of goods, it remains valid until the final judgment of the case, which is conducted between the applicant and the receiver representing the debtor.[27] In other cases, the impact of the debtor's bankruptcy depends on the nature of the creditor's claim, its relation to the bankruptcy property, and the decision of the receiver.

24. Rokas, *On Bankruptcy* (10th ed.), p. 27.
25. Rokas, *op. cit.*, p. 136; Levantis, *On Bankruptcy*, p. 97.
26. Supreme Court Judgment No. 137/77, 25 November, 1145.
27. Rokas, *op. cit.*, p. 158.

Provision of guarantee

In the event that the debtor has provided a guarantee by depositing funds or bonds/shares with the "Deposits and Loans Fund", his bankruptcy is irrelevant since the creditor is vested by statute (Article 166, CPC) with the right of pledge on the funds/bonds/shares, and therefore he can pursue his claim outside the bankruptcy procedure.

In the event of a bank guarantee, unless the court's judgment is suitably qualified as to the bankruptcy of the debtor to render the guarantee invalid and ineffective, the general rule is that the bankruptcy of the primary debtor does not affect the effectiveness and validity of the guarantee.[28] The possibility of such qualified judgment is, of course, remote, and it is not intended to deal with this theoretical point in this chapter; it suffices to say that such a judgment appears never to have been requested or granted, and it may require that the request for such a qualification is made by the applicant, which, in ordinary cases, seems extremely unlikely.

Provisional adjudication of a debt

The bankruptcy of the debtor does not affect the validity of the provisional payment of a claim by the debtor made before the "suspect period". The same also applies, according to the prevailing view, when the provisional payment was made within the "suspect period".[29]

Provisional regulation of a relationship

The impact of the debtor's bankruptcy on the validity of the orders granted for the regulation of a relationship is not capable—due to the multiplicity of the orders—of being specifically defined. The issue depends on the nature and scope of the judgment and its relation to the bankruptcy property, and generally on the scope of the bankruptcy procedure. The same apply *mutatis mutandis* to seal, unseal, inventory, and public deposit.

INTERIM RELIEF AND THE JUDGMENT CREDITOR

Can a judgment creditor apply for interim relief?

It is almost unanimously accepted that a judgment creditor is not entitled to apply to the court for a security measure. The reasoning is that a judgment creditor is free to proceed to fully satisfy his claim on the basis of the final judgment issued on the merits of the case, and there is no need to apply for interim relief.[30]

However, in some exceptional cases, the court may entertain a judgment creditor's application for a security measure. This is normally, if not exclusively, the case where

28. Rokas, *op. cit.*, p. 139.

29. Anastasiadis, *On Bankruptcy*, p. 224; Supreme Court Judgment No. 444/59, *Commercial Law Review*, 11, p. 210.

30. Beis, *op. cit.*, vol. V, pp. 24–28; Tzifras, *op. cit.*, p. 8, Piraeus Court Judgment No. 72/72, D 4, 187; Piraeus Court Judgment No. 917/1974, *Case Law Archives* KE, 575.

the judgment creditor seeks to seize and auction a Greek flag vessel. If the vessel is trading outside Greece (and therefore the auction procedure cannot take place), the judgment creditor is allowed to apply for conservative attachment of the vessel and this is entered in the Registry so that the vessel cannot change its legal status.[31]

Absence of traceable assets

It is not unusual that a judgment creditor may not be able to enforce a final judgment due to the lack of apparent assets of the debtor. In such a situation, the judgment creditor may take either of the following steps, which may possibly lead to a recovery of his claim:

Taking an oath on the existence/particulars of assets

Greek law provides that a judgment creditor, where the debtor does not have traceable assets, may request the court to order the debtor to appear before the court and submit a list of all his assets (immovables, movables, claims against third parties), taking an oath that the list is exhaustive and accurate. If the debtor fails to appear before the court or refuses to take the oath, he is liable to personal detainment (Articles 986, 861–866, CPC).

Personal detainment of the debtor

Greek law provides that one of the means of enforcement of civil judgments is the personal detainment of the debtor. More specifically, the CPC provides, in Article 1047, that:

> Personal detainment is ordered ... against merchants in respect to commercial claims. Personal detainment also may be ordered in respect to claims on tort ... The duration of the personal detainment may be up to 12 months ... Personal detainment is not ordered on persons over 65 years of age ... The court judgment must be final, not subject to appeal. ...

Therefore, a foreign judgment creditor, having obtained an enforceable judgment from a Greek court or having a foreign judgment declared enforceable in Greece, may enforce the judgment through the detainment of the debtor, provided the debtor is a merchant and the claim is commercial. The court has the duty to order the personal detainment of the debtor, provided the above preconditions are fulfilled. In respect to claims based on tort, the court has only a discretion (and not a duty) to order the personal detainment.

It should be noted that, according to the prevailing view, personal detainment may be ordered only where the *lex causae* of the case contains provisions regarding the personal detainment of the debtor as a means of enforcement of civil judgments.[32]

NIKOS ANAGNOSTOPOULOS

31. Piraeus Court Judgment No. 542/71, D 3, 291.
32. Athens Court of Appeal Judgment No. 6471/73, *Shipping Law Review*, 2, p. 481.

CHAPTER 13

HONG KONG

INTRODUCTION

This chapter examines provisional remedies available to foreign claimants and the recognition and enforcement of foreign judgments in Hong Kong.

Foreign judgments may be enforced in Hong Kong either at common law or by way of registration with the Supreme Court of Hong Kong in the manner prescribed in the Judgments (Facilities for Enforcement) Ordinance (Chapter 9 of the Laws of Hong Kong) and Foreign Judgments (Reciprocal Enforcement) Ordinance (Chapter 319 of the Laws of Hong Kong). For the sake of brevity, the former Ordinance will be referred to as Cap. 9 and the latter as Cap. 319.

This chapter deals with the modes by which a foreign judgment can be given effect in Hong Kong and the methods by which such a judgment can be enforced there.

MODES OF RECOGNITION OF A FOREIGN JUDGMENT

Common law

Enforceable judgment

Not all foreign judgments can be enforced at common law in Hong Kong; those which are enforceable include judgments for the recovery of a debt or a definite sum of money, but not for taxes or penalties. In addition, the judgment must be final and conclusive as between the parties. This is basically a matter of fact, as was decided in the case of *Caffall Brothers Forest Products Inc.* v. *Chie Ku-yin trading as Sin Lie International Enterprises.*[1] A foreign judgment, notwithstanding its being subject to an appeal in the foreign country where the judgment was given, may still be regarded as final and conclusive by the Hong Kong courts where appropriate. However, the Hong Kong courts will also, where appropriate, exercise their inherent jurisdiction to order a stay of execution pending the outcome of such appeal.

In addition to the foregoing matters, the original court must be shown to have had jurisdiction to grant the judgment in the first place; and there must be no defence at common law available for the judgment debtor against enforcement.

At common law, the rule that the foreign court in question must have acted with proper jurisdiction is quite well settled. Where the judgment debtor is an individual,

1. [1987] 1 HKLR 92.

his residence in the foreign country will normally suffice to give that country jurisdiction. But where the judgment debtor is a corporation, the test on jurisdiction is whether the company has carried on its business in the foreign country concerned. However, the test is not as strict as it may look; it may be adequate if there has been some carrying on of business in a definite, and to some reasonable extent, permanent, place within the foreign country.

As regards defence to the enforcement of a foreign judgment which is capable of enforcement having passed all the previously mentioned "tests", it appears that there are only two possible defences available against enforcement at common law, namely: that the foreign judgment was obtained by fraud, or that the enforcement of the judgment would be contrary to public policy in Hong Kong.

Enforcement

At common law, a foreign judgment has no direct application in Hong Kong. As a general rule, the judgment creditor is entitled to bring a fresh action against the judgment debtor in Hong Kong based on the foreign judgment. Normally, the Hong Kong proceedings will commence with the issuance of a writ, which would then be followed as soon as possible by an application to the court for summary judgment under Order 14 of the Rules of the Supreme Court, on the ground that the defendant, i.e., the original judgment debtor, has no defence against the claim of the judgment creditor. Methods of execution of such a judgment are discussed below.

Security for costs

In certain cases, a defendant to an action or other proceedings in the Hong Kong courts is entitled to apply for an order that the plaintiff should give security for costs of the pending litigation. Order 23 of the Rules of the Supreme Court stipulates that the court has a discretion, having considered all the circumstances in each case and having been satisfied that it is just to do so, to make such an order. One of the situations where the court may consider making the order is that "the plaintiff is ordinarily resident out of the jurisdiction".

While there is no longer any inflexible rule or practice that a plaintiff resident abroad or a foreign judgment creditor intending to enforce the foreign judgment at common law will be ordered to give security for costs, in practice security will almost invariably be ordered. As a rule of thumb, the amount of security will be about two-thirds of the likely costs of the adversary in defending the proceedings, but again, the amount of security ordered is a matter for the discretion of the court.

Statute

Applicability

Some foreign judgments may also be enforced in Hong Kong by way of registration procedures contained in Cap. 9 and Cap. 319.

Cap. 9 contains provisions for registration in the Supreme Court of Hong Kong by a judgment creditor of any judgment obtained in a superior court in the United Kingdom within a duration of 12 months from the judgment date. The Governor is empowered by Cap. 9 to make orders in council to extend the provisions for registration set out therein to other Commonwealth countries on the condition that he is satisfied that reciprocity would be afforded by the courts of the country concerned. However, while Cap. 9 is still part of the laws of Hong Kong, by virtue of certain orders in council applying the provisions of sections 3 and 9 of Cap. 319, Cap. 9 has practically ceased to have effect, with the notable exception that it remains available for the registration of judgments of superior courts of the United Kingdom.

Cap. 319 was introduced in 1960. Pursuant to section 3, the Governor in Council may direct that its provisions shall extend to a particular foreign country, provided that it is satisfied on the question of reciprocity. Section 9 provides that the Governor may by order in council direct that the provisions of Cap. 319 shall apply "to every part of the Commonwealth and to judgments obtained in the superior courts of any such part". "The Commonwealth" is defined by the Interpretation and General Clauses Ordinance (Cap. 1) to mean collectively:

(1) the United Kingdom;
(2) the Channel Islands;
(3) the Isle of Man;
(4) the countries mentioned in Schedule 3 to the British Nationality Act 1981, namely:

Antigua and Barbuda	Malta
Australia	Mauritius
The Bahamas	Nauru
Bangladesh	New Zealand
Barbados	Nigeria
Belize	Pakistan
Botswana	Papua New Guinea
Brunei	Saint Lucia
Canada	Saint Vincent and the Grenadines
Republic of Cyprus	Seychelles
Dominica	Sierra Leone
Fiji	Singapore
The Gambia	Solomon Islands
Ghana	Sri Lanka
Grenada	Swaziland
Guyana	Tanzania
India	Trinidad and Tobago
Jamaica	Tuvalu
Kenya	Uganda
Kiribati	Vanuatu
Lesotho	Western Samoa
Malawi	Zambia
Malaysia	Zimbabwe

(5) the British Dependent Territories mentioned in Schedule 6 to the British Nationality Act 1981, namely:
Anguilla
Bermuda
British Antarctic Territory

British Indian Ocean Territory
Cayman Islands
Falkland Islands and Dependencies
Gibraltar
Montserrat
Pitcairn, Henderson, Ducie and Oeno Islands
Saint Christopher and Nevis
Saint Helena and Dependencies
The Sovereign Base Areas of Akrotiri and Dhekelia (i.e., the area mentioned in section 2(1) of the Cyprus Act 1960)
Turks and Caicos Islands
Virgin Islands

In addition to these Commnwealth countries, section 9 of Cap. 319 also provides that its provisions "apply to foreign countries and judgments obtained in the superior courts of foreign countries". For this purpose and by order in council, the provisions of Cap. 319 apply and extend to the following countries:

Belgium
France
Germany
Italy
Austria
The Netherlands
Israel.

Notable exceptions from this list include some of Hong Kong's important trading partners, such as The People's Republic of China, Japan and the United States.

It is perhaps worth noting that section 9 also stipulates that, upon the making of such an order in council, the provisions of Cap. 9 shall cease to have effect except in relation to such part of the Commonwealth to which it extends at the date of the order. In the event that an Order is made under section 3 at any time after a direction has been given under section 9(1) extending the provisions of Cap. 319 to any part of the Commonwealth to which Cap. 9 extends, Cap. 9 shall cease to have effect in respect of that particular part of the Commonwealth.

It has been submitted that Cap. 9 still operates in relation to judgments obtained in the United Kingdom, but only to such judgments, and that registration of foreign judgments obtained elsewhere should be registered under the provisions of Cap. 319. Judgments obtained in the United Kingdom are nonetheless often registered under Cap. 319; indeed, Order 71 of the Rules of the Supreme Court, deals solely with applications for registration under Cap. 319.

Enforceable judgments

Only foreign judgments which are final and conclusive between the parties and which are for money other than taxes or fines or penalties are enforceable under Cap. 9 and Cap. 319.

The Foreign Judgments (Restriction on Recognition and Enforcement) Order provides that a foreign judgment shall not be registered or enforced in Hong Kong if the foreign judgment was contrary to a valid and binding agreement under which the dispute was to be settled otherwise than by proceedings in the courts of the foreign country giving the judgment, provided that the person against whom the judgment was given did not bring or agree to the bringing of proceedings in that country and did not submit to its jurisdiction.

It should also be noted that, as regards judgments given after 28 June 1985, if the judgment is enforceable or entitled to registration in Hong Kong, no proceedings may be brought on the original cause of action in the foreign proceedings. In other words, any enforcement proceedings must be based on the foreign judgment itself, and the old right to an alternative claim on the original cause of action is to that extent abrogated.

Cap. 319 specifically includes in the definition of "judgment" a judgment or order given or made by a court in any criminal proceedings for the payment of a sum of money in respect of compensation or damages to an injured party.

Cap. 319 provides that, although a judgment must be final and conclusive as between the parties to be capable of registration under it, a foreign judgment shall be deemed to be final and conclusive, notwithstanding that an appeal is pending against it or that it may still be subject to appeal in the courts of the country of the original court.

As at common law, a creditor of an enforceable foreign judgment may still have to overcome the jurisdictional hurdle as well as to establish that the judgment debtor is not assisted by any possible defence against enforcement.

Cap. 319 regards non-jurisdiction of the original courts as one of the grounds on which the defendant may apply to set aside the registration of the foreign judgment. Cap. 319 also provides that the original court will be deemed to have had jurisdiction if the judgment debtor, being the defendant in the original court, was at the time when proceedings were instituted resident in, or, being a body corporate, had its principal place of business in, the country of that court and the proceedings in that court were in respect of a transaction effected through or at that office or place. It also provides that a judgment debtor shall be deemed to have submitted to the jurisdiction of the foreign court by voluntarily appearing in the proceedings, either by being the plaintiff in or counter-claiming in the proceedings in the original court or by expressly agreeing to so submit before the commencement of the proceedings.

As regards possible defences against the enforcement of foreign judgments, only two are available for the judgment debtor concerned, which are:

(1) that the foreign judgment was obtained by fraud; and
(2) that the enforcement of the judgment would be contrary to public policy in Hong Kong.

Registration

Foreign judgments are enforced by way of registration under both Cap. 9 and Cap. 319 in the Supreme Court of Hong Kong. Upon registration, the judgment concerned will be deemed to have the same force and effect as a judgment obtained in the Hong Kong court, so that the usual methods of execution will be equally available for the judgment creditor. These various methods of execution will be detailed below.

An application to register a foreign judgment under Cap. 319 can be made within six years of the date of the judgment. Unless the court in Hong Kong directs that an *inter partes* summons be issued, such an application can be made on an *ex parte* basis as provided by Order 71 of the Rules of the Supreme Court. The application must also be supported by an affidavit of facts and, other than exhibiting and stating the same matters as are required under Cap. 9, must also set out the name, trade, or business and usual or last known place of abode or business of the judgment creditor and the judgment debtor, respectively. In addition, the deponent must also state that, to the best of his information and belief, the judgment creditor is entitled to enforce the judgment, that the judgment has not been satisfied and can be enforced by execution in the original country, and that it is not liable to be set aside in the courts of the original country. The affidavit must also set out the amount of interest (if any) due on the judgment in the original court.

Order 71 of the Rules of the Supreme Court also provides that the applicant for registration may be ordered to give security for the costs of the application. Notice of the registration must be served on the judgment debtor, and may be served out of the jurisdiction if necessary.

Other matters

INTEREST AND COSTS

Both Cap. 9 and Cap. 319 provide for the recovery of reasonable legal costs of and incidental to the registration as if they were payable under the foreign judgment.

CURRENCY

If a foreign judgment is expressed in Hong Kong currency, it is registrable and enforceable in Hong Kong currency. However, if the foreign judgment is expressed in its local currency, then, under Cap. 319, it must be registered as if it were a judgment for such sum in the Hong Kong currency as is equivalent to the foreign currency sum so payable thereunder on the basis of the rate of exchange prevailing at the date of registration. Cap. 9, however, is silent on this point.

If enforcement is by way of common-law action, in the light of the *Miliangos* decision in England,[2] the Hong Kong court has a wide discretion on whether to allow a foreign judgment expressed in its local currency to be enforced in such foreign currency.

METHODS OF ENFORCEMENT

Foreign judgments, once registered in or recognised by Hong Kong courts, will be deemed to have the same force and effect as a judgment obtained in the Hong Kong court so that the following methods of enforcement of a local judgment will also be available to the judgment creditor of a foreign judgment:

(1) writ of *fieri facias* (in High Court) or writ of execution (in District Court);
(2) examination of judgment debtors and prohibition orders;
(3) garnishee proceedings;

2. *Miliangos* v. *George Frank (Textiles) Ltd* [1975] 3 All ER 801, HL.

(4) charging orders;
(5) winding up of a limited company; and
(6) bankruptcy proceedings.

In addition, there are two provisional remedies available in the courts of Hong Kong which can be of assistance if there is sufficient evidence to support the contention that a substantial debtor is likely to abscond from the jurisdiction with intent to defeat the claims of his creditors or to dispose of his assets:

(1) *Mareva* injunction; and
(2) Order 44A of the Rules of the Supreme Court.

Writ of *fieri facias* and writ of execution

Essentially, this is a court direction to the bailiff to enter the premises of the judgment debtor and to seize and sell the goods belonging to him.

If the bailiff successfully executes the judgment against the judgment debtor's goods, the goods seized are then sold by the bailiff by public auction after the expiry of seven days. The proceeds will be paid to the judgment creditor in diminution of the judgment debt after deduction of the court expenses and other administrative expenses incidental to the execution and the sale. Nevertheless, the bailiff must retain the proceeds of the public auction for 14 days before he is permitted to pay them to the judgment creditor.

The execution will be regarded as completed after the proceeds have been paid over to the judgment creditor. This can be important particularly where the judgment debtor is being wound up or made bankrupt by some other creditors, since if a winding-up or bankruptcy petition is presented before a judgment creditor has completed his execution, he will lose the benefit of his execution in the event of a winding-up or bankruptcy order subsequently being made. Accordingly, if a creditor knows that another creditor is about to levy execution against the debtor's goods, he may be able to thwart that creditor from securing any advantage over other creditors by initiating winding-up or bankruptcy proceedings.

In addition, an execution against a debtor's goods, whether they be stock, machinery, or office furniture, may often be frustrated because the debtor may have charged all or some of his assets to a financial institution to secure his borrowing of funds. Such a charge will normally have priority to the judgment creditor's claims.

Examination of judgment debtors and prohibition orders

A judgment creditor is able to examine a judgment debtor as to his income, assets and liabilities by invoking the Order 49B procedure with a view to determining the means of the debtor to pay off the judgment debt, in particular by way of instalments. The application must be supported by an affidavit stating the reasons why such an examination is useful. If the court is satisfied with the reasons given in the affidavit, it will issue an order directing the judgment debtor to appear before the court to make full disclosure of his financial position and give details of the way in which he has disposed of any of his assets or income. Personal service of the order on the judgment debtor is required save in the most exceptional cases.

At the hearing, the court will give directions as to the disclosure to be made by the judgment debtor or, if he is absent from the hearing, the court may make an order for the arrest of the judgment debtor. As a consequence, the matter will be adjourned to a further date on which the judgment debtor will be examined on oath by the judgment creditor, or a solicitor or a barrister on his behalf.

In extreme cases, the court may order the imprisonment of the debtor for a period not exceeding three months if it is satisfied after the examination that the judgment debtor:

(1) is able to satisfy the judgment, wholly or partly; or
(2) has disposed of the assets with a view to avoiding satisfaction of the judgment wholly or partly; or
(3) has wilfully failed to make full disclosure of his assets and/or income or properly to answer any question put to him at the examination.

In addition, if the court is satisfied that there is probable cause for believing that the debtor is about to leave Hong Kong and, by reason thereof, satisfaction of the judgment is likely to be obstructed or delayed, then it may impose a prohibition order prohibiting the judgment debtor from leaving Hong Kong. Such an order must be served on the Director of Immigration, the Commissioner of Police, and, if possible, the judgment debtor. Non-compliance with the order may render the judgment debtor arrestable by any immigration officer, police officer, or court bailiff. A prohibition order lasts initially for only one month, which, however, is extendable or renewable up to a total period of three months upon application by the judgment creditor; in appropriate cases, subsequent prohibition orders may be granted.

Generally, the court has power to order the arrest of the judgment debtor as soon as the Order 49B proceedings are commenced. However, the court will require very strong evidence before making such an order. In the event that the application for the prohibition order is based on insufficient grounds, the court may award damages to the judgment debtor for loss caused by the order.

It is important also to note that where a judgment debtor is arrested and subsequently committed to prison, the judgment creditor must pay the judgment debtor's subsistence fees while he is in prison, though the sum will ultimately be added to the judgment debt.

Following the enactment of the Bill of Rights Ordinance in 1991, the validity of a prohibition order has been subject to judicial scrutiny, in particular in the light of Article 8 of the Bill of Rights Ordinance which stipulates that freedom of movement both in or out of Hong Kong is a basic human right that cannot be contravened. However, in a recent Court of Appeal decision, all of the three presiding judges were of the opinion that the prohibition order offers the necessary protection for the rights of the others as opposed to the person being prohibited; accordingly, they allowed an appeal against a single-judge decision in the District Court that the prohibition order is in contravention of Article 8 of the Bill of Rights Ordinance, and also remitted the proceedings in question "to the judge below to reconsider the application (of the prohibition order) and decide whether any and if so what order should now be made".[3]

Therefore, the legal position of the prohibition order appears quite well settled at

3. *Tam Hing Yee* v. *Wu Tai Wai* Civil Appeal No. 118 of 1991: 19–21 November 1991.

the moment, and a judgment creditor should give serious consideration to seeking such an order as a useful device to enforce a judgment.

Garnishee proceedings

If a judgment creditor has knowledge that the judgment debtor is owed some money by a third person and he is in a position to swear an affidavit specifying the identity of the person owing money to the judgment debtor, he can apply for a garnishee order to have the debt attached, the effect of which will be to compel such third person to pay his debt owing to the judgment debtor directly to the judgment creditor in order to reduce the judgment debt. A common example would be where there are sums standing to the judgment debtor's credit in bank accounts.

There is a two-stage procedure. The application is initially made on an *ex parte* basis after judgment has been obtained. The court will first make a garnishee order to show cause (often known as a garnishee order nisi) about four days after the date of application, which is then served on the garnishee, i.e., the third-party debtor. Upon service of the garnishee order nisi, the garnishee is barred from paying the debt to anyone. Then, a hearing will take place not less than seven days after the garnishee order nisi, at which the garnishee and the judgment debtor can attend and, unless they can show cause why the garnishee order nisi should be discharged, the garnishee order absolute will be made directing the garnishee to pay the money direct to the judgment creditor.

This remedy does not extend to debts accruing after the date the order nisi was served, and therefore salary not yet due is not covered. There is unfortunately no facility in Hong Kong for the attachment of earnings of an employee.

Charging orders

If the judgment debtor owns land or shares or has money in court standing to his credit, the judgment creditor may consider applying for a charging order against his assets. Like garnishee orders, charging orders are also obtained in two stages. On an *ex parte* application, the court can make a charging order to show cause (i.e., a charging order nisi) which, in the case of land, should be registered with the Land Office, and, in the case of shares in a company, should be lodged at the registered office of that company. In the case of a charging order in respect of shares in a company, either the judgment debtor or a representative from the company may attend on the second hearing to show cause why the shares should not be charged. In the case of a charging order on land, any person interested in the land may show such cause.

In the case of land, the charging order operates to give the judgment creditor a security interest in the land, although, of course, it has priority subject to any prior interests. If the property is sold, and if the sum realised is sufficient, the judgment debt will be paid out of the proceeds of sale. If the property is not sold, it may be possible to enforce the charging order by sale or the appointment of a receiver.

In the case of shares in a private company, a carefully-drafted memorandum and articles of association will normally include provisions precluding any disposition of shares without the consent of the directors, and therefore it is very difficult, if not impossible, to enforce the charge. In addition, a charging order over shares will not prevent the company from diminishing the value of the shareholding which is charged, either by disposing of the comapny's assets or by resolution to increase its share capital substantially.

It is to be noted, in connection with both garnishee and charging order proceedings, that the execution must be completed (by payment over of the money to the judgment creditor in the case of garnishee proceedings, and by registration of the order absolute in the case of charging orders) before either a winding-up or bankruptcy petition is presented; otherwise the fruits of the proceedings may be lost if a winding-up or bankruptcy order is subsequently made.

Winding-up of a limited company

A petition to wind up a limited company can be presented to the court when the company has failed to satisfy a judgment against it. The winding-up petition should be served on the company and on the official receiver. The petition must be advertised in the English and Chinese press and the Government *Gazette*.

If a winding-up order is made against the company, then a liquidator is appointed, and this will usually be the official receiver, although it is quite possible to appoint outside liquidators. The liquidator will call for all the creditors to file their proofs of debt, which are formal documents verifying the debts which the company owes to them.

It is the task of the liquidator to wind up the affairs of the company, to collect in all its debts, and to realise its assets. The assets are then distributed amongst the creditors in order of priority. The secured debts will be paid first, next will come the preferential debts, these being principally staff wages and tax, and last the unsecured debts. If there are insufficient assets to meet the unsecured debts in their entirety, then the liquidator will declare a dividend of so many cents on the dollar, and the unsecured creditors will be paid in accordance with that dividend. Where there is evidence that the company's assets are in jeopardy, the court may appoint a provisional liquidator (who, in practice, is invariably the official receiver) upon the presentation of the winding-up petition to protect and preserve the assets until a winding-up order is made.

Bankruptcy proceedings

When a judgment has been obtained against an individual and is unsatisfied, a bankruptcy notice may be served on the judgment debtor pursuant to that judgment requiring him to pay the judgment debt within seven days. If he fails to pay the judgment debt accordingly, a bankruptcy petition may be presented to the court and served on the bankrupt and the official receiver in the same way as a winding-up petition, but there is no requirement to advertise a bankruptcy petition.

If a receiving order in bankruptcy is made on the hearing, and no composition or agreement is reached between the debtor (and later the bankrupt upon the making of an adjudication order) and his creditors, his property vests in his trustee in bankruptcy (usually, though again not necessarily, the official receiver) to be distributed amongst his creditors. Again, the same priorities apply as in winding up.

Mareva injunction and Order 44A

There are two procedures available in the courts of Hong Kong which can be of assistance if there is reason to suppose that a substantial debtor is likely to abscond from the jurisdiction with intent to defeat the claims of his creditors or to dispose of his assets, although applications for these procedures have proved to be difficult and are expensive to be approved.

A *Mareva* injunction is an injunction restraining a debtor, whether an individual or limited company, from disposing of or dealing in any way with his/its assets. Once such an order is obtained, it can be served upon the parties holding assets of the debtor, for instance banks, and will operate to preclude them from any dealings with the debtor's assets. In view of the very serious nature of the injunction, it is not lightly granted by the courts, and even where it is, the party applying must give an undertaking to the court to pay damages to the party injuncted if it is later held that he was not entitled to an injunction. The creditor may also have to pay the costs reasonably incurred by third parties affected by the injunction.

An order under the Order 44A procedure of the Rules of the Supreme Court can only be obtained against an individual defendant. Again, there must be evidence that the defendant is about to leave Hong Kong or dispose of his assets in Hong Kong and by reason thereof the enforcement of a judgment against him may be obstructed or delayed.

An order may be obtained prohibiting the debtor from leaving Hong Kong and, if he attempts to do so after service of the order on him, he may be arrested and brought before the court. Where assets are at risk, an order may be made in effect executing the plaintiff's claim against him, i.e., by seizure of his goods and chattels by the bailiff or by the imposition of a charging order on land or shares, pending a hearing at which the defendant may apply for the discharge of the order, or provide security for the plaintiff's claim or provide bail to the satisfaction of the court by a surety or sureties.

CONCLUSION

It is beyond contention that both Cap. 9 and Cap. 319 (and the various orders made thereunder) provide a relatively simple and effective procedure for foreign money judgments to gain recognition and thus seek enforcement in Hong Kong by way of the registration procedure. However, the notable exceptions of judgments obtained in China, Japan, and the United States from the list of countries which benefit from the two Ordinances means, no doubt, that these judgments can only resort to the common law for assistance with respect to their enforcement in Hong Kong. Of course, there always remains a possibility that creditors of those overseas judgments which are not enforceable in Hong Kong, both by statute and at common law, will be permitted to sue on the original cause of action all over again in Hong Kong, provided that the jurisdictional issue is resolved.

As regards the choice of the various methods of execution of judgments available, a prudent judgment creditor, both local and foreign, should make his selection only after the financial standing of the judgment debtor has been thoroughly checked, and only when he is satisfied that the judgment debtor is worth pursuing.

ZEKE C. W. MOK

CHAPTER 14

IRELAND

INTRODUCTION

This chapter surveys issues of relevance to foreign creditors seeking provisional or interim remedies or long-term relief through the courts and against debtors located in Ireland.

JURISDICTION

Foreign creditors may gain access to Irish courts under two separate sets of jurisdictional rules:

(1) rules outlined in the Brussels Convention 1968 (as amended by the Accession Conventions of 1978, 1982 and 1989) and the Lugano Convention 1988 "on Jurisdiction and the Enforcement of Judgments in Civil and Commercial matters", which were adopted into Irish law by the Jurisdiction of Courts and Enforcement of Judgments Acts 1988 and 1993 respectively; and

(2) rules of Private International Law as applied in Ireland.

The rules of the Brussels Convention apply solely between the Contracting States to the Convention which are the Member States of the European Union (EU) other than Sweden, Finland and Austria. Following its success, its principles were extended by the 1988 Lugano Convention which applies between members of the EU and of the European Free Trade Association (EFTA) (Austria, Finland, Iceland, Norway, Sweden and Switzerland). The conventions are almost identical, the Lugano Convention differing only slightly from the Brussels Convention. The main difference between them is that the former contains no provision for its interpretation by the European Court of Justice (ECJ). The remainder of this article will refer to the Brussels Convention except where the Lugano Convention differs.

The rules are applicable only in commercial and civil matters (Article 1) and a number of matters are specifically excluded. Among other things, the Brussels Convention specifically excluded from its ambit bankruptcy proceedings relating to the winding-up of insolvent companies or other legal persons, judicial arrangements, compositions and analogous proceedings (Article 1(2)). Hence, if the debtor is bankrupt, a foreign creditor may not proceed under these rules.

As is implied in the name of the Convention, it has two principal elements:

(1) A set of rules governing the basis of jurisdiction of the national courts in civil and commercial matters.

(2) A set of rules forming the basis for the recognition and enforcement of judgments given in one Member State by the Court of another Member State.

Article 2 of the Brussels Convention outlines the basis on which jurisdiction is founded:

> Subject to the provisions of this Convention persons domiciled in a Contracting State shall whatever their nationality, be sued in the courts of that State.
>
> Persons who are not nationals of the State in which they are domiciled shall be governed by the rules of jurisdiction applicable to nationals of that State.

"Domicile" for the purposes of the Act is described in the case of an individual in the Fifth Schedule, Part I as meaning "ordinary residence" and an individual is domiciled in a place in Ireland if, but only if, he is domiciled in Ireland and is ordinarily resident or carries on any profession, business or occupation in that place. In the case of a corporation or an association, the relevant considerations as to whether it has its seat in Ireland are whether:

(1) it was incorporated under the laws of Ireland; or
(2) its essential management and control is exercised in Ireland.

Paragraph 4, Part III of the Fifth Schedule provides that a corporation or association shall not be regarded as having its seat in a contracting state other than Ireland if it has its seat in Ireland because it was incorporated or formed under the laws of Ireland or it is shown that the courts of that other state would not regard it as having its seat there for the purposes of Article 16.2 which deals with exclusive jurisdiction in proceedings dealing with the validity of the constitution, the nullity or the dissolution of companies.

The legislation also provides for cases of special jurisdiction and exclusive jurisdiction in Articles 5 and 16 respectively. Contracting parties should note that special jurisdiction is outlined in Article 5(1) for matters relating to contracts:

> A person domiciled in a contracting state may be sued in another contracting state in matters relating to a contract in the courts for the place of performance of the obligation in question.

Furthermore exclusive jurisdiction is granted, regardless of domicile "in proceedings which have as their object, rights *in rem* in, or tenancies of a movable property", to the courts of the contracting state in which the property is situated (Article 16(1)). If, however, a tenancy is for less than six months, it is for private use and the parties are natural persons domiciled in the same contracting state, that state also has jurisdiction (Article 16(1)(a) as inserted by the 1989 Accession Convention).

In situations where the Brussels Convention jurisdictional rules are not applicable, Irish private international law rules apply. The basis of these rules concentrates on procedural matters rather than on any connecting factors. Jurisdiction exists in Irish courts if the originating summons has been duly served in accordance with procedural rules with regard to issue and service. In this sense, no distinction is made between the requirements for Irish-based plaintiffs and foreign plaintiffs. Exceptions to jurisdiction exist and Irish courts will not deal for example with foreign revenue laws, foreign penal laws and aspects of family law. The basis for actions within Irish jurisdiction are:

(1) personal presence of the defendant in the jurisdiction; or

(2) temporary presence of the defendant in the jurisdiction.

SERVICE

Service is effected by delivering a copy of the summons to the defendant in person, or it can be delivered to the defendant's residence or place of business. Alternatively, no service is required where the defendant's solicitor accepts service and agrees to enter an appearance.[1]

In the case of companies, service is governed by the Companies Acts 1963 to 1990. For companies incorporated within the State, the originating summons is delivered to the registered office. For companies not incorporated within the State, but with an established place of business in the State, the originating summons must be served on a person within the company nominated to accept such a summons. If no such person exists or cannot be found, then it is adequate to serve the document at the place of business.

If a foreign creditor finds that the debtor has left the jurisdiction, it may be possible under Order 11 of the Rules of the Superior Courts to obtain leave from the court to serve proceedings outside the jurisdiction. This is so, if it can be shown that Ireland is the most appropriate forum, given the nature of the proceedings. Of particular interest to the foreign creditor may be Order 11, rule 1(a), dealing with actions, the whole subject matter of which is land situate in the jurisdiction. In addition under rule 1(e)(i), service outside the jurisdiction may be allowed where the contract was made within the jurisdiction. Furthermore, service may be granted where the contract was made by/through an agent residing in the jurisdiction (Order 11 rule 1(e)(ii)), or where the terms of the contract imply that Irish law should govern the contract (Order 11, rule 1(e)(iii)).

Order 11(A) of the Rules of the Superior Courts 1989 deals with similar cases which are governed by the Brussels Convention. Service outside of the jurisdiction in Brussels Convention cases differs from other Order 11 cases in that leave of the court is not required but certain preconditions which must be complied with are laid out in Order 11(A):

(1) The case must fall within the scope of the Jurisdiction of Courts and Enforcement of Judgments Act 1988. This precondition excludes questions of revenue, bankruptcy status and arbitration. However, maintenance payments auxiliary to divorce decrees have been held to be within the bounds of the Convention.[2]

(2) *Lis alibi pendens* must not arise. According to Article 21 of the Brussels Convention, any court other than the court first seized of the matter must decline jurisdiction. Article 21 operates where there is the same cause of action in all proceedings. In *Gubisch* v. *Palumbo*,[3] the ECJ interpreted "*lis pendens*" as being broad enough to cover a case where one party seeks to rescind a contract and the other party seeks to enforce the same contract. It is held that the proceedings had the same cause of action. This broad

1. Rules of the Superior Courts 1986 Order 9, rule 1.
2. *De Cavel* v. *De Cavel (2)* case No. 120/79 [1980] ECR 731.
3. [1987] ECR 4861.

interpretation is reflected by the Irish Supreme Court in *International Commercial Bank plc* v. *Insurance Corporation of Ireland plc and Meadows Indemnity Company*.[4]

(3) The defendant must either be domiciled in a contracting state or exclusive jurisdiction under Article 16 must apply or the defendant must be a party to an agreement conferring jurisdiction to which the provisions of Article 17 apply.

Finally, Order 11(A), rule 6 maintains the distinction made between Irish citizens and non-citizens in Order 11 of the 1986 Rules of the Superior Courts. For non-citizen defendants, notice of the summons rather than the summons itself is served.

SECURITY FOR COSTS/POSTING A BOND

A plaintiff who is not resident within the State may often have to give security for costs. Different rules exist under the Brussels Convention and under private international law for non-Convention cases.

In cases involving the enforcement of foreign judgments, Article 45 of the Jurisdiction of Courts and Enforcement of Judgments Act 1988 does not require any security:

> No security, bond or deposit, however described, shall be required of a party who in one contracting state applies for the enforcement of a judgment given in another contracting state *on the ground that he is a foreign national* or that he is not *domiciled or resident in the state* in which enforcement is sought.

Article 45 was introduced into Irish law under Order 29 of the Rules of the Superior Courts of 1989.

Although Article 45 refers specifically to enforcement, the main policy basis for such a rule is the ease with which an order for costs could be enforced under the Brussels Convention. It is arguable that this position can be directly applied to situations where a plaintiff is seeking audience in the jurisdiction of another contracting state. Such is the view expressed by Browne-Wilkinson V-C in *Porzelack KG* v. *Porzelack (UK Limited)*.[5] It is submitted that the view of the English court is in keeping with the *spirit of the Convention* and would be favoured by the Irish courts.

In non-Convention cases, plaintiffs residing outside this State may be required to give security for costs. This rule is based on policy considerations which have the protection of the defendants as their rationale.[6] An exception to this basic rule is the case of the maintenance creditor seeking enforcement of an order. He or she cannot be forced to give security on the basis that he or she is not residing in the State.[7]

Difficulties arise when the court seeks to "nominate" the parties as plaintiff and defendant respectively. The person who takes the action is considered to be the plaintiff and the party who defends himself against attack is considered to be the defendant. A defendant resident abroad is not required to give security.[8] It should be

4. [1989] IRLM 788.
5. [1987] 1 All ER 1074.
6. *White* v. *Carroll* [1874] IR 8 CL 296.
7. Maintenance Orders Act 1974, s. 12
8. *In the Goods of Twomey deceased; O'Leary* v. *Stack* (1800) 2 IR 560.

noted that in bankruptcy cases, the creditor who is forced to come to court to defend his rights is considered to be in the position of defendant and thus is not required to give security for costs.[9]

PROVISIONAL AND INTERIM REMEDIES FOR CREDITORS

A series of provisional remedies is available for the creditor in Irish law. The primary purpose of such remedies is to maintain the "status quo" until the court has time to hear and adjudicate upon the matter at hand. Furthermore, the availability of such short-term remedies may protect the plaintiff from damage to his interests.

The injunction is the most important form of interim remedy. An injunction is a discretionary court order obliging a party to do or refrain from doing a certain act or actions. The exercise of the court's power with regard to injunctions is regulated by Order 50, rule 6 of the Rules of the Superior Courts. Injunctions are differentiated according to the duration of their validity (provisional or perpetual) and according to the function (mandatory, prohibitory).

Of provisional injunctions, there are three types:

(1) *Interim injunctions* are sought in situations of great urgency and can be granted on an *ex parte* application. Such an injunction continues in force for a short period specified by the court and until the defendant can have an opportunity to be heard by the court. An undertaking as to damages must be given by the plaintiff.

(2) *Interlocutory injunctions* are also provisional court orders. They are generally longer in duration than interim injunctions. However, if it is practical to have an early hearing, then the application for an interlocutory injunction may be treated as a trial of the action.

(3) *Quia timet injunctions* may be granted where the plaintiff can show "a strong probability" that his rights are about to be infringed. In such cases, no actual damage has yet taken place. Such injunctions are rarely granted.

Provisional injunctions are usually not granted unless the plaintiff gives an undertaking as to damages to the court. These damages include those that the court may order in the event that the injunction proves to have been unwarranted.[10] The undertaking is made to the court, not to the defendant, and therefore failure to pay amounts to contempt of court.

The test used by the courts for granting injunctions is whether there is a "serious question" at stake.[11] Once it has been recognised that a serious question is at issue, the courts look at the "balance of convenience". By this is meant whether the granting of an injunction is just, given the circumstances of all the parties. The plaintiff or plaintiffs must be able to show that they will suffer an "irreparable loss" if the injunction is not granted.[12]

In terms of function, prohibitory rather than mandatory injunctions are more

9. *Re Ring, a bankrupt* [1869] IR 3 Eq 507.
10. *Keenan Brothers Limited* v. *CIE* [1963] 97 ILT 54.
11. *Campus Oil Limited* v. *The Ministry for Industry and Energy and Others (No. 2)* [1983] IR 88.
12. *Moore* v. *The Attorney General* [1927] IR 569.

Examinaton order

Granted upon an *ex parte* application, this order calls on the defendant to file a statement regarding his means and obliges him to appear in court to support such evidence. The defendant can be subjected to cross-examination. The examination order, like the other execution orders must be applied for in the District Court of the area where the debtor is ordinarily resident.

Instalment order

An instalment order is a court order specifying payments to be made by instalments by the debtor to the creditor. An instalment order may be granted following on an examination order, depending on the financial circumstances of the debtor. If the debtor ignores the instalment order, the creditor has the right to demand the full sum, in one payment. As this is often unrealistic, the creditor may take the procedure a step further and file an application for a committal order.

Committal order

This is issued for failure to comply with the instalment order. Should nothing come of the committal order, then a warrant may be executed by the Garda (Police Force), on foot of a committal order which involves the arrest of the defendant creditor.

Garnishment

The garnishment procedure is similar to an execution order and is governed by the Circuit Court Rules 1950, Order 37. Garnishment may be used if a creditor has been unsuccessful with a judgment order. If the creditor is aware that there is another party within the jurisdiction who is indebted to the debtor, he may seek an order that all debts owing to the debtor be intercepted and attached to the plaintiff's judgment against the debtor. The third party is called the garnishee. The garnishee has a right of appeal against the attachment of such an order.

Judgment mortgage

A judgment mortgage is a mortgage created by the court, over property owned by the debtor, when the debtor fails to pay under a judgment order. All remedies available under a legal mortgage are available to the mortgagee of a judgment mortgage. These rights are subject, of course, to any previously existing rights such as those of a mortgage or charge holder. If there are no existing rights, the creditor can apply to the court for sale of the property. A judgment mortgage can only be registered against an interest in real estate which the debtor can alienate without the consent of another.

***Mareva* injunction**

Although this type of injunction has previously been discussed as an interim remedy for a creditor, it is important to note that the *Mareva* is a useful mechanism to hold assets in place, thus allowing the creditor to pursue more permanent means of collecting the debts owed to him.

Ownership reservation

Ownership reservation with respect to goods is recognised according to Danish law, but foreign creditors should be especially aware that a number of requirements must be complied with. In order for an ownership reservation to be valid, it is thus required that the following conditions exist:

(1) a clear agreement,
(2) made not later than at the delivery of the goods,
(3) concerning specified and identifiable objects.

If the goods are sold to a consumer, a further requirement in order to make the ownership reservation valid is that at least 30% of the purchase price is paid before the delivery.

Special notice should be made of the claim for specification and identification of the goods supplied. Supply of a stock of goods in the form of products which cannot be identified individually once they are in the receiver's stock will not be a valid ownership reservation according to Danish law, and the stock will be included as a free asset in the event of a subsequent bankruptcy. An ownership reservation may thus only be made with valid effect with respect to individual, identifiable objects, e.g. machines and equipment.

It should also be noted that ownership reservation may not be used to cover old debt. Ownership reservation will only be valid to the extent it is made as a condition for payment of the service supplied.

In the case of supplies of operating equipment, there is a further risk. According to the Danish Registration Act, machines and operating equipment which are built-in by the owner in real estate to be used by a company will be comprised by the mortgage on the property with the result that the property right of a third party in the operating equipment lapses. A supplier of machines to be erected in a company may thus run the risk that an otherwise valid ownership reservation will lapse if the machine is erected in a property owned by the company. If, on the other hand, the operating equipment is installed in a property where the company is merely a lessee, the reservation is valid.

Mortgaging and pledging

A creditor may seek security through mortgaging and pledging of assets belonging to the debtor. Generally speaking, almost any asset in a commercial business may be mortgaged, but different rules apply to the different kinds of assets. For example, real estate and operating equipment are mortgaged by way of official registration of a mortgage deed.

In such case, I would, however, only recommend banks that are familiar with handling and valuing such mortgages to accept that kind of security. It is very important that a creditor makes sure that the appropriate formalities are complied with. If at all possible the supplier should preferably claim that security is provided by way of a banker's guarantee against the mortgage being placed at the disposal of the debtor's bank.

CHAPTER 7

DENMARK

INTRODUCTION

As in most other countries in the Western world, creditors' access in Denmark to proceedings against a debtor may be divided into two main areas:

(1) Individual legal proceedings by creditors whereby a creditor seeks only to satisfy his own claims.

(2) Universal proceedings by creditors whereby arrangements are made for the total assets of a debtor to be applied for equal distribution among the creditors of the debtor.

In both situations, the creditor may in advance have tried to secure his position in the best possible manner by way, for example, of a mortgage, charge, lien, or ownership reservation to protect himself against any loss. I will start by describing the guidelines that exist under Danish law for a creditor to establish what may be called "original securities". Next, I will survey creditors' options within the two main areas. Finally, I will explain to what extent foreign legal decisions are recognised under Danish law.

Since this contribution is not an exhaustive description of the Danish legal system and its rules, this should naturally only be taken as a very broad outline of the Danish system. It should, therefore, be stressed that this outline is to serve as a guideline for either the creditor personally or possibly for his national adviser but should not be used as basis for independent advice. If it is intended to establish securities, or in any other manner to try to act on the proposals set out below, it must be advised that a Danish lawyer be approached to assist in the procedure.

ORIGINAL SECURITIES

A company which is asked to supply on a credit basis or to give a loan to a company or another legal entity in a foreign country will normally make a natural reservation and carry out in-depth investigations. If at all possible, suppliers as well as banks involved should be provided with security.

I would recommend that the foreign creditor who is in doubt about his customer's ability to meet payments receives a banker's guarantee rather than security by way of a mortgage on one or more of the assets of the debtor.

If security provided by the debtor is the only possibility, the kinds of security discussed below are those that the debtor may typically be able to provide.

Legislation

Legislation provides remedies for creditors of both corporate and individual debtors. In a situation where the debtor is a company, the creditor may be successful by using legislative provisions to collect debts owed; he may seek to declare the company insolvent and apply for liquidation by Court Order. Section 213 of the Companies Act 1963 outlines the circumstances in which a company may be wound up by Order of the Court. In particular, sub-section (e) states that the court is so empowered if "*the company is unable to pay its debts*".

Section 214 of the 1963 Act, as amended by section 123 of the Companies Act 1990 outlines the circumstances in which a company is deemed unable to pay its debts. Based on the parameters of the above section, section 215 states:

> ... an application to the court for the winding-up of a company shall be by petition presented, subject to the provisions of this section, either by the company or by any creditor or creditors (including any contingent or prospective creditor or creditors), contributory or contributories, or by all or any of those parties, together or separately ...

A creditor must prove that a prima facie case exists and (in the case of contingent or prospective creditors security *must* be given (section 215(c)).

The disadvantage for a creditor in having to resort to a petition for winding-up his corporate debtor as the means of recovering debts is that in a liquidation, creditors are paid according to statutory priorities. Some such priorities are outlined in the Bankruptcy Act 1988 (as incorporated into the Companies Act 1963 in section 284). Creditors with mutual (set-off) debts, those benefiting from retention of title clauses and those owed specifically secured debts (e.g., a mortgage, lien or charge other than a floating charge) are paid in preference to creditors without such security. Furthermore, section 285 of the Companies Act 1963, as subsequently amended by various legislation, lists a set of preferred debts which are given preference over and above all other debts on the grounds of public policy. These include certain rates, taxes and employee remuneration.

Because the liquidation of companies works on the basis of these preferences, using this mechanism in an attempt to recover a debt may not be beneficial for all creditors. This is, of course, unless the creditor is certain that there are sufficient assets to meet all debts or if it is clear that the threat of liquidation and the personal implications that may arise for the directors of the debtor company would spur the debtor to repay the debt owed.

Where the debtor is an individual, the pursuance of the debtor to bankruptcy is governed by the Bankruptcy Act 1988. A person may be adjudicated bankrupt following a creditor's petition or by a petition of the debtor himself.

The principal distinction between company insolvency and individual insolvency is that an individual must commit an "act of bankruptcy" to be eligible for adjudication in bankruptcy. Although acts of bankruptcy tend to be indications of insolvency, it is not necessary to be insolvent in order to commit an act of bankruptcy.

The main acts are:

(1) a voluntary declaration of insolvency;
(2) an assignment of assets for general benefit of one's creditors;
(3) a fraudulent conveyance or fraudulent preference;
(4) creditor avoidance;

(5) an execution pursuant to an execution order levied or attempted; and
(6) a bankruptcy summons.

A creditor may petition the court, within a three-month period, following any of the above acts. The debtor must, however, come within the bankruptcy jurisdiction, i.e., he must be ordinarily resident in Ireland. Alternatively, he must possess a place of business or a dwelling place within the jurisdiction. The commission of the act while temporarily present does not found jurisdiction. The debt being sought must be not less than IR£1,500 (section 11(i)(a)) and it must be legally enforceable.

Equity

Equity may intervene on behalf of secured creditors through the equitable right and power of a debenture holder to appoint a receiver. The court also has an equitable jurisdiction to appoint a receiver. A receiver takes control of the debtor company's assets and he may also be appointed as manager with the right to carry on or manage the business of the debtor company. A receiver or receiver and manager is primarily concerned with the debenture holder's interests in the company,[15] but is subject to statutory priorities equivalent to those in a winding-up.

RECOGNITION OF FOREIGN JUDGMENTS

In a domestic case, the principle of *res judicata* applies, i.e., once a matter has been decided upon, the cause of action is extinguished and the matter cannot be adjudicated upon again.

In the case of a foreign judgment, *res judicata* does not apply and, therefore, a person with a foreign judgment may choose to sue in an Irish court (under the jurisdiction rules) or may seek to have the foreign judgment recognised (and enforced) in this jurisdiction. Although this latter course of action is theoretically cheaper and less time consuming, the rules for recognition must be met.

In Irish law, there are two different sets of rules for the recognition of foreign judgments or claims. As well as the traditional recognition rules, the Jurisdiction of Courts and Enforcement of Judgments Acts 1988 and 1993 allow for the recognition of the judgments that fall within the terms of the Brussels and Lugano Conventions respectively.

For a foreign judgment to be recognised outside the terms of these Conventions in Ireland, the foreign court must have jurisdiction according to private international law rules as applied in Ireland. For jurisdiction to exist, the defendant must be resident or present in the foreign jurisdiction, i.e., must be in a position to be under the protection of its laws. For the purpose of enforcing a maintenance order, jurisdiction can exist even if the defendant does not reside or is not present in that foreign jurisdiction provided that the claimant was resident there at the commencement of the proceedings (Maintenance Act 1994, section 22(b) which gave force of law to the 1990 Rome Convention and the New York Convention 1956 designed to simplify the enforcement of foreign maintenance orders). A foreign court will be considered to

15. *Lynch* v. *Ardmore Studios (Irl) Ltd* [1966] IR 133.

have jurisdiction only if the party has submitted to the court by appearing as a plaintiff or as a defendant. Furthermore, if the parties have contracted to submit to a foreign jurisdiction, then that court will be considered to have jurisdiction, by Irish rules of private international law.[16]

In the case of companies, a foreign court will be considered to have jurisdiction (and its judgment recognised) if the company is registered or has an established place of business in that jurisdiction. The temporary presence of directors in a jurisdiction will not suffice.[17] An agency is not considered to amount to a definite place of business.

Not only must a judgment meet the above requirements to be recognised under private international law, a judgment must be final and conclusive in nature. The *lex fori* decides what constitutes "final and conclusive". A foreign judgment however will be recognised even if there is a possibility that the judgment may be appealed in the foreign courts.

Foreign judgments must be for a definite monetary amount.[18] This pre-condition has given rise to considerable difficulties for maintenance creditors in the past. However Part IV, section 22(a) of the Maintenance Act 1994 now allows for the recognition of a foreign maintenance order even if the court which made it retains power to vary or revoke it.

Finally, a court cannot examine the merits or mistakes made by a foreign court when recognition is sought.

The Jurisdiction of Courts and Enforcement of Judgments Acts 1988 and 1993 are underpinned by the presumption that judgments falling within the ambit of the legislation should be recognised and enforced within this jurisdiction. Non-recognition and non-enforcement are considered to be the exception to the rule. Title III, section 1 of the 1988 Act covers recognition and Article 26 states that "a judgment given in a contracting state shall be recognised in the other Contracting States without any special procedure being required".

Article 27 outlines the grounds upon which a foreign judgment will not be recognised. These include judgments that are contrary to public policy, where the defendant has not been duly served and where the judgment is "irreconcilable with a judgment given in a dispute between the same parties in the state where the recognition is sought".

Furthermore, where the judgment of the foreign court is based on a preliminary question of status or matrimonial property rights which conflicts with domestic private international law rules, then that judgment will not be recognised (Article 27(4)).

CONCLUSION

The Brussels Convention as adopted in Ireland by the 1988 and 1993 Acts together with the adoption of the Lugano, Rome and New York Conventions have, where applicable, radically altered the rules for the recognition and enforcement of civil and

16. *International Alltex Corporation* v. *Lawler Creations Limited* [1965] IR 264.
17. *Dennis* v. *Leinster Paper Company* [1901] 2 IR 337.
18. *McDonnell* v. *McDonnell* [1921] 2 IR 148.

commercial judgments of a foreign court. However, these exist side by side with the traditional rules of private international law where these Conventions are inapplicable, so that it is important to ascertain early on in a dispute which has a transnational dimension, whether the Conventions do apply or not so that a decision can be made on the most advantageous jurisdiction in which to issue proceedings and to enforce a resulting judgment.

JOHN A. GLACKIN

SOURCES OF LAW

Legislation

Brussels Convention 1968: adopted into Irish law by:
Jurisdiction of Courts and Enforcement of Judgments Act 1988 and 1993
Rules of the Superior Courts 1929, 1986, 1989
Companies Acts 1963–1990
Maintenance Orders Act 1974
Courts (Supplemental Provisions) Act 1961
Circuit Court Rules 1950
Courts Act 1981
Irish Bankrupt and Insolvent Act 1857
Irish Bankruptcy Act 1988
Courts (No. 2) Act 1991

Case law

De Cavel v. *De Cavel (No. 2)* Case No. 120/79 [1980] ECR 731
The Nordglimt [1988] QB 183
Porzelack KG v. *Porzelack UK Limited* [1987] 1 ER 1074
White v. *Carroll* [1874] IR 8 CL 296
In the Goods of Twomey, deceased; O'Leary v. *Stack* (1800) 2 IR 560
Re Ring, a Bankrupt [1869] IR 3 EQ 507
Keenan Bros. Limited v. *CIE* [1963] 97 1 LT 54
Campus Oil Limited v. *Minister for Industry and Energy and Others (No. 2)* [1982] IR 88
Moore v. *AG* [1927] IR 569
Fleming and Others v. *Ranks (Irl) Limited and Another* [1982] ILRM 541
Z Limited v. *A-Z and AA-LL* [1982] 1 QB 574
International Alltex Corporation v. *Lawlor Creations Limited* [1965] IR 264
Dennis v. *Leinster Paper Company* [1901] 2 IR 337
McDonnell v. *McDonnell* [1921] 2 IR 148

CHAPTER 15

ISRAEL

INTRODUCTION

A foreign creditor of an Israeli debtor may be one who had already litigated his matter and had won a judgment in his favour in a foreign court, or one who considers the institution of legal proceedings against his adversary in the Israeli courts.

In order to be able to attack the Israeli defendant's assets situated in Israel, the former (the judgment creditor) will have to take steps to introduce the foreign judgment into the Israeli legal system; otherwise, the foreign judgment will not be operative in Israel on its own strength. Thus, it must be recognised and enforced by the Israeli courts.

The giving of local effect to the foreign judgment by way of regarding it as valid is the recognition of the foreign judgment: the furnishing of the judgment creditor with means for its local execution against the defendant's assets is its enforcement.

This chapter will deal with the recognition and enforcement of a foreign judgment, the procedure relating to the initiation of a claim in the Israeli courts, and the various interim remedies and reliefs provided by the Israeli legal system to the litigant who wishes to secure his chances of recovery, or to the winner in a trial who wishes to enjoy the fruits of his victory and collect his judgment.

RECOGNITION AND ENFORCEMENT OF A FOREIGN JUDGMENT

The governing law

The normative source of law applicable to these issues is the Foreign Judgment Enforcement Law 1958, which sets the framework of rules regarding recognition and enforcement of foreign judgments.

Where the law leaves certain matters to the court's discretion, or where the provisions of the law are too laconic, these concepts will be amplified in accordance with the standards formed by Supreme Court judgments and with reference to the English common law, as a persuasive source, unless the Israeli law expressly deviates from the arrangement of the English law.[1]

1. CA 499/79, *Ben-Dayan and ors* v. *IDS International Ltd*, PD 38(2), 99, pp. 104–105.

A foreign judgment—definition

A foreign judgment is defined in section 1 of the Law as:

A judgment given by a court in a foreign state in a civil matter, and includes a judgment for the payment of compensation or damages to an injured party even though it may not have been given in a civil matter.

As prescribed by the Law, the document should be one rendered by a "court" and which is considered as a "judgment", both in the eyes of the foreign legal system and in the eyes of the Israeli jurisprudential criteria.[2] In addition, the judgment should be in a "civil matter", i.e., as distinguished from a criminal, public, religious, or military matter.

Conditions of enforcement

According to section 3 of the Law, the court may declare a foreign judgment enforceable if it meets all the four following conditions:

The judgment was given in a state, the courts of which were, according to its law, competent to give it

The foreign judgment creditor has to establish that the judicial system of the foreign country had general internal jurisdiction.

According to section 6(a)(3) of the Law, if the foreign court lacked international jurisdiction to render the judgment, then the enforceability of the judgment can be challenged by way of defence. As a result, as a condition of enforcement, the foreign judgment should, at the same time, be given by a competent court according to the rules of private international law prevailing in Israel.

Although this section refers expressly to the enforcement of a foreign judgment, the Supreme Court applies the same condition of competence and its international jurisdiction as a requirement for recognition of the foreign judgment, as well.[3]

The judgment is no longer appealable

As long as an appeal can still be lodged on the foreign judgment in its country of origin, it will not be enforced in Israel. Neither will an interim judgment for interlocutory relief be enforced.[4] However, as an exception to this condition, a foreign maintenance judgment can be enforced even though still appealable. This exception is embodied in section 8 of the Law. The court may, if it considers that the circumstances of the case justify its doing so, enforce a foreign provisional judgment or interim order in a matter of maintenance even though such judgment or order may still be appealed, so long as the other conditions imposed by this Law are fulfilled in respect thereof. The reasons for this exception are social and humane, and express the legislative concern for those

2. A. Shapira, "Recognition and Enforcement of Foreign Judgments", *Tel Aviv University Studies in Law* (1977), Vol. 3, p. 181.

3. CA 499/79, *Ben-Dayan*, note 1 *supra* at p. 106.

4. CA 72/69, *Gross* v. *Express Service*, PD 23(2), 807.

who are in need of support to be able to have local enforcement of foreign provisional judgments and interim orders.[5]

The fact that the foreign judgment can still be modified or annulled by the same court does not break the unappealability condition. The Israeli Law's concern was limited to the question of appeal to a higher chamber, and in that it deviated from the rule applied by the English common law. Under the common law, effect is given to a foreign judgment only if it is "final and conclusive"—if the judgment requires additional proceedings to be finalised, or if it is subject to modification by the rendering court so that its result may be altered, it is not considered as final and conclusive, and in consequence it will not be given effect in England.[6]

The obligation imposed by the judgment is enforceable according to the law relating to the enforcement of judgments in Israel, and the tenor of the judgment is not contrary to public policy

By this condition, the legislator indicates that a foreign decree for which the Israeli execution laws do not provide a mechanism for the enforcement thereof, will not be enforceable. In addition, a foreign judgment is not enforceable if the contents thereof are contrary to Israeli public policy.

The term "public policy" lacks a definition, and hence it requires interpretation by the court. It may be expected that a judgment which collides with such basic values as public safety or decency will not be enforced in Israel. This yardstick will be employed very carefully, and only in very extreme circumstances will the foreign judgment be denied enforcement, as stated by the court[7]:

> But there are instances—though exceptional—where giving effect to a foreign law and to the consequence resulting therefrom will actually impinge upon our public policy, and only where a foreign law violates the sentiments of justice and morals of the Israeli public should it be barred.

Among the interests and principles which can be taken into consideration in this context are principles of equality under the Women's Equal Rights Law,[8] welfare of the child,[9] and other fundamental values of justice, morality, freedom, and decency. State interests, such as security, sovereignty, and relations with friendly foreign countries, are also included.

The judgment is executory in the state in which it was given

Any limitation existing in the country of origin, such as time prescription, would bar the foreign judgment from enforcement. This condition relates only to enforcement of the jurisdiction and not to its recognition in Israel.

5. CR 227/83, *Goldberg* v. *Goldberg*, PD 37(2), 778; CA 619/89, *Kason* v. *Kason*, PD45(2), 656.
6. *Nouvion* v. *Freeman* (1889) 15 App Cas 1.
7. HC 143/62, *Schlezinger* v. *Minister of Interior*, PD 17, 225 at p. 256. See also CA 1137/93 *Ashkar* v. *Hymes*, PD 48(3), 641.
8. Section 2 of the Law, SH, 1951, 248.
9. For example: A foreign decree determining the custody of a child will be subject to an independent examination by the Israeli court as to whether it conforms with the welfare of the child; HC 268/80 *Jensen Zohar* v. *Jensen*, PD 35(1), 1 at p. 31. See also HC 71/80 *Sleich* v. *Arshied*, PD 35(1), 100, 106; HC 635/79 *Miller* v. *Miller*, PD 34(2), 673; HC 836/86 *Bachar* v. *Bachar Davis*, PD 41(3), 701.

Supplementary considerations

When considering the fulfilment of the above conditions, the Israeli court may weigh the circumstances prevailing at the time of rendering the judgment and also relevant facts and subsequent events, such as a waiver or settlement of the obligation thereof.[10]

Reciprocity of enforcement

According to section 4 of the Law, a foreign judgment shall not be declared enforceable if it was given in a state the laws of which do not provide for the enforcement of judgments of Israeli courts. Nevertheless, the court may, on the application of the Attorney-General, enforce such a foreign judgment.

To satisfy this condition of reciprocity, it is not necessary to show an international convention for the mutual enforcement of judgments with the country of origin, but of course such a convention, if existing, fulfils the required element. It should be noted that the reciprocity requirement applies only to enforcement and not to the recognition of a foreign judgment.

Period of enforcement

A judgment creditor should file his application for the enforcement of the foreign judgment within five years from the day on which the judgment was given, unless a different period has been agreed upon between Israel and the state in which the judgment was given, or unless the court considers that there are special reasons justifying the delay (section 5 of the Law). This condition also applies only to enforcement and not to recognition of a foreign judgment.

As to the discretion of the court regarding the justifying circumstances, it was decided by the Supreme Court that the fact that a judgment creditor did not know in which state to file his application was a justification for an applicant who filed his request beyond the five-year period.[11]

Recognition of judgments

Section 11 of the Law states as follows:

11(a) A court or tribunal in Israel shall recognise a foreign judgment which fulfils all the following requirements:
(1) an agreement with a foreign state applies to it
(2) Israel has undertaken by that agreement to recognise foreign judgments of the same kind
(3) the undertaking applies only to judgments capable of enforcement under the law in Israel
(4) it fulfils the conditions of the agreement.
(b) In dealing with and for the purpose of a matter within its jurisdiction, a Court or tribunal in Israel may recognise a foreign judgment even if sub-section (a) does not apply to it, if it considers it lawful and just to do so.

For example, a German succession order is not enforceable in Israel due to an express

10. CA 555/84, *Fucs* v. *Manchik*, PD 39(3), 386.
11. CA 257/88, *Hochman* v. *Raveh*, PD 38(3), 639.

provision in the Convention between Israel and Germany.[12] Nevertheless, in view of its power under sub-section (b), the court examined the possibility of its recognition upon considerations of "law and justice". In view of the defects which were found in the foreign proceedings, e.g., the judgment was obtained by fraud, the respondent was not afforded a reasonable opportunity to present his arguments and, at the time the action was brought in Germany, a suit in the same matter and between the same parties was pending in Israel, the foreign decree was not recognised.[13]

The section also provides:

(c) In proceedings in relation to recognition of foreign judgments under this law will apply the provisions of section 6(b) and 6(c).

Section 11 provides for the recognition of foreign judgments as a matter of right by a direct declaratory judgment affirming its validity (section 11(a)) and as a matter of judicial discretion of the Israeli court as an incidental recognition limited to the matter in question and thus creating a confined *res judicata* between the parties in the specific case only (section 11(b)).

The recognition of the foreign judgment is usually requested for defensive purposes by a party sued in the local court—he may wish to show that the same claim was determined by a foreign court in his favour or that he had already fulfilled his obligation under the foreign judgment.

The foreign judgment will be recognised in Israel even if the parties thereto are not identical to the litigants in Israel. As to the condition of "lawful and just" stated in section 11(b), the Supreme Court held that, if a foreign judgment satisfies the requirements for being enforced, then it may also be recognised and hence receive the validity of an Israeli judgment for all purposes except for its being enforced.[14]

Defences against enforcement and recognition

Five defences are set forth in section 6:

6(a)(1) The judgment was obtained by fraud.
(2) The defendant was not afforded a reasonable opportunity to present his arguments and to produce his evidence before the judgment was given.
(3) The judgment was given by a court not competent to give it according to the rules of private international law applicable in Israel.
(4) The judgment contradicts another judgment given in the same matter between the same parties and which is still valid.
(5) At the time the action was brought in the foreign court, a suit in the same matter and between the same parties was pending before a court or tribunal in Israel.

These defences, if established, may bar the foreign judgment from enforcement.

Section 6(a)(3) deals with the issue of international jurisdiction. The Israeli rules of international jurisdiction are based on the English common law, in which "residence" as a ground for international jurisdiction encompasses mere presence of the defendant in the foreign state when served with process. "Presence" in the rendering court's jurisdiction can be even a temporary one at the time of service or, for a company, the carrying on of a business.[15] However, if the presence was merely in order to deny or

12. KA 897 vol. 26, p. 667 (Treaty Series).
13. CA 587/85, *Stark* v. *Birnberg and ors*, PD 41(3), 227.
14. CA 499/79, *Ben-Dayan*, note 1 *supra*.
15. *Ibid.*, Shapira, note 2 *supra*, p. 203.

contest the court's jurisdiction, the law would not consider it as an adequate basis for acquisition of jurisdiction (section 6(b) and 6(c)) and, hence, the rendering court would not be considered as a competent court as provided in section 6(a)(3).

By an express amendment to the Law, the defences set forth in section 6(b) and 6(c) apply also to recognition of a foreign judgment.[16]

Results of enforcement and recognition

A foreign judgment which has been declared enforceable shall, for the purposes of execution, have the effect of a judgment validly given in Israel (section 10(a)).[17] A foreign judgment which has been recognised will be considered valid and serve as *res judicata* but will not be executed in Israel.

Procedure

The procedure for enforcement of foreign judgments is stated in regulations 352–359 of the Civil Procedure Regulations 1984, according to which the judgment creditor should apply to the court by way of motion. This will specify the name and address of the rendering court and the date of the judgment, and will have attached to it a certified copy of the judgment. If required by the court, the applicant should submit to the court a translation to Hebrew certified by a consular representative of the rendering state or by an Israeli consul who acts in the country of origin.

The respondent should lodge an answer within 30 days from receipt of the motion, and, in case of a dispute in the fulfilment of the conditions set forth in section 3, must give a sworn affidavit to that effect.

Conventions

Israel is a party to several conventions for the enforcement and recognition of foreign judgments:

(1) The Convention between Israel and the Republic of Austria for the Reciprocal Recognition and Enforcement of Judicial Decisions in Civil and Commercial Matters.[18]

(2) The Convention between the Government of Israel and the Government of the United Kingdom and Northern Ireland, providing for the Reciprocal Recognition and Enforcement of Judicial Decisions in Civil Matters.[19]

(3) The Convention between the State of Israel and the Federal Republic of Germany for the Reciprocal Recognition of Court Decisions in Civil and Commercial Matters and for the Enforcement of Such Decisions.[20]

(4) The Convention between the State of Israel and the Kingdom of Spain for the Mutual Recognition and Enforcement of Judgments in Civil and Commercial Matters.[20a]

16. s. 11(c) of the Enforcement of Foreign Judgments Law.

17. If the foreign judgment was rescinded by the rendering court after its being declared enforceable in Israel, the enforcing judgment will be annulled as well. See CA 282/79, *Dankner* v. *Spilsky*, PD 36(1), 775.

18. Signed on 6 June 1966, KA 701, vol. 21, p. 147.

19. Signed on 28 October 1970, KA 750, vol. 22, p. 55.

20. Signed on 20 July 1977, KA 897, vol. 26, p. 667.

20a. Signed on 30 May 1989, KA 1016, vol. 30, p. 707.

INSTITUTION OF AN ACTION IN ISRAEL

The jurisdiction of the Israeli courts applies to persons present in Israel and immovables located therein, and is assumed by the service of summons to the defendant.

No relevancy is attached to the residence or the location of the plaintiff, except for the requirement of a bond to secure the defendant's costs—a requirement which is discretionary and exercised upon a motion filed by the defendant. In determining whether to impose on the plaintiff a duty to provide a bond, the court may take into consideration whether the plaintiff has assets in Israel from which the costs may be collected, or any circumstances relevant to the possibility of collecting the costs.

According to rule 519 of the Civil Procedure Regulations 1984, failure to post the bond in time as ordered results in the dismissal of the action unless the plaintiff convinces the court that the delay was caused by a justified reason.

However, a foreign plaintiff who is a citizen and resident of one of the countries which is a signatory to one of the Hague Conventions (Convention Rélative à la Procedure Civile),[21] to which Israel became a party in 1952 and 1968, will be exempted from the duty to provide a bond or a guarantee to secure court costs. Section 17 of the Hague Convention states the reciprocal exemption from this obligation which will apply to all the participating countries. According to sections 18 and 19 of the Convention, a judgment which obliges such an exempted plaintiff (or intervenes) to pay costs to the defendant will be executory by the local authorities upon a request transferred through the diplomatic channels.[22]

It should be noted here that the court's powers to impose the duty to secure the defendant's costs is not confined to foreigners, and the court may decide to oblige an Israeli plaintiff to do so as well.[23]

Upon filing the action, the plaintiff has to pay court fees to the court (in monetary actions the subject matter of which can be valued in amounts of money, 2.5% of the claimed amount; in other actions, according to a table specified in the Court Regulations—Court Fees), and has to submit to the court, together with the statement of claim, a summons in which the defendant will be required to file his statement of defence within 30 days.[24]

An action relating to real estate will be filed in the court most proximate to where the real estate is located.[25] Other actions will be filed in the court, *inter alia*, in whose region one of the following is found: residence or place of business of the defendant; location where the obligation was created or the place in which the obligation was intended to be fulfilled.

21. KA 125, at p. 93.

22. The states which are parties to the 1905 Convention are: Austria, Belgium, Czechoslovakia, Denmark, Estonia, Finland, France, Germany, Holland, Hungary, Israel, Italy, Latvia, Luxembourg, Norway, Poland, Portugal, Romania, Russia, Spain, Sweden, Switzerland, and Yugoslavia. In 1954, another Convention was signed in The Hague which Israel joined in 1968. The participating states are mainly identical, except for the USSR which signed instead of Russia, Estonia and Latvia, and the inclusion of the Vatican.

23. CA 432/78, *Weiler* v. *Chekaber*, PD 34(2), 775.

24. In actions lodged in summary procedure, the defendant should request leave to defend and is not entitled to file a defence as a matter of right.

25. Rule 4 of the Civil Procedure Regulations 1984.

The particulars of the claim and the various proceedings are administered by the Civil Procedure Regulations 1984.

The Israeli court may also issue a summons to a defendant who is out of the jurisdiction. According to rule 500 of the Civil Procedure Regulations 1984, leave for an out-of-jurisdiction service of process may be granted in one of the following circumstances: a relief is sought against a person whose usual place of residence is within Israel; the subject matter of the claim is real estate situated in Israel; the claim is for the enforcement or the rescission of a contract or for compensation for the breach thereof and the contract was made in Israel, either directly or through an agent residing or dealing in Israel, or when the contract is expressly or impliedly subject to the Israeli laws; the claim is for breach of a contractual obligation committed in Israel, regardless of the place of making the contract; an injunction is sought regarding a matter done or about to be done in Israel; a claim which is based on an act or omission committed in Israel; the action is for the enforcement of a foreign judgment or a foreign arbitration judgment; the action is under the Law of Dissolution of Marriage (special cases), or the person out of the country is a proper or necessary party to an action duly filed and served in Israel against another person.

If the foreign defendant is served with summons, while temporarily present in Israel or abroad (or even through his representative or lawyer in Israel), according to the regulations this service establishes the court's jurisdiction over him.[26] Lack of such jurisdiction can be cured by the waiver of the defendant, i.e., by his express or implied submission to the Israeli court's jurisdiction.[27]

INTERIM RELIEFS

Once the foreign creditor has instituted a claim in Israel, he is entitled to the same remedies and reliefs available under the Israeli system. In order to preserve the status quo pending the final judgment, or to preserve the defendant's assets and secure the possible collection therefrom at the end of the litigation, the law provides the plaintiff with interim reliefs. These reliefs are given on a prima facie basis, upon affidavits and without a full hearing, and their effect is provisional and does not create final findings as to the rights and duties in dispute.

Attachment and garnishment

Attachment

A temporary attachment order places a procedural bar upon the defendant's assets by preventing the defendant from any transaction in regard to the attached asset, and thus ensuring its preservation for the execution of the judgment which might be rendered.[28]

26. BRA 156/73, *Uniroyal* v. *Zion Ltd*, PD 25(1), 229.
27. CA 23/83, *Jochimak* v. *Kedem*, PD 38(4), 309, 316.
28. CA 533/87, *Hapoel Hamizrahi* v. *Wallach*, PD 43(2), 864; CA 1226/90, *Bank Leumi LeIsrael Ltd* v. *The American Rabbinical Organization and Others* (unreported).

The procedure and conditions relating to temporary attachment are stated in rules 360–375 of the Civil Procedure Regulations 1984, and their main provisions are as follows:

(1) The attachment may be placed on assets belonging to the defendant, including movable or immovable property, and on any debt or right whether already mature or not.[29]

(2) The giving of an attachment order is subject to the discretion of the court and is usually conditional on the plaintiff's guaranteed undertaking to indemnify the defendant for damages sustained if the claim is subsequently dismissed or the attachment annulled.[30]

(3) The action upon which the court may grant the temporary attachment order should be an action for an amount of money[31] which is supported by a document or other reliable evidence to the satisfaction of the court. Although the evidence required for the interim order is prima facie, nevertheless, the court may not render the order where the validity of the cause of action in the claim is seriously doubted.[32] For example, a cause of action which is conditional on a written document which is non-existent will not form a basis for attachment, even though reliable evidence (an affidavit) was provided to support the application for the temporary attachment.[33]

(4) A claim for damages for breach of contract, or claims based on written undertakings or admissions, are the main types of claims upon which a temporary attachment may be granted. Declaratory claims or tortious causes of action cannot serve as a basis for this remedy.[34]

(5) The temporary attachment may also be ordered by the court upon Israeli or foreign arbitration proceedings. The appointment of an arbitrator is equivalent to the submission of a claim.[35]

(6) In an action for a specific asset, an attachment may be placed on the asset.

(7) The request for the attachment is heard by the court *ex parte*, but the court may order that it be heard in the presence of both parties. The applicant may be a plaintiff and a defendant in a counterclaim, who is also a counter-plaintiff.[36] The application should be lodged in writing[37] and be supported by a sworn affidavit verifying the facts which form the cause of action.

29. Not a mere hope or expectation, BRA 232/75, *Ataba* v. *Ratsabi*, PD 30(1), 477.

30. For the rationale of the undertaking as to damages, see CA 732/80, *Arens* v. *Beit El*, PD 38(2), 645, at pp. 658–661.

31. A conditional action to indemnify a guarantor for an obligation which might be imposed on him is still an action for an amount of money. See CA 551/73, *Marioca Shipping Co.* v. *Sela Insurance Co.*, PD 28(2), 136.

32. RA 490/86, *Johan* v. *McMillan*, PD 40(4), 115.

33. CA 146/72, *Levi* v. *Goldman*, PD 27(1), 321; CA 558/85, *Ilien* v. *Rothenberg*, PD 40(1), 553.

34. A rare case of tortious action in which a temporary attachment was ordered: see CA 364/65, *Tabashi* v. *Shaki*, PD 19(4), 104, where the plaintiff alleged in his action that fire escaped from the premises of the defendant and the court held that, for the purposes of the temporary attachment, the plaintiff can be assisted by the presumption of liability which imposes on the defendants the duty to prove that they were not negligent. See also Goren, *Issues in Civil Procedure* (Israel Bar Association 1987), p. 165.

35. s. 16 of the Arbitration Law 1968; see RA 102/88, *Ma'adanei; Avaz Hakesef* v. *Cent Or*, PD 42(3), 201; CA 603/80 *Establishment Nahal* v. *Holiday Inns Inc.*, PD 35(3), 393.

36. Rule 360(4) of the Civil Procedure Regulations 1984.

37. But can be requested orally: (1) at the time of rendering the judgment; (2) in summary procedure when a motion for leave to defend is filed; (3) under s. 29 of the Arbitration Law 1968.

(8) A temporary attachment may be granted, in urgent cases, before the filing of the statement of claim, but it will expire if the claim is not lodged within seven days from the date of the attachment order.

(9) The defendant whose asset was put under a temporary attachment *ex parte*, may apply to the court with a request to cancel the order within 30 days from the date of its being served. The defendant should submit an affidavit which verifies the facts included in his application, and the motion is heard in the presence of both parties. A defendant may also seek to remove the attachment from a certain asset, and exchange it for another asset or guarantee.[38]

(10) The attachment order expires in each of the following cases:
  (a) the plaintiff failed to submit to the court, within seven days, all the documents necessary for service to the defendant;
  (b) the order was rendered before filing of the claim, and the plaintiff failed to file it within seven days; or
  (c) the action was subsequently dismissed or struck out, or the judgment was executed.

(11) No attachment will be placed over assets which are protected as unattachable according to any law. For example, under the Law for the Protection of Salary 1958, a certain amount of a salary should be left for living expenses of the employee and is exempt from attachment.[39]

Usually, the financial ability of the defendant is not taken into consideration, but banks, insurance companies, and similar institutions are presumed to have financial ability and liquidity, and unless this presumption is rebutted, the court will not grant an attachment order on their assets. Thus, a request for a temporary attachment on the assets of three insurance companies pending final judgment against them was dismissed by the court in respect of two, and granted in respect of the third company in view of the appointment of a special supervisor over its business, a fact which was prima facie evidence to rebut the financial ability presumption.[40]

It should be noted that the attachment does not establish any material right in the asset, and its effect is merely procedural. It is not identical to a lien on the property, and other creditors may place additional attachments on the same asset or join an existing one. The chronological order of the various attachments does not establish a priority in the division of the sale redemption.

Garnishment

The court may grant a garnishment order on assets of the defendants held by a third party, "the holder".[41] For example, banks, upon money in the defendant's account; employer of the defendant, upon future salaries.

After such an order is issued, a notice should be delivered to the holder, in which he

38. See RA 490/86, *op. cit.*, p. 116.

39. The same protection is given to an independent worker who is not salaried, in the same amount as the employee: CA 711/84, *Discount Bank* v. *Fishman*, PD 41(1), 369.

40. RA 246/85, *Arad Insurance Co. Ltd* v. *M.B.I. Ltd*, PD 41(1), 586.

41. RA 383/86, *Batarsa* v. *Iash*, PD 41(2), 100, 103.

is required to respond to the court in writing whether the garnished assets are held in his possession.

If the holder admits possession of the garnished assets, he is barred from withdrawal of his admission. If the holder does not admit possession or has not responded at all, or if he objects to the garnishment on any other grounds, the plaintiff may apply for affirmation of the garnishment or give up. The application for affirmation of the garnishment will be in writing and is considered as a statement of claim, and the holder, respectively, as a defendant.

At the end of this claim, the court may either dismiss the claim or otherwise affirm the garnishment. An attachment placed directly on the defendant's assets is affirmed by the court in its judgment if such judgment is rendered in favour of the plaintiff.

After the affirmation, the plaintiff can carry on with the proceedings of realising attached assets according to the Execution Law 1967. The holder may not deliver the garnished asset or otherwise give it to the debtor. The delivery of the asset or payment of the amount to the Execution Office discharges the holder from his duty towards the debtor.[42]

Temporary receivership

The court may, if it considers it just and convenient, appoint a receiver to any property before or after a judgment is given.[43] In its order, the court may decide to remove any person from the possession or custody of the property; place the property under the possession, custody or administration of the receiver, or grant the receiver all the powers of the owner of the property, such as filing claims and defending them, realisation of the property, its administration, safekeeping and its betterment, collection of rent or profits out of the property and their use.

In past practice, the court appointed a receiver only in certain cases, such as where the property was the subject matter of the claim and it seemed necessary to take measures to preserve the property pending the final determination of the rights therein, or where the property was in danger of extinction or damage. Recent Supreme Court judgments led to a wider scope for this remedy.[44]

A plaintiff who filed a monetary claim is entitled to apply for a temporary receivership of the defendant's assets whenever other reliefs are not efficient[45] or not available.[46]

The appointment of the receiver will be published in the official government gazette or in the newspaper, but the court may decide in special cases to prohibit publication.[47]

The receiver should provide a security for his responsibility for the assets over which he was appointed, and will be liable for any loss caused to the assets due to his deliberate or negligent acts.

It should be noted that the appointment of a temporary receiver pending the final

42. s. 51 of the Execution Law 1967.
43. Rule 388 of the Civil Procedure Regulations 1984.
44. CA 846/75, *Onisson* v. *Deutsch*, PD 30(2), 398 (performance of a building contract), CA 689/74, *Basmat* v. *Eilat Municipality*, PD 20(20), 281.
45. BRA 7/89, *Rotem* v. *Nesher*, PD 42(4), 683.
46. This relief is considered as a residual one; see CA 132/77, *Genish* v. *Palmer*, PD 32(2), 64.
47. Rule 390 of the Civil Procedure Regulations 1984.

judgment is obviously limited and aimed, as any other interlocutory relief, at the preservation of the assets. However, when a judgment is given, this proceeding is available under the Execution Law 1967 and its objective is the fulfilment of the judgment.[48]

Provisional injunction

The court is authorised to order a provisional or temporary injunction pending the judgment to be given at the end of litigation whenever it considers it necessary to do so, in view of the following considerations:

(1) The necessity of the court's interference before the hearing of the claim in order to avoid frustration of the plaintiff's rights and to preserve the status quo.

(2) Whether the plaintiff has prima facie proved his cause of action which forms the basis for the application for injunction.[49]

(3) The balance of inconvenience of the plaintiff if the order is not given as weighed against the inconvenience of the defendant should the order be granted.[50]

(4) Considerations of equity whereby the applicant should apply to the court with no delay and clean-handed[51] and, as in other temporary reliefs, the order is conditional on the submission of a security for indemnification of the defendant for damage which he might sustain by the order in case the claim is dismissed or the order expires for any other reason.

Mareva injunction

In a recent District Court decision,[52] the court issued a *Mareva* injunction (which is an *in personam* order), preventing the defendant removing his assets which were being held out of Israel. The sanction for breach of such an injunction (as any other *in personam* order) is being held liable for contempt of court.

Under this injunction, the defendant was prevented from any action regarding moneys held in his bank accounts abroad, and as a condition for that order the court required reliable evidence in support of the claim and proof of the necessity of the order to avoid the concealing of the assets and thus frustration of the expected judgment.

This remedy, too, is subject to the security of the plaintiff's undertaking as to possible damage to the defendant.

Stay of exit

According to rule 376 of the Civil Procedure Regulations 1984, the court may prevent the defendant from leaving the country by issuing a writ of stay of exit, or may

48. See Chapter 5 of the Execution Law 1967, ss. 53–60.

49. See CA 40/87, *Shukha* v. *Shukha*, PD 41(3), 614. See also G. Ginat, "New Principles in the Issue of Provisional Injunction", *Iyunei Mishpat* 5, 413.

50. RA 10/87, *Gadir* v. *Gaber*, PD 41(5), 553, 559.

51. CA 121/65, *Nechmad* v. *Bijou*, PD 19(2), 578; CA 512/73, *Mery* v. *The Histadrut*, PD 27(2), 670; R (Jer) 307/62 (District Court) *Baruch* v. *Elias*, DCJ 36, 107.

52. CC:TA 2233/90, *Okon* v. *Sachs* (District Court) DCJ 1992 (A) 184.

condition his leaving the country on various stipulations, such as a guarantee for his return or guarantee for the fulfilment of a judgment when given.

The conditions upon which the court may grant a stay of exit are:

(1) a statement of claim has been filed; and

(2) it was proved to the satisfaction of the court that:

(a) the defendant intends to leave the country permanently or for a long time,[53] and

(b) the defendant's absence from Israel might put a burden on the conduct of the trial or on the execution of the judgment.[54]

The plaintiff must prove these elements in a strict manner since a stay of exit places a severe restriction on the freedom of movement of the defendant. It is at the court's discretion whether to issue a stay of exit and to consider whether the plaintiff has other means less drastic which may prevent the frustration of the proceedings by the defendant.

Usually, the court will not order a stay of exit against a defendant whose permanent residence is not in Israel, since the objective of such a writ is not a means of pressure against the defendant, and thus the court will prefer other securities.[55]

The court will not order a stay of exit when the amount of the claim is less than NIS 10,000, unless the claim is for alimony.

According to rule 383, the court may order a stay of exit after a judgment has been given in order to prevent the frustration of its execution.

A plaintiff applying for a stay of exit against a defendant must provide a guarantee to the satisfaction of the court, to insure the damages which might be caused to the defendant or a third party. In addition, the plaintiff must deposit a sum of money which is not less than NIS 1,000 and does not exceed NIS 100,000. This can be forfeited to the benefit of the defendant if it becomes apparent that the application for a stay of exit was unreasonable, or that it was not meant to serve the purposes of rule 376, as stated above. The forfeiture does not depend on proof of any damage. For damages, the defendant will be compensated out of the guarantee.

Stringent requirements in view of Basic Law: Human Dignity and Liberty

It should be noted that pursuant to the Basic Law: Human Dignity and Liberty,[55a] many rights such as the right to personal property, freedom of movement, etc. became "constitutional rights". Although the Basic Law is not effective retroactively, and therefore does not apply to the Civil Procedure Regulations, 1984, the current President of the Supreme Court in Israel, Judge Barak, stated that laws which were enacted before the enactment of the Basic Law, should be interpreted in light of the latter.[55b]

Therefore, it can be expected that the Courts will be less willing to grant interim reliefs by virtue of the Civil Procedure Regulations, than they were prior to the enactment of the Basic Law. These reliefs are given prior to the actual hearing and final

53. RA 451/85, *Adin* v. *Plato Sharon*, PD 39(3), 303.
54. CA 703/70, *Somech* v. *Ozer*, PD 24(2), 799.
55. CA 565/62, *Hirshenberg* v. *Hirshenberg*, PD 16, 2851; CA 219/64, *Rozov* v. *Duda*, PD 18(3), 412.
55a. LB 1391, 5752 (25 May 1992), p.150.
55b. HC 3914/92, *Lev* v. *The Regional Rabbinical Council in Tel Aviv*, PD 48(2), 491.

judgment, and before determination of liability. In such a case the interim reliefs may be seen as an infringement of the "constitutional rights".

For example, Rule 376 of the Civil Procedure Regulation provides that for the purpose of granting a Stay of Exit Order, it is enough to show that the defendant's absence from the country *might* frustrate the possible collection at the end of litigation. However, in HC *Lev*,[55c] Judge Barak stated that pursuant to Basic Law: Human Dignity and Liberty, the plaintiff must first show that there is a *true and serious fear* that the defendant's absence will frustrate a future collection, before a Stay of Exit order will be granted.

With respect to attachments, it was stated by Supreme Court Judge Dorner[55d] that it is possible that although the Civil Procedure Regulations do not require, for the granting of an attachment order, to show that the defendant might smuggle his assets out of the country, nevertheless pursuant to the Basic Law: Human Dignity and Liberty this requirement may be read into the Regulations as an implied requirement.

Supreme Court Judge Levin also stated[55e] that pursuant to the enactment of Basic Law: Human Dignity and Liberty which acknowledged the right to personal property as a constitutional right, hence, before an attachment order is granted the Court should give more weight to the quality and quantity of the evidence presented by the plaintiff in support of the request for an attachment order.

As in the past, Civil Procedure Regulation No. 360 requires a document, or other reliable evidence, to support the request, but today the tendency of the Court will be to examine the *prima facie* evidence presented to its merits and not to accept it as a matter of course.

EXECUTION

A creditor who has received a judgment against a debtor, and the foreign judgment creditor who has a judgment which has been declared enforceable in Israel, can execute the judgment through the Execution Office. According to section 81 of the Execution Law 1967, this Law also applies to other documents and decisions which any other law has stated can be executed like a judgment. Such documents include, for instance, realising a pledge according to section 18 of the Pledge Law 1967, and realising a mortgage according to section 90 of the Real Estate Law 1969.

When a file for the execution of a judgment is opened, the debtor should be served with a warning, requiring payment of the judgment. When the period set in the warning elapses (10 days), the winner may start execution proceedings against the debtor and his assets. These proceedings include an arrest order against the debtor and attachments on the debtor's assets and their subsequent sale. Some of the defendant's assets cannot be attached: those necessary for the daily living of the debtor, such as food, beds, linen, dishes, and other necessary items, including tools which the debtor needs for his profession.[56]

55c. *Ibid.*

55d. CR 4475, 4459/94, *Solomov* v. *Sharabani* (unreported).

55e. RCA 5242/95, *Signal Electronics Services (1975) Ltd.* v. *Denbar Ltd.* (handed down in September 1995; unreported).

56. s. 22 of the Execution Law 1967.

The attachment placed by the Execution Office may apply to real estate, bank accounts, movables, rights, and debts. With regard to assets which require formal registration, the attachment is placed by registration. The attachment can apply to the debtor's assets held by third parties ("the holder").

The attachment and garnishment described above, under the Civil Procedure Regulations, have the same nature and effect as the attachment under the Execution Law. After an attachment has been placed on the asset, or at the same time of the application for an attachment, the creditor may apply for the sale of the asset by auction, or its realisation in any other way prescribed by law.

BANKRUPTCY AND LIQUIDATION

Bankruptcy of an individual

Besides the regular system of legal claims in court and subsequent execution through the Execution Office, the creditor who seeks to attack his debtor's assets is provided with a parallel system of proofs and enforcement, which is administered according to the laws of bankruptcy. This system was formed to answer the needs of creditors who face a debtor whose assets are worth less than his due liabilities; hence, the regular execution process may lead to the satisfaction of only a few of his creditors and leave the rest with no assets from which to collect. In a bankruptcy, all the unsecured creditors should file their proof of debts and, at the stage of enforcement, all property of the debtor is accumulated, sold, and divided by rules of priorities among all the creditors.[57]

A creditor who has located sufficient assets belonging to the debtor and has taken actions to preserve them pending the litigation by interim reliefs, would usually prefer the individual proceedings through the Execution Office, which may lead to the full satisfaction of his judgment. However, a creditor who is unable to locate such assets or fears that the debtor has taken actions to conceal his assets would need a more drastic process which, although administered for the benefit of all the creditors, may reveal fraudulently conveyed assets and lead to their accumulation and seizure and subsequent sale for the satisfaction of the debts.[58]

In order to initiate bankruptcy proceedings, the Israeli law (as similar to other common law systems) requires the creditor to show that the debtor is in a state of insolvency, not by proof relating to the debtor's financial position but by indications relating to his actions and behaviour which are considered by the law as "acts of bankruptcy". Section 5 of the Bankruptcy Ordinance states seven such acts:

(1) A fraudulent transfer of property.
(2) Conveyance of property or creating a charge on the property in favour of a creditor, thus creating fraudulent preference of creditors.
(3) Departure from Israel, disappearance from residence or business place, with the intent to evade or delay the creditors.
(4) An attachment and sale by the Execution Office of an asset of the debtor.

57. See M. Mautner, *An Act of Bankruptcy—Whether the End Proves the Beginning* (Lowenberg Book Israel Bar Association 1988), pp. 108–137.

58. S. Levin, *Bankruptcy* (1984), p. 11.

(5) The submission of a formal statement by the debtor of his insolvency.
(6) The sending of a notice by the debtor to his creditor that he has suspended payment of his debt.
(7) Non-payment of debt despite the service of bankruptcy notice requiring such payment.[59]

Besides these acts, the Ordinance states several other actions which will be considered as equivalent to an act of bankruptcy: the filing of a petition by the debtor for bankruptcy; the issuing of a receiving order upon an application for a creditor to arrest the debtor, and a notice to the successors of a debtor or to the administrator of his estate on the filing of an application for an order to administer the estate according to the Bankruptcy Ordinance.

All the acts of bankruptcy should occur not later than three months prior to the submission of the application for bankruptcy. The debt should be a liquidated sum not less than 1,000 shekels payable immediately or at some definite future date.[60]

It should be noted that bankruptcy proceedings will not apply to property of the debtor from which the creditor has already collected by finalising the execution process prior to the initiation of the bankruptcy proceedings, whereas ongoing execution proceedings will be stopped by the bankruptcy proceedings, if not already terminated.[61]

A secured creditor does not usually need to apply to the court or to the trustee in bankruptcy proceedings but may execute his security individually in accordance with the terms provided in his security agreement.[62] Nevertheless, the Law provides, in section 8, that such a creditor has the option to join these proceedings for the amount beyond the value of his security. In such a case, the secured creditor will have to state in his application whether he is willing to give up his security for the benefit of the creditors, or give an estimate of the value of the security. If he chose to do so, he will be admitted as an unsecured creditor for the balance due to him beyond the value so estimated.

According to an application for bankruptcy, the court may make an order for the protection of the property of the debtor, a receiving order. By that order, the official receiver will be the receiver of all the debtor's property. The debtor will be required to make out and submit to the official receiver a statement of his affairs, showing the particulars of his assets, debts and liabilities, his creditors, and the securities held by them.

Before a receiving order is rendered, the debtor may submit an official proposal for composition and arrangement of his affairs with his creditors. The court will not approve a proposal unless a reasonable security for immediate or short-term payment of 50% of the unsecured debt is given.

59. Under s. 3 of the Ordinance, a creditor who has obtained a final judgment against a debtor to pay a sum of money, and where its execution has not been stayed, may apply for service of bankruptcy notice on the debtor by which the latter will be required to pay the determined debt according to the judgment or secure its payment or settle with the creditor.

60. Levin, note 58 *supra*, pp. 68–69.

61. See ss. 91–94 of the Bankruptcy Ordinance (New Version) as to which proceedings will be considered as finalised.

62. HC 42/64, *Bank Hapoalim* v. *The Execution Office*, PD 18(3), 116.

Winding-up of a company

The liquidation or winding-up of a company is a process whereby the company property is administered in order to pay all its debts to its creditors, and the remaining assets, if there are any, are divided among the members. The company's existence is then brought to an end.

A creditor of a company may initiate winding-up proceedings against it in order to collect his debt.

The laws of winding-up have a double goal: one is ensuring a fast dissolution of the company's business by receivership of its assets, including realisation of the company's rights, and the other is their just and equal division between the creditors and shareholders according to an order of priorities set by the law.

Section 266 of the Companies Ordinance provides that a liquidation order acts in favour of all creditors and participants of a company as if given according to a joint application of a creditor and a participant. When a liquidation order is given, all claims and other legal proceedings against the company are stayed.

One of the grounds for the winding-up of a company is its insolvency.[63] A company is deemed to be insolvent if one of the following occurs:

(1) If a creditor, to whom an amount in excess of NIS 5 is due under a cheque or in any other way, delivers to the company at its registered office a demand to pay its debt and the company, during three weeks after the demand, did not pay the debt or provide a guarantee, or breached an arrangement that reasonably satisfied the creditor.

(2) If an execution or other court process issued on a judgment or an order of a court in favour of a creditor is wholly or partly not satisfied.

(3) If it is proved to the court's satisfaction, after it has taken its conditional and future liabilities into account, that the company is unable to pay its debts.

However, where the company disputes the alleged debt on real grounds and in good faith, the application for winding-up will be dismissed, and the creditor will be referred to ordinary proceedings in order to prove his right.[64] But an admission by the directors that the company has no assets from which the creditors can collect debts can serve as the prima facie evidence of insolvency.[65]

The company may rebut this evidence by proving otherwise, but if it fails to do so, the winding-up order may be given in spite of the dispute on the specific debt. In any case, the insolvency is not limited to insolvency in the balance sheets, but includes inability to pay debts due to lack of liquidity.

In comparison with the criteria for bankruptcy of the individual, which focus on the behaviour of the debtor and not on his position, a company will be considered insolvent when it is shown to the court that it is unable to pay its debts in view of its future and conditional liabilities. Where the company's position as a whole shows lack of liquidity and inability to pay its debts which are due, a creditor can apply for its winding-up by the court.[66]

63. s. 257 of the Companies Ordinance.

64. CA 138/79, *Tomer* v. *Levinsky*, PD 35(1), 409.

65. R. Pennington, *Company Law* 1979, 4th ed., p. 691, cited in CA 138/79.

66. CA 577/74, *Bank E.I. Britania* v. *Attorney-General*, PD 29(2), 6; CA 174, 173/75, *The State of Israel* v. *Ben Zion*, PD 30(1), 119.

As in bankruptcy, the liquidation proceedings stay all regular proceedings against the company, and the creditors are required to submit proof of debts to the liquidator. The advantage is also similar to the possibility of locating an accumulation of fraudulently conveyed property and the rescission of improper transactions carried out by the previous management.

The law relating to the winding-up of the company is based on the English law, and the principles relating to the divison of the company's assets among the various creditors and the possible arrangements are dealt with according to English company law.

Rate of exchange—foreign currency

It should be noted that a foreign creditor is entitled to receive payment according to the rate of exchange prevailing on the date of actual payment, and the fact that the company is wound-up does not alter this right.

Although the debts of the company crystallise on the date of the winding-up, the court will view a debt in foreign currency as an undertaking to pay the actual money, with an option for the debtor to repay his debt in Israeli currency, according to the rate of exchange on the actual payment day.[67]

RACHEL LEVITAN
PEGGY SHARON

67. CA 173/75, *supra*.

CHAPTER 16

JAPAN

INTRODUCTION

The Japanese law relating to provisional remedies is contained in a new law which came into force in January 1991 (*Minji Hozen Hou*, Law No. 91 of 1989, hereafter referred to as Civil Action Preservation Law, "CAPL"). The law itself is technical and complex, and there are no provisions dealing specifically with international cases or other situations where litigation might be continuing outside Japan at the same time as applications are made for provisional remedies under the Act. The complete lack of applicable provisions, plus the vagueness and inadequacy of Japanese legal theory relating to the interaction of Japanese with foreign law, along with the seeming inability of many Japanese judges to grasp even the most elementary principles of private international law, make any definitive explanation of the law in this area impossible. All that can realistically be achieved is an outline of the basic principles and an explanation of the main problem areas.

When a foreign plaintiff tries to bring an action in Japan, even if it is a minor action, such as seeking provisional remedies against a defendant to secure assets against which a foreign judgment is later to be enforced, he faces a number of problems. There are problems which can be defined as strictly "legal": What is the law? How can I make use of it? What does it allow me to do? However, there are also a great number of problems which are not "legal", in the strict sense, but which are nevertheless just as important, if not more important, for the foreign plaintiff to understand and appreciate if he is to be successful in obtaining what he wants at the end of the day.

The way in which the Japanese legal system operates in practice, and some of the practical problems faced by a foreign plaintiff are often amongst the most difficult aspect of litigation that will be faced by a foreign plaintiff or lawyer. The provisions of the law itself are often not so difficult to understand. Of course, for the foreigner in Japan, language is a key problem and, where law is concerned, can remain a problem even for those with fairly fluent Japanese. This is particularly so with some of the older laws written in old style language. Translations into English are available but need to be used very warily and only in conjunction with the up-to-date Japanese version.[1]

In order to give some guidance to both the "legal" and "non-legal" aspects of litigating in Japan, this chapter is divided into two sections. The first section deals with the law, setting out the basic provisions relevant to obtaining provisional remedies

1. See note 7.

against a defendant with assets in Japan. The second section gives a brief overview of some of the practical issues involved: lawyers, costs, and time.

LEGAL ISSUES

Availability of Japanese courts to foreign plaintiffs

Foreign plaintiffs are free to bring actions in Japan and, in general, there are few legal problems relating to the legal status of a foreign plaintiff as a non-Japanese party. However, there are occasionally problems relating to whether or not a person has standing to sue, which in practice have made it impossible for foreign plaintiffs to sue on certain occasions. One of the most notable of these is illustrated by the *Novo* case.[2] In this case, a foreign company, Novo, entered into a contract with a Japanese company which contained a number of contractual restrictions on the Japanese company. The Japanese Anti-Monopoly Commission issued an order addressed to the Japanese company, stating that these restrictions were contrary to the Japanese Anti-Monopoly Law and were therefore void. Novo attempted to challenge this decision, but the Supreme Court held that, since the order was not addressed to Novo, it had no standing to challenge the decision of the Anti-Monopoly Commission. The court's reasoning is quite surprising since Novo was the only party adversely affected by the order. Obviously, the Japanese company was not going to make any challenge since it had collected a windfall bargain through the deletion of the restrictions.

In this case, Novo clearly had the capacity to bring actions in general in Japan. The issue was simply whether it was entitled to bring this action against the Commission. The effect of the court's decision was to make the order unchallengeable in practice. This was greatly to the disadvantage of the foreign company.

Capacity to bring an action

This refers to the capacity of a party to litigate in general. The basic rules relating to the capacity of a foreign plaintiff to bring an action in Japan are contained in the Code of Civil Procedure (*Minji Soshou Hou,* CCP) and the Civil Code (*Minpou,* CC). Under CCP, Article 45, the capacity of foreign parties to litigate is governed by the general rules of capacity in the CC. Foreign individuals have the same private rights as Japanese persons unless otherwise prohibited (CC, Article 2). However, this only applies to natural persons. CC, Article 36, states that no foreign legal persons shall be recognised except for foreign states, administrative divisions of states, and trading companies. Therefore, foreign plaintiffs who are individuals or companies have the capacity to litigate in Japanese courts.

Foreign plaintiffs who are neither natural persons nor companies (e.g., foreign plaintiffs who are unincorporated associations) cannot bring actions in their own name but must use a representative, who sues as an individual on behalf of the association. Even where such representative action cannot be brought under the national law of the association, it may still be brought in Japan under Japanese law, which provides that, where a party has no capacity to sue under its own national law,

2. *Novo Industry SA*, Supreme Court, 28 November 1975, Minshu, 29.10.1592.

if such a party would have capacity under Japanese law, then Japanese law applies (CCP, Article 51). The usual means for an association to bring an action in Japan is by means of a representative.

Security to bring an action

When a plaintiff who has no domicile, office, or place of business in Japan brings an action, the court must order security for costs to be deposited on application by the defendant (CCP, Article 107). Once the defendant makes such an application, he is entitled to refuse to appear until such security has been offered by the plaintiff (CCP, Article 109). The court will determine the amount of security based on the legal costs which will be incurred by the defendant (CCP, Article 110(2)).[3] Security may be made by depositing cash or negotiable securities, or by any other means deemed suitable by the court and allowed under the Rules of the Supreme Court (CCP, Article 112). However, the parties are free to agree between themselves that any other means of offering security is acceptable, and in the case of such an agreement the agreement prevails (CCP, Article 112).

If the defendant makes an application demanding security, which he invariably will, the court must fix a period within which the plaintiff must offer security. If he fails to comply within this period, then the court may dismiss the action without making any decision on the merits (CCP, Article 114). Once security is given, the defendant obtains a right of a pledgee[4] over the security. This gives him a priority over everyone else to claim against the property.

Plaintiffs resident in countries which are parties to the Hague Convention 1954 do not have to give security.[5]

Provisional remedies

Availability

The plaintiff can apply for provisional remedies in Japan before any action, either in Japan or abroad, has commenced. In addition, even in the case of a contractual dispute with a valid foreign exclusive jurisdiction or arbitration clause, as long as he can satisfy the requirements for obtaining the provisional remedy, the plaintiff can obtain provisional remedies notwithstanding such clauses.

In theory, provisional remedies can be enforced immediately once the relevant court order has been obtained. However, in practice, the defendant will usually pay money into court to prevent immediate enforcement. Thereafter, the plaintiff must wait until the Japanese or foreign judgment on the merits has become final before he can actually obtain final execution over the assets attacked by obtaining an "execution judgment" from a Japanese court. This is a decision which comes at the enforcement stage and which converts the temporary seizure of assets into a permanent transfer to the plaintiff.

If the provisional remedy is to be used to enforce an award on the merits made by a

3. This will not include the cost of the defendant's lawyers: see text relating to litigation costs.
4. *Tampousha*.
5. The Hague Convention 1954 is one of several multilateral agreements which may have significant impact on the rights of the parties.

foreign court, the foreign action must comply with the provisions on recognition and enforcement of foreign judgments in Japan (see below). Special care must be taken when there are two defendants in Japan.[6]

Background to current law

The law dealing with provisional remedies was first introduced as part of the CCP nearly 100 years ago. It was based on the German rules and remained almost intact for the whole of that period.

One of the peculiarities about the Japanese system is that the law governing the application and issue of an order is completely separate from the law governing the enforcement of that order (the rules relating to obtaining an "execution judgment"). This separation created a number of technical difficulties. However, with the increasing speed of transactions in Japan and the need for faster and more effective methods of dispute resolution through the courts, it was felt that a revision of the law was necessary.

The purposes of the revision included establishing quicker procedures for obtaining a provisional remedy and the clarification of the necessary procedures to make clear the validity, effectiveness, and enforceability of frequently used measures, and to unify as far as possible the interpretation and procedure for applications and subsequent enforcement.

The revised law is only partially successful in meeting these objectives. Application and enforcement are still governed by separate laws: the CAPL and the Civil Enforcement Law (CEL), respectively. This chapter deals almost exclusively with the problems of obtaining the order and only briefly with problems relating to execution of it.

Types of provisional remedy

There are two types of provisional remedy available under Japanese law: provisional attachment (*kari sashiosae*) and provisional disposition (*kari shobun*). The law setting out the main provisions relating to these remedies is the Civil Action Preservation Law (CAPL, *Minji Hozen Hou*, Law No. 91 of 1989).

This is a new law which came into effect on 1 January 1991, and it replaces the provisions relating to provisional remedies which were contained in the CCP, Articles 737–747 and 755–765.[7] The principles of the new law remain similar to the old law but are not identical.[8] The new law uses a generic term of "civil action preservation

6. See text relating to parent and subsidiary as joint defendants.

7. To the author's knowledge, there is no official translation of this law available at the date of writing. As a word of caution, the English translations of Japanese law, including those issued under the authorisation of the Ministry of Justice, are not always reliable and should not be used for the purposes of advising clients. For example, the 1988 edition of the CCP still contains provisions in the English translation that were, in fact, repealed in 1979.

8. The new law has been enacted as part of an on-going revision process whereby the CCP (*Minji Soshou Hou*) is being split into three separate laws governing civil litigation procedure (CCP, *minji soshou*), civil execution (*shikkou*), and civil action security (*minji hozen*), respectively. The CCP is, therefore, gradually getting shorter. Finally, it is to be rewritten in more simple and up-to-date Japanese.

(CAP) order" to refer to orders in respect of both kinds of remedy mentioned above that can be granted under the new law.

PROVISIONAL ATTACHMENT

Provisional attachment is a procedure which allows the plaintiff to obtain an order from the court which prevents the defendant from disposing or otherwise dealing with his property. The order can be made in respect of any kind of property, both tangible and intangible, owned by the defendant. Orders can also be obtained in respect of conditional and/or prescriptive rights owned by/owed to the defendant (CAPL, Article 20(2)).

The purpose of provisional attachment is to preserve assets so that they can later be sold or otherwise converted into money in order to prevent a monetary claim becoming impossible or very difficult to execute at a later date (CAPL, Article 20). For most claims, this kind of order will be the most appropriate.

When a provisional attachment order is issued, the defendant is able to have the order cancelled by paying a sum of money into court. When the court issues the order, the court must serve notice on the defendant and must state the amount of money which the defendant must pay into court in order to stay execution. Obviously this amount is directly related to the amount of the plaintiff's claim.

PROVISIONAL DISPOSITION

Orders for provisional disposition serve a different purpose. They are used to protect claims relating to rights which are not convertible into money. There are two circumstances in which an order for provisional disposition can be granted by the court, one of which relates to property which is the subject of a dispute (CAPL, Article 23(1)) and the other to the status of the parties in relation to each other (CAPL, Article 23(2)).

A provisional disposition order relating to property (*Keisoubutsu ni kansuru kari shobun*) prevents a party from dealing with or changing property which is the subject matter of the dispute, to ensure that execution of an award is not made more difficult or impossible. For example, in a dispute over land, it would prevent the owner of the land from granting building rights over it, making the transfer of it to the claimant difficult at a later stage. Its purposes, therefore, is to preserve the nature of property which is in dispute in order to protect the claimant by ensuring that the right he is claiming remains realisable at the time of any award (CAPL, Article 23). It differs from a provisional attachment in that provisional attachment relates to property that is not in itself the subject matter of the dispute but which is either money or can be converted into money by compulsory sale and used to satisfy a monetary claim.

A provisional disposition order relating to the state of affairs in dispute (*Kari no chii o sadameru kari shobun*) is a temporary declaration by the court that a particular status or legal relationship is deemed to exist unless and until the court decides otherwise. It involves ordering the parties to continue to behave as if a particular state of affairs existed, and therefore requires the supervision of the court. For instance, in a dispute about the legality of the dismissal of an employee, the court can order the employer to continue to pay the employee until a decision on the merits is completed. Because it is an order with far reaching consequences and which requires supervision, it is more difficult to obtain. This kind of order usually requires a hearing with both parties represented, and can only be obtained *ex parte* in very exceptional circumstances.

Both kinds of provisional disposition are usually only appropriate for disputes relating to rights over property or to long-term on-going relationships taking place in Japan, such as employment. In general, a foreign plaintiff will be more likely to want to obtain an order for provisional attachment to secure a money claim. Therefore, the remainder of this chapter will concentrate on the issues relating to the obtaining of an order for provisional attachment.

Bringing an action

Jurisdiction

There are no separate rules governing the jurisdiction of Japanese courts over international as opposed to domestic disputes. Therefore, jurisdictional issues are, in theory, governed by the domestic rules which set out which domestic court has jurisdiction *vis-à-vis* other domestic courts. This causes numerous problems, because these rules were never designed to apply to questions of international jurisdiction, and therefore create totally inappropriate results at times. These inappropriate results can be mitigated by the judiciary through the application of principles of natural justice, but such applications are vague, inconsistent, and difficult to predict. Also, unfortunately, they often seem in practice to have the effect of working very much to the injustice of foreign parties. This should not be too surprising for those with experience of the Japanese judiciary. Their decisions tend to be pro-government, bureaucratic, archly conservative, and show scant regard for the consistent application of legal theory.

The Japanese court system comprises one Supreme Court,[9] eight High Courts,[10] 50 District Courts,[11] 50 Family Courts[12] and 439 Summary Courts.[13] In most commercial cases, the relevant court of first instance will be the District Court[14] which has jurisdiction under these domestic rules.

Applications for Civil Action Protection (CAP) orders may be made to the court which has jurisdiction to hear the action on the merits (whose jurisdiction will be based on the rules in the CCP), or to a court given jurisdiction under the CAPL (CAPL, Article 12(1)). The plaintiff, therefore, has a choice. If the plaintiff is going to bring an action on the merits in Japan, it will usually be more appropriate to make all applications to the court where the action on the merits will be brought, even before the main action has actually commenced. If, on the other hand, the purpose of the

9. *Saikou saibansho.*
10. *Kotou saibansho.*
11. *Chihou saibansho.*
12. *Katei saibansho.*
13. *Kan i saibansho.*
14. The choice of Summary or District Court depends on the amount of money involved in the claim. Summary Courts deal with all claims involving less than 900,000 yen. All claims which cannot be converted into monetary claims are deemed to exceed this sum and, therefore, the relevant court will usually be the District Court (CCP, Art. 22). In cases where a foreign plaintiff is bringing an action, it will invariably be in the District Court. One exception to the rules is that actions based on the Anti-Monopoly Law must be brought at the Tokyo High Court, which has exclusive jurisdiction to hear all such actions.

application is to seize assets to satisfy a foreign judgment, the issue becomes slightly more complicated. It seems that a plaintiff can apply either to the court that would have jurisdiction on the merits or make the application to any court given jurisdiction under the CAPL.[15]

In either case, the plaintiff must consider general rules of jurisdiction contained in the CCP, as well as the rules especially laid down for provisional remedies under the CAPL.

Jurisdiction under CCP

The basic rules relating to jurisdiction of the court in main actions on the merits are contained in CCP, Articles 1–20, which set out the forum where it is possible to bring an action. The forum is simply an indication of the geographical place where an action may be commenced, and is not a reference to a particular court or kind of court. Therefore, once the relevant place has been located under the rules, it is still necessary to decide which particular court within the location has jurisdiction, i.e., District Court, Summary Court, High Court or Family Court.

In commercial cases (excluding cases brought under the Anti-Monopoly Law[16]) and all other non-family civil cases, the Summary Court has jurisdiction over all claims for money or which can be converted into money and which involve sums of less than 900,000 yen.[17] The District Court has jurisdiction over all claims which exceed 9000,000 yen or which involve immovable property.[18] For the purposes of calculation, all claims made under the same action are added together,[19] but claims which are merely incidental to the main object of the action are excluded from the calculation.[20] Claims which are not convertible into money (e.g. injunction) are deemed to be monetary claims in excess of 900,000 yen[21] and therefore go to the District Court.

The CCP provides for two kinds of forum: general and special. The basic starting point for jurisdictional questions is to locate the general forum of the defendant. The relevant court of the general forum of the defendant is the court with general jurisdiction.[22] This court will have jurisdiction to hear an action on the merits and any procedural matter relating to such an action, unless there is a special law which creates

15. See text relating to jurisdictional rules in the CAPL. It is unclear from Art. 12(1) whether an application can be made to the court that would have jurisdiction on the merits if the plaintiff is, in fact, not going to bring a merits action in Japan. There are no cases on this point to date. It is clear that a plaintiff in this situation can bring an action based on the jurisdictional rules under the CAPL and, in many cases, the relevant court(s) under these provisions will be the same courts as would be arrived at using the CCP rules. For instance, the defendant is most likely to have movables which are located in the same place as is his permanent residence. Whether one obtains jurisdiction because of place of residence or location of the assets often gives the same results. But the results will not always be the same. For a Japanese plaintiff who will, in any event, be bringing a merits action in Japan, the difference is not important. It only becomes important for a foreign plaintiff who is bringing a merits action abroad. This, plus the fact that the law is so recent, accounts for the lack of any reported decisions on this point.

16. For an action brought under the Anti-Monopoly Law the Tokyo High Court has exclusive jurisdiction to hear all claims.

17. Court Law (*Saiban Hou*), Art. 33(1)i.

18. *Ibid.*, Art. 24(1).

19. CCP, Art. 23.

20. CCP, Art. 23(2).

21. CCP, Art. 22(1).

22. CCP, Art. 1.

an exception to the general rule by declaring that a particular court has exclusive jurisdiction.[23] If there is a special law which gives exclusive jurisdiction to a particular court, then the general rules of jurisdiction cease to apply.[24]

For natural persons, the general forum of the defendant is determined by his/her permanent residence.[25] If the defendant has no permanent residence or if it is unknown, then the general forum is determined by the defendant's current actual residence, and if the residence is unknown, by his/her last permanent residence[26] or by his current place of abode.[27]

For legal persons (e.g., companies), the general forum is determined by the place of the principal office or place of business[28] or, if there is no principal office or place of business, then by the permanent residence of the principal person in charge of its affairs.[29] For groups which are not legal persons, such as associations, the general forum is the general forum of the legal representative of the association, ascertained under the rules for individuals.

As was stated earlier, the jurisdictional rules give rise to certain problems in cases with an international dimension. One of these problems is that the basic rule is very wide, giving jurisdiction to courts in Japan more frequently than might be expected. When attacking assets, this is to the advantage of the plaintiff. In theory, it is possible to bring an action even if the case has no connection with Japan other than the fact that the defendant has a permanent residence there.[30]

There are also certain special rules of jurisdiction[31] which allow a plaintiff to bring an action in a place other than the general forum where appropriate. The rules giving special jurisdiction operate in addition to and alongside the general jurisdiction rules and give a plaintiff a choice of where to initiate proceedings. The most important special bases of jurisdiction are: contract, place of performance of a property right (Article 5); cheques, place of payment of a cheque or other instrument (Article 6); claims against ships, place of registry of the ship (Article 10); and tort, place where the wrongful act was committed.[32] There are a number of other special bases of jurisdiction.

23. For example, the Anti-Monopoly Act which gives exclusive jurisdiction to the Tokyo High Court for all actions brought under it.

24. CCP, Art. 27.

25. CCP, Art. 2.

26. CCP, Art. 2(2).

27. CCP Art. 22.

28. CCP Art. 4.

29. All companies in Japan are required to register certain things in the companies register kept by the registry having jurisdiction over the seat or place of business (Commercial Code, Art. 9). These items must also be registered at the registry having jurisdiction over any branch of the company (Commercial Code, Art. 10), and they include: *Kabushiki Kaisha*—their principal place of business (Commercial Code, Art. 188(2)2); full name and permanent residence of representative director (Commercial Code, Art. 188(2)8); *Gomei Kaisha* (commercial partnership)—principal place of business (Commercial Code, Art. 64(2)), and full name and permanent residence of each partner (Commercial Code, Arts. 63(3) and 64(1)). Foreign companies with a place of business in Japan are also required to register this place of business (Commercial Code, Art. 479).

30. Therefore, a Japanese court will have jurisdiction over an action based on a contract entered into by a Japanese resident and an English company, made and performed in England, governed by English law, and where all the evidence and witnesses are in England. Whilst there is now a tendency for courts to refuse to accept jurisdiction in a case such as this on the grounds of inconvenience and injustice, the legal basis for such refusal remains vague.

31. CCP, Arts. 5–20.

32. This includes either where the act was committed or where the damage was suffered.

Jurisdictional rules in the CAPL

For provisional remedies, either the courts which have jurisdiction over the main action, or the courts which are given jurisdiction under the CAPL have jurisdiction to deal with claims for provisional remedies relating to the main action.[33] Jurisdiction in this sense relates to the issue of which domestic court has jurisdiction. Obviously, a defendant may well have assets which are located in more than one district; therefore, in a purely domestic case, the plaintiff will usually apply to the court which has jurisdiction over the main action. Otherwise, he may have to make multiple applications in multiple districts, which would be expensive and time consuming.

However, one of the effects of the CAPL is that it is not necessary for the court to have jurisdiction over the main action on the merits in order to grant provisional remedies. All the court needs is jurisdiction under the CAPL. Therefore, a court may in certain circumstances be able to grant a provisional attachment order relating to property located within that court's district even if no Japanese court would have jurisdiction to hear the main action (for example, because of a valid foreign exclusive jurisdiction or arbitration clause, or because the property is movable property belonging to a non-resident foreigner and the claim has no other connection whatsoever with Japan).

The jurisdictional rules in the CAPL are quite problematic and not very clear or easy to understand. Which court has jurisdiction to issue an order depends upon the location or, in some cases, the deemed location of the asset which is being attacked, or the place of its registration. If the asset is a right owed to the defendant by a third party, or property in or over which third parties have rights (e.g., mortgage), then the jurisdiction may depend on the location of the general forum[34] of the third party.[35]

It should be obvious that, when a plaintiff wishes to attack a number of different assets, of different kinds, located in different places, he may well end up having to make applications to various courts. The rationale behind these provisions seems to be to protect third-party rights and to promote the effective execution against attached assets at the enforcement stage. However, it seems that these provisions make the application stage much more difficult and expensive than is really necessary, especially when the plaintiff wishes to attack a number of assets simultaneously without bringing an action on the merits in Japan. Not only will such an attack be more expensive (involving lawyers in different locations), but the advantage of surprise may well be lost as soon as the first application is made. The making of simultaneous applications in a number of different locations will be demanding to co-ordinate in any event, and for a foreign plaintiff even more difficult.

A full account of the rules under CAPL, Article 12, relating to the location of assets is not given here. However, the following provisions may be helpful.

(1) Immovables[36] are located in the district where they exist.

33. CAPL, Art. 12.

34. General forum under the basic rule of the CCP, Art. 2 (individuals), or Art. 4 (legal persons).

35. There are no provisions relating directly to what happens when such rights are owed or owned jointly by more than one third party with general forums in different places. Presumably, the plaintiff must pick one and have the other third party joined as a proper party.

36. "Immovables" are defined in CC, Art. 86, which states that land and all things firmly attached thereto are immovables. All other things are movables (CC, Art. 86(2)). "Things" means corporeal things (CC, Art. 85), except that obligations payable to bearer are deemed to be movables (CC, Art. 86(3)).

(2) Rights in or over immovables which are required to be registered are deemed to exist at the place of registration.
(3) For rights owed to the defendant by third parties, the court is the relevant court of the general forum of the third party, except when the object of the attachment is to transfer rights in or mortgages over ships,[37] or movables,[38] in which case the place is the relevant court of the place where those things exist (CAPL, Article 12(3)).

The main advantage under the new law is that it is now possible for a court to make a general order attaching all of the movables of a defendant located within that court's district (CAPL, Article 21). Under the old law, the plaintiff was required to specify each and every asset which he wanted to attach. This meant that the plaintiff had to supply descriptions of individual assets plus indications of their whereabouts. Such requirements made attachments much more difficult and expensive to obtain in practice.

For all other kinds of assets (assets which are not "movables"), the plaintiff is still required under the new law to submit descriptions and other evidence relating to the whereabouts and kind of right which he wants to attach. In some cases, this involves also having to give details of any rights which third parties have over such assets, and this in particular can be extremely difficult to ascertain. However, at least it is now possible to get a general attachment of a defendant's movables.[39]

Evidential requirements

Once the plaintiff has found the appropriate court, CAPL, Article 13, sets out the items which must be included in the application for an order.

The plaintiff must explain in his application the basis of his claim and either the rights that should be protected or the legal relationship, and the reasons why protection by means of an order is necessary.[40] The explanation must be made clearly, and giving security and/or swearing to the fact that there is a good basis to the claim are not substitutes for an explanation.[41] For provisional attachment orders, the requirement of necessity is elaborated in CAPL, Article 20, which states that an order can be issued when there is a risk that money will not be able to be paid to satisfy a claim, or a risk that the execution of any judgment will become very difficult.

The plaintiff must also submit evidence of ownership by the defendant, and the location and value of the property he wishes to be attached (CAPL, Articles 19–20).

37. As defined in CEL, Art. 112.
38. As defined in CEL, Art. 122.
39. Subject to certain exemptions which prevent the seizure of assets such as clothes up to a certain value and tools of trade.
40. CAPL, Art. 13(1) and (2).
41. Under the old law, instead of having to show cause the plaintiff used to be able to give security or swear to the truth of the claim where there was a lack of cogent evidence to support it (CCP, Art. 267(2)). Sometimes, the plaintiff was able to obtain provisional remedies without giving any evidence as to the necessity for them but simply by furnishing security. The new law makes it clear that the plaintiff must give an explanation as to why any such order is necessary, and cannot use CCP, Art. 267(2), to avoid doing this.

Recognition and enforcement of foreign judgments

Recognition and enforcement of foreign judgments is a fairly complicated subject, and only a brief outline is given here.

Foreign judgments can be enforced in Japan if a Japanese court recognises and renders an "execution judgment" in favour of the plaintiff. Once the execution judgment is obtained, enforcement proceeds using the same rules that apply to domestic awards.

Recognition

The requirements which must be satisfied for a Japanese court to recognise a foreign judgment are set out in CCP, Article 200, which lists five conditions that must be fulfilled. These conditions are cumulative, so that failure to meet any one condition will result in non-recognition. They are as follows:

(1) Final and conclusive (CCP, Article 200). The foreign award must have reached a stage of finality which makes it unappealable under the laws of the foreign state. Therefore, the plaintiff should wait until any time limits for an appeal under the rules of the foreign jurisdiction have expired. Interlocutory orders cannot be enforced in Japan, but default judgments may be enforceable as long as the service requirements (see below) have been complied with.

(2) Jurisdiction of the foreign court is not contrary to Japanese law (CCP, Article 200(1)). This condition will normally be satisfied where the foreign court would have had jurisdiction under the Japanese rules. Since Japanese rules on jurisdiction are wide, this condition is unlikely to give rise to many problems unless a Japanese court is given exclusive jurisdiction under Japanese law, or if the foreign court has accepted jurisdiction in spite of a foreign exclusive jurisdiction clause which a Japanese court would have held to be applicable. In any event, responding on the merits by the defendant to the foreign jurisdiction will satisfy this requirement.

(3) Service (CCP, Article 200(2)). If the defendant is a Japanese national or company, then the defendant must have either made an appearance (an appearance simply to contest jurisdiction is adequate), or must have been served by a means which complies with the Japanese rules relating to service. Service should, therefore, be effected under the relevant convention[42] or judicial co-operation agreement and should not be done by post or personal service.

(4) Public order and good morals (CCP, Article 200(3)). The judgment of the foreign court must not be contrary to public order and good morals under Japanese law. Enforcement of a judgment which directly conflicts with a previous judgment of a Japanese court is not possible.[43] Foreign judgments

42. For example, the Hague Convention 1954; Japan/UK Consular Convention, Art. 25; Japan/US Consular Convention, Art. 17(1)e.

43. This was the case in the *Kansai Tekko* case, see text relating to parent and subsidiary as joint defendants.

whose enforcement requires the defendant to perform an act which is prohibited under Japanese law are not necessarily against public order and good morals.[44] Each case must be considered on its own, and infringement of criminal or administrative laws does not necessarily effect private rights and their enforcement.

(5) Reciprocity (CCP, Article 200(4)). There must be reciprocal treatment of the enforcement of Japanese judgments in the foreign jurisdiction. This condition is interpreted relatively loosely and "substantialy similar treatment" is sufficient.[45] However, if the foreign jurisdiction would review a Japanese judgment on the merits, the requirement of reciprocity will not be met.[46]

Enforcement

As stated above, the plaintiff wishing to enforce a foreign judgment must first obtain an "execution judgment" from the relevant Japanese court. The rules governing which court has jurisdiction to hear such an application are set out in CEL, Article 24, which states that the relevant court is the District Court of the defendant's general forum[47] or, if no general forum exists, then the District Court with jurisdiction over the subject matter of the claim or attachable property belonging to the defendant.

In deciding whether or not to grant an execution judgment, the Japanese court cannot review the merits of the case but must ensure that the requirements in CCP, Article 200, are satisfied[48] and that the foreign judgment has become final and binding (CEL, Article 24(3)).

Once an execution judgment had been obtained, it is enforced as a domestic judgment using any or all of the procedures applicable to domestic cases.

PRACTICAL ISSUES

Court orders to commence proceedings

One major problem area is Article 37 of the new law. Under Article 37(1), on application by the defendant the court has the power to order the plaintiff to commence an action on the merits within a given period or face cancellation of the attachment order. It is not at all clear whether or not the commencement of an action against the defendant in a foreign jurisdiction would be held to satisfy the requirements of this Article.

Under Article 37(5), there are provisions which enable the commencement of arbitration proceedings to be recognised as "bringing a main action" for the purposes of preventing the cancellation of the order. Again, however, there is no reference to the

44. For example, payment of money in a foreign currency in breach of the Foreign Exchange and Foreign Trade Control Law was held to be enforceable (Tokyo District Council, 3 *Kokusai torihiki hanreishu* 538, 28 May 1970).

45. Great Court of Judicature, 3670 *Shinbun* 16, 5 December 1933.

46. For example, a Belgian judgment was denied recognition on the grounds that, under the Belgian law then in force, the Belgian court had to review the merits (Tokyo District Court, 11 *Kaninshu* 1522, 20 July 1960).

47. See the basic rule of jurisdiction under the CCP.

48. CEL, Art. 24(3).

status of a foreign arbitration proceeding. On the one hand, since the plaintiff is required to give documentary evidence that proceedings have commenced, there are good reasons to suppose that a Japanese court should recognise that starting an action or an arbitration proceeding abroad and providing proof of such, should be sufficient to prevent the cancellation of the attachment order. However, on the other hand, there is a similar provision dealing with stays of actions which has been held to apply only to domestic actions, and which cannot be used to grant a stay of proceedings in Japan on the basis that an action between the same parties about the same issue has already commenced abroad.[49]

Finding assets

This is the most important and difficult part of making a successful application. In practice, locating the assets which can be attached will always be the most difficult task that a plaintiff has to achieve. In most cases, it will be this stage which will be decisive in the decision as to whether or not to make the application.

In order to obtain an attachment order, the plaintiff has to be able to provide exact details of the asset which he wants the court to attach. It is not possible to get a general order attaching all the property of the defendant[50] or an order restraining the defendant *in personam* from dealing with his assets in general.

In addition, Japanese lawyers will not usually find the details of assets of the defendant. The plaintiff will be expected to provide this information to the lawyers. This means that either the plaintiff must already know such details (unlikely) or must discover them. This will involve such activities as instructing Japanese private investigators, which will be costly[51] and, in any event, may not bring the desired information to light.

Details

The extent to which details will be required is such that it is often practically impossible to supply them. For instance, when trying to attach money held in a bank account, the plaintiff will be required to supply details of the bank, the branch where the account is located, the number of the account, and probably the amount of money in the account which the plaintiff wishes to attach. This last detail obviously means that the plaintiff needs to know with some degree of accuracy the balance of the account. Even when all these details are available, the plaintiff will seldom be able actually to attach all (or any) of the money for reasons that will be explained later.[52]

Companies

The first place to start will be the company's registered office. All Japanese companies are required to register their principal place of business. This must be done in the district where the office is located. There is no national registry of principal offices, but

49. Therefore, there is no international doctrine of *lis alibi pendens* in Japan.
50. Except for the limited exception relating to movables discussed earlier.
51. In addition, this cost will probably not be recoverable: see text relating to litigation costs.
52. See text relating to bank accounts.

this should not be a major problem, since there will usually be some indication on company stationery.

Once located, all of the principal assets of the company that are required to be registered can be pinpointed quickly and easily; however, it will be very unlikely that any of these assets will be appropriate for attachment. This is because these assets will inevitably have prior charges over them to an extent which will cover their value completely.

Japanese companies usually work from a group or a *keiretsu* structure. These are not legal terms, nor do they have any definite meaning. However, they are generally used to describe slightly different aspects of business structures. In general, "group" indicates a number of different companies which operate around a central bank or central company. All members of the group will usually have extensive cross shareholdings and interlocking directorships. Groups may have large numbers of companies, and the activities of these companies may be quite different. One company may be involved in automobile manufacture, another in real estate development, a third in tourist hotels. In contrast, *keiretsu* is usually used to refer to companies that are locked together by some means (contract, shares, directorships, bank) and which also share a common business activity. In large structures, both methods will usually be used, with each member company in the group heading its own *keiretsu* of other companies whose business activities are closely related to its own and who are in practice controlled by it.

Both such structures will involve a central bank to which all of each company's major assets will be charged. The companies usually operate on the basis of a series of short-term loans from the bank. These will be granted and paid off on a revolving basis. One of the effects of this is that companies will usually not have assets which can be attached, since the previous bank charges will take priority over any attachment order.

Where a main action is taking place abroad, it is more likely to involve a subsidiary set up by a parent, or a company other than the central group parent or bank. Therefore, the chances of its being part of this kind of parent-bank-subsidiary relationship will be especially high.

Bank accounts

As was mentioned earlier, the extent of information regarding a bank account needed to obtain a provisional attachment order is fairly high. Even when the information has been obtained, however, there is often little chance of actually attaching the money contained in it. This is because of the ability of a bank to set off the deposit held against loans made or credit given to the company. These set-off clauses are generally contained in the contracts for deposit accounts. Therefore, if the bank holds three million yen on deposit but has extended a loan of two million yen, it can set off the two million yen against the three million yen, and this set off again takes priority over any provisional attachment order. Thus, in the above example, the plaintiff will be able to attach only one million yen.

Thankfully, this kind of set off applies only to moneys and credits actually held by the bank, and not to cash which it has transferred to the company, which can be attached as a movable (if it can be located). However, on a practical level, this advantage is not very useful since cash will usually be difficult to locate or will have been used. In addition, loans will usually take the form of an extension of credit. This is very disadvantageous since, if the credit has been extended, then the bank can set off up to the level of the credit even if it has not been used. Further, if the bank is a group bank and also holds the companies' immovable property as security, it may well have extended credits which are worth considerably more than the deposits held. This will leave a minus sum after the set off, which obviously means that there will be nothing left to attach.

Attacking the parent company

In most cases, it will be impossible to attack the parent company, since the separation of legal persons is very much respected under Japanese law. In most cases, even where the defendant is owned as a 100% subsidiary, the court will continue to treat the parent and the subsidiary as strictly separate legal entities, and it will not be possible to make the parent liable for the acts of its subsidiary.[53] If the parent might be separately liable and is a second defendant abroad, there are very limited interim remedies against the parent in Japan.[54]

Japanese tactics

The difficulties faced by a company wishing to attach assets of another company apply to Japanese as well as to foreign companies. It is helpful, therefore, to look at what Japanese companies do in such situations.

Generally, if the plaintiff cannot locate sufficient company assets, his most likely next target will be the personal assets of the company officers.[55] Of course, in any major litigation, these assets will generally not be sufficient to cover the claim. The main purpose of such attachments is to create personal inconvenience to produce some leverage for the plaintiff. In this way, assets which commonly might be sought to be attached would be the house, car, and other personal property belonging to the company president and other directors. Sometimes, such assets will be owned by the company and might be difficult to attach for all of the reasons given above. At other times, attachment may be possible and may produce considerable inconvenience. This tactic has been made easier by the change in the law allowing attachment of movables in general.[56]

Bankruptcy

If the defendant goes bankrupt after a provisional attachment order has been obtained but before it has been executed, the attachment order will become unenforceable and the plaintiff will rank as an ordinary creditor.[57]

53. The one notable exception to this is contained in the 1991 antitrust guidelines, which state that where a parent owns more than 50% of the subsidiary, the two companies may be treated by the Federal Trade Commission as the same economic entity. This is a very new concept in Japanese law and is very unlikely to be applied in any other area.

54. See text relating to parent and subsidiary as joint defendants.

55. *Torishimari yakuin.*

56. See Law No. 91 of 1989.

57. Bankruptcy Law 1922 (Law No. 71 of 1922), Art. 70.

Assignment of assets

Under the rules governing the assignment of assets, written assignments which take place by means of a notarised deed are binding on all third parties with or without notice of the assignment (CC, Article 467(2)). Consequently, where an attachment order in respect of a particular asset has been granted by the court but has not yet been served on the defendant, such an assignment by the defendant to a third party will frustrate the order. If the assignment takes place on the same day as notice of the order is served, the assignment will still be effective if it takes place before the notice is received.[58]

Given the fact that consideration is not necessary under Japanese law, proving that an assignment took place at an undervalue for the purpose of frustrating an attachment order which the defendant suspected to be imminent will be problematic. As in most other jurisdictions, speed in obtaining such orders is essential. Since orders restraining a defendant *in personam* from dealing with his assets in general are not available, and since general attachment orders are only available for movables, the scope for this kind of behaviour by unscrupulous defendants is wider in Japan than in some other jurisdictions.

Parent and subsidiary as joint defendants

As was mentioned previously,[59] it will not be possible to attack the parent company unless it has become a party to the main action for some reason. If the parent has been made a party to the main action abroad, or where there is a second defendant, there are certain aspects of Japanese law which require that special care must be taken.

The problem is one which relates to the eventual enforceability of any final award which might be obtained in the foreign jurisdiction.

The problem is illustrated by the following example.[60] P sues D1 in a foreign country. P or D1 joins D2 who was a party to the transaction further up the line. D2 sues D1 in Japan for a declaration that D2 has no liability. D2 obtains the declaration. When P tries to enforce his award in Japan against D2, he is met with a finalised contrary decision by a Japanese court which prevents his being able to enforce his award in Japan.

If D1 and D2 are parent and subsidiary, it is unrealistic to expect that the action for a declaration in favour of D2 will be effectively opposed by D1. The same will probably apply where the two companies have a close trading relationship (which will usually be the case). For example, in the *Kansai Tekko* case, the Japanese defendants had a close trading relationship and D1 did not defend the case on the merits in Japan.

This problem is a major one which has to be kept in mind. First, the plaintiff may not even know that such an action is taking place, since he will not be a party. Secondly, even if he does know, there is considerable doubt as to whether he can join himself as a party to the Japanese action. Thirdly, Japan has no doctrine of *lis alibi pendens* which applies to cases which are proceeding in a foreign jurisdiction. On the

58. Supreme Court, 4 October 1983, Hanji 1095/95.

59. See text relating to attacking the parent company.

60. This example is a simplified version of the facts in the case *Kansai Steel (Kansai Tekko)*, interlocutory judgment, Osaka District Court, 9 October 1973; final judgment, 22 December 1977.

contrary, in the leading case on this issue,[61] the court stated that the fact that such an action prevented the eventual enforcement of the foreign judgment against one of the parties would be a valid reason for him to bring the action.

Therefore, it would appear that the plaintiff's best option will be to try to obtain an order from the foreign court, restraining this kind of parallel proceeding. Since the enforceability of such an order in Japan is questionable, if possible, it will be a very wise precaution to try to persuade the first defendant to give undertakings in the foreign court to inform the plaintiff of any actions being brought in Japan relating to the liabilities of the defendants as between themselves.

Choosing lawyers

A word of caution is necessary here about choosing a law firm. Most Japanese companies of any size will have a number of lawyers on retainer in their local area. Due to the small number of law offices in general in Japan, it may well be the case that the defendant company retains at least one lawyer from all of the local law firms of any size, i.e., the kind of law firm which a foreign company will want to employ. While it is possible for two lawyers from the same firm to represent opposing clients, it may be that a foreign plaintiff will feel uncomfortable about this. The problem is not so relevant in Tokyo, where the number of law firms is relatively high, but it will need to be considered there, as well. It will be wise to check on whether any lawyer in the firm is on retainer to the defendant company.

Often, law firms in Japan do not work as firms *per se* but work independently, sharing office space and facilities but not clients. The disadvantage for the foreign plaintiff is that he may have to use non-local lawyers to make his application. This can result in higher fees which will not be recoverable.[62] It may also turn out that the element of surprise in gaining an *ex parte* provisional attachment order could be lost.

Costs

Litigation costs

The general rule in Japan under CCP, Article 89, is that the loser pays the legal costs of the winner. However, a peculiarity of the Japanese system is that lawyers' fees do not count as litigation costs. Since everyone has the right to represent himself in court, the use of a lawyer and the costs which arise from such use are not regarded as "necessary" and are not, therefore, included in the calculation of costs. The only exception to this rule is a limited one relating to tort actions. Under CC, Article 709, a person who intentionally or negligently violates the rights of another is bound to make compensation for the damage arising therefrom. The Supreme Court has held that, where it becomes unavoidable for a person who has suffered loss to litigate in order to protect his rights, and so instructs a lawyer for that purpose, the lawyers' fees count as damage caused by the unlawful act and can, therefore, be claimed as damages to the extent that such fees are reasonable.[63]

61. See note 54.
62. See text relating to litigation costs.
63. Supreme Court, 27 February 1969, Minshu 23.2.441.

CHAPTER 17

KOREA

INTRODUCTION

The purpose of the following chapter is to examine the ability of a foreign creditor to seek interim or provisional relief towards securing collection on a claim in the Republic of Korea (hereinafter referred to as "Korea").

Western legal concepts and institutions were introduced to Korea in the early-20th century. Korea has adopted a so-called civil law system, whereby most laws have been codified, in contrast to the common law system. Accordingly, statutes are the most important source of law, while unwritten customary law and practice also supplement any gaps in the written laws.

Pursuant to the Korean Code of Civil Procedure (hereinafter referred to as the "CCP"), the Korean courts are equally available to Korean and to foreign creditors and litigants. Thus, there is no limitation with respect to foreign creditors.

PROVISIONAL REMEDIES

All provisional and interim remedies are issued or granted by the courts. The following remedies are available to creditors in Korea, irrespective of whether these creditors are Korean or foreign:

(1) pre-judgment attachment, pursuant to Articles 696 to 713 of the CCP; and

(2) pre-judgment injunction, pursuant to Articles 714 to 723 of the CCP.

These remedies include all possible types of remedy against the assets of the debtor, such as movables, bank deposits, and real property.

Pre-judgment attachment

Pre-judgment attachment is broadly accepted in Korea in order to freeze specific assets of the defendant for partial or full satisfaction of any future judgment, and to put pressure on the defendant by demonstrating the plaintiff's intent to complete the action and enforce any judgment which may be obtained.

The court with jurisdiction over a pre-judgment attachment proceeding is the court that has jurisdiction over either the subject matter or dispute in connection with which the pre-judgment attachment is being sought, or the location of the asset being sought to be attached.

Notwithstanding the jurisdiction agreement or the pending litigation outside judgment of the Australian Supreme Court for lack of reciprocity. This decision was based on both the Australian statutes and the common law.

Korean legal commentators take the position that, in the modern world, Korean courts should recognise judgments rendered by the courts of other countries as long as they meet the basic requirements of Article 203 of the CCP and afford roughly equivalent treatment to the judgments of the Korean courts. They dismiss the technical approach which would require an item-by-item comparison of the two systems of jurisprudence.

Lower courts have apparently accepted this approach in reported cases. For example, the Seoul Civil District Court recognised a Massachusetts state court judgment with respect to a family law matter on 12 September 1984, citing *Hilton* v. *Guyot, Conflict of Laws* (1971) as grounds for finding the existence of reciprocal treatment. Further, the Seoul Appellate Court has recognised a New York divorce case (11 January 1988, 87 Re 203, 204).

We note, however, that these cases have not been tested by the Korean Supreme Court and, therefore, it is not entirely certain that there exists full reciprocity between these foreign courts and Korea. Moreover, since the cases cited above are family law cases, it is not clear whether a foreign monetary judgment would enjoy the same reciprocity. As a general matter, however, the CCP does not distinguish enforcement between different kinds of judgments.

ENFORCEMENT OF ARBITRAL AWARDS

In 1973, Korea became a party to the United Nations Convention on the Recognition and Enforcement of Foreign Arbitral Awards ("New York Convention"). In addition, Korea has entered into bilateral conventions, regarding institutional arbitration organisations, with a number of countries, including the United States, Japan, The Netherlands, the Republic of China (Taiwan), Thailand, India, Ghana, Indonesia, Denmark, Egypt, Hungary, Romania, and Bulgaria.

According to the Korean Arbitration Law, "compulsory execution of an arbitral award may be made only when its lawfulness has been declared in an enforcement judgment by a court". This requirement is applicable to both Korean and foreign arbitral awards. The court considers such enforcement in a procedure in which the losing party is given an opportunity to present its views. The enforcement judgment is usually rendered within several months after filing a complaint for such judgment. The enforcement judgment is subject to appeal. Approximately one-half of 1% of the amount of the arbitral award should be paid to the court as stamp tax at the time of filing a complaint for the enforcement judgment to the first level court.

An enforcement judgment may not be made if a ground exists for requesting cancellation of the arbitral award. The party against whom enforcement of the award is sought, when notified of the request for enforcement, may commence a procedure for cancellation of the award. A lawsuit for enforcement and a legal request for cancellation are two quite separate procedures but may practically be joined in one and the same proceeding. An enforcement judgment will normally include a declaration that provisional execution may be made.

Appeal against an enforcement judgment can be made to a higher court. The decision of the latter is subject to review by the Supreme Court in accordance with the CCP.

FORECLOSURE OF THE JUDICIAL MORTGAGE

In order to obtain security in maritime cases, a foreign creditor may arrest a vessel in Korea on the basis of a maritime lien or a mortgage through court proceedings. The procedure for arresting a vessel is relatively simple and a court order is easily obtainable. However, it is very costly and time consuming to have the vessel released subsequently. In case of the arrest of a vessel based on the maritime lien or mortgage, although no security is required, auction fees and appraisal costs must be paid to the court at the time of the application because an arrest under a maritime lien or mortgage aims at proceeding with a sale by auction.

It will take a few days to prepare the documents to be submitted to the court, and all the documents prepared in a foreign language must be translated into the Korean language. It will take at least two working days to obtain the court order after all the documentation is completed. A court order granting an auction sale will be served upon the master who will represent the owner (the arrest thereby becoming effective), and on the port authority.

The arrest order only directs the owner/master of the vessel to have the vessel berthed at the present place. It is possible that the vessel could escape notwithstanding the court order. In order to secure the arrest of the vessel, the creditor may wish to obtain a court order for the maintenance and preservation of the vessel, and thereby physically arrest the vessel. In such a case, the court sheriff will take possession of the vessel. The creditor would be required to pay the costs for such maintenance and preservation of the vessel in advance. The amount of these costs varies depending on the location and the size of the vessel.

Although theoretically a foreign creditor may also arrest an aeroplane on the same basis as described above, this would obviously be more complicated in practice and is less likely to happen.

LEGAL IMPACT OF BANKRUPTCY OF THE DEBTOR

In the case of bankruptcy of a debtor, we may distinguish the following three different situations:

(1) the debtor is *de facto* bankrupt, but he is not yet adjudged bankrupt;
(2) the debtor is adjudged bankrupt; and
(3) the debtor is in the process of being reorganised and rehabilitated.

With respect to the first situation, there is no limitation regarding the creditor's claims against the debtor. With respect to the second and third cases, we note the following. In these cases, the creditor can only be paid in accordance with the court approved plan, subject to the nature of the claims. Interim remedies may be stayed in such cases.

CONCLUSION

The laws of Korea offer sufficient means to a foreign creditor to seek interim or provisional relief towards securing collection on a claim. As described above, provisional remedies are broadly available in Korea.

However, in the case of a foreign judgment which is rendered outside Korea, the creditor should first investigate whether enforcement of the judgment in Korea is (easily) obtainable. The reciprocity requirement pursuant to the CCP is rather important in this regard, as the court may not enforce the foreign judgment if reciprocity is not secured between Korea and the foreign country with regard to this issue.

In the case of the enforcement of an arbitral award rendered in a country which is party to the New York Convention, the court is likely to enforce such an award without great difficulty.

YOUNG MOO KIM

CHAPTER 18

THE NETHERLANDS

INTRODUCTION

This overview is limited to a discussion of the substantive and procedural requirements pertaining to the attachment of assets in The Netherlands as these requirements came into effect on 1 January 1992.[1]

ACCESS TO COURTS BY FOREIGN CLAIMANTS

Foreign parties are competent to litigate before the Dutch courts, assuming that they satisfy the same subject matter and venue requirements imposed for Dutch litigants in order to be admitted as a party in a litigation before one of the various Dutch courts.

There are four types of court in The Netherlands: the cantonal courts (*kantongerechten*), district courts (*arrondissementsrechtbanken*), courts of appeal (*gerechtshoven*), and the Supreme Court (*Hoge Raad*).[2] The cantonal courts act as the court of first (and, in some cases, last) instance in a very limited number of matters.[3] In all other matters, the district courts act as the exclusive court of first instance, and as the court of first appeal of decisions by the cantonal courts.[4] The court of appeal and the *Hoge Raad* function, respectively, as courts of subsequent and final appeal for all decisions of the district courts.[5]

The appropriate venue for instituting litigation in The Netherlands is the court with jurisdiction over the place where:

(1) the defendant legally resides;
(2) the defendant actually resides; or
(3) the plaintiff resides if the defendant has no known place of residence in The Netherlands.[6]

1. The attachment of assets in connection with family law matters is not treated here.
2. Art. 1, Wet op de Rechterlijke Organisatie (Judicial Organisation Law) (hereinafter cited as the "Wet RO").
3. See, e.g., Arts. 38–42, Wet RO. These matters include, for example, claims valued at less than Dfl. 5,000, all labour law disputes and landlord/tenant cases.
4. Arts. 53 and 54 3°, Wet RO.
5. Arts. 69, 91, and 94. Wet RO.
6. See e.g., Art. 126, Wetboek van burgerlijke rechtsvordering (Code of Civil Procedure) (hereinafter cited as "Rv"). Arts. 2 and 3, Europees jurisdictie- en executieverdrag (EEC jurisdiction and execution treaty).

Where both a Dutch and a foreign court can claim jurisdiction over a dispute, the Dutch conflict of laws rule provide that the Dutch court is competent to adjudicate the matter—although not to the exclusion of the foreign court—where statute or treaty so provides. The European Economic Community (EEC) Jurisdiction and Execution Treaty (hereinafter "EEX Treaty") contains, for example, both substantive and procedural provisions governing when a citizen of one EC country can sue or be sued in a court of another EC country.

In the absence of a specific statutory or treaty provision granting jurisdiction to a Dutch court, the normal Dutch competence rules will be used to determine whether a Dutch court can exercise jurisdiction and, if so, which one.[7]

Must a bond be posted?

At the request of a Dutch defendant, a foreign plaintiff or foreign intervenor can be ordered to provide security for the payment of any legal costs, damages, or other compensation it may ultimately be ordered to pay to the Dutch defendant. Such a request can be made at any point during a proceeding, including prior to the filing of any arguments or defences by the Dutch defendant. This request, however, does not constitute an acceptance of the competence of the court.[8]

The amount and form of security to be provided by the foreign plaintiff need not be specified by the Dutch defendant but shall instead be determined by the court.[9] A demand to provide security can be made again upon appeal, provided, however, that the foreign appellant was also plaintiff or intervenor before the lower court.[10]

No bond can be required of a foreign defendant,[11] nor can any bond be demanded of a party who is a citizen of a country that is a party to the Rechtsvorderingsverdrag of 1954.[12]

Where a party seeks conservatory attachment of assets or demands that assets attached be held in judicial safekeeping, the petitioning party can also be required by the court to provide security for the payment of any damages caused by (incorrect) seizure and transfer of assets, regardless of whether the party seeking attachment is foreign.[13]

PROVISIONAL OR INTERIM REMEDIES

There are three forms of "conservatory" measures, in addition to the option of temporary injunctive relief, which are available to a litigant either prior to submitting a claim to litigation or pending resolution thereof.

The most common interim remedy is the conservatory attachment of assets or

7. W. Hugenholtz and W.H. Heemskerk, *Hoofdlijnen van Nederlands Burgerlijk Procesrecht* (Utrecht 1996), nr. 12 (hereinafter cited as "Hugenholtz/Heemskerk").

8. Art. 152, Rv. Rb Rotterdam, 31 March 1937, NJ 1937, nr. 974.

9. Hugenholtz/Heemskerk, nr. 152. Art. 153, Rv.

10. Arts. 353 (court of appeal) and 414 (Supreme Court), Rv.

11. Hugenholtz/Heemskerk, nr. 152.

12. Arts. 17 and 19, Rechtsvorderingsverdrag 1954. Most of the European countries, including The Netherlands, are signatory to this treaty.

13. Arts. 701 and 709(4), Rv.

intangible rights (*conservatoir beslag*). Permission to use this remedy will only be granted where:

(1) the claim which the plaintiff alleges to have against the defendant is or will be due and fully enforceable by the time judgment is issued in the main litigation[14];
(2) the assets in question can be legally attached[15]; and
(3) in the case of assets under the control of the defendant or a third party, the plaintiff has reason to fear that the defendant will attempt to remove or dispose of said assets in order to prevent recovery of the plaintiff's claim.[16]

In addition to the remedy of conservatory attachment, it is possible to demand that goods already attached be handed over for safekeeping by an officer of the court (*gerechtelijke bewaring*). In contrast to the remedy of conservatory attachment, only certain kinds of tangible assets can be placed into judicial safekeeping,[17] and even that only after all interested parties have been heard.[18]

In lieu of conservatory attachment and/or judicial safekeeping, a plaintiff can petition the court to appoint a guardian who will be charged with the management and supervision of the subject assets.[19] This can be useful in the case of assets such as a company, real estate, or investment portfolios.[20]

All three forms of provisional measure require the prior permission of the president of the district court with subject matter jurisdiction.[21] The three conservatory measures—attachment, judicial safekeeping and guardianship—are available only if the plaintiff has already submitted its claim for adjudication before a court (Dutch, foreign, or arbitral) or such a claim will be filed within a certain period of time.[22] This term can be extended where, for example, the claim in question must be submitted to an arbitration panel or a foreign court for adjudication.[23] Where, however, the plaintiff fails to initiate litigation within the period prescribed, permission to employ such measures will automatically expire and the effects of such a measure be nullified.[24]

Temporary injunctive relief is available in those cases where the urgency of the matter and the interests of the parties concerned dictate that a litigant be compelled to take or refrain from taking certain actions until such time as the legal rights of the parties can be determined.[25]

14. Hof 's-Gravenhage, 8 June 1982, NJ 1984, nr. 407: Pres. Rb. 's-Hertogenbosch, 12 June 1981, NJ 1981, nr. 634.

15. Goods which cannot be attached include assets used for public services and basic living necessities. Arts. 703, 447, and 448, Rv. Assets owned by a defendant but in the possession of a third party, by contrast, can be attached. Art. 718, Rv.

16. Arts. 711(1) (tangible assets other than registered assets such as aeroplanes or ships), 714 (certain securities and other commercial paper), and 725 (real estate), Rv.

17. Art. 709, Rv.

18. *Ibid.*, subsection 3.

19. Art. 710, Rv.

20. Hugenholtz/Heemskerk, nr. 286.

21. Arts. 700(1) (conservatory attachment: the court where the assets are located or where the party resides under whom the lien is imposed); 709(1) (judicial safekeeping; the same court that granted permission to attach the goods or where the assets are located), and 710(1) (guardianship: the court where the assets are located or before whom the principal case is pending), Rv.

22. The statutory period is at least eight days. Arts 700(3), 709 and 710(2) Rv.

23. Hugenholtz/Heemskerk, nr. 285.

24. See, e.g., Arts. 700(3) and 710(2), Rv.

25. Arts. 289 and 292 Rv.

Permission to employ this remedy must be obtained by engaging in a separate emergency proceeding (*kort geding*). Temporary injunctive relief is, by definition, a mere stop-gap measure to avoid irreparable injury to either of the parties during the pendency of the main litigation.

Where judgment has already been rendered by a foreign court, provisional measures can also be sought and obtained during the pendency of a proceeding before a Dutch court seeking recognition and enforcement of that judgment in The Netherlands (*exequatur*). The degree to which a judgment must be perfected in order to be recognised in The Netherlands will be dictated by the specific statutory or treaty provisions which govern the *exequatur* procedure, as described further below.

RECOGNITION OF FOREIGN JUDGMENTS

The general rule is that condemnatory judgments pronounced by a foreign court can be recognised and/or executed in The Netherlands only to the extent explicitly permitted by statute or treaty.[26] In the absence of such a provision, the issue must be retried on the merits before a Dutch court, although a Dutch court can recognise certain aspects of the foreign judgment or accord evidentiary value thereto.[27]

The Dutch statutory provisions pertaining to the recognition of foreign condemnatory judgments for purposes of enforcement are set forth in Articles 985–994, Rv. There are no provisions under Dutch law for the recognition of declaratory judgments which require no enforcement measures.[28] Pursuant to Articles 985 *et al.*, a foreign judgment can only be enforced once permission to do so (*exequatur*) has been granted by a Dutch court. In determining whether or not to grant *exequatur*, no substantive retrial of the issue is required.[29] Instead, the Dutch court need only determine whether enforcement of the judgment in question would violate the public order.[30]

An *exequatur* is obtained by filing a request with the district court. This request must include an authentic copy of the foreign judgment and, at the request of the court, authentication of these documents and an official translation thereof.[31] The party against whom enforcement is being sought has the right to be heard.[32] Unless otherwise specified by the court, the *exequatur* is immediately and fully enforceable upon grant thereof.[33] The decision to grant *exequatur* can be appealed.[34]

The aforegoing procedural requirements governing the *exequatur* process are also applicable where recognition and/or enforcement of a foreign judgment is governed by treaty, provided that this treaty does not prescribe procedural requirements of its

26. Art. 431, Rv.
27. HR, 14 September 1924, NJ 1925, cited in Council of Europe, *The Practical Guide to the Recognition and Enforcement of Foreign Judicial Decisions in Civil & Commercial Law* (1975: Strasbourg), p. 119 (hereinafter cited as "Council of Europe").
28. Hugenholtz/Heemskerk, nr. 261.
29. Art. 985, Rv. The Dutch court with jurisdiction over an *exequatur* proceeding is either the court where the defendant resides or the court where enforcement of the judgment is being sought.
30. Council of Europe, p. 120.
31. Art. 986, Rv.
32. Art. 987, Rv.
33. Art. 988(2), Rv.
34. Arts. 989 and 990, Rv.

own.[35] The EEX Treaty, for example, contains its own *exequatur* provisions. In addition to this treaty, The Netherlands is also party to a number of bilateral treaties, many of which have since been superseded by the provisions of the EEX Treaty.[36]

REMEDIES AVAILABLE TO FOREIGN CREDITORS

The same legal remedies available to a Dutch litigant are equally available to the foreign litigant properly admitted as a party to a Dutch proceeding. These remedies include the following:

(1) Where the defendant fails to comply with a legal obligation, the court can authorise the plaintiff to do so and/or to undo any acts taken by the defendant in violation of its obligations, all at the expense of the defendant.[37]

(2) Where the defendant refuses to execute a document or to issue a declaration, the court can order that its judgment in the case act in place of that document or declaration.[38]

(3) Where the defendant refuses to deliver tangible assets to the plaintiff which the plaintiff has a right to receive, the court can seize those goods and return them to the plaintiff.[39]

(4) Where the defendant fails to pay moneys due to the plaintiff, any or all of its assets can be seized and sold in public by the court, with the proceeds being used to render payment to the plaintiff.[40]

(5) In order to encourage a defendant to comply with the judgment of the court, a court can provide in its judgment that any such failure shall result in the imposition of a fine (*dwangsom*), the amount of which shall be determined by the court[41] or, under extraordinary circumstances, imprisonment (*lÿfsdwang* or *gÿzeling*) for a maximum term of one year.[42] As both of these remedies are intended to induce compliance, use of either does not prevent a party from availing itself of one or more of the other forms of execution.[43]

Regardless of which remedy is involved, a party seeking enforcement of that remedy in The Netherlands must first obtain the authorisation of a Dutch court to execute judgment. This authorisation (*executoriale titel* or title of execution) exists in many forms, including a judgment or other decision issued by a Dutch court, a written settlement agreement, a decision by an arbitration panel together with the *exequatur* of a Dutch court, or a judgment issued by a foreign tribunal together with an *exequatur*.[44] A title of execution issued by a Dutch court is most readily recognisable by its caption: *In naam der Koningin* (In the name of the Queen).[45]

35. Art. 992, Rv; F.M.I. Jansen, *Executie- en Beslagrecht* (1990: Zwolle), p. 281 (hereinafter cited as "Jansen"), nr. 984.
36. *Burgerlijke Rechtsvordering*, vol. *Verdragen* (Deventer, looseleaf).
37. Art. 3:299, Burgerlijk Wetboek (Dutch Civil Code) (hereinafter cited as "BW").
38. See, e.g., Art. 3:300, BW.
39. Art. 491, Rv.
40. Art. 435, Rv.
41. Arts. 611a–i, Rv.
42. Arts. 585–611, Rv.
43. Art. 598, Rv.
44. Hugenholtz/Heemskerk, 1996, 238.
45. Art. 430(2), Rv.

In addition to obtaining a title of execution, a party seeking enforcement must serve the party being compelled to comply with a copy of the title of execution, incorporating a written demand for compliance within a specified period of time.[46] Only if the opposing party fails to comply within the terms specified can the party seeking execution proceed with enforcement measures.[47] Failure to serve notice renders any execution measures null and void.[48]

Where the remedy being enforced involves the attachment of goods (whether for public sale or return to the rightful owner), the process of execution can be begun even though the time for filing appeal of the underlying judgment has not yet expired. However, unless the title of execution explicitly states that it is immediately enforceable (*uitvoerbaar bij voorraad*), the filing of an appeal suspends but does not undo any execution measures already taken.[49] To the extent, for example, goods have already been attached pending public auction, the writ of attachment need not be withdrawn.[50]

Prior service of process and a separate waiting period are also required where execution of an attachment remedy requires the co-operation of a third party. The party seeking execution must serve such a third party not only a copy of the title of execution, but also a statement from the clerk of the court confirming that no appeal of the decision has been filed.[51] The minimum statutory waiting period for all attachment remedies to be enforced against third parties is eight days.[52] This waiting period is intended to ensure that the losing party has adequate opportunity to appeal the decision of the court.[53]

Once the minimum waiting period has elapsed, attachment can begin. Attachment is accomplished by serving a separate bailiff's writ or other form of notice upon the party being compelled to comply.[54] In principle, any and all of the assets of the losing party, including bank accounts and wages, can be attached/garnished for purposes of executing judgment.[55] As in the case of conservatory attachment of assets, however, assets used for public services, basic living necessities and one's livelihood cannot be attached.[56] Similarly, garnishment of wages is limited to that amount in excess of a statutory minimal sum reserved to cover the living expenses of the garnishee.[57]

Thereafter, assets attached can be sold publicly or returned to the rightful owner, in accordance with the provisions of the judgment of the court. Cash and securities attached must be placed into judicial safekeeping pending final disposition[58]; other

46. Art. 430(3), Rv.
47. The statutory minimum waiting period imposed varies, depending upon the remedy being enforced and, in the case of attachment, upon the type of asset involved. See, e.g., Art. 439(1) (two-day waiting period: attachment of tangible assets); 502(1) (two days: attachment of real property); 563(1) (24 hours: attachment of ships), and 599(1) (one day: imprisonment), Rv.
48. HR, 9 March 1939, NJ 1939, nr. 1012 and Hugenholtz/Heemskerk, nr. 246.
49. Art. 350(1), Rv.
50. HR, 18 June 1915, NJ 1915, nr. 891.
51. If appeal has been filed, any obligation of a third party to co-operate with execution is also suspended. HR, 20 March 1913, NJ 1913, nr. 636.
52. Arts. 86 (default judgments) and 432 (all other judgments), Rv.
53. Hugenholtz/Heemskerk, nr. 247.
54. Art. 440, Rv.
55. Art. 435(1), Rv.
56. Arts. 436, 447, and 448, Rv.
57. Arts. 475d–475f, Rv.
58. Art. 445, Rv.

assets can also be placed into judicial safekeeping or under court guardianship at the request of the party seeking execution.[59]

The public sale of tangible and intangible assets must be conducted by a bailiff of the court[60]; the public sale of real property is conducted by a public notary.[61] These officials are responsible for distributing the proceeds of the sale in accordance with the court judgment.[62] Notices must be posted in the municipality(ies) where the sale is to occur and where the assets are located, as well as published in a local newspaper prior to the sale.[63] Of the assets attached, only those assets can be sold which are needed to produce the amount of the judgment to be paid and the execution costs incurred.[64] Special additional rules apply to the sale of goods such as those normally sold on official exchanges, real estate and ships.[65]

Virtually all phases of the execution of a judgment are performed by a bailiff of the court (*deurwaarder*), who is also charged with serving the various notices of process upon the parties involved. Simple delivery of the title of execution to the bailiff is sufficient to authorise him to carry out all of the execution measures described above, other than imprisonment.[66] Execution by imprisonment is permitted only where the judgment of the court expressly grants this remedy, and the party seeking execution has furnished the bailiff with an explicit power of attorney authorising him to perform.[67] If necessary, a bailiff can also enlist the assistance of the so-called "strong arm" (e.g., police or other government officials).[68]

INTERNATIONAL TREATIES

Among more important treaties affecting the ability of foreign parties to recover claims in The Netherlands is the EEX Treaty. For arbitration judgments, the New York Convention of 10 June 1958 is relevant.

BANKRUPTCY

The conservatory lien placed on assets owned by a debtor ceases to exist once that debtor has been declared to be bankrupt. The state of bankruptcy imposes, by operation of law, a lien on all of the assets of the bankrupt for the benefit of all his creditors.[69] In the event that the state of bankruptcy is withdrawn, any conservatory liens earlier imposed will be automatically reinstated.[70] Notably, in the case of goods

59. Arts. 446 and 506(2), Rv. See also Arts. 491–500, Rv, for procedures governing the return of assets attached.
60. Art. 463(1).
61. Art. 514, Rv.
62. Arts. 474 and 524, Rv.
63. Arts. 464, 466, and 516, Rv.
64. Arts. 470 and 522, Rv.
65. Arts. 463, 514–529, and 562a–582, Rv.
66. Art. 434, Rv.
67. Art. 589; Hugenholtz/Heemskerk, nr. 248.
68. Hugenholtz/Heemskerk, nr. 244.
69. Art. 33(2) Faillissementswet (Bankruptcy Act) (hereinafter cited as "Fw").
70. HR, 25 January 1935, NJ 1935, nr. 1509.

attached while under the control of a third party, the bankruptcy of this third party does not affect the validity of the lien.[71] The conservatory measure of judicial safekeeping would, by definition, also fall in view of the fact that it is based upon the proper imposition of a conservatory lien.

Court guardianship over an asset belonging to a bankrupt, or a temporary injunction imposed upon a bankrupt to take or refrain from taking certain action, would no longer be necessary, in view of the fact that a bankrupt is no longer considered to be legally competent to dispose of or otherwise manage his properties.[72] Instead, a trustee in bankruptcy, also appointed under supervision of the court, is charged with the administration of the affairs of the bankrupt.

KAREN KAO
ISMAËL EL MECKY

71. HR, 15 January 1960, NJ 1960, nr. 174; HR, 7 January 1983, NJ 1983, nr. 542.
72. Art. 23, Fw.

CHAPTER 19

NEW ZEALAND

INTRODUCTION

New Zealand has a variety of legal procedures which can successfully be used in order to attack foreign assets. The following is an outline of the various procedural remedies available in the New Zealand courts to ensure that foreign assets can be preserved or charged pending the outcome of substantive proceedings in that jurisdiction. The procedures referred to are usually in the first instance, interlocutory pre-judgment applications that are commenced prior to determination of the substantive proceeding or trial of the matter on its merits.

The main procedures are obtained from the High Court Rules, which specifically set out the procedural guidelines in the High Court and grounds for any approach about attacking foreign assets. Depending on the urgency of the situation to be addressed and the likelihood of assets being dissipated or not, the application to "attack" any asset would probably be *ex parte* in the first instance with a right to review that order upon notice.

The New Zealand courts which would deal with any applications to attach to assets would be the High Court, which has unlimited jurisdiction. The District Court is the lower court and on 1 July 1992 increased its jurisdiction to NZ$200,000. This chapter will concentrate primarily on assets to be attached, although enforcement procedures (which may relate to foreign assets) may also be invoked against individuals, including remedies involving arrest and security to be provided by individuals in certain circumstances.

A foreign plaintiff does not need to have an actual judgment in the foreign jurisdiction before commencing proceedings in New Zealand in order to "attack" the asset in New Zealand. Provided there is a bona fide claim or a good arguable case, then proceedings can be issued in New Zealand to attack the asset in New Zealand. Issues about whether New Zealand was the proper jurisdiction for hearing of the substantive claim would be the subject of later applications to establish the proper *forum conveniens*. This would be by way of an application for a stay of proceedings, which may be considered if the defendant applied to the court to set aside the interim orders that may be made against the defendant's assets.

This chapter will first consider the procedures that are available to register a judgment or claim in New Zealand, although it is not necessary to have a formal judgment before considering one's right to claim against assets in New Zealand.

ENFORCEMENT OF FOREIGN JUDGMENTS

These procedures are available for enforcing a foreign judgment in New Zealand. At common law, the judgment of a foreign court creates a debt which can be sued on in New Zealand. A common-law action is possible unless the judgment is enforceable under Part I of the Reciprocal Enforcement of Judgments Act (see below). The procedural approach is to file an originating application supported by an affidavit giving details of the judgment. The affidavit must comply with the High Court Rules (as recently amended) and care should be taken to ensure that all necessary points are covered in the affidavit.

Judgments from other territories having Queen Elizabeth as their sovereign can be filed in court under the Judicature Act, section 56. Unless the judgment debtor persuades the court that it should not be recognised, the judgment is enforceable as if handed down by the High Court. This procedure is an alternative to a common-law action.

The other statutory means of enforcement is by registration under Part I of the Reciprocal Enforcement of Judgments Act. The judgment debtor will usually have 30 days to oppose registration, after which the judgment is enforceable in the High Court.

Registration is possible only if the foreign court is a superior court of the country to which the Act applies by Order in Council. A list of these countries is available. If registration is available, it excludes both the common law and the Judicature Act procedures.

A fourth procedure is contained in the Law Reform (Miscellaneous Provisions) Bill. It is proposed to enact a Part IA to the Reciprocal Enforcement of Judgments Act. That Part would allow direct enforcement of Australian orders under section 46A of the Trade Practices Act (Commonwealth), relating to misuse of trans-Tasman market dominance. It would not be necessary to seek the High Court's sanction for enforcing a judgment of this class.

Under each procedure, a six-year limitation period applies. Time starts to run when the judgment is delivered by the foreign court. A foreign debt is a simple contract within the meaning of section 4(1) of the Limitation Act 1950.[1]

At common law, the High Court will recognise a foreign judgment as creating an actionable obligation to pay the judgment debt.[2]

A foreign judgment does not merge with the original cause of action. The law was changed in 1982 by statute in the United Kingdom but remains unchanged in New Zealand, apart from judgments which must be enforced under the Reciprocal Enforcement of Judgments Act 1934.

A foreign judgment will found a claim at common law if:

(1) the foreign court had jurisdiction;
(2) the judgment was final; and
(3) the judgment debtor cannot impeach the judgment by means of the few defences available.

There is no difficulty where judgment is to be enforced against the party who chose the foreign jurisdiction, or where the defendant fought a case on its merits, or appealed

1. *Berliner Industriebank AG* v. *Jost* [1971] 2 All ER 1513 at p. 1517.
2. *Obrist* v. *Reudi* (unreported, Supreme Court, Hamilton, 14 July 1977; A202/73; Richardson J).

from a default judgment by arguing on the merits. Difficulties arise where the defendant has appeared to dispute the foreign court's jurisdiction. It was previously thought that such an appearance was voluntary, unless it was to save property which had already been seized in the foreign jurisdiction. It is now established that an appearance merely to dispute the existence of jurisdiction does not form a sufficient basis for jurisdiction. The New Zealand position is similar to the English Court of Appeal's ruling that an appearance to request the court in its discretion not to exercise its jurisdiction constitutes an appearance, but will leave open the effect of an appearance to dispute the actual existence of the jurisdiction.

There is also no difficulty in establishing a submission in New Zealand jurisdiction by agreement, particularly if the express words of a contract provide that disputes shall be tried in a certain jurisdiction. Such agreement shall not be inferred from a choice of law clause, and such an agreement to submit cannot be created by implication.

FOREIGN JURISDICTIONS AND ENFORCEMENT OF JUDGMENTS

It is necessary to consider those circumstances where the asset to be attacked is in New Zealand but there is a foreign defendant who must be served or procedures followed in New Zealand regarding service of the proceeding upon the foreign defendant.

If an intended defendant cannot be served within New Zealand with a notice of proceeding, the High Court may not have jurisdiction to hear the action or might decline to exercise jurisdiction. If jurisdiction exists and is exercised and the action is successful, it may be necessary to execute judgment against the defendant's assets overseas. A brief overview of procedural considerations arising is set out below.

Service

The first step in bringing an action before the court is obviously to serve the defendant with notice of the case against him. Service may be effected without leave if the defendant is served within New Zealand, or is served outside New Zealand under rule 219. The instances in which rule 219 will permit overseas service without leave may be summarised by cases where either the subject matter of the action or the defendant has a close connection with New Zealand, or where the defendant has submitted to the jurisdiction of the New Zealand court. In all other cases of service overseas, an application for leave must be made under rule 220.

Various conventions relating to the international service of documents are in force. The procedure offered is optional. It is set out in rule 224. A request for service in Form 18 is filed with the document for service (with a translation if necessary), and a duplicate of each. The registrar seals the document and translation and forwards them to the Secretary for Justice. In return, the registrar receives a certificate of service.

Enquiries concerning the existence from time to time of conventions should be directed to the Treaty Officer, Legal Division, Ministry of Foreign Affairs, Wellington.

Existence of jurisdiction

The defendant may dispute the existence of jurisdiction either after service or, if the plaintiff seeks leave under rule 220, at the hearing of the application for leave to serve overseas.

Such an appearance may be made under rule 131. This rule permits an appearance to be made to argue the non-existence of jurisdiction. Previously the defendant ran the risk of such an appearance being construed as a voluntary submission to the court, thereby providing the court with an independent basis for jurisdiction. An appearance under rule 131 is deemed not to constitute a submission to the court.

Exercise of jurisdiction

The court may decline to exercise jurisdiction because the New Zealand court is not an appropriate forum (a plea of *forum non conveniens*), whether the defendant is served in New Zealand or not. This may be argued at an application under rule 220 for leave to serve the defendant overseas; by a condition appearance under rule 131[3]; or as an interlocutory matter. The leading cases on *forum non conveniens* are *McConnell Dowell Constructors Limited* v. *Lloyd's Syndicate 396*,[4] and *Club Mediterranée NZ* v. *Wendell*.[5]

Assuming that a plaintiff has a claim and/or wishes to register and enforce a foreign judgment, then the following pre-judgment remedies and forms of execution by way of interlocutory applications can be invoked prior to determination of the substantive issues.

MAREVA INJUNCTION AS A PRE-JUDGMENT REMEDY

The *Mareva* injunction restricts a defendant's access to his assets so that he may not render himself judgment-proof. This form of attack is available upon any foreign assets within the New Zealand jurisdiction. The nature of the relief sought is an application for an interim injunction, commonly termed a *Mareva* injunction, and requires the usual undertaking as to damages to be filed by the plaintiff.

If a foreign plaintiff wishes to obtain a *Mareva* injunction, then it may be necessary on a subsequent application to the court by the defendant to provide security for costs. The court in its discretion may order under the relevant High Court Rules that, because the plaintiff is a foreign plaintiff, it should pay into court the costs that may otherwise be awarded at trial if the plaintiff's claim is ultimately successful. This rule concerning security for costs applies to any claim or proceeding that a foreign party may have in the New Zealand jurisdiction.

In New Zealand, the *Mareva* jurisdiction was recognised in *Hunt* v. *BP Exploration Co. (Libya) Ltd*.[6] Reliance was placed on the inherent jurisdiction of the court and section 16 of the Judicature Act 1908. That case also referred and relied upon the

3. See *Kuwait Asia Bank EC* v. *National Mutual Life Nominees Limited* (1990) 5 NZCLC 66, 509 (PC); [1989] 2 NZLR 43 (HC), 50 (CA).
4. [1988] 2 NZLR 257.
5. [1989] 1 NZLR 216.
6. [1980] 1 NZLR 104.

founding cases for this principle, being *Mareva Compania Naviera SA* v. *International Bulkcarriers SA*[7]; and *Lister* v. *Stubbs*,[8] which had held that a defendant could not be prevented from dealing with assets before judgment, was distinguished.

In addition, there is now the statutory power given by rule 236B of the High Court Rules. The applicant is required to give notice of third parties who would be affected by the injunction.

To obtain the injunction, the plaintiff must show that he has a good arguable case in the substantive proceeding. He must also show that there is a risk of the defendant dissipating his assets, either within or outside the jurisdiction.[9] The defendant must have the appropriate assets within the jurisdiction.[10]

The plaintiff must make full and frank disclosure of all facts which are relevant to the court's decision to issue the injunction. There is a duty to make all proper enquiries.[11] The plaintiff must also be prepared to give an undertaking as to the defendant's or any third party's costs or damages resulting from the injunction.

The granting of the injunction is discretionary. The injunction will not issue where it would interfere unduly with third-party rights, would be impracticable or unduly inconvenient. Hardship to the defendant will be taken into account.

The injunction will not be allowed to operate so as to prevent a legitimate use of the defendant's funds[12] or affect third-party rights.[13]

A *Mareva* injunction can be combined with an *Anton Piller* order, an order for the defendant to surrender his passport, or similar orders.[14]

A recent judgment in the New Zealand courts concerning the scope of a *Mareva* injunction is *Zietlow* v. *Simon*.[15] This decision allowed orders to be made concerning disclosure of assets world-wide, and *Anton Piller* orders were made in association with wide-ranging *Mareva* orders for the purpose of preserving evidence, assets and locating assets in other jurisdictions. The case is of considerable importance in considering *Mareva* injunctions and the nature of the orders that can be made in certain circumstances. Accordingly, *Anton Piller* orders are not necessarily confined to intellectual property areas. This follows from the basic justification for the jurisdiction in New Zealand which is to ensure that justice is ultimately done in a case by providing an effective remedy to discover and preserve assets and any necessary evidence associated with the substantive claim.

The approach of the court to an application for discharge will vary depending upon the time of the application. If an application is brought prior to execution of the *Mareva* injunction or an *Anton Piller* order, then it would seem proper that this be dealt with on the same basis as any other application to discharge an *ex parte* order, i.e., there should be no presumption in favour of the order. However, as it would be

7. [1980] 1 All ER 213.
8. (1890) 45 ChD 1.
9. *Z Limited* v. *A* [1982] 1 All ER 556.
10. *BNZ* v. *Hawkins* (1989) 1 PRNZ 451.
11. *Brinks-MAT Limited* v. *Elcome* [1988] 3 All ER 188.
12. *PCW (Underwriting Agencies) Limited* v. *Dixon* [1983] 2 All ER 158.
13. *Cretanor Maritime Co. Ltd* v. *Irish Marine Management Ltd* [1978] 3 All ER 164.
14. *Bayer AG* v. *Winter* [1986] 1 All ER 733; *Hydrox Corporation Limited* v. *Moreau* (unreported, High Court, Auckland, CP 2037/87; 7 December 1987, Barker J); *Allied Arab Bank Ltd* v. *Hajjar* [1987] 3 All ER 739.
15. High Court, Auckland, CP 1336/91, 23 August 1991.

usual for an application for discharge to be heard by the same judge who has made the order, the absence of such a presumption may be a legal rather than factual reality. It would seem that the strongest grounds for setting aside an order prior to execution would be:

(1) it had been obtained *mala fide*; or
(2) as a result of material non-disclosure; or
(3) if there were other special circumstances which clearly demonstrated a need for immediate relief; or
(4) if, implicitly, there was an abuse of process, or
(5) self-incrimination, though there is limited scope for that objection in New Zealand (this ground is more applicable to the *Anton Piller* type orders which may be made in conjunction with a *Mareva* order).

PRESERVATION OF PROPERTY UNDER RULE 331 HIGH COURT RULES

Rule 331 of the High Court Rules concerns preservation of property, and this rule effectively can be invoked against any asset in the New Zealand jurisdiction. The rule provides as follows:

(1) In any proceeding, the court may make orders for the detention, custody, or preservation of any property.
(2) An order under subclause (1) may authorise any person to enter any land or to do any other thing for the purpose of giving effect to that order.
(3) In a proceeding concerning the right of any party to a fund, the court may order that the fund be paid into court or otherwise secured.

There are three points of interest. The meaning of "property", the meaning of "fund", and whether the discretion to grant an order under the rule should be exercised. The definitions of "property" and "fund" affect the scope of the court's jurisdiction under this rule. Unless the thing which the court is asked to deal with comes within the definition of one of these terms, the court does not have jurisdiction under this rule.

Once it is shown that the subject of the intended order is "property" or a "fund" within the meaning of the rule, the applicant need only satisfy the court that there is a serious triable issue in the substantive proceedings. Once this threshold is met, whether the order is granted is a matter for the court's discretion.

"Property"

A helpful case is *Rapid Metal Development (NZ) Limited* v. *Rusher (No. 2)*.[16] There, McGechan J held that the general purpose of this rule was that a claim should not be rendered nugatory before judgment could be entered. Nevertheless, the rule should not be read so widely as to swallow up the court's *Mareva* jurisdiction nor that relating to charging orders under rule 567. The intention is to enable preservation of property or a fund involved in litigation or preservation of evidence relating to litigation. The rule is not intended to provide a means of security for the plaintiff against assets of the defendant which are unrelated to the litigation.

16. [1984–1988] BCLD 1005 (1987).

Property must be understood to be property involved in the litigation, although the contrary was held in *Steel* v. *Australian Guarantee Corporation (NZ) Limited*,[17] where Chilwell J considered that the procedure under rule 331 could be used against property which was not the subject of the proceedings.

Property must be regarded as tangible property. Thus, a cheque might be made the subject of an order under rule 331, but the debt evidenced by the cheque would not come within the scope of the rule. Preservation of an intangible debtor/creditor relationship must be achieved under rule 331(3) if it is to be achieved at all.

Examples of application of the rule are as follows:

(1) A caveat is not property within rule 331(1).[18]

(2) An application seeking to appoint a manager to operate a restaurant run by a company, to preserve property, namely shares, assets and profits, was held to be misconceived. In effect the applicant was seeking control of the company, that is its ongoing business and operation which was not within the meaning of the term "property".[19]

(3) A preservation order was made over shares notwithstanding that they were in a public listed company and were therefore effectively negotiable property. There was evidence that these shares were subject to a trust.[20] In *Neale & Haddow Limited* v. *Strawbridge*,[21] the proceeds of an intended sale were held to be not property; in any case, they do not yet exist.

"Fund"

McGechan J held that "fund" for the purposes of rule 331(3) is to be given a traditional rather than a liberal interpretation: "The underlying feature of a 'fund' so exemplified is that it is an aggregation of money or an accounting device directing money to a particular purpose, and that such money is still so held or still so allocated for that purpose." Examples are, "trust funds, benevolent funds, sinking funds, reserve funds, maintenance funds, and the like". The two elements of a "fund" are, therefore, deliberate allocation and identity.

Examples of the nature of the word "fund" are as follows:

(1) A preservation order was sought over the purchase price of certain shares, part of which could be traced into an identified bank deposit. It was held that no "fund" existed.[22] Surplus moneys accumulated by receivers following the realisation of assets and the discharge of the receivers' obligations was not money held, set aside, or allocated for a particular purpose.[23]

(2) "Fund" must be a fund directly the subject of a proceeding. Doubt was expressed as to whether the jurisdiction can be extended to proceedings which, although not referring expressly to any fund, concern it in a practical way.[24]

17. Unreported, High Court, Auckland, 5 June 1987, CP 54/87.
18. *Profile Developments Limited* v. *Contractors Bonding Limited* [1989] BLC 559.
19. *Moffat* v. *Chambers* [1989] BCL 2132.
20. *Hurst* v. *Alexander* (1987) CCA (2nd) H–129.
21. [1984–1988] BCLD 1132.
22. *Rapid Metal Developments (NZ) Limited* v. *Rusher (No. 2)* [1984–1988] BCLD 1005; (1987) 10 TCL 22/7.
23. *Lewis* v. *Poultry Processors (Holdings) Limited* (1988) 4 NZCLC 64, 508.
24. *Ellison* v. *Bolton Enterprises Limited* (1986) 10 TCL 4/6; CCA (2nd) H–128.

(3) In a claim for damages for misrepresentation against an estate, the estate did not form a "fund".[25]

The court's discretion

The rule still requires the court to exercise its discretion. The plaintiff must show that there is a serious triable issue in the substantive proceeding.[26] The plaintiff must also show that the defendant possesses the item which it is sought to preserve.[27]

Having fulfilled those two requirements, an order may be made in the court's discretion. The factors that the court takes into account are as follows.

(1) The fact that the defendant had relied on having the funds available for purchase of a property should be taken into account; absence of an order would not endanger the plaintiff's claim; a condition imposed that the defendant undertake to apply the fund only to the purchase of a particular property and that the property would not be on-sold or further encumbered.[28]

(2) Where damages would be an adequate remedy there was no reason to prevent the defendant from exercising its right to realise its security over shares.[29]

(3) Preservation order refused where the defendant filed a declaration of assets showing that he was judgmentworthy.[30]

The *Marketing Management* v. *NZI Securities* case recognises that the defendant's right to the fund or property at stake in the proceeding continues until judgment is entered against him. It appears that good reason will be required to justify interference with the defendant's rights. Exactly what will be required is not clear. Undoubtedly, factors similar to those that would justify a *Mareva* injunction would be relevant.

The purpose of the rule is to preserve property, not to give pre-judgment security. The effect of an order once made, however, is to give pre-judgment security, limited to those cases where title to property or a fund is disputed.

An application for the preservation of property may result in an order that the property be valued[31] or in the defendant being offered the option of putting up an equivalent value in security.[32]

FORMS OF EXECUTION

There are numerous forms of execution within the New Zealand jurisdiction, and these are considered under Part VI of the High Court Rules. These are also available in certain circumstances before judgment.

Rule 547 provides that judgment may be enforced by any one or more of:

25. *St Heliers Bay Coffee Lounge Limited* v. *Klass* (1987) 10 TCL 41/4; CCA (2nd) A–17.
26. *Marketing Management Holdings* v. *NZI Securities Ltd* [1989] BCL 1674.
27. *Wilder* v. *Wilder* (1912) 56 SJ 571.
28. See *Rapid Metal Developments (NZ) Ltd* v. *Rusher (No. 2)*, n. 22 *supra*.
29. See n. 26 *supra*.
30. *Proco Holdings Ltd* v. *C.W. Thompson* [1989] BCL 350.
31. Rules 335 and 437; *Barton* v. *Wells* (unreported, High Court, Auckland, 14 August 1987, CP 1233/87, Master Gambrill).
32. *Ridpath & Ridpath* v. *Zachner* (1893) 9 TLR 538.

(1) a charging order;
(2) a writ of sale;
(3) a writ of possession;
(4) a writ of arrest; and
(5) a writ of sequestration.

Writs

The writ of possession is the mechanism whereby a judgment for possession of land or chattels is enforced (rules 550 and 606).

The writ of arrest authorises the arrest of a person for failure to comply with a court order to do or abstain from doing any act—not being the payment of a sum of money (rules 551 and 608).

The writ of sequestration is to enforce a direction by the court to pay money into court or to do any other act in a limited time or to abstain from doing any thing. It authorises the court officer to take possession of real and personal property and to get into his hands the rents and profits therefrom until the person against whom it is directed clears his contempt of court (rules 552 and 610).

In contrast to the other three writs, the writ of sale deals with execution against the judgment debtor. It may be issued at any time after judgment has been sealed (rule 558). It authorises the seizure and sale of the judgment debtor's chattels and real property in satisfaction of the judgment debt (rule 549).

In summary, the writs authorise and direct the seizure of personal property to enforce a variety of court judgments or orders. The writ of sale is the instrument for use by the judgment creditor against a judgment debtor.

Charging orders

Charging orders before judgment and after judgment are available in the New Zealand jurisdiction. Whereas the writs authorise the seizure of personal property, the charging order is simply a charge on the property of the person against whom it is issued for payment of the amount for which judgment has or may be obtained (rule 548). The word "charge", however, is not entirely accurate. Its effect is not to create a charge in the conventional sense but to halt dealings with the property until the plaintiff/judgment creditor has the opportunity to seize and sell the property in satisfaction of the judgment debt.

Charging orders are akin to garnishee proceedings in the sense they are intended:

(1) initially, to restrain third parties from paying or transferring to the defendant or his order money or property payable or held on behalf of the defendant by the third party; and
(2) ultimately, to have the money or property applied by the third party not to the judgment debtor but direct to the judgment creditor in satisfaction of the judgment.

Interests in land held in the defendant's own name may be the subject of a charging order and are therefore an exception to the general rule that charging orders involve money or property owing or held by third parties for the defendant/judgment debtor. This topic will be dealt with further below.

Except in the case of land held in the defendant's own name (referred to above), one must first obtain a charging order nisi (limited) which achieves the restraint of third parties disposing of the moneys or property discussed in (1) above. One may then apply to have the charging order nisi made absolute so as to be in a position to enforce judgment against the property in question or against the third party to the extent of the debt or property ((2) above).

With the exception of land held in the defendant's own name, the property over which a charging order may be obtained is set out in rule 579. Items (a) and (b) deal with debts or sums of money due or accruing due to the defendant. Item (c) covers the right or interest of the defendant in any partnership. Item (d) covers shares held by the defendant/judgment debtor in any company incorporated in New Zealand or having an office in New Zealand in which transfers of shares may be registered. Item (e) covers interests in land, money, shares or other chattels held under any express or implied trust for the defendant/junior debtor. Notable by their absence are most forms of personal property possessed by the defendant/judgment debtor himself.

The charging order must be nisi in the first instance, and is served on the "person it is intended to affect thereby", i.e., the third party (rule 580(2)(a)). Its effect is to restrain the person served (rule 581):

(1) from paying over any debt, income, interest, dividends, bonus, profits or other money due or accruing due to the defendant/judgment debtor;

or

(2) from making, or concurring in making or permitting any conveyance, transfer, assignment or disposition of any estate, right, or interest or of any share in a partnership or company, of the defendant/judgment debtor.

Upon being served with a charging order nisi, the third party may:

(1) pay into court money affected by the order (rule 583); or
(2) at any time before judgment, apply to the court for an order that property affected by the charging order be sold and the proceeds paid into court (rule 584).

The third party may then await the result of the proceeding or order of the court.

Where the third party fails to comply with the charging order, he may be ordered to pay to the plaintiff the money paid or the value of property disposed of in contravention of the charging order, sufficient to satisfy any judgment the plaintiff may obtain (rule 582).

In summary, the effect of the charging order nisi is to keep property or debts due to the defendant/judgment debtor out of his hands and available to the plaintiff/creditor. This is achieved either by freezing the position as between the defendant/judgment debtor and third party, or by having the third party pay the money into court or, with the leave or by the direction of the court, sell the property affected by the order and pay the proceeds into court.

At any time after judgment has been sealed, the judgment creditor may apply to have the charging order nisi made absolute. At that time, the court may give directions as to the disposal of moneys paid into court pursuant to rules 583 or 584 (rule 585).

Upon the charging order being made absolute, the judgment creditor may issue a writ of sale on the property of the third party (rule 586). Where a debt is charged, he may proceed in the same manner as if judgment had been sealed by the judgment debtor against the third party. In respect of property referred to in rule 579(c) to (e) (being partnership interests, shares, interests in land), he should follow as nearly as possible the procedure for sale of land.

It can be seen, therefore, that drastic consequences follow for the third party upon a charging order being made absolute in the event that he disputes the claimed liability to the defendant/judgment debtor. The opportunity to raise any such dispute is given by rule 570. That rule provides in substance that any person (including, of course, the third party) may at any time apply to the court for relief, in which case the court may vary or rescind the charging order.

From the judgment creditor's point of view, it is desirable that the application to make the charging order nisi absolute be served on the third party, having regard to the serious ramifications for the third party upon the order becoming absolute. Service of the applicant is also likely to pre-empt any application for relief by the third party under rule 570 after the charging order nisi has been made absolute.

The procedure for service of the charging order nisi on the third party followed by the application to make the order absolute gives both the plaintiff and the third party the protection each requires. In the plaintiff's case, it preserves the assets of the defendant in the third party's hands and ensures that they are available to satisfy any judgment he may obtain. In the case of the third party, it protects him against liability to the defendant/judgment debtor and against liability to pay more than is due from him to the defendant/judgment debtor.

There is one type of property which is subject to the charging order procedure which does not involve third parties. That is an interest in land held by the defendant in his own name (rule 573). The charging order may be registered against land transfer land (rule 574) or against Deeds Registry land. Since third parties are not involved, the charging order nisi procedure is unnecessary, and the charging order is absolute in the first instance (rule 573). Here, the charging order acts not against disposal of property or moneys due to the defendant *by* third parties but against disposal of the defendant's land *to* third parties. This protection is afforded the plaintiff because of the system of registration of title to land in New Zealand.

The charging order is notice of the plaintiff's interest. Equities which arise after registration of the charging order take effect subject to the charging order. Equities, however, which arise before the charging order, even though unregistered, are unaffected by the charging order. So, for instance, an agreement for sale and purchase of the land, notwithstanding that it is unprotected by a caveat, will nevertheless not be affected by a charging order registered after the agreement for sale and purchase but before settlement. In those circumstances the buyer may require removal of the charging order.[33] For this reason, therefore, charging orders should be registered at the earliest opportunity.

Charging orders over land lapse after two years. The court, may, however, where justice so requires, extend the effect of a charging order for such period as may be necessary (rule 578). Accordingly, a writ of sale should be issued well before the two-year period expires. The jurisdiction to grant an extension is not limited to any particular period. If the charging order does lapse there is nothing to prevent the issue of a second charging order against the same land for the same debt.[34] It would,

33. *Firth Concrete Industries Limited* v. *Duncan* [1973] 1 NZLR 188.
34. *Nicholl* v. *Official Assignee* [1966] NZLR 779.

however, be undesirable to rely on the issue of a second charging order, as any equities which had arisen in the intervening period would take priority over the charging order.

As indicated earlier, a charging order is not in itself a form of execution. It is in the nature of a stop order. The writ of sale is the enforcement procedure whereby land or chattels are seized and sold and the proceeds applied in satisfaction of the debt. Before a writ of sale may issue, judgment must have been obtained and sealed (rule 588).

Where land is concerned, in the event that a charging order may not be obtained before judgment, it is nevertheless desirable that a charging order should be obtained immediately after judgment, notwithstanding that a writ of sale has also been filed. This is so having regard to rule 576, which provides:

> Until registration of a charging order in respect of land, no sale of transfer or the land or of any part thereof under a writ of sale shall have any effect as against a purchaser for valuable consideration, notwithstanding that the writ of sale may have been actually delivered for execution at the time of purchase, and that the purchaser may have had actual or constructive notice of the delivery of the writ of sale for execution.

A charging order may be obtained either before or after judgment, although a charging order nisi may not be made absolute until after judgment, nor may a writ of sale issue until after judgment.

Issue of a charging order nisi

Rule 567 deals with the issue of charging orders before judgment. It provides:

> Leave to issue a charging order before judgment shall be granted only on proof that the opposite party, with intent to defeat either his creditors or the party applying or both—
> (a) Is making away with his property; or
> (b) Is absent from or about to quit New Zealand.

Examples of charging orders

Examples of charging orders in the New Zealand jurisdiction are as follows:

(1) *Pond* v. *Glover*,[35] followed in *Nelson & Robertson Pty Limited* v. *Niue Products Limited*.[36]

(2) *Easton* v. *Hannan*,[37] evidence of the defendant's intention to make away with property must amount to more than conjecture, or even a very positive opinion.

(3) *Campion* v. *Campion*,[38] the application must be supported by concrete evidence; an affidavit in support was required. An order was refused in *Marac Finance Limited* v. *Martin*,[39] on the grounds that there was no indication that the defendant was making away with his money.

(4) *Jones* v. *Poffenroth Smellie J.*,[40] it was held that, like the *Mareva* injunction, rule 567 should not be used to tie up the defendant's funds as security; the

35. [1933] GLR 358.
36. Unreported, High Court, Auckland, 31 August 1983, A853/83, Chilwell J.
37. [1924] GLR 401.
38. (1986) 9 TCL 16/5; CCA (2nd) H–169.
39. [1988] BCL 304.
40. [1986] BCL 516; (1986) 9 TCL 16/5; CCA (2nd) H–167.

correct purpose of an order under the rule is to prevent the removal of the defendant's goods from the jurisdiction. The judge should be satisfied that the action is likely to succeed before granting the order. In the instant case, His Honour in his discretion decided not to make an order under rule 567: the substantive action smacked of champerty. In any case, there was insufficient evidence that the defendant was trying to defeat his creditors.

(5) *Bank of New Zealand* v. *Hawkins*,[41] an *ex parte* charging order was rescinded; while the applicant had proved that there was a risk of dissipation of the defendant's assets, he had not proved that the defendant intended to defeat his creditors.

(6) *D.F. Hammond Land Holdings Limited* v. *Elders Pastoral Limited*,[42] it was held that the possible withdrawal of money from a solicitors' trust account did not give rise to anything more than a "surmise" that the defendant would attempt to defeat his creditors.

(7) *National Mutual Finance (1988) Limited* v. *Shaw*,[43] the plaintiff had obtained an *ex parte* charging order over the defendant's house. The house had been sold before the order was granted, and the plaintiff sought to have the order transferred to the proceeds of sale. The court discharged the order, holding that the sale of the house was apparently a genuine transaction. An intention to defeat creditors could not be proved. In any case, granting a charging order over the proceeds of sale would prevent the purchase of a new house, and prejudice third parties. The new house was to be in the defendant's wife's name, and the defendant was to lend half the purchase price to her and receive an acknowledgement of debt. Tipping J held that the defendant had impliedly undertaken on his affidavit not to weaken his wife's debt to himself until the current action was completed. The conditions for an order under rule 567 were not made out.

Affidavit in support for charging order absolute

It is apparent from rule 556 that leave to issue a charging order after judgment has been entered is unnecessary. In that case, the documentation required for the issue of a charging order or a writ of sale or possession is *a praecipe*; an affidavit by the applicant or his solicitor deposing that paragraphs (c) to (e) of subclause (2) of rule 556 do not apply (rule 556(3)), together with the appropriate form of charging order or writ (rule 558).

As indicated, the necessary affidavit may be sworn by the solicitor for the plaintiff, the substance of which may simply be expressed as follows: "Paragraphs (c) to (e) of subclause (2) of rule 556 of the High Court Rules do not apply to the parties entitled or liable to execution under the judgment in favour of the plaintiff against the defendant dated the [insert date of judgment] nor to the assets against which execution is sought."

Chattels owned by and in the possession of the defendant/judgment debtor may not

41. (1989) 1 PRNZ 451.
42. [1989] BC 2026; (1989) 12 TCL 42/5, 7.
43. [1989] BCL 882.

be the subject of a charging order. These may be preserved before judgment by way of *Mareva* injunction and after judgment by way of writ of sale.

District Court charging orders

As of 1 January 1989, a similar charging order regime was introduced in the District Court by section 96A of the District Courts Act 1947 and rules 244A–W of the District Courts Rules 1948. There are three significant differences under the District Court procedure:

(1) Debts or sums of money due or accruing due from third parties to the defendant/judgment debtor are not included in the property which may be the subject of a charging order in the District Court, except in the case of money held under or by virtue of any express or implied trust for the defendant/judgment debtor. The property thus excluded from the charging order procedure in the District Court corresponds with that included by way of rule 579(a) and (b) in the charging order procedure permitted by the High Court Rules. The reason for the exclusion of those items in the District Court is because there the garnishee procedure performs the same task (see section 96 of the Act and rules 264 to 278A of the Rules).

(2) The charging order procedure is not available before judgment.

(3) Discovery is now available in aid of execution of a judgment.

As from 1 July 1992, the new District Court Rules 1992 came into effect. These rules have replaced the old procedures and are similar to the High Court Rules, particularly with regard to execution procedures.

Part X, rules 564 to 668, now upgrade the mode of execution and creditors' rights in this jurisdiction to include attachment orders, interpleader proceedings under executions, and a range of other remedies not previously available.

CONCLUSION

There are numerous remedies available in the New Zealand jurisdiction which can attack assets, as outlined in this chapter. The matters addressed are not intended to be exhaustive of all the remedies available in the New Zealand courts. In particular, recognition should be given to rights against companies under the Companies Act 1955 concerning provisional liquidations and, equally, under the Insolvency Act against individuals and their assets.

MICHAEL C. BLACK

CHAPTER 20

NIGERIA

INTRODUCTION

Most commercial transactions entered into in Nigeria are governed by Nigerian law, which is derived from the received English law, local statutes, and court decisions. With the growth of foreign trade, a substantial part of commercial contracts in Nigeria now have a foreign element. The interplay of activities between Nigerian citizens and companies with foreign entrepreneurs and business has, in no small measure, contributed to this phenomenon. For instance, a contract may be entered into between A in Germany for importation of goods from Thailand to be delivered in Nigeria. In any of these instances, there is a potential conflict of laws, and the question is whether the Nigeria court has jurisdiction to hear an action brought on such contracts. Can the court apply the law of another country, especially in a situation where the contract stipulates the law that governs it? Does it matter where the subject matter of the contract is situated, or where the contract is to be performed, if outside Nigeria? Can the foreigner seek redress in a Nigerian court and, if so, which Nigerian court?

The rapid industrial development which the Nigerian Federal Military Government has been pursuing, and the gradual relaxation of fiscal restraints, added to other measures calculated to attract foreign investors and funds, have in the main encouraged foreign governments, companies, and individuals to take a second look on Nigeria and do business with all sectors of the Nigerian community.

ACCESS TO NIGERIAN COURTS

As the nature of a claim or issue determines which court a litigant has to approach for a remedy, it is therefore pertinent that the foreign investor should know if and which of the Nigerian courts are open to him should the need arise. Generally, the Nigerian courts are available to foreign creditors and litigants. Access to the courts is guaranteed and safeguarded by the 1979 Constitution of the Federal Republic of Nigeria.

The accessibility of the Nigerian courts to individuals or groups, whether they be citizens of the Federal Republic or not, is further governed by rules and regulations of the various courts, as amended from time to time. At the apex of the Nigerian court system is the Supreme Court, which superseded the West African Court of Appeal,

point to a foreign court, the Nigerian courts will assume jurisdiction. This was the position taken in a case involving a claim for non-delivery where the question was which of four countries (Nigeria, Thailand, Liberia, and Germany) had the closest and most intimate connection with a claim for non-delivery before a Nigerian court.[7]

Once the foreign litigant has access to the Nigerian court, he can bring any action for redress in the court subject only to the rules and regulations of that particular court.

SECURITY FOR COSTS

A foreign litigant or a plaintiff not ordinarily resident in Nigeria may be ordered to give security for costs. The court *suo muto* may order security for costs, or may do so on the application of either the plaintiff or the defendant at any time during the course of proceedings. The security may be either by deposit or by bond. The rule is that security for costs should not be imposed on a party who is being compelled to litigate. Thus, the defendant is not usually asked to provide security. Where the order is for a bond, the litigant concerned may instead pay money into court.

Money or part thereof standing in the name of a person resident outside Nigeria, can only be used as security for costs after it has been converted into foreign currency in the name of that person and paid into a special account, as may be agreed by the parties or as may be ordered by the court.[8]

REMEDIES AVAILABLE

During the course of proceedings, a party may apply for any of the following orders, which may be issued interlocutory until the final determination of the suit:

(1) An order for an injunction.
(2) An order for a stay of execution.
(3) An order for a particular act in the nature of an injunction for the purpose of preserving the property in dispute or for its better management.
(4) An order for the appointment of a receiver or manager of such property.
(5) An order for the accelerated hearing of the suit.

These remedies, and indeed other interim remedies, are available to both the plaintiff and defendant, and the courts do grant them whenever it is just or convenient to do so.

Usually, interim remedies are applied for after the exchange of pleadings, but they could be sought at an earlier stage, depending on the nature of the subject matter and the type of remedy sought. As was stated by the Supreme Court:

> the premise for an application for an interlocutory injunction is the claim before the court. An interlocutory injunction is usually granted with the object of keeping matters in status quo until the question at issue before the parties is determined. So also is an order of stay of execution and an order of stay of proceedings. It is not available in respect of issues not raised in the action or proceedings before the court unless such issues or matters are directly related to the issues raised.[9]

7. *Swissair* v. *A.C.B. Ltd* (1971) INNLR 213.
8. *Sommar (Nig.) Ltd & Anor* v. *Partenreederei M.S. Norwind & Anor*, SC 38/1986, p. 121.
9. *Norwood (Nig.) Ltd & Ors* v. *Tahiban GMBN* (1988) 4 NWLRP 495.

Injunction is the main interim remedy and an application for such order is usually by motion on notice. The applicant must establish by affidavit evidence a prima facie case for the existence of his right and that it is just and convenient for the court to intervene. Note that, in all suits commenced by writ of summons, every interlocutory proceeding shall be commenced by a motion, except in Lagos state where it shall be commenced by summons. The motions are supported by affidavit and served on the parties, and must state the order sought.

RECOGNITION OF FOREIGN JUDGMENTS

By virtue of the Foreign Judgments (Reciprocal Enforcements) Act 1960 ("an act to make provision for the enforcement in Nigeria of judgments given in foreign countries which accord reciprocal treatment to judgments given in Nigeria for facilitating the enforcement in foreign countries for judgments given in Nigeria and for other purposes in connection with matters aforesaid"), foreign judgments are given due recognition in Nigeria. The Minister of Justice periodically looks into the matter of reciprocity.[10]

For a foreign judgment to be enforced, it must be a judgment of a superior court of a foreign country included on the enforcement list. The judgment creditor and the judgment debtor must be those who, in accordance with the law of the country where the judgment was given, are entitled to levy execution or against whom execution may be levied, respectively, in the judgment. In order to enforce the judgment, the judgment creditor must also have the judgment registered in the register of foreign judgments.[11]

An application shall be made within six years after the judgment date, or thereafter at the court's decision. This application shall be brought by *ex parte* motion supported by affidavit verifying the facts, including the names of the parties, value and nature of the transaction, and places of abode of the judgment creditor and debtor. Attached to the affidavit shall be an authenticated copy of the judgment to be enforced. The local currency equivalent of the judgment sum should also be mentioned in the affidavit. There is a fee to be paid for the registration of the foreign judgment. Where the judgment is in a language other than English, a translation thereof into English shall also be attached and verified in the affidavit.

Once leave to register the judgment is granted by the court, the registrar draws up the order and registers the judgment in the prescribed register. A notice of the registration, together with a copy of the order granting leave for the registration, is served on the debtor. A foreign judgment registered in any High Court in Nigeria becomes a judgment of that High Court. Once registered, the foreign judgment may be enforced as if it were the judgment of the registering court entered on the date of registration.

A foreign judgment will not be registered by a Nigerian court if:

(1) The foreign court acted without jurisdiction.

10. *Vaswani* v. *Savalak* (1972) 12 SC, p. 77.
11. s. 12(1) of the Foreign Judgments (Reciprocal Enforcements) Act 1960.

(2) The judgment debtor was not ordinarily resident or carrying on business in the jurisdiction and did not volunteer submission to the jurisdiction of the court.
(3) The judgment debtor was not served with the process of the original court and did not appear.
(4) The judgment was obtained by fraud.
(5) An appeal is pending or the debtor shows an intention to appeal against the judgment.
(6) The judgment was in respect of a cause of action which, on grounds of public policy, could not have been entertained by the registering court.

Note that where a judgment creditor is unable to apply for registration under the Act, the judgment may be sued upon, the Supreme Court having ruled that a suit brought on a foreign judgment ought not to be struck out merely on the ground that there is no treaty guaranteeing reciprocal treatment.[12]

The enforcement of a foreign arbitration award is governed by Nigerian law, the *lex fori*, as modified by the New York Convention of 1958.[13] Legislation which may be of great interest to the foreign litigant includes the National Office of Industrial Property Act 1979 and the Arbitration and Conciliation Decree 1988, section 4(d).

National Office of Industrial Property Act 1979

The National Office of Industrial Property Act 1979, section 4(d) provides:

The registration of all contracts or agreements having effect in Nigeria on the date of the coming into force of this decree and of all contracts and agreements hereafter entered into for the transfer of foreign technology to Nigerian parties and without prejudice to the generality of the foregoing, every such contract or agreement shall be registrable if its purpose or intent is in the opinion of the National Office wholly or partially for or in connection with any of the following purposes, that is to say;

1. The use of trademarks
2. The right to use patented inventions
3. The supply of technical expertise in the form of the preparation of plans, diagrams, operating manuals or any other form of technical assistance or any description whatsoever
4. The supply of basic or detailed engineering
5. The supply of machinery and plant and
6. The provision of operating staff or managerial assistance and the training of personnel.

Section 5(2) provides:

As from the commencement of this Decree every contract or agreement entered into by any person in Nigeria with another person outside Nigeria in relation to any matter referred to in section 4(d) of this Decree shall be registered with the National Office in the prescribed manner not later than 60 days from the execution or conclusion thereof.

Section 7 declares:

. . . for the purposes of the Exchange Control Act 1962 and subject to section 8 of this Decree no payment shall be made in Nigeria to the credit of any person outside Nigeria by or on the authority of the Federal Ministry of Finance, any licenced bank in Nigeria in respect of any

12. *Ibid.*, s. 3(1).
13. *Alfred C. Toepper Inch of New York* v. *Edokpolor* [1965] 1 All NLRP 292.

payments due under a contract or agreement mentioned in section 4(d) of this Decree unless a certificate of registration issued under this Decree is presented by the party or parties concerned together with a copy of the contract or agreement certified by the National Office in that behalf.

Note that registration is not automatic, under this section 6(2).

Arbitration and Conciliation Decree 1988

The Arbitration and Conciliation Decree 1988, section 1(2) provides: "Any reference to a document containing any arbitration clause constitutes an arbitration agreement if such contract is in writing and the reference is such as to make that clause part of the contract."

Under section 31(1) of the Decree, it is provided that: "An arbitral award shall be recognised as binding and subject to this section and section 32 of this Decree shall upon application in writing to the court be enforced by the court." Section 31(2) declares that the party relying on an award or applying for its enforcement shall supply the duly authenticated original award or a duly certified copy thereof and the original arbitration agreement or a duly certified copy thereof.

According to section 31(3), an award may, by leave of the court or a judge, be enforced in the same manner as a judgment or order to the same effect.

Under section 32 any of the parties to an arbitration agreement may request the court to refuse recognition or enforcement of the award.

Section 51 states that an arbitral award shall, irrespective of the country in which it is made, be recognised as binding subject to this section, and provides that section 32 shall, upon application in writing to the court, be enforced by the court. Section 52(2) gives instances when the court may refuse enforcement.

Under section 54 it is provided:

Subject to sections 51 and 52, where the recognition and enforcement of any award arising out of an international commercial arbitration are sought, the Convention on the Recognition and Enforcement of Foreign Awards (hereinafter referred to as "The Convention") set out in Schedule 2 to this Decree shall apply to any award made in Nigeria or in any contracting state provided:

a. that such contracting state has reciprocal legislation recognising the enforcement of arbitral awards made in Nigeria in accordance with the provisions of the convention
b. that the convention shall apply only to differences arising out of legal relationship which is contractual.

REMEDIES AND PROCEDURE

One of the attributes of a court of law is its competence to enforce its judgment. This is established in section 251(I–III) of the 1979 Constitution, which reads as follows:

I. The decisions of the Supreme Court shall be enforced in any part of the Federation by all authorities and persons and by courts with subordinate jurisdiction to that of the Supreme Court.

II. The decisions of the Court of Appeal shall be enforced in any part of the Federation by all authorities and persons, and by courts with subordinate jurisdiction to that of the Federal Court of Appeal.

III. The decision of the High Court and of all other courts established by this constitution shall be enforced in any part of the Federation by all authorities and persons and by other courts of law with subordinate jurisdiction to that of the High Court and those other courts respectively.

Thus being invested with judicial powers of the Federation and all the inherent powers and sanctions of a court of law, any of the listed courts has powers not only to enforce its judgments and orders but also to punish for contempt.

A party to a proceeding who wishes to invoke the judicial powers of the court to enforce an order or judgment must take the initial step by filing an application before the court. Among the orders frequently invoked are the orders for injunction, specific performance, and delivery of goods. The Sheriffs and Civil Process Law of the Federation contains details of the procedure to be employed to enforce orders to do or to abstain from doing an act.

Enforcement, unless stipulated by the Act, may be made by a writ of attachment or by committal. Section 71 of the Sheriffs and Civil Process Law, provides:

> If a person refuses or neglects to comply with the order made against him other than for payment of money, the court, instead of dealing with him as a judgment debtor may order that he be committed to prison and detained in custody until he has obeyed the order in all things that are to be immediately performed and given such security as the court thinks fit to obey the other parts of the order, if any, at the future times thereby appointed, or in case of his no longer having the power to obey the order then until he has been imprisoned for such time or until he has paid such fine as the court directs.

The Judgment (Enforcement) Rules explain the procedure to be followed by a judgment creditor who wishes to have the debtor committed to prison. On the application by the judgment creditor, the order is prepared by the registrar. The original of the order, together with a notice, is served on the debtor. If the debtor within two days fails to comply with the order, the judgment creditor may apply to the court by motion for the debtor to show cause why he should not be committed to prison for failure to obey the order. If the debtor or the appointed day fails to satisfy the court, the court shall commit him to prison.[14]

Garnishment and writ of execution

Garnishee proceedings and writs of execution are among the major remedies which are available to successful litigants. Under Order 47(2) of the Imo State High Court (Civil Procedure) Rules 1988, "All fines, forfeitures pecuniary penalties and costs ordered to be paid may be levied by distress, seizure and sale of movable and immovable property of the person making default in payment".

Procedures in regard to execution of judgment and orders, including the recovery of penalties and costs, are laid down in the Sheriffs and Civil Process Law of each state and in the Sheriffs and Civil Process Act in respect of the Federal High Court. The Sheriffs and Civil Process Law, Imo State, section 52.05 (similar to that of the other states of Nigeria) reads as follows:

> 1. Any sum of money payable under a judgment of a court may be recovered, in case of default or failure of payment thereof forthwith or at the time or times and in the manner thereby directed by execution against the goods and chattels and the immovable property of the judgment debtor in accordance with the provisions of this law.

14. *Murmansk State Steamship Line* v. *Kano Oil Olillen Ltd* (1974) NCLR, p. 1; *J.O. Anakwenze* v. *Loius Aneke & Ors* (1985) Lose, pp. 41–61.

2. The registrar on the application of the judgment creditor shall cause to be issued a writ of attachment and sale whereby the sheriff shall be empowered to levy or cause to be levied by distress or sale of goods and chattels wherever they may be found within the division or district of the court, the money payable under the judgment and the costs of the execution.

With respect to interim attachment of property, Order 16 of the High Court (Civil Procedure) Rules, Imo State, provides:

16 (1) Where the defendant in any suit with intent to obstruct or delay the execution of any decree that may be passed against him, is about to dispose of his property, or any part thereof, or to remove any such property from the jurisdiction or where in any suit founded on contract or for detinue or trover in which the cause of action arose within the jurisdiction:

a. The defendant is absent from the jurisdiction or there is probably cause to believe that he is concealing himself to evade service; and
b. The defendant is beneficially entitled to any property in the state in the custody or under the control of any other person in the state, or such person is indebted to the defendant,

then in either case the plaintiff may apply to the Court either at the time of the institution of the suit or at any time thereafter until final judgment to call upon the defendant to furnish sufficient security to fulfil any decree that may be made against him in the suit and on his failing to give such security, or pending the giving of such security, to direct that any property movable or immovable belonging to the defendant shall be attached until the further order of the court.

(2) The application shall contain a specification of the property required to be attached, and the estimated value thereof so far as the plaintiff can reasonably ascertain the same, and the plaintiff shall, at the time of making the application declare that to the best of his information and belief the defendant is about to dispose of or remove his property with such intent as aforesaid.

If the court is satisfied with the application, it may order the defendant either to furnish security in such sum as may be specified in the order, to produce and place at the disposal of the court the said property or the value of the same or such portion thereof as may be sufficient to fulfil the decree, or to appear to show cause why he should not furnish security.

Pending the defendant's compliance with the order, the court may by warrant direct the attachment until further order of the whole or any portion of the property specified in the application. If the defendant fails to show cause or to furnish the required security within the time fixed, the court may direct that the property specified in the application, if not already attached, or such portion as shall be sufficient to fulfil the decree, be attached until further order.

Note that where an order requires any party to give security for costs, the security shall be given in such manner at such time and on such terms (if any) as the court may direct.

Garnishment proceedings are directed against a debt due to the judgment debtor. The debt must be recoverable within the jurisdiction. Proceedings are initiated by the filing of an affidavit in a form provided for in the schedule to the law. The affidavit must comply with the Evidence Act. A copy of the judgment is attached and verified by the affidavit, which must also verify the grounds upon which the court could exercise jurisdiction.[15]

The filing of the affidavit constitutes an *ex parte* application for an order nisi, which

15. *Raccah-Wahab* (1958) NNLR 58.

is issued by the registrar for service on the garnishee. The order calls upon the garnishee to show reason why he cannot be compelled to pay that debt over to the judgment creditor. The order informs the garnishee, *inter alia*, that the debt stands attached. The order is served on the garnishee as well as the judgment debtor.

A garnishee who does not dispute his liability to the judgment debt shall, within eight days of service of the order nisi, pay into court the amount due from him.

A judgment creditor who has obtained a garnishee order absolute may enforce such order against the garnishee by writ. The writ of *fi. fa.* (*fieri facias*) is a common form of enforcement of judgment for payment of money. The writ is available to a litigant in whose favour a monetary award is made in a proceeding. The procedure is straightforward. The judgment creditor or his solicitor files *a praecipe* using the appropriate form and pays the fees. The registrar completes the second half of the form.

A writ of *fi. fa.* is only valid for execution in a particular judicial division, so separate writs must be issued for every judicial division in which the property of the judgment debtor may be found and for which an application has been made. The writ is signed by the judge or magistrate and endorsed by the registrar. Execution of the writ is the responsibility of the sheriff or bailiff.

Order 10 procedure and the undefended list

The foreign litigant could initiate an action for summary judgment for recovery of a loan under Order 10 of the High Court of Lagos State (Civil Procedure) Rules. This procedure is available to the plaintiff whose claim is unarguable in law and where facts are undisputed. According to Whyte JSC in *Macaulay* v. *NAL Merchant Bank Ltd*[16]: "*Interest rei publicae ut sit finis lituim* is the mother of this procedure as in all forms of action which seek to reduce the volume of litigation."

Order 10, rules 1, 2, and 3, provide as follows.

> 1.a. Where the defendant appears to a writ of summons specially endorsed with or accompanied by a statement of claim under Order 3, rule 4, the plaintiff may, on affidavit made by himself or by any other person who can swear positively to the facts verifying the cause of action and the amount claimed (if any liquidated sum is claimed) and stating that in his belief there is no defence to the action except as to the amount of damages claimed, if any, apply to a judge in chambers for liberty to enter judgment for such remedy or relief as upon the statement of claim the plaintiff may be entitled to. The judge thereupon, unless the defendant shall satisfy him that he has a good defence to the action on the merits or shall disclose such facts as may be deemed sufficient to entitle him to defend the action generally, may make an order empowering the plaintiff to enter such judgment as may be just having regard to the nature of the remedy or relief claimed.
>
> b. If on the hearing of any application under this rule, it shall appear that any claim which could not have been specially endorsed under Order 3, rule 4 has been included in the endorsement on the writ, the judge may if he shall think fit, forthwith amend the endorsement by striking out such claim, or may deal with the claim specially endorsed as if no other claim had been included in the endorsement and allow the action to proceed as respects the residue of the claim.
>
> c. Where the plaintiff's claim is for the delivery up of a specific chattel (with or without a claim for the hire thereof or for damages for its detention) the judge may make an order for the

16. *Macaulay* v. *NAL Merchant Bank Ltd* (1990) 4 NWLR 324.

delivery up of the chattel without giving the defendant any option of retaining the same upon paying the assessed value thereof, and such order if not obeyed may be endorsed by a writ of attachment or a writ of delivery.

2. The application by the plaintiff for leave to enter final judgment under rule 1 of this Order shall be made by summons returnable in chambers not less than four clear days after service accompanied by a copy of the affidavit and exhibits referred to therein.

3.a. The defendant may show cause against such application by affidavit or the judge may allow the defendant to be examined upon oath.

b. The affidavit shall state whether the defence alleged goes to the whole or to part only and (if so) to what part of the plaintiff's claim.

c. The judge may, if he thinks fit, order the defendant or, in the case of a corporation, any officer thereof, to attend and be examined upon oath or to produce any leases, deeds, books or documents or copies of or extracts therefrom. In summary judgment procedure under Order 10 a judgment is given without taking the defence of the defendant.

In *Nishizawa Limited* v. *Strichand N. Jethwani*, the defendant had guaranteed payment to the plaintiff, a Japan-based company, of a debt owed by a motor company should it default. Any payment was to be on an instalment basis. The motor company defaulted in payment and the defendant failed to meet his obligation under the guarantee. The total amount outstanding was the equivalent of N3,123,466.22. The plaintiff sued on the debt.

Under Order 10 procedure, the plaintiff would file a writ specially endorsed with a statement of claim. On the entry of appearance by the defendant after service, the plaintiff would by motion on notice apply for an order empowering the plaintiff to enter judgment against the defendant as upon the writ of summons and statement of claim. The affidavit in support must verify the facts pleaded in the statement of claim.

The affidavit should be made by the plaintiff or any other person who can swear positively to the facts verifying the cause of action and the amount claimed, and stating that in his belief there is no defence to the action. Unless the defendant can satisfy him that there is a good defence to the action, the judge may make an order empowering the plaintiff to enter judgment as per his statement of claim.

Note that the operation of Order 10 excludes claims based on libel, slander, malicious prosecution, false imprisonment, and allegation of fraud, but covers most other actions where there is no real defence.

As was stated by Aniagolu JSC in *Nishizawa Limited* v. *Strichand N. Jethwani*: "a defendant who has no real defence to the action should not be allowed to dribble and frustrate the plaintiff and cheat him out of the judgment he is legitimately entitled to by delay tactics."[17]

The procedure could still be available to the plaintiff, even after the defendant has failed his statement of defence.

Order 10 procedure is peculiar to Lagos State. The High Court (Civil Procedure) Rules of other states have provision for what is known as the undefended list. Only claims for debt or liquidated money demands are maintainable under the list (see Order 23 of the High Court (Civil Procedure) Rules 1988, Imo State).

To bring an action under the undefended list, the litigant files the summons in the ordinary way. Attached to the summons is an affidavit verifying the facts upon which the claim is based. It is essential that the points raised in the affidavit contain sufficient

17. *Nishizawa Limited* v. *Strichand N. Jethwani* (1984) 12 SC, p. 234.

facts that would lead the court to belief that, prima facie, there is no defence to the claim. If the court is not satisfied, the suit will not be listed in the undefended list.

If the defendant wishes to defend a suit commenced in the undefended list, he must notify the court of his intention to do so. Where a defendant fails to notify the court within the specified time, he may still be allowed to do so, provided he files an affidavit containing enough or sufficient reasons to justify his being allowed to do so.

The hearing of suit in the undefended list simply implies that the court shall enter judgment for the plaintiff on the date fixed for hearing without calling upon him to lead evidence in proof of his case.

Order 23 of the High Court (Civil Procedure) Rules 1988, Imo State, provides as follows:

> 1. Whenever application is made to a court for the issue of a writ of summons in respect of claim to recover a debt or liquidated money demand and such application is supported by an affidavit setting forth the grounds upon which the claim is based and stating that, in the deponent's belief, there is no defence thereto, the court shall, if satisfied that there are good grounds for believing that there is no defence thereto enter the suit for hearing in what shall be called the "undefended list" and mark the writ of summons accordingly and enter thereon a date for hearing suitable to the circumstances of the particular case.
>
> 2. There shall be delivered to the Registrar, upon the issue of the writ of summons as aforesaid, as many copies of the above-mentioned affidavit as there are parties against whom relief is sought, and the Register shall annex one such copy to each copy of the writ or summons for service.
>
> 3.(i) If the party served with the writ of summons and affidavit delivers to the registrar a notice in writing that he intends to defend the suit, together with an affidavit disclosing a defence on the merit, the court may give him leave to defend upon such terms as the court may think just.
>
> (ii) Where leave to defend is given upon this rule the action shall be removed from the undefended list and placed on the ordinary cause list, and the court may order pleadings or proceed to hearing without further pleadings.
>
> 4. Where any defendant neglects to deliver the notice and affidavit prescribed by rule 3(i) or is not given leave to defend by the court, the suit shall be heard as an undefended suit and judgment given thereon without calling upon the plaintiff to summon witnesses before the court to prove his case formally.

EFFECT OF BANKRUPTCY

The Nigerian community exhibits an ambivalent attitude towards bankruptcy and related matters. However, under the Bankruptcy Act 1979, where a creditor has issued execution against the property of a debtor or has attached a debt due to him, he shall not be entitled to retain the benefit of the execution or attachment against the trustee in bankruptcy of the debtor unless he has completed the execution or attachment before the date of the receiving order and before petition by or against the debtor or of the commission of any available act of bankruptcy by the debtor.[18]

JOSEPH DOZIE

18. Ban' ıptcy Act 1979, s. 43(1).

CHAPTER 21

NORWAY

INTRODUCTION

Attacking assets in Norway will be discussed with respect to ordinary enforcement proceedings and obtaining arrests or injunctions. These aspects are addressed only with respect to the civil procedure rules regarding seizing, attaching, or otherwise attacking assets of economic value in Norway. Enforcement of criminal or family (i.e., child allocation) decisions falls outside the scope of this chapter. In addition, certain enforcement rules regarding eviction from property are not covered.

On 26 June 1992, a new Norwegian Enforcement Act (EA) was adopted, effective from 1 January 1993. No major changes were made relative to the prior act. The enforcement provisions are not subject to contract (i.e., the creditor cannot stipulate more stringent enforcement measures).

This chapter is only a survey of the main aspects of enforcement, with particular emphasis on aspects of special interest to foreign creditors or debtors and their representatives.

ORDINARY ENFORCEMENT PROCEDURES

The Norwegian legal system follows the general civil law system, with law primarily being derived from Acts passed by the Norwegian Parliament (*Storting*) and regulations made pursuant to such Acts. Precedents (chiefly Norwegian Supreme Court decisions) are of particular importance in deciding what is law. Other important sources of law are preparatory reports proposing Acts of Parliament, legal commentaries, and other court decisions.

International law and treaties are not *per se* binding on the courts, unless incorporated into specific Acts passed by Parliament (which is the normal procedure). Norwegian law is generally presumed to be in conformity with international law and treaty obligations and will, in case of doubt, be so interpreted.

The court system consists of three tiers: the lower court, the court of appeals, and the Supreme Court. There are no particular courts for commercial, admiralty, criminal, tax, or administrative cases. The same court system (under a different name) also handles disputes regarding enforcement, injunctions, or arrests. Actual enforcement is handled by the public enforcement authorities (*namsmyndighetene*). In the cities, there is a special organisation apart from the police (which will have to obtain the police's assistance if enforcement is forcibly resisted), whereas the enforcing official in the countryside is the local sheriff (who also has police powers). In this chapter he will be referred to as the "sheriff". His decisions—in so far as they can be appealed—can be appealed to the lower court (*namsrett*), and then through the court system.

The fees to be paid to the court are nominal. The main rule under the Norwegian Civil Procedure Act (CPA), chapter 13, is that the prevailing party shall be compensated for his costs (including his lawyer's fee), but there are many exceptions to the rule and decisions as to costs may appear discretionary.

Position of the plaintiff

Any person or legal entity (duly represented by its authorised representatives) may appear as plaintiff. Parties may appear in court on their own behalf (i.e., without a lawyer), although that is not recommended.

According to CPA, section 182, a plaintiff who is not resident in Norway may— if so required by the defendant—have to provide security (in the form of a bank guarantee or cash deposit) in advance for the defendant's legal fees as estimated by the court. (This is not a problem at the enforcement stage.) However, by treaty, notably the Hague Convention of 1 March 1954, Article 17, Norway has waived such requirement for citizens of the countries which are signatory to the treaty. These countries include most of Europe, Russia, Japan, Argentina, Lebanon, Israel, Morocco, and Surinam. There is also a separate treaty with the UK (of January 1931) (cf. Article 11).

Beyond this, there is no restriction on foreign parties. There are no longer any relevant currency restrictions in Norway.

Position of the defendant

Any person or legal entity can be a defendant. Of particular importance is that, if the defendant is not resident in Norway, he may nevertheless be sued in any jurisdiction in Norway where he has any asset or where the disputed asset is located (CPA, section 32) (cf. however, the restriction following from the Lugano Convention, Article 3).

Basis for enforcement

Bankruptcy

Although technically not an "attack on assets", it should be mentioned that, under some circumstances, the non-payment of moneys (whether determined by a court decision or not) may entitle a creditor to threaten—and then demand—that the debtor be put into bankruptcy. This will in due course lead to the creditor receiving his share of dividends from the bankruptcy estate. The threat of bankruptcy will, in some instances, be effective to obtain payment.

Enforcement of "enforceable documents"

According to EA, sections 7–2 and 11–2, a promissory note which specifies that enforcement can be made without prior court decision and which has been correctly witnessed may be presented to the sheriff for enforcement if not paid when due. (The same applies for cheques, bills of exchange, and Norwegian mortgages.) A "sales lien" ("right of retention") made as recognised by Norwegian law will give the seller the right to repossess the asset without court proceedings.

Enforcement of Norwegian decisions

Once a final Norwegian court decision (i.e., a decision where no further appeal is possible or the appeal period has expired without an appeal being filed; or a settlement is filed with the court) is at hand, the party entitled thereunder can demand enforcement. The same applies to arbitration awards made in accordance with CPA, chapter 32, cf. EA, section 4–15.

Execution of foreign court decisions

Certain countries have treaties with Norway regarding mutual recognition and enforcement of court decisions:

(1) Norway has signed and ratified the Lugano Convention (1988).
(2) Decisions pursuant to the EEA Treaty.
(3) The Nordic countries (Sweden, Denmark, Finland, and Iceland), as per Treaty of 11 October 1977 (also according to earlier treaty);
(4) Great Britain, as per Treaty of 12 June 1961;
(5) Germany, as per Treaty of 17 June 1977; and
(6) Austria, as per Treaty of 21 May 1984.

The treaties specify how the decision to be enforced must be documented and presented to the enforcing country's authorities. Such foreign decisions (properly documented and presented) may be enforced directly by the enforcement authorities in Norway (EA, section 4–17).

Furthermore, final court decisions made by a foreign court agreed on by the parties can in most cases also be directly enforced (cf. CPA, section 168a).

Court decisions from other countries cannot be directly enforced in Norway. They can, however, be presented before an ordinary Norwegian court as evidence and will be given such weight as the Norwegian court finds correct. The Norwegian court will first establish which law properly applies to the matter. If that should be the law of the jurisdiction of the decision that is sought to be enforced in Norway, then the foreign decision will, of course, have considerable weight, particularly regarding the application of such law. The Norwegian court may wish to reassure itself that ordinary procedural safeguards have been observed in the foreign jurisdiction and that the evidence has been properly considered. If the evidence could only be considered in full by the foreign court—for instance, due to the need for inspection *in situ* or considering of evidence which has since disappeared or become worthless—then the Norwegian court is likely to put considerable emphasis on the evaluation of the evidence made by the foreign court, even if it would otherwise be inclined to review the merits of the case itself.

The Norwegian court is in such cases, in principle, free to come to an opposite—or modified—conclusion on the evidence, and even on law.

A foreign judgment *in absentia* (judgments *in absentia* are otherwise recognised in Norway) will carry little weight.

A Norwegian court will not enforce a decision which would be in violation of *ordre public*, a reservation also taken in the treaties mentioned above.

Even if accepted in full, the legal basis for enforcement becomes the Norwegian decision, not the foreign decision that forms its foundation.

Enforcement of international arbitral awards

Norway has ratified the New York Convention (1958), and arbitral awards covered by it will be enforceable in accordance with EA, section 4–1(f).

Other foreign arbitral awards must be considered under the conditions as set out above relating to court decisions from other countries.

The enforcement procedure

The procedure for enforcement is governed by the EA. If the decision is foreign, it should be checked in the appropriate treaty how the foreign decision should be documented and presented to the enforcement authorities in Norway.

Prior to demand for forced execution, the debtor must have at least two weeks' warning and the possibility of complying voluntarily.

The creditor sends a written application to the sheriff (or court, if the basis is a foreign decision), enclosing the basis for the application (e.g., the decision with a certificate from the court that the decision is final) and also, if known, a direction as to which assets should be sought to cover the amount due.

If the decision is foreign, the court will, after having given the debtor a chance to state his view on the attachment demanded by the creditor, rule on the matter. If the application to have the foreign decision is accepted, the matter will be sent to the sheriff.

The sheriff will approach the debtor and attach such assets as are deemed sufficient, upon sale, to cover the amount due. If the asset to be considered is already encumbered, this must be taken into account in deciding whether attaching it serves any purpose for the creditor.

The debtor may not claim set-off, unless the claim for which set-off is demanded is recognised by final decision of the courts or is accepted by the creditor.

The debtor may, under some circumstances, however, have the sheriff or the lower court consider whether the enforcement proceedings should be delayed pending resolution of some dispute relating to the enforcement of the claim or, in some circumstances, relating to the claim that constitutes the basis for the enforcement proceedings.

The main rule is that all assets of value belonging to the debtor that can be converted to money can be attached. However, there are exceptions regarding personal effects, household goods of modest value, and tools and equipment needed for the continued exercise of trade. Specific exceptions are also made for compensation for personal injury, inheritance that has not fallen due, stipends and support, reasonable wages and pensions (unless the debtor wilfully does not pay amounts he is able to) and moneys needed to support the debtor and his family for two months. If the enforcement is directed at the debtor's residence, the court may make it a condition that the forced sale only be completed provided a reasonable lodging be provided for the debtor.

The attachment is notified to the debtor, and he is forbidden to dispose over it. If the asset is registrable (for instance, land and buildings, and ships), the attachment will also be registered to avoid sale to a buyer in good faith. If it is a bank account or claim, the attachment will be notified to the bank or person owing the amount, forbidding them to pay to the debtor.

If the attached asset is a chattel, it shall be taken out of the possession of the debtor if so demanded by the creditor.

By the attachment, the creditor receives a lien on the attached asset, with priority from the date of attachment. If the debtor goes bankrupt or opens composition proceedings within three months of the attachment being made, the attachment has no effect.

To retain the attachment of a chattel, the creditor must demand sale of the attached asset within three years.

If the basis for the enforcement is a registered mortgage (see *Enforcement of "enforceable documents"*, above), the enforcement proceedings do not have to go through this "attachment" stage.

Once the creditor is granted the attachment (or has registered a mortgage which is in default), he can demand that the attached asset shall be sold. The sale is normally made by ordinary sale or by forced auction held by the court. The holding of such auction is minutely regulated by law.

A sale cannot be confirmed by the court unless the purchase price cover costs, prior ranking encumbrances (statutory liens and prior registered mortgages), and is accepted by the creditor. Lower ranking encumbrances will be deleted by the forced auction (but remain the payment obligation of the debtor).

If the creditor fears that the purchase price will not reflect the true value of the asset (so that he consequently will not receive enough to cover his claim), he may himself bid up to the value of costs and prior lien and, if he has the highest bid, purchase the asset (to keep or sell subsequently at a private sale at, it is hoped, a better price). The amount bid will reduce the amount owed by the debtor by the like amount. Within the amount of his lien, the creditor does not need to pay out the amount he has bid. However, if there are costs and/or prior ranking encumbrances, these must be paid. The creditor may, of course, also bid higher than his (and prior) liens and encumbrances but must then pay the excess amount in cash.

Acceptance of bids at forced auctions can be denied by demand of the debtor, a lower ranking holder of a lien or encumbrance or other interested party, who can make it likely that the highest bid made is inadequate relative to market value.

The enforcement authorities may more generally postpone enforcement if the debtor has temporary liquidity problems without this being intended to give more time to debtors who cannot be expected to pay.

Ready cash value chattels (cash, accounts, money claims, quoted shares, and bonds) may be turned into cash by the sheriff without auction. In some instances, the creditor may, instead of a forced sale, demand that the asset be subjected to forced use.

If the creditor has a possessory lien (for instance right of retention on goods sold to the debtor in accordance with agreement and to the extent recognised by Norwegian

information. It is recommended—although not by law necessary—that legal assistance be sought before any direct steps are taken.

KNUT BOYE

CHAPTER 22

THE PHILIPPINES

INTRODUCTION

As a general rule, foreign citizens (natural and juridical) have access to the Philippine judicial and legal system in the same manner and extent as Filipino citizens. As an exception in the case of foreign corporations, the Corporation Code[1] incapacitates a foreign corporation doing business in the Philippines without the required licence, or its successors or assigns, from maintaining or intervening in any action, suit, or proceeding in any court or administrative agency of the Philippines. However, such corporation may be sued or proceeded against before Philippine courts or administrative tribunals on any valid cause of action recognised under Philippine laws.[2]

The Corporation Code defines a foreign corporation as one formed, organised or existing under any laws other than those of the Philippines, and whose laws allow Filipino citizens and corporations to do business in its own country or state.[3] Under the Corporation Code, foreign corporations have the right to transact business in the Philippines only after obtaining a licence so to do.[4]

It is not the lack of prescribed licence to do business in the Philippines, but rather doing business in the Philippines without the required licence, that bars a foreign corporation from access to Philippine courts.[5] Otherwise stated, a foreign corporation which does not have the required licence to transact business in the Philippines, and which is in fact not doing business in the Philippines, may bring suit in the Philippines.[6] Likewise, a foreign corporation performing an isolated transaction in the Philippines, not constituting "doing business", is not barred from seeking redress in Philippine courts.[7]

The term "doing business" implies a continuity of commercial dealings and arrangements, and contemplates to that extent the performance of work or the exercise of some of the functions normally incident to, and in the progressive prosecution of, the purpose and object of its organisation.[8] When a single act or transaction is not merely casual or incidental but indicates the foreign corporation's

1. Batas Pambansa Blg. 68.
2. Corporation Code, s. 133.
3. *Ibid.*, s. 123.
4. *Ibid.*, ss. 123–126.
5. *Home Insurance* Co. v. *Eastern Shipping Lines*, 123 SCRA 424 (1983).
6. *Eastboard Navigation Ltd* v. *Juan Ysmael & Co., Inc.*, 102 Phil. 1 (1957).
7. *Marshall-Wells* Co. v. *Elser and Co.*, 46 Phil. 70 (1924).
8. *Mentholatum* Co. v. *Mangaliman*, 72 Phil. 524 (1941).

intention to do other business in the country, that single act or transaction constitutes "doing business" in the country.[9] Thus, where a foreign corporation enters into a contract with a local corporation to manufacture and market its products and equipment, thereby carrying out the purpose for which it was created, it is deemed to have established in the Philippines a continuous, not merely temporary, business in the country.[10]

In particular, "doing business" includes:

(a) soliciting orders, purchases (sales) or service contracts. Concrete and specific solicitations by a foreign firm, not acting independently of the foreign firm, amounting to negotiation or fixing of the terms and conditions of the sales or service contracts, regardless of whether the contracts are actually reduced to writing and even if the enterprise has no office or fixed place of business in the Philippines;

(b) appointing a representative or distributor who is domiciled in the Philippines, unless said representative or distributor has an independent status; and

(c) opening offices, whether called "liaison" offices, agencies or branches, unless provided otherwise.[11]

Thus, an air carrier maintaining a general sales agent in the Philippines who is engaged in: (i) selling and issuing tickets; (ii) breaking down the whole trip into series of trips—each trip in the series corresponding to a different airline company; and (iii) consequently allocating the various airline companies on the basis of their participation in the services rendered through the mode of interline settlement as the IATA agreement is considered "engaged in business" in the Philippines. These activities are in the exercise of the functions which are normally incident to, and are in progressive pursuit of, the purpose and object of its organisation as an international air carrier.[12]

EFFECT OF FOREIGN JUDGMENTS

A judgment of a tribunal of a foreign country, having jurisdiction to pronounce the judgment, has the following effects under Philippine law:

(a) in case of a judgment upon a specific thing, the judgment is conclusive upon the title to the thing;

(b) in case of a judgment against a person, the judgment is presumptive evidence of a right as between the parties and their successors in interest by a subsequent title; but the judgment may be repelled by evidence of want of jurisdiction, want of notice to the part collusion, fraud, or clear mistake of law or fact.[13]

A writ of execution will not be issued by Philippine courts for foreign judgments. An action to enforce the judgment must first be brought before Philippine courts, and it is, in effect, the judgment of the Philippine court which will be enforced.[14] A foreign judgment against a person is merely presumptive evidence of a right between the

9. *Far East International Import & Export Corp.* v. *Nankai Kogyo Co.*, 116 Phil. 1053 (1962).
10. *Top-Weld Manufacturing, Inc.* v. *ECED, SA, et al.*, 138 SCRA 118 (1985).
11. *Facilities Management Corp.* v. *dela Rosa*, 89 SCRA 131 (1979).
12. *Commissioner of Internal Revenue* v. *British Overseas Airways Corp., et al.*, 149 SCRA 395 (1987).
13. Rules of Court, rule 39, s. 50.
14. *Perkins* v. *Benguet Consolidated Mining Corp.*, 93 Phil. 1034 (1953).

parties, and Philippine courts may reject it on the ground, among others, of evidence of want of jurisdiction.[15] In *Nagarmull* v. *Binalbagan-Isabela Sugar Co., Inc.*,[16] the Supreme Court refused to enforce a decision of the Tribunal of Arbitration of the Bengal Chamber of Calcutta, on the ground that it was rendered upon a "clear mistake of law". In *Arca and Javier* v. *Javier*,[17] the Supreme Court refused to recognise and enforce the effects (the right to receive and the duty to give support) of a foreign divorce decree on the ground that divorce is contrary to Filipino morals, customs, and traditions.[18]

PROVISIONAL REMEDIES ON A COLLECTION SUIT

The provisional remedies available and relevant to a collection suit are preliminary attachment and receivership.

Preliminary attachment

The writ of attachment is a process issued at the commencement or during the progress of an action commanding the sheriff or other proper officer to attach property, rights, credits, or effects of the defendant to satisfy the demand of the plaintiff. There are three kinds of attachment under Philippine law—preliminary attachment, garnishment and levy on execution.

Technically, preliminary attachment and garnishment are differentiated in that in the former the property attached is actually taken into the custody of the officer holding the writ, and is under his custody and control, while in garnishment, the property remains with the garnishee, or the third person owing money to or holding property of the defendant. However, in practice, the term "preliminary attachment" is used in either or both senses. Levy on execution is an attachment issued to enforce a judgment that has become final and executory.

A writ of preliminary attachment may be applied for by the plaintiff, at the commencement of the action or at any time thereafter. The application must be supported by the affidavit of the plaintiff or some other person who personally knows the facts, and by a bond executed to the adverse party.

The affidavit must show: (i) that a sufficient cause of action exists; (ii) that there is no other sufficient security for the claim sought to be enforced by the action; (iii) the amount due the plaintiff or the value of the property the possession of which he is entitled to recover above all legal counterclaims[19]; and (iv) that the case is one of the following:

(a) an action for recovery of money or damages on a cause of action arising from contract, express or implied, against a party who is about to depart from the Philippines with intent to defraud his creditors;

(b) an action for money or property embezzled or fraudulently misapplied or converted to his own use by a public officer, or an officer of a corporation, or

15. *Borthwick* v. *Castro-Bartolome*, 152 SCRA 229 (1987).
16. 33 SCRA 46 (1970).
17. 50 OG 3583 (1954).
18. To the same effect is *Querubin* v. *Querubin*, 87 Phil. 124 (1950).
19. Rules of Court, rule 57, s. 1.

an attorney, factor, broker, agent, or clerk, in the course of his employment as such, or by other persons in a fiduciary capacity, or for a wilful violation of duty;

(c) an action to recover the possession of personal property unjustly detained, when the property, or any part thereof, has been concealed, removed, or disposed of to prevent its being found or taken by the applicant or an officer;

(d) an action against a party who has been guilty of a fraud in contracting the debt or incurring the obligation upon which the action is brought, or in concealing or disposing of the property for the taking, detention or conversion of which the action is brought;

(e) an action against a party who has removed or disposed of his property, or is about to do so, with intent to defraud his creditors;

(f) an action against a party who resides out of the Philippines, or on whom summons may be served by publication.[20]

To be entitled to a writ of preliminary attachment, the plaintiff posts a bond in an amount to be fixed by the judge, not exceeding the plaintiff's claim, conditioned that the plaintiff will pay all the costs which may be adjudged to the adverse party and all damages he may sustain by reason of the attachment, if the court shall finally adjudge that the plaintiff was not entitled thereto.[21]

If the judge finds the application sufficient in form and substance, he shall issue an order of attachment, requiring the sheriff or other proper officer of the province to attach all the property of the party against whom it is issued within the province not exempt from execution, or so much thereof as may be sufficient to satisfy the plaintiff's demand, besides costs, unless such party makes deposit or gives bond in an amount sufficient to satisfy such demand, besides costs, or in an amount equal to the value of the property to be attached.[22]

At the time of service upon them a copy of the order of attachment and notice, all persons having in their possession or under their control any credits or other similar personal property belonging to the party against whom attachment is issued, or owing any debts to the same, shall be liable to the plaintiff for the amount of such credits, debts or other property, until the attachment is discharged, or any judgment recovered by him satisfied, unless such property is delivered or transferred, or such debts are paid, to the clerk, sheriff, or other proper officer of the court issuing the attachment.[23]

At any time after an order of attachment has been granted, the party whose property has been attached may apply to the judge who granted the order, or the judge of the court in which the action is pending, for an order discharging the attachment wholly or in part on the security given. The judge may order the discharge of the attachment if a cash deposit is made, or a counter-bond executed to the attaching creditor is filed, on behalf of the adverse party, with the clerk of judge of the court where the application is made, in an amount equal to the value of the property attached as determined by the judge, to secure the payment of any judgment that the attaching credit may recover in the action.[24]

20. *Ibid.*, rule 57, s. 3.
21. *Ibid.*, rule 57, s. 4.
22. *Ibid.*, rule 57, s. 2.
23. *Ibid.*, rule 57, s. 8.
24. *Ibid.*, rule 57, s. 12.

If judgment is recovered by the attaching creditor and execution issue thereon, the sheriff or other proper officer may cause the judgment to be satisfied out of the property attached, if it is sufficient for that purpose, in the following manner:

(a) by paying to the judgment creditor the proceeds of all sales of perishable or other property sold in pursuance of the order of the judge, or so much as shall be necessary to satisfy the judgment;
(b) if any balance remain due, by selling so much of the property, real or personal, as may be necessary to satisfy the balance, if enough for that purpose remain in the officer's hands, or in those of the clerk of court;
(c) by collecting from all persons having in their possession credits belonging to the judgment debtor, or owing debts to the latter at the time of the attachment of such credits or debts, the amount of such credits and debts as determined by the court in the action, and stated in the judgment, and paying the proceeds of such collection over to the judgment creditors.[25]

If after realising upon all the property attached, including the proceeds of any debts or credits collected, and applying the proceeds to the extinguishment of the judgment, any balance shall remain due, the officer must proceed to collect such balance as upon ordinary execution.[26]

Receivership

A receiver is a person appointed by the court to assume custody and control of property, and to preserve and sequester the same, pending litigation concerning its disposal.

One or more receivers of the property, real or personal, which is the subject of the action, may be appointed by the judge of the Regional Trial Court in which the action is pending, or by a Justice of the Court of Appeals or of the Supreme Court, in the following cases:

(a) when a corporation has been dissolved, or is insolvent, or is in imminent danger of insolvency, or has forfeited its corporate rights;
(b) when it appears from the complaint or answer, and such other proof as the judge may require, that the party applying for the appointment of receiver has an interest in the property or fund which is the subject of the action, and that such property or fund is in danger of being lost, removed, or materially injured unless a receiver be appointed to guard and preserve it;
(c) when it appears in an action by the mortgagee for the foreclosure of a mortgage that the property is in danger of being wasted or materially injured, and that its value is probably insufficient to discharge the mortgage debt, or that the parties have so stipulated in the contract of mortgage;
(d) after judgment, to preserve the property during the pendency of an appeal, or to dispose of it according to the judgment, or to aid execution when the execution has been returned unsatisfied or the judgment debtor refuses to apply his property in satisfaction of the judgment, or otherwise, to carry the judgment into effect;

25. *Ibid.*, rule 57, s. 15.
26. *Ibid.*, rule 57, s. 16.

(e) whenever in other cases it appears that the appointment of a receiver is the most convenient and feasible means of preserving, administering, or disposing of the property in litigation.[27]

If a receiver is appointed upon an *ex parte* application, the court, before making the order, may require the person applying for such appointment to file a bond executed to the party against whom the application is presented in an amount to be fixed by the court, to the effect that the applicant will pay such party all damages he may sustain by reason of the appointment of such receiver in case the applicant shall have procured such appointment without sufficient cause; and the court may, in its discretion, at any time after the appointment, require an additional bond as further security for such damages.[28]

The application for the appointment of a receiver may be denied, or the receiver already appointed may be discharged, when the party opposing the appointment makes it appear by affidavit(s) that such appointment was secured without sufficient cause, or when the party opposing the appointment files a bond executed to the applicant in an amount to be fixed by the court, to the effect that such party will pay the applicant all damages he may suffer by reason of the acts, omissions, or other matters specified in the application as ground for such appointment.[29]

Subject to the control of the court in which the action is pending, a receiver shall have power to bring and defend, as such, actions in his own name; to take and keep possession of the property in controversy; to receive rents; to collect debts due to himself as receiver or to the fund, property, estate, person, or corporation of which he is receiver; to compound for and compromise the same; to make transfers; to pay property that shall remain among the persons legally entitled to receive the same; and generally to do such acts respecting the property as the court may authorise. But funds in the hands of a receiver may be invested at interest only by order of the court made upon the written consent of all the parties to the action.[30]

Whenever the court, of its own motion or that of either party, shall determine that the necessity for a receiver no longer exists, it shall, after due notice to all interested parties and hearing, settle the accounts of the receiver, direct the delivery of the funds and other property in his hands to the persons adjudged entitled to receive them, and order the discharge of the receiver from further duty as such. The court shall allow the receiver such reasonable compensation as the circumstances of the case warrant, to be taxed as costs against the defeated party, or apportioned, as justice requires.[31]

EFFECT OF THE INSOLVENCY OF THE DEBTOR ON THE PROVISIONAL REMEDY OF ATTACHMENT

The insolvency of the debtor will, in certain cases, affect the provisional remedy of attachment.

Insolvency is primarily governed: (i) by the Civil Code, specifically its Articles

27. *Ibid.*, rule 59, s. 1.
28. *Ibid.*, rule 59, s. 3.
29. *Ibid.*, rule 59, s. 4.
30. *Ibid.*, rule 59, s. 7.
31. *Ibid.*, rule 59, s. 8.

CHAPTER 23

PORTUGAL

INTRODUCTION

This chapter surveys the provisional or interim relief and post-judgment actions which may be available in Portugal to foreign creditors.

The Portuguese Civil Procedure Code of 1939, Article 4, along with simple examination, condemnation, constitutive and executive actions, also provided for conservatory actions. In the system of the Civil Procedure Code of 1961, still in force, the proceedings previously denominated "preventive and conservatory" were eliminated. Since 1961 they are regarded as simple preliminary actions, devoid, therefore, of autonomy in relation to lawsuits already instituted or about to be instituted.[1]

NATURE OF PROVISIONAL RELIEF

The juridical regime of provisional relief is defined in Articles 381 *et seq.* of the Civil Procedure Code. An essential aspect of this subject is the circumstance that the provisional relief is no more than a simple measure intended to prevent *periculum in mora* in the judgment or in the course of any lawsuit.[2] In fact, the concepts of curatorship and defence that the law makes available to the parties are frequently not sufficient, without provisional relief, to avoid the disadvantages of delay in the declarative or executive action. Such disadvantages are particularly aggravated in cases where the creditor is a foreigner or the condemnation or execution is conducted from outside Portugal. In such event, while the declarative, condemnation, or execution action is pending the risk of a change in the situation that might impair the effect of a judgment favourable to the creditor increases significantly. This is an obvious consequence of the usual delays caused by distance and by the eventual recognition processes and execution of foreign judgments. Yet one of Portugal's major procedural principles stipulates that delay in the judgment of a lawsuit shall cause no harm to the party having a right.[3] The jurisdictional accomplishment of the law aims at giving the creditor a satisfaction identical to that he would obtain by way of a

1. Artur Anselmo de Castro, *Direito Processual Civil Declaratório*, Almedina, Coimbra, 1981, Vol. I, p. 129.

2. *Ibid.*, p. 130; Antunes Varela, Miguel Bezerra, Sampaio e Nora, *Manual do Processo Civil*, 2a ediçao revista e actualizada, Coimbra Editora, Coimbra, p. 24.

3. Anselmo de Castro, note 1 *supra*, p. 130.

peaceful and punctual realisation of his rights.[4] This is the goal envisaged by provisional relief.

Let us imagine that, in the course of a condemnation action, or even before it has been instituted, a creditor sees his debtor rapidly deplete his assets. To avoid the serious and irreparable losses that the debtor's conduct can cause to the creditor, the law permits the anticipation—though not the realisation or concretisation—of everything that the creditor might be entitled to receive by according him, for instance, the right to petition for the arrest of the debtor's assets.[5]

In line with its specific objective, provisional relief is ruled by a structure rather more simplified than that involved for other types of lawsuits. Such structure is identical whether the petitioner is Portuguese or a foreign citizen. It is necessary—in the same manner as when a lawsuit is instituted—to effect payment of court costs and tax in the terms defined in the Code of Judicial Costs.[6]

On examining the premises of provisional relief, the judge cannot require that the existence and violation of the petitioner's right, or the demonstration of the risk of damage that the provisional relief is designed to avoid, be proved to the same degree that is usually required for a lawsuit. As the law itself states (Article 401, Civil Procedure Code), the judge must be satisfied with the strong probability of existence of the right, namely with the proof of a *fumum boni iuris* (Article 400, No. 1, Civil Procedure Code).

The hearing of the other party may be waived if the observance of the principle of contradiction would risk the purpose of the provisional relief (Article 400, No. 2, Civil Procedure Code). For relief to be given, it will be sufficient for the petitioner to demonstrate that the fear of harm is justifiable, understandable, and well-founded, although it may never occur (Article 401, No. 1, Civil Procedure Code). It is incumbent upon the judge to reach only a *summaria cognitio*; on this basis, he may grant the provisional relief.

However, at the defendant's request, and the creditor having been heard, the provisional relief may be replaced by an adequate pledge whenever such remedy appears to be sufficient to prevent the harm (Article 401, No. 3, Civil Procedure Code).

In the event that the provisional relief would cause to the defendant a damage higher than the loss that the petitioner seeks to avoid, the judge must deny the petition (Article 401, No. 1, Civil Procedure Code).

Inasmuch as it constitutes a simple procedural incident, provisional relief is always dependent upon a principal lawsuit, pending or to be instituted immediately by the petitioner. If the lawsuit has not yet been instituted, the provisional relief is a mere preliminary measure, and will become null and void if such lawsuit is not instituted within 30 days following the notification that the provisional relief has been accorded (Article 382, No. 1, al. (a), Civil Procedure Code). If the lawsuit is pending, the provisional relief will constitute a mere incident thereto.[7]

As the provisional relief depends upon the lawsuit whose beneficial effect it seeks to

4. *Ibid.*
5. See *infra.*
6. No discrimination exists as to the citizenship of the petitioner for the preventive injunction. The payment of the tax and court fees is owed by Portuguese and foreign citizens alike.
7. See Varela et al., note 2 *supra.*

defend, it will become null and void if the principal lawsuit is held to be groundless (Article 382, No. 1, Civil Procedure Code).[8]

IMPACT OF FOREIGN LITIGATION

The regime described above was based on the premise that both the provisional relief and the principal lawsuit were brought before the Portuguese courts. In the event that the provisional relief is sought in Portugal but the principal lawsuit falls within the competence of a foreign court, some difficulties could arise, the solution of which appears to be difficult.

In such an event, what impact has the rule that the provisional relief must always be dependent on a principal lawsuit? What of the requirement formulated in Article 384, Nos 2 and 3, Civil Procedure Code, according to which the provisional relief must apply appended to the principal action? Two situations must be distinguished:

(1) The first occurs if, at the time when the provisional relief is petitioned in Portugal, the principal lawsuit—whose beneficial effect the provisional relief is designed to defend—is already in process abroad.

(2) The second occurs whenever the provisional relief is petitioned prior to the principal lawsuit being instituted abroad.

Principal lawsuit in process abroad

In the case where the principal lawsuit is in process abroad, it appears, at first glance, that the competence for decreeing the provisional relief should also be incumbent upon the foreign court. This solution, however, does not stand up to closer analysis. Foreign courts cannot order acts in the Portuguese juridical sphere. Based on this principle, as well as on the rule that provisional relief must always arise in connection with a principal action, Portuguese jurisprudence has upheld the impossibility of provisional relief being accorded in situations such as those under analysis herein.[9]

However, it is submitted that such a view is not acceptable. Procedural law is adjective. Whatever its interpretation, it cannot, in the issue under discussion, imply the reduction of the guarantees that ensure the substantive rights of the parties. Yet this can only be ensured if we accept the possibility for the Portuguese court to autonomise the provisional relief in relation to the principal lawsuit which is in process abroad.

This solution is expressly sanctioned in two international conventions to which Portugal is party. They are the Brussels Convention concerning the Judicial

8. The inverse situation, however, is not true. The denial of the preventive injunction does not impair the petitioner's right. Even if the *periculum in mora* does not exist as grounds for granting the preventive injunction, the right invoked by the petitioner could actually exist, as well as the violation against which he wishes to protect himself. For this reason, the legislator has sanctioned in Art. 386 of the Civil Procedure Code the rule that the decision taken in the preventive injunction shall have no influence in the examination of the principal lawsuit.

9. *Sentence of the Appellate Court of Oporto of 4 December 1986* in *Colectânea de Jurisprudência*, 1986, Vol. V, pp. 234 *et seq*. The foreign court lacks competence to order the practice of authority in Portugal. Thus, the injunction cannot be ordered by it. The Portuguese court would also be unable to accord the preventive injunction. If it orders the injunction, it would violate, according to some jurists, the rule that the preventive injunction must always arise in connection with a principal lawsuit.

Competence and the Execution of Decisions on Civil and Commercial Matters, and the Lugano Convention concerning the Judicial Competence and the Execution of Decisions on Civil and Commercial Matters. In both Conventions, it has been established in an unequivocal manner[10] that the provisional or preventive measures prescribed by the law of a signatory country can be petitioned to the judicial authorities of that country, even though, by force of such conventions, a court in another signatory country is competent for examining the central issue.

Thus, there is no room for doubt. If the principal lawsuit is run in one of the states signatory to the Brussels or Lugano Conventions, and if the provisional relief is petitioned in Portugal, the rule of the dependence between the lawsuit and the provisional relief is broken. Portuguese courts are competent to decree the provisional relief though they lack competence for the principal lawsuit. Furthermore, the solution just described must, consequently, apply to all cases where the principal lawsuit takes place outside Portugal and the provisional relief is sought in this country. A different solution would lead to the reduction of the guarantees ensuring the rights of the parties on the basis of a purely formal interpretation of the adjective rules, which is by no means justified.

Relief sought prior to litigation

In cases where the provisional relief is petitioned in Portugal prior to the institution of the principal lawsuit abroad, the solution of the problem will not be very different. If the courts competent for deciding the central issue are from countries signatories to the Brussels Convention or the Lugano Convention, no difficulties will arise. Article 24 of the Conventions will apply. Thus, in those cases falling within the scope of the Conventions, the competence of the Portuguese courts to decree provisional relief is not impaired by the rule according to which such provisional relief must occur in connection with a principal lawsuit. The solution is, therefore, absolutely identical to the one that must hold for the case where the principal action has already been instituted abroad.

The issue, however, becomes more complicated when the jurisdictional authorities who must decide the principal action are not from a Convention country. Will, in such event, the Portuguese courts be able to decree the provisional relief, or must they abstain from ordering any measures? The key to this question must be found in the reading of Article 2 with Article 65, No. 1 al. (d) of the Civil Procedure Code.

In Article 2 the principle is established according to which every right—unless the law determines otherwise—encompasses the ability to seek its recognition, as well as measures necessary to safeguard the beneficial effect of the action. Article 65, No. 1 al. (d) accords international competence to the Portuguese courts when the right cannot become effective unless by way of a lawsuit instituted in Portugal, provided that a significant connection exists between the lawsuit and Portugal.

These rules allow us to conclude that:

(1) Inherent in every law, there is an action and a set of measures to ensure the beneficial effect of that action. The fact that the principal lawsuit has been

10. See Art. 24 of the Brussels and Lugano Conventions.

instituted abroad must not, in any way, impair the guarantees accorded by Portuguese law.

(2) If a right cannot become effective unless by way of a lawsuit instituted in a Portuguese court, the Portuguese judicial authorities have international competence to decide the dispute. The provisional relief will only take its beneficial effect in Portugal if ordered by a Portuguese court.

Thus, the Portuguese courts must consider themselves competent to decree provisional relief, even if the central issue is to be decided in a country which has neither sanctioned nor adhered to the Brussels Convention or the Lugano Convention.

Furthermore, as the provisional relief becomes null and void if the principal lawsuit is not instituted within 30 days—and in the absence of other mechanisms capable of preventing the situation—the Portuguese court must also consider itself competent to examine the principal lawsuit. Otherwise, the beneficial effect of the provisional relief would be impaired.

TYPES OF REMEDY

Having defined, in general terms, the juridical regime of provisional relief and having studied the question as to what extent must the Portuguese courts consider themselves competent to decree provisional remedies, a short reference must now be made to the various types of provisional remedy.

It is possible to distinguish between:

(1) inhibitory provisional remedies;
(2) restitutive provisional remedies; and
(3) anticipatory provisional remedies.

Inhibitory remedies

Suspension of deliberations

Among the inhibitory provisional remedies, it is worth mentioning the suspension of corporate deliberations (Article 397, No. 4, Civil Procedure Code). Through this process, the shareholders of a company can petition for the suspension of any deliberations of the general assembly that are contrary to legal or statutory provisions. For that purpose, they must furnish proof of their capacity as shareholders and give evidence that a significant damage may result from the execution of the deliberation (Article 396, No. 1, Civil Procedure Code).

As from the date of summons and up to the time the petition for suspension is decided, the company is not permitted to execute the contested deliberation.

Enrolment

Included in the category of inhibitory provisional relief is enrolment. This is a measure destined to remove the danger of a right not being satisfied due to delay in the final decision. This danger of non-satisfaction is characterised by Article 421 of the Civil Procedure Code requiring fear of deviation or dissipation of the assets, either chattels or real property, or documents.

If someone claims to have the right to certain assets and gives evidence that some facts or circumstances give rise to a well-founded fear that the respective holder or owner could deviate or dissipate them before the claimed right to the said assets is recognised and sanctioned by the court, a petition may be made for enrolment.

If the enrolment is urgent, and there is no possibility of effecting it immediately or concluding it on the day it was begun, the law provides for the sealing of the doors of the buildings or cupboards in which the assets are kept, and measures necessary to their safety must be adopted (Article 425, Civil Procedure Code).

Enrolment makes it impossible for the owner of the assets to dispose of them, and their administration must be carried out through a trustee (Article 423, No. 2, and Article 424, Nos. 1 and 2, Civil Procedure Code).

Arrest and embargo

For a purpose identical to enrolment, one must mention arrest and embargo.

The arrest consists of the judicial apprehension of assets (Article 402, Civil Procedure Code). It may occur when the creditor has a justifiable fear of the debtor's insolvency or of depletion of assets (Article 403, No. 1, Civil Code, and Articles 614, 622, 819, and 822, Civil Procedure Code). It aims at eliminating the danger that the creditor may suffer loss before the attachment is decreed. The arrest appears, therefore, as an anticipated form of attachment. They both produce the same substantial effect: the immobilisation of the assets upon which they fall.

Embargo may be decreed when one undertakes a work or service bringing offence to any *jus in rem* or the ownership of another. Should this occur, the court may recognise the injured party's right to embargo the activity (Article 412, No. 1, Civil Procedure Code).

Restitutive remedies

A restitutive preventive injunction is the provisional restitution of ownership. This is a measure having to do with *jus in rem*. It takes place in the case of violent dispossession (Article 393, Civil Procedure Code). By this measure, the dispossessed person is immediately restored to ownership.

Anticipatory remedies

In the third category of the preventive measures, the anticipatory preventive injunction, is included the provisional supply of food. This measure relates to a lawsuit in which, as a principal or accessory claim, the providing of food is requested. Should it be petitioned, the judge must fix the monthly amount the petitioner should receive as a pension of provisional alimony (Article 388, No. 1, Civil Procedure Code).

Preventive injunctions characterised

Some preventive injunctions are designed to ensure obligations of a pecuniary nature. Such is the case of the arrest and the provision of alimony.

In the case of arrest, the assets upon which it falls are entrusted to a trustee to be sold later. With the proceeds of sale, the creditors are paid the amounts due to them. The provision of alimony is also designed to ensure a pecuniary credit.

Other preventive injunctions are designed to ensure and guarantee rights to things or obligations for the supply of things. Such is the case with enrolment, embargo, and provisional restitution of ownership.

The suspension of corporate deliberations is a third category. It is not intended to guarantee the right to a pecuniary supply or to a thing or fact, but rather the protestative right to cancellation of a faulty deliberation.

Portuguese law also provides that other non-specified or denominated preventive measures may be petitioned and decreed. These arise when someone shows a well-founded fear that another, prior to the institution of the principal lawsuit or even during its course, may cause serious and irreparable harm to his rights, and none of the measures specifically designed by law is appropriate. These measures function as a cover for the system: the initiator may petition the measure he deems adequate for avoiding the harm.

BANKRUPTCY

In the event that the subject of a preventive injunction becomes bankrupt, all the actions relating to the bankrupt estate must be appended to the bankruptcy process, except where they are dependent on an appeal of a final judgment. In that case, the appending takes place only after the final judgment takes full force and effect (Article 1198, No. 1, Civil Procedure Code).

Once the bankruptcy has been decreed, the apprehension of the whole estate of the bankrupt is done, even if the estate had been arrested, attached, detained, or seized, with the safeguarding of the creditors' rights paramount (Article 1205, No. 1, Civil Procedure Code).

The court decreeing the bankruptcy must ask the court or the competent authority to remit the processes where the arrest, attachment, apprehension, or detention of the bankrupt estate was made (Article 1205, No. 2, Civil Procedure Code).

The rules enunciated above also apply, according to Article 1315 of the Civil Procedure Code, in the case where the defendant is subject to the rules of insolvency, not of bankruptcy, due to the fact that he is not a company.

PEDRO DE ALBUQUERQUE

CHAPTER 24

SINGAPORE

INTRODUCTION

Having litigated and won a case, the successful plaintiff has won nothing more than moral appeasement unless he can enforce his judgment. For the foreign claimant who has received money judgment, the next step is to find money or assets against which to satisfy the judgment. More often than not, to enforce the judgment debt, the judgment creditor must take the judgment issued by the original court and enforce it in the defendant's own country. This chapter will deal with matters of procedure and substance relating to provisional remedies, enforcement of foreign judgments, and defences against enforcement in Singapore.

In private international law, there are two main modes of enforcement of foreign judgments; namely, under common law and statute. Under the common-law method, the foreign creditor must relitigate the case where the foreign judgment is not recognised or enforceable.

COMMON LAW

If the foreign litigant brings a claim under common law, the jurisdiction of the Singapore High Court to hear such claims is governed by the Supreme Court of Judicature Act (Cap. 322). Section 15 of the Act deals with criminal jurisdiction, and sections 16 and 17 deal with civil jurisdiction.

Once the question of jurisdiction is satisfied, the foreign plaintiff may apply for summary judgment under Order 14 of the Rules of Court, based on the judgment he has obtained in the foreign court and on the contention that there is no valid defence to his claim. The application for summary judgment is based on the "doctrine of obligation" in that, where a foreign court of competent jurisdiction has adjudicated a certain sum to be due from one person to another, the liability to pay that sum becomes a legal obligation that may be enforced in this country by an action of debt.

Once the judgment is proved, the burden lies on the defendant to show why he should not perform the obligation. He can do so by raising various defences[1] normally available in private international law, including where there is allegation of fraud,[2] the original court had no jurisdiction,[3] the judgment is contrary to public policy, the

1. *United Malayan Banking Corporation Bhd* v. *Soo Lean Tooi & Others* [1984] 1 MLJ 47.
2. *Cheah Wong Nyan* v. *Palaniappa* [1935] MLJ 31.
3. *United Overseas Bank Ltd* v. *Tjong Tjui Njuk* [1987] 2 MLJ 295.

judgment is already wholly satisfied,[4] and the judgment seeks to enforce foreign penal or revenue law. However, an Order 14 judgment based on a final foreign judgment will still be allowed in a proper case if the fraud alleged is clearly frivolous.[5]

Statute

Under statute, the foreign judgment may be treated in the same way as a judgment obtained in the court of receiving jurisdiction, based on the concept of reciprocity. The relevant enactments governing the registration and enforcement of foreign judgments in Singapore are:

(1) Reciprocal Enforcement of Commonwealth Judgments Act (Cap. 264) (CJA);
(2) Reciprocal Enforcement of Foreign Judgments Act (Cap. 265) (FJA); and
(3) Arbitration (Foreign Awards) Act (Cap. 10A).

INTERIM REMEDIES

Interim remedies in the jurisdiction of Singapore are regulated by Order 29 of the Rules of Court. Normally, they are available on application by any party to a cause or matter before or after trial, whether or not such a claim is included in that party's writ, originating summons, counterclaim or third party notice, as the case may be. In cases of urgency, such application may be made *ex parte* by originating summons supported by an affidavit, but otherwise application must be by originating motion.

For a foreign claim brought under common law, Order 29 would apply, and the foreign judgment is irrelevant in so far as proceedings in Singapore are concerned, as it involves a fresh re-examination of the issues in accordance with Singapore law. The general principles for the grant of interlocutory injunctions will follow those of the *American Cyanamid* v. *Ethicon* case. Such grant is usually accompanied by an undertaking as to damages by the applicant. This means that, in effect, any foreign claims can, if required, utilise interim remedies under the Singapore rules. There is no need for a foreign claim to be perfected in terms of a judgment before it can utilise the interim remedies in Singapore.

With respect to foreign claims which are already perfected in the form of judgments, the relevant Singapore statutes in relation to recognition and enforcement of the same do not expressly include nor preclude powers of the High Court to make provisions for interim remedies. The implication is that, if the situation is one of urgency, the interim remedies can always be utilised on the normal basis, whilst the foreign judgment is in the process of being registered or recognised in the Singapore courts.

Section 6 of the CJA and section 8 of the FJA provide for the power of the Supreme Court to make rules regulating practice and procedure under the Acts. These provisions may allow the use of the Rules of the Supreme Court in relation to recognised foreign judgments.

4. *KS Das* v. *P Suppiah* [1988] 2 MLJ 445.
5. See *Hua Daily News Sdn Bhd* v. *Tan Thien Chin & Others* [1986] 2 MLJ 107.

RECOGNITION OF FOREIGN JUDGMENTS

In order for a foreign judgment to be recognised, much will depend on under which enactment it is sought to be enforced and whether it falls foul of concepts of private international law. We shall deal with each Act separately for easier reference.

Reciprocal Enforcement of Commonwealth Judgments Act, Cap. 264

This Act basically provides for reciprocal enforcement of judgments obtained in a superior court of the United Kingdom and Northern Ireland.[6] The Minister of Law may, however, extend this Act to any part of the Commonwealth if satisfied that reciprocity of Singapore High Court judgments is provided for by legislation of that part of the Commonwealth.[7]

To date, this Act has been extended to Australia,[8] Negara Brunei Darussalam,[9] Sri Lanka,[10] Hong Kong,[11] India[12] (except the states of Jammu and Kashmir), Malaysia,[13] New Zealand,[14] Pakistan,[15] Papua New Guinea,[16] and the Windward Islands.[17]

In this Act, judgment is defined only as any judgment or order given or made by the court in any civil proceedings whereby any sum of money is made payable. It includes arbitration awards,[18] although that will now fall under the Arbitration (Foreign Awards) Act.

Registration of Commonwealth judgments is not a matter of right, it being requisite that the High Court shall "in all the circumstances of the case ... think it just and convenient[19] that the judgment should be enforced in Singapore".[20]

To enforce a Commonwealth judgment, the foreign creditor (or his successors and assigns) may apply to the High Court any time within 12 months from the date of judgment or such longer period allowed, to have the judgment registered in the court.[21] However, no judgment would be ordered to be registered if[22]:

(1) The original court acted without jurisdiction.
(2) The judgment debtor, being a person who was neither carrying on business nor ordinarily resident within the jurisdiction of the original court, did not

6. s. 3.
7. s. 5(1).
8. Western Australia GN 729/25; South Australia GN 1206/25; New South Wales GN 1580/25, Victoria GN 42/27; Territory of Norfolk Island GN 335/27; Territory of North Australia GN 1581/27; Territory of Central Australia GN 1582/27; Queensland S 188/72; Tasmania S 194/72.
9. S 5/55.
10. GN 1322/25.
11. GN 151/25.
12. S 342/68.
13. S 100/50.
14. S 877/25.
15. S 1444/54.
16. S 303/56.
17. S 5/53.
18. s. 2(1).
19. *Bank of India* v. *Trans Continental Commodity Merchants Ltd & Anor* [1986] 2 MLR 342.
20. s. 2(1).
21. s. 3(1).
22. s. 3(2).

voluntarily appear or otherwise submit or agree to submit to the jurisdiction of that court.[23]

(3) The judgment debtor, being the defendant in the proceedings, was not duly served with the process of the original court and did not appear notwithstanding that he was ordinarily resident or was carrying on business within the jurisdiction of that court or agreed to submit to the jurisdiction of the court.

(4) The judgment was obtained by fraud.

(5) The judgment debtor satisfies the registering court that an appeal is pending or that he is entitled and intends to appeal against the judgment.

(6) The judgment was in respect of a cause of action which for reasons of public policy or some other similar reason could not be entertained by the registering court.

Once registered, judgment will be of the same force and effect as if it had been judgment ordinarily obtained in a Singapore court; and in so far as execution of the judgment is concerned, the Singapore court will have the same control and jurisdiction over the judgment as it has over the judgment given by itself.[24] The costs of and incidental to registration of the judgment will be recoverable in the same manner as sums payable under the judgment.[25]

Reciprocal Enforcement of Foreign Judgments Act, Cap. 265

This Act makes provision for the enforcement in Singapore of judgments given in foreign countries which afford reciprocal treatment to judgments of Singapore courts. The Act gives the Minister of Law power to extend the Act to foreign countries if he is satisfied that substantial reciprocity of treatment will be assured as respects the enforcement in that country of judgments given in the High Court of Singapore,[26] or to judgments obtained in Commonwealth countries.[27] The Act, however, has yet to be extended either way, so the following discussion is purely academic.

A foreign creditor may, as of right, apply to the High Court any time within six years from date of judgment or after determination of appeal, to have the judgment registered in the High Court; and the High Court shall, subject to proof of prescribed matters and to other provisions of the Act, order judgment to be registered.[28]

As with the CJA, Cap. 264, procedure for such application falls under Order 67 of the Rules of the Supreme Court.

This Act differs from the CJA in many respects. For example, "judgment" is construed more widely to include a judgment or order made by a court in any criminal proceedings for payment of a sum of money in respect of compensation or damages to the injured party.[29] The Act does not include an arbitration award, but this is now covered by separate legislation, as mentioned above.

23. *Sun-Line (Management) Ltd* v. *Canpotex Shipping Services Ltd* [1986] 2 MLJ 348.
24. s. 3(3)(a).
25. s. 3(3)(c).
26. s. 3(1).
27. s. 9(1).
28. s. 4(1).
29. s. 2(1).

The judgment must be final and conclusive,[30] but judgment is deemed final and conclusive notwithstanding that an appeal is still pending against it, or that it may be subject to appeal.[31] It must also not be for a sum payable for taxes or other damages of a like nature, or for a fine or other penalty.[32]

If the sum payable is expressed in foreign currency, the Act expressly provides that the judgment shall be registered as if it is a judgment for such sum in the Singapore currency on the basis of the rate of exchange on the date of judgment of the original court.[33] Partially satisfied judgments can only be registered in respect of the balance payable at the date of application.[34]

Registration of judgment must be set aside on the following grounds[35]:

(1) It is not registered in accordance with provision of the Act.
(2) The original court had no jurisdiction.
(3) The judgment debtor did not receive notice of those proceedings in sufficient time to enable him to defend.
(4) The judgment was obtained by fraud.
(5) Enforcement of the judgment is contrary to public policy.

The court may also set aside registration if it is satisfied that the matter under dispute in proceedings of the original court had been the subject matter of a final and conclusive judgment by another court having jurisdiction.[36]

Arbitration (Foreign Awards) Act, Cap. 10A

This Act gives effect in Singapore to the New York Convention on the Recognition and Enforcement of Foreign Arbitral Awards, to which both Singapore and the US are signatories.

The Act provides that a foreign award made in a convention country, may be enforced in the High Court either by action or in the same manner as an award made in Singapore which is enforceable under the Arbitration Act, Cap. 10.[37]

Section 20 of the Arbitration Act provides that an arbitral award may, by leave of court, be enforced in the same manner as a judgment, and that judgment may be entered in terms of the award. It should be noted that enforcement under this section is discretionary. Any foreign award thus enforceable shall be recognised as binding for all purposes upon the persons to whom it was made.[38] The procedural rules for enforcement of such foreign awards in Singapore are straightforward. The foreign creditor is required to produce to the court[39]:

(1) the duly authenticated original award or a certified copy of it;
(2) the original arbitration agreement or a certified copy; and

30. s. 3(2)(a).
31. s. 3(3).
32. s. 3(2)(b).
33. s. 4(3).
34. s. 4(4).
35. s. 5(1)(a).
36. s. 5(1)(b).
37. s. 5(1).
38. s. 5(2).
39. s. 6.

(3) a certified translation of the award or arbitration agreement where applicable.

However, enforcement may be refused if the judgment debtor proves to the satisfaction of the court that[40]:

(1) a party to the arbitration agreement in pursuance of which the award was made was, under the law applicable to him, under some incapacity at the time when the agreement was made; or
(2) the arbitration agreement was invalid under the law to which the parties subjected it or under the law of the country where the award was made; or
(3) he was not given proper notice of the appointment of the arbitrator or of arbitration proceedings, or was otherwise unable to present his case; or
(4) subject to section 7(3), the award dealt with a difference not contemplated by or not falling within the terms of submission to arbitration, or contained a decision on the matter beyond the scope of submission to arbitration; or
(5) the composition of the arbitral authority or the arbitral procedure was not in accordance with the agreement of the parties or with the law of the country where arbitration took place; or
(6) the award has not yet become binding on the parties, or was set aside or suspended by a competent authority of the country in which the award was made.

Enforcement of a foreign award may also be refused if the subject matter is not capable of settlement by arbitration under Singapore law, or if enforcement is contrary to public policy of Singapore.[41]

PROCEDURE FOR REGISTRATION

Such application must be made by originating summons *ex parte* supported by an affidavit[42]:

(1) exhibiting the judgment or a certified copy and a certified translation, if applicable;
(2) stating the name, trade or business and usual or last place of abode or business of the judgment creditor and debtor;
(3) stating to the best of the information or belief of the deponent:
    (a) that the judgment creditor is entitled to enforce his judgment;
    (b) either that at the date of application the judgment is not satisfied or the amount remaining unsatisfied;
    (c) that the judgment does not fall within any cases in which judgment is not registrable; and
    (d) that, at the date of application, judgment is enforceable by execution in the country of the original act and registration is not liable to be set aside; and
(4) specifying the amount of interest due until the time of registration.

An order giving leave to register the judgment must stipulate the period within which

40. s. 7(2).
41. s. 7(4).
42. Order 67, rules 2 and 3.

registration may be set aside. This period may be extended on application by any competent party. Application to set aside registration judgment is made by summons supported by affidavit.[43]

SECURITY FOR COSTS

Whether under common law or statute, the foreign creditor may be required to furnish security for costs under the Rules of Court. However, such an order is discretionary in nature, and the court will only make such order if in all the circumstances of the case, it thinks it just to do so.

Factors that will be taken into consideration include the ease of reciprocal enforcement in relation to countries for which such reciprocity exists, the substantial assets of the plaintiff company, and no suggestion of likely dissipation and other relevant factors laid out in *Sir Lindsay Parkinson & Co. Ltd* v. *Triplan Ltd.*[44]

ENFORCEMENT OF REGISTERED JUDGMENTS

Once a foreign judgment is registered, the judgment will be of the same force and effect as if it is a judgment originally obtained in a Singapore court.

The execution of a duly registered judgment will only be issued after the expiration of the period or extended period within which an application may be made to set aside the registration or if there is such an application to set aside registration, after the final determination thereof.[45]

The judgment or order for the payment of money may be enforced by one of the following means, all of which are governed by the Rules of the Supreme Court[46]:

(1) writ of seizure and sale;
(2) garnishee proceedings;
(3) stop notice;
(4) appointment of receiver; and
(5) bankruptcy and winding-up proceedings.

Writ of seizure and sale

This mode of enforcement is provided for in Orders 46 and 47 of the Rules of Court.

Issue of a writ of seizure and sale takes place on its being sealed by an officer of the Registry of the High Court.[47] Before such issue, *a praecipe* in the prescribed form must be filed and the proceedings must be signed by the person entitled to execution or by his solicitors.[48]

Before the writ can be sealed, the foreign creditor must produce to the Registry of the court:

43. Order 67, rule 9.
44. [1973] QB 609.
45. Order 29, rule 10.
46. Order 45.
47. Order 46, rule 4(1).
48. *Ibid.*, rule 4(2) and (3).

(1) the foreign judgment or a certified copy of it;
(2) the leave of court to issue such writ (where applicable); and
(3) the written permission of the Controller of Foreign Exchange under Order 49, rule 5, of the Rules of Court.[49]

The writ is valid for 12 months and may be extended for further periods of 12 months by application.[50] After issue of the writ, the sheriff is empowered to seize and sell property of the judgment debtor.

Order 46, rules 14 to 21, lay down the duties of the sheriff, including the times allowed for execution, form of notice to be given to judgment debtor, list of inventory taken by him, date of arrest, and maintenance of proper statements of accounts by him. Where the value of the property exceeds S$2,000, sale must be conducted by a licensed auctioneer, and the sale must be publicly advertised by the sheriff or auctioneer at least two days prior to the sale.[51]

Garnishee proceedings

Governed by Order 49 of the Rules of Court, the court may order any person within the jurisdiction indebted to the judgment debtor to pay the foreign claimant the amount of any debt "due or accruing due" to the judgment debtor.[52]

Application for such an order must be made *ex parte* by summons supported by affidavit in the prescribed form[53]:

(1) identifying the judgment or order to be enforced and stating the amount remaining unpaid at the time of application; and
(2) stating to the best of the information and belief of the deponent, that the garnishee (naming him) is within the jurisdiction and is indebted to the judgment debtor, and stating the sources of information or grounds of belief.

The order must be served on the garnishee personally and on the judgment debtor.[54] If the garnishee does not dispute the debt due, the order will be made absolute.[55]

However, it is important to note that such an order will not be made unless the foreign creditor produces a certificate to the effect that the Controller of Foreign Exchange has given permission under the Exchange Control Act for such payment, whether conditionally or unconditionally.[56]

Stop notice

This measure is governed by Order 50 of the Rules of Court.

The claimant will use this remedy if he wishes to be notified of any proposed transfer of payment of the securities in which he is interested or beneficially entitled. As such,

49. *Ibid.*, rule 4(4).
50. *Ibid.*, rule 6.
51. *Ibid.*, rule 24.
52. Order 49, rule 1.
53. *Ibid.*, rule 2.
54. *Ibid.*, rule 3.
55. *Ibid.*, rule 4.
56. *Ibid.*, rule 7.

this is not really an enforcement but rather more of a means of preserving status quo until the other methods of enforcement can be utilised.

Appointment of receiver

This is governed by Order 51 and Order 30 of the Rules of Court.

The appointment of a receiver by way of equitable execution is discretionary and is made if the court thinks it just or convenient, having regard to the amount claimed by the foreign creditor, the amount likely to be obtained by the receiver and the probable costs of his appointment.[57]

In addition, the foreign creditor must obtain the permission of the Controller of Foreign Exchange and comply with conditions imposed (if any).[58]

An application for the appointment of a receiver may be made by summons or motion.[59] Such application may include an injunction ancillary or incidental to an order appointing a receiver.[60] Where the injunction sought is of urgency, application may be made *ex parte* by summons supported by an affidavit.[61]

The receiver must give security approved by the court in order to be appointed. Such security is usually in the form of a guarantee or undertaking in the prescribed form.[62]

An appointed receiver must submit accounts to the court at prescribed intervals, together with an accompanying affidavit.[63]

Bankruptcy and winding-up proceedings

Strictly speaking, these are not modes of execution of judgments. However, the threat of them will often produce payments. The procedure and effect of such proceedings are dealt with in the next section.

EFFECT OF BANKRUPTCY OF DEBTOR

Where a foreign judgment has been recognised by the Singapore court, but the judgment debtor has been adjudicated bankrupt, the Bankruptcy Act will apply. On the making of a receiving order under the Act, the Official Assignee will be made receiver of the judgment debtor's property, and thereafter no creditor to whom the debtor is indebted in respect of any debt provable in bankruptcy shall have any remedy against the property or person of the debtor in respect of the debt. Such creditor will also be unable to commence any action or legal proceedings except with the leave of court and on such terms, if any.[64] However, the Act does not in any way affect a secured creditor.[65]

57. Order 51, rule 1(1).
58. *Ibid.*, rule 1(2).
59. Order 30, rule 1(1).
60. *Ibid.*, rule 1(2).
61. *Ibid.*, rule 1(3).
62. *Ibid.*, rule 2.
63. *Ibid.*, rule 4.
64. s. 76(6)(ii).
65. s. 76(3).

The court may, at any time after the presentation of a bankruptcy petition, stay any action, execution or legal process against the property or person of the debtor.[66]

The foreign creditor, unless he is a secured creditor, will be affected by the Act and will rank as an unsecured creditor who has to lodge proof of debt along with other unsecured creditors.

Where the foreign creditor has managed to register his judgment, the Act will affect him only in so far as he has not been able to complete execution of the judgment. Under section 105(1) of the Act, where the foreign creditor has issued execution against the grounds or lands of the judgment debtor, or has attached any debt due or property belonging to the debtor, he will not be entitled to retain the benefit of such execution or attachment against the Official Assignee unless he has completed it before the date of receiving order and before notice of the presentation of a bankruptcy petition or of the commission of any available act of bankruptcy by the debtor.

The Act also sets out what is meant by completion as follows[67]:

(1) Execution against grounds or land is completed by seizure and sale, or in the case of an equivalent interest in land, by appointment of a receiver.
(2) Attachment of debt is completed by receipt of debt.
(3) Attachment of property is completed by the sale of such property and satisfaction of the costs of execution out of the proceeds of sale.

Where the foreign creditor has issued execution but has not completed it in accordance with the Act, the proceeds of sale or property as yet unsold will vest in the Official Assignee, subject to a first charge for the costs of execution.[68]

EFFECT OF WINDING-UP OF DEBTOR

Where the judgment debtor is a company being wound-up, whether voluntarily or compulsorily, the Companies Act (Cap. 50) applies.

Winding-up is deemed to commence where:

(1) a provisional liquidator is appointed[69]; or
(2) the resolution for voluntary winding-up is passed[70]; or
(3) the petition for winding-up is presented.[71]

In the case of winding-up by the court, a stay of proceedings pending against the company may be obtained any time after the presentation of the petition and before the winding-up order is made.[72] Once the winding-up order is made, no action or proceeding may be commenced against the company or proceeded with except with the leave of court and on such terms as the court may impose.[73] The same is true of voluntary winding-up.[74]

66. s. 74(1).
67. s. 105(2).
68. s. 106(1) and (2).
69. s. 291(6)(a).
70. s. 255(1).
71. s. 255(2).
72. s. 258.
73. s. 262(3).
74. s. 299(2).

After commencement of winding-up, a judgment creditor may not enforce his judgment against a company that is in liquidation. This applies only to winding-up by the court[75] and to a creditors' voluntary winding-up[76] but apparently not to a members' voluntary winding-up.

If a judgment creditor has initiated but not completed execution or attachment against the company before the commencement of winding-up (whether by the court or voluntarily), he may not retain the benefit of his execution as against the liquidator.[77] "Completion" under the Act is defined in the same way as in the Bankruptcy Act.[78]

In such a case, the bailiff may be ordered to hand over to the liquidator any goods taken in execution that have not been sold, or money seized or received in part satisfaction of the execution.[79] The court may, however, give the creditor the benefit of an uncompleted execution.[80]

If the foreign creditor is unable to register judgment or complete execution of judgment against the debtor company, he has to lodge proof of debt along with other creditors unless he is a secured creditor.

The secured creditor is the first on the list of priority of claims settled out of realised assets of the company, and the other creditors are paid in the following order:

(1) Preferential creditors who have priority over floating chargeholders.
(2) Floating chargeholders or those creditors whose debts are secured on the book debts of the company.
(3) Preferential creditors who do not have priority over floating chargeholders.
(4) Unsecured creditors.
(5) Shareholders.

CONCLUSION

Recognition and enforcement of foreign judgments and application for provisional remedies involve an understanding of another country's laws, confidence that these laws have been given full effect, and an examination of whether these laws are similar, so as to enable judgments entered or pronounced according to them, to be maintained in the country where registration and enforcement are sought.

At present, there are 43 countries in the Commonwealth, and Singapore has reciprocal arrangements with only 10, i.e. 23%.

The difficulty here lies with foreign claimants who obtain judgment in a country with no reciprocal arrangement with Singapore. For such claimants, it is necessary to examine and identify common areas of law, procedure (before and during trial), and execution to ascertain and identify a type of judgment satisfying all requirements.

As can be seen, Singapore subscribes to principles of private international law, most if not all of which are incorporated into its legislation.

SEI BEE TAN

75. s. 260.
76. s. 299(1).
77. s. 334(1).
78. s. 334(2). See also note 67.
79. s. 335(1).
80. s. 334(1)(c) and s. 335(3).

CHAPTER 25

SOUTH AFRICA

INTRODUCTION

Generally, when one considers the judicial attachment of property, South African law draws a sharp distinction between the rights of the creditor who is armed with a judgment granted in his favour against the debtor by a competent South African court and one who simply alleges a claim against a debtor and desires, prior to obtaining a permanent judgment, to enhance his prospects of recovery by attaching assets in South Africa belonging to the debtor. This is a principle which applies with equal force whether the creditor is himself domiciled in South Africa or not. Apart from Exchange Control Regulations, which still exist in South Africa and which could place difficulties in the path of the foreign creditor attempting to remove from South Africa the proceeds of his claim, there is virtually no difference, once a South African court judgment has been obtained, between the execution and attachment rights accruing to a creditor who is an *Incola* of South Africa and a creditor who is a *Peregrinus* or personally resident outside South Africa.

There are, as will be demonstrated later in this chapter, certain common-law and statutory impediments which can make it more difficult for a foreign creditor to obtain in the South African courts a competent judgment against his debtor than it would be for a creditor domiciled in South Africa to obtain the same judgment, but, once that final judgment had been obtained, then the rights of the judgment creditor, in so far as attachment of his debtor's property is concerned, are not in any way dependent upon his being a South African resident.

In considering the rights of the foreign creditor who is not armed with a competent South African court judgment, distinction must be drawn between the creditor who has already had granted in his favour judgment in a foreign court against the debtor, and one who has as yet no judgment at all against the debtor. In the first instance, it must be stressed at the outset that, although at the moment South Africa has no effective statutory procedure for the registration or automatic admission of foreign judgments, there are procedures whereby foreign judgments can be made judgments of a South African court which do not involve a complete rehearing by the South African court of the merits of any dispute between the creditor and debtor which gave rise to the foreign judgment. The common-law principle under which such judgment will in effect be made a judgment of the South African court, certain statutory limitations thereon, and the procedure which must be adopted by the foreign judgment creditor will be examined later in this chapter.

Against that background, this chapter will endeavour to provide an answer—of necessity in very summarised form—to the following questions:

(1) With special reference to foreign claimants, how does a creditor obtain a South African court judgment in his favour against a debtor resident in South Africa?

(2) Assuming the foreign creditor already to have a judgment in his favour granted by a court outside South Africa, what are the special procedures whereby that judgment can in fact be converted into a judgment of the South African courts?

(3) What special remedies are there which can be used by a creditor, with special reference to a foreign creditor, to "attack" or "attach" assets of the debtor which may be in South Africa in order to protect or secure his claim, or to prevent removal of those assets, in circumstances where the creditor has not yet obtained a South African judgment in his favour in respect of the claim?

(4) What are the normal execution and attachment remedies open to a South Arican judgment creditor, i.e., a creditor who has already obtained against his debtor a judgment in the South African courts, in order to recover amounts due to him under that judgment?

OBTAINING A SOUTH AFRICAN COURT JUDGMENT

Structure of South African Civil Courts

The Supreme Court of South Africa, assuming it has jurisdiction in other respects which are dealt with below, has unlimited jurisdiction as to causes of action to determine civil disputes and give enforceable judgments in respect of civil claims, whether of a monetary nature or not. There are four provincial divisions of the Supreme Court, the jurisdiction of which coincides with the territorial limits of the four provinces which came together in 1910 to form the then Union of South Africa—the Cape Provincial Division which sits in Cape Town; the Orange Free State Provincial Division which sits in Bloemfontein; the Transvaal Provincial Division which sits in Pretoria; and the Natal Provincial Division which sits in Pietermaritzburg. In three of the four provinces, there are also local divisions of the Supreme Court, whose area of jurisdiction within a particular province is defined and whose courts have within that area jurisdiction concurrent with that of the provincial division. Of the local divisions, by far the largest is the Witwatersrand Local Division, which covers the whole of the Witwatersrand area and sits in Johannesburg, which is South Africa's largest city and the centre of South Africa's commercial activities. There are more legal practitioners practising in the Witwatersrand area than in any other part of the country and, amongst those who do practise there, there are a number of firms which specialise in international work and in the representation of foreign clients.

With the advent in 1994 of a new government fully representative of all the peoples of South Africa, the divisions of the Supreme Court are now under review, and a new

"Constitutional Court" has been created to protect and uphold the principles of the country's new constitution.

Although, as mentioned above, the Supreme Court has an unlimited jurisdiction, creditors who have claims which amount to less than R100,000 are better advised to bring those claims in the lower civil courts (magistrates' courts) which are scattered throughout South Africa and each of which has an area of jurisdiction corresponding to that of the particular town or district. The legal costs incurred in magistrates' court proceedings are, generally speaking, considerably less than those incurred in the Supreme Court, part of the reason being that South Africa still maintains the English system of having a two-tier legal profession. In the Supreme Court, therefore, it is still usual, although no longer essential, to use the services both of an attorney and of an advocate, just as in the High Court in England the services of both a solicitor and a barrister must be engaged.

The decision in a magistrates' court can be taken on appeal to a provincial, and sometimes to a local, division of the Supreme Court, and there is a further and final appeal to the highest court in the country, the Appellate Division of the Supreme Court, which sits in Bloemfontein. From an initial decision of the Supreme Court, an appeal can be brought either to a full bench of that Division, consisting of three judges, or once again directly to the Appellate Division.

Of course, the court hearing such issues must not only have jurisdiction as regards the cause of action or the remedy claimed but also over the person of the defendant. Generally, a civil court can exercise jurisdiction over any defendant who is physically within the area of its jurisdiction, and it can exercise jurisdiction over any defendant elsewhere in South Africa if it is shown that the cause of action upon which the plaintiff relies arose within its area of jurisdiction. If it has jurisdiction on that ground, then—provided it can be shown that the defendant has assets which are physically attachable and within the court's jurisdiction—even a defendant who is outside South Africa may by means of a process called edictal citation and by attachment found or confirm the jurisdiction issued in the South African court.

The limitations on jurisdiction as summarised above would apply to any case where a foreign creditor wished to obtain judgment against his debtor in a South African court. Either the debtor must be physically within the jurisdiction of the court, or the cause of action must have arisen within the area of jurisdiction of that court and the debtor must be somewhere in South Africa, or, if the debtor is not in South Africa, he must have attachable assets in South Africa which can be used to found or confirm jurisdiction.

Court proceedings

Legal proceedings, either in the Supreme Court or in the magistrates' court, commence by way of issue of what is called a civil summons, which is issued out of the court and served upon the defendant by an official called the Sheriff. That document sets out the cause of action and requires the defendant to indicate whether he intends to defend the proceedings and, if so, to serve and file a plea which sets out the nature of his defence. Failure to give notice of intention to defend will normally entitle the plaintiff in either court to apply for a default judgment, and the court then grants such a judgment. Evidence is not usually required, save to establish the quantum of damages. The obtaining of a judgment in an undefended matter and on a simple claim is therefore a comparatively swift and inexpensive procedure in either court, and provided there are no difficulties as to service and the matter takes its normal course, the judgment may be expected within a month of the issue of summons. A default judgment is a valid and competent judgment of the court upon which attachment and execution proceedings can be founded, but it has not quite the finality of a judgment granted after a defended hearing. There are procedures whereby a default judgment can be set aside at the instance of the debtor by means of an application for rescission of that judgment, for example in circumstances where the defendant alleges that the summons was never really properly served upon him and that he has a good defence to the claim.

Where the defendant, having been served with a summons, gives notice of intention to defend, the matter takes on a completely different aspect and becomes a defended action. Rules of court in both courts set out the subsequent procedure before the matter can be enrolled for trial. Thereafter, it has to be formally enrolled and special rules complied with in connection with discovery of documents, expert witnesses and the like. The matter eventually comes before a trial court, evidence is given on both sides, and the court determines the issue.

It can take up to two years (depending upon the state of the roll and the particular division in which the action is instituted) from the date of service of the summons to the date on which the matter comes before the court for trial in a defended action, and, particularly in the Supreme Court, this will involve the creditor in a substantial outlay of moneys for legal costs, including advocates' and attorneys' fees. It also should be borne in mind that there can be further and lengthy delays occasioned by the use of the appeal procedure which is outlined above.

If, at the end of the defended trial hearing, or of the appeal proceedings, the court has made a determination in favour of the plaintiff, then that is a final judgment of the Supreme Court or magistrates' court, as the case may be, and can be used for the pursuit of the execution remedies, including attachment, which are outlined below.

Civil judgments in the South African court normally carry with them an award as to legal costs, and a creditor who succeeds in his claim can expect an award in his favour for costs. However, it must be borne in mind that these costs, which are based on a tariff applicable to party and party costs (i.e. costs awarded against the other side), are generally taxed and determined at a figure which is substantially lower than the actual costs and expenses that the creditor may have had to incur in pursuing the proceedings in South Africa.

Practical difficulties for the foreign creditor

What has been set out above applies broadly to all creditors, but, where the creditor is a *Peregrinus*, or foreign based, the following should be noted.

Where the defendant is an *Incola* of South Africa, and the plaintiff is a *Peregrinus* and has no assets of substance in South Africa, then in terms of the rules of court the defendant may call upon the plaintiff to give security for the defendant's costs incurred in defending the action. The action may be stayed, or in certain circumstances even dismissed, if such security is not given.

This security can take the form of moneys actually paid into the registrar of the court in question, or of an adequate and recognised banker's guarantee, or of money being paid and held in a trust account pending the outcome of the action.

In the magistrates' court, security can be given by means of a security bond with two satisfactory guarantors, and these would probably have to be South African residents.

The amount of security, if it cannot be agreed between the parties, is determined by the registrar of the Supreme Court or the clerk of the magistrates' court and is usually based upon what the defendant's party and party costs would be up to the end of the first day of trial of the matter. If the trial continued beyond that, then further security would be awarded. It is beyond the scope of this chapter to give detailed, accurate estimates of the actual amount of security that could be asked for and granted in a particular case, but, assuming no particular complications, the average security figure in a Supreme Court action for legal costs incurred up to the end of the first day of trial could be between R20,000 and R30,000. In a case involving complications and senior advocates or expert witnesses, the amount of security ordered could be correspondingly higher.

If the foreign creditor eventually wins his case, then his security is returned to him, but, if he loses it, the amount of the security is devoted towards payment of any legal costs which the court may have awarded in favour of the other side and against the creditor.

PROCEDURES FOR CONVERTING A FOREIGN JUDGMENT

What is the position when someone has obtained a judgment in his favour in a court outside South Africa and wants to have that judgment recognised or enforced in South Africa? The object of such recognition or enforcement will almost inevitably be to assist in obtaining payment from the judgment debtor who may be in South Africa, or in levying execution against his movable or immovable property in South Africa, or both.

There was, in fact, a statute which was passed by the South African Parliament in 1966 under the title of the Reciprocal Enforcement of Civil Judgments Act, and this Act contains provisions whereby under certain circumstances judgments of foreign courts could be registered in South Africa and treated as though they were judgments of the local courts. It has recently been replaced by a similar statute, said to be intended to make enforcement of judgments granted in the "homeland" states easier. There are, unfortunately, two impediments to the use of this statute: the first is that it has never been brought into operation, and the second is that it was intended by regulation to designate certain countries to which its provisions would apply, and no such regulations have been made. With the disappearance of the "homelands" in the new South Africa, this statute now falls away.

Another recent statute, the Protection of Businesses Act of 1978, as amended in 1981, has, however, had a very practical effect on the question of recognition of foreign judgments in that, in terms of section 1(a) of the Act, the recognition or enforcement of certain foreign judgments is made conditional upon the prior approval of the Minister of Economic Affairs.

The wording of the section is as follows:

(1) Notwithstanding anything to the contrary contained in any law or other legal rule, and except with the permission of the Minister of Economic Affairs—

(a) no judgment, order, direction, arbitration award or letters of request delivered, given or issued or emanating from outside the Republic and arising from any act or transaction contemplated in subsection (3), shall be enforced in the Republic; ...

(3) In the application of subsection (1)(a) an act or transaction shall be any act or transaction which took place at any time, whether before or after the commencement of this Act, and is connected with the production, importation, exportation, refinement, possession, use or sale of or ownership to [sic] any matter or material, of whatever nature, whether within, outside, into or from the Republic.

From that wording, it will be readily appreciated that there are few, if any, foreign judgments which would fall outside its scope, and from a practical point of view, therefore, an essential preliminary in South Africa at the moment to the recognition or enforcement of a foreign judgment is the obtaining of the Minister's permission. In practice, the Minister adhered to what he said in Parliament when the proposed Act was under consideration, which was that he did not intend to interfere with the normal rights of creditors and that the legislation was intended to protect South African citizens and companies against the effects of overseas sanctions legislation or judgments having a political aspect. With the disappearance of sanctions, the attitude of the Minister may be based on different consideration in future.

Another section of the same Act puts into statutory form what was probably part of South African common law beforehand. It effectively precludes the court, whether or not the permission of the Minister has been granted, from recognising or enforcing foreign judgments which contain an element of penalty damages or double damages, or any amounts under the head of damages which exceed the actual loss sustained by the judgment creditor in the matter in question.

Apart from the provisions of the Protection of Businesses Act, the whole question of recognition or enforcement of foreign judgments is, therefore, still governed by South African common law.

Under Roman Dutch law and in summary, the judgment of a foreign court will be recognisable and enforceable in South Africa if, and only if:

(1) the foreign court has international competence, i.e., proper jurisdiction, to determine the matter and to give a judgment on it;
(2) the foreign judgment was a final and conclusive one;
(3) the foreign judgment is not against natural law or does not disregard the concept of natural justice, or is not obtained by fraud or based on an unconscionable agreement; and
(4) the foreign judgment is not in respect of a fiscal matter, such as a tax or a penalty imposed by a foreign state, or one which gives assistance in enforcing foreign exchange control regulations.
(5) the defendant was afforded proper notice of the foreign proceedings, and given an opportunity to defend them.

Jurisdiction

The question as to whether the foreign court had effective jurisdiction is judged, not by its own concepts of jurisdiction, but by South African concepts. In other words, the mere fact that, according to its own rules, the foreign court had jurisdiction would not suffice to satisfy the rule as to international competence. The South African court will hold that the foreign court had jurisdiction only if such jurisdiction would have been enjoyed by the foreign court under South African rules. United States "long arm" statutes will, therefore, not suffice to create jurisdiction from a South African point of view, nor will South African courts be prepared to uphold judgments which were obtained, for example, in the absence of the defendant where no notice of the proceedings was afforded to him, or where he was neither physically present nor resident nor domiciled within the foreign country at the time when the foreign proceedings against him were commenced.

It is possible, of course, under South African law, for a person to consent to the jurisdiction of a particular court, even though it would not otherwise have had jurisdiction. If it can be shown that the defendant did in fact consent to the jurisdiction of the foreign court, then the South African courts will uphold that jurisdiction.

What amounts to such a consent to jurisdiction can sometimes be a difficult legal matter, since consent may be by conduct as well as by words or in writing. It has been held, for example, that if the defendant in foreign proceedings attempts to defend the proceedings on the merits instead of challenging the jurisdiction of the court, then this would amount to a consent to that court's jurisdiction. For this reason, a South African defendant who is served with the process of a foreign court often must consider very carefully whether he should ignore that process or attempt to defend the matter in the foreign court: if he does the latter, he may in fact give it a jurisdiction which it did not previously enjoy and so enable the plaintiff, if successful in the foreign court, to have the foreign court's judgment recognised in South Africa.

Finality

The finality of the foreign judgment is a question of fact, and a South African court will not enforce a provisional judgment which has not yet become final. The mere facts that the foreign judgment was subject to an appeal and that no appeal had actually been noted against it have been held not to affect the finality of the foreign judgment.

Natural justice

The broad concept of natural justice covers a fairly wide variety of matters.

Just as a South African court will not recognise a foreign judgment where there has been no proper service of the proceedings upon the proposed defendant, so it will refuse to recognise it if the defendant did not get a fair hearing in the foreign court, if the cause of action was not a recognised one, if the action was based on an unconscionable agreement, or if the enforcement of the judgment would be *contra bonos mores*, i.e., against public policy. Under these heads also fall the concepts of penalty damages and double damages dealt with in the Protection of Businesses Act mentioned earlier. Actions based on fraud or deceit would also fall under these heads.

No retrial on the merits

What is clear, however, is that, provided that the foreign judgment falls within the rules summarised above, the South African court will not reopen the dispute which the foreign court, in fact, decided. In other words, if the foreign court had jurisdiction, if the judgment was final, and if it cannot be attacked on the grounds of natural justice or associated grounds, then the South African courts will recognise and enforce it even if, under South African law, a South African court would not have come to the same conclusion on the merits of the case.

Procedure

The usual method by which it will be sought to recognise or enforce a foreign judgment will be by means of a summons issued out of one of the divisions of the Supreme Court of South Africa asking the court to recognise and enforce the foreign judgment.

Frequently, a provisional sentence summons (a procedure dealt with below) is followed in this type of case because a foreign judgment is a liquid document in terms of the rules of court and a provisional sentence matter usually comes before the court more quickly than proceedings instituted by an ordinary summons, particularly if the proceedings are defended.

The plaintiff's case will have to be supported by a properly authenticated copy of the judgment which it is sought to recognise, and the plaintiff will have to show that the other requisites are present and, where the Act applies, that the permission of the Minister as required by the Protection of Businesses Act has been obtained.

In most cases the plaintiff will be a *Peregrinus* or a person resident or domiciled outside South Africa, and this will enable the defendant to call upon the plaintiff, in terms of the rules of the Supreme Court, to furnish security for the defendant's costs in opposing the action (see above).

If the South African court does recognise the foreign judgment, then that judgment is treated exactly as if it were a judgment of a South African court, and all the remedies normally open to a successful litigant by way of execution and attachment become available to the foreign judgment creditor.

REMEDIES AVAILABLE TO FOREIGN CREDITORS

As a general rule, a creditor, including a foreign creditor, can under South African law attach his debtor's assets in South Africa only once he is armed with a judgment and has become a judgment creditor. However, there are a number of exceptional circumstances in which to a greater or lesser extent a creditor can achieve attachment of the debtor's assets or can prevent the debtor from disposing of those assets before that creditor has, in fact, obtained a final judgment in South Africa against the debtor. Some cases where this is possible are summarised in the following paragraphs. The list is not put forward as being comprehensive but gives examples of various remedies which may be available and various circumstances which may render attachment or protection possible.

Security

The first set of circumstances is where the creditor's claim is such that, under South African law, the debt actually enjoys some form of security which affects the property of the debtor in South Africa which the creditor wishes to "attack", or "attach" or preserve for his benefit.

A creditor, including a foreign creditor, who is the holder of a mortgage bond over immovable property belonging to the debtor in South Africa, or to whom movable property has been properly pledged or to whom incorporeal rights have been properly ceded already enjoys security over those assets. This will normally operate to prevent disposal by the debtor, and will also often provide quicker avenues for obtaining a judgment in a South African court of law against the debtor combined with an order that the hypothecated property be attached to satisfy the creditor's claim.

Contract

Again, certain contractual relationships between creditor and debtor can bring about a situation in South African law where the creditor who is actually in possession of an asset of the debtor has a lien or right of retention over that asset until the debtor has discharged his liability.

Examples of this sort of situation are contracts of letting and hiring of immovable property, where goods belonging to the tenant on the leased property form some sort of security for outstanding rental; creditor and debtor lien, where the creditor who has worked on a particular property of the debtor in terms of a contract and has that property still in his possession may retain it pending payment of what is due to him; salvage and improvement lien, which affords a creditor who has incurred expense in preserving or improving the debtor's property the right under certain circumstances to hold the property as against payment of what is due to the creditor; storage lien, and construction lien, where a construction contractor may enjoy a lien over a contract works.

Provided the correct legal relationship exists, giving rise to these liens or rights of retention, it makes no difference to the efficacy of such lien that the lien holder happens to be a foreigner.

Maritime statutes

Attention must also be drawn to maritime law.

South Africa has maritime statutes similar to those in other countries, providing for special remedies and the immediate attachment of a ship and actions *in rem* against a ship where it is alleged the owners of the ship are, in fact, liable to a creditor, which would include a foreign creditor. To go into details of these rights would involve a dissertation on South African maritime law, which is beyond the scope of this chapter, but where the claim has a maritime element to it, the preliminary attachment of the debtor's ship in South African waters pending maritime proceedings is a very common feature.

Claim linked to particular assets

Another case where preliminary attachment is possible before a judgment is where the claim of the creditor is intimately bound up with the very assets which the creditor is seeking to attack or attach. A creditor claiming to be entitled to the delivery of specific goods belonging to the debtor could, in circumstances where it could be shown that the debtor is threatening to dispose of the goods, claim an interdict preventing the disposal and possibly the interim attachment of the goods.

A creditor claiming that his debtor is in unlawful possession of assets in South Africa which are, in fact, alleged to be the property of the creditor, could in similar circumstances obtain an order from the court attaching the property, or an order preventing disposal of the property pending the outcome of the claim. Here it should be added, of course, that, where the creditor is a foreign creditor, this means the institution of preliminary legal proceedings, which in turn give the debtor the right to demand security for the cost of his opposition to those proceedings on the basis already discussed above.

Provisional sentence

The nature of the creditor's claim may be such that, if the claim falls within the jurisdiction of the Supreme Court, he can adopt a remedy called provisional sentence, which gives him a provisional judgment under which he can proceed to attachment of the debtor's assets. Provisional sentence proceedings can be taken in South Africa on a "liquid document", and a liquid document generally includes any document which on the face of it demonstrates the debtor's liability and bears the defendant's signature or that of his duly authorised agent. Claims founded upon negotiable instruments, written acknowledgements of debt, mortgage bonds, notarial bonds, architect's or engineer's certificates in construction contracts and, as indicated above, on foreign judgments duly certified all fall within this category.

By a special form of summons in the Supreme Court recently extended to operate also in Magistrate Courts, the debtor is called upon to admit or deny his liability and to acknowledge his signature on the document in question where applicable, and to appear in court on a particular day in order to have the matter provisionally determined. The procedure is much quicker than the general procedure for determination of actions which has been outlined above, and if the plaintiff, including a foreign plaintiff, is successful he will get a provisional judgment from the court upon which he can execute against assets of the defendant immediately and which in the absence of final opposition can become a final judgment. The procedure is somewhat technical and the summons has to be carefully drawn and prepared so as to comply with the rules of court, but it nevertheless constitutes an avenue open to the foreign creditor who enjoys the right type of claim.

Absence from jurisdiction

There are circumstances where the debtor is not himself in South Africa which could justify the creditor (including a foreign creditor) obtaining, in order to institute proceedings against the debtor, an attachment of the debtor's property in South Africa either to found or to confirm jurisdiction. In order to achieve this, it might be necessary to show that the cause of action arose in South Africa and/or that South African law applied, because the South African courts would be chary of allowing an action between two foreigners, neither of whom was domiciled in South Africa, in regard to a cause of action which did not arise in South Africa and has nothing to do with South

Africa, and which is possibly governed by a legal system other than the South African legal system, simply because one of the parties has assets in South Africa.

Attachment by court

There is a procedure open to a creditor under South African law, and this will include a foreign creditor, whereby a debtor himself or his movable property may be made subject to a formal attachment by the court *tamquam suspectus de fuga*. In order to obtain this sort of an order and the attachment of the debtor's person or property, it is essential that the creditor is able to show the debtor is about to flee the country and in appropriate cases to remove his property, for the purpose of defeating the claims of his creditors generally or of that particular creditor.

The court will not lightly grant such an order, and a creditor could attract severe damages to himself if the facility is abused. Given the right circumstances, however, this remedy could be open to the foreign creditor.

Non-disputed debt

Where the debt which is owing to the creditor is more than R400 and where there is no reason to suppose it will be disputed by the debtor, one last method of achieving an earlier attack upon or attachment of the debtor's property is to consider the possibility of insolvency proceedings against the debtor if the debtor is a natural person, or liquidation proceedings if the debtor is an artificial person such as a limited liability company.

The creditor bringing such an application to the Supreme Court must show that he has an undisputed claim for R400 or more, and also on the balance of probabilities that the debtor either has committed one of a number of "acts of insolvency" provided for in the Insolvency Act or is in fact insolvent in that, fairly valued, his liabilities exceed his assets.

An application for the compulsory sequestration of the debtor's estate or the placing of an artificial person into liquidation is a fairly complicated legal exercise and, of course, has the disadvantage that, even if successful, although it will result in the placing of the debtor's assets in South Africa into the hands of a liquidator or trustee, it will be for the benefit not simply of the applicant creditor who has brought about the insolvency but of all other creditors of the debtor. Unless, therefore, the particular foreign creditor enjoys particular security or preference, he will find himself in a queue of concurrent creditors lining up for a dividend which will simply represent his alloquot share of the debtor's assets, or such of them as are not secured or possibly reserved to preferent creditors who, as a matter of interest, include the Receiver of Revenue of South Africa.

While the possible insolvency of the debtor is under discussion, it should be noted that if the foreign creditor seeks a South African judgment or to convert a foreign judgment and there is an intervening application for insolvency, either by the debtor himself (who can make himself insolvent by a procedure called voluntary surrender) or by any of his other creditors, to place the debtor into insolvency as above, the result is the same. The insolvency will divest the debtor of all his assets, will put the foreign creditor who has patiently been trying to establish his claim in a position where he no longer has or can possibly be expected to enjoy any rights over any particular assets of the debtor unless he had those rights by virtue of security or lien or one of the other circumstances mentioned earlier in this section, and where he simply stands in the queue of creditors.

EXECUTION AND ATTACHMENT REMEDIES

South African law permits several methods whereby a judgment creditor may attempt to enforce the judgment which the court has granted in his favour against the debtor and thereby achieve payment of what is owed to him in terms of that judgment. The remedies include garnishee proceedings, under which income or other moneys accruing to the debtor may be attached in the hands of an employer or a person who owes the debtor money and be in fact paid over to the creditor; and financial inquiry, by virtue of which the debtor may be compelled to attend court and provide a full statement of his income and expenditure and financial affairs, and be ordered to pay the creditor a monthly sum. The most usual remedy, and the only one which directly affects property or assets of the debtor, and therefore falls within the scope of this chapter, is the issue as a result of a judgment of a process which is called a writ of execution.

A writ of execution is a formal document issued by the registrar of the court which granted the judgment at the instance of the judgment creditor, and is addressed to an official called the Sheriff. It requires and authorises the Sheriff to seek out the judgment debtor to demand payment of what is owing under the judgment. If he does not receive payment, he will place under attachment, and thereafter, if necessary, proceed to a sale of, sufficient of the debtor's assets to satisfy the judgment debt.

The method of execution requires the Sheriff first to attempt to make an attachment of movable property belonging to the debtor. Only if insufficient movable property is available to satisfy the full amount of the writ may the Sheriff proceed to the attachment of immovable property.

Generally, all classes of movable property, whether corporeal or incorporeal, are subject to attachment by the Sheriff in terms of a properly issued writ, save that protection is given to the judgment debtor in respect of ordinary household goods, clothes and, in certain circumstances, jewels. The debtor must be left with sufficient assets to enable him, if not to live comfortably, at least to have the basic minimum. Television sets, video machines, "luxury" furniture, artistic works, jewellery, and the like are subject to attachment.

The right to attach is, of course, limited to property which is owned by the judgment debtor, or in which he has some sort of interest which may be less than ownership. Goods such as motor vehicles and furniture are frequently sold on the basis that credit is given but the seller retains ownership until the item is paid for in full, and under those circumstances it is only the debtor's interest in such goods which can be attached, if it is worth attaching. Goods and assets which are the property of another member of the defendant's household are not normally subject to attachment for judgment debts owing by the debtor himself.

If the judgment creditor so requires, the Sheriff will, against the provision of security by the judgment creditor, remove the goods attached and keep them in storage pending the formal sale in execution. This sale must be properly advertised in terms of the provisions of the relevant statute and is an auction in which the goods are knocked down to the highest bidder, the sale being conducted by the Sheriff or his authorised representative.

The proceeds of the sale, after deduction of all costs and expenses, are then paid over to the judgment creditor, or to as many judgment creditors as have writs which are participating against the debtor. There is nothing to prevent another creditor with a judgment, once he sees that there is an attachment and sale in execution pending, lodging his writ and thereby also participating *pro rata* in the proceeds of the sale of the goods attached.

Where immovable property is attached under a writ of execution, the steps taken by the Sheriff are similar to those set out above, but notice also must be given to the Registrar of Deeds and to bondholders. Since most immovable properties are subject to mortgage bonds, the judgment creditor arranging a sale of such property in execution of a writ runs the risk that he may not, in fact, get any return out of the sale if not enough is achieved to pay outstanding mortgages, rates or other preferent claims.

Until recently, a judgment debtor ordered to pay his debt in instalments and failing to comply with the order, could be sentenced to undergo civil imprisonment. This remedy has been successfully challenged in the Constitutional Court.

CASES AND AUTHORITIES

This chapter of necessity covers a wide field of law and procedure, rendering it almost impossible and, at any rate, impracticable to quote hundreds of case authorities and the details of many statutes. However, following are Schedules A and B, which list, respectively, some of the statutes referred to in this text and some commentaries on particular topics.

M. J. M. BENNETT

CHAPTER 26

SPAIN

AVAILABILITY OF SPANISH COURTS TO FOREIGN CREDITORS AND LITIGANTS

Under Spanish law, all persons are explicitly granted the right to effective jurisdictional protection of their legitimate rights and interests.[1] From a subjective viewpoint, this right applies to all types of persons, whether public- or private-law, Spanish or foreign, individuals or juristic persons.[2] From an objective viewpoint, the right is protected by the courts, before whom such persons may appear, i.e., they are entitled to be parties to proceedings and to judgments in law.[3]

In certain circumstances the right of foreign persons to be parties to legal proceedings, which has thus been recognised, is subject to the requirement of posting a bond.[4] The required bond, called bond for court costs or *cautio judicatum solvi*, has often been criticised by many authors as a "truly outdated" procedural institution[5] or even an "untenable punishment to foreign plaintiffs",[6] on the ground that it is clearly an exception to the rule of equality among Spanish and foreign citizens under Spanish law.[7]

Therefore, under the provisions of section 534 of the Code of Civil Procedure (CCP), foreign plaintiffs may be required to post such bond if a similar requirement applies to Spanish citizens under the procedural laws of the plaintiff's country.[8] The burden of proving that Spanish citizens are granted reciprocal treatment in the plaintiff's country is up to the defendant, according to an old Supreme Court decision

1. In the Spanish Constitution (s. 24.1); in Basic Act No. 6/1985, of 1 July 1985 on the Judiciary (ss. 7 and 21.1); in Basic Act No. 7/1985 of 1 July 1985 on the Rights and Freedoms of Foreign Citizens in Spain (s. 29.1). Also, in Article 6 of the European Treaty for Protecting Human Rights and Basic Freedoms (Rome, 4 November 1950), which was ratified through the Instrument of 26 September 1979; in Article 14 of the International Treaty of Civil and Political Rights of 19 December 1966, which was ratified through the Instrument of 13 April 1977. And in s. 27 of the Civil Code.

2. Constitutional Court Decision (CCD) No. 64/1988 of 12 April 1988.

3. CCD No. 115/1984 of 3 December 1984; CCD No. 164/1984 of 17 December 1984; CCD No. 9/1981 of 31 March 1981, CCD No. 60/1982 of 11 October 1982.

4. Code of Civil Procedure (CCP) (s. 534); and Code of Criminal Procedure (CCrP) (s. 281).

5. *Inter alia*, Ferri Lopez-Bonilla, Ana, "La condición procesal de extranjero y la excepción de arraigo en juicio" (a propósito de la AT Madrid S. 11 November 1981), *La Ley*, 1984, 1, p. 1,070.

6. Cortes Dominguez, V., *Derecho Procesal Civil Internacional* (*Ordenamiento Español*) (1981: Madrid) p. 48.

7. Decision of the Territorial Court of Justice of Burgos of 15 February 1983.

8. Puente Egido, J., *Derecho Internacional Privado Español: Doctrina Legal del Tribunal Supremo* (Barcelona 1981), p. 949.

of 30 June 1887, which raises the difficult problem of specifying the terms for applying it.[9]

In the last analysis, different kinds of political and legal criteria are used by the courts and authors, with varying degrees of success, in connection with that requirement, in order to justify the institution.[10] Among the political criteria, we should mention that of nationality, in which case the requirement is used as a clearly precautionary measure, to protect the Spanish party against the foreign party; and reciprocity, as foreseen in section 534 of the CCP mentioned above.[11] Among the legal criteria, we should mention that of domicile which, as in the case of nationality, discriminates against foreign parties, or against Spanish parties having their domicile in another country, in favour of those whose country of domicile is Spain; and the property or real estate which exempt a foreign party from posting the bond where such property and real estate are deemed to suffice by the judge or court that has to decide on the matter.[12]

The foregoing notwithstanding, the courts and authors, being aware of the wrong involved by the bond for court costs, have tended to construe the relevant provisions in a restrictive way,[13] in order to reduce their negative impact on foreign parties to legal proceedings. They have done so partly because of the fact that the requirement of posting such bond is being dropped by way of the growing number of bilateral and multilateral treaties to which Spain has become a party in recent years.[14]

9. Gonzalez Campos, Julio, "Régimen del proceso. Las partes: caución de arraigo en juicio", *Revista Española de Derecho Internacional* (REDI), Vol. XXXIII, No. 2, 1981, p. 657.

10. See, Espinar de Vicente, José María, *Derecho Procesal Civil Internacional* (Madrid 1988), p. 9. Also, the Supreme Court Decision of 20 June 1959 and the Decision of the Territorial Court of Burgos of 15 February 1983, among many others.

11. See note 4 *supra*. The grounds of reciprocity have been mentioned in, among other decisions, those of the Territorial Court of Santa Cruz de Tenerife of 21 September 1962 and of the Territorial Court of Burgos of 15 February 1983, and have been criticised by some authors such as Mariano Aguilar Benitez de Lugo who believe that such view "clashes with the attempt to provide rational grounds for the institution": see Aguilar Benitez de Lugo, Mariano, "Actualidad de la caución de arraigo en juicio", *La Ley*, 1990, 2, p. 1104.

12. However, sometimes that is not enough according to some Decisions, such as that handed down by the Territorial Court of Burgos of 15 February 1983, which in addition requires reciprocal treatment of Spanish citizens under the laws of the foreign country in question.

13. Aguilar Benitez de Lugo, note 11, *supra*, p. 1103. Also, a Decision of the Territorial Court of Madrid of 11 November 1981.

14. The *bilateral treaties* include those with *Switzerland* (19 November 1896) on enforcing state court decisions or arbitration awards, on civil and commercial matters, and on acts of communication; with *Colombia* (30 May 1908) on enforcing civil decisions; with *France* (28 May 1969) on recognising and enforcing court decisions, arbitration awards and plaintiffs' right of execution; with *Italy* (22 May 1973) on judicial assistance and recognising as well as executing decisions on civil and commercial matters; with *Germany* (14 October 1983); with *Austria* (8 February 1984) on recognising and enforcing foreign decisions; with *Mexico* (6 February 1987) on recognising and enforcing court decisions and arbitration awards on civil and commercial matters; with *Czechoslovakia* (4 May 1987) on legal advice as well as on recognising and enforcing decisions on civil matters; with *Uruguay* (4 November 1987) on legal co-operation (not yet in force); with *Brazil* (13 April 1989) on legal co-operation on civil matters; as well as with *Israel* (30 May 1989) on common recognising and enforcing decisions on civil and commercial matters. The *multilateral treaties* include that of *The Hague* on civil procedure of 14 October 1896, 17 July 1905 and 1 March 1954; that of *Brussels* on judicial competence and enforcing decisions on civil and commercial matters of 27 September 1968; that of *Luxembourg* on interpretation by the Court of Justice of the Treaty of 27 September 1968, already mentioned; as well as that of *The Hague* on facilitating international access to justice of 25 October 1980.

GRANTING OF PROVISIONAL OR INTERIM REMEDIES

In Spanish law, there is a precautionary, provisional justice, which includes measures similarly called precautionary, provisional measures. As one author correctly points out, that does not mean to say there is a specific concept of precautionary, provisional measures as such. Rather, the concept is developed in a scattered way through different laws such as the CCP, the Real Estate Mortgage Act (REMA), the Commercial Code (CommC), and the Civil Code (CivC).[15]

According to the same author, these may be defined as measures that are approved in a process already under way or which is about to begin within the statutory term for doing so, for the purpose of securing the effectiveness of pending or future judgments which may have a financial content or may call for a party to do or refrain from doing something, or of providing or preserving a necessary or legally appropriate position in the relevant proceedings.[16]

The basic reason for these measures is to prevent a debtor who is acting in bad faith to escape performing a liability, becoming insolvent or hiding away the things to which the process refers, squandering his wealth or even disappearing. Therefore, these measures are aimed at protecting the creditor's rights and, at the same time, preventing the debtor from doing anything that might hamper execution of the relevant judgment.[17]

The precautionary measures mentioned above are mainly provisional measures, as they last only as long as the main process which is under way or is to be held. As such, these measures anticipate the final result of the main process, making timeliness prevail over security considerations, on the grounds that a belated judgment may in many cases involve a denial of justice.[18]

The foregoing notwithstanding, these measures are normally conditional on the party that requests them providing security in the form of a bond, to answer eventually for any damages that may be caused thereby to the other party, particularly where the party who requested the measures loses the main suit. Sometimes, the requirement of posting a bond is so radical, as in the case of provisionally executing a judgment which is pending appeal for dismissal or reversal (section 1722, CCP), that it may prevent the precautionary measure from being ordered.[19]

The actual type of precautionary measure is normally chosen according to the purpose it is intended to serve, which, as we have seen, is to guarantee the effectiveness of judgments having a financial content or which call for doing or not doing something, to be handed down in pending or future processes, or else to provide or preserve a necessary or legally appropriate position in such proceedings.

Apart from the breakdown of precautionary measures given above, which is certainly one of the most typical, there are others in which the measure known as precautionary embargo is set apart, in a category of its own, with the rest falling under

15. Prieto-Castro, L, *Tratado de Derecho Procesal Civil* (2nd ed.), Vol. II (Pamplona 1985), pp. 848–849.

16. *Ibid.*, pp. 850, 852.

17. Kisch, W., *Elementos de Derecho Procesal Civil* (Madrid 1940, 2nd ed.), p. 375.

18. Ramos Mendez, Francisco, *Derecho Procesal Civil* (Barcelona 1980), pp. 899 et seq. Also, Ramos, Mendez, Francisco, *Arbitraje Internacional y Medidas Cautelares* (Barcelona 1987), p. 186.

19. Prieto-Castro, note 15 *supra*, p. 854.

the general description of provisional security measures[20] without any further methodological distinctions.

Types of precautionary measures

Among the precautionary measures which guarantee the effectiveness of judgments, the main ones are preventive embargo (sections 1397 *et seq.*, CCP),[21] provisional annotation of a complaint at the Real Estate Registry (section 42.1, REMA) and seizure (section 499, CCP, and section 1785, CivC). Among those which provide or preserve a given position in the proceedings, there is the appellant's bond for securing leave of appeal to both effects where permission to appeal has been granted to a single effect (section 1476, CCP), provisional execution of judgment (section 1722, CCP) and stay of execution of a judgment pending review (section 1803, CCP).

The provisions governing preventive embargoes, which should briefly be mentioned on account of the significance of this specific measure, are found in sections 1397 *et seq.*, CCP. These require that a document providing that the debt exists be submitted on requesting a preventive embargo (section 1400.1, CCP; Decision of the Territorial Court of Barcelona of 30 September 1985), and that the debtor is a foreign person who has not acquired Spanish citizenship by naturalisation, or that the place of domicile of the foreign non-naturalised person is unknown, or that such person does not own any real estate, or a farming, manufacturing or commercial enterprise at the place where payment of the debt may be claimed (section 1400.2, CCP; Decision of the Territorial Court of Caceres of 2 March 1975).

Even given these circumstances, a precautionary embargo may be ordered where the debtor has disappeared from his place of residence or of business without leaving anyone in charge or where, having left someone in charge, such person is not aware of the debtor's whereabouts. Also, where the debtor hides away, or there are reasons to believe that he will hide away or squander his assets in prejudice of his creditors (section 1400.2, CCP).[22]

Thus, the fear of a person escaping or the fact that the person is foreign are two important considerations when it comes to interpreting the above-mentioned subjective requirements and ordering a preventive embargo, as the case may be. Where a creditor's request for an embargo is based on prima facie evidence of his claim, such as a public document, a bill of exchange, a promissory note or a cheque, or any lawful bearer or registered securities or written commercial contracts, such subjective requirements are not necessary pursuant to the provisions of section 1401 of the CCP, read together with the provisions of Act No. 96/1966 of 23 July 1966, on the competence of municipal or local judges.[23]

20. Kisch, note 17 *supra*, p. 380.

21. The wording of section 1397 was modified through Act No. 10/1992 of 30 April 1992 on Urgent Measures of Procedural Reform.

22. See Cordon Moreno, Faustino, "Breve examen jurisprudencial del embargo preventivo", *Revista General de Legislación y Jurisprudencia*, 1983, No. 5, pp. 497–510. Decisions of the Territorial Courts of Seville of 9 December 1960, Oviedo of 8 May 1962, Madrid of 28 September 1966, Majorca of 7 May 1968, and Madrid of 5 May 1977.

23. The wording of s. 1428 of the 1966 Act was altered later on through Act No. 34/1984 of 6 August 1984, under which the need to meet one of the requirements mentioned in the first three paragraphs of s. 1429 has been replaced by "partial proof in writing clearly reflecting the transaction", as mentioned in the Decision of the Territorial Court of Barcelona of 30 September 1985.

Where the above requirements are met and the preventive embargo is granted, this is not put into effect if, at the time of doing so, the party against whom the embargo has been ordered pays, deposits the sum owing or posts a bond covering the sum being claimed (section 1405, CCP). Otherwise, the embargo is put into effect and then the main process is undertaken, at which time the creditor shall request that the embargo be confirmed (section 1411, CCP) by filing the relevant demand within a term of 20 days after the embargo becomes effective, and the debtor may oppose it on the grounds that it is contrary to law and not admissible (section 1416, CCP).

Status of foreign parties

The plaintiff or the defendant can be foreign. In either case, they may appear before ordinary Spanish courts, which are the only competent ones for hearing civil cases arising in Spanish territory among Spanish persons or among foreign and Spanish persons (sections 51 and 71, CCP). Spanish procedural laws are the only ones which apply in cases tried in Spanish territory, without prejudice to the court eventually referring to foreign laws in respect of procedural acts taking place outside of Spain (sections 8.2 and 27, CivC).

In that connection, for foreign documents to carry the same weight in Spanish courts as those executed in Spain, they must meet the following requirements: the subject matter of the act or contract must be lawful and permitted under Spanish laws; the parties who have executed the instruments must be legally competent and have the necessary legal capacity for entering into commitments according to the domestic laws of their respective countries; the document must have been executed according to the formalities and solemnities required in the country of origin; and, finally, the document must contain the required elements for being valid in Spain (section 600, CCP).

RECOGNITION AND EXECUTION OF FOREIGN JUDGMENTS

Spanish provisions on recognising and executing foreign judgments have been strongly criticised by some authors, who consider them not only insufficient, incomplete, and hollow[24] but also unsystematic, because the rules on recognising and executing such judgments are not grouped together in a single code of law.[25]

Besides, the lack of clear rules leads these authors to consider that the term "judgments" used in the applicable Spanish laws has to be construed broadly, as meaning not only "judgments" as such but also "writs of execution", "decisions" and "decrees", as well as those delivered by jurisdictional courts and courts of arbitration.

In the same sense, these authors take the view that any other similar foreign instruments proving a right of execution should carry similar weight in Spain, provided only that they carry the relevant "executive clause".[26] Then, taking into

24. Prieto-Castro, note 15 *supra*, p. 924.
25. *Ibid.*, p. 924.
26. *Ibid.*, p. 925.

account both Spanish legislation and the international treaties which are effective in Spain, the authors give the following list of judgments, writs of execution, decisions and decrees which may be recognised in Spain:

(1) Final, non-appealable judgments handed down by foreign courts or in foreign countries.[27]

(2) Decisions on court costs.[28]

(3) Arbitration decisions.[29]

(4) Decisions handed down by jurisdictional courts or courts of arbitration, emergency or precautionary measures and documents which provide prima facie evidence of a claim.[30]

(5) Final, non-appealable decisions.[31]

In order for such foreign judgments, decisions, and decrees to be fully effective for procedural purposes in Spain, i.e., in order to be recognised and executed, Spanish laws call for them to meet the requirements foreseen in any of the *exequatur* systems in force: the conventional system (section 951, CCP), the reciprocity system (sections 952 and 953, CCP) and the conditions system (section 954, CCP).[32]

These three systems are ranked, with the conventional system prevailing over the other two, and the reciprocity system prevailing over the conditions system. Despite being the lowest-ranking and of a supplementary nature, the conditions system is generally considered the most practical of the three.[33] It dates back to 1881, but has hardly changed over time, save for the amendments introduced by way of conventions.[34]

27. s. 951, CCP.

28. Convention of The Hague on Civil Procedure of 1 March 1954.

29. Geneva Convention on International Transport Carriage of Goods by Road (CMR) of 19 May 1956; New York Convention on Recognising and Executing Foreign Arbitration Awards of 10 June 1958; Geneva Convention on International Commercial Arbitration of 21 April 1961; Berne Convention on Transport of Passengers and Baggage by Railway (CIV) of 7 February 1970; Berne Convention on International Transport of Goods by Railway (CIM) of 7 February 1970.

30. Treaty between Switzerland and Spain on executing judgments of state courts or arbitration awards in civil or commercial matters and on acts of communication of 19 November 1896; Treaty between Colombia and Spain on executing civil judgments of 30 May 1908; Treaty between France and Spain on recognising and executing judicial and arbitrators' decisions as well as executive titles of 28 May 1969; Treaty between Italy and Spain on judicial assistance and on recognising as well as executing decisions on civil or commercial matters of 22 May 1973; Treaty between Germany and Spain on recognising and executing foreign judgments of 14 October 1983; Treaty between Austria and Spain on recognising and executing foreign judgments of 8 February 1984; Treaty between Mexico and Spain on recognising and enforcing court decisions and arbitration awards on civil and commercial matters of 6 February 1987; Treaty between Czechoslovakia and Spain on legal advice and on recognising as well as executing judgments on civil matters of 5 May 1987; Treaty between Uruguay and Spain on legal co-operation (not yet in force) of 4 November 1987; Treaty between Brazil and Spain on legal co-operation on civil matters of 13 April 1989; and Treaty between Israel and Spain on common recognising and enforcing decisions on civil and commercial matters of 30 May 1989. Also, the Brussels Convention on judicial competence and enforcing decisions on civil and commercial matters of 27 September 1968; that of Luxembourg on interpretation by the Court of Justice of the Treaty of 27 September 1968, already mentioned, as well as that of The Hague on facilitating international access to justice of 25 October 1980.

31. ss. 369 and 374, CCP.

32. Supreme Court Decision of 25 February 1985.

33. See Calvo Caravaca, A.L., *La Sentencia Extranjera en España y la Competencia del Juez de Origen* (Madrid 1986), p. 101. Also Gonzalez Campos, J.D., et al., *Derecho Internacional Privado, Parte Especial*, Vol. I (Oviedo 1984), p. 392. Remiro Brotons, A., *Ejecución de Sentencias Extranjeras en España* (Madrid 1974), pp. 81 and 114. Against, Espinar Vicente, José M., note 10, *supra*, pp. 163 and 164.

34. Espinar Vicente, note 10, *supra*, p. 162.

Conventional system

In the first place, we shall discuss the conventional system, which applies under section 951 of the CCP. Under the provisions of section 951, final, non-appealable judgments handed down in foreign countries shall have such force in Spain as is foreseen in the respective treaties. Thus, the duty of the judge or court that has to decide on the matter[35] is to examine the requirements foreseen in the convention on which the petition for recognising and executing the foreign judgment is based, and then decide whether or not the petition, or more specifically the decision which according to the petition should be recognised and executed, meets such requirements.

Having already mentioned those conventions,[36] we shall not repeat them here, or go into complex doctrinal considerations of their nature, which may be simple or imperfect, or double or perfect. Rather, we shall merely point out that there are very few such conventions, and their number has grown modestly since 1945 as a result of the growing cross-border flows of persons and property and the underlying need to regulate these flows, and shall stress the fact that under virtually all of the conventions recognition of the foreign decision is conditional on the court in which the decision originated having the necessary competence.[37]

In any case, it is advisable to clarify the meaning of three key terms mentioned in section 951 of the CCP, by reference to section 369 thereof. The three terms are: "judgment" (*sentencia*), "final, non-appealable judgment" (*sentencia firme*), and "writ of execution" (*ejecutoria*). In that sense, a "judgment" is a court decision that finally decides the questions raised in a suit; a "final, non-appealable judgment" is one that is not or may not be appealed, and a "writ of execution" is a public and solemn document in which the final, non-appealable judgment is set forth.

Thus, in the face of a foreign final, non-appealable judgment and of a petition that the judgment be recognised and executed in Spain, the judge or court which has to decide on the matter reviews the document carrying the judgment to determine if it meets the requirements foreseen in section 600 of the CCP, and particularly the most problematic of all, that of legislation. Since The Hague Convention of 5 October 1961 was ratified, thus eliminating the requirement that foreign documents be legalised, however, the question is much simpler: all that is required is an apostil by the relevant authority of the country of origin.

Reciprocity system

Apart from the conventional system there is the reciprocity system, governed by the provisions of section 952 of the CCP, according to which, where there is no special treaty with the country in which the judgment in question has been handed down, this judgment shall have similar force in Spain to that which a writ of execution issued in Spain has in the other country.

Apart from that positive reciprocity there is a negative reciprocity, provided for in

35. Normally, Section One of the Supreme Court: s. 56 of the Basic Act on the Judiciary (BAJ) and s. 955 of the CCP.

36. s. 951, CCP.

37. Calvo Caravaca, note 32 *supra*, pp. 104, 119, and 122.

section 953 of the CCP, under which, if writs of execution issued by Spanish courts are not recognised in the decisions handed down by the courts of the other country, the writs of execution from that country shall have no force in Spain.

Conditions system

Finally, the conditions system applies once it has been shown that there is no treaty with the country of origin, that the positive reciprocity system does not apply, and that the writ of execution comes from a country whose courts do not recognise writs of execution issued by Spanish courts. In that case, the foreign judgment shall be recognised if it meets the requirements laid down in section 954 of the CCP, which are as follows:

(1) That the writ of execution has been issued as a consequence of a personal action being brought.
(2) That it has not been issued in default.
(3) That the liability to be performed under the writ of execution is lawful in Spain.
(4) That the writ of execution shall meet the requirements in force in the country in which it has been issued in order to be considered authentic, and shall meet the requirements of Spanish laws for being a valid document in Spain.[38]

Authors, in general, take a rather dim view of the Spanish *exequatur* system, not only because it is not well suited to the characteristics of current legal practice but also because of the problems found in applying it, particularly in the case of the reciprocity system, in both its positive and negative or retortion forms, on account of the former being a vestige of the past and the latter playing an unjustified role in the system[39]

Procedural aspects

Besides these problems, which in most cases have to be solved by resorting to the doctrine of authors and previous court decisions, the procedure for recognising and executing foreign judgments in Spain is comparatively simple. Thus, a written petition for a judgment to be recognised and executed is addressed to Section One of the Supreme Court (section 955, CCP), accompanied by a document attesting to the decision, which must carry the apostil set out in The Hague Convention. These documents shall be duly translated (section 956, CCP), either before they are filed with the Supreme Court (section 601, CCP) or later on during the proceedings.

In line with the rule that parties must furnish the evidence necessary to a decision, the condemned party or the party affected by a declaratory judgment is given nine days in which to appear before the court to be heard (section 956, CCP). For the said party to be able to appear, the relevant certificate is issued to the responsible Spanish and foreign authorities according to the relevant judicial assistance arrangements.[40] Once the term has elapsed, the court shall go ahead with the proceedings even if the person who has been summoned does not appear.

38. s. 600, CCP.
39. Espinar Vicente, note 10, *supra*, pp. 118 *et seq*.
40. s. 957, CCP. Also, the Convention of The Hague of 15 November 1965 on Notification or Transfer Abroad of Judicial and Nonjudicial Documents in Civil and Commercial Matters.

After hearing the Government attorney, the court declares whether the writ of execution shall be recognised or not. If the court does not recognise the writ of execution, this is returned to the party who has filed it. If recognised, it is forwarded to the High Court (*Audiencia*) which orders the judge of first instance of the district where the condemned party has his domicile or the judgment is to be executed to put this into effect (section 958, CCP).

The procedure for recognising the writ of execution has an erroneous consequence in the view of some authors, as it only provides for the inexorable result of execution (*exequatur*) and, in sum, for condemnatory judgments, leaving aside merely declarative judgments, constitutive judgments, and decisions on taking precautionary and provisional measures. Thus, the provisions of section 958 of the CCP have to be interpreted as appropriate in case the petition is not to the effect that a judgment be recognised, but to some other effect.[41]

REMEDIES AVAILABLE TO FOREIGN CREDITORS

According to the provisions mentioned above, as well as those of section 24.1 of the Constitution, sections 7 and 21.1 of the Basic Act on the Judiciary No. 6/1985 of 1 July 1985, of section 29.1 of Basic Act No. 7/1985 of 9 July 1985 on the Rights and Freedoms of Foreign Citizens in Spain, and in sections 8.2 and 28 of the Civil Code, foreign creditors are practically on an equal standing with Spanish creditors when seeking performance of an obligation of giving, doing or not doing something.

The foregoing notwithstanding, it should be borne in mind that, according to other provisions which have also been mentioned, such as those of sections 534 and 951 *et seq.* of the CCP, the possibility of foreign creditors exercising their rights may be partly restricted from the procedural viewpoint, although not from the substantive point of view.

Ordinary executory proceedings

In order to be able to exercise his rights, the foreign creditor must have an instrument which proves his right of execution of a claim or of execution of judgment, the liability to be performed must be liquidated, due, demandable and for more than 50,000 pesetas, and the debt must require that the liability be performed. When the creditor has a right of executing a claim, he may bring executory proceedings of a declaratory nature, and when he has a right of execution of judgment he may bring proceedings for execution of judgment of an executory nature. In either case, the obligation, as we have seen, must be liquidated, i.e., must be for a specific sum or liable to be estimated in money terms, without depending on any further consideration due by the creditor or to any choice on the part of the debtor, and must be for more than 50,000 pesetas (sections 1435 *et seq.*, CCP).

Starting with the executory instruments, we should bear in mind that, under section 1429 of the CCP, these are the following: a public document; any private document recognised under oath before the judge who has competence for handling the

41. Prieto Castro, note 15 *supra*, p. 933.

execution; a confession rendered before the competent judge; a bill of exchange, a promissory note or a cheque; any bearer or registered securities which have been lawfully issued and represent liabilities which have become due, as well as coupons carried by such securities which are due for payment; and the original copies of commercial contracts, executed by the parties concerned and witnessed by a stockbroker or registered broker.

The latter are really executive, and therefore give way to outright execution where the debtor does not oppose them in any way and pays up on payment merely being demanded by the creditor. If the debtor does not pay and, instead, objects to the claim, execution does not take place on the basis of the instrument itself but as a result of a definitive judgment handed down at the end of the ordinary executory proceedings which the creditor will have to undertake in that case. The scope of the execution is ultimately determined by this judgment, which certifies the creditor's rights.[42]

Thus, where the creditor has no option left but to undertake ordinary executory proceedings, he must do so before the judge of first instance to whose jurisdiction the parties have explicitly agreed to submit. If there is no explicit agreement to that effect, the creditor may choose between the judge of the district where the obligation is to be performed according to the executory instrument,[43] the judge of the district in which the party has his domicile, or that of the district in which the real estate is situated in the case of mortgaged property (section 1439, CCP).[44] The judge of first instance may even decide of his own accord whether he has the necessary territorial jurisdiction (section 1440, CCP), which leads some authors to conclude that the territorial jurisdiction system is a mixed system, in which explicit choice of jurisdiction is allowed and tacit choice of jurisdiction is forbidden.[45]

For the judge to accept to handle the complaint or, what amounts to the same thing, to order the execution to be dispatched, the creditor's claim must be based on any of the documents mentioned in section 1429 of the CCP, paying special attention to the fact that these have no voiding defects and meets the necessary formal requirements, and that the underlying obligation is liquidated, due for payment, demandable and for more than 50,000 pesetas. Once the judge orders the execution to be dispatched and payment is demanded from the debtor, the debtor may or may not agree to pay: if he does, the sum is handed over to the creditor, the costs are paid, and the proceedings come to an end (section 1445, CCP); if he does not, the debtor's property will be attached in an amount sufficient to cover the principal, interest and costs (section 1447, CCP), and he will be summoned to attend the public sale (sections 1459 and 1460, CCP).

If the debtor duly declares that he intends to oppose the complaint, he has a term of four days, which may not be extended, in which to bring his exceptions and propose such evidence as he feels necessary (sections 1463 *et seq.*, CCP). The debtor's response to the complaint is served on the creditor who has a term of four days to reply to it and, in turn, propose evidence (section 1468, CCP). Then there is a period of 10 days during which the judge will take the relevant evidence (section 1469, CCP) and, at the

42. See Prieto-Castro, note 15 *supra*, p. 689.

43. Supreme Court Decisions of 21 May 1957 and 23 March 1977.

44. The Act No. 10/1992 of 30 April on Urgent Measures of Procedural Reform has amended section 1439, CCP, and declared inapplicable the rules on explicit or tacit submission.

45. Cortes Dominguez, V. et al., *Derecho Procesal*, Vol. I (Book II) (Valencia 1986), p. 140.

end of the 10-day period, the evidence is made available to the parties at the clerk's office for a term of four days. Once the parties are informed, the judge summons the parties to judgment (section 1472). The debtor may be condemned or absolved, or the proceedings may be declared void (section 1473, CCP), and the judgment may be appealed to both effects.

If the debtor does not appear, he is declared to be in default (section 1462, CCP), and the proceedings go ahead without the debtor being summoned again or given any notices other than those specified by law, until the definitive judgment. This will normally be condemnatory, will carry an order to proceed with the execution, which will be carried out by legal means of collection, and will state the sum to be paid to the creditor. In such case, the debtor being adjudged will be ordered to pay the court costs, as laid down in section 1474 of the CCP.

Special executory proceedings

Besides ordinary executory proceedings, there are special executory proceedings, such as those based on bills of exchange, cheques, and promissory notes, or for collection by legal means in commercial transactions. Those based on bills of exchange are governed by the provisions of sections 66 to 68, 96 and 153 of the Bill of Exchange and Cheque Act,[46] through which certain changes have been introduced in the executory proceedings laid down in section 1429 of the CCP, such as doing away with the need for judicial inspection of the signatures at the time of the judge agreeing to handle the complaint, which, as mentioned in due course, makes this a summary declaratory process.

Executory proceedings based on cheques also have certain special features. Such proceedings may only be based on the credits mentioned in section 1544 of the CCP and on the documents mentioned in section 1545 thereof. In addition, such credits must be liquidated according to the relevant instrument, as otherwise they will not be allowed until they are liquidated. The notice of public sale is served unless the debtor brings his exceptions against collection by legal means within a term of three days (sections 1549 and 1550, CCP).

As mentioned above, a creditor may not only claim his rights on the basis of an executory instrument, but may also request execution of judgment in order to recover a sum owing to him. We must bear in mind that documents which entitle creditors to file claims in proceedings for execution of judgment also call for giving, doing or not doing something, and the requirements that the liability be liquidated, due for payment and demandable apply to these as they do to executory instruments. Therefore, the above comments on the requirements to be met by such instruments also apply here.

Nature of the proceedings

The foregoing notwithstanding, there are significant differences between executory instruments and the documents on which proceedings for execution of judgment are

46. Act No. 19/1985 of 16 July 1985 on the Bill of Exchange and Cheque.

based, starting with the breakdown of such documents. These are divided into two main categories, jurisdictional and non-jurisdictional documents.

Jurisdictional documents include final condemnatory judgments, whether Spanish or foreign ones which have been recognised in Spain (sections 919 and 951, CCP); provisionally executable judgments; and certain decrees to be carried out by way of execution, such as orders to pay court costs (section 421, CCP), to pay compensation to the defendant for the plaintiff's failure to appear in oral hearings (section 728, CCP), and to pay compensation for damages on a preventive embargo being lifted (sections 1417 and 1427, CCP).

Non-jurisdictional documents include arbitration awards, whether domestic or foreign awards recognised in Spain (sections 52 *et seq.*, Arbitration Act 36/1988 of 5 December 1988); judicial settlements (section 1815 of the Civil Code and Supreme Court Decision of 10 July 1969); mortgage deeds and pledge instruments which do not call for handing over possession; settlement agreements (during process: section 692, CCP; pre-trial: section 476, CCP). Other documents which may be considered to fall under this description are court orders to advance funds to the procurator and pay his duties, as well as to pay the lawyer's fees,[47] even though some authors include these among jurisdictional documents.[48]

In principle, under Spanish law, only final condemnatory judgments are liable to be executed, as provided in section 191 of the CCP. In certain circumstances, however, this general rule does not apply, and is replaced by another according to which judgments other than final, non-appealable judgments may be executed, albeit provisionally. These include judgments which have been appealed, where the appeal has been accepted only to a devolutive effect (section 381, CCP), or to both the devolutive and suspensive effects (section 385, CCP); also, where the appeal is for dismissal or reversal (section 1722, CCP).

With reference to provisional execution of judgments which have been appealed, where the appeal has been accepted to several effects, section 385 of the CCP sets out three different cases: judgments whereby a debtor is condemned to pay a liquidated sum, or one which can be liquidated by carrying out simple arithmetic operations as specified in the judgment; and judgments whose subject or nature is not that of condemning a debtor to pay a liquidated sum, such as doing, not doing or giving a certain thing, as well as those condemning the debtor to pay a sum which is liquidated.

From the point of view of the procedure in force, we should note that the court having competence for the purpose is the one that handed down the judgment which has been appealed. In addition, that execution may only be ordered at the request of the party concerned, normally that against whom the appeal has been filed, and that in order for the appeal to be carried out, the party filing the appeal must post bond in order to guarantee reimbursement, if the judgment is reversed as a result of the appeal, of what has been obtained through execution.

According to some authors, there is a significant vacuum in the provisions of the CCP governing this procedure, as even though it is true that said provisions specify that the petition for execution must be filed within a term of six days after being advised that the appeal has been accepted for trial, and that upon execution being

47. Cortes Dominguez, V. et al., note 43 *supra*, p. 366.
48. e.g. Prieto-Castro, note 15 *supra*, p. 689.

allowed the applicant must post a sufficient bond within a term of three days, it is also true that there are no provisions to the effect that the other party should be heard on whether execution is advisable or the bond suffices.[49]

At the time of executing, the executor is entitled to take exception to the relevant judicial decrees, where the judge does not agree to dispatch the execution. The party who is executed on may also do so, when an embargo affects property which is not eligible for the purpose. And third parties may also take exception to the judicial decrees, and seek to have certain items excluded from the embargo, or to be paid with preference to the executor. The embargo may be opposed through a motion to set aside (sections 376 *et seq.*, CCP), an appeal (sections 949 and 153, CCP), and an appeal for dismissal or reversal, as the case may be (section 1687, CCP). This also may be opposed through a motion for dismissal, when the party being executed on intends to attack the execution as a nullity (section 949, CCP), or through third-party intervention where those who intend to do so are third parties (sections 1532 *et seq.*, CCP).

Apart from these provisional executions, there are other executions strictly speaking or, as they are called by some authors, specific executions, which are those consisting of doing, not doing or delivering a given thing other than money. There are also monetary executions in which, as opposed to what is the case with the previous type, the debtor does not have to do or refrain from doing something, and must instead hand over to the creditor a certain sum of money by realising those assets which can be sold off for cash.[50]

Executions which consist of doing something are governed by the provisions of section 924 of the CCP. Under these provisions, the debtor must carry out a tangible or juridical activity. The claim is brought by the party concerned, by filing a petition before the judge or court which is to decide on the matter; once the proceedings begin, the judge or court orders the debtor to carry out the activity in question, without previously hearing him. If the debtor complies with the order within the term fixed for the purpose, the execution proceedings end; otherwise they continue.

In the case of executions which consist of not doing something, the obligation is performed by refraining from a certain behaviour, or else giving permission for doing so. If the party condemned not to do something breaches the decision, he will be taken to choose to pay compensation for damages to the party holding the writ of execution, as recognised in section 925 of the CCP.

Executions which involve delivering something are governed by the provisions of section 926 of the CCP. These may consist of handing over movable or immovable property, whereupon the party who has won the suit is given possession of the property and the relevant fixtures. This obligation is closely related to the nature of the property, which may be specific and certain, or generic and indeterminate. The manner of execution is contingent on this circumstance, particularly if the property is *in natura*.

Monetary executions, which are substantially different from those mentioned so far, take place when this type of obligation is specified in the document on which the claim is based, or when the property cannot be delivered *in natura* and an equivalent

49. Cortes Dominguez, V. et al., note 43 *supra*, p. 371.
50. *Ibid.*, pp. 384 *et seq.*

way of performing the liability has to be sought. In that case, the proceedings start with a petition for a writ of execution and go on with the attachment and realisation of the attached property.

Monetary executions start with a request filed by the party concerned before the judge handling the execution proceedings, for the judge to order the dispatch of the execution and issue an attachment order. In the request, the party must naturally mention the sum being claimed. If this is liquidated, the property of the condemned party is attached (section 921, CCP); otherwise, the sum has to be fixed.

In the case of a judgment condemning a debtor to pay a liquidated sum, this includes any given interest on the principal that has been fixed in the judgment on the basis of the rate at which interest has accrued and the time during which it has accrued (section 921, CCP). Interest accrues on the liquidated sum, to the benefit of the creditor, from the moment that judgment is handed down by the first instance court until the judgment is fully executed, at an annual rate equal to the statutory rate of interest plus two percentage points,[51] or at whatever rate has been agreed between the parties or arises from special provisions, save that the judgment be wholly reversed on appeal.

If the judgment orders a liquidated sum to be paid along with another unliquidated sum, the former may be paid without waiting for the latter to be liquidated (section 927, CCP). And if the condemnatory judgment orders a compensation for damages to be paid without fixing the sum as a liquidated amount, the party who has been awarded damages shall file a list of the damages and the corresponding amounts along with the request for payment of the compensation (section 928, CCP).

In the case of a judgment ordering payment of a debt in foreign currency, the peseta equivalent has to be fixed at the official selling rate of exchange on the day when the liability became due or the dealing day immediately before that, in order to be used as a basis for the purposes of attaching the debtor's property and in taking further steps (sections 1436 and 1440, CCP). The rate of exchange to be used in computing the peseta equivalent must be proven by referring to the official exchange rates published in the *Official National Government Gazette*, and the party concerned must also prove that the liability denominated in foreign currency has been duly authorised and is legally permitted (section 1436, read together with section 1435, CCP).

Once the request for execution has been filed, the judge handling the execution proceedings has decided that he has competence for ordering execution and territorial jurisdiction for doing so, and all the legal requirements have been met, such as the basis for executing the obligation therein contained, the legal capacity and standing of the executor and the party being executed on, as well as the personality of the procurator, the judge shall dispatch the execution and order attachment of the debtor's property in an amount sufficient to cover the sum to be executed and the court costs, without any need for serving prior notice demanding payment on the debtor personally (sections 1440 and 1442, CCP).

Once the execution has been dispatched, the order is handed to a court official, who makes a formal demand for payment from the debtor before the clerk. When the debtor's domicile or his whereabouts are unknown, the judge may order, at the plaintiff's request, that the attachment be carried out without previously and formally

51. At the time of this writing, the statutory rate fixed under Act No. 31/91 of 30 December 1991, is 10%, so the rate would be 12%.

demanding payment, or by demanding payment from whoever may be in charge of the property.

If the debtor fails to pay immediately, the relevant attachment will be carried out; if he does, the sum paid by the debtor shall be handed over to the plaintiff and the judge shall wind up the proceedings, putting it down in the records of the case and having the clerk issue a receipt (sections 1442 and 1445, CCP).

In the case of a foreign currency liability, the relevant sum shall be paid in the currency in which the liability has been incurred, or in pesetas provided that these are accepted as being convertible into the agreed foreign currency. If not proven or if the debtor seeks to pay the principal and the interest, as the case may be, in Spanish currency, such payment may only be made if the creditor explicitly accepts it; otherwise, the sum being offered in Spanish currency may be attached (section 1445, CCP).

The embargo applies to given property items, provided that these belong to the debtor and are in his possession or in the hands of a third party, that they are of economic value and are liable to be realised, and are neither wholly nor partly ineligible for attachment, either on account of their low economic value, or of being in the public domain or for public use, or on grounds of public, social or humanitarian interest, or on account of the sale of such items being banned, or on account of being insolubly tied to other property.

The decision on which property items to attach may be up to the creditor, the court official or clerk, or the party being adjudged. From the outset, the creditor may report the debtor's items he is aware of, for these to be attached. In that respect, the CCP provides for a certain order of preference to be observed for attachment purposes, for the benefit of both the party being executed on, so that the execution is not so burdensome, and the executor, so that he can collect as soon as possible.

In that respect, section 1447 of the CCP mentions the types of assets which may be attached in the following order of preference:

(1) Cash, if any is found.
(2) Securities listed at a stock exchange.
(3) Jewels made of gold, silver, or precious stones.
(4) Credits which can be realised immediately.
(5) Fruits[52] and income of all kinds.
(6) Movable property and animals.
(7) Immovable property.
(8) Balances or pensions.
(9) Credits and rights which cannot be realised immediately.
(10) Commercial or manufacturing operations.

In order to prevent the debtor from disposing of any property attached for execution, Spanish laws provide for various safeguarding measures, such as deposit (sections 968, 1069, 1175, 1179, 1409 and 1442, CCP), receivership (sections 966, 1007, 1010, 1179, and 1450, CCP), and preventive annotation in public registries (section 1453, CCP, and section 86, Mortgage Act,[53] as well as section 199, Mortgage Act Regulation[54]).

52. Fruits, i.e., products of the earth, animal offspring and other animal by-products.
53. Real Estate Mortgage Act of 8 February 1946.
54. Real Estate Mortgage Act Regulation of 14 February 1947.

In the course of the attachment proceedings, certain property may be included which, despite being in the hands of the party being executed on, actually belongs to third parties. These may then request that their property be released from attachment by bringing a third-party claim of ownership. This is an action that may be brought in proceedings for executing judgment, or in any other proceedings which involve attaching and selling off property (section 1543, CCP).

Under the provisions of section 488 of the CCP, the third-party claim of ownership does not suspend the executory proceedings to which it is incidental, and is heard separately in such declaratory proceedings as may be in order according to the sum involved. The jurisdictional body that has competence for hearing the claim is that handling the execution, provided that it also has objective competence on account of the value of the attached property in question. And the person who has legal standing for filing the claim is the person whose property has been affected in executing another's liability.

Once the claim is filed along with the document on which it is based, without which the claim shall not be heard (section 1537, CCP), the legal proceedings for collection may be suspended in respect of the property concerned, until the claim is decided (section 1535, CCP). A judgment by virtue of which a third-party claim of ownership is upheld shall include an order lifting the embargo on the unduly attached items and the safeguarding measures taken in respect of these, and shall declare that the third party concerned is the owner. This judgment may be corrected, and may be appealed to both effects (section 1541, CCP).

Once the debtor's property is attached, under the provisions of section 922 of the CCP the property is appraised and sold off according to the rules laid down for legal proceedings for collection (sections 1481 to 1531, CCP). The property is normally sold off at auction, which is the method used for assets other than money (section 1447.1, CCP), salaries, pensions or credits which can be realised immediately (section 1481, CCP) or securities listed on an official secondary market (section 1482, CCP).

The auction proper begins with the procedure for appraising the attached property. The appraisal is carried out by experts appointed by the parties concerned and by a third party (section 1483, CCP), in the case of both movable and immovable property, in order to establish a fair price and the minimum required bid. Then notices are published announcing the auction to prospective bidders, and a public sale is held. In order to take part in the public sale, bidders are required to make a deposit in cash for the equivalent of 20% of the minimum required bid for the property to be auctioned off.

The judge presides over the public sale, with the clerk in attendance. After reading out the list of properties and the bidding terms, the bidding begins. The bids must cover two-thirds of the appraisal value of the properties. If there are no bidders prepared to bid up to the required amount, the judgment creditor may request to be awarded the properties for two-thirds of the appraisal value, or that the properties be tendered for sale at auction once again, in which case the procedure described above, which includes posting the 20% bid-bond, is repeated.

If the bids received at the second auction are still below the required level, the judgment creditor may request to be awarded the properties for two-thirds of the minimum required bid, or that the properties be handed over to him for administrating, or, simply, that a third auction be held with no minimum required bid. In any case, at the end of the whole process, once the judge reaches the conclusion that no higher bids will be forthcoming, the sale price and the name of the highest bidder will be announced to the public. The sale is approved, the properties are delivered to the buyers, and these must pay the remaining part of the price within a term of three or eight days, depending on whether the property is movable or immovable.

An interesting point here is that a public sale may be held "in bankruptcy", which is a situation that arises where the highest bidder fails to pay the price he bid at the auction within the specified period, or is responsible for the property failing to be sold off. In such case, a new auction "in bankruptcy" is held, unless the bid bonds cover the principal and interest owing to the judgment creditor as well as the court costs (section 1513, CCP).

Among the extrajudicial instruments that give rise to enforcement of judgment proceedings there are those that prove a real encumbrance created on movable or immovable property, which is thus tied to performance of a liability (sections 1587 *et seq.*, Civil Code; sections 104 and 138, Mortgage Act, and sections 1, 2, 19, and 52, Chattel Mortgage Act). These real security rights are basically mortgages and pledges which do not involve transferring possession of the pledged items, whose main features are that they are secondary and indivisible rights of realising the value of a thing, on one hand, and on the other hand that the thing which has been mortgaged or pledged belongs to the person in whose favour the thing has been mortgaged or pledged, while the person who mortgages or pledges the thing may freely dispose of it or is duly authorised to do so (Supreme Court decisions of 25 March 1925, 23 April 1957, 19 December 1964, and 3 July 1987).

Performance of a liability guaranteed through a mortgage on real property may be enforced by bringing an executory process of the type foreseen in the CCP (sections 1429 and 1447); by undertaking another executory process and, in the context of this process, bringing foreclosure proceedings (sections 126 and 127, Mortgage Act); by resorting to an out-of-court procedure before a public notary with a view to realising the value of the property (section 129, Mortgage Act); or, finally, by seeking enforcement of judgment before the courts and realising the immovable property through summary judicial proceedings (sections 129 and 130 to 135, Mortgage Act).

In summary judicial proceedings, foreclosure proceedings are brought on real property which guarantees performance of a liability. The court having territorial jurisdiction is the court of first instance to which the parties may have agreed to submit in the mortgage deed or, failing that, the court of first instance of the district in which the property is situated. If the property is situated in more than one district, or there are several properties situated in various districts, the case may be brought before the judge of first instance of any of those districts (section 131.1, Mortgage Act).

The proceedings begin by filing a complaint stating the facts and legal grounds according to which the credit is certain, outstanding and exigible, and specifying the exact amount being claimed on all accounts (section 131.2, Mortgage Act). The written complaint must be accompanied by the instrument or instruments which bear out the credit and a notarial requisition of payment to have been sent to the debtor and the third possessor 10 days earlier (section 131.3, Mortgage Act).

Thirty days after a writ is issued to the real estate registrar ordering him to provide a certificate quoting the latest entries concerning ownership and possession, as well as listing any mortgages, annuities, encumbrances, and real rights on the property, and notice of the proceedings is served on the latest owner, the plaintiff, the debtor, and the third possessor, a request may be filed for the property to be auctioned off without previously being appraised.

If a suitable bid is received at the auction, the judge approves it and then the buyer has a term of eight days in which to pay the difference between the bid bond he has posted and the bid price for which he has been awarded the property. Where the winning bidder is the creditor himself, he only has to pay the difference between the bid price and the principal, as well as the interest owing under the mortgage (section 131.15, Mortgage Act). The auction price is used for settling the plaintiff's credit under the mortgage, and the remainder is handed over to any other creditors or to whoever is entitled to it.

IMPACT OF A DEBTOR'S BANKRUPTCY

A creditor, whether Spanish or foreign, may file a petition for the debtor to be declared bankrupt. Under section 876 of the Commercial Code, the petition must be based on a writ of execution or a judicial order of collection, and may only be filed if the attachment has not produced sufficient unencumbered assets for settling the debt.

A declaration of bankruptcy has significant implications for both the bankrupt person and the creditors: in the case of the former, it involves a restriction on his rights of disposing of and administrating his assets, and in the case of the latter, their credits are ranked by type in a certain order of preference and according to certain terms. The breakdown, ranking and payment of the credits is governed, in Spanish law, by a "confused set of provisions of different nature and different rank", as some authors have put it,[55] which involve a "difficult task of construing highly heterogeneous provisions".[56]

In order to settle the outstanding credits, the creditors are broken down into "specially privileged" and "privileged" creditors, according to the order of preference in which they are entitled to be paid. The order of preference depends on whether the privilege is in respect of movable or immovable property.

In the case of movable property, the preference consists of being entitled to be paid ahead of other creditors out of the value of the personal property to which the preference refers (section 912, CommC, read together with sections 1922 and 1926, CivC), and in the case of immovable property, it consists of a similar right to the value of the real property to which the preference refers (section 912, CommC, read together with sections 1923 and 1927, CivC).

Privileges in respect of movable property are equal to real rights on account of their immediacy and of being effective "erga omnes", like a pledge; and privileges in respect of immovable property can, in turn, be likened to privileged mortgages, such as credits in favour of the Government, credits in favour of insurers, credits on mortgages and credits for money advanced to builders, credits on which a precautionary annotation

55. See Majada, Arturo, *Práctica Concursal* (Madrid 1983), p. 22.

56. *Ibid.*, p. 23. Also the Civil Code (ss. 1921 *et seq.*); the Commercial Code (ss. 908 *et seq.*); the Suspension of Payments Act of 26 July 1922 (*Gazette* No. 257 of 11 September 1922) (ss. 113 *et seq.*); CCP (ss. 1378 *et seq.*).

has been made in the Real Estate Registry, and credits of financial backers on real property which have not been registered or annotated.[57]

As mentioned above, the order of preference among creditors is fixed according to whether their credits are to be settled with the proceeds of the bankrupt person's movable or immovable property. Those whose credits are to be settled with the proceeds of movable property are in turn ranked according to the following order:

(1) Specially privileged creditors.[58]
(2) Privileged creditors having a preferential right under the Commercial Code.[59]
(3) Privileged creditors pursuant to civil law, and mortgage creditors having preference, pursuant to civil law, over those whose credits are based on movable property.[60]
(4) Creditors whose claims are evidenced in a public deed, as well as those evidenced in mercantile instruments attested to by a registered broker or dealer.[61]
(5) General creditors by virtue of commercial transactions.[62]
(6) General creditors by virtue of agreements subject to civil law.[63]

For their part, creditors falling into the second group, i.e., those whose credits are to be paid out of the proceeds from real property, are paid off in the following order of preference: in the first place, creditors having real rights, in the terms and according to the order of preference foreseen in the Mortgage Act[64]; followed by specially privileged creditors and the others mentioned in section 913 of the Commercial Code, in the order specified in said section.

For such credits to be recognised, creditors must produce to the receivers the instruments evidencing their credits within a term of not more than 60 days. Such credits then have to be examined and recognised at the creditors' meeting,[65] with the relevant meeting to be held at least 12 days after the end of the term given to the creditors for producing the relevant instruments.[66] After the credits are examined, should any creditor believe that he has been prejudiced by the resolution taken at the creditors' meeting, he may claim their rights before the judge handling the bankruptcy proceedings within a term of 30 days, which may not be extended.[67]

The creditors' demands concerning both the examination and recognition of the

57. Albacar, José Luis, and Santos Briz, Jaime, *Código Civil. Doctrina y Jurisprudencia*, Vol. VI (Madrid 1991), p. 1131.

58. Specially privileged creditors are broken down, pursuant to the provisions of s. 913.1, Commercial Code, into those who have: claims for burial, funeral and probate expenses; claims for alimony; claims for wages owing for the six months prior to bankruptcy (s. 32 of the Basic Labour Act No. 8/1980 of 10 March 1980), and claims arising from mandatory social insurance and social benefit systems as well as mandatory mutual worker association systems.

59. s. 913.2, Commercial Code, read together with ss. 98, 196, 208, 276, 320, 340, 372, 375, 376, 580, 581, 667, 704, and 730, Commercial Code.

60. s. 913.3, Commercial Code; s. 1922, Civil Code, and s. 168, Mortgage Act.

61. s. 913.4, Commercial Code.

62. s. 913.5, Commercial Code.

63. s. 913.6, Commercial Code.

64. s. 914.1, Commercial Code, and ss. 25, 50, 51, and 63, Mortgage Act.

65. s. 1100, Suspension of Payments Act.

66. s. 1378, CCP.

67. s. 1381, CCP.

credits and the ranking of the credits, must be made according to the procedure set forth in the bankruptcy proceedings.[68]

ANTONIO VINAL

68. s. 1382, CCP, read together with ss. 1273 and 1277, CCP.

CHAPTER 27

SWEDEN

INTRODUCTION

All forms of provisional measures are founded on two conflicting interests. On the one hand, the plaintiff has a justified interest to protect himself against a defendant inclined to "sabotage" or to collude; on the other hand, the defendant has a justified interest—within the framework of a "mere" summary proceeding—not to be subjected to a measure which would actually bar him from obtaining a worthwhile material test of the issue at hand in a subsequent full hearing.

A proceeding aiming to achieve only a provisional measure holds many advantages for the plaintiff. The advantages are so important that it may, in many cases, be tempting to contemplate whether such a proceeding could even be a substitute for a full trial. These advantages are, *inter alia*, the relative swiftness of the procedure, the cost, and, above all, that the plaintiff may often achieve the "end" result he seeks at this early stage. This "prejudicial" importance is perhaps often exaggerated in theory, since the primary aim of a provisional measure is to hinder a defendant from sabotaging a possible subsequent enforcement. One cannot, however, disregard that the court in the provisional proceeding makes an assessment of the plaintiff's chances of success in a possible subsequent full hearing, and that the plaintiff thereby, in practice, gains a significant advantage.

In this chapter, we will analyse and comment on the different possibilities to obtain provisional measures offered by Swedish law. This practical viewpoint means also that we have not made reference to doctrine (which is almost exclusively in Swedish).

The particular problems which can arise for a foreign, i.e., non-Swedish, creditor/plaintiff, will be stressed. The chapter will comment briefly on the courts' handling of, *inter alia*, provisional remedies. The discussion concentrates on sequestration, the dominating provisional measure, which can be used in principle for all types of claims and cases, regardless of the status of the parties and the nature of the property or goods concerned.

Distraint, garnishment, general rules on enforcement of foreign judgments and orders, as well as certain special forms of provisional measures will also be considered.

Where we refer to "person" or "persons", this includes both natural and legal persons, unless otherwise specified. "Foreign" means, as indicated above, non-Swedish.

SEQUESTRATION

According to the Swedish Code of Judicial Procedure (*rattegångsbalken*), a plaintiff must meet the following requisites in order to have his claim for sequestration approved. He must:

(1) show that there is probable cause that he has a claim which can be tried in a judicial process as regulated by the Code, or in another similar fashion;
(2) show that there is a risk that the defendant will avoid the claim; and
(3) put up sufficient security to cover indemnification to the defendant for damages which might result from the application for and the granting of provisional relief.

For certain foreign plaintiffs—those who are not exempted because of convention regulations or because of the nature of the case—there is a further requisite, namely that such plaintiff must put up security for such litigation costs as he might be ordered to pay to the defendant. This last requirement, which is general in the sense that it applies in practically all kinds of cases and matters, is, however, applicable only if the defendant—at the latest when he should first have replied in the case—demands such security from the plaintiff. The three other requisites are tried by the court *ex officio*. They will be individually commented on below.

Sequestration can be granted as a provisional measure for various types of claim. Claims for payment are the most frequent. Through a sequestration order, the creditor assures that the debtor's property is "taken care of" or otherwise withdrawn from the latter's disposable sphere, pending a possible enforcement. So much of the debtor's property which is deemed to cover, upon distraint, the plaintiff's claim, is sequestrated. It is incumbent upon the Enforcement Services Authority (*kronofogdemyndigheten*) to enforce the order. Usually, it is the Enforcement Services Authority, the bailiffs, which decides what property shall be "taken". The plaintiff is, however, at liberty to indicate or direct certain specified property to be the object of enforcement.

Sequestration can also be ordered in disputes concerning better rights to certain property. If there is reason to fear that a defendant will, to the plaintiff's detriment, hide, diminish, or otherwise dispose of property being the subject matter of a case regarding superior right, the court can—if the plaintiff can show that he has probable cause for his claim and if indemnification security has been put up—order the property in dispute to be sequestrated pending the outcome of the case.

In addition to sequestration to secure future enforcement or to secure property being the subject of a dispute of superior right, sequestration can also be ordered, says the Code, "in other cases". Thus, the courts have been given a general authority to order suitable provisional measures. Still, the plaintiff must show that he has probable cause for his claim and that a risk is at hand. He must also put up an indemnification security. Again, if these requisites are fulfilled, the court can, on the plaintiff's demand, e.g., prohibit the defendant from conducting certain business or a certain activity.

The defendant's activity can consist of either positive or negative actions. "Positive actions" are, for instance, divulging of trade secrets to a third party, contravention of a competition clause by conducting business or other activities, becoming employed by a competitor, improper use of a company name, or conducting activity on real estate which causes a nuisance. Examples of "negative actions" are failure to leave the plaintiff's premises upon the occurrence of an obligation to do so, and failure to take actions to maintain property which is in the defendant's possession but to which the plaintiff claims a superior right. Negative actions also embrace failure concerning documents, such as bonds or shares, to which the plaintiff claims superior right, to take action on which the value of the documents is substantially dependent. The court will impose a fine in case of breach of the order.

A case[1] from the Swedish Supreme Court (*Högsta Domstolen*) illustrates the use of the court's authority in practice. Invoking a competition clause in an agreement, the plaintiff succeeded in having a former managing director of a large company prohibited from competing with the former employer. The plaintiff had demanded that the fine attached be set at SEK 1,000,000, a sum of which the District Court and the Court of Appeal approved. The Supreme Court, however, found it reasonable to set the fine at SEK 200,000. It should be noted that, in general, fines and damages ordered by Swedish courts are still comparatively very small, even if slight changes in this practice have been seen in recent years.

If the debtor unlawfully handles or in any way disposes of sequestrated property, he commits a criminal offence.

The sequestration order does not give a right of priority if the debtor is subjected to distraint for another debt or put into bankruptcy. The sequestrated property can, in such cases, be used to cover the claims of any other creditors, including the state, having right of priority.

A sequestration order can be rendered even if the case as such is to be tried in another manner than by a public Swedish court, for instance in accordance with the Arbitration Act or by a foreign court (see the text below relating to "International legal situations" and the "Recognition and enforcement of foreign judgments and orders").

Prognosis assessment

An order for a provisional measure is built, *inter alia*, on a prognostic assessment as to how the full case as such will end. If the plaintiff's chances of winning the full proceeding are deemed to be good, the court will most likely approve the plaintiff's demand for sequestration (or other provisional measure). The level of evidence which the plaintiff must produce is obviously lower than in a full proceeding.

This relatively low level of evidence, "probable cause", means that the courts will usually not disapprove a sequestration application on the grounds that the plaintiff has not produced sufficient evidence that he will win the full case. In the leading commentary on the subject, it has been stated that the "probable cause" level of evidence should not be stringently applied when making the prognosis assessment.

Avoidance risk

Unlike in other countries, the courts in Sweden have no formal authority to make a "balance of convenience", or as it is called in Sweden, a "proportionality assessment". Traditionally, the requisite of avoidance risk has, therefore, been one of the foremost

1. NJA 1991, p. 200.

means to prevent abuse of provisional measures. Many sequestration applications have failed on this requirement. The difficulty in proving that there is an avoidance risk at hand should, however, not be exaggerated. The requirement that a risk of avoidance "can reasonably be feared" is, in fact, less harsh than the "probable cause" requisite. It is sufficient that the plaintiff proves that the actions or failure of the defendant *can* lead to avoidance. There is thus no requirement to prove that the defendant acts with an *intention* to avoid enforcement.

This said, it should be added that a recent case[2] from the Swedish Supreme Court shows that there now may be a general inclination towards the adoption of a proportionality assessment in more complex cases. Accordingly, it is likely that Swedish courts in the future will balance the damage a provisional measure may bring about, against the arguments invoked by the plaintiff in support of his application for sequestration. Only if the latter arguments outweigh the inconveniences of the defendant will sequestration be granted.

Requirement of indemnification security

A sequestration order can usually be granted only if the plaintiff puts up an indemnification security. In a few very special cases, freedom from this obligation can be obtained. The security must consist of either a guarantee or a pledge/mortgage. The courts have significant duty of investigation to find out whether the security is sufficient.

It is, of course, practically impossible to state generally the amount of security required in relation to the claim of the plaintiff. Experience indicates that the lower courts seem principally inclined to request that the security at least corresponds to 50% of the value of the subject matter. In larger claims, the requirement is sometimes lower. It is not uncommon to find open-ended guarantees being submitted in these cases, but this of course presupposes that the plaintiff has very good contacts with, for example, a bank.

The advantage of an open-ended guarantee, i.e., "for all damage that may be caused to the defendant by the plaintiff's application for sequestration and subsequent sequestration order", is, of course, that there will then be no dispute in court as to whether the security is sufficient or not, which in turn expedites the provisional measure proceeding.

Interlocutory orders

An order for a provisional measure shall, in principle, be preceded by a hearing. If, however, there is danger in delay, a sequestration order may be given immediately. It is common that a sequestration application is combined with an interlocutory demand. Since the documentation and material of the proceeding will then not be very large, the demand on the level of evidence required should, in reality, and at least according to the prevailing doctrine on procedural law, be lower than otherwise. An interlocutory order is usually retried as soon as the court has received a reply from the defendant.

2. NJA 1993, p. 182.

Requirement of security for costs from foreign plaintiffs

If the defendant, when replying for the first time in the case, and provided he replies within the time set by the court, demands that a foreign plaintiff put up security for costs, the plaintiff must do so (*cautio judicatum solvi*). This duty applies not only in proceedings for provisional measures but in almost every case or matter where the plaintiff is a foreign person.

If the defendant's demand for security is not timely produced, his possibilities to obtain such are precluded. The security shall consist of a guarantee or a pledge/mortgage. If the security offered is not accepted by the defendant, the court will decide on the size of the security. The possibility to demand security for costs applies only to a Swedish person appearing as a defendant and, according to convention regulations, French persons.

If the action is brought in the form of a counterclaim, or if it is a "bill of exchange" or "cheque" case (according to Swedish legal terminology), or a case in the Market Court or Administrative Court, in most real estate cases, in cases concerning labour disputes, or cases tried under the Water Rights Act, the plaintiff need not put up security for costs.

Sweden is signatory to conventions freeing Danish, Icelandic, and Japanese nationals from the obligation to put up security for costs. Furthermore, according to the Hague Conventions of 17 July 1905 and 1 March 1954, nationals of member states do not have to put up security for costs in certain types of cases. The same principle applies in the New York Convention of 20 June 1956.

Most EC/EFTA countries are signatories to one of the Hague Conventions. However, Greece, the UK and Ireland have not signed either of the Conventions, and in practice this has meant that legal persons from these countries have been under an obligation to put up security for costs, if requested so to do. Whether this, in fact, is contrary to EC law and the provisions on free movement of workers, on the right to establishment and the right to provide services, is an issue of contention. A Swedish District Court and Svea Court of Appeal have found that the requirement that UK, Greek and Irish legal persons put up security for costs if requested is contrary to the EEA Agreement (the matter was tried before Sweden became a member of the EC). A reference to the EFTA Court has been made by the Swedish Supreme Court and the answer provided will be of great interest.

According to a special Swedish Act on cases regarding maintenance allowance to children, citizens of certain states are also free from the duty to put up security for costs. Plaintiffs in cases emanating from freight contracts tied to the Geneva Convention of 19 May 1956 and to the Treaty of 9 May 1980 on international railway traffic are also exempt. Finally, persons residing in a state signatory to the Hague Convention of 25 October 1980 on international legal aid are free from the obligation to put up security for litigation costs.

Procedural rules

When a provisional measure has been granted under the Code of Judicial Procedure, the plaintiff will be ordered to institute his action within a month from the date of the order of the provisional measure (unless, of course, the request for the measure is part of a full writ already lodged). If the order is interlocutory, the leave starts from the day on which the interlocutory order was given. If the action is not initiated within this period, the provisional measure shall immediately be revoked.

By "instituting an action" is meant the submission to court of the summons applications. In arbitration cases, it is sufficient that arbitration is called for within the time limit. According to a judgment of the Supreme Court,[3] it is also sufficient that the action is initiated at a competent foreign court.

The rules in provisional measure cases regarding proper forum are the same as for civil cases in general. The main rule is that the court of the defendant's residence (*forum domicili*) is competent, but the place where an agreement or contract was entered into (*forum contractus*) can also be used to create proper forum in Sweden. There are also forum rules founded on the location of property (*forum rei sitae*) and on damaging acts (*forum delictum*).

In disputes concerning real estate, there are special forum rules. A person conducting business from a permanent establishment in Sweden can be sued for a claim arising out of the business activity where the establishment is located, regardless of whether the person is a foreign company having its registered office abroad. In addition, there are many special rules in Swedish legislation creating jurisdiction for specific Swedish courts. It is beyond the scope of this chapter to enumerate them all here but, as one example, we can mention that, in cases where the creditor has or can successfully claim to have a maritime lien for his claim in a vessel, the court having jurisdiction in maritime cases over the port where such vessel (regardless of the nationality of the vessel) lands is the proper forum.

International legal situations

On 1 January 1993 the Lugano Convention entered into force in Sweden. In cases where Swedish courts are to apply this Convention, the provisions on proper forum contained therein will prevail over the national rules discussed above. The main rule in such cases will be that the court in the country in which the defendant is resident is competent—the *forum domicili* rule is, in other words, the main rule here too. In addition to this rule, there is a number of alternative forum provisions which the plaintiff may choose to invoke. Thus, in contractual disputes, the plaintiff can bring an action against the defendant not only in the latter's country of residence, but also in the country where the contractual obligation was or is to be fulfilled (*forum solutionis*). Meanwhile, if the dispute concerns damages in tort, the court of the place where the damage occurred will be competent. There are several other provisions creating competence for specific courts to hear cases involving a certain kind of dispute. Some of these provisions give exclusive competence to one court. This is the case as regards certain disputes involving real estate. Such cases are only to be examined by the court in the country where the property is located.

Accordingly, a plaintiff wishing to apply for an interim measure, is to approach the court which is competent to try the whole case. This court will then grant or refuse a preliminary measure applying its own domestic law.

However, this is not the only way a plaintiff can proceed. Article 24 of the Lugano

3. NJA 1983, p. 814.

Convention gives the plaintiff further facilities to secure a sequestration order or a similar preliminary measure. The article stipulates that preliminary measures may be ordered in each of the signatory states pursuant to applicable national law, even if the courts of the country in issue are not competent to try the material issues of the case and the main action thus is to be brought in another signatory state.

In Sweden an interim measure can be obtained for a claim that is to be materially tried by a foreign court if the judgment of the foreign court can be enforced in Sweden. This follows from a case[4] which has become of great practical significance as a result of the entry into force of the Lugano Convention.

A rule similar to the one established in the 1983 Supreme Court case probably applies to provisional measures in connection with arbitration proceedings outside of Sweden. As indicated above, the requirement that the action be brought within a month from the date of the provisional measure order is fulfilled if such action is initiated in a timely way at the competent foreign court or by calling for arbitration.

The Code of Judicial Procedure contains a rule that a defendant who has property in Sweden also has proper forum in the court of the place where the property is located. An application for sequestration is probably not justified if there is no property in Sweden which can be sequestrated. Since the rule on *forum rei sitae* means that a competent court is almost always at hand in Sweden as long as there is property belonging to the defendant located in Sweden, a foreign plaintiff can very often apply for a provisional measure and also institute other proceedings. This forum rule is sometimes considered as exorbitant, especially as it gives a foreign plaintiff the opportunity also to attack property in Sweden belonging to a foreign defendant (see text below relating to "Recognition and enforcement of foreign judgments and orders").

OTHER PROVISIONAL MEASURES

Marketing and intellectual property law

For a "marketing right", supported by some form of intellectual property right or otherwise under the Swedish Marketing Act, and for intellectual property rights, there are various methods available to stop infringements in Sweden. We will first say a few words on Swedish jurisdiction, and thereafter we will comment on the most important rights in this context and the possibilities of obtaining orders for provisional measures.

Swedish jurisdiction

Special rules on a court's competence to try cases concerning the registration or the validity of a patent, a trademark or a similar right can be found in the Lugano Convention, which, as previously mentioned, entered into force in Sweden on 1 January 1993. According to Article 16, item 5 of the Convention, such cases may only be tried by the courts in the country in which a deposit or a registration has been applied for or has been effected or should be deemed to have been effected. It should be

4. *Ibid.*

noticed that the scope of the provision is limited to the said cases, i.e., to cases concerning registration or validity. Other cases involving intellectual property rights, e.g., cases relating to infringement of such rights etc., fall outside the ambits of Article 16, item 4, and are to be tried by the court which is competent pursuant to the general forum rules of the Convention (see above).

In cases where the Lugano Convention does not apply, there are other rules at hand. If the right in dispute is Swedish—and Sweden is a member, *inter alia*, of the Paris Convention—an action concerning the creation of the right, its legal meaning, and its validity can be tried in Sweden. Only in special circumstances, for example in prejudicial matters, can the right be tried in Sweden if it is foreign. A Swedish court ought also to be competent to try an action regarding compensation for infringement of a foreign right.

When it comes to enforcement, intellectual property rights, including "marketing rights", are equated with property located in the country. It is, however, not possible to distrain foreign intellectual property rights.

Trademarks

Intentional infringement of trademarks is a criminal offence and is prosecuted by the General Prosecutor after having been reported by the "injured person", i.e., anybody suffering or caused detriment by the (ab)use of the mark. The injured person thus reports the use to the prosecutor for the area in which the infringement occurs or is about to occur. The prosecutor can then prosecute the infringer, and he might be punished for the infringement with fines or imprisonment. In this proceeding, the court can decide that marks unlawfully attached to products shall be deleted. The court can also, as a provisional measure, order a seizure or confiscation, prior to trying materially whether a punishable infringement exists.

If a trademark, following assignment or licensing, is misleading in the hands of the new owner or licensee, the court can, to the extent found appropriate, prohibit its use and sanction the prohibition with a fine. The court can also order such an injunction in other cases of infringement. If the plaintiff shows probable cause for the existence of an infringement and if it can be feared that the infringement will depreciate the value of the trademark, an interlocutory injunction can be issued. However, the plaintiff will have to offer security for costs to obtain such an interim order.

There are no restrictions on foreign plaintiffs in suing for damages because of trademark infringement, other than those already mentioned regarding jurisdiction and the duty to put up security for litigation costs in certain cases.

In Sweden, there is also a special court, the Market Court, which, on actions normally instigated by the Consumer Ombudsman, can prohibit the use of misleading trademarks under section 7 of the Marketing Act.

If the owner of a trademark registered in Sweden is not resident in Sweden, he must have a representative residing in Sweden and empowered to represent him in all regards concerning the mark.

The proper forum for actions regarding trademark infringement, including for provisional measures, is usually the court having jurisdiction over the residence of the defendant (see the text above relating to procedural rules).

Copyright

The Swedish Copyright Act applies to works by persons who are Swedish nationals or who usually reside in Sweden, and to works first published in Sweden or simultaneously in Sweden and abroad. It does, however, also give certain reciprocal and convention protection to foreign works. In addition, in copyright infringement cases, there is criminal law protection available. The most important sanction, however, as in trademark infringement cases, is damages, which can be ordered regardless of negligence. To prevent abuse, the court can, if it finds that a copyright infringement has occurred, order property destroyed or changed in a certain manner, or that other measures shall be taken to prevent abuse.

Following recent changes in the Swedish Copyright Act, the rightholder can now also obtain an injunction from the court, prohibiting further infringement of his right. As in trademark cases, the court also has authority to issue an interlocutory injunction.

Company names

The rules governing infringement of company names are very similar to those governing infringement of trademarks, including the provisional measures available. It is, however, interesting to note that an action under the Company Names Act can be brought at a court where the defendant has its registered office or, if no court is competent according to the Code of Judicial Procedure, at the District Court of Stockholm in the first instance.

Design protecton

Again, the rules and possibilities applicable and available as to design protection are similar to those for trademarks and company names. In addition, owners of Swedish design rights not being resident in Sweden must have a representative living in Sweden authorised to do everything in regard to the design, including to receive service of summonses, notifications, and other documents in cases and matters concerning the design.

Patents

The Swedish Patents Act contains a prohibition sanction. It is possible to apply at the District Court of Stockholm for an order prohibiting infringement. The infringer can be ordered to stop his actions, and the order can be sanctioned by fines. Under certain circumstances, the order can also be interlocutory, namely if there is probable cause that an infringement is at hand. To obtain an interlocutory order, the plaintiff must put up an indemnification security with the court. Here, however, there is a certain possibility to obtain leave not to put up the security if one has no means to do so.

Both a patent owner and a licensee can bring an action for a provisional measure. For most patent cases, the District Court of Stockholm is the proper forum.

Maritime and aviation law provisional measures

Following Sweden's accession to the Lugano Convention, there are now new forum rules in international cases involving maritime law. In connection with the accession to this Convention, Sweden also signed and ratified the so-called Arrest Convention, which contains more detailed provisions on appropriate forum. The latter Convention entered into force in Sweden on 30 October 1993.

Article 7 of the Arrest Convention grants authority to courts in signatory states to examine disputes involving so-called maritime claims (*sjöfordringar*), provided that a vessel belonging to the defendant has been subject to interim measures in the country in issue. The fact that the vessel is within the territory of the country in question is accordingly not enough. For the plaintiff to be able to raise an action, it is necessary that the vessel to which the claim/debt pertains, or another vessel owned by the defendant, has been subject to a sequestration order or a similar preliminary measure in the country, aiming at securing the plaintiff's claim.

Chapter 4 of the new Swedish Maritime Act gives the Swedish rules on sequestration of vessels in cases with foreign elements. A vessel can only be sequestrated for so-called maritime claims and only provided that the basic requirements for sequestration in general (*cf.* above) are fulfilled. It should be noted that certain foreign state vessels are exempted from the application of the chapter.

Enforcement

An application for enforcement of the provisional measure is made at the Enforcement Services Agency where the property in question is situated (Chapter 16, section 10 of the Enforcement Code, *utsökningsbalken*). A registered ship is deemed to belong to the debtor if he is registered as owner, provided it is not evident that the property belongs to somebody else. Mortgaged vessels can be sequestrated even if the ship owner himself is not personally responsible for payment.

A ship registered in Sweden can be sequestrated even if there is reason to believe that there is a hindrance against enforcing the sequestration. This means that a ship can be sequestrated even if it is in line traffic between domestic ports.

Aircraft

Generally, aircraft can be sequestrated, but there are certain exceptions. The exceptions pertain to foreign aircraft only if Sweden has entered into agreement with the foreign state in question. Aircraft owned or used by the Swedish state, aircraft used in regular traffic for "common" purposes, or aircraft intended for carrying persons or goods against payment cannot, when the aircraft is ready to take off, be sequestrated. Where the sequestration application pertains to debt made in order to carry out the actual journey, it cannot be approved.

If the defendant puts up security equal to the amount claimed, plus costs, sequestration is cancelled.

RECOGNITION AND ENFORCEMENT OF FOREIGN JUDGMENTS AND ORDERS

Traditionally, the main rule in Swedish law was that foreign judgments could not be recognised nor enforced in the absence of a statute permitting such enforcement or recognition. Statutory support for the recognition and enforcement of foreign judgments was only available in respect of judgments issued by Swiss and Austrian courts, and courts in the other Nordic countries.

The Lugano Convention

The provisions on recognition and enforcement enshrined in the Lugano Convention accordingly brought about a great deal of change to the state of the law, when incorporated into Swedish law. From the entry into force of the Convention, Sweden is under an obligation to recognise and enforce judgments issued in EFTA and EC countries. Not only must Swedish authorities recognise and enforce judgments issued by a court of another signatory state when this court has based its competence on the provisions in the Lugano Convention. The rules on recognition and enforcement also apply when a court in a signatory state has examined a dispute relying solely on domestic provisions on jurisdiction. Enforcement can only be refused in a very limited number of cases.

In Sweden Svea Court of Appeal has been designated to deal within applications for enforcement of foreign judgments under the Convention.

Recognition and enforcement in other situations

Needless to say, there are situations where the rules of the Lugano Convention are to little avail. This is, for instance, the case when a judgment is issued by a court outside the EC/EFTA or when it covers a subject matter outside the ambits of the Convention, such as tax or custom duties. As mentioned earlier, the main rule in these cases will be that a foreign judgment cannot be enforced or recognised unless there is support in Swedish law for such recognition or enforcement.

It would, however, be wrong to think that a foreign judgment only is of value in Sweden if it can be enforced, or if it is granted positive or negative legal force in Sweden. The foreign judgment always has effect as evidence in a Swedish proceeding, since Swedish courts apply a so-called "free evidence valuation".

The rules on enforcement of foreign judgments and orders are closely connected with jurisdiction rules. The two sets of rules often serve to "fill in" for each other, for example, so that a refusal to acknowledge and enforce foreign judgments necessitates a wide jurisdiction in order to avoid a legal vacuum. In this context, we repeat what was said above regarding *forum rei sitae*, according to which rule someone who does not have a known residence within Sweden may be sued in Sweden anyway in a dispute regarding a payment obligation, if he owns any property situated in Sweden. The property need not have any connection with the dispute nor have a value of any reasonable proportion to the value of the subject matter of the dispute. In practice, thus, the ownership of a Swedish share or a few Swedish Kronor deposited in a

Swedish bank account can make a Swedish court competent regardless of the value of the claim and without other reference points to Sweden.

There are still a few provisions in Swedish law on recognition and enforcement of foreign judgments in situations where the applicant cannot invoke the Lugano Convention. Such provisions can be found in Swedish family law, in legislation on rights of succession and in a number of Acts dealing with very specific topics. Among the latter can be mentioned the Nuclear Responsibility Act and the International Railway Traffic Act.

Finally, it is worth noticing that there are situations where a foreign judgment can be recognised and enforced in Sweden despite lack of support in codified law. This is the case, for instance, when contractual parties have included a valid so-called prorogation clause in their agreement, i.e., a clause empowering a certain court to settle disputes between them. There are also certain provisions for judgment regarding real estate situated outside of Sweden, and for certain resolutions pertaining to aircraft and air traffic as well as patents.

Recognition and enforcement of foreign arbitration awards

The Swedish Arbitration Act takes into account the international conventions to which Sweden is a party. Under this Act, a foreign arbitration award shall be valid in Sweden provided that the following conditions are met:

(1) The arbitration clause is valid according to the law applicable.
(2) The arbitration proceeding has been conducted in a formally correct manner.
(3) The arbitration award does not comprise a resolution which according to Swedish law must be tried by a public court.
(4) Application of the arbitration award does not contravene Swedish *ordre public.*

Enforcement presupposes an application for *exekvatur* with the Svea Court of Appeal.

DISTRAINT AND GARNISHMENT

For these measures to be taken by the Enforcement Services Authority, one must have a judgment or order, be it a judgment or order issued by a Swedish court or by a court in an EC/EFTA member state. It should be stressed that before a judgment issued by a court in an EC or EFTA state can be enforced by the Enforcement Services Authority, it must undergo the enforcement procedure provided for in the Lugano Convention (Articles 31 *et seq.*). Accordingly, an application for a declaration to the effect that the judgment is enforceable must be lodged with the Svea Court of Appeal. It is worth noting in the context of this chapter that the Swedish Enforcement Code in certain cases allows for enforcement of judgments and orders even prior to their coming "into force", i.e., before the leave to appeal time has lapsed or, indeed, even if an appeal has been made. To avoid enforcement, the debtor must then put up security, pending the final, legally definitive outcome of the case.

BANKRUPTCY AND LIQUIDATION

The Swedish Bankruptcy Act permits an application for bankruptcy to be tried in Sweden if the debtor has forum in Sweden. Normal Swedish forum rules apply, which means that, for instance, *forum rei sitae* constitutes competence also for a bankruptcy petition. It is worth noticing that the forum rules of the Lugano Convention do not apply to bankruptcy.

Swedish law distinguishes between so-called "domicile" and so-called "special" bankruptcy. A domicile bankruptcy is founded on the debtor having his permanent residence in Sweden. Such a bankruptcy comprises property situated outside of Sweden,[5] whilst a special bankruptcy, founded for instance on *forum rei sitae*, comprises only Swedish assets.

In a domicile bankruptcy, the Swedish bankruptcy receiver is, of course, dependent on international procedural law in the countries where the debtor has assets, in order actually to make these part of the Swedish bankruptcy estate. According to a special Act applying to the Nordic countries, the universality principle prevails, which means that a domicile bankruptcy in any of the Nordic countries is, in principle, recognised throughout the Nordic countries.

It is of interest to mention bankruptcy here, since a bankruptcy petition, or even a notice under the Swedish Bankruptcy Act, Chapter 2, section 9—that unless payment of a clear and due debt is made within one week from the notice having been served upon the debtor, a bankruptcy petition may follow—is one of the strongest "provisional measures", or at least pressures, one can use. Especially where the debtor is a large company, perhaps even quoted on the Stock Exchange, the mere threat of a bankruptcy petition being lodged, if the formalities required therefor are fulfilled, usually gives good results without a proper action or an application for a real provisional measure having to be lodged. Often, whilst of course having to be prepared to do so, one need not actually lodge the bankruptcy petition.

In addition, the bankruptcy actually occurring means, of course, that the creditor, at least indirectly, through the receiver, can access the property of the debtor. To succeed with a bankruptcy petition, the creditor must prove that the debtor is insolvent. The Bankruptcy Act contains certain rules of assistance regarding this evidence. A debtor who is under an obligation to keep books, i.e., conducts a business, and who has been urged (by the form of notice described above) to pay a clear and due debt but has omitted to do so within a week from being served, is presumed to be insolvent.

Naturally, one must observe that in the bankruptcy the possibility for the creditor applying for the bankruptcy to get paid will depend, *inter alia*, on the priority his claim enjoys as compared to the priority rights enjoyed by other creditors.

We would also like in this context to stress the difficult position of suppliers in Sweden, Swedish dynamic third-party protection, right *in rem*, being very restrictive in upholding retention of title clauses. Many foreign creditors take losses in Swedish bankruptcies as their arrangements made with the purpose of retaining title are often disallowed, in spite of the same measures possibly being valid in the supplier's own country. This also often, quite naturally, leads to disputes as to what country's law

5. NJA 1956, p. 1.

shall be applied. The Swedish Supreme Court has, in two cases[6] applied Swedish law because the property at the time of the bankruptcy was situated in Sweden. The rights *in rem* are thus usually decided by *lex rei sitae*.

CONCLUSION

We hope that the foregoing discussion may be of use to and benefit readers, whether they are "foreign creditors", their advisers and consultants, or generally interested readers. We stress, however, that, by necessity, the brief outline above is not comprehensive, and we take no responsibility for actions taken on the grounds of what can be found in this chapter. We strongly recommend that, before any action of any sort in any legal matter is taken in Sweden, Swedish legal experts be consulted.

LENNART KANTER
JENS TILLQVIST
MARIA-PIA MIDENBÄCK

6. NJA 1978, p. 593; NJA 1985, p. 879.

CHAPTER 28

SWITZERLAND

INTRODUCTION

The competence of Swiss courts to deal with claims emanating from foreign creditors and litigants is based on the Federal Law of 18 December 1987 on Private International Law (hereafter "PIL"), which entered into effect on 1 January 1989.[1] Those matters which are subject to an international treaty are primarily regulated in the treaties themselves.[2]

JURISDICTION AND PROCEDURAL ASPECTS

How jurisdiction is established

In the absence of specific rules in the PIL or in international treaties, the competence of Swiss courts and other governmental authorities is based on the domicile of the defendant (Article 2, PIL). Domicile is the place where an individual is staying with the intention of doing so permanently, or where a company has the centre of its business activities.

If a forum in Switzerland is not provided for either specifically by the applicable law or based on the domicile of the defendant, and litigation abroad is either impossible or unreasonably difficult, the PIL designates the courts or authorities of that place as competent with which the claim has its closest connection (Article 3, PIL). The definition of the circumstances giving rise to this forum is left to the courts.[3]

The plaintiff who has successfully blocked a defendant's assets in Switzerland by

1. For a French, German, Italian, and English edition, see LDIP-IPRG-LDIP-CPIL, Editions Payot, Lausanne 1989.

2. The Federal Court endorsed an extensive application of the Franco-Swiss Treaty on 21 December 1989, i.e., after the PIL entered into force, in a bankruptcy matter, *Bundesgerichtlicher Entscheid* (hereafter "BGE") 115 III 148, and of the Spanish-Swiss Treaty on 15 February 1990 in a divorce matter, BGE 115 II 390. Considerations of a general nature are found in an earlier decision on the applicability of the Warsaw Convention, BGE 113 II 262.

3. Hans Ulrich Walder, *Einführung in das Internationale Zivilprozessrecht der Schweiz* (Zurich 1989), p. 165, and reference in note 8, suspects that this formula may lead to forum shopping. The Supreme Court of the Canton of Zurich applied rather strict criteria and denied jurisdiction on 27 August 1990 in a divorce matter, *Blätter für Zürcherische Rechtsprechung* (hereafter "BlZR"), vol. 89, Nr. 65. The Rome Convention of 1980 on the Law Applicable to Contractual Obligations contains certain rebuttable presumptions in this respect.

placing an order of attachment (see below) may pursue his claim before the courts of the place where the blocked assets are located (Article 4, PIL).[4] Such *quasi in rem* jurisdiction is subsidiary to the main forum based on domicile, and non-exclusive, as the parties may have agreed to submit the claim to another court or an arbitration tribunal. On 18 February 1992 the Federal Court confirmed that the *quasi in rem* jurisdiction is non-exclusive.[5]

The parties may have agreed on jurisdiction by a Swiss court.[6] Such an agreement must be in writing and is limited to disputes over monetary claims. If either party has its domicile or a sustained presence in the respective canton, or if Swiss law is applicable to the dispute (which again the parties may agree), the court seised may not deny jurisdiction (Article 5, PIL). Even if the Swiss court is prepared to accept jurisdiction, however, this may not be the final criterion: in order to obtain a valid judgment, it is important that the competence of such Swiss court is recognised wherever execution of the judgment is being sought.[7]

If the defendant voluntarily enters into the proceedings, the effect is the same as that of an agreed choice of jurisdiction (Article 6, PIL).

The court seised with a claim is also competent to adjudicate a counterclaim, provided that there is a sufficiently close material connection (over and above a simple set-off) between claim and counterclaim.

Jurisdiction for the various categories of claims

(1) Contractual claims may be pursued at the defendant's domicile (Article 112, paragraph 1, PIL), including a foreign company's Swiss place of business (Article 112, paragraph 2, PIL), or in the absence thereof at the proper place of performance of the contractual obligation (Article 113, PIL).[8] An employee may sue his employer at the normal place of work or at his own domicile or ordinary residence (Article 115, paragraphs 1 and 2, PIL).

(2) Actions in tort may be brought before the court at the defendant's domicile, ordinary place of stay, or place of business and—in their absence—at the location where the tortious act was committed or had its principal effect (Article 129, PIL). Special rules apply to claims resulting from traffic accidents which have an international dimension.

(3) Claims based on company law are brought before the courts of the company's legal domicile (Article 151, PIL).

(4) In the matter of forced execution in Switzerland, the forum is created by the special laws pertaining thereto, even if one of the parties is domiciled abroad. The PIL does not apply.[9]

4. On 15 January 1991, the Federal Court stated that the PIL has, in fact, adopted the concept prevalent in cantonal law and that therefore no minimum amount of assets blocked was required to obtain jurisdiction, BGE 117 II 90.

5. BGE 118 II 190.

6. Choice of forum, now exclusively governed by the PIL, BGE 116 II 624.

7. Walder, note 3 *supra*, p. 167.

8. In a decision rendered 10 days after the PIL went into effect, the Federal Court confirmed its earlier practice regarding letters of credit, BGE 115 II 67.

9. Walder, note 3 *supra*, p. 184.

Procedural aspects

The PIL is a Swiss Federal Law; compliance is subject to appellate review by the Swiss Federal Court.[10]

Parties domiciled abroad may be required, when filing a claim or an appeal in a Swiss court, to provide security for the cost of proceedings, including the reimbursement of the counterparty's legal expenses. Unless an international treaty, such as the Hague Convention of 1 March 1954 or 25 October 1980 applies, the details of guarantee deposits or bonds are regulated by the cantonal laws on procedures.

The need for imposing such a security is obvious: if judgment is rendered against the foreign party, the winning defendant can collect immediately against the security. If such collection is facilitated by a treaty, the guarantees may not be required.

PROVISIONAL REMEDIES

An application for provisional remedies (sometimes also referred to as interim remedies) is normally but not exclusively made to the court which is competent to decide on the merits of the matter (Article 10, PIL) and must establish a prima facie case that the applicant has a valid claim and would suffer irreparable prejudice if the remedy were denied. Available remedies are contained in a number of laws, and the procedure is entirely governed by cantonal law. Of particular interest are blocking measures, such as orders of attachment.[11]

Provisional and interim measures of a foreign authority are recognised in Switzerland based on the very criteria used for the recognition and enforcement of foreign judgments.[12]

Whether and how the decision of a court to impose the measures may be appealed, is again subject to cantonal law; after local means have been exhausted, the Federal Court may be addressed if principles of due process have been violated.

The court may require the applicant to put up a security. A claim for damages would have to be brought under the law based on which the provisional remedy was being imposed in the first place.

RECOGNITION OF FOREIGN JUDGMENTS

The fundamental requirement for the recognition of a foreign judgment is the competence of the foreign court to decide the case. Recognition in Switzerland is based on the rules of Swiss law on international jurisdiction.

10. The traditional reticence of the Federal Court to review matters with a foreign connection is no longer appropriate when it comes to recognition and execution based on the provisions of the PIL.

11. See the discussion of attachment below.

12. As contained in Arts. 25 to 27 PIL. The Geneva District Court, in a decision rendered on 8 February 1990 and upheld by the Appellate Court, ruled to the contrary; *Semaine Judiciaire*, Vol. 112, p. 196.

The basis for recognition

An international treaty may allocate the jurisdiction of the courts in a manner binding on the parties; the courts must accept jurisdiction based on the treaty (this is referred to as "*convention double*").

Alternatively, the treaty may regulate the mutual enforcement of judgments only and say nothing on which courts are to exercise jurisdiction, as this is left to the parties' internal law ("*convention simple*").

Where no such treaty applies, Swiss law on the recognition of foreign judgments is contained in various parts of the PIL (Article 1, paragraph 2, PIL). The law determines the basis of recognition as well as the implementing procedure (PIL, Articles 25 to 32).

Recognition based on treaties

The Warsaw Convention of 1929[13] allows contractual claims against an air transport carrier to be brought at the domicile of the carrier, or at the carrier's place of business where the ticket was purchased, or at the point of destination of the journey. The Uniform Rules on International Rail Transport of 1980 provide for jurisdiction by the courts of the railroad's country of domicile for claims other than personal injury claims which may be brought before the court at the place of accident. Further multilateral treaties structured as *conventions doubles* were concluded by Switzerland to unify the rules applicable to collisions between ships in 1952, and for the protection of minors in 1969.

The Lugano Convention on Jurisdiction and on the Enforcement of Judgments in Civil and Commercial Matters, which was signed between the member states of the European Community (EC) and the European Free Trade Association (EFTA) in September 1988 and has become the most important treaty after entering into effect in January 1992, will be dealt with below.

Bilateral treaties in the form of *conventions doubles* are in force between Switzerland and France (1869/1935, but see below) and the US (1855, estate matters only).

The New York Convention of 1958 (limited to arbitral awards), The Hague Conventions of 1905 and 1954 (on civil procedural law), of 1958 (concerning decisions on child support), of 1970 (regarding marital separation and divorce), of 15 November 1965 (on service of documents), of 18 March 1970 (on taking of evidence), and of 25 October 1980 (concerning access to courts), are multilateral *conventions simples*.

Spain (1896), Czech Republic (1926), Slovakia (1926), Germany (1929), Italy (1933), Sweden (1936), Belgium (1959), Austria (1960) and Liechtenstein (1968) have each concluded a bilateral *convention simple* with Switzerland.

Recognition based on the PIL

Recognition and ensuing execution of foreign awards in Switzerland presupposes a decision (in a civil matter) which emanates from a court of law or any other competent public office (Article 26, PIL, refers to "authority"). A settlement in court and the

13. See BGE 113 II 262, note 2 *supra*.

acceptance or withdrawal of the claim before a court are considered the equivalent of a judgment if that is also the case at the place where the suit was filed and decided, settled, or terminated by acquiescence. The same is true for decisions resulting from non-contentious jurisdiction (Article 31, PIL).

Although provisional remedies are not mentioned in the PIL, the following stipulations would apply to them by analogy.[14]

The competence of the court or authority, a prerequisite for the recognition of its decision, may be established on any of the following bases:

(1) the defendant has its domicile in the state where the decision was rendered, or the PIL itself specifically refers to the particular jurisdiction;

(2) the parties to a dispute in a pecuniary matter have agreed on such jurisdiction in due and proper form;

(3) the defendant, again in a pecuniary matter, accepts service without reservations; or

(4) a counterclaim is properly connected with the claim brought before the same court.

To be recognised, a judgment or decision must have the following characteristics:

(1) It must be final, i.e., not subject to any ordinary legal remedy such as an appeal (Article 25, lit. b., PIL).[15]

(2) It has to be compatible with the Swiss *ordre public* (Article 27, paragraph 1, PIL).[16]

(3) It must result from due process (Article 27, paragraph 2, PIL, lists as violations thereof lack of proper service, refusal to give the defendant his day in court,[17] or failure to consider an objection based on *res iudicata*).[18]

Recognition will be sought at the court which is competent to rule on execution; moreover, it may be raised in another court as a preliminary question if the result has an impact on the proceedings before it (Article 29, paragraph 3, PIL). If the statutory requirements are met, the plaintiff has a right that the foreign award is recognised.[19]

Special stipulations provide for the recognition of foreign decisions if they were rendered (a) at the place of proper performance in contractual matters (but only if the defendant was not domiciled in Switzerland, Article 149, paragraph 2, lit. a., PIL); or (b) at the ordinary place of work if an employment contract is at issue (Article 148, paragraph 2, lit. c., PIL); or (c) at the place of registration of a business if the claim

14. See note 12 *supra*.

15. Supreme Court of the Canton of Zurich of 11 July 1989, BlZR, vol. 88, Nr. 37, point 3.

16. *Ibid.*, point 5. In an interesting decision, the Basle Civil Court ruled, on 1 February 1989, that punitive damages were not incompatible with the Swiss *ordre public, Basler Juristische Mitteilungen 1991*, p. 31; The Swiss *ordre public* is violated, *inter alia*, if process is served on the Swiss defendant one day before the hearing takes place (Decision of the Federal Court of 17 October 1991, BGE 117 Ib 350). In contrast, an award that was rendered in absentiam is compatible with the Swiss *ordre public* although the final award does not contain the reasoning of the court (Decision of the Federal Court of 19 December 1990, BGE 116 II 631).

17. See note 15 *supra*, point 5.

18. The Zurich Commercial Court decided, on 19 October 1990, that if, as, and when the foreign court has accepted jurisdiction at the time that the claim was submitted to a Swiss court, the latter must not accept the case, BlZR vol. 89, Nr. 58.

19. On 19 January 1994 the Federal Court recognised the final award by the Superior Court of California for the County of Los Angeles since the award satisfied the requirements set forth in Art. 27, paras. 1 and 2, PIL. The Court opined that the number of requirements referred to therein is exhaustive as a matter of statutory law, BGE 120 II 85.

results from the operation of that business (Article 148, paragraph 2, lit. d., PIL); or (d) for claims based on tort at the place where the act was committed or the damage resulted (again only if the defendant was not domiciled in Switzerland, Article 148, paragraph 2, lit. f., PIL). Decisions in matters of company law are recognised if they were rendered at the company's domicile and are recognised there, and provided that the defendant was not domiciled in Switzerland (Article 165, paragraph 1, PIL).

Procedural matters

Only judgments which are properly certified and documented as final and resulting from due process are eligible (Article 29, PIL), and their recognition and execution must be pronounced by the court at the defendant's domicile or at the place where a claim which gave rise to an order of attachment was being properly pursued.

Proceedings in a foreign court—even before the rendering of a final award—will cause the suspension of a claim on the same grounds and between the same parties in Switzerland, if the foreign decision when rendered is apt to be recognised.[20]

Decisions on the recognition of a foreign judgment are either based on a treaty or a federal law (the PIL), and are therefore subject to full appellate review by the Swiss Federal Court, even if they were not themselves based on Swiss (federal) law. Execution, by contrast, is based on cantonal law and subject only to limited review (violation of the stipulations on due process contained in the Federal Constitution).

DEBT COLLECTION

The Swiss Federal Law on Debt Collection and Bankruptcy of 1889 (hereafter "DCB") applies to monetary obligations only. For our purposes, it constitutes the centre piece of statutory law on legal remedies in Switzerland against debtors. It not only provides the remedies for the enforcement of judgments, but also facilitates the collection of debts which are properly documented in qualified writing (Article 82, DCB).

Cantonal statutes governing civil procedure designate the judicial authorities competent to deal with certain actions provided for in the DCB.

Concerning the enforcement of foreign awards, the DCB contains, however, only one stipulation, in Article 81, paragraph 3, determining that if a judgment was rendered in a foreign country with which a treaty on the mutual enforcement of judgments is in force, the judgment debtor may avail himself of the defences provided for in such treaty (the countries with whom Switzerland has entered into bilateral or multilateral enforcement treaties are listed above). Generally, this clause is interpreted to make all foreign monetary awards just like domestic money judgments subject to the DCB.

20. See Oscar Vogel, President of the Zurich Supreme Court, in *Schweiz Juristenzeitung*, Vol. 86 (1990), pp. 77 *et seq.*; on 18 January 1992 the Federal Court held that the suspension of the court proceedings in Switzerland will be ordered unless there is reason to believe that the pertinent proceedings in a foreign court in the foreseeable future will not result in an award that is apt to be recognised, BGE 118 II 188.

Disputes arising out of cross-border enforcement, however, tend to be settled out of court, which leaves comparatively little scope for judge-made law.

The procedure

The cantonal authorities carrying out the actions under the DCB are designated in the law itself, which also requires one or two supervisory authorities whose decisions are in turn subject to review by the Federal Court's Bankruptcy Division (Articles 17 to 21, DCB). The procedure is characterised by an intricately interwoven assortment of administrative and judicial authorities and remedies.

The provisional attachment or garnishment, hereafter referred to as "attachment", often a preliminary step in a creditor's efforts to seek or enforce a judgment, is regulated by the DCB in Articles 271 *et seq.* When it comes to "attacking foreign assets" in Switzerland, it may be the only means of first obtaining jurisdiction and subsequently successfully executing a favourable award.

The DCB, and in particular its provisions regulating the attachment, have been amended recently. The amendments are scheduled to go into effect on 1 January 1997. The changes in part reflect current case law and the policies of most courts issuing orders of attachment. In addition to codifying existing practices, the new statutory language strengthens the position of the debtor.

The request for an order of attachment is made in summary proceedings, depending upon the jurisdiction involved either verbally or in writing, to the court in whose territory the assets are located. In order to obtain an order of attachment, the creditor must meet the following requirements:

(1) The creditor has to establish in a manner plausible to the court that he has a liquid claim for money (Article 272, paragraph 1, DCB). The price to be paid if the attachment is ultimately held to have been unjustified is compensation due to the defendant.[21]

(2) The creditor further has to establish one of several grounds for an attachment of assets (Article 272, paragraph 1, DCB).

An attachment is granted in particular if the debtor removes himself or his assets from Switzerland in order to escape his obligations or if successful earlier procedures of execution have ended up in a certified loss (Article 271, paragraph 1, DCB). Under the new statutory language it will become more difficult to invoke the ground that hitherto was resorted to most frequently: The fact for the debtor to have no domicile or place of business in Switzerland as such and in itself will no longer be a sufficient ground. The absence of a Swiss domicile will be a sufficient ground only provided the debt is evidenced in a written document in due and proper form or if the debt has a *nexus* with Switzerland (Article 271, paragraph 1, DCB, as amended).

(3) The creditor finally has to establish that assets belonging to the debtor are available (Article 272, paragraph 1, DCB).

Under the current regime the possibilities for the debtor to oppose the attachment are

21. Art. 273, DCB; Federal Court in BGE 115 III 125 and 112 III 112. If the attachment is outright abusive, it will upon appeal be disallowed, BGE 112 III 47.

limited. He may lift the attachment by providing his own security (Article 277, DCB). The debtor further may lodge a complaint with the Federal Court if the authority in granting the attachment has acted arbitrarily or has violated an international treaty or the immunity of a foreign government.[22] If there were no grounds for the order or if the debt is secured by a pledge or mortgage, the debtor may file a motion to lift the attachment. It must be filed within five days of receipt of the order and it results in a ruling on a mere procedural issue subject to appeal to the Federal Court for violation of due process only.[23]

Under the new statute, the debtor and any party whose rights the attachment affects may lodge, within ten days, an opposition against the attachment order (Article 278, DCB, as amended). The cognisance of the court is meant to be large: The debtor or the third party may submit, e.g., that there are no valid grounds for the attachment, that the claim is without merit, or that the claim is otherwise secured. A complaint with the Federal Court to the effect that the authority in granting the attachment has acted arbitrarily or has violated an international treaty or the immunity of a foreign government continues to be possible.

In order to prevent the attachment from lapsing, the creditor must pursue his claim within 10 days of the attachment order having been executed (Article 278, DCB; Article 279, DCB, as amended).[24]

For the pursuit of his claim, the creditor has several options. If he has not already done so, he would ask for the execution of his claim in administrative proceedings (*Betreibung* in German, *poursuite* in French, a device peculiar to the DCB), and if opposed by the debtor, pursue his claim within 10 days in summary judicial proceedings (Article 278, paragraph 2, DCB: *Rechtsöffnung/mainlevée*). If execution is not granted, the creditor has again 10 days to deposit a claim in ordinary proceedings.

If the creditor is successful at any one of the stages outlined above, the assets under attachment may be used to satisfy his claim.

If the debtor obtains a ruling that either the creditor has no valid claim or there were no grounds for an attachment of his assets, he may claim compensation for damage suffered in his credit standing or resulting from the blocking of the assets (Article 273, DCB).[25] Negligence or wilful misconduct on the creditor's part is not a prerequisite, but—if proven—may lead to additional compensation due.

If the defendant has removed his assets before the creditor is in a position to attach them, the creditor may, subject to certain conditions, obtain a ruling from the court which seeks to restore the *status quo ante*. The action is based on the disposal of assets

22. Switzerland has signed but not yet ratified the European Convention on the Immunity of States, and it has no explicit statutory provisions on sovereign immunity. Nevertheless, when performing governmental functions serving a public purpose, a state or governmental entity may invoke sovereign immunity based on public international law which is upheld by Swiss courts.

23. Federal Court in BGE 97 I 683.

24. This may be done in a foreign court (Federal Court in BGE 114 II 188). Where the Lugano Convention or a bilateral treaty applies, the pursuing action must be brought in a foreign court.

25. The duration of the non-availability of the assets and the cost of borrowing an equivalent amount, as well as the interest the blocked assets may be producing during this period will be considered (Federal Court in BGE 113 III 102, point 11a) and b)). If both parties to the attachment procedure agree on how the blocked assets are to be invested, the office holding them has to comply with such instructions provided they contain all the necessary elements (Supreme Court of Zurich on 10 December 1990, BlZR, vol. 89, Nr. 119).

by an over-indebted defendant by way of donation, by fraudulent preference of creditors or by other actions designed to cause prejudice to the creditor (Article 288, DCB).[26]

Whether or not the creditor resorts to an attachment of the debtor's assets, actual execution commences when he requests the competent authority to issue an "order to pay" to the debtor (Article 69, DCB), who may formally oppose the order within 10 days (Article 74, DCB).[27] If he does not,[28] or if the debt is evidenced by a written document in due and proper form, execution will be pursued in summary proceedings; in all other cases, the claim is relegated to the ordinary court. A last resort of the debtor against execution through summary proceedings is an ordinary court action for declaratory judgment that there is no valid debt or claim.

If all defences of the debtor in summary or ordinary proceedings have been overcome, the creditor will either seek to realise security he may have in hand, or seize specific assets of the debtor, or commence bankruptcy proceedings if the debtor is registered in the commercial register (Article 39, DCB).

If a debt is secured by assets, whether movables or immovables, the debtor may insist that execution be carried out only by first utilising such assets. The creditor may nevertheless seek to execute by other means if the debt consists of interests or annuities secured by a mortgage, or if the debt results from a cheque or bill of exchange, or if the creditor releases the security, or if he pursues ordinary execution with the debtor's agreement.

In the forced execution of an unsecured debt, the creditors will seek to seize assets the sale of which will satisfy their claim, or institute bankruptcy proceedings which will result in all of the debtor's assets being sold off. The law determines the sequence in which assets are to be sold (Article 95, DCB)[29] and that part of income or property which the debtor and his family need in order to survive (Article 93, DCB).[30]

For every unpaid claim, the creditor receives a certificate of loss (Article 115, DCB).

THE LUGANO CONVENTION

The Convention on Jurisdiction and the Enforcement of Judgments in Civil and Commercial Matters of 16 September 1988 has been signed by 10 EC countries and five members of EFTA; as of 1 March 1995 the Convention had entered into force for Germany, Spain, France, The Netherlands, Luxembourg, Great Britain, Portugal, Italy, Sweden, Finland, Norway, Ireland, and Switzerland.[31]

26. The right of action under Art. 288, DCB, expires if the creditor could have attacked a transfer of assets between spouses under Art. 188, Civil Code, but decided not to do so (Federal Court in BGE 111 III 43).

27. No strict formal criteria are applied to this "opposition", which simply has to make clear that the alleged debtor does not acknowledge the debt (Federal Court in BGE 108 III 6).

28. Even if the debtor erroneously failed to register opposition, there is no remedy against the follow-up by summary proceedings (Federal Court in BGE 113 III 2).

29. Assets that had been attached are sold off last, Art. 95, para. 3, DCB.

30. There is ample jurisprudence on this aspect; see, for a succinct analysis of the purpose of this provision, the Federal Court's decision rendered on 5 September 1989, BGE 115 III 45.

31. For a detailed analysis, see Ivo Schwander (ed.), *Das Lugano-Uebereinkommen* (St. Gallen 1990).

Superseding treaties and the PIL

The Lugano Convention will supersede, in all subject matters it covers, the treaties between Switzerland and those countries which have ratified the Convention; thus far, this applies to the Franco-Swiss Treaty of 1869/1935.

The PIL will continue to govern issues of jurisdiction and enforcement outside the scope of the Lugano Convention, and will remain fully applicable in disputes relating to countries which are not (yet) a party to or have not (yet) ratified the Convention.

The issue of domicile

There is no definition of "domicile" in the Convention. The court seised with an action under the Lugano Convention must first apply its own national law; if the defendant is found not to be domiciled in the forum country, the national laws of the other member states of the Convention will be applied in order to determine this issue.

Although the Lugano Convention maintains the basic principle that proceedings shall be brought before the courts of the defendant's domicile, the exceptions to that rule have the effect of significantly curtailing the constitutional privilege of a debtor in Switzerland to be sued at his domicile (Article 59 of the Federal Constitution).[32]

From a commercial perspective, the most important designations of a place of jurisdiction other than the defendant's domicile are:

(1) the proper place of performance of a contractual obligation;
(2) the place where a tort was committed;
(3) the place where criminal proceedings are taking place, if the same court is competent to deal with civil claims resulting from the acts being tried;
(4) the place of establishment of a branch office, agency and the like; and
(5) under specific rules, the place of action for certain insurance claims and consumer protection rights.

If the court has jurisdiction over a particular dispute, it will be competent to deal with an action against a joint defendant, with counterclaims and third-party actions based on the same legal grounds.

Before Lugano, any defendant without domicile in Switzerland could be sued there, namely at the place where his assets were found and attached. Such long-arm jurisdiction is no longer admitted where the defendant is domiciled in a member state of the Lugano Convention.[33] However, the Convention does not bar the plaintiff to pursue the attachment, in a first stage, by requesting the competent authority to issue an "order to pay" to the creditor.[34]

The parties may confer exclusive jurisdiction to the courts of their choice by agreement in writing which conforms to general usage in international commerce or to their own established practice.[35] Such choice must not, however, conflict with any

32. Even before the Lugano Convention, any forum clearly established by federal law, whether in a statute or developed by jurisprudence, could effectively deactivate this constitutional guarantee (Federal Court in BGE 109 Ia 53).

33. Art. 3 of the Convention contains an explicit reference to the Swiss forum based on an attachment.

34. See Decision of the Federal Court of 1 July 1994, BGE 120 III 92.

35. Lugano Convention, Art. 17, para. 1.b). Compare Art. 5, PIL, which simply refers to an agreement "in writing, by telegram, telex, telecopier, or by any other means of communication which evidences the terms of the agreement by a text".

of the Convention's rules on exclusive jurisdiction. If a defendant accepts service other than for the purpose of moving for dismissal for lack of jurisdiction, jurisdiction is established.

Exclusive jurisdiction is reserved for the courts:

(1) of the place where property is located for disputes over rights *in rem*.[36]
(2) of the place of registration for patent and trademark matters and proceedings concerning public registers[37]; and
(3) of the place of enforcement for all matters concerning the enforcement of judgments.

The first court in which an action is filed having accepted jurisdiction, all other courts will have to decline to deal with the same cause of action between the same parties.[38]

Recognition and enforcement of foreign awards

To the extent that the Lugano Convention applies, foreign judgments (including interlocutory and provisional measures not obtained *ex parte*) will be recognised and enforced upon simple application by a party and without special procedure.

Recognition and enforcement may, however, be opposed as being in violation either of *ordre public*, or of the principle of due process, or of an earlier judgment in the same matter and between the same parties which is capable of enforcement in the same state.

Swiss reservations

Until the end of 1999, Switzerland will not be obligated under the Lugano Convention to recognise or enforce foreign judgments rendered against a defendant domiciled in Switzerland, if such jurisdiction is claimed at the place of contractual performance and the defendant had not waived his constitutional right to be sued at his domicile.[39]

Switzerland will not allow service of foreign official documents in a manner other than that provided for in the applicable cantonal and federal law (which, as a rule, means communications through diplomatic channels).[40]

CONCLUSION

The special debt collection procedures under Swiss law, when combined with an attachment order, the use of which has vastly increased over the last two decades,

36. Lugano Convention, Art. 16, para. 1.a), compare Art. 97, PIL.

37. Lugano Convention, Art. 16, para. 3; compare Arts PIL, 109, 110 and 111, para. 2, PIL, and the interesting considerations in the Supreme Court of Zurich's decision of 15 October 1990, BlZR Vol. 89, Nr. 103.

38. See note 18 *supra*.

39. Gerardo Broggini in Schwander, note 31 *supra*, p. 130.

40. Art. 271 of the Swiss Criminal Code, which prohibits acts performed in Switzerland on behalf of a foreign state and in violation of the jurisdiction of the competent Swiss authority, will remain in force.

render an attack on assets in Switzerland comparatively easy to accomplish. Indeed, if the assets of a party not domiciled in Switzerland can be found and blocked by attachment, a Swiss forum for the underlying claim can thereby be created.

The most significant change in this context will be brought about by the Lugano Convention as it is being ratified by more and more signatory states and becoming applicable to an increasing portion of Europe. Under the Convention, the forum created by an attachment may no longer be imposed on parties domiciled in a member country.

DANIEL URECH

SANDRO VISINI

CHAPTER 29

TAIWAN

INTRODUCTION

This chapter will provide a brief note on the attacking of assets by a foreign creditor in Taiwan, Republic of China (ROC), from the following perspectives:

(1) What is the nature of the ROC court system? To what extent are the courts available to foreign creditors and litigants?

(2) What devices are available under ROC law to provide remedies to the creditors on debt collection?

(3) To what extent are foreign judgments recognised in this jurisdiction?

(4) What types of remedy are available in this jurisdiction to foreign creditors?

THE COURT SYSTEM

The ROC court system is quite different from the common-law courts, and many of the procedures which exist in the common-law courts either do not exist or are not often used in the ROC courts. The following synopsis of procedures in the ROC courts is intended to give a brief overview of such procedures and thereby demystify the litigation process for those who have never litigated in the ROC. It is not, however, intended to be, and is not, a complete summary of the entire ROC Code of Civil Procedure, and the way in which the procedures can be used will obviously vary from case to case.

ROC litigation—preliminary matters

The ROC court system consists of the District Courts, the High Courts, and the Supreme Court. The District Court is the trial court and is a court of general jurisdiction. Appeals to the High Court are a matter of right in the ROC. Appeals to the Supreme Court are limited by statute and require that the judgment made by the High Court be contrary to law or ordinances.[1]

The legal system in the ROC is a civil law system, based on the German model. The law is set forth in a series of codes which collectively are called the "Six Books of the Law". Legal matters are decided by reference to the codes and to the writings of

1. Code of Civil Procedure, Art. 467 provides that: "No appeal may be made against a judgment passed by the court of first appeal, unless it is based on the ground that the judgment is contrary to laws or ordinances."

scholars and judges who interpret the codes. There is very little judge-made law in the ROC.

The ROC court system also follows the German model. Procedures are inquisitorial rather than adversarial, and judges are active participants in the trial process.

The most important requirements to note in connection with the commencement of any litigation in the ROC are the requirement of a court bond and a power of attorney in favour of the attorneys who will be handling the case.

Under Article 2 of the ROC Code of Civil Procedure Fees, the plaintiff in a civil action in the ROC is required to pay a fee to the court in the amount of 1% of the value of the claim. The fee is refunded in the event that the defendant loses and pays the court fees pursuant to the order of the court. Court fees are usually paid in cash, though they can be posted in the form of cash equivalents such as negotiable certificates of deposit and ROC government securities.[2] Court fees must be denominated in New Taiwan Dollars.

A lawyer may appear in court only pursuant to a power of attorney executed in the lawyer's favour by his client.[3] If the party is a foreign person, the power of attorney must be notarised by someone who is authorised to take oaths in the relevant jurisdiction, and then legalised by the relevant ROC governmental entity in the jurisdiction of execution. In the United States, for example, a power of attorney would have to be legalised by the ROC Co-ordination Council for North American Affairs.

A party commences litigation in the ROC court system by filing a complaint with the relevant District Court. The complaint must be accompanied by supporting documentation.[4] In the event that the supporting documentation is in a language other than Chinese, translations must be provided. The court does not translate documents; all translations must be provided by the parties.

A verdict may be secured in approximately four to six months from the commencement of the action. An appeal may be filed by either party with the High Court within 20 days after the date on which a judgment is served on the party.

The High Court usually reaches a decision in approximately four to six months. Likewise, a dissatisfied party may institute an appeal with the Supreme Court within 20 days upon receipt of a decision from the High Court.[5] The Supreme Court may finally decide the case in merit or remand the case to the High Court for reconsideration. If the case is finally decided by the Supreme Court, the decision is final and binding. However, if the case is remanded, it may also take approximately four to six months for the High Court to amend the original decision.

If either party is dissatisfied with the High Court's decision upon remand from the Supreme Court, again, appeal may be made to the Supreme Court. This process may be repeated several times.

2. *Ibid.*, Art. 102.

3. *Ibid.*, Art. 69.

4. According to Art. 116 of the Code of Civil Procedure, the complaint of a party shall specify the following particulars: (1) the full name, age, occupation, and place of domicile, or place of residence, of the party; in case of a legal entity or corporate body, its name and the place of its office or business establishment; (2) the full name, age, occupation, and place of domicile, or place of residence, of the statutory agent or agent *ad litem*, if any; (3) the subject matter of the action; (4) the allegations or statements required to be made therein; (5) the evidences to be used as proof or explanation; (6) the annexed documents and the number thereof; (7) the court; (8) the date.

5. See Code of Civil Procedure, Art. 440.

It is worth noting that a court award is in New Taiwan Dollars and is generally not repatriable.

ROC litigation and the foreign plaintiff

In a case which involves a foreign plaintiff, the following issues are often raised by the defendant.

Additional court fees

At the first hearing, the defendant has the right to demand that a foreign plaintiff which has no domicile, residence, or business establishment in the jurisdiction be required to post a bond in the amount of an additional 3% of the claim.[6] The purpose of the additional bond is to secure court fees for potential appeals to the High Court (1.5%) and Supreme Court (1.5%). Once the defendant makes this motion, it is generally granted and the plaintiff is generally not given the opportunity to argue, except to refute the contention that it has no presence in the jurisdiction. On the other hand, some attorneys fail to move for an increase in the bond. If the defendant's attorney begins arguing the case prior to making the motion for an increased bond, the defendant is deemed to have waived the issue.[7]

In the event that the plaintiff is ordered to post an additional bond for court fees and fails to do so, the defendant is no longer required to argue the case. The court then issues an order for the posting of the bond. The proceedings will be adjourned until the plaintiff posts the additional bond.[8] If the bond is not posted within a reasonable time, the complaint is dismissed.

Status of the plaintiff

Another argument which is sometimes encountered at the first hearing is that the plaintiff has no legal existence and that it has no standing to bring the lawsuit. For example, the defendant may argue that the plaintiff is not in good standing in its jurisdiction of incorporation. The defendant may also argue that the plaintiff has no standing to bring this particular lawsuit.

In the event that the defendant raises these arguments, the court would probably require the plaintiff to provide the court with documentary evidence that the plaintiff is in good standing and that it has standing to bring the lawsuit. Examples of evidence which would be sufficient to rebut these allegations might be a good standing certificate from the country of incorporation or a legal opinion from an attorney who is licensed to practice law in the country of incorporation.

Status of the plaintiff's "statutory representative"

The "statutory representative" of the plaintiff is the person who signs the power of attorney in favour of the law firm handling the matter. The defendant may argue that

6. *Ibid.*, Art. 96.
7. *Ibid.*, Art. 97.
8. *Ibid.*, Art. 98.

said person is not the statutory representative and that the power of attorney is therefore invalid. Again, the plaintiff would be required to provide documentary evidence that the person who signed the power of attorney had the power to do so under the laws of the country of incorporation.

Counterclaims

The defendant may present counterclaims at the first hearing, either orally or in writing. The defendant may also allege a set-off, though a set-off can be alleged at any time prior to the end of proceedings at the first level of appeal. The counterclaim must be presented to the court prior to the conclusion of oral argument at the first hearing or it is deemed to have been waived. The defendant must post a bond in the amount of 1% of the amount of its counterclaim as security for the court costs involved in litigating the counterclaim. The plaintiff is not required to post any bond in connection with the counterclaim.

Applicable law and settlement

The two other issues which are often raised at the first hearing relate to the applicable law and settlement of the case. With regard to the former, the choice of applicable law is determined in accordance with the ROC Law Governing the Application of Laws to Civil Matters Involving Foreign Elements. With regard to the latter, it is not unusual for the judge to request the parties to settle the case at the first hearing, in accordance with Article 377 of the ROC Code of Civil Procedure.[9] Judges in complicated cases are often anxious to have the parties settle.

Payment order

In the event that an action of debt collection is considered to be simple in nature and the creditor has a reasonable chance to win the case, a possibly simpler and more economic proceeding can be adopted. Article 508 of the ROC Code of Civil Procedure states that:

> If the claim of the creditor is one for the payment or delivery of a definite amount or quantity of money or other fungibles, or valuable securities, an application may be made to the court, praying that an order for payment be issued in accordance with the provisions relating to hortatory proceedings.

Under the above Article, the court shall give a ruling to the application for an order for payment without examining the debtor. If the debtor does not file an objection within 20 days after his receipt of the order, the court order for payment would become final and conclusive. However, if the debtor files an objection within the statutory period, the court order for payment will lose its effect and the application by the creditor for the order for payment shall be deemed as the institution of an action.[10]

9. Art. 377 of the Code of Civil Procedure states that: "Irrespective of the stage of the proceedings reached, the court may, in the course of oral proceedings, attempt to bring the parties to a compromise or cause a commissioned judge or a requested judge to do the same, when it is considered that there is hope for compromise."

10. *Ibid.*, Arts. 508–521.

In the event that no motion of objection is made, the next step to be taken is to request the Enforcement Department of the District Court to attach the assets of the debtor.

ATTACHMENT OF PROPERTY

Prior to the commencement of the civil litigation, to safeguard against the possibility that there are no assets from which to obtain satisfaction, a plaintiff may apply for provisional attachment of the defendant's assets.[11] Such an attachment requires the posting of a bond in an amount equal to one-third of the claim. No difference will be made between local and foreign creditors in the application for a provisional attachment, except that a higher bond may be required if the applicant is a foreigner with no assets in the ROC.

Provisional attachment of the property

A provisional attachment may be filed against any property of the defendant which is found in the ROC. A provisional attachment may generally be obtained within three to seven days of the filing of the request for provisional attachment with the court. A request for provisional attachment may generally be filed, and may generally be issued by the court, without notice to the defendant.

In addition to filing a request for a provisional attachment, the ROC courts usually require that a bond be posted by the applicant. The amount of the bond, which must be denominated in New Taiwan Dollars, can range from a nominal amount to the entire value of the claim. If a foreigner with no assets in the ROC applies for a provisional attachment, it is possible that an ROC court would require a bond in the full amount of the claim. In practice, the amount of the bond is generally about one-third of the claim.

The form of the bond which must be posted is somewhat different from that which is acceptable in Western courts. Since insurance companies are not permitted to post bonds in the ROC, it is usually necessary to obtain a certificate of deposit or other such security from a local bank or the local branch of a foreign bank.

In the event that the applicant does not have an existing relationship with a local bank, it may be possible to obtain the necessary security from the local branch of a foreign bank by pledging a deposit in the requisite amount with an offshore branch of the foreign bank and having the onshore branch issue the necessary security.

The applicant is generally given a certain amount of time to post the bond. An ROC court will not issue an order for provisional attachment in the absence of a bond. Moreover, if the provisional attachment proceeding is filed prior to the filing of an *in personam* action against the owner of the attached property, the court may, upon the application of the owner, order that the *in personam* action be filed within a short time after the issuance of the provisional attachment. If the *in personam* action is not filed within the requisite time frame, the attachment will terminate.[12]

11. *Ibid.*, Art. 522 states that: "With a view to safe-guarding the compulsory execution of a money claim or of a claim convertible to a money claim the creditor may apply for provisional seizure. The application above provided may also be made with regard to a claim not yet due for performance."

12. *Ibid.*, Art. 529.

Filing of the *in personam* action

The documents required for the filing of an *in personam* action are the following:

(1) power of attorney in favour of the legal representative (the attorneys handling the litigation); and

(2) statement of facts setting forth a very general statement of the claim against the defendant and the relief sought.

The plaintiff in an *in personam* action is also required to deposit with the court an initial court fee in the amount of 1% of the amount of the claim. If the plaintiff prevails, he will be able to recover the court fees from the defendant. Attorneys' fees are not recoverable unless provided for by contract between the plaintiff and the defendant.

The initial court fees for both levels of appeal in the ROC court system are 1.5% of the amount of the claim. If the plaintiff is a foreigner with no office, residence or assets in the ROC, the defendant can request that the plaintiff be required to deposit an additional 3% of the amount of the claim. This deposit represents security for court fees in the event that the foreign plaintiff is successful in the District Court but fails to prevail on the subsequent appeal.

A civil suit in the ROC begins in the District Court and usually results in an initial verdict within four to six months of the filing of the action. The ROC court system is inquisitorial rather than adversarial and the judges are generally not licensed attorneys. Once a verdict has been reached, the losing party has 20 days to appeal to the High Court. Appeals are also permitted from the High Court to the ROC Supreme Court.

ENFORCEABILITY OF FOREIGN COURT JUDGMENTS

Pursuant to Article 43 of the Compulsory Execution Law, a final foreign judgment creditor may apply to the ROC court for a judgment permitting the enforcement of the foreign judgment. The enforcement may be carried out only when the requirements of Article 402 of the Code of Civil Procedures are satisfied.

Article 402 of the Code of Civil Procedures states that a foreign judgment must fulfil the following requirements to be enforceable in the ROC:

(1) The foreign court rendering the judgment shall have jurisdiction over the dispute in question according to the laws of the ROC.

(2) If the party defeated is a national of the ROC, he must have responded to the action brought against him; however, this does not apply where service is made in the country where the court rendering the judgment is located, or where service is effected through the judicial assistance of the ROC.

(3) The foreign judgment is not contrary to the public order or good morals of the ROC.

(4) Judgments given by ROC courts are reciprocally recognised by the foreign country concerned.

Does a foreign court have jurisdiction?

The ROC courts would apply the jurisdictional tests set forth in Articles 1 to 15 of the Code of Civil Procedure in determining whether or not a foreign court has jurisdiction; the foreign court's jurisdictional rules are irrelevant for these purposes.

As the ROC courts' view of jurisdiction is quite broad, except under unusual circumstances, it is unlikely that an ROC court would conclude that a foreign court did not have jurisdiction.

Was there effective service of process?

Section 2 of Article 402 of the Code of Civil Procedure provides that a foreign judgment is unenforceable if the defendant is a citizen of the ROC and did not respond to the action. However, this principle does not apply where summons or orders necessary for the commencement of action have been served on the parties themselves in that country or have been served on them in the ROC through the judicial assistance of the ROC. By "judicial assistance of the ROC" it is meant that service has been effected through diplomatic channels pursuant to the ROC's Law Governing the Extension of Assistance to Foreign Courts.

Public order and good morals

It is unlikely that any case involving a commercial transaction for recovery of a debt will give rise to a defence based on public order or good morals.

Note that there is a Supreme Court precedent in the ROC which provides that since gambling is contrary to the public order and good morals of the ROC, any claim arising out of gambling is unenforceable in the ROC courts.

Reciprocity

Recognition by a foreign court of ROC court judgments can be proved by the existence of treaties, custom or a foreign country's law. The precise scope of recognition need not be the same as that granted by ROC courts to foreign judgments, but the major principles should be the same. Formal diplomatic relations or treaties are not a requirement for meeting the reciprocity requirement.

Article VII of the 1948 Treaty of Commerce, Friendship and Navigation between the ROC and the US provides that the nationals, corporations and associations of either party "shall enjoy freedom of access to the courts of justice ... in the territories of the other party". Notwithstanding this provision, recognition of US judgments is presumably still subject to the rule of reciprocity. However, US judgments have been recognised in Taiwan in the past, even after the withdrawal of diplomatic recognition of the ROC.[13] Past experiences also reveal that it is unlikely that a US court judgment would be denied recognition by ROC courts for lack of reciprocity.

With respect to the United Kingdom and Hong Kong, the ROC High Court has refused to recognise a Hong Kong judgment because it was found that England (Hong Kong) has neither diplomatic relations nor reciprocal recognition treaties with the

13. See Judgment (63) Tai Shang Tse No. 426.

ROC (Letter of Ruling (69) Yuan Tai-T'ing Tze No. 03938, 15 November 1980); also, according to a letter from the Ministry of Foreign Affairs, the courts of Hong Kong have not recognised civil judgments of the ROC courts (Letter of Ruling (69) Wai Tiao Tze No. 24039, 6 November 1980).

When the requirements of Article 402 are met, the recognition of the foreign judgment will be finalised and request can be made to the Civil Execution Department of the District Court for attachment of the assets of the ROC debtor. The attachment process usually requires two weeks.

In the case of immovable or high value assets, the period from the filing for attachment to the moment when the assets are ready for auction is approximately two months. In the case of bank accounts, the minimum execution period is about one and a half months.

With respect to the cost of enforcing a foreign judgment, court fees amount to 1% of the claim for the District Court (trial court), 1.5% for appeal to the High Court, and 1.5% for appeal to the Supreme Court. The execution fee is 0.5% of the value of the claim, and the attaching party must post a bond with the court. While the amount of the bond can vary from case to case, it typically amounts to one-third of the value of the property to be attached.

The losing party is liable for the court fees and the fees paid by the winning party may be recovered. However, if the complainant is a foreigner or a foreign company without residence or offices in Taiwan, upon request of the defendant, he must post a bond for the 3% of appellate court fees in addition to paying the 1% District Court fee. In general, court fees, attachment fees and execution fees may be posted as a bond and repatriated from Taiwan after successful conclusion of the case. The bond must be posted in cash or a cash equivalent, however.

REMEDIES AVAILABLE TO FOREIGN CREDITORS

In terms of judicial remedies, no difference will be made between local and foreign creditors so far as the creditors have obtained any one of the so-called "execution titles". Article 4 of the ROC Compulsory Execution Law provides that:

> A compulsory execution shall be carried out by virtue of the following execution titles:
>
> (1) An irrevocable final judgment.
>
> (2) A ruling authorising a provisional seizure, provisional disposition or provisional execution and other rulings upon which compulsory execution may be made in accordance with the provisions of the Code of Civil Procedure.
>
> (3) A compromise or a mediation reached in accordance with the provisions of the Code of Civil Procedure.
>
> (4) A notarial deed made in accordance with the Public Notarisation Law; provided, however, that this shall apply only to the case where the subject matter of the creditor's claim is the prestation of money or substitutes therefor or valuable securities in a certain number or amount and it was specified in the notarial deed that default in making such prestation shall be directly subject to compulsory execution.
>
> (5) A ruling of the court authorising a compulsory execution in response to an application for permission to sell the mortgaged property by auction filed by the mortgagee in accordance with the provisions of Article 873 of the Civil Code.
>
> (6) Other grounds which may be taken as executive titles in accordance with the provisions of other laws.

Several kinds of execution methods are available on various properties.

Compulsory execution of *personal property* is effected by means of attachment, auction or sale.[14] Attachment is confined to such property as is sufficient in value to meet the amount of the judgment, and any auction would be discontinued as soon as proceeds were sufficient to meet the judgment.[15]

Compulsory execution against *real property* is effected by means of attachment, auction or compulsory administration. The attachment is carried out by proclamation, sealing of the property, or ordering the surrender of the deed. The court may allow the debtor limited use of the property or may entrust its safekeeping to an autonomous chamber of commerce or trade union.[16]

Compulsory execution also may be ordered against a debtor's claim for payment of money from a third person. Pursuant to this procedure, the court prohibits the debtor from collecting the money and otherwise disposing of his claim and prohibits the third party from paying the debtor. The court may allow the creditor to collect the money or may transfer the right of claim to the creditors. It also may order the third party to make payment to the court for transmission to the creditors.[17]

If the claim is against a third party for delivery of movable property or for transfer of the right to immovable property on the basis of a right of claim or a right over things, the court may prohibit the debtor from making dispositions of, and the said third party from delivery of or transferring, the movable or immovable property, by a garnishment order. The court may further order, when it is deemed to be appropriate, such third party to turn over such movable or immovable property to the execution court.

The Compulsory Execution Law further stipulates that execution may be applied to claims for delivery or for feasance and non-feasance. Furthermore, in the case of the debtor's failure to furnish an adequate security, the execution court may arrest the debtor and place him under custody under specific circumstances.

SHELLY CHEN

14. See Compulsory Execution Law, Art. 45.
15. *Ibid.*, Art. 72.
16. *Ibid.*, Arts. 70 and 79.
17. *Ibid.*, Art. 115.

CHAPTER 30

UNITED STATES

INTRODUCTION

There are several different litigation procedures that a creditor or claimant located outside the United States (a "foreign claimant") may follow to pursue a monetary recovery on a claim against a party located in the United States (a "US defendant"). Each procedure presents the foreign claimant with a particular set of alternatives for seeking interim or provisional relief, while the litigation is pending, to ensure that the US defendant will have assets available to satisfy the claim when all the necessary litigation is concluded.

One way for a foreign claimant to pursue a monetary recovery on a claim against a US defendant is for the foreign claimant to sue the US defendant in a US court located in the section of the US (i.e., a particular state) in which that defendant resides or does business, and to obtain a full adjudication of the claim on the merits in that court, leading to a final judgment which is generally enforceable anywhere in the United States under the "full faith and credit" clause of the United States Constitution (see US Const. Article 4, § 1; 28 USC § 1738).

In this regard, the US courts are generally open to foreign litigants who wish voluntarily to commence legal proceedings in the United States[1] and, although certain jurisdictions in the US may require foreign litigants to register as doing business there in order to initiate judicial proceedings, they generally do not require that foreign litigants, merely because they are located outside the United States, post bonds or make other substantial payments in order to commence legal proceedings in the US courts (although bonds may be required of all litigants in order to obtain certain equitable remedies such as temporary or preliminary injunctions, or, in some states, in order to appeal).

Another procedure that a foreign claimant can follow to pursue a monetary recovery on a claim against a US defendant is to:

(1) commence legal proceedings against the US defendant in the courts of the foreign claimant's own country (or in the courts of a third country where the claim arose);
(2) obtain a judgment on the merits against the US defendant in the foreign court; and

1. See *Banco Nacionale de Cuba* v. *Sabbatino*, 376 US 398, 408–409 (1964).

(3) petition a US court in the state where the US defendant resides or does business to "recognise" the foreign judgment, and issue its own judgment enforcing that foreign judgment.

Given the increasing tendency of US courts to recognise foreign judgments when the procedures followed in the foreign courts comport with traditional American concepts of fairness and "due process" of law, this method of pursuing recovery on a claim against a US defendant has become increasingly attractive to foreign claimants.

A third procedure is also available where the foreign claimant's claim arises out of a contract with a US defendant that expressly provides for mandatory arbitration of all disputes arising out of it. In that situation, the foreign claimant can commence an arbitration proceeding on its claim whenever and however the contract permits, have the claim adjudicated on the merits in that arbitration, obtain an award from the arbitrator(s), and then petition a US court in the state where the US defendant resides or does business to render a judgment "confirming" that award, and rendering it enforceable as a US judgment, pursuant to federal or state statutes authorising this procedure (see, e.g., Federal Arbitration Act, 9 USC § 1 *et seq*.).

In each of these situations, it may be critical to the foreign claimant to obtain some kind of interim or provisional relief, prior to the entry of an enforceable US court judgment, limiting the transfer or disposal of the US defendant's assets so as to ensure that those assets will be available to satisfy the foreign claimant's US judgment when it is ultimately obtained. This chapter addresses the alternative strategies available to the foreign creditor, in each situation, for seeking such relief against US defendants.

STRUCTURE OF THE US COURT SYSTEM

At the outset, it is important that any foreign claimant seeking to recover from a US defendant has a basic understanding of the US judicial system, which operates at two distinct levels, federal and state, and consists of federal and state courts that frequently have overlapping jurisdiction.

The US federal courts constitute the judicial branch of the national government of the United States. They consist of trial courts located throughout the country (in all 50 states); regional appellate courts, each covering a different geographic region of the United States; and the United States Supreme Court. These federal courts interpret and apply the federal law of the United States (such as the provisions of the United States Constitution and the various federal statutes enacted by the US Congress), and, in connection with disputes between citizens of different states, or between US citizens and foreign entities or individuals, the laws of individual states (whose choice of law rules may, in turn, require application of the law of some other jurisdiction in particular cases). To the extent that the federal courts are called upon to apply state or foreign law, they rely on the decisions of the state or jurisdiction whose law they are being asked to apply. Where that law conflicts in any way with federal law that is specifically applicable to the dispute in question, however, federal law governs, as it is the "supreme law of the land".

The state courts, by contrast, constitute the judicial branches of the individual states in which they are located. Each state has its own body of statutory law enacted by its legislature, and its own body of common law consisting of the historical opinions of its courts. Typically, each state has trial courts located throughout its territory, and one or more levels of appellate courts, usually including a "supreme court" or "court of appeals" constituting the highest state court of that jurisdiction. These state courts interpret and apply the statutory and common law of their own state, and, where necessary, any federal law (such as federal constitutional questions) or other state or foreign law that they determine to be applicable to disputes brought before them.

Although the laws of each individual state frequently differ from the laws of other states, there is significant uniformity in the overall approach of the different states to a wide variety of legal issues. In some areas, this consistency in approach is reflected in similar decisions by the courts of different states addressing the same issues. In other areas, this consistency is reflected in the enactment of similar statutes by different states addressing the same issues, such as statutes providing litigants with prejudgment attachment and garnishment remedies, and statutes governing the enforcement of foreign judgments and arbitration awards.

This consistency in approach to many legal issues among the various states makes it possible to draw some useful general conclusions about the availability of interim and provisional relief under state laws to secure expected judgments in favour of foreign claimants against US defendants. It remain essential to examine the specific laws of the states in question, however, to determine the appropriate strategy in each individual case.

In this regard, the law of the state in which a foreign claimant's US defendant is located or does business is important to the foreign claimant because it is primarily that state law, rather than federal law, that will determine:

(1) the availability of specific interim or provisional attachment or garnishment remedies to secure assets of the US defendant; and

(2) the enforceability of a judgment rendered by a foreign court.

This is true even if the case is pending in federal court, because in "diversity" cases (i.e., those involving disputes between citizens of different states or between citizens of one state and a foreign country) the federal courts are obliged to apply the laws of the state in which they are located to all parts of a dispute before them not governed by federal law.

On the other hand, federal law is also important to the foreign claimant because there are special rules in federal court governing the issuance of preliminary injunctions, which provide another way to try to "freeze" the assets of US defendants. In addition, certain federal statutes, such as the Federal Arbitration Act, 9 USC § 1 *et seq.*, can prove very helpful to a foreign claimant seeking to enforce an arbitration award.

The following sections describe the interplay between state and federal laws dealing with the availability of provisional remedies to secure a defendant's assets pending final judgment, and the impact of those laws on a foreign claimant in each of the three different situations in which a foreign claimant may be pursuing a monetary recovery from a US defendant.

ATTACKING ASSETS OF US DEFENDANT WHERE FOREIGN CLAIMANT'S CLAIM IS BEING ADJUDICATED ON THE MERITS IN A US COURT

If a foreign claimant chooses to pursue an ajudication of its claim against a US defendant on the merits in a US court, the foreign claimant can generally elect whether to commence its action:

(1) in a state court located in a state in which the US defendant resides or does business; or

(2) in a federal court in the state in which the US defendant resides or does business.

If such an action is commenced in state court, however, the defendant may nevertheless have the right to "remove" it (i.e., have it transferred) to a federal court located in that state (see 28 USC § 1441 *et seq.*).

In either event, the availability of interim or provisional relief to secure assets of the US defendant pending final adjudication of the claim will fall into two categories:

(1) specific interim procedural orders or writs, expressly authorised by the law of the state in which the court (whether it be a state or federal court) is located, that are designed to secure specific assets pending final adjudication of claims—such as writs of attachment, garnishment, replevin, sequestration, or other seizure of assets; and

(2) more general, temporary restraining orders and preliminary injunctions ordering the US defendant to take certain actions, or to refrain from taking certain actions, concerning all or portions of its assets.

The availability of specific interim writs varies considerably from state to state, and the requirements for obtaining such remedies, where they are available, also varies widely. The types of specific remedies most frequently permitted by state law include writs of attachment or sequestration authorising the local sheriff to take possession of personal property or real estate owned by the defendant, either by taking actual physical possession or simply recording the writ with the appropriate Registry of Deeds for Land; and garnishment of assets owed to the defendant by third parties through the issuance of a writ to such third parties commanding them to hold those assets in order to satisfy the defendant's obligation to the claimant.

In general, a claimant seeking prejudgment relief in the form of an attachment or garnishment pursuant to state law must at least satisfy the US court in which the action is pending that it has a strong likelihood of success on the merits of its claim, and that the judgment likely to result will at least equal or exceed the value of the assets sought to be attached.[2] Some states also require that the claimant demonstrate that the provisional remedy of an attachment or garnishment is "necessary" to ensure that the defendant will have sufficient assets to satisfy the expected judgment when it is

2. See, e.g., NY Civ Prac Law & R 6212, 6223.

rendered,[3] and/or that there is no insurance available that would satisfy such a judgment.[4]

In this regard, although specific interim writs (such as for attachment and garnishment of specific assets) are creatures of state law, they are also available in the federal courts of each state that authorises their issuance, because these courts are required by law to make available to litigants all provisional and interim remedies for the seizure of assets prior to judgment that are available under the laws of the state in which they are located. On this issue, Fed R Civ P 64 ("Seizure of Person or Property") specifically provides that:

> At the commencement of and during the course of an action [in federal court], *all remedies providing for seizure of person or property for the purpose of securing satisfaction of the judgment ultimately to be entered* in the action *are available* under the circumstances and *in the manner provided by the law of the state in which the district court is held*, existing at the time the remedy is sought, ... The remedies thus available include *arrest, attachment, garnishment, replevin, sequestration* and other corresponding or equivalent remedies, however designated and regardless of whether by state procedure the remedy is ancillary to an action or must be obtained by an independent action. [emphasis added]

Accordingly, even where a foreign claimant is planning to have its claim ajudicated on the merits in a US federal court, it must still closely examine the law of the state in which that federal court is located to determine what specific interim writs may be available to it to secure the assets of its US defendant prior to entry of a final judgment.

Generally speaking, writs of attachment or garnishment can be obtained without the claimant having to post a bond or other security, so if the requirements for such remedies are met, they can be often obtained with relatively little cost. Accordingly, the availability of these specific state law procedures should be explored before the broader remedy of a preliminary injunction application is considered.

Even when such state law remedies are available, however, they may not prove useful to a foreign claimant, because they generally authorise the service of writs only within the boundaries of the state in which the court is located.[5] Obviously, although a US defendant may reside in that state, it may have substantial assets located elsewhere in the United States.

In these or other situations where provisional state law remedies are inadequate, the only alternative to a claimant in a US court seeking provisional relief to preserve assets is some kind of a temporary injunction directly ordering the defendant to preserve its assets pending the results of the litigation on the merits of the claim.

The provisional remedy of a preliminary injunction or temporary restraining order (which is essentially a preliminary injunction that lasts no more than 10 days and can be granted *ex parte* under appropriate circumstances) is a well-established equitable

3. See *Nippon Emo-Trans Co. Ltd* v. *Emo-Trans, Inc.*, 744 F Supp. 1215, 1218 (EDNY 1990)—"In order to prevail on a motion to confirm [an attachment], ... [the claimant] must show ... the need for continuing the levy".

4. See Mass R Civ P 4.1, providing that the party seeking attachment must demonstrate "that there is a reasonable likelihood that the plaintiff will recover judgment in an amount equal to or greater than the amount of the attachment over and above any liability insurance known or reasonably believed to be available".

5. See, e.g., Massachusetts General Laws, chapter 223, § 42 (Property Subject to Attachment); *Cheshire Nat'l Bank* v. *Jewett*, 119 Mass. 241 (1876).

remedy that is generally available in both state and federal courts throughout the United States. Its basic purpose is twofold: first, to ensure that, where necessary, the parties preserve the status quo pending resolution of their dispute so as to ensure that the court's resolution of that dispute will be meaningful and enforceable; and, secondly, to protect the claimant from irreparable harm when it has shown a strong likelihood of success on the merits of its claims, and can demonstrate that it is likely to be harmed unless some specific interim order concerning those claims is entered immediately.

Typically, a preliminary injunction is sought in those situations where the claimant's ultimate remedy is at least in part equitable in nature—that is, where the claimant is seeking some kind of permanent injunction prohibiting the defendant from taking particular actions (such as infringing on a patent or trademark, violating a valid non-competition agreement, or making unlawful use of a claimant's trade secrets), or requiring the defendant to take certain action (such as to convey real property to the claimant).

It is well-established in both the state and federal courts, however, that preliminary injunctions can also be issued to preserve the assets of a defendant where it is likely that the claimant will succeed in obtaining a monetary judgment against that defendant, and where, in the absence of a preliminary injunction, there is a clear risk that the defendant will not have sufficient assets to satisfy the expected monetary judgment by the time it is obtained, whethere because the defendant is likely to dissipate those assets deliberately, or because other creditors may get to the assets first.[6]

In these situations, a preliminary injunction remedy is sometimes referred to as an "equitable attachment", in that it accomplishes the purpose of freezing assets without following specific statutory procedures for the actual seizure of such assets.[7] As the US Court of Appeals for the First Circuit held in *Teradyne, Inc.* v. *Mostek Corp.*[8]:

> The question raised here is *whether injunctive relief restraining the transfer of assets* can be granted when the District Court finds that the *defendant may be insolvent before a final judgment is entered* and, if so, whether such a finding was warranted in the circumstances of this case. *The Supreme Court has held that a preliminary injunction, designed to* freeze the status quo and *protect the damages remedy is an appropriate form of relief when it has shown that the defendant is likely to be insolvent at the time of judgment* ... under these circumstances, we affirm the District Court's conclusion that the possible hardship to ... [the claimant] of having a $3–4 million judgment prove worthless, outweighed the inchoate hardship to Mostek of having $4 million of its assets tied up in an interest bearing account pending judgment. [at pp. 52–53; emphasis added]

Significantly, both the state and federal courts frequently require that any party seeking a preliminary injunction be prepared to post security (i.e., cash deposit, bond, pledge of assets) in an amount sufficient to compensate the defendant for the costs and damages it is expected to incur as a result of the injunction. Actual compensation will only be ordered, of course, if it is subsequently determined that the claimants are not

6. See *Deckert* v. *Independence Shares Corporation*, 311 US 282 (1940).
7. See *Anderson Foreign Motors* v. *New England Toyota, et al.*, 475 F Supp. 973, 977–978 (D Mass. 1979).
8. 797 F 2d 43 (1st Cir. 1986).

entitled to prevail on their claim, or that the injunction should not have been issued, but the security must nevertheless be posted by the claimant if the court so orders. Although the requirement is sometimes waived on a showing of good cause, the rules generally assume that some kind of security will be required (see Fed R Civ P 65(c) (Security)—"No restraining order or preliminary injunction shall issue except upon the giving of security by the applicant, in such sum as the court deems proper, for the payment of such costs and damages as may be incurred or suffered by any party found to have been wrongfully enjoined or restrained"). This may involve significant cost for a foreign claimant if the assets to be "frozen" are substantial.

Once issued, however, the preliminary injunction is binding on the defendant, and can be drafted by the claimant's own counsel so as to incorporate whatever specific asset-preservation terms seem appropriate in each particular case. Violation of such an injunction is also punishable by contempt orders and heavy fines. Thus, it can be a very effective tool for preserving assets.

These are the basic provisional remedies to secure assets that are available to any claimant, including a foreign claimant, pursuing its claims on the merits in the US courts. The two primary factors that determine whether a US court will grant such relief are:

(1) The apparent likelihood that the claimant will succeed on its claim, and that the defendant will not have any plausible defences (e.g., recovery of money due on a promissory note admittedly executed by the defendant would generally be considered a strong claim).

(2) The risk that in the absence of some kind of provisional relief securing assets of the defendant, the plaintiff will be unable to enforce any money judgment it obtains from the US court.

ATTACKING ASSETS OF US DEFENDANT WHERE FOREIGN CLAIMANT'S CLAIM IS BEING ADJUDICATED ON THE MERITS IN A FOREIGN COURT

If a foreign claimant chooses to pursue an adjudication of its claim against a US defendant on the merits in a foreign court, it will be difficult for it to obtain effective interim relief securing the US assets of that US defendant until it first obtains a final judgment from the foreign court. The reason for this is that interim or provisional orders of foreign courts are not generally recognisable or enforceable in US courts, and it will generally be difficult for a foreign creditor to convince a US court to grant it such interim relief prior to the entry of a final judgment in the foreign court.

Once a final judgment in the foreign court is obtained, however, even if it is subject to appeal, the foreign creditor may petition a US court to "recognise" that judgment, and simultaneously ask the US court to issue interim or provisional relief of the same type that the US court could issue if it were adjudicating the claim on the merits. In this situation, there is sound authority under US law for the issuance of such interim relief by the US court. Before reviewing this authority, however, it is helpful to understand the overall US approach to dealing with actions by foreign courts that purport to affect US defendants.

Obtaining "recognition" of foreign court judgments in US courts

The question of when and under what circumstances the US courts will recognise and give effect to the actions of foreign courts is governed not by federal law but by state law.[9] Thus, the question of whether such judgments should be recognised in individual cases is governed by the law of the state in which the court being asked to recognise them is located.[10]

Although there are 50 different states in the United States, each of which could theoretically apply its own unique body of law to the question of whether and under what circumstances foreign country judgments could be enforced there, there is considerable uniformity in approach to enforcing such judgments throughout the 50 states, although there are some variations. Eighteen states in the US have adopted (either by legislative enactment or court decisions adopting the approach of the statute) some variation of a "uniform" statute, known as the Uniform Foreign Money-Judgments Recognition Act (the "Uniform Act"), to deal with this issue. These states include Alaska, California, Colorado, Connecticut, Georgia, Illinois, Maryland, Massachusetts, Michigan, Minnesota, Missouri, New York, North Dakota, Ohio, Oklahoma, Oregon, Texas, and Washington.

Basically, the Uniform Act, in those states that have adopted it, codifies the recent common-law decisions of the majority of US courts (both state and federal) relating to the recognition and enforcement of foreign judgments in the United States (see *Commissioner's Preparatory Note to the Uniform Foreign Money-Judgments Recognition Act*). These common-law decisions originated with an 1895 decision of the United States Supreme Court in *Hilton* v. *Guyot*,[11] in which the Court held that:

> [w]here there has been opportunity for a *full and fair trial abroad before a court of competent jurisdiction*, conducting the trial upon regular proceedings, after due citation or voluntary appearance of the defendant, and under a system of jurisprudence likely to secure an impartial administration of justice between the citizens of its own country and those of other countries, and there is nothing to show either prejudice in the court, or in the system of laws under which it was sitting, or fraud in procuring the judgment, or any other special reason why the comity of this nation should not allow if full effect, *the merits of the case should not*, in an action brought in this country upon the judgment, *be tried afresh*, as on a new trial or on appeal upon the mere assertion of the party that the judgment was erroneous in law or in fact. [at p. 202, emphasis added]

In *Hilton*, the US Supreme Court was asked to give conclusive effect to a judgment of a French court. Although, as the above-referenced quote indicates, the Supreme Court believed that enforcement of such judgments in the United States was generally appropriate if the aforesaid criteria could be satisfied, it declined to enforce the particular French judgment in question on the ground that the French courts at that time did not, under similar circumstances, grant conclusive effect to valid judgments of American courts.

This rule that a foreign judgment otherwise meeting the requirements for recognition in the United States should be denied such recognition if the foreign courts

9. See *Banque Libanaise Pour Le Commerce* v. *Khreich*, 915 F 2d 1000 (5th Cir. 1990)—"state law governs the recognition and enforcement of foreign country judgments".

10. See *De La Mata* v. *American Life Ins. Co.*, 771 F Supp. 1375, 1380 (D Del. 1991)—"A foreign judgment must first be recognised and reduced to a judgment in the enforcing United States court".

11. 159 US 113 (1895).

rendering that judgment declined to recognise valid judgments of US courts came to be known as the "reciprocity" requirement for recognising foreign judgments.[12]

Although most of the requirements set forth in *Hilton* for recognition of foreign judgments in the US were approved of and adopted by state courts throughout the United States in the years following that decision, there was considerable controversy surrounding the "reciprocity" requirement, and some states declined to follow that rule in their own court.[12a] Other states simply interpreted the *Hilton* decision narrowly as imposing a reciprocity requirement only where the foreign judgment was sought to be enforced in US courts against an American citizen.[13]

In this regard, although decisions of the United States Supreme Court such as *Hilton* are ordinarily deemed the "supreme law of the land", binding upon state as well as federal courts, the US Supreme Court held after *Hilton* that disputes being litigated in federal courts between citizens of different states, and between citizens of foreign countries and citizens of the United States, were to be decided according to the law of the state where the federal court in question was located (including the choice of law rules of that state), unless application of federal law is mandated by the US Convention or by federal statute.[14]

Since no federal statute governs the recognition and enforcement of foreign judgments, subsequent federal court decisions have held that the specific requirement of reciprocity imposed by *Hilton* is not binding on states that do not wish to follow it. As one United States District Court held in recognising and enforcing a default judgment obtained by a British corporation in the courts of the United Kingdom against a US defendant:

> in its brief . . . and supporting affidavit, *defendant argues that the English judgment should not be recognised* and enforced by this Court *because an English court would not enforce an American judgment under similar circumstances.* The position that [such] reciprocity is an essential element in determining whether or not to enforce a foreign judgment was first annunicated in 1895 by the Supreme Court in the *Hilton* case. However, we do not find the teaching of *Hilton* on reciprocity to be controlling in this case. The Hilton decision was a *pre-Erie R.R. Co.* v. *Tompkins* case and it has never been suggested that it was constitutionally dictated and therefore binding on the states. It is clear, and this Court has so stated earlier in this opinion, that the law governing *the enforceability of foreign judgments by a federal court is the law of the state where the court is located.* Therefore, the issue, as this Court perceives it, is whether the courts of Pennsylvania would hold that reciprocity is a necessary precondition to the enforcement of foreign judgments. [*Somportex Limited* v. *The Philadelphia Chewing Gum Corp.*, 318 F Supp 161, 167–169 (ED PA 1970), emphasis added]

12. See *Venezuelan Meat Export Co.* v. *United States*, 12 F Supp. 379 (DC Md. 1935), refusing to give effect to a French judgment on grounds that the reciprocity requirement was not satisfied; *Harrison* v. *Triplex Goldmines*, 33 F 2d 667, 671 (1st Cir. 1929)—"The principle of comity is extended by the courts of this country to the judgments of the courts of a foreign country *to the same extent that courts in the foreign country* extend the principle to judgments of the courts in this country" [emphasis added].

12a. See *Johnston* v. *Compagnie Generale Transatlantique*, 242 NY 381, 152 NE 121 (1926) declining to apply the *Hilton* reciprocity requirement to case pending in the New York state courts involving enforcement of foreign judgments; *Nicol* v. *Tanner*, 310 Minn. 68, 256 NW 2d 796 (Minn. 1976)—"It is clear that reciprocity does not achieve that goal [of protecting Americans abroad and encouraging foreign nations to enforce US judgments] because it does not look to the fairness or persuasiveness of the foreign judgment"; but see *Hager* v. *Hager*, 1 Ill.App. 3d 1047, 274 NE 2d 157 (1971), requiring reciprocity as a precondition to recognising foreign judgment.

13. See *Bata* v. *Bata*, 39 Dl. Ch 258, 163 A 2d 493, 503 (Del. 1960), *cert. denied*, 366 US 964 (1961).

14. See *Erie R. R. Co.* v. *Tompkins*, 304 US 64 (1938); *Klaxon Co.* v. *Stentor Elec. Mfg Co.*, 313 US 487 (1941).

See also *Svenska Handelsbanken* v. *Carlson*[15]

Thus, it is now well settled in the United States "that state law governs the recognition and enforcement of foreign country judgments".[16] As the Supreme Court of the State of Washington recently held:

> Federal and state court judgment within the United States are enforced state-to-state pursuant to the full faith and credit clause of the United States Constitution, Article 4, § 1, and 28 USC § 1738 (1988). For such judgments, the standard for recognition is federal in nature.
>
> ... However, foreign country judgments are not vested with the protections of the full faith and credit clause or 28 USC § 1738 and no federal law in the absence of treaty or federal statute governs the recognition or execution of foreign country judgments in the United States. Thus, *the recognition of such judgments is governed by applicable state law, even when that recognition is sought in federal court.* [*Tonga Air Services Ltd* v. *Wayne Fowler*, 1992 Wash. Lexis 78 (Supreme Court of Washington State, Appeal No. 58057–0, Opinion dated 26 March 1992, emphasis added)]

Under the laws of most states today, reciprocity is not a requirement for the recognition and enforcement of foreign judgments (see Restatement (Third) of the Foreign Relations Law of the United States, § 481, Reporter's Note 1 (1987)). A small minority of states (including, for example, Texas, Massachusetts, and Georgia) do impose a reciprocity requirement, however, either by statute or common law. Accordingly, a foreign creditor must examine the law of the particular state in which its US defendant resides before determining whether to pursue its case on the merits in the courts of a foreign country which does not recognise and give conclusive effect to US judgments.

Assuming that reciprocity is not a problem, however, either because the court issuing the foreign judgment recognises similar US judgments, or because the state in which the foreign claimant will seek to have its foreign judgment recognised does not demand reciprocity, the foreign claimant still needs to establish the following facts in order to obtain recognition and enforcement of its foreign judgment in the US:

> Summarised the criteria [for recognition and enforcement of a foreign judgment] are:
> (1) Opportunity for a full and fair trial [in the foreign jurisdiction].
> (2) Trial before a court of competent jurisdiction [in the foreign country].
> (3) Proceedings following due citation or voluntary appearance of adversary parties.
> (4) Trial conducted upon regular proceedings.
> (5) Trial under a system of jurisprudence likely to secure an impartial administration of justice between the citizens of its own country and those of other countries.
> (6) No evidence to demonstrate
> (a) fraud in the procuring of the judgment
> (b) prejudice in the system of laws in which the court was sitting
> (c) prejudice in the court
> (d) any other special reason why comity of the United States should not allow full effect [of the foreign judgment]. (*De La Mata* v. *American Life Ins. Co.*, 771 F Supp 1375, 1381 (D Del 1991))

In setting forth these basic criteria for the recognition of foreign judgments, most US

15. 258 F Supp. 448, 450 (D Mass. 1966)—"Plaintiff's first contention is that the judgment of the Swedish Court should be given conclusive effect and judgment entered upon it ... Massachusetts rather than federal law seems to be properly applicable here [to the question of recognition]".

16. *Banque Libanaise Pour Le Commerce* v. *Khreich*, 915 F 2d 1000, 1003 (5th Cir. 1990). See also *Pariente* v. *Scott Meredith Literary Agency, Inc.*, 771 F Supp. 609, 615 (SDNY 1991)—"New York law governs actions brought in New York to enforce foreign judgments".

courts have adopted all the requirements for recognition set forth in *Hilton* other than reciprocity, and the following language of the *Hilton* decision is frequently quoted as an early recitation of those requirements:

When an action is brought in a court of this country, by a citizen of a foreign country against one of our own citizens, to recover a sum of money adjudged by a court of that country to be due from the defendant to the plaintiff, and *the foreign judgment appears to have been rendered by a competent court having jurisdiction of the cause and of the parties, and upon due allegations and proofs and opportunity to defend against them, and its proceedings are according to the course of a civilized jurisprudence, and are stated in a clear and formal record*, the judgment is prima facie evidence, at least, of the truth on the matter adjudged; and *it should be held conclusive upon the merits tried in the foreign court, unless some special ground is shown for impeaching the judgment*, as by showing that it was effected by fraud or prejudice, or that by the principles of international law and by the comity of our own country it should not be given full credit and effect. [*Hilton* v. *Guyot*, 159 US 113 at 218 (1895) [emphasis added]]

See also *Somportex Limited* v. *Philadelphia Chewing Gum Corp.*[17]

In determining whether a foreign judgment is the product of an impartial and civilised system of jurisprudence, US courts do not require that proceedings in the foreign court have mirrored the procedures and substantive law that would have been applied to the dispute in a US court.[18] As a New York federal court recently observed:

"In order for comity to be extended, the foreign court must abide by fundamental standards of procedural fairness." *Cunard, supra* 773 F 2d at 457. *However, it is well established that mere divergence from American procedure does not render a foreign judgment unenforceable. ...* "Under New York law, ... *foreign decrees and proceedings will be given respect ... even if the result under the foreign proceeding would be different than under American law.*" [Citing cases]

Differences in evidentiary standards have been treated similarly. In *Hilton*, the Supreme Court upheld enforcement of a French judgment, *despite the fact that*

> One of the plaintiffs was permitted to testify not under oath, and was not subjected to cross-examination by the opposite party, and ... the defendants were therefore deprived of the safeguards which are by our law considered essential to secure honesty and to detect fraud in a witness, and ... documents and papers were admitted in evidence, with which the defendants had no connection, and which would not be admissible under our own system of jurisprudence.

Hilton, supra, 159 US at 204–05, 16 S Ct. at 159. In so ruling, the *Hilton* Court stated:

> It having been shown by the plaintiffs, and hardly denied by the defendants, that the practice followed and the method of examining witnesses were according to the laws of France, *we are not prepared to hold that the fact that the procedure in these respects differed from that of our own courts is of itself a sufficient ground for impeaching the foreign judgment.*

Hilton, supra, 159 US at 205, 16 S Ct. at 159; *see also Tahan, supra*, 662 F 2d at 866 n. 18 ("*Hilton* ... stands for the proposition that Amercian courts have been signally reluctant to deny recognition to foreign judgments by virtue of mere difference of procedure"). *Pariente* v. *Scott Meredith Literary Agency, Inc.*, 771 F Supp 609, 616–617 (SDNY 1991) [emphasis added]

US courts are fairly stringent, however, in requiring that a foreign claimant seeking recognition of a foreign judgment demonstrate that the foreign court's exercise of personal jurisdiction over the US defendant comported with US notions of due process, which require that a defendant have certain "minimum contacts" with a

17. 453 F 2d 435, 440–441 (3rd Cir. 1971), *cert. denied* 405 US 1017 (1972) (citing *Hilton*).

18. See *Ackermann* v. *Levine*, 788 F 2d 830, 842 (2nd Cir. 1986)—"As Judge Cardozo so lucidly observed: 'We are not so provincial as to say that every solution of a problem is wrong because we deal with it otherwise at home.' "

given jurisdiction (including a foreign country) before the courts of that jurisdiction can assert personal jurisdiction over it.[19]

Generally speaking, the kind of "minimum contacts" sufficient to support a finding that a foreign court had personal jurisdiction over a US defendant include the defendant being licensed or registered to do business in that foreign country, maintaining offices or agents in that country, entering into contracts with the citizens of that country, and/or shipping goods into that country. In *De La Mata* v. *American Life Ins. Co.*,[20] for example, a Delaware federal court concluded that a Bolivian court's exercise of personal jurisdiction over a US life insurance company defendant was appropriate, and that the requirement that the foreign court have personal jurisdiction in order to have its judgment against the company enforced in the US was satisfied, where the following facts about that insurance company, referred to in the opinion as "ALICO", were demonstrated:

> ALICO *registered with the Bolivian Registry of Commerce and engaged in the business of selling insurance policies in Bolivia*. The certificate from the Registry of Commerce reveals that ALICO at one time *appointed a legal representative in Bolivia* and that appointment had not been revoked as late at 1990. From 1982 until 1985, ALICO *maintained at the very least one Bolivian insurance agent* ... who sold insurance policies on behalf of ALICO. ALICO was responsible for payment to at least two Bolivian beneficiaries if the terms for payment under the whole life policy were met. According to the certificate from the Registry of Commerce, *ALICO had at one time in the 1980s a headquarters for its Bolivian operations in La Paz*. Given the preceding undisputed contacts of ALICO with Bolivia, it would not be unfair or unreasonable to require ALICO to appear with defendant Bolivia against the plaintiff. [emphasis added]

Although contacts as substantial as these are not essential to support a conclusion that a foreign court had a right to exercise personal jurisdiction over a US defendant in an individual case,[21] they are the kinds of contacts that are relevant to a conclusion that a foreign court's exercise of personal jurisdiction was appropriate.

In addition to examining this personal jurisdiction issue, the US courts are also particularly sensitive to whether the US defendant had fair and adequate notice of the commencement of proceedings against it in the foreign court, and specifically whether service of process on the US defendant pursuant to the foreign country's laws comported "with traditional American notions of due process".[22] In this regard, the United States Supreme Court has held that in order for service of process in any given situation to satisfy the requirements of due process, it must provide notice to the defendant which is "reasonably calculated, under all the circumstances, to apprise interested parties of the pendency of the action and afford them an opportunity to present their objections".[23] The importance of foreign service of process meeting these

19. See *International Shoe Co.* v. *Washington*, 326 US 310 (1945); *World-Wide Volkswagen Corp.* v. *Woodson*, 444 US 286, 291–292 (1980), holding that defendants should not be subject to the burden of defending litigation in a forum with which the defendant had little or no contact; *Hanson* v. *Denckla*, 357 US 235, 253 (1958), assertion of personal jurisdiction is only appropriate where the defendant has "purposefully availed itself of the privilege of conducting activities within the forum state, thus invoking the benefits and protections of its laws".

20. 771 F Supp. 1375 (D Del. 1991).

21. See *McGee* v. *International Life Insurance Co.*, 355 US 220 (1957), where the US Supreme Court approved the exercise of personal jurisdiction over a defendant insurance company which had only one contact with the state in which the court was located, namely the mailing of an offer of reinsurance to a resident of that forum.

22. *De La Mata*, 771 F Supp. At 1386.

23. *Mullane* v. *Central Hanover Bank & Trust Co.*, 339 US 306 (1950).

requirements cannot be understated. In *De La Mata*, for example, the federal court concluded that the exercise of personal jurisdiction over the US defendant by the Bolivian courts would have been appropriate, *but* that in this case the

> purported service [of process] upon ALICO [the US defendant] through Aviles [the US defendant's former agent] fails to comport with American fundamental notions of due process *resulting in the inability to enforce the judgment in this court.* [*De La Mata*, 771 F Supp. at 1388, emphasis added]

Thus, foreign claimants pursuing their claims against US defendants on the merits in foreign courts must ensure that those US defendants receive fair and adequate notice of the proceedings in the foreign court—otherwise, the judgment of the foreign court will not be recognised in the US.

Absence of fraud in the procurement of the foreign judgment, and absence of prejudice against the US defendant in the foreign forum, are also important requirements for recognition of a foreign judgment. With regard to fraud,

> [C]ourts have held that *only extrinsic, as opposed to intrinsic, fraud will bar the recognition of a foreign judgment.* If fraud relates to matters other than those that were litigated and was committed upon the foreign court, then it is extrinsic fraud. [*De La Mata*, 771 F Supp. at 1388, emphasis added]

In *De La Mata*, the US defendant had not appeared to defend the action, and the foreign claimant had apparently deliberately not apprised the Bolivian court of the fact that she had executed a legal document that arguably barred her claims. Based on this fact, the US court being asked to recognise the Bolivian judgment concluded that:

> Since the waiver was not an issue litigated before the Bolivian courts, the plaintiff's failure to refer to the document or explain the circumstances of its execution *is fraud extrinsic to the Bolivian proceedings and of sufficient magnitude to preclude enforcement of the Bolivian judgment.* [*De La Mata*, 771 F Supp. at 1389, emphasis added]

Thus, a foreign claimant must necessarily be concerned that any foreign court whose judgment it may subsequently ask a US court to enforce is fully apprised of all facts relevant to the dispute in question.

Finally, with regard to issues relating to the impartiality of the proceedings in a foreign court, the US courts generally will assume that the foreign court has acted impartially in the absence of specific evidence to the contrary. In fact, in *De La Mata*, although the US court found that the foreign claimant had committed extrinsic fraud which precluded enforcement of the Bolivian judgment, it nevertheless concluded that

> ... The record does not reveal any irregularity in the Bolivian proceedings (other than fraud), prejudice in the system of law in which the Bolivian courts were sitting or prejudice in either the District Court or the Superior Court.
>
> Further, *there has been no showing that the Bolivian proceedings were conducted under a system of jurisprudence unlikely to secure an impartial administration of justice* between the citizens of its own country and those of other countries. Bolivia is a nation with which the United States maintains friendly relations. One United States court has expressly recognised that Bolivia has a civilized system of jurisprudence. ... There has been no indication Bolivian jurisprudence does not exhibit impartiality with regard to non-Bolivians. ...
>
> Indeed, *it appears the impartiality criteria [for the enforcement of foreign judgments] only comes into play where a plaintiff seeks to enforce a money judgment from a country whose foreign policy manifests express hostility to the United States and whose jurisprudence has been molded to reflect that hostility. See Carl Zeiss Stiftung* v. *V.E.B. Carl Zeiss, Jena*, 293 F Supp. 892 (SDNY 1968), *modified* 433 F 2d 686 (2nd Cir. 1970), *cert. denied*, 403 US 905, 91 S Ct

2205, 29 LEd 2d 680 (1971) (involving East German jurisprudence). [*De La Mata*, 771 F Supp. at 1389–1390, emphasis added]

Thus, lack of impartiality should not generally be a problem in connection with most foreign judgments as to which recognition is sought in a US court.[24]

In trying to reconcile and codify these various common-law requirements for the enforcement of a foreign judgment, the Uniform Foreign Money-Judgments Recognition Act sets forth a basic rule that any foreign judgment that is final and conclusive and enforceable where rendered, even though an appeal therefrom is pending or it is subject to appeal, will be deemed conclusive between the parties to the extent that it grants or denies recovery of a sum of money, and will be enforceable in US courts in the same manner as the judgment of a sister state which is entitled to full faith and credit. The Uniform Act then provides, however, that:

(a) A foreign judgment is not conclusive if
   (1) the judgment was rendered under a system which does not provide impartial tribunals or procedures compatible with the requirements of due process of law;
   (2) the foreign court did not have personal jurisdiction over the defendant; or
   (3) the foreign court did not have jurisdiction over the subject matter.
(b) A foreign judgment need not be recognized if
   (1) the defendant in the proceedings in the foreign court did not receive notice of the proceedings in sufficient time to enable him to defend;
   (2) the judgment was obtained by fraud;
   (3) the (cause of action) (claim for relief) on which the judgment is based is repugnant to the public policy of this state;
   (4) the judgment conflicts with another final and conclusive judgment;
   (5) the proceeding in the foreign court was contrary to an agreement between the parties under which the dispute in question was to be settled otherwise than by proceedings in that court [if, for example, there was a forum selection clause in the parties' contract stipulating that the courts of another jurisdiction would be employed to resolve the dispute, or that the dispute would be resolved by arbitration]; or
   (6) in the case of jurisdiction based only on personal service, the foreign court was a seriously inconvenient forum for the trial of the action. (Uniform Foreign Money-Judgments Recognition Act (1962 Act), § 4(a) (Grounds for Non-Recognition))

From a procedural standpoint, a foreign claimant seeking to secure recognition and enforcement of a foreign judgment against a US defendant in the US court needs to commence a lawsuit against that US defendant in the US court, and present evidence, either by affidavit or otherwise, establishing that a foreign judgment was rendered against the US defendant after a proceeding in a foreign court meeting all of the requirements for recognition set forth by the state in which the US court is located. The foreign claimant then requests that the US court recognise the foreign judgment, and enter its own judgment incorporating the terms of that foreign judgment.

In virtually all of the US cases that have addressed the issue of whether a foreign judgment should be enforced, the courts have resolved the matter through a US court procedure known as "summary judgment", in which both parties submit sworn affidavits concerning the facts necessary to support their respective positions. If the

24. See *Parsons* v. *Bank Leumi Le-Israel, B.M.*, 565 So 2d 20, 25 (Alabama 1990)—"Our review of the record does not indicate that the proceeding conducted against Parsons [in Israel] was unfair; in fact, the record indicates the opposite".

affidavits conflict with one another in material respects, then a trial becomes necessary in which a finder of fact, either a jury or a judge, weighs the credibility of each side's evidence and determines which party's version of the facts is true. In the typical case where a foreign claimant is seeking recognition of a foreign judgment, however, the facts relating to the foreign proceeding are not disputed, often because there is a detailed record of that proceeding available to all parties and to the US court.

For this reason, a foreign claimant seeking recognition and enforcement of a foreign judgment should accompany its complaint with a motion for summary judgment supported by detailed affidavits attaching certified copies of the foreign judgment, transcripts of the foreign proceeding (if available), and describing in detail all steps taken to apprise the US defendant of that proceeding, and the basis for the personal and subject matter jurisdiction exercised by the foreign court.[25]

The advantage of employing the summary judgment procedure is that evidence can be submitted in the form of affidavits, which do not require the personal presence of witnesses in the US jurisdiction; and assuming the court finds that there are no material facts relating to the proceeding in dispute, and that it is simply a question of whether, under the agreed-upon facts relating to the foreign court proceeding, the foreign judgment can be given legal effect, the US court can decide that issue as a matter of law without convening a jury and holding a trial. This process can be completed in a matter of weeks or months, depending on the court's schedule, whereas it frequently takes years before a full trial to resolve disputed facts in a civil case can be held (criminal cases are given priority).

Using "recognition" of the foreign judgment to obtain provisional relief securing assets of US defendant

Once a US court rules that a given foreign judgment should be recognised, the foreign claimant who holds that judgment can persuasively argue to the US court that it has a likelihood of success on the merits of obtaining a final judgment from the US court in the amount of its foreign money judgment. This likelihood of success, in turn, entitles the foreign claimant to pursue the full range of provisional remedies available to any litigant in the US court who can demonstrate a likelihood of success on the merits, plus a risk that in the absence of provisional relief, its opponent may conceal or dissipate assets and render any ultimate judgment unenforceable.

In addition, even where the foreign judgment in question is still subject to appeal in

25. See, e.g., *Tahan* v. *Hodgson*, 662 F 2d 862, 863 (DC Cir. 1981)—"Plaintiff brings this action for enforcement of a default judgment entered against the [US] defendant by an Israeli court. The matter is before this court on cross motions for summary judgment . . ."; *Pariente* v. *Scott Meredith Literary Agency, Inc.*, 771 F Supp. 609, 614 (SDNY 1991)—"Plaintiffs have moved for summary judgment seeking enforcement of the [foreign] judgment; SMLA [US defendant] has cross-moved for summary judgment, seeking dismissal of the complaint in this action and thus non-enforcement of the judgment . . ."; *Overseas Inns SA PA* v. *United States*, 911 F 2d 1146, 1147–1148 (5th Cir. 1990)—"Overseas [a Luxembourg corporation] moved for summary judgment, asserting that the Luxembourg judgment was binding on the IRS . . ."; *Panama Processes* v. *Cities Service Co.*, 796 P 2d 276, 281 (Oklahoma 1990)—"Cities then moved for partial summary adjudication in the Tulsa trial court on the breach of contract theory, asserting that the Brazilian judgment should be recognised and enforced ... the district court sustained Cities' [summary judgment] motion on the basis of comity. The following July it gave summary judgment to Cities on both of Panama's theories of liability."; *Parsons* v. *Bank Leumi Le-Israel B.M.*, 565 So 2d 20 (Ala. 1990), affirming grant of summary judgment against US defendant for the amount of a foreign judgment against that defendant plus accumulated interest.

The *Nippon* court thus concluded that it had to determine whether the Japanese Judgment appeared to be recognisable and enforceable under New York state law. In this regard, the court noted[33] that "[a]s a general matter, New York courts have long maintained a strong policy of giving preclusive effect to foreign country judgments."

The court also noted that New York law provided two alternative avenues for recognising foreign judgments:

(1) recognition under Article 53 (the Uniform Act); and
(2) recognition under the common law of New York, which does not require reciprocity but otherwise applies the *Hilton* criteria (full and fair trial in foreign court, adequate notice to the defendant, absence of fraud or partiality).[34]

Since the *Nippon* opinion does not explicitly address such questions as whether the Japanese Judgment was the result of a fair and impartial trial, whether adequate notice of the trial was given to the US defendant ETI, or whether the Japanese court had subject matter jurisdiction over the dispute, these issues were apparently not contested by ETI. The question of whether the Japanese court's exercise of personal jurisdiction over ETI had been appropriate, however, was sharply contested by ETI, and the *Nippon* decision contains an extensive discussion of whether the exercise of such personal jurisdiction was appropriate in that case.

In this regard, the *Nippon* court not only addressed the extent to which the exercise of personal jurisdiction by the Japanese court over ETI was consistent with American due process requirements but also the extent to which the Japanese court's *own determination* on the question of whether it could exercise personal jurisdiction over ETI, in the face of ETI's objection to that claim of jurisdiction, was itself binding on the US court and preclusive on the jurisdictional issue. As to these latter questions, the *Nippon* court noted that "[t]he [New York] case law shows a clear reluctance to blindly accept a foreign court's assertion of jurisdiction without an examination of the basis therefore" (744 F Supp., at 1222) and the court concluded that "[n]either Article 53 nor New York's common law principles of recognition would prevent [US] Court from re-examining a foreign court's determination of a jurisdictional issue".[35]

The court did opine, however, that "in appropriate circumstances" its examination of a foreign court's decision on a contested jurisdictional issue "might be cabined within narrow limits",[36] and it expressed approval of an approach to this question in which US courts would defer to the factual determinations relating to personal jurisdiction made by foreign courts, but more closely scrutinise a foreign court's resolution of mixed fact/law questions relating to jurisdiction:

> The Restatement (Third) of the Foreign Relations Law of the United States suggests an approach which takes into account both the grounds of the foreign court's jurisdiction and the nature of the determination made by the foreign court:
>
> "If the defendant appeared in the foreign court to challenge the jurisdiction of the court and failed to prevail, it is not clear whether such determination will be considered *res judicata* by a court in the United States asked to recognize the resulting judgment. If the determination of jurisdiction depended on a finding of fact to support an otherwise objectionable basis of

33. 744 F Supp. at 1226.

34. See 744 F Supp. at 1226: "A New York court may recognise a [foreign] judgment based on grounds other than those articulated in Article 53."

35. 744 F Supp. at 1229.

36. *Ibid.*

jurisdiction—for example, whether X was an agent through whom the defendant did business in the forum state—the determination after contest ordinarily will be respected ... If the determination depended on a question of law or a mixed law/fact question—for example, whether a nonresident corporation is present in the forum state by virtue of having an 'alter ego' subsidiary there—the court asked to recognize the resulting judgment will scrutinize the jurisdictional determination on its merits ..." (Restatement (Third) of the Foreign Relations Law of the United States § 482 comment c (1986))

The court is of the view that such an approach would generally be consistent with the goals of New York's statutory and common law principles of recognition [of foreign judgments]. [*Nippon*, 744 F Supp. at 1229]

Applying these principles, and the provisions of New York's Uniform Act, to the jurisdictional question, the *Nippon* court concluded that although "neither of the bases of jurisdiction [expressly] articulated by the Tokyo Court would support jurisdiction under New York Law",[37] it was nevertheless the case that:

In view of the volume and continuity of activity initiated by ETI and directed toward Japan, the court concludes that, were it necessary to re-examine the facts to determine whether ETI is amenable to personal jurisdiction in Japan, it would find that, judged by the standards of section 301, a New York court would conclude that ETI was doing business in Japan on a substantial, continuous and permanent basis, and that as a result the Tokyo court could properly have asserted a jurisdiction over it. [744 F Supp. at 1233]

This conclusion was supported by the undisputed fact that ETI had an agent in Japan performing business activities on its behalf, derived approximately US$600,000 in gross revenues from shipments to Japan each year during the time period in question, and engaged in "continuous" activity directed at Japan with a "fair measure of permanence and continuity".[38] As a result, the *Nippon* court concluded that:

Whether under ... [New York statutory law] or under common law, NET has demonstrated a probability of success on the question of the Tokyo court's jurisdiction, and thus [since personal jurisdiction was apparently the only disputed issue relating to recognition of the foreign judgment] on the merits of this action. [*Nippon*, 744 F Supp. at 1233]

Having reached that conclusion, however, the *Nippon* court explained that:

It remains to be seen whether NET has demonstrated a need to continue the levy, as required by sections 6212(a) and 6223(b) of the New York Civil Practice Law and Rules, N.Y. Civ. Prac. Law and R. §§ 6212(a), 6223(b) (McKinney 1980). NET mounts two arguments here. First, it asserts that in cases where the ... [party seeking attachment] is already a judgment creditor by virtue of the decision of a fair and impartial foreign tribunal, nothing more need be shown to justify an attachment than the existence of the foreign judgment and the fact that it remains unsatisfied. Second, it argues that ETI, as a judgment debtor, has a strong incentive to conceal its assets, that it has made no effort to satisfy the judgment, has refused to post alternative security, and has, by its own admission, transferred assets to third parties since the Japanese judgment was entered. [*Nippon*, 744 F Supp. 1233, emphasis added]

In examining these arguments, the *Nippon* court explained that New York's statutory provisions allowing for the provisional remedy of attachment:

... are designed to serve two basic purposes: acquiring jurisdiction over the defendant and making provision, where necessary, to secure any judgment which plaintiff eventually recovers. ... In this case, ETI, as a New York corporation, is subject to the jurisdiction of the court; thus, an attachment would appear to be warranted only if there is a need to secure the judgment NET hopes to obtain in this Court. [*Nippon*, 744 F Supp. 1233–1234]

37. 744 F Supp. at 1230.
38. 744 F Supp. at 1232.

On this issue, the court noted that NET argued that the requirement of showing a "need" for the attachment arose only out of cases dealing with prejudgment attachments, and that in postjudgment cases the showing of an unsatisfied foreign judgment should be sufficient under New York state law to support issuance of an attachment.[39] The *Nippon* court could not accept this argument, however, and after extended discussion stated that:

[t]he court is of the view that in cases where jurisdiction is not at issue, the standard ... [for upholding an attachment] *requires that the plaintiff makes some showing of a need to secure the sought-after judgment*, both at the time an attachment is sought *ex parte* and on the motion to confirm albeit a lesser showing than would be required ... [under statutes dealing purely with prejudgment attachment requirements]. [*Nippon*, 744 F Supp. 1235, emphasis added]

Based on this analysis, the *Nippon* court explained that:

[t]hus the question for the court [in determining whether to grant a foreign claimant an attachment based on a foreign judgment] is not merely whether there exists a foreign judgment, likely to merit recognization, and remaining unsatisfied; rather, it is whether NET has shown that confirmation is necessary to secure payment of the Japanese Judgment. The court concludes it has not. It must be conceded that if ETI's statements regarding its revenues and assets are credited, ETI would have no difficulty satisfying the Japanese Judgment. NET has not presented the court with any information which tends to cast doubt on ETI's assertions, although it bears the burden of proof on this issue and has had the opportunity to conduct limited discovery. Similarly, in view of the nature and history of ETI's business, it appears unlikely that it would attempt to "flee" the jurisdiction ...

The Court concludes that NET has not met its burden of proof regarding the need to continue the attachment; as a result, the motion to confirm is denied ... [744 F Supp. 1236]

Although the *Nippon* court denied the foreign claimant's motion for confirmation of the attachment, however, it did take into account the rights of the foreign claimant by leaving NET's attachments in effect until the US defendant posted a bond for the full amount of the Japanese judgment. In doing so, the court fashioned its own unique remedy based on its conclusion that:

(1) if ETI owned any assets in Japan, it would have had to post a bond while the Japanese appeal was pending to fend off enforcement action against those assets; and
(2) New York state law contained the same policy of requiring the defendant to post a bond before judgment creditors were prevented from enforcing their judgments against assets located in New York during the pendency of any appeals there.

The *Nippon* court's discussion of its reasoning in this respect is instructive, and demonstrates the sensitivity of US courts to the legitimate rights of foreign judgment creditors:

Notwithstanding the vacatur of the order of attachment, in the absence of a stay NET would be able to move for summary judgment on its claim for recognition of the Japanese Judgment; in view of the discussion of the jurisdiction of the Tokyo court, it appears likely that, absent compelling new evidence, summary judgment would be granted in NET's favor, and it could enforce that judgment immediately. If, subsequently, ETI were to prevail on its appeal in Japan, in whole or in part, the soundness of this court's judgment would be called into question. *The parties have advised the court that it may well take a year or more before the appeal process is exhausted in Japan. On NET's behalf, it must be recognized that this is a considerable time to*

39. 744 F. Supp. at 1234.

> *wait, without security, for a judgment which under Article 53 might be granted and enforced forthwith.* If ETI had any assets in Japan the only way it could fend off enforcement pending appeal would be to post a bond; and while this court does not sit as a court of appeal from the Japanese Judgment, the same policy of requiring a bond in order to postpone enforcement is reflected in New York law, *see* N.Y. Civ. Prac. Law and R. § 5519(a)(2) (McKinney 1978), and in the Federal Rules *see* Federal Civil Procedure 62(d). In view of these competing considerations, ... in order to avoid creating any incentive for "strategic behavior" on ETI's part [with respect to its assets], *the effective time of the vacatur of this court's order of attachment shall be postponed until such time as ETI posts the bond described above.* [*Nippon*, 744 F Supp. 1236, emphasis added]

Clearly, the results in *Nippon* provided the foreign claimant with the ideal kind of provisional remedy to secure the collectability of its expected judgment against the US defendant. Although the same result would not necessarily obtain in all US courts, the *Nippon* decision provides an important road map concerning how much relief should be sought in the US courts in situations where the foreign claimant already has a foreign judgment against its US defendant.

ATTACKING ASSETS OF US DEFENDANT WHERE FOREIGN CLAIMANT'S CLAIM IS BEING ADJUDICATED ON THE MERITS IN ARBITRATION

If a foreign claimant chooses to pursue an adjudication of its claim against a US defendant on the merits in an arbitration proceeding, either within or outside the United States, there are a number of alternatives available to it for seeking preliminary relief securing assets of the US defendant located in the United States.

First, it can try to persuade the arbitrators themselves, while the arbitration is pending, to issue some kind of interim order directing the US defendant to preserve specific assets, or provide some other kind of security, to guarantee the enforceability of any subsequent award. Effective enforcement of such an interim order would depend on the willingness of a US court to enforce it, however, and that in turn would depend on the extent to which the US court concluded that the foreign claimant was:

(1) likely to succeed in obtaining an arbitration award in its favour;
(2) likely to obtain a US court judgment based on that award; and
(3) in genuine need of security in the form of an attachment or other provisional relief.

A second alternative would be for the foreign claimant to commence an action in a US court, prior to the arbitration or while it was pending, seeking provisional relief directly from that court without first obtaining an interim order in the arbitration.[40]

Where the arbitration involves an admiralty dispute, such provisional relief, in the form of attachments of maritime vessels, is expressly authorised by federal statute (see 9 USC § 8).

Outside of the admiralty area, however, US courts are generally somewhat reluctant to become involved in any detail in the substance of factual issues being adjudicated in arbitration, or to prejudge how those factual issues may be resolved by issuing

40. cf. *C.T. Shipping Ltd* v. *DMI (USA) Ltd*, 774 F Supp. 146 (SDNY 1991)—"To secure execution of any eventual judgment on the arbitration award, DMI successfully commenced attachment proceedings against CT in the United States District Courts".

attachments in favour of one party or the other. Some US courts have even concluded that, in connection with international arbitrations subject to enforcement pursuant to the Convention on the Recognition and Enforcement of Foreign Arbitral Awards (to which the US is a party), pre-award attachments by a US court are not permissible,[41] although not all US courts agree with that view.[42]

In any event, in light of the confusion in this area, a foreign claimant should expect that a US court will be reluctant to grant it this kind of pre-award relief in the absence of:

(1) overwhelming proof that it will prevail in the arbitration, and that the US defendant cannot even raise a colourable defence;
(2) a showing of compelling need for such preliminary relief; and
(3) assurance that granting such relief will not in any way interfere with the ongoing or upcoming arbitration.

A third alternative for pursuing interim relief to secure assets to satisfy an arbitrable claim is for the foreign claimant to press ahead with the arbitration as quickly as possible, obtain an arbitration award, commence litigation in the US courts to confirm the award, and seek interim relief in that litigation based on the argument that the material factual issues relating to the underlying dispute have already been resolved in its favour.

Clearly, a US court is likely to be far more receptive to a claim for interim relief to secure assets in this type of situation, where the party seeking relief has already obtained an arbitration award in its favour. This is because awards resulting from arbitration of commercial disputes are specifically enforceable in the United States.

In this regard, where the dispute in question involves interstate or foreign commerce (as would be the case in connection with disputes between US defendants and foreign claimants), the arbitrability issue is governed by federal law (see Federal Arbitration Act, 9 USC § 1, *et seq.*). Where the dispute is limited solely to commerce *within* a single state of the United States, the issue is governed by the law of that state, and many states in the US have adopted another "uniform" statute, the Uniform Arbitration Act, which (like the Federal Arbitration Act, with some differences) renders arbitration clauses and arbitration awards specifically enforceable in their courts.

Before addressing some of the relevant issues concerning when a foreign claimant involved in an arbitration with a US defendant can seek to obtain interim relief to secure assets of that defendant, it is helpful to understand the overall US approach to dealing with arbitration issues between US residents and foreign parties.

Since 1947, the Federal Arbitration Act, 9 USC § 1, *et seq.*, has provided that mandatory arbitration clauses in commercial contracts affecting interstate or foreign commerce are specifically enforceable, and it has provided a procedure whereby US courts, after an examination of the arbitration clause in the parties' contract, can make a summary determination as to whether the dispute is "arbitrable", and thereafter order the parties to proceed to arbitration. In this regard, the Act provides that:

> A party aggrieved by the alleged failure, neglect, or refusal of another to arbitrate under a

41. See, e.g., *McCreary* v. *CEAT*, 501 F 2d 1032 (3rd Cir. 1974).
42. cf. *Carolina Power & Light* Co. v. *Uranex*, 451 F Supp. 1044, 1051 ND CA (1977)—"This court... does not find the reasoning of *McCreary* convincing".

written agreement for arbitration *may petition any United States district court* which, save for such agreement, would have jurisdiction ... of the subject matter of a suit arising out of the controversy between the parties, *for an order directing that such arbitration proceed* in the manner provided for in such agreement. ... The court shall hear the parties, and upon being satisfied that the making of the agreement for arbitration or the failure to comply therewith is not in issue, *the court shall make an order directing the parties to proceed to arbitration in accordance with the terms of the agreement.* [9 USC § 4, emphasis added][43]

The Federal Arbitration Act also provides that where a party is sued in a US court with respect to a dispute that is subject to a mandatory arbitration clause, that party can move to stay the litigation pending the results of an arbitration conducted pursuant to that clause:

If any suit or proceeding be brought in any of the courts of the United States upon any issue referable to arbitration under an agreement in writing for such arbitration, the court in which such suit is pending, upon being satisfied that the issue involved in such suit or proceeding is referable to arbitration under such an agreement, shall on application of one of the parties *stay the trial of the action until such arbitration has been had* in accordance with the terms of the agreement, providing the applicant for the stay is not in default in proceeding with such arbitration. [9 USC § 3, emphasis added][44]

It has also been well-settled, since the Federal Arbitration Act went into effect, that "[t]his Act applies to arbitration proceedings which are to take place in a foreign jurisdiction".[45] It is also clear that it applies to contracts between US citizens and foreign claimants.[46]

In addition to enforcing agreements to arbitrate, the Federal Arbitration Act expressly provides that a US court must confirm an arbitration award unless the award is vacated, modified, or corrected on the narrow grounds permitted by that statute (see 9 USC § 9, "Award of Arbitrators; Confirmation; Jurisdiction; Procedure"). In this regard, the grounds upon which a US court is permitted to vacate an arbitration award under the statute are quite limited:

In either of the following cases the United States court in and for the district wherein the award was made may make an order vacating the award upon the application of any party to the arbitration—

43. See *Joseph Muller Corp. Zurich* v. *Commonwealth Petro Chemicals, Inc.*, 334 F Supp. 1013, 1018 (SDNY 1971)—"A motion to compel arbitration under section 4 [of the Federal Arbitration Act] is simply a request for an order compelling specific performance of part of a contract"; *Sprague* v. *Rhodes Commodity Corporation*, 566 F 2d 861, 862 (2nd Cir. 1977)—"Judge Pierce held that Sprague and Rhodes had failed to make a showing that any written agreement which contained an arbitration provision existed between the parties ... [and] denied the petition for arbitration".

44. See *Moses H. Cone Memorial Hospital* v. *Mercury Const. Corp.*, 460 US 1 (1983), where it was held that both state and federal courts are obliged to grant stays of litigation where the litigation involves arbitrable disputes.

45. *Ford Motor Company Ltd* v. *M/S Maria Gorthon*, 397 F Supp. 1332, 1336 (D Md.).

46. See *Genesco, Inc.* v. *T. Kakiuci & Co. Ltd*, 815 F 2d 840 (2nd Cir. 1987), enforcing arbitration clause in contract between Japanese seller and American buyer; *Sedco, Inc.* v. *Petroleos Mexicanos Mexican Nat. Oil Co.*, 767 F 2d 1140 (5th Cir. 1985), enforcing arbitration clause in contract between Mexican boat charterer and American owner of drilling vessel; *Al-Salamah Arabian Agencies Co. Ltd* v. *Reece*, 673 F Supp. 748 (MDNC 1987), enforcing arbitration clause in marketing services contract entered into in Saudi Arabia; *Pioneer Properties, Inc.* v. *Martin*, 557 F Supp. 1354, appeal dismissed, 776 F 2d 888 (DC Kansas 1983), enforcing arbitration clauses in joint venture agreements between Kansas corporation and Canadian venture.

already been entered in favour of the claimant, and was likely to be confirmed shortly as a judgment of the US court. In a single decision, the court concluded that although the arbitration award should be confirmed, an attachment based on it should be denied, on grounds that:

> ... [p]rejudgment attachment is not favored in the law. A plaintiff must show a likelihood of difficulty enforcing a judgment. Plaintiff has not done so. ...
>
> For the foregoing reasons, I deny petitioner's application for an attachment. I do, however, grant the petition to confirm arbitration ... [*Ibid.*, at pp. 23–24]

Nevertheless, particularly in admiralty cases, many US courts take the position that "attachment... serves only as a security device in aid of the arbitration",[51] and that its use is fully consistent with the broader US policy favouring arbitration in both domestic and foreign disputes.

In addition to state law attachments, preliminary injunctions to preserve the status quo pending the results of arbitration can also be sought in the US courts[52] and where an arbitration award has already been rendered, and a risk that the defendant will dissipate its assets to avoid paying that award can be shown, this flexible equitable remedy should be considered.

Effect of US defendant declaring bankruptcy

The filing of bankruptcy by a US defendant will almost always substantially disrupt the efforts of a foreign claimant to attach that defendant's assets, or even to pursue a judgment against it. The practical reason for this is that whenever a US defendant files a petition for bankruptcy, or is forced into bankruptcy by the filing of an involuntary petition by its creditors, US federal law imposes an "automatic stay" which immediately prohibits the following:

> (1) *The commencement* or continuation, including the issuance or employment of process, *of a judicial, administrative, or other action or proceeding against the [US defendant] debtor* that was or could have been commenced before the commencement of the case under this title, or to recover a claim against the debtor that arose before the commencement of the case under this title;
>
> (2) *The enforcement*, against the debtor or against property of the estate [of the US defendant debtor], *of a judgment* obtained before the commencement of the case under this title;
>
> (3) *Any act to obtain possession of property* of the estate [of the US defendant debtor] or of property from the estate or to exercise control over property of the estate;
>
> (4) *Any act to create, perfect, or enforce any lien* against property of the estate;
>
> (5) Any act to create, perfect, or enforce against property of the debtor any lien to the extent that such lien secures a claim that arose before the commencement of the case under this title;
>
> (6) *Any act to collect, assess, or recover a claim* against the debtor that arose before the commencement of the case under this title;
>
> (7) *The set off of any debt* owing to the debtor that arose before the commencement of the case under this title against any claim against the debtor, and
>
> (8) The commencement or continuation of a proceeding before the United States Tax Court concerning the debtor. [11 USC, § 362(a) (emphasis added)]

Thus, where a US defendant is forced into bankruptcy in the United States, the foreign claimant is precluded, subject to certain narrowly defined exceptions, from employing

51. *Atlas Chartering Services* v. *World Trade Group*, 453 F Supp. 861, 863 (SDNY 1978).
52. See, e.g., *Guinness-Harp Corp.* v. *Jos. Schlitz Brewing*, 613 F 2d 468 (2nd Cir. 1980).

judicial process anywhere to seek or enforce a money judgment against the US defendant, unless it first obtains an order from the governing bankruptcy court "lifting" the automatic stay for good cause.

In this regard, the exceptions to the "automatic stay" provisions of US bankruptcy law are quite narrow, and in general apply only to criminal proceedings; the collection of certain alimony, maintenance or support payments; the filing of documents to perfect security interests whose perfection will be retroactive to a date preceding the filing of the bankruptcy; the prosecution of actions by governmental units to enforce their police or regulatory powers; the assertion of specified rights of set-off by certain stockbrokers, commodities brokers, and financial institutions; the commencement of proceedings by certain federal agencies to foreclose property or issue tax deficiency notices; the repossession of commercial property leased to the debtor where the state lease term has expired; the presentment of a negotiable instrument and the giving of notice of and protesting dishonour of such an instrument; and the commencement of certain actions by the Secretaries of Transportation and Commerce to foreclose specified ship mortgages (see 11 USC § 362(b); see also 11 USC §§ 1110, 1168).

Even where none of the foregoing exceptions applies, however, a foreign claimant (like any other creditor or claimant) may make a specific request for relief from the automatic stay at any time during the course of a bankruptcy proceeding. This is done by filing the appropriate motion, as a "party in interest" (i.e., a creditor of the bankrupt party), with the bankruptcy court having jurisdiction over the case, and the following provisions of the US Bankruptcy Code apply to such motions:

> (d) On request of a party in interest and after notice and a hearing, the court shall grant relief from the stay provided under subsection (a) of this section, such as by terminating, annulling, modifying, or conditioning such stay—
>
> (1) for cause, including the lack of adequate protection of an interest in property of such party in interest; or
>
> (2) with respect to a stay of an act against property under subsection (a) of this section, if—
>
> (A) A debtor does not have an equity in such property; and
>
> (B) Such property is not necessary to effective reorganization.
>
> (e) *Thirty days after a request* under subsection (d) of this section *for relief from the stay* of any act against property of the estate under subsection (a) of this section, *such stay is terminated* with respect to the party in interest making such request, *unless the court, after notice and a hearing, orders such stay continued in effect* pending the conclusion of, or as a result of, a final hearing and determination under subsection (d) of this section. ...
>
> (f) *Upon request of a party in interest*, the court, with or without a hearing, *shall grant such relief from the stay* provided under subsection (a) of this section *as is necessary to prevent irreparable damage to the interest of an equity in property*, if such interest will suffer such damage before there is an opportunity for notice and a hearing under subsection (d) or (e) of this section.
>
> (g) In any hearing under subsection (d) or (e) of this section concerning relief from the stay of any act under subsection (a) of this section—
>
> (1) The party requesting such relief has the burden of proof on the issue of the debtor's equity in property; and
>
> (2) The party opposing such relief has the burden of proof on all other issues. [11 USC § 362(d–g), emphasis added]

In response to a specific request for relief from the automatic stay, a bankruptcy court may, for example, permit a foreign claimant holding an arbitration award or a foreign judgment against a US defendant to commence a lawsuit in the US courts against the

US defendant to confirm the arbitration award, or to obtain recognition of the foreign judgment, during the pendency of the bankruptcy proceeding. It also may limit the foreign claimant's right to take any enforcement action against the US defendant's assets, however.

In another situation, if insurance were available to satisfy the US defendant's debt to the foreign claimant, the bankruptcy court might well lift the automatic stay to the extent necessary to allow the foreign claimant to bring suit against the US defendant solely to reach and apply that defendant's insurance coverage to satisfy the claim, so long as no steps were taken directly to attack the defendant's own assets (which become part of the bankrupt "estate").

In still another case, if a foreign claimant had already attached certain assets of the debtor which were depreciating in value, the bankruptcy court might order the assets sold and the proceeds deposited in escrow to secure the foreign claimant's claims. Alternatively, the bankruptcy court could require the debtor to make periodic payments, either to the foreign claimant or into an escrow account, during the pendency of the bankruptcy proceedings, with provisions for the automatic stay to terminate as to the foreign claimant in the event the payments are not made.

Thus, even where the US defendant has declared bankruptcy, there are procedures available to allow a foreign claimant to seek limited relief from the "automatic stay" in order to obtain recognition and enforcement of any foreign judgment or arbitration award that it may hold, and in certain instances to obtain security for its claim. In the absence of such a ruling from the bankruptcy court, however, no such action can be taken.

In general, once a US party files for bankruptcy, the bulk of its assets become part of the bankrupt "estate", and only those who hold "claims" against the debtor or the estate can share in the distribution of those assets as creditors. In this regard, the term "claim" under US bankruptcy law is defined as a:

> (A) right to payment, whether or not such right is reduced to a judgment, liquidated, unliquidated, fixed, contingent, matured, unmatured, disputed, undisputed, legal, equitable, secured, or unsecured; or
>
> (B) right to an equitable remedy for breach of performance if such breach gives rise to a right to payment, whether or not such right to an equitable remedy is reduced to judgment, fixed, contingent, matured, unmatured, disputed, undisputed, secured, or unsecured ... [11 USC § 101]

Significantly, it is not necessary in bankruptcy for a claimant's claim to have been reduced to a judgment in order to be allowed; rather:

> (a) A claim or interest, *proof of which is filed* under §501 of this title, *is deemed allowed, unless a party in interest*, including a creditor of a general partner in a partnership that is a debtor in a case under chapter 7 of this title, *objects*.
>
> (b) ... if such objection to a claim is made, the court, after notice and a hearing, shall determine the amount of such claim ... [11 USC § 502, emphasis added]

The required "proof" of claim is not the kind of evidentiary submission that would be required during a formal trial or arbitration proceeding. Rather, it is simply a form issued by the US Supreme Court, a copy of which is set forth in the appendix to Title Eleven of the United States Code, which requires the claimant to specify the nature and amount of the claim.[53]

53. See Bankruptcy Rules 3002, 3003; 11 USC Appendix, Official Forms No. 10.

Depending on the nature of the bankruptcy proceeding, and the relative interest of the various participants, it sometimes happens that no one objects to a particular proof of claim, such as that of a foreign claimant, and in that case the foreign claimant stands in line with other creditors (secured creditors have priority) to share in whatever assets remain to be distributed at the conclusion of the bankruptcy proceeding. On the other hand, the trustee or debtor in possession appointed by the bankruptcy court to run the estate during the bankruptcy proceeding may object if he or she has a basis for arguing that the claim is unenforceable (for reasons other than it being contingent or unmatured), or otherwise falls within a particular category of disallowable claims (see 11 USC § 502(b)).

If the foreign claimant's claim is disputed, it will either be decided on the merits in the bankruptcy court, or the automatic stay will be lifted to allow for substantive proceedings on the merits of that claim to go forward in another court in order to liquidate and resolve the matter. If there is likely to be substantial opposition to the foreign claimant's proof of claim in the bankruptcy proceeding, it may be advisable for a foreign claimant to obtain permission from the bankruptcy court to pursue or conclude litigation on the merits of its claim in the courts of its home country (if those courts have jurisdiction over the US defendant), obtain a judgment there, and then file its proof of claim in the bankruptcy proceeding.

In this regard, if the foreign claimant ever wishes to enforce its claim against the US assets of a US defendant, it is highly advisable, in the event that the US defendant declares bankruptcy, for the foreign claimant to observe and abide by the "automatic stay" provisions of the US Bankruptcy Code, even if there is some question in the foreign claimant's mind as to whether such "automatic stay" provisions apply to its actions in its own country. This is particularly true where the foreign claimant is in any way amenable to personal jurisdiction in the United States, because violation of the automatic stay is punishable by citations for contempt of court, and contempt orders can impose substantial fines that will eventually have to be paid by the foreign claimant if it appears anywhere in the United States.

In re McLean Industries Inc.[54] provides a good example of why foreign claimants should observe the automatic stay in cases where they have claims against a bankrupt US defendant. In *McLean*, a US shipping company had filed for bankruptcy in November of 1986, and the automatic stay provided by §362(a) of the US Bankruptcy Code had gone into effect at that time. Ten days later, a United Kingdom corporation, GAC Marine Fuels Ltd (GAC), which was fully aware of the bankruptcy and the "automatic stay" rule, nevertheless commenced an *in rem* admiralty action against the US company in the Supreme Court of Hong Kong, seeking to recover US$173,750 in moneys allegedly owed to it for fuel oil that it had delivered in October of 1986 to a vessel owned by the US company and then docked in the United Arab Emirates. Thereafter, on 9 December 1986, at the specific request of GAC, the Hong Kong court issued a warrant of arrest against that vessel, which was docked in Hong Kong at the time, restraining it from leaving Hong Kong harbour.

During the same time period, GAC commenced another admiralty proceeding against the US company in the High Court of Singapore, seeking to recover another US$69,500 allegedly owed to it for fuel oil it had supplied to another vessel owned by

54. 68 BR 690 (Bkrtcy SDNY 1986).

the US company in November of 1986. On 8 December 1986, the Singapore court issued a warrant of arrest restraining that vessel from leaving Singapore.

In response to these actions by GAC, the US company promptly (on 16 December 1986) commenced an action against GAC for contempt and injunctive relief in the US bankruptcy court where its bankruptcy petition had been filed, claiming that GAC had wilfully violated the "automatic stay" provisions of US law. The US bankruptcy court agreed, concluding that:

GAC Marine took these actions *with knowledge of* the debtor's [the US company's] filing of its reorganization petition [in bankruptcy] and *the resultant automatic stay* provided by §362 of the Code, *and, after being informed by the debtor that such actions would be improper*. ... [*In re McLean Industries, Inc.*, 68 BR at 692, emphasis added]

In issuing the requested preliminary injunction, citing GAC for contempt, and imposing a fine (pursuant to the contempt citation) of US$5,000 per day until the foreign attachments and arrests were dissolved, the court noted that:

... [i]t is undisputed here that in causing the issuance of the Hong Kong and Singapore warrants, the [foreign claimant] defendant took steps to proceed on a pre-[bankruptcy] petition claim *in violation of 11 USC §362(a)(1)* and disturbed the debtor's possession of its property in violation of 11 USC §362(a)(3). ... *It matters not that the property of the estate was located beyond the territorial borders of the United States.* Section 541(a) [of the Bankruptcy Code] makes clear that property of the estate is not so confined but consists of all property "wherever located" in which the debtor has an interest. [68 BR at 694, emphasis added]

The court also addressed, and rejected, GAC's claim that the court did not have personal jurisdiction over its actions:

GAC Marine, although essentially admitting the underlying facts, opposes these motions, declaring that it, *as a non-domiciliary corporation organized under the laws of the United Kingdom and with a principal place of business in London, is not subject* to the *in personam* jurisdiction of this Court. ...

Two grounds for the exercise of such [in personam] jurisdiction consistent with due process are asserted here: (i) transactional jurisdiction ... and (ii) general "doing business" jurisdiction ...

Here it is clear that *the [foreign claimant] defendant transacts business in the United States.* It regularly affords, in the United States, quoted prices and terms for delivery of bunkers abroad. Agreements for the same are reached in the United States upon the acceptance of the quoted prices and terms. Its representative in the United States is apparently empowered to sign letters and to deliver documents on its behalf with respect to US customers. *It repeatedly holds itself out to the world as having an office in the United States.*

It is also clear that the second half of the test, *i.e.*, that *the cause of action asserted arose from business done here*, has also been satisfied even though the acts complained of, the procuring of the Hong Kong warrant and the Singapore arrest, took place abroad.

...

The defendant [GAC] is thus subject to *in personam* jurisdiction here on those claims. [68 BR at 691, 697–699, emphasis added]

McLean and other US bankruptcy court cases make it reasonably clear that foreign claimants who commence or continue legal process abroad against US defendants, after being informed that those US defendants have filed for bankruptcy in the United States, act at their peril, particularly to the extent that they themselves do business or have assets in the United States. Not only can they be subjected to contempt proceedings and fines, but they may also adversely affect their ability to participate effectively in the US bankruptcy proceeding when the time comes to try to satisfy their claims out of any remaining US assets of bankrupt defendants.

Thus, when confronted with the question of whether to commence or continue legal proceedings *outside* the US against a US defendant that has filed for bankruptcy *in* the US, it will generally be more prudent for a foreign claimant first to ask the US bankruptcy court to modify its automatic stay to permit the commencement or continuation of such proceedings. Although direct attempts to attach assets may not be permitted, merely pursuing dispute resolution mechanisms such as arbitration often will be. In *Société Nationale Algérienne Pour La Recherche, La Production, Le Transport, La Transformation et La Commercialisation des Hydrocarbures* v. *Distrigas Corporation*,[55] for example, a US district court allowed a foreign claimant's motion to modify the automatic stay, as to claims against a US defendant that had filed for bankruptcy in Massachusetts, so to allow the foreign claimant to commence an international arbitration against the US defendant pursuant to an arbitration clause in a prior contract between those two parties.

In that case, the foreign claimant was Sonatrach, the National Energy Corporation of the Algerian government. It sought to pursue international arbitration in order to determine the damages it had incurred as a result of the US defendant's rejection (which is permitted under the Bankruptcy Code, but is considered a breach of contract for which compensatory damages may be sought from the bankrupt's estate) of a 20-year supply contract for the purchase and sale of Algerian liquified natural gas. After an extended discussion of the issues, the court held as follows:

> For the reasons discussed below, *this Court rules that Sonatrach is entitled to commence international arbitration, pursuant to the parties' contractual agreement*, to resolve any outstanding questions of liability and damages in its breach of contract claim against Distrigas and *directs that the automatic stay be modified accordingly*. ...
>
> In weighing the strong public policy favoring international arbitration with any countervailing potential harm to bankruptcy policy upon the present facts, this Court finds the scales weighted in favor of arbitration. ... *While international arbitration will require a temporary and limited incursion into the Bankruptcy Court's exclusive jurisdictional bailiwick, no bankruptcy policies will suffer adverse impact*. Conversely, the very image of the United States and the international business community stands to be tarnished. *It is important and necessary for the United States to hold its domiciliaries to their bargains and not allow them escape their commercial obligations by ducking into statutory safe harbors*. Rather, our country should take special pains to project those qualities of honesty and fairness which are essential parts of the traditional American character and be perceived as a fair and equal player in the global market place, particularly in our commercial relations with the underdeveloped world.
>
> Therefore, *Sonetrach's motion to Modify the Stay and proceed with international arbitration is Allowed* for the reasons stated above. [*Ibid*., at pp. 867, 874–875, emphasis added]

Thus, although the *Société Nationale* court noted that "[t]here may be disputes where arbitration is decidedly unsuitable" in these situations, it allowed the foreign claimant's motion to lift the automatic stay in that case. Clearly, therefore, such motions are given serious consideration in the US courts, and a willingness on the part of foreign claimants to abide by US bankruptcy procedure will generally result in a greater likelihood that they can utilise that procedure to maximise their recovery on claims against bankrupt US defendants.

55. 18 Collier Bankruptcy Cases (2nd Series) at p. 865, Civil Action No. 86–2012–Y (D Mass. 1987).

CONCLUSION

The extent to which a foreign claimant can obtain interim or provisional relief securing the assets of a US defendant pending final resolution of a dispute between them necessarily depends on the choices that the foreign claimant has made with regard to how to pursue its overall claims on the merits, i.e., either through litigation in the United States, litigation in foreign courts, or through arbitration. Although the discussion in this chapter is by no means an exhaustive account of all the factors to be considered on this issue, it does make clear that in situations where it is important to the foreign claimant to obtain interim or provisional relief securing assets of its US defendant, the foreign claimant must take this concern into account in its overall decision on how to pursue its substantive claims on the merits. It is also clear that in cases where the US defendant declares bankruptcy, a foreign claimant should carefully consider the impact of US bankruptcy law on any collection efforts it is undertaking outside the United States.

ROBERT J. KALER

INDEX

Remedies and common processes and procedures are not duplicated under national headings

Admiralty *see* Shipping
Aeroplanes
  Greece, 207
  Korea, 287
  Norway, 330–331
  Sweden, 408
Algeria, treaties and conventions, and Belgium, 48, 49, 54
Alimony *see* Family matters
Anton Piller orders
  Australia, 16–17
  Cayman Islands, 107
  England and Wales, 142, 143
  Ireland, 236–237
  New Zealand, 301
Arbitration
  and Australia, 10–13
  and Canada, 85–86
    Quebec, 96–97
  and Cayman Islands, 113–114
  and Denmark, 129–130
  and Germany, 197–198
  and Korea, 286–287
  and Nigeria, 317
  and Norway, 326
  and Singapore, 355–356
  and Sweden, 410
  and United States, 455–460
Arrest
  New Zealand, 305
  Norway, 328–333
  Portugal, 348, 349
Assets
  Cayman Islands, 107–110
  Greece, 217
  Hong Kong, 227
  Israel, 258
  Japan, 275–277, 278
  The Netherlands, 291, 295
  removal,
    Australia, 14–15
    see also Mareva injunctions
  South Africa, 371
  Switzerland, 421
Attachment
  Australia, 7
  Belgium, 59–60
  Cayman Islands, 115
Attachment—*cont.*
  Denmark, 131–132
  Finland, 162, 167
  France, 175–176
  Germany, 180–195
  Israel, 252–254, 258
  Japan, 266, 267, 272, 275, 276–277
  Korea, 283–285
  The Netherlands, 290–291, 294
  Norway, 326–327, 328
  The Philippines, 337–339, 340–342
  South Africa, 370, 373, 374
  Spain, 393, 394–396
  Switzerland, 419–420
  Taiwan, 429–430, 433
  United States, 438–439, 455, 460
  see also Arrest; Garnishment/garnishee proceedings
Attachment, conservative, Greece, 205–208, 215, 217
Attorney, power of, Taiwan, 426, 427–428, 430
Australia, 3–23
  enforcement of foreign judgments within, 4–10
    registration, 6–7
    transitional provisions, 5
  equitable relief, 13–17
  insolvency, 18–23
    Australian debtors, 18–21
    foreign orders, 21–23
  question of internal enforcement, 3–4
  treaties and conventions,
    and Cayman Islands, 111
    and England and Wales, 157
    and Hong Kong, 221
    and New Zealand, 6, 7, 298
    and Singapore, 353
    and United Kingdom, 6
Austria, 25–42
  and bonds, 27–28
  costs, damages and penalties, 28–29, 36–37
  execution to secure a claim, 37–38
  and injunctive orders, 36
  preliminary injunctions, 30–33, 34
  procedure, 34–36, 39–41
    appeals, 36, 40–41
  remedies as to particular assets, 33–34
  requirements, 38–39
  selection of proper forum, 26–27

Austria—*cont.*
treaties and conventions, 25, 43–44
and Belgium, 48, 53, 54
and Finland, 161, 167
and Germany, 197, 198
and Hong Kong, 222
and Israel, 250
and Norway, 325
and Sweden, 409
and Switzerland, 416

Bailiff
Cayman Islands, 114
Hong Kong, 225
Bank accounts
Austria, 33
Greece, 208
Japan, 275, 276–277
Korea, 284
Taiwan, 432
Bankruptcy
Australia, 7, 8–9
Austria, 41–42
Belgium, 63–65
and Brussels Convention, 231
Canada, 82–83, 86–88
Cayman Islands, 116, 119
Denmark, 126, 131, 133–135
England and Wales, 153, 158–160
Finland, 166
France, 176–177
Germany, 194
Greece, 214–216
Hong Kong, 228
Ireland, 235, 237, 239–240
Israel, 259–262
Japan, 277
Korea, 287
The Netherlands, 295–296
Nigeria, 322
Norway, 324, 327, 331
Portugal, 349
Singapore, 359–360
Spain, 396–398
Sweden, 411–412
United States, 460–465
see also Liquidation; Winding up
Belgium, 47–65
and bankruptcy, 63–65
characteristics of foreign claim, 50–51
conservatory remedies, 59–60, 62
and domicile, 47–48
procedure, 55–62
treaties and conventions, 52–54, 62–63, 197
and Austria, 43
and Germany, 197, 198
and Hong Kong, 222
and Switzerland, 416
and United Kingdom, 149
types of remedy, 54
Bonds
posting *see* Costs, security for
remedies regarding, Austria, 33–34
Brussels Convention on Recognition and Enforcement of Foreign Judgments in Civil and Commercial Matters
and Austria, 30, 38
and Belgium, 48, 53–54
and England and Wales, 138–139, 144, 146–150, 155–156
and France, 170, 172
and Greece, 213, 214
and Ireland, 231, 243
parties and scope, 62–63, 155, 186
and Portugal, 345–346
Bulgaria
treaties and conventions,
and Belgium, 48, 49
and Greece, 213
and Korea, 286

Canada, 67–98
British Columbia, 67, 89, 90–91
legislation, treaties and conventions, 44, 83–86
and Cayman Islands, 111
and Hong Kong, 221
and United Kingdom, 83–84
and United States, 85
nature of jurisdictions, 67
Quebec, 67, 75, 92–98
remedies, 97–98
recognition procedure, 69–77
procedural issues, 74–75
Quebec, 93–97
remedies, 78–83
priority of unsecured creditors, 81
Cayman Islands, 99–123
availability of courts to foreign litigants, 101–110
confidentiality, 107–108, 122–123
extracts from legislation, 119–123
fraudulent dispositions law 1989, 110
legal structure, 99–100
methods of execution of judgments, 114–115
registration, 112
treaties and conventions, and Hong Kong, 222
Charging orders
Canada, 82
England and Wales, 152–153
Hong Kong, 227–228, 229
New Zealand, 305–310
China, People's Republic, treaties and conventions, and Hong Kong, 222
Commonwealth
and Singapore, 353–354, 361
treaties and conventions, and Hong Kong, 221
Copyright
Belgium, 49, 61–62
Nigeria, 312
Sweden, 407
Costs
and arbitration, Denmark, 129
and bankruptcy, Denmark, 134
litigation and lawyers' fees, Japan, 279–281

Costs—*cont.*
question of,
Austria, 28–29, 41
Denmark, 128
security for,
Austria, 27–28
Belgium, 49
Cayman Islands, 104
Denmark, 128
England and Wales, 140
Germany, 182–183
Hong Kong, 220
Ireland, 234–235
Japan, 265
The Netherlands, 290
New Zealand, 300
Nigeria, 314
The Philippines, 338
Singapore, 357
South Africa, 366–367
Sweden, 403
Taiwan, 427
United States, 435, 439, 440–441
and US/Japan case, 454
Currency
court awards,
Canada, 74–75
Hong Kong, 224
Taiwan, 427
exchange rate, Spain, 392, 393
offences, Nigeria, 312
Cyprus, Republic of
treaties and conventions,
and Greece, 213
and Hong Kong, 221, 222
Czechoslovakia/Czech Republic/Slovakia
treaties and conventions,
and Belgium, 48, 54
and Greece, 213
and Switzerland, 416

Debt and debts
Denmark, 129, 130
Greece, 212
South Africa, 370, 373
Switzerland, 418–421
Denmark, 125–136
individual legal proceedings by creditors, 127–132
obtaining a basis of execution, 129–130
judgment by a Danish court, 127–129
original securities, 125–127
treaties and conventions, 135, 197
and Korea, 286
and Norway, 325
and Sweden, 403
universal proceedings by creditors, 132–135
Design
protection,
Nigeria, 312
Sweden, 407
Distraint
Belgium, 50, 60–61
Sweden, 410
Documents
removal,
Australia, 16
see also Anton Piller orders
Domicile
Belgium, 47–48
France, 170
Greece, 200
Ireland, 232
Lugano Convention, 422–423
Spain, 380
Switzerland, 417, 419

England and Wales, 137–160
appeals, 150–152
common law, 145
courts' availability to foreign creditors, 137–140
interim relief, 141–144
interlocutory injunctions, 141
judgments under 1968 Convention, 146–150
proceedings, 145
remedies available to foreign creditors, 152–154
treaties and conventions, 138–139, 140–141, 154–158
see also United Kingdom
Equitable execution
Canada, 81–82
Quebec, 98
Equitable relief, Australia, 13–17
Equity
Cayman Islands, 119
Ireland, 240
Execution
New Zealand, 304–310
Spain, 391–393
Execution judgments, Japan, 280–281
Execution, levy on, as provisional remedy, The Philippines, 337
Execution orders, Ireland, 237–238
Execution, writ of
England and Wales, 152
Hong Kong, 225
Nigeria, 318–320
South Africa, 374
Spain, 385, 386, 387

Family matters
alimony/maintenance,
Canada, 86
Ireland, 233, 234
Portugal, 348–349
Sweden, 403
United States, 461
Australia, 8–9
Cayman Islands, 119
Fieri facias, writ of
England and Wales, 151–152
Hong Kong, 225
Nigeria, 320

Finland, 161–167
  proceedings on substance, 167
  provisional measures, 162–166
    attachment, 163
    proceedings for, 164–166
  appeal, 165
  treaties and conventions, 421
    and Austria, 43
    and Lugano Convention, 161, 165, 167
    and Norway, 325
France, 169–177
  enforcement of foreign decisions, 171–174
  enforcement measures, 175–176
  jurisdictional rules, 169–171
  provisional or interim measures, 174–175
  remedies available to foreign creditors, 174–176
  treaties and conventions, 197, 421
    and Austria, 43
    and Belgium, 49, 53
    and Hong Kong, 222
    and Quebec, 92
    and Sweden, 403
    and Switzerland, 416
    and United Kingdom, 149
Fraud
  Canada, 72
  France, 173
  Hong Kong, 223
  Israel, 249
  Singapore, 351, 354, 355
  United States, 447

Garnishment/garnishee proceedings
  Australia, 7
  Belgium, 49–50, 60
  Canada, 78–80
    Quebec, 97
  England and Wales, 153
  Germany, 193–194
  Hong Kong, 227, 228
  Ireland, 238
  Israel, 254–255
  The Netherlands, 294
  New Zealand, 305
  Nigeria, 318–320
  The Philippines, 337
  Singapore, 358
  South Africa, 373–374
  Sweden, 410
  United States, 438–439
  see also Attachment
Germany, 179–198
  cost of litigation, 198
  influence on Taiwan, 425–426
  provisional attachment proceedings, 180–195
    obtaining writ, 188–195
  recognition and enforcement of foreign judgments, 195–197
  treaties and conventions, 197
    and Austria, 43
    and Belgium, 49, 53, 54
    and Hong Kong, 222
Germany—*cont.*
  treaties and conventions—*cont.*
    and Israel, 250
    and Switzerland, 416
    and United Kingdom, 149
Ghana
  treaties and conventions,
    and Hong Kong, 221
    and Korea, 286
Goods and chattels *see* Immovable goods; Movable goods
Great Britain *see* England and Wales; United Kingdom
Greece, 199–217
  interim relief, 201–205
    and judgment creditor, 216–217
    procedure, 204–205
  question of sovereign immunity, 201
  specific measures, 205–213
  treaties and conventions, 213–214
    and Germany, 197, 198
    and Sweden, 403
Guarantees, Greece, 210–211, 216
Guardianship, court, The Netherlands, 294, 296

Hong Kong, 219–229
  methods of enforcement, 224–229
    examination of judgment debtors, 225–226
    Order 44A, 229
    prohibition orders, 226–227
  modes of recognition, 219–224
    enforceable judgments, 219–220, 222–223
  treaties and conventions,
    and Singapore, 353
    and Taiwan, 431–432
Hungary
  treaties and conventions,
    and Belgium, 49
    and Greece, 213
    and Korea, 286

Iceland
  treaties and conventions,
    and Norway, 325
    and Sweden, 403
Immovable property
  Austria, 34
  Canada, 69–70, 80–81
    Quebec, 93, 98
  Cayman Islands, 114
  Denmark, 126, 130, 131
  Finland, 164
  France, 170, 176
  Greece, 208–209, 210
  Hong Kong, 227
  Israel, 251
  Japan, 269, 271–272
  New Zealand, 305, 307
  Sweden, 404
  Taiwan, 433
  see also Attachment
India
  treaties and conventions,
    and England and Wales, 157
    and Hong Kong, 221

India—*cont.*
  treaties and conventions—*cont.*
    and Korea, 286
    and Singapore, 353
Injunction proceedings, Austria, 28
Injunctions
  Ireland, 235
  Korea, 285
  Norway, 329–333
Injunctions, preventive, Portugal, 348–349
Injunctions, provisional, Israel, 256
Injunctive relief
  Austria, 27–28, 37
  The Netherlands, 291–292
Insolvency
  Australia, 8–9, 18–23
  England and Wales, 153–154
  Ireland, 239–240
  The Philippines, 340–342
  see also Bankruptcy; Liquidation
Ireland, 231–242
  jurisdiction, 231–233
  remedies for creditors, 235–240
    legislation, 239–240
  service, 233–234
  treaties and conventions, 421
    and Sweden, 403
Isle of Man
  treaties and conventions,
    and England and Wales, 157
    and Hong Kong, 221
Israel, 245–261
  Basic Law: Human Dignity and Liberty, 257–258
  execution, 258–259
  institution of an action, 251–252
  interim reliefs, 252–257
  procedure, 250
  treaties and conventions, 250, 324
    and Austria, 43
    and England and Wales, 157
    and Germany, 197
    and Hong Kong, 222
Italy
  treaties and conventions, 197, 421
    and Austria, 43
    and Belgium, 53
    and Germany, 197, 198
    and Hong Kong, 222
    and Switzerland, 416
    and United Kingdom, 149

Japan, 263–281
  assignment of assets, 278
  legal issues, 264–274
    bringing an action, 268–272
  practical issues, 274–281
    finding assets, 275–277
    lawyers, 279, 280
    and parent companies, 277, 278–279
    timescale, 281
  treaties and conventions, 324
    and Belgium, 49
    and Hong Kong, 222
    and Korea, 286

Japan—*cont.*
  treaties and conventions—*cont.*
    and Sweden, 403
    and United States, case, 450–455
Judgment mortgages, Ireland, 238
Judgment orders, Ireland, 237
Judgment, summary, United States, 448–449

Kenya
  treaties and conventions,
    and Belgium, 49
    and Hong Kong, 221
Korea, 283–288

Land *see* Immovable property
Lebanon
  treaties and conventions, 324
    and Greece, 213
Liechtenstein
  treaties and conventions,
    and Austria, 43
    and Switzerland, 416
Liquidation
  Cayman Islands, 117–118
  England and Wales, 153, 158, 159–160
  Israel, 260–261
  Sweden, 411–412
  see also Winding up, Bankruptcy
Liquidation orders, Australia, 22–23
Lithuania, treaties and conventions, and Belgium, 48, 49
Lugano Convention on Jurisdiction and Enforcement of Judgments in Civil and Commercial Matters
  and Austria, 25, 30
  and England and Wales, 138, 156–157
  and Finland, 162, 166, 167
  and Ireland, 231
  and Norway, 325
  parties and scope, 38, 156, 421, 422–423
  and Portugal, 345–346
  and Sweden, 404–406, 409, 410
  and Switzerland, 416, 423
Luxembourg
  treaties and conventions,
    and Austria, 43
    and European Convention on the Enforcement of Civil and Commercial Judgments, 197
    and Lugano Convention, 421

Maintenance *see* Family matters
Malaysia
  treaties and conventions,
    and Hong Kong, 221
    and Singapore, 353
Mareva injunctions
  Australia, 14–15, 16–17
  Canada, 78
  Cayman Islands, 105–107
  England and Wales, 141–142, 143
  Hong Kong, 229
  Ireland, 236, 239
  Israel, 256
  New Zealand, 300–302

Morocco
treaties and conventions, 324
and Belgium, 54
Movable property
Canada, 69–70, 80–81
Quebec, 93, 98
Denmark, 126, 131
Finland, 164
Greece, 210, 213, 216
Taiwan, 433
see also Attachment

Netherlands, The, 289–296
conservatory measures, 291–292
procedure, 293–294
treaties and conventions, 197, 290, 292–293, 295
and Austria, 43
and Belgium, 53
and Germany, 197, 198
and Hong Kong, 222
and Korea, 286
and United Kingdom, 149
New Zealand, 297–310
and Australia, 6
procedure, 299–300
question of preservation of property, 302–304
and registration of foreign judgments within Australia, 7
treaties and conventions,
Australia, 298
and Hong Kong, 221
and Singapore, 353
writs, 305
Nigeria, 311–322
court system, 311–314
remedies available, 314–315
remedies and procedure, 317–322
treaties and conventions, and Hong Kong, 221
Norway, 323–333
procedures, 323–328, 331–332
treaties and conventions, 325, 421
and Austria, 43
and Germany, 197

Pakistan
treaties and conventions,
and England and Wales, 157
and Hong Kong, 221
and Singapore, 353
Papua New Guinea
treaties and conventions,
and Hong Kong, 221
and Singapore, 353
Patents
Belgium, 49, 61–62
Lugano Convention, 423
Nigeria, 312, 316
Sweden, 407
Personal property *see* Movable property

Philippines, The, 335–342
provisional remedies, 337–340
Poland
treaties and conventions,
and Austria, 43
and Greece, 213
Portugal, 343–349
time limit, 344, 347
treaties and conventions, 345–346, 421
types of remedies, 347–350
restitutive remedies, 348
Public policy
Australia, 12–13
Canada, 71–72
Cayman Islands, 110
England and Wales, 147
France, 173
Hong Kong, 223
Ireland, 241
Israel, 247
Japan, 273–274
Nigeria, 316
Singapore, 351, 354, 355, 356
Taiwan, 431

Real property *see* Immovable property
Receivership
Australia, 7
Canada, 79, 82
England and Wales, 142
Israel, 255–256
The Philippines, 339–340
Singapore, 359
Reciprocity
Austria, 39
Japan, 274
Korea, 285
Taiwan, 431–432
United States, 442–444
Republic of China (Taiwan) *see* Taiwan
Residence
Japan, 270
The Netherlands, 289
Romania
treaties and conventions,
and Belgium, 54
and Greece, 213
and Korea, 286

Safekeeping, judicial, The Netherlands, 291, 294
Secured debts, enforcement, Canada, 68
Security
Austria, 30–31, 35, 41
Finland, 163–164
Germany, 187, 190–191
Greece, 201, 209
The Netherlands, 290
Norway, 332, 333
see also Costs, security for
Sequestration
Australia, 7, 19–20
Greece, 210, 215
New Zealand, 305
Sweden, 400–405

Shipping
  Australia, 17–18
  Belgium, 61
  Cayman Islands, 119
  England and Wales, 143
  Greece, 207, 217
  Japan, 270
  Korea, 287
  Nigeria, 312
  Norway, 328, 330–331, 333
  South Africa, 371
  Sweden, 408
  Switzerland, 416
  United States, 455, 460
Singapore, 351–361
  enforcement, 357–359
  procedure, 356–357
  treaties and conventions, and Hong Kong, 221
South Africa, 363–377
  court system, 364–367
  procedures, 367–370
  remedies, 370–374
    absence from jurisdiction, 372
    provisional sentence, 372
Soviet Union, former
  treaties and conventions, 324
    and Germany, 198
    and Greece, 213
Spain, 379–398
  conditions system, 386
  procedure, 386–387
  treaties and conventions,
    and Austria, 43
    and Germany, 197
    and Switzerland, 416
Sri Lanka
  treaties and conventions,
    and Hong Kong, 221
    and Singapore, 353
Surinam
  treaties and conventions, 324
    and England and Wales, 157
Sweden, 399–412
  bankruptcy and liquidation, 411–412
  intellectual property law, 405–407
  procedure, 403–404
  treaties and conventions, 404–406, 409, 410, 421
    and Austria, 43
    and Norway, 325
    and Switzerland, 416
Switzerland, 413–424
  procedure, 415, 418, 419–421
  treaties and conventions, 416, 421, 423
    and Austria, 43
    and Belgium, 53
    and Germany, 197, 198
    and Sweden, 409

Taiwan (Republic of China [ROC]), 425–433
  court system, 425–429
  procedure, 431
  treaties and conventions, and Korea, 286
Trademarks
  Lugano Convention, 423
  Nigeria, 312, 316
  Sweden, 406
Tunisia
  treaties and conventions,
    and Austria, 44
    and Germany, 197, 198
Turkey
  treaties and conventions,
    and Austria, 44
    and Belgium, 49

United Kingdom
  and Australia, 6
  treaties and conventions, 421
    and Austria, 44
    and Belgium, 49, 53
    and Canada, 83–84
    and Cayman Islands, 111
    and European Convention on the Enforcement of Civil and Commercial Judgments, 197
    and Germany, 197
    and Hong Kong, 221
    and Israel, 250
    and Norway, 325
    and Singapore, 353
    and Sweden, 403
    and Taiwan, 431–432
  see also England and Wales
United States, 435–466
  court system, 436–437
  question of South African jurisdiction, 368
  treaties and conventions,
    and Belgium, 49
    and Canada, 85
    and Cayman Islands, 111
    and Germany, 198
    and Hong Kong, 222
    and Korea, 286
    and Switzerland, 416
    and Taiwan, 431
  US defendant—foreign court, 441–455
    question of due process, 445–446
    Uniform Act, 442, 448, 450
    view of Japanese litigation, 450–455
  US defendant—US court, 438–441

Wales *see* England and Wales
Winding up
  Australia, 20, 22
  England and Wales, 159
  Hong Kong, 228
  Singapore, 359, 360–361
  see also Bankruptcy; Liquidation

Yugoslavia
  treaties and conventions,
    and Belgium, 49, 53, 54
    and Greece, 213